online resource centre
www.oxfordtextbooks.co.uk/orc/watt/

An Online Resource Centre accompanies this book, providing additional support for both students and lecturers.

Resources

- Video clips giving an introduction to equity and trusts along with three mini-lectures presented by Gary Watt
- General guidance on answering essay questions and problem scenarios
- Sample essay questions & problem scenarios, along with answer guidance
- Key legal developments since publication
- Web links
- Flashcard glossary

Trusts and Equity

Sixth Edition

GARY WATT

Professor of Law, University of Warwick

OXFORD

UNIVERSITY PRESS

OXFORD
UNIVERSITY PRESS

Great Clarendon Street, Oxford, OX2 6DP,
United Kingdom

Oxford University Press is a department of the University of Oxford.
It furthers the University's objective of excellence in research, scholarship,
and education by publishing worldwide. Oxford is a registered trade mark of
Oxford University Press in the UK and in certain other countries

Third edition 2008
Fourth edition 2010
Fifth edition 2012

Impression: 1

Published in the United States of America by Oxford University Press
198 Madison Avenue, New York, NY 10016, United States of America

British Library Cataloguing in Publication Data
Data available

Library of Congress Control Number: 2013955891

ISBN 978–0–19–967893–8

Printed in Great Britain by
Ashford Colour Press Ltd, Gosport, Hampshire

To Emma

Contents

Part III The Regulation of Trusts

New to this edition

A wide range of new case law, including:

- *Futter v. HMRC Commissioners; Pitt v. HMRC Commissioners* (2013) UK Supreme Court on the review of trustee discretions
- *Prest v. Petrodel* (2013) UK Supreme Court on resulting trust and statutory formalities
- *Day v. Royal College of Music* (2013) Court of Appeal on the rule in *Strong* v. *Bird*
- *AIB Group (UK) Plc v. Mark Redler & Co Solicitors* (2013) Court of Appeal on trustee liability
- *Smith v. Bottomley* (2013) Court of Appeal on detrimental reliance as basis for constructive trust of home
- *Santander UK Plc v. RA Legal Solicitors* (2014) Court of Appeal on relief under Trustee Act s.61
- *Federal Republic of Brazil v. Durant International Corp* (2013) Jersey Court of Appeal on tracing
- *Lawie v. Lawie* (2012) on rectification
- *Araci v. Fallon* (2011) Court of Appeal on specific performance
- *Byrnes v. Kendle* (2011) High Court of Australia on intention to create trust
- *Re Bogusz (Deceased)* (sub nom *Vallee v. Birchwood*) on *donatio mortis causa*
- *Curtis v. Pulbrook* (2011) on constitution of trusts
- *Rubin v. Dweck* (2012) on trusts for the purpose of defrauding creditors
- *Re St Andrew's (Cheam) Lawn Tennis Club Trust (sub nom Philippe v. Cameron)* (2012) on private purpose trusts and the beneficiary principle
- *Re E A Scott (1991 Children's Settlement N1); Scott v. Scott* (2012) on removal of trustees
- *Towers v. Premier Waste Ltd* (2011) Court of Appeal on fiduciary duties
- *Relfo Ltd (In Liquidation) v. Varsani* (2012) on the equitable liability of strangers to the trust
- *Goldspan Ltd v. Patel* (2012) on liability for knowing receipt of trust property
- *Armstrong DLW GmbH v. Winnington Networks Ltd* (2012) on liability for knowing receipt
- *Joyce v. Epsom* (2012) Court of Appeal on remedial satisfaction of proprietary estoppel
- *Suggitt v. Suggitt* (2012) Court of Appeal on remedial satisfaction of proprietary estoppel

- *Aspden v. Elvy* (2012) on proprietary estoppel and constructive trust
- *Omojole v. HSBC Bank Plc* on resulting trust
- *Crossco No. 4 Unlimited v. Jolan Ltd* (2011) Court of Appeal on the *Pallant v. Morgan* equity
- *Kearns Brothers Ltd v. Hova Developments Ltd* (2012) on the *Pallant v. Morgan* equity
- *AG v. Charity Commission* Upper Tribunal (Tax And Chancery Chamber) (2012) on poverty charities
- *Khaira v. Shergill* (2012) Court of Appeal on religious charities
- *R (on the application of Hodkin and another) v. Registrar General of Births, Deaths and Marriages* [2013] UKSC 77 Supreme Court decision recognizing scientology to be a religion
- *Williams v. Central Bank of Nigeria* (2014) Supreme Court on limitation acts and third parties

Coverage of recent legislation, including:

- The Trusts (Capital and Income) Act 2013
- Estates of Deceased Persons (Forfeiture Rule and Law of Succession) Act 2011
- Expanded coverage of The Perpetuities and Accumulations Act 2009
- Expanded coverage of The Charities Act 2011

Plus references to recent scholarship and the work of relevant commissions, including:

- Charity Commission's 2013 official guidance on public benefit

Preface

The student approaching the subject of trusts and equity for the first time is faced with a constellation of textbooks from which to choose. It is a range of choice that testifies both to the dynamic nature of the subject and to the diverse opinions that it engenders in those who teach it. One commentator has even suggested that books on trusts may be a '*song without end*'. The present book is not the end of the song, but, hopefully, it contributes a new verse that is consonant with the needs of students and their tutors. The aim has been to produce a lucid and readable text of medium length, which provides comprehensive coverage of the subject matter of typical undergraduate courses in trusts and equity. At the same time, it is hoped that the student reader will be stimulated to engage in critical reflection upon the ever-shifting frontiers of the subject. For further inspiration, the reader is directed throughout the pages of this book to specialist academic works on particular aspects of the subject, many of the most influential of which are published by Oxford University Press.

My greatest satisfaction in more than two decades of teaching trusts and equity has been to demonstrate that a subject that students sometimes expect will be archaic, insignificant, and impenetrable is, in fact, highly relevant to contemporary commercial and family life—and, most importantly, is interesting and can be clearly understood. Accordingly, trusts in commerce, insolvency, pensions, and cohabitation figure prominently; a full third of the book is devoted to the nature of trusteeship and the consequences for trustees and third parties of breaches of trust. Special attention is reserved for the exercise of trust discretions, including the trustees' choice of investments, and to problems arising from the misapplication of trust property. It is not only trusts that are examined, but also 'trust-like', or fiduciary, relationships. Reference is also made to international trusts, to trusts based in foreign jurisdictions, and to the comparative law of trusts.

Every system of law must find a way in which to enable property to be held by one person for the benefit of another person—not least in the event of death or insolvency—and every system must find a way to enable a fund to be held for the advancement of purposes that are beneficial to the public. Jurisdictions not based on the English model have tended to find solutions in the laws of property and of obligations, but the English solution was to recognize a legal institution that is a genuine hybrid of property and obligation. That institution is the trust.

The unique feature of the trust is that the trustee does not merely possess or control the trust property for the purpose of fulfilling his personal obligations; he actually owns it in law, subject to the duties of his trust. Likewise, the beneficiary of the trust is not restricted to a mere personal right to take action against the trustee for breach of trust obligations; the beneficiary is the owner in equity of a beneficial interest in the trust property, and, in certain circumstances, may even bring the trust to an end and take the property absolutely. This distinctive ability of the trust to combine property owner-ship with personal obligation has rendered it uniquely flexible and uniquely effective as a method of protecting beneficiaries' interests. Today, the trust fulfils the function of collective investment in fields as diverse as pensions and charity, and it is employed to manage the distribution of estates when people die, or become bankrupt, or are inca-pacitated. It follows that the reader will profit greatly from an understanding of trusts, regardless of whether or not he or she intends one day to practise as a lawyer.

Each chapter advances certain key perspectives on its subject matter, with a view to challenging students to think critically, to stimulating discussions in tutorials, and, of course, to setting out the author's own opinions on the subject. The key perspectives provide a conceptual hub around which the relevant law is arranged within each chapter, but they also provide core concepts and perspectives that link one chapter to the next. If there is a strand that spans the length of the book it is the author's view that the trust is primarily an institutional mode of holding property, onto which trust obligations are overlaid. The image of the trust as property overlaid with obligations is particularly apt to describe expressly created trusts, but even non-express trusts are properly understood as being, first and foremost, modes of property ownership rather than forms of obligation.

Trust obligations are fluid. In an expressly created trust of the traditional sort, obliga-tions laid down by the general law are subject to the specific terms of the particular trust instrument and, in commercial contexts, general trust obligations are subject to, and sometimes submerged beneath, the terms of the parties' contractual deal. Nevertheless, although the obligations attached to a trust may change and although some may even be removed, or at least suspended for a while, underneath there will always be a trust as a matter of property law as long as the legal owner of certain property is entitled to less than the whole beneficial ownership in it.

Each chapter of the book begins with an introduction to the main themes of that chapter. Indeed, the reader may find it useful, before reading the substance of any one chapter, to read the introductions to all of the chapters. In this way, the reader will acquire an overview of the concepts that underpin the book and some insight into the subject as a whole.

The 16 chapters are arranged within five parts. In Part I, we examine the historical and conceptual foundations of trusts and equity, and we place trusts in their social context and in the context of other bodies of law, such as contract, tort, and restitution. A signifi-cant feature of the first chapter is an explanation of the symbiotic, functional relationship that exists between equity and law, including an argument in favour of a more rigorous, limited version of the doctrine of 'unconscionability' (the traditional basis of equitable intervention and invention). The first chapter also invites the reader to orientate his or her study of trusts and equity by means of four compass points, or perspectives: prece-dent, principle, policy, and pragmatism. Legal precedent and principle go only part of the way to determining the outcomes in the cases; wider policy and practical considerations continue to exert a great influence on the development of trusts and equity, and the law cannot be understood without a firm grasp of background policy concerns, and some appreciation of the way in which judges and lawyers work in practice.

In Part II, there are two chapters devoted expressly to key policy influences on the creation and recognition of trusts. Those influences have resulted in formality requirements, limitations on the duration of trusts, prohibition of illegal trusts, and recognition of trusts for charitable purposes. Also in this part, we consider the factors—which are often pragmatic—that lead courts to decide whether a disposition is a trust, an outright gift, or a mere power. We consider the requirements that must be met before a trust will be fully constituted and the consequences of failure to dispose of property effectively. Competing theoretical analyses of the resulting trust and of its (arguably illegitimate) offspring, the '*Quistclose* trust', are considered at length. A resulting trust is an example of a trust that is not created expressly; another, the constructive trust, can be described as the polar opposite of an express trust and is the main subject of the final chapter in this part.

Part III concerns the regulation of trusts. In a chapter on the flexibility of benefit, we examine the potential of a trust beneficiary to enjoy the trust property even when his or her interest in the trust property has not yet fully vested and even though that interest may never fully vest. The possibility of varying a trust is also examined, as are the motivations (usually tax avoidance) for doing so. The remainder of this part identifies the duties to which trustees are subject in the discharge of their office when exercising the powers that are theirs as an incident of their legal ownership of the trust property. There is a focus upon the tension that exists between insistence upon strict compliance with trust duties and ensuring that there is always someone willing to assume the office of trustee. The fiduciary duty, which is the defining duty of trusteeship and the basis for the recognition of other fiduciary ('trust-like') relationships, has a chapter to itself. It is suggested that the fiduciary duty is strictly applied for reasons of public policy in order to set an example and to encourage good behaviour in all who hold positions of trust. A chapter is also devoted to trust investment. It provides a context in which to examine the interplay of a number of significant trustee duties, including the duty of care, the duty to act fairly, the duty to exercise a sound discretion, and even the fiduciary duty. Investment is where obligation and property meet, but not every trust involves a fund in need of investment. Accordingly, much of the chapter on trustees' personal liability for breach of trust is concerned with bare trusts in commercial contexts, and the practical interplay in that context of the remedies of compensation and account. The classic bare trust is a bi-party trust in which the trustee holds the trust property on trust for a single beneficiary and it is perhaps because of its simple, bi-party character that notions of causation, remoteness of damage, and contributory negligence borrowed from the common law of tort are increasingly being introduced to determine trustees' liability for breaches of bare trusts in commercial contexts.

In Part IV, our attention turns to situations in which trust property has passed into the hands of a third party, and so must be followed and recovered, or its value traced and recovered. We will see that the beneficiary is entitled to assert a proprietary claim even when his property has been mixed with other property in the defendant's hands. However, the proprietary claim will fail if neither the claimant's property, nor its substitute, is presently in the defendant's possession or under his control. There are, in addition, defences available to the defendant in reply to such a claim: an unanswerable defence being that he purchased the claimant's property in good faith and without notice of the claimant's interest in it. If the defendant received trust property, but has not retained it, the beneficiary's proprietary claim will fail. In such a case, the beneficiary may be able to bring a claim against the defendant personally if the defendant's receipt was wrongful. The final part of this book, Part V, contains a single chapter devoted to equitable maxims, doctrines, and remedies.

Consistent with the primary aim of writing a lucid and readable text, I have not adopted any special convention on gender usage in this book, so the male gender is the default usage throughout. I have chosen not to use he/she or s(he) and I have tried to avoid 'their' and 'they' in reference to an individual. However, I have found the clarity of certain passages to be enhanced by referring to trustees in the male gender and beneficiaries in the female gender, and I have adopted that approach throughout the text wherever appropriate. It is true that the trustee has formal powers over the trust assets, but it is the beneficiary who has the substantial rights, so I hope I cannot be accused of perpetuating any stereotype. In practice, of course, trustees and beneficiaries are no more likely to be of one sex than the other; indeed, many modern trustees are, in fact, corporations.

The reader will observe that, throughout this book, there are numerous footnotes to the text. These footnotes serve at least three functions: first, they provide authority for the points made in the text; second, they identify fruitful sources of material for further reading; third, they identify useful cross-references between different chapters and sections of the text. Occasionally, a footnote is also useful for explaining technical, and especially non-English, terminology. The disadvantage of footnotes is that they can tend to disrupt the flow of a chapter, which can be a very significant disadvantage when a reader approaches a new book on a new subject for the first time. With this in mind, the author has endeavoured to ensure that the main body of the text makes sense without having to refer to the footnotes. On a first read-through, the student might even prefer to ignore the footnotes entirely so as to ensure that the trees do not obscure the forest.

The tree is a common metaphor for law. Law has deep roots, and many branches . . . and it never stops growing! Since the last edition, significant new laws have added several new leaves to this book. Important statutory developments and decisions of superior courts are considered as well as the latest Law Commission reform proposals and academic commentary. For a fuller list of recent developments, see the 'new to this edition' page.

Some things, however, do not change. I would, as ever, like to record my thanks to the many staff at Oxford University Press who have had a hand in the production of this new edition, and to thank my wife Emma and my sons, Jamie and Michael, for their encouragement and patience every time I have disappeared to my study.

Gary Watt
University of Warwick
April 2014

Table of cases

Table of statutes

Canada

Cayman Islands

France

New Zealand

USA

Table of statutory instruments

Table of conventions and treaties

PART I

Introduction to Trusts and Equity

1

Foundations

The aim of this chapter is to reveal the historical and conceptual foundations of trusts and equity. If it were possible to produce a permanent, definitive floor plan of our subject we might not need to consider its foundations; we could simply enter it and find our way around according to the map, but the law of trusts and equity is constantly being extended and added to: an established wall knocked through here; an extra level added there. Only with a firm understanding of the foundations of our subject will we know whether or not the present state of the law is sound and fit for its purpose, and how, if at all, it ought to be developed further. The student who understands the historical and conceptual foundations of the law, the processes by which it develops, and the political and practical pressures that influence the form it takes, will fare much better than the one who simply takes the law as read.

The first part of this chapter is an examination of the history of the relationship between law and equity, including the historical origins of the trust. It proceeds to explain the idea of equity and the symbiotic way in which equity and the common law function. The term 'equity' can be used to describe social fairness, or a branch of morality, or even an aspect of divine justice,[1] and all such uses are apt to shine a critical light upon the law.[2] For the purpose of this book, however, the term 'equity' simply connotes an established aspect of law and legal reasoning. Nowadays, when a judge hears a case, he or she has authority to administer the common law rules with equity. Equitable remedies, doctrines, and principles (many in the form of maxims) are considered in detail in the last chapter of this book.

The second part of this chapter is a preliminary introduction to the modern trust. The trust will be contrasted with concepts such as gift and contract, with which the reader will already have some everyday, if not technical, familiarity. We will see that the trust developed in response to equity's special concern to ensure that legal rights are not used in bad conscience, but that it later became a sophisticated institution governed by established rules, with the result that most problems concerning deliberately created trusts can now be resolved without recourse to equity's flexible, discretionary approach.

---

[1] Psalm 98:9: 'he cometh to judge the earth: with righteousness shall he judge the world, and the people with equity' (The Bible, King James version).

[2] See, further, G. Watt, *Equity Stirring: the Story of Justice Beyond Law* (Oxford: Hart Publishing, 2009).

Historical foundations

In the twelfth century, the royal court was largely itinerant. The majority of cases were heard locally by shire courts, hundred courts, and local lords.[3] Effective government required the King and his courtiers to travel the length and breadth of the realm collecting taxes, dispensing justice, and generally asserting royal authority. Thus the itinerary of Henry I took him as far afield as Carlisle, Norwich, Southampton, and Normandy, all within the years 1119–23, while still allowing time to campaign war in Wales. The King's Chancellor was one of the chief members of this travelling court. He was a learned cleric, usually a bishop, whose role was to advise the King as a member of his private ('privy') council. The Chancellor was keeper of the King's Great Seal, and beneath him were the Chancery scribes who were responsible for the King's paperwork (or parchment work, as it was then). The manuscripts of early Chancery proceedings helped to establish coherence in the law, and they also helped to standardize the English language, where previously there had been great regional variation.[4] Most other written material of the time was in Latin; hence Chancery became known as the English jurisdiction.[5] Writs bearing the royal seal were issued out of Chancery to deal with any matters of law and justice falling within the King's special concern or 'prerogative'. The *Leges Henrici Primi* (Laws of Henry I)[6] contain a long list of such matters, including murder, treason, governance of the forests, and such like. Most significant for us is that the King's prerogative included the power to deal with 'unjust judgment' and 'default of justice'.[7] Here, in the King's authority to issue writs out of Chancery to address the unjust judgments of his courts, is the seed of English equity.

By the early thirteenth century, certain royal writs could be purchased cheaply and directly from the Chancery,[8] and by the early fourteenth century, the forms of writ and the form of the King's common law had become very well established, even to the point of rigidity and inflexibility. In fact, as early as *The Provisions of Oxford 1258*, it was established that Chancery had no authority to issue novel writs without the prior approval of the King's council, so thereafter claimants had to show that the facts of their case fell within some existing form of writ in order to gain a remedy. Accordingly, petitions to the Chancellor became routine in the late thirteenth and early fourteenth centuries, as a way of escaping the rigidity of the common forms of writ and the judgments of the common law courts. It became an important function of the Chancellor, through his Chancery scribes, to exercise the King's prerogative of 'grace' or 'mercy' to grant special relief in particular cases. '*Mercy*' Shakespeare wrote, '*is enthroned in*

---

[3] See A. Harding, *The Law Courts of Medieval England* (London: Allen & Unwin, 1973) and J. Hudson, *The Formation of the English Common Law* (London: Longman, 1996) esp. 27–31.

[4] It is arguable that '[t]he geneology of modern Standard English goes back to Chancery, not Chaucer' (D. Crystal, *The Cambridge Encyclopedia of the English Language* (Cambridge: Cambridge University Press, 1995) at 41).   [5] F. W. Hardman, 'Equity and the Latin side of Chancery' (1952) 68 LQR 481.

[6] A miscellany of laws laid down c. 1100–35.

[7] *Leges Henrici Primi* 10.1 (L. J. Downer, ed. and trans.) (Oxford: Oxford University Press, 1972) at 108. See J. Hudson, op. cit, at 29.   [8] Hudson, ibid. at 136.

the hearts of kings, It is an attribute to God himself; And earthly power doth then show likest God's When mercy seasons justice.'[9] The establishment of the Chancellor's court depended upon a simple hierarchy typical of medieval thought: the King was accountable to God for the righteousness of his laws and the Chancellor, as 'keeper of the king's conscience', would act in particular cases to admit 'merciful exceptions' to the King's general laws, to ensure that the King's conscience was right before God. By extension of this hierarchy, the basis for granting relief became concern for the personal 'conscience' of the defendant in Chancery. The defendant would not be permitted to enforce a common law right or rely upon a lack of common law formality if to do so would be 'unconscionable'.[10] One common form of relief was an injunction granted by the Court of Chancery against the unconscionable enforcement of a common law judgment, with the threat of imprisonment for breach of the injunction.[11] This inevitably produced a rivalry between Chancery and the common law courts.

By the end of the fourteenth century, the Chancellor was dispensing justice on his own authority from his base at Westminster Hall (in the middle of that century, litigation caused by the 'Black Death' had caused the common law courts to be overwhelmed). As petitions to the Chancellor grew in number throughout the fifteenth and sixteenth centuries, the Court of Chancery expanded and records of the Chancellor's decisions gradually acquired the status of a separate body of legal authority distinct from the common law. The rivalry between Chancery and the common law courts came to a head in the early seventeenth century as exemplified by *The Earl of Oxford's Case*.[12] Judgment had been awarded against a defendant to a common law action who had then taken the not unusual step of applying to the Lord Chancellor for an injunction to prevent the enforcement of the common law judgment. The defendant claimed that the common law judgment entered against him had been obtained by fraud. The head of the common law courts, Sir Edward Coke,[13] Lord Chief Justice of the King's Bench, promptly indicted the defendant, but Lord Ellesmere granted the injunction in favour of the defendant, with the result that the common law and Chancery were at loggerheads. Coke argued that the Lord Chancellor was guilty of illegally hearing appeals from common law judgments, but Ellesmere reasoned that his injunction did not offend the common law courts. He argued that it merely operated *in personam* against the conscience of the person who had been successful at common law:

> The office of the Chancellor is to correct men's consciences for frauds, breach of trust, wrongs and oppressions, of what nature soever they be, and to soften and mollify the extremity of the law.[14]

[9] *The Merchant of Venice* (1597) IV:1.

[10] Macnair argues that unconscionability is the remnant of a test of conscience that was devised, not as a matter of principle, but as practical supplement to the shortcomings of common law processes of proof and evidence (Mike Macnair, 'Equity and Conscience' (2007) 27(4) OJLS 659).

[11] Even today, breach of an injunction is a contempt of court that may be punished by imprisonment. See, for example, *Patel v. Patel* [1988] 2 FLR 179. A further example is *Shalson v. Russo* [2003] EWHC 1637 (Ch), in which a fraudster was imprisoned for two years for breaching an equitable injunction that had frozen his assets.

[12] (1615) 1 Ch Rep 1.   [13] Pronounced 'Cook'.   [14] (1615) 1 Ch Rep 1 at 6, 7.

According to Lord Ellesmere, Chancery leaves the common law judgment in peace and is only concerned with the corrupt conscience of the party.

In 1616, the dispute between the Chief Justice and the Lord Chancellor was finally referred to King James I. On the advice of his Attorney General, Sir Francis Bacon, the King resolved the matter in favour of Lord Ellesmere.[15] The real reason underlying the King's decision to side with Chancery was not jurisprudential, but political. Bacon was a firm defender of the royal prerogative over the common law, whereas Sir Edward Coke favoured the supremacy of the common law over the royal prerogative. So Chancery, like that other peculiarly English institution, the Church of England, traces its independence and pre-eminence as much to a clash of political wills as to any doctrinal dispute. Coke was dismissed from office shortly after *The Earl of Oxford's Case* and, the following year, Bacon succeeded Lord Ellesmere as Lord Chancellor. Less than 30 years after *The Earl of Oxford's Case*, the issue of royal prerogative was to become a prime cause of the English Civil War.

Confident in its new status, equity matured through the seventeenth century like a good port wine of the sort so popular at the time. One of the Chancellors of this period was Sir Heneage Finch, Earl of Nottingham,[16] who has rightly been called the father of modern equity.[17] The doctrine of clogs on the equity of redemption, which enabled borrowers to redeem their mortgaged land free from unconscionable conditions, and the modern rule against perpetuities[18] find their source in his judgments. However, it was a frequent criticism of Chancery in the sixteenth and seventeenth centuries that the Chancellor's discretion to dispense justice ad hoc on the ground of 'conscience' produced justice that varied markedly in quality from one Lord Chancellor to the next. Thus one sixteenth-century lawyer asked whether '*it be meet that the Chancellor should appoint unto himselfe, and publish to others any certaine Rules & Limits of Equity*'.[19] In the mid-seventeenth century, such criticism had become a standing joke, hence John Selden's famous observation that the official measure of justice might as well be the foot, because it varies according to the length of the Chancellor's foot.[20] In fact, even that assessment may have been overgenerous in so far as it suggests that each Chancellor always acted consistently with his own previous judgments. In truth, the imprint of the Chancellor's foot would frequently vary from case to case.

In the eighteenth century, Enlightenment philosophy helped to free equity from its early association with the royal prerogative and ecclesiastic notions of conscience, so that it became, in Enlightenment terms at least, a 'rational' feature of the law. This was followed in the nineteenth century by a period of consolidation and development,

---

[15] Hence the maxim 'where equity and law conflict equity prevails'. See Chapter 16.

[16] Lord Chancellor, 1675–82.

[17] Sir W. Holdsworth, *History of English Law* (London: Methuen, 1966) vol. VI at 547.

[18] See Chapter 6.

[19] W. Lambarde, quoted in S. F. C. Milsom, *Historical Foundations of the Common Law*, 2nd edn (London: Butterworths, 1981) at 94.   [20] *Table Talk of John Selden* (ed. F. Pollock, 1927) at 43.

culminating in the procedural unification of the Court of Chancery with the courts of common law (this is considered in the next section). The late nineteenth century can also be regarded as the golden age of the settlement trust.

By the twentieth century, it was generally accepted that 'equity's naked power of improvisation' had long since been 'spent'.[21] One judge even asserted that '[i]n the field of equity the Chancellor's foot has been measured or is capable of measurement', although his Lordship added the following caveat:

> This does not mean that equity is past child-bearing; simply that its progeny must be legitimate—by precedent out of principle.[22]

Reform of Chancery procedure

A victim of its own success, by the early nineteenth century, the Court of Chancery had become hopelessly busy. The creation at this time of strict rules preventing trustees from entering certain species of transaction,[23] which rules still survive today,[24] has been attributed to the fact that the courts were frantically busy, and were therefore unable to examine the rights and wrongs of individual transactions in any detail.[25] The appointment, in 1729, of the Master of the Rolls (the chief Chancery Master) to sit as a second judge in certain cases had done little to reduce the burden on the Chancellor, because any decision of the Master of the Rolls could still be appealed to the Chancellor. It was not until 1833 that the Master of the Rolls had a true concurrent jurisdiction. In 1813, a Vice-Chancellor was appointed to assist the Chancellor and the Master of the Rolls. Yet when, in 1816, Sir Launcelot Shadwell VC was asked by a Commission of Inquiry whether the three judges could cope, he is said to have replied: '*No; not three angels*'.[26]

The Chancery judges were, indeed, overworked and increasingly unable to cope with the demands made upon them. In 1616, the supremacy of equity had been established as a means of escaping the common law jurisdiction, but by the nineteenth century, because of the backlog of administration in the Court of Chancery, escape was often sought in the other direction. Even as late as 1852, it appears that claimants were attempting to avoid the queue to the Chancellor's door by asserting concurrent common law rights arising out of facts that ought to have been the exclusive concern of the Court of Chancery. Thus in *Edwards v. Lowndes*,[27] Lord Campbell CJ had to remind

---

[21] R. P. Meagher, W. M. C. Gummow, and J. R. F. Lehane, *Equity, Doctrines and Remedies*, 2nd edn (Sydney: Butterworths, 1984) at 68–9. [22] *Cowcher v. Cowcher* [1972] 1 All ER 943, *per* Bagnall J at 948.
[23] *Keech v. Sandford* (1726) Sel Cas Ch 61. [24] See Chapter 10.
[25] J. H. Langbein, 'Questioning the trust law duty of loyalty: sole interest or best interest?' (2005) 114 Yale L J 929, 987–90.
[26] Cited in G. R. V. Radcliffe and G. Cross, *The English Legal System*, 3rd edn (London: Butterworths, 1954) at 153, n. 1. Note that, under the Constitutional Reform Act 2005, the Vice-Chancellor is renamed 'Chancellor of the High Court'. [27] (1852) 1 El & Bl 81.

litigants that a trustee is accountable to the beneficiaries of his trust in equity, but not at common law:

> no action at law for money had and received can be maintained against him, though he has money in his hands which under the terms of the trust he ought to pay over to the cestui que trust.[28]

The Court of Chancery Act 1850 and the Court of Chancery Procedure Act 1852 were early attempts to wrestle with the procedural problems in the Court of Chancery, the latter appearing in the same year as the first instalment of *Bleak House*, Charles Dickens's great satire on delays in Chancery.[29] However, the major step towards expediting the procedure of Chancery did not come until Lord Chancellor Selborne introduced the Judicature Act 1873 into Parliament. Ironically, it was due to administrative delays that the statute did not, in fact, come into force until 1875, when it was re-enacted with amendments. We now refer collectively to the Judicature Acts 1873–75. By these enactments, the Supreme Court of Judicature was established with concurrent jurisdiction to administer the rules of equity and law within a unified procedural system. Today, the same judges administer both law and equity.

The historical development of the trust

The progenitor of the trust was the 'use'.[30] Later, we will examine the shared history of the use and the trust in detail, but in simple terms we can say that the trust of land began its life when medieval monks wished to enjoy the benefit of land without infringing their vow of poverty by actually being owners of the land.[31] A more colourful account suggests that the trust originated when early medieval landowners went abroad on religious crusades and pilgrimages, leaving behind their families and their lands.[32] Before he 'took up the cross', the crusader would make a legal transfer of his lands to a trusted friend. The trusted friend, or 'trustee', would then be the legal owner of the land, with all the legal rights and powers that entails, but he would be aware that his duty was to re-convey the land to the crusader on his return and, in the meantime, to hold the land for the benefit of the crusader's family. If the trustee, asserting his legal entitlement to the lands, refused to account to the crusader's family for rents received on the lands, or otherwise exercised his legal entitlement in bad conscience, the crusader's family

---

[28] (1852) 1 El & Bl 81 at 89. *Cestui que trust* (pronounced 'settee key trust') is an archaic description of a trust beneficiary. Translated from the medieval French, it means 'the one who trusts'. It is hard to find a case within the past 30 years in which the term has been used.

[29] The novel, which was published in serialized form during 1852 and 1853, was an historical critique of Chancery procedures, which had already been, in large part, reformed by the time the novel was written. See W. S. Holdsworth, *Charles Dickens as a Legal Historian* (New Haven: Yale University Press, 1928).

[30] See, generally, N. G. Jones, 'Uses, trusts and a path to privity' [1997] 56(1) CLJ 175.

[31] Holdsworth, op. cit., vol. IV, at 415.

[32] For an interesting argument that the crusaders might have brought the idea of the trust back from the crusades see M. M. Gaudiosi, 'The influence of the Islamic law of Waqf on the development of the trust in England: the case of Merton College' (1988) 136 U Pa L Rev 1231.

(the 'beneficiaries' of the trust as we would call them today) had no rights at law, but could petition the King for justice in the light of the circumstances of their particular case. If he was moved to, the King would exercise his royal prerogative and order the recalcitrant trustee to do his duty, and if the trustee had wrongfully paid away the rents to a third party, the King would make an order against the third party. In every case, the order operated '*in personam*' against the personal conscience of the trustee or the third party, but initially the beneficiaries of the trust had no property right in the trust assets.[33] We will now turn to consider the historical relationship between the trust and the use.

As early as the seventh and eighth centuries, the common law had a form of 'use' in relation to chattels and money, under which money had and received by A 'for the use of B' subjected A to common law obligations in relation to the use of the money. If A refused to account to B, B could bring an action to account which came to resemble something like a modern action for breach of trust.[34] This common law 'trust' for the payment of money was enforced long before Chancery recognized trusts of land.

It was in relation to land that '[t]he use simply could not be fitted into the common law scheme of things, for the doctrine of estates and the doctrine of seisin left no place for the separation of beneficial enjoyment from legal title'.[35] (The doctrines of estates and seisin merely contemplated the state of a feudal tenant's legal entitlement relative to that of his overlord.) However, the Chancellor was prepared to recognize the use of land and, as early as the beginning of the thirteenth century, it was acknowledged to be a practical device for separating legal title from beneficial enjoyment. Thus if Sir Guy de Pends were about to depart for the crusades, he might choose to convey the estate in his land (the 'feoffment to uses') to his trusted friend Sir Richard de Livers (the 'feoffee to uses') 'for the use and benefit of Lady de Pends and her children'. Sir Richard would thereby become solely entitled to the land at law, but with an obligation to exercise his entitlement for the exclusive benefit of Lady de Pends and her children, and to re-convey the land to Sir Guy on his eventual return from the crusades. The use in this form did not bind the land itself so as to confer a property right on Lady de Pends and the children; rather, it was conceived as a personal confidence reposed in Sir Richard de Livers, binding upon his conscience and the conscience of any third party (other than a bona fide purchaser of the legal estate for value without notice of the use) into whose name Sir Richard might choose to pass the legal title.[36] The Chancellor ensured that Sir Richard did not place unconscionable reliance upon his legal title to the detriment of Sir Guy, Lady de Pends, and their children. From the King's point of view, there was a significant downside to the recognition of the use. The King was entitled, as supreme overlord in the medieval feudal system of land ownership, to levy valuable feudal 'fines'

---

[33] P. Vinogradoff, 'Reason and conscience in the fifteenth and sixteenth centuries' (1908) 29 LQR 373, 379.

[34] *Taillour v. Medwe* (1320) Year Books of Edward II, 14 Edward II (London: Selden Society, 1988) vol. 104, at 39 and xi.

[35] A. W. B. Simpson, *An Introduction to the History of the Land Law*, 2nd edn (Oxford: Clarendon Press, 1986), esp. ch. 8 on 'Uses and the statute' at 175.   [36] Simpson, op. cit., at 170.

or 'incidents' whenever land was inherited or an owner died without an heir. The use provided a way of circumventing these feudal incidents by allowing the owner of land to place his legal title in a number of persons who could be replaced periodically, so ensuring that the land always had a living legal owner and that legal title would never be inherited or left without an heir. In the meantime, the true beneficiary of the land was able to continue in occupation of the land and to reap the benefits of the land, so that the use can be regarded as an early 'tax avoidance scheme'. The use was also subject to the complaint that, because of it, *'no man can know his title to any land with certainty'*.[37] In response to these various objections to the use, Henry VIII enacted the Statute of Uses 1536.[38] The effect of the statute was to transfer legal title to the beneficiary of the use (the so-called *cestui que use*), thereby bringing the use to an end or 'executing' it. By means of this statute, Henry VIII executed a great many uses, but as with his wives, he did not execute them all. The only uses that were executed were those concerning land for which there was a single named beneficiary, usually the original absolute owner, and which therefore represented a sham device for avoiding feudal incidents. Eventually, of course, inventive legal draftsmen found creative ways of avoiding the statute entirely. One such was a 'use upon a use' in the generic form: 'to A to the use of B to the use of C'. It was supposed that the effect of the Statute of Uses would be to execute the first use by vesting legal title in B, who would then be obliged to hold it to the use of the intended beneficiary, C. This supposition was confirmed by the routine enforcement in Chancery of B's conscientious obligation to observe the use upon a use in favour of C. In the seventeenth century, the Chancellors *'began to enforce the use upon a use as a trust'*,[39] leading one commentator to observe that a *'bastardly use'* had started up *'by the true name which the use had at first—which is "trust and confidence"'*.[40] By the end of the seventeenth century, it was not even necessary for A to be mentioned at all: Chancery was content to enforce a form of conveyance 'to B, unto and to the use of B, in trust for C'.[41] Chancery was doubtless comforted in this approach by the enactment of the Tenures Abolition Act of 1660, which removed the feudal incidents that the Statute of Uses had been introduced to protect. The interest of C, the *cestui que trust*, could only be defeated by a bona fide purchaser of the legal estate for value without notice of C's interest, and so the modern form of equitable ownership[42] and the modern trust were conceived.[43]

It is something of a mystery how and why a mere personal right against a particular defendant, based upon his possession of a thing and the corresponding burden on his

---

[37] T. Audley, *Reading on Uses* (1526) (a reading on 4 Hen. 7, c. 17) cited in J. H. Baker and S. F. C. Milsom, *Sources of English Legal History: Private Law to 1750* (London: Butterworths, 1986) at 103.

[38] 27 Hen. 8, c.10.

[39] Sir W. Holdsworth, *History of English Law*, 2nd edn (London: Methuen, 1937) vol. VI, at 641.

[40] H. Sherfield, *Reading on Wills* (1623) at 32. (This publication is a commentary on the Statute of Wills 1540, Hen. 8, c.1.) See, generally, M. Lupoi, 'Trust and Confidence' (2009) 125 LQR 253.

[41] Simpson, op. cit., at 187–8. Baker and Milsom, op. cit., at 125–6.

[42] *Sinclair v. Brougham* [1914] AC 398, HL, *per* Lord Parker of Waddington at 441–2.

[43] Sir W. Holdsworth, *A History of English Law*, 3rd edn, vol. IV (London: Methuen, Sweet & Maxwell, 1945) at 433.

conscience, became a property right in the thing enforceable by the beneficiary against the whole world, apart from the bona fide purchaser for value of a legal estate without notice. The answer may lie in the pragmatism and economy of the equity judges. As we know, there never were many equity judges in the old Court of Chancery and those few were hopelessly overburdened. They could not have failed to appreciate the savings on their time that could be achieved if, instead of having to examine the conscience of each alleged trustee or recipient of trust property on a case-by-case basis, they were to protect trust beneficiaries generally by recognizing them to have proprietary rights in the trust assets. The Chancery judges would have been familiar with the relatively efficient common law system of proprietary entitlement and, by adopting a version of it, they 'followed the common law'. Crucially, though, equity's idea of property was not as extensive as that of the common law; hence the recognition of the superiority of legal title by means of the 'bona fide purchaser' exception (according to which, the proprietary title of a mere 'equitable owner' does not bind the good faith purchaser of legal title who paid value and had no notice of the equitable interest). Had equitable property been made coextensive with legal title, equity would have effectively undermined the common law of proprietary title. It is because of these inherent limitations of equitable property that it cannot properly be said to confer true rights '*in rem*',[44] although that term (somewhat unhelpfully adopted from the Roman law, which has no concept of division between legal and equitable property)[45] is still often used as shorthand to describe a beneficiary's proprietary right in the trust property.

Whatever the explanation for how and why the beneficiary's mere personal right against a particular defendant became a property right in the trust asset, it is now clear that when the absolute owner of an asset transfers it to trustees on express trusts for certain beneficiaries, the effect is to vest legal title to the property in the trustees and equitable title (also called equitable or beneficial 'ownership') in the beneficiaries. Of course, when we use the language of equitable 'title' and equitable 'ownership', this is just convenient shorthand to describe the most distinctive and potent feature of the beneficiaries' interest under a trust, which is its proprietary status, i.e. its ability to bind third parties other than the trustee. One must not be confused by the shared shorthand into thinking that equitable title is the mirror-image of legal title.[46] Equity's operation and proprietary effect is, as we will see, very different to that of law.

Professor Lionel Smith has suggested that the most significant and surprising step in the evolution of the use to the trust was not that the use came to bind strangers who wrongfully accepted a transfer of the feoffment from the feoffee, but that the court decided that it should bind those who had *innocently* inherited the feoffment from the feoffee. This is a strong argument, for an innocent successor commits no wrong, unless it is the wrongful *retention* of property to which someone else has better title.

---

[44] 'In the thing'.   [45] D. Johnston, *The Roman Law of Trusts* (Oxford: Clarendon Press, 1988).
[46] This warning is reiterated in James Edelman, 'Two Fundamental Questions for the Law of Trusts' (2013) 129 LQR 66.

It would have been understandable had equity declined to recognize any burden on the conscience of the innocent inheritor. According to Professor Smith, the decision of the Chancery judges to enforce such a burden was the decision that transformed a personal right over a thing in the hands of the feoffee[47] into a proprietary right in the thing[48] binding on the whole world (other than innocent purchasers without notice). The crux of Smith's argument is that the step to recognizing the proprietary right was made possible because the personal right already had a *negative* proprietary aspect, in so far as every person in the world was already under an obligation not to commit any wrongful interference with the beneficiary's personal right against the feoffee.[49] We will return to this argument in later chapters.

Conceptual foundations

The purpose of this section is to introduce the modern concepts of equity and trust; with a special focus on how equity relates to the common law and how the trust relates to other legal institutions, such as company and contract. The relationship of equity to common law is considered further throughout the book, and especially in Chapters 14 and 16. Chapter 16 contains a very detailed examination of equitable principles (maxims), doctrines, and remedies. The relationship of the trust to other legal institutions is considered further throughout the book, and especially in Chapter 2, where the trust is contrasted with such legal institutions as contract, corporation, and charge.

Equity

Equity is a body of principles, doctrines, and rules, developed originally by the old Court of Chancery in constructive competition with the rules, doctrines, and principles of the common law courts, but now applied, since the Judicature Acts 1873–75, by the unified Supreme Court of England and Wales. The abolition of the old Court of Chancery and courts of common law has led to the suggestion that the distinction between law and equity is now obsolete; that the two systems of law have become 'fused'. The better view is that the common law and equity remain distinct, but mutually dependent, aspects of law.[50] They 'are working in different ways towards the same ends, and it is therefore as wrong to assert the independence of one from the other as it is to assert that there is no difference between them'.[51]

---

[47] A *jus in personam ad rem*.   [48] A *jus in rem*.

[49] L. Smith, *Transfers in Breach of Trust* (P. Birks and A. Pretto, eds) (Oxford: Hart Publishing, 2002) at 123.

[50] The term 'common law' is here used in contrast with 'equity', but it should be borne in mind that 'common law' and 'equity' are both parts of the common law, as that term is used to distinguish the English precedent-based system of law from code-based or 'civil' systems of law derived from the Roman model. To confuse matters still further, the term 'common law' can be used in a third sense, to describe English case law in contradistinction to English statutory law.

[51] Radcliffe and Cross, op. cit., at 116.

The difficulty with asserting the independence of law from equity is inherent in Professor Ashburner's attempt to describe equity and law as different streams running in the same channel without mingling their waters.[52] The metaphor does not work: it is no more sensible to suppose that two streams of water could be kept separate within the same channel than to suppose that the same judges sitting in the same courts could dispense two truly independent forms of justice. However, the assertion that equity and the common law are identical is equally inaccurate. Lord Diplock was no doubt correct to observe, in *United Scientific Holdings Ltd v. Burnley Borough Council*, that the waters of Ashburner's confluent streams have mingled,[53] but his Lordship was surely guilty of the so-called 'fusion fallacy' if he meant to suggest that there is no longer any substantial functional difference between equity and the common law. The learned authors of the Australian textbook *Meagher, Gummow, and Lehane on Equity* took the view that their Lordships, in *United Scientific*, had been guilty of that very error, indeed they described their Lordships' decision as '*the low water mark of modern English jurisprudence*'.[54] Professor Peter Birks took a more charitable view of Lord Diplock's intent, observing (with yet another aquatic metaphor) that:

> it is dangerous, not to say absurd, almost 120 years after the Judicature Acts, to persist in habits of thought calculated to submerge and conceal one or other half of our law.[55]

This brings us back to our initial view, surely the correct one, that the common law and equity are mutually dependent aspects of all law:

> Neither law nor equity is now stifled by its origin and the fact that both are administered by one Court has inevitably meant that each has borrowed from the other in furthering the harmonious development of the law as a whole.[56]

The functional distinction between equity and law

The distinction between equity and law must be understood at the level of function, not form. The eminent legal historian, Professor J. H. Baker, has observed that:

> If, for reasons of history, equity had become the law peculiar to the Court of Chancery, nevertheless in broad theory equity was an approach to justice which gave more weight than did the law to particular circumstances and hard cases.[57]

It is because equity is functionally distinct from the common law that both approaches to law survived the Judicature Acts, which brought about the physical and jurisdictional unification of the old Court of Chancery with the courts of common law.

---

[52] Professor Ashburner, *Principles of Equity*, 1st edn (1902) at 23.
[53] *United Scientific Holdings Ltd v. Burnley Borough Council* [1978] AC 904, *per* Lord Diplock at 924–5.
[54] Op cit. at xi.
[55] *Civil Wrongs: A New World, The Butterworth Lectures, 1990–91* (London: Butterworths, 1992) at 55.
[56] *Elders Pastoral Ltd v. Bank of New Zealand* [1989] 2 NZLR 180, *per* Somer J at 193.
[57] Op. cit. at 132–3.

The function of the common law is to establish rules to govern the generality of cases; the effect of those rules is to recognize that certain persons will acquire certain legal rights and powers in certain circumstances. Legal rules allow the holders of legal rights and powers to exercise them in the confidence that they are entitled to do so. But *'in some cases it is necessary to leave the words of the Law, and follow that* [which] *Reason and Justice requireth, and to that intent Equity is ordained; that is to say, to temper and mitigate the rigor of the Law'.*[58] The function of equity is to restrain or restrict the exercise of legal rights and powers in particular cases, whenever it would be unconscionable for them to be exercised to the full. It is also said that equity 'supplements' the shortcomings of the common law, but if that is correct, it is nevertheless the case that equity only supplements the common law when, by doing so, it can prevent unconscionable reliance on the shortcomings of the common law.

'Unconscionable' cannot be defined in the abstract; it can only be understood in connection to the facts of particular cases.[59] The question is always whether it would be unconscionable to exercise *this* legal right or power in *this* factual context.[60] Unconscionable conduct *'is not by itself sufficient to found liability'.*[61] The most that can be said of a general nature is that unconscionability *'will commonly involve the use of or insistence upon legal entitlement to take advantage of another's special vulnerability or misadventure . . . in a way that is unreasonable or oppressive to an extent that affronts ordinary minimum standards of fair dealing'.*[62]

Even the legal rights that accompany the legal title to a fee simple absolute in possession, the most complete form of ownership known to land law, are not beyond equity's jurisdiction to restrain an unconscionable abuse. So, for example, if the legal owner of the fee simple title to land invites a stranger to build a house upon it, having raised in that stranger a legitimate expectation that the stranger will thereby acquire a beneficial interest in the land, and the stranger duly builds the house in reliance on the assurance given by the legal owner, equity restrains the legal owner from asserting the absolute quality of his legal title. The legal owner will not be able to exercise his usual legal right to evict trespassers in order to evict the stranger.[63]

It may be true, as Millett LJ suggested in *Jones & Sons (a firm) v. Jones*,[64] that the common law itself has sometimes had regard for considerations of conscience, but if the common law has ever prevented a person from placing unconscionable reliance upon a legal rule or right or power, it was then performing an equitable function.

---

[58] Christopher St German, *Dialogue in English between a Doctor of Divinity and a Student in the Laws of England etc* (London: Treverys, 1530) (ch. XVI).

[59] *National Westminster Bank plc v. Morgan* [1985] AC 686, *per* Lord Scarman at 709.

[60] *Royal Brunei v. Tan* [1995] 3 WLR 64, *per* Lord Nicholls at 76B–D.

[61] Sir Nicolas Browne-Wilkinson, Presidential Address of the President of the Holdsworth Club (Holdsworth Club, University of Birmingham, 1991) at 7.

[62] *The Commonwealth v. Verwayen* [1990] 170 CLR 394, *per* Deane J at 441.

[63] See 'Proprietary estoppel', discussed in Chapter 8. See, generally, E. Cooke, *The Modern Law of Estoppel* (Oxford: Oxford University Press, 2000).

[64] [1996] 3 WLR 703, at 710E, CA ('It would . . . be a mistake to suppose that the common law courts disregarded considerations of conscience').

Equity does not always consider it to be unconscionable for a party to take advantage of a legal right in a way that is 'sharp', or even oppressive and unfair. So, for example, in *Liverpool Marine Credit Co v. Hunter*,[65] the defendants (the owners of a ship subject to a mortgage) deliberately sent the ship to Louisiana knowing that Louisiana did not recognize mortgages of ships. The plaintiff argued that the defendant had committed a positive fraud. The judge held that the defendant owed no duty to the plaintiff:

> I do not...see how Equity could properly interfere to restrain the actions which, however oppressive...arose out of remedies employed by the plaintiff for the recovery of his debt, of which the law entitled him to avail himself.[66]

It is not uncommon for a judge to express his disapproval of the way in which a party has exercised a legal right or power and to conclude, nevertheless, that equity is powerless to do anything about it.[67] The court will even *insist upon* morally dubious conduct, such as breaking a non-contractual 'gentleman's agreement' entered into by a trustee, if the financial interests of the beneficiaries require it.[68]

The essential point is that equity is meant to regulate and supplement the general law; it is not meant to undermine the general law with exceptions. In short, 'equity follows the law'.[69] Having said that, the former Chief Justice of Australia, Sir Anthony Mason, is not alone in taking a different view. He has suggested that:

> by providing for the administration of the two systems of law by one supreme court and by prescribing the paramountcy of equity, the Judicature Acts freed equity from its position on the coat-tails of the common law and positioned it for advances beyond its old frontiers.[70]

From this starting point, his Lordship contends that the neighbourhood principle in the common law tort of negligence might conceivably have been developed in equity, rather than in the common law tort of negligence.[71] This writer would respectfully disagree. It is not, and should not be, equity's task to determine which forms of social behaviour ought to give rise to justiciable obligations; equity should be concerned with one form of wrongful behaviour, and one only; namely, the unconscionable abuse of rights and powers established by the common law. Equity follows the law, '*coat-tails*' and all. The distinction between common law and equity is predicated on an immutable distinction between their functions. The function of the common law is to lay down rules for society, generally—to regulate society one might say—whereas the function of equity is to regulate the common law.[72] Remove this distinction and one entirely removes any meaningful distinction between common law and equity, leaving one with

---

[65] (1868) LR 3 Ch App at 479.   [66] Ibid. at 487.

[67] See, for example, *Re McArdle* [1951] 1 Ch 669 at 676 (in Chapter 4).

[68] *Buttle v. Saunders* [1950] 2 All ER 193.   [69] See Chapter 16.

[70] 'The place of equity and equitable remedies in the contemporary common law world' (1994) 110 LQR 238 at 239.   [71] Ibid.

[72] 'The daily relations of man and man are governed by the common law, tempered but slightly with equity': Sir Owen Dixon, *Jesting Pilate*, at 13 (cited by The Hon. Mr Justice G. A. Kennedy, 'Equity in a commercial context', in *Equity and Commercial Relationships* (P. Finn, ed.) (Sydney: The Law Book Co, 1987) at 1).

no distinction apart from that based on the bland historical observation that equity is the form of law developed in the old Court of Chancery prior to the Judicature Acts.

Unconscionability, morality, and social values

Chris: 'We took a contract.'

Vin: 'It's not the kind any court would enforce.'

Chris: 'That's just the kind you gotta keep.'

This dialogue between the characters played by Yul Brynner and Steve McQueen in the MGM classic, *The Magnificent Seven*,[73] expresses the fundamental incompetence of courts to deal with matters of private moral conscience and social obligation. Sir Anthony Mason made substantially the same point when sitting as the Chief Justice of Australia:

> The breaking of a promise, without more, is morally reprehensible, but not unconscionable in the sense that equity will necessarily prevent its occurrence or remedy the consequent loss.[74]

Equity's concern with unconscionability is a concern for only a limited branch of immoral or antisocial behaviour—namely, the immoral or antisocial abuse of legal rights. Attempts to use equity as a vehicle for the promotion of morality and social justice must be sensitive to this limitation or they will fail. Thus Margaret Halliwell is right to observe that '*conscience, as represented by the body of law we all know as equity, contributes a key "morality" to the legal system in general*'[75] and that equity '*operates as an anti-legal element* via *the judicial modification of existing rules of law by reference to current conditions and circumstances*'[76] (or '*matches established principle to the demands of social change*'[77] as one senior judge put it). But Halliwell overestimates equity's functional capacity when she suggests that, in the context of trust law, equity '*prescribes optimum standards of behaviour in social relationships of trust*'.[78] Equity doubtless exemplifies or demonstrates a legal form of trusting through its enforcement of the trust, and the legal paradigm might influence social perceptions. In fact, a person who wants to entrust assets to another will often rely on an equitable trust (the sort a court will enforce) precisely because mere moral trust will not guarantee performance of the obligation.[79] However, it is going too far to suggest that equity 'prescribes' standards of social behaviour. If that is a legal function, it is a function of the general law we call the 'common law'.

Caution must be exercised before notions of social and moral wrongdoing are introduced into the interpretation of unconscionability. Judges can do no more than promote

---

[73] John Sturges (dir.) Metro Goldwyn Meyer, 1960.

[74] *The Commonwealth v. Verwayen* (1990) 170 CLR 394 at 416.

[75] *Equity and Good Conscience in A Contemporary Context* (London: Old Bailey Press, 1997) at 1–2.

[76] Ibid. at 5.   [77] Waite LJ in *Midland Bank v. Cooke* [1995] 2 FLR 915 at 927D.

[78] Op. cit. at 142.

[79] *Ullah v. Ullah* [2013] EWHC 2296 (Ch) joins a long line of cases in which an owner claimed to have trusted someone (in this case his son) but found to his cost that he had failed to create a trust that a court could recognize.

their own 'reasonable', 'objective' ideas of morality and society.[80] It was observed long ago that even when a judge is conscious that he has no right to '*Dictate according to his Will and Pleasure*', he will nevertheless look to his own moral ideas and perceptions of society, to what he perceives to be 'that infallible Monitor within his own Breast'.[81]

One should not lose sight of the relatively narrow sphere within which unconscionability and equity operate. Equity is singularly uncritical of a vast range of behaviour that might be regarded as immoral or antisocial. No court of law, not even the old Court of Chancery, is in any moral sense a court of conscience.[82] In 1594, a leading scholar of English law made the following telling observation:

> There is a difference between Equitie and Clemencie: for Equitie is always most firmly knit to the evil of the Law which way soever it bends, whether to clemency, or to severity.[83]

And it is a myth to suppose that courts of law (and equity) are concerned with social justice per se. If 99 per cent of all wealth were in the hands of 1 per cent of the population, this would be a great social inequality, but equity would have nothing to say on the matter. Equity, especially in the context of trusts law, is concerned with supporting or vindicating private rights to property; it is not its business to reassess the political correctness or moral 'righteousness' of wealth.

Equity hardens into rights

It has been suggested that one way of describing the difference between common law and equity is to say that common law seeks to achieve justice in the generality of cases, through certainty, whereas equity seeks to prevent injustice occurring in individual cases as a result of the application of general legal rules. Of course, such a simple statement could never be the whole story. For one thing, although equity is, in theory, unconcerned with the generality of cases, in that it does not share the common law's concern to lay down rules for the general governance of society, equity is a pragmatic and efficient system of law, and the equity judges have always been concerned to respect precedents laid down by other equity judges. So, if a judge has restrained the unconscionable exercise of a legal right in one particular case, future judges will tend to apply equity to restrain the unconscionable exercise of a legal right in every like case. Over time, this means that awarding equitable relief in certain common types of case tends to be routine. Hence the rhetorical question posed by Lord Eldon, the Lord Chancellor, in *Muckleston v. Brown*:[84]

> Is the court to feel for individuals and to oblige persons to discover in particular cases and not to feel for the whole of its own system and compel a discovery of frauds that go to the root of its whole system?[85]

---

[80] See, generally, G. Teubner (ed.), *Autopoietic Law: A New Approach to Law and Society* (Berlin, 1988); G. Watt, 'Giving unto Caesar: rationality, reciprocity and legal recognition of religion' in *Current Legal Issues: Law and Religion* (R. O'Dair and A. Lewis, eds) (Oxford: Oxford University Press, 2001) at 45–64.

[81] R. Francis, *Maxims of Equity* (Fleet Street: J. Stephens, 1727).

[82] *Re Telescriptor Syndicate* [1903] 2 Ch 174, *per* Buckley J at 196.

[83] W. West, *Symboleography* (London, 1594) section 28.

[84] (1801) 6 Ves Jun 52.   [85] Ibid. at 69.

When, over time, equitable relief is routinely granted to restrain unconscionability in certain types of case, it might make sense to say that the equitable claimant is *entitled* to his relief and therefore that he has an equitable *right* to a remedy. This tendency of equity to become rule-bound over time has been called the '*the decadence of equity*'.[86] One case in which this has clearly occurred is the recognition that trust beneficiaries have equitable proprietary rights in, or 'equitable title' to, trust property. Nowadays, with the possible exception of the constructive trust,[87] there really isn't very much equity in the trust, at least not that flexible equity which is functionally distinct from the common law. Bernard Rudden was correct to observe that the traditional distinction between law and equity '*provides only an historical and not a rational account of the trust*'.[88]

Trust

The trust is a unique way of owning property under which assets are held by a trustee for the benefit of another person, or for certain purposes, in accordance with special equitable obligations. The trust should be contrasted with absolute ownership, because a person who is solely and absolutely entitled to an asset is entitled to the exclusive and unrestricted right to possess, use, and otherwise enjoy the asset for his *own* benefit (he is even at liberty to abuse and destroy it), subject only to limitations imposed by statute as a matter of public policy[89] and limitations imposed to take account of the rights of others to enjoy the assets they own absolutely.[90]

It is helpful to contrast the trust with other legal ideas, such as absolute gift and contract, with which the reader may already be familiar.[91] If the owner of this book wishes to make an absolute gift of it to one of next year's students, he or she simply has to transfer possession of the book in circumstances which indicate that an absolute gift is intended. Words such as 'happy birthday', 'this is for you', or 'I don't need this any more' will suffice. Transferring possession of an ordinary moveable asset is sufficient to transfer legal title[92] and, where an absolute gift is intended, the transfer of legal title also has the effect of conferring the exclusive right to the beneficial use and enjoyment of the asset on the transferee. In contrast, transfer of legal title to a transferee to hold on trust for someone else has the quite different effect of constituting the transferee a trustee of the property for the designated beneficiary. A related distinction between an absolute gift and a trust is that it is possible to create a trust for the benefit of beneficiaries who, because of some legal incapacity such as infancy or mental illness, cannot take an absolute interest in the asset in question. Land, for example, cannot be held absolutely by

---

[86] R. Pound 'The decadence of equity' (1905) 5 Columbia LR 20.

[87] See Chapter 8.

[88] 'Things as things and things as wealth' (1994) 14 OJLS 81 at 89.

[89] Such as the rule that a landowner is not entitled to oil and coal discovered under his land.

[90] Such as the common law tort of nuisance, which prevents the owner of land from using his land in a manner detrimental to his neighbour's land.

[91] Such comparisons occupy a significant part of Chapter 2.

[92] See Chapter 4.

any person under the age of 18, but it is possible to transfer land to a competent adult to hold on trust for an infant. It is even possible to create a trust for the benefit of persons who have not yet been born: there is nothing to prevent an 18-year-old from establishing a trust for his grandchildren. Nevertheless, for all of their differences, absolute gifts and trusts do have some significant features in common. Indeed, the express trust has been described as '*a gift projected on the plane of time and, meanwhile, in need of management*'.[93] Perhaps their most important common feature is the fact that the transfer of benefit is irrevocable whether made by outright gift or by trust. So if, having read it from cover to cover, the owner of this book declares that she holds it on trust for her friend, the generous student is now a trustee and is no longer entitled to use the book for her own benefit.

It has been suggested that the trust is '*functionally indistinguishable from the modern third-party-beneficiary contract*',[94] in other words that the trust is merely a form of contract between the settlor and the trustees entered into for the benefit of the third-party beneficiary. Langbein argues that:

> even in the law of donative transfers the trust functions as a deal, in the sense that what trust law does is to enforce the trustee's promise to the settlor to carry out the terms of the donative transfer.[95]

It is true that a trust usually originates in the consensual disposition of the trust property by the settlor in favour of a trustee who consents to receive it,[96] but such consent need not be contractual. It is certainly hard to see the contractual 'deal' where the court appoints a trustee[97] or where the trust comes into effect on the testator's death.[98] (The reader should note that the term 'settlor' is used to describe the creator of a trust—called an *inter vivos* trust—that comes into effect during the settlor's lifetime, whereas the term 'testator' or 'testatrix' is used to describe the creator, male and female respectively, of a trust—called a 'testamentary' trust—that comes into effect when the creator of the trust dies.)

There are a number of reasons why it does not make sense to regard the arrangement entered into between settlor and trustee as being contractual in nature. For one thing, whereas a contracting party always has the right to enforce his contractual rights against the other party, the power of enforcing trusts lies with the beneficiaries of the trust, so the settlor of a trust has no power to enforce it against the trustees unless he happens to nominate himself to be a beneficiary or becomes a beneficiary under

---

[93] F. H. Lawson and B. Rudden, *The Law of Property*, 2nd edn (Oxford: Clarendon Press, 1982) at 55; Rudden (1981) 44 Mod LR 610 (book review of *Gifts and Promises* by J. P. Dawson).

[94] J. H. Langbein, 'Contractarian basis of the law of trusts' (1995) 105 Yale LJ 625 at 627. The quotation is followed by the even bolder assertion that '[t]rusts are contracts'.

[95] 'The secret life of the trust as an instrument of commerce' (1997) 107 Yale LJ 165 at 185.

[96] Professor Kevin Gray has observed that every trust 'has its origins in some arrangement of consent or assent': 'Property in thin air' [1991] 50(2) CLJ 252 at 302.

[97] See Chapter 8.

[98] *Re Duke of Norfolk's Settlement Trust* [1981] 3 All ER 220, *per* Fox LJ at 228h–j.

a resulting trust.[99] Otherwise, the settlor of a trust drops out of the picture just as the donor of an absolute gift drops out of the picture when he has made his gift. Of course, many settlement trusts do not come into effect until the death of the testator, so the testator patently 'drops out' of the picture in those cases.

The most significant distinction between a trust and a contract, even a contract entered into for the benefit of a third party, is the nature of the beneficiary's rights. In some ways, the beneficiary's rights resemble contractual rights, in that they are enforceable against the trustee personally, but the beneficiary's right is not merely a personal right against the trustee; it is also a proprietary right in the asset itself. This is the feature that most clearly distinguishes the English trust from concepts that perform similar functions in other jurisdictions.[100] The significance of the proprietary status of the beneficiary's right under the trust is essentially twofold. First, the beneficiary's right under the trust can be enforced not only against the trustee, but also against the trustee's successors in title. This is useful where the trustee has wrongfully transferred trust property into the hands of a third party and is particularly useful if a trustee dies or becomes insolvent. At no time does the beneficiary's property become part of the trustee's personal estate, so, when a trustee dies, the beneficiary's proprietary right in the trust assets is binding on the trustee's personal representatives[101] and, when a trustee becomes insolvent, the beneficiary's right is binding on the 'trustee in bankruptcy', or, if the trustee was corporate (as many trustees are), on its successor in insolvency.[102] Second, the proprietary status of the beneficiary's right under the trust means that the beneficiary is free to alienate the property wholly (by selling it or giving it away, for example) or partially (by leasing it or subjecting it to a charge such as a mortgage, for example). It is even possible for a beneficiary to declare a trust of her equitable interest, thereby creating a sub-trust, although that possibility is somewhat controversial.[103]

Creating a trust

The deliberate or 'express' creation of trusts, and the necessary prerequisites to constituting an express trust completely, are discussed in depth in Chapters 3 and 4. Here, we will take a brief moment to outline the basics.

Declaring oneself to be a trustee

The simplest way to create a trust is for the absolute owner of an asset to declare that he holds the asset for the benefit, at least in part, of someone else. He might say: 'See this book I am holding? I declare that I hold it with immediate effect on trust for my room-mate.' Such a 'declaration of trust' will make the original absolute owner a trustee for his room-mate. The room-mate will be the sole beneficial owner or 'equitable' owner of the

---

[99] See Chapter 5.   [100] Compare, for instance, the French law of *La Fiducie* (see later).
[101] Officers, such as executors and administrators, who administer a deceased person's estate.
[102] The 'administrator', the 'administrative receiver', the 'liquidator', or the 'provisional liquidator', as the case may be (Insolvency Act 1986, ss. 234–236).   [103] See Chapter 6.

book and, as such, she is entitled, assuming that she is a competent adult, to insist that the book be transferred to her.

Transferring property to trustees on trust

The more usual method of creating a trust is slightly more complicated. It arises when an absolute owner does not retain legal title to the asset, but instead transfers it to a trustee to hold on trust for a designated beneficiary. Of course, a trust may have several trustees[104] and several beneficiaries. Under a traditional settlement trust, the trustee would typically hold the asset on trust for one beneficiary, for the duration of that beneficiary's life, and for another beneficiary after the first has died. The first beneficiary is called the 'life beneficiary' or 'life tenant' and has an immediate interest in the benefit of the asset, which means that she can possess it, take income from it, and so on, whereas the second beneficiary is called the 'remainderman' or 'remainder beneficiary', because she is primarily interested in what remains of the trust assets when the first beneficiary has died. The interest of the life beneficiary is said to vest 'in possession' the moment the trust is created, whereas the interest of the remainder beneficiary merely vests 'in interest' at that point and does not vest in possession until the death of the life beneficiary. Naturally, there may be several life tenants, followed by several remaindermen. No remainderman will be entitled to an interest in possession until all of the life tenants have died. Settlement trusts of this sort are typically created by will. The life tenant will usually be the settlor's surviving spouse and the remaindermen are typically the children of the marriage.

The right of beneficiaries to terminate the trust

When the absolute owner of certain assets subjects them to a private (as opposed to a charitable) trust, absolute ownership of the assets is not so much destroyed as postponed. There are even rules designed to limit the period of the postponement.[105] Eventually, the trust will terminate and the asset will be owned absolutely once again. If a trust is established 'for A for life and B in remainder', B will become the absolute owner of the asset when A dies. Of course, until the trustee actually transfers legal title into B's name, there will still be a form of trust, but, assuming that B is an adult, the trustee's only duty under such a 'bare trust' is to transfer the trust property to B and, in the meantime, to account to B for any income arising from the trust property. By extension of this principle, once A has died B can demand the trust property even if her interest is subject to a contingency that has not yet been met. The trust might have been established 'for A for life and B in remainder *when B reaches the age of 30*'. If, when A dies, B is a competent adult and is solely entitled to the benefit of the trust property, she is entitled to demand that the trustee transfer the property to her even though she has not yet reached the age of 30. This rule was laid down in the case of *Saunders v. Vautier*.[106]

---

104 Subject to certain limits, see Chapter 11.
105 The rules against perpetuity are considered in Chapter 6.   106 (1841) 10 LJ Ch 354.

The fact that B must be 'absolutely entitled' means that the property can only be transferred to B if (continuing our example) any person expressed to be entitled to the trust property in the event of B's death before the age of 30 consents.[107] It is also required that the trustees have power to transfer the particular assets which make up the fund.[108] By extension of the so-called 'rule in *Saunders v. Vautier*', it is now established that a trust can be terminated even if there is more than one beneficiary interested in it,[109] as would be the case if a trust were established 'for my nephews'. If all the nephews are of full age and between them absolutely entitled to the trust property, they can agree to bring the trust to an end. The rule can also be relied upon to terminate a trust under which competent adult beneficiaries are entitled to successive interests, as in a trust for 'A for life, to B in remainder', even though A has not yet died.[110] However, the rule has no application where potential beneficiaries (e.g. 'grandchildren') do not yet exist, even if their interests are remote and might be unlikely ever to vest.[111]

The principle underlying the rule also lies behind the statutory provision that allows adult beneficiaries to change the trustees of the trust without actually bringing the trust to an end,[112] although the beneficiaries are not permitted to dictate to the trustees how they should conduct trust business in the meantime.[113] The statutory jurisdiction to vary beneficial interests under a trust without bringing the trust to an end is also based on the principle behind the rule in *Saunders v. Vautier*.[114] The principle is simply this, that '[f]idelity to the settlor's intention ends where equitable property begins'.[115] In the USA, by way of contrast, the courts have taken quite a different approach to the problem of balancing the settlor's intentions against the beneficiaries' proprietary rights. The rule in *Saunders v. Vautier* failed to acquire a foothold in the USA, so the rule there is that no trust may be terminated or modified by the beneficiaries if termination would defeat a 'material purpose' of the settlor or testator.[116]

Trust assets

A trust asset does not have to be a tangible thing such as a plot of land or a book; it can be an intangible asset such as a debt, a trademark, or the right to the proceeds of an

---

[107] *Gosling v. Gosling* (1859) Johns 265.

[108] Where 'the subject matter of the trust is a non-assignable contract and there are outstanding obligations to be performed by the trustee' the trustee cannot assign it to the beneficiary, even though the beneficiary wishes to compel the assignment: *Barbados Trust Co Ltd v. Bank of Zambia* [2006] EWHC 222 (Comm); *Don King Productions Inc v. Warren* [2000] Ch 291; *Re Brockbank* [1948] Ch 206.

[109] *Re Smith* [1928] Ch 915.

[110] *Brown v. Pringle* (1845) 4 Hare 124.

[111] *Thorpe v. Revenue and Customs Commissioners* [2009] EWHC 611 (Ch).

[112] Trusts of Land and Appointment of Trustees Act 1996, ss. 19–20. See Chapter 11.

[113] *Stephenson (Inspector of Taxes) v. Barclays Bank Trust Co Ltd* [1975] 1 All ER 625, *per* Walton J at 637e–f.

[114] Variation of Trusts Act 1958, see Chapter 9.

[115] J. W. Harris, *Variation of Trusts* (London: Sweet & Maxwell, 1975) at 2.

[116] *Claflin v. Claflin* (1889) 20 NE 454; American Law Institute, Restatement of the Law of Trusts (3rd) §65(1), and Uniform Trust Code (2000), s. 411(b). In *Tod v. Barton*, 20 February 2002, Chancery Division (unreported), the difference between the English and US approaches gave rise to a dispute over governing law. The case concerned the will of an Englishman who had died when domiciled in the USA.

insurance policy. Of course, even in the case of a book or a plot of land, the true asset is not the thing itself, but the intangible right to benefit from the use and enjoyment of the thing. Usually, the trust 'property'—or the 'estate' as it is sometimes referred to in the case of traditional settlement trusts—consists of a number of different assets that together make up a 'fund'. Eventually, the trust fund must be distributed to the beneficiaries, or the proceeds of sale of the fund must be distributed, but, in the meantime, the fund must be managed and invested.[117]

Equitable rights under a trust

An equitable proprietary right under a trust does not 'bind the whole world' in quite the same way that legal title is binding on the whole world or in quite the same way that *in rem*[118] property rights in a civil (Roman law-based) jurisdiction are binding on the whole world (*'erga omnes'*).[119] The most important limitation on the binding nature of equitable proprietary rights under a trust is the fact that a bona fide ('good faith') purchaser for value of a legal estate will not be bound by any beneficial interest under a trust affecting the vendor's legal title unless the purchaser had, or ought reasonably to have acquired, notice of the equitable interest.[120] ('Notice' is not quite the same thing as 'knowledge', but that distinction can wait until later.)[121] The bona fide purchaser for value of a legal estate without notice is sometimes, even today,[122] referred to as 'equity's darling', because a beneficiary's equitable interest under a trust cannot be enforced against him. In fact, the bona fide purchaser for value without notice is, in reality, the darling of the common law, because the reason equity does not enforce its property rights against the innocent purchaser of legal title without notice is that it would undermine the common law rules for acquiring 'good title' to property if it did.[123]

Separation of legal and equitable ownership

It is this writer's contention that the separation of legal title to an asset from equitable property *in the same asset* will always produce a trust in English law, even though a trust might conceivably be produced without separation of legal and equitable ownership. In other words, separation of legal and equitable ownership is a sufficient, but not a necessary, feature of trust creation. Separation does not require that different persons hold the legal and equitable 'titles': it is sufficient to create a substantial separation of legal and equitable ownership for certain persons to hold legal title on trust for themselves, provided that they have distinguishable interests under the trust. The equitable proprietary interest may be divided sequentially, as in the case of a trust 'for A for life and B

---

[117] See Chapter 12.   [118] See earlier.

[119] *Webb v. Webb* [1994] 3 WLR 801, European Court of Justice, *per* Mr Advocate-General Darmon at 816B.

[120] *Pilcher v. Rawlins* (1872) LR 7 Ch App 259, *per* Sir W. M. James LJ at 268–9.   [121] See Chapter 15.

[122] See, for example, *Griggs Group Ltd v. Evans* [2005] EWCA Civ 11, CA, *per* Jacob LJ at para. 7.

[123] J. Hackney, *Understanding Equity and Trusts* (London: Fontana, 1987).

in remainder' or contemporaneously, as in the case of a traditional trust 'for A and B for life'.

Separation of legal and equitable ownership without a trust

It cannot be denied that my claim (that a trust is necessarily created whenever legal title is separated from equitable property in the same asset) conflicts with Lord Browne-Wilkinson's observation (made obiter in *Westdeutsche Landesbank Girozentrale v. Islington LBC*) that '[e]*ven in cases where the whole beneficial interest is vested in B and the bare legal interest is in A, A is not necessarily a trustee*'.[124]

His Lordship's best examples in support of that statement are the example of land acquired by estoppel against a legal owner and the example of a mortgagor who has fully discharged the mortgage debt. It is respectfully submitted that neither example truly supports his Lordship's point of view.

Estoppel is considered in depth in Chapter 8, but suffice to say that estoppel is a cause of action that prevents the legal owner of an asset from asserting his absolute beneficial ownership of the asset and which, having been raised, must be satisfied by a final remedial award in favour of the claimant. It is true that, before the award is made, there can strictly speaking be no trust, but by the same token, neither is there any split in beneficial ownership before the remedial award is finally made. It might turn out that the estoppel can be remedied by a simple award of damages, leaving the defendant's beneficial ownership of the asset unaffected. The most that can be said is that the legal owner is not permitted to act as if he were entitled to 100 per cent of the beneficial ownership, because it might turn out that he is not. If, in the event, the estoppel is satisfied by recognizing the claimant to have a beneficial ownership interest in the defendant's asset, the defendant will, from that moment, be a trustee. In short, there is no point in the process of raising and satisfying an estoppel when the claimant has an established equitable interest without there being a trust.

The second example, of the landowner who has repaid a loan secured by mortgage over his land, is also unconvincing. It is true that so long as the mortgagee (lender) holds the legal title to the mortgage, the mortgagor (borrower) is said to have an equitable interest in his land, known as the 'equity of redemption'.[125] Crucially, though, the mortgagee's legal title is in the mortgage charge and the mortgagor's equitable interest is in the estate subject to the charge, so there is no sense in which there is any division between legal and equitable ownership of the *same* asset. Perhaps his Lordship had in mind the old form of mortgage, in which legal title to the land was actually placed in the

---

[124] *Westdeutsche Landesbank Girozentrale v. Islington LBC* [1996] AC 669 at 707A. Followed in *Don King Productions Inc v. Warren* [2000] Ch 291, 295, Ch D, *per* Lightman J at 317 (affirmed by the Court of Appeal [2000] Ch 291, 327), but doubted by Lord Millett writing extra-judicially, 'Restitution and constructive trusts' (1998) 114 LQR 399 at 403: 'a trust exists whenever the legal title is in one party and the equitable title in another'.

[125] For an argument that it is unhelpful to regard the so-called 'equity of redemption' as a distinctive equitable estate, see G. Watt, 'The lie of the land: Mortgage law as legal fiction' in *Modern Studies in Property Law* (E. Cooke, ed.) (Oxford: Hart Publishing, 2007) vol. IV at 73.

name of the mortgagee until it was redeemed, with the mortgagor retaining an equity of redemption in the meantime. In such a case, it is true, as his Lordship observes, that the mortgagor's action to recover the mortgaged property takes the form of an action for redemption and not an action for breach of trust,[126] but it does not follow that the split between the mortgagee's apparent formal ownership of the land and the mortgagor's beneficial ownership of the land is not a trust—merely that there is no need to refer to it as such, the usual remedy for redemption of the mortgage being sufficient. We can say that, in the old form of mortgage by conveyance and reconveyance, there was a trust as a matter of property, but a mortgage as a matter of obligation. A comparable case is the trust that arises when X formally contracts to purchase land from Y. Equity is prepared to grant specific performance of such contracts almost as a matter of course and, because equity sees as done that which ought to be done, the result is that X becomes the equitable owner of Y's land from the moment of contract. Y's legal title does not pass to X until the completion of a deed in favour of X, so, in the meantime, Y holds his bare legal title on trust for the sole beneficial owner, X. There is a trust, but it is rarely referred to as such precisely because there is a contract between the parties and the primary cause of action between the parties will be for breach of the contractual terms. We will see in the next chapter that it is perfectly possible to conceive of a trust running alongside (or underneath) a contractual relationship such as a debt. Provided that the contractual remedies are adequate to fulfil the parties' intentions, there may never be a need to refer to the underlying trust. To put it another way, whenever there is a split between legal and beneficial ownership there will inevitably be a trust as a matter of *property law*, but as a matter of *obligations law*, the parties will frequently be bound by sets of obligations, whether established by contract or statute, more sophisticated than the crude obligation of a bare trustee to account to his beneficiary for the trust property on demand.

The creation of trusts must be distinguished from their effects on third parties. The separation of legal title from equitable property necessarily creates a trust —it might be helpful to picture trust creation as the process of splitting the formal/external legal title from the beneficial/inner equitable interest, as if one were peeling the skin off a banana. It does not follow, however, that the mere passing of bare legal title to a third party will make them a trustee. That would be an unfair presumption, since legal title brings powers and responsibilities without the benefits that equitable property brings (bare legal title is in this respect like a banana skin: one can slip up on it, but one can't eat it). This means that there might be cases in which a third party might come to hold bare legal title without being a trustee. In such a case, whether or not A can be called a trustee cannot be determined without an inquiry into A's state of knowledge or notice of the pre-existing trust.[127]

---

[126] *Westdeutsche Landesbank Girozentrale v. Islington LBC* [1996] 2 WLR 802 at 707A.

[127] These issues are considered in Chapters 14 and 15. See, also, the discussion in *Allan v. Rea Brothers Trustees Ltd* [2002] EWCA Civ 85, Court of Appeal, *per* Robert Walker LJ at paras 43–6. See, generally, G. Watt, 'Personal liability for receipt of trust property: allocating the risks' in *Modern Studies in Property Law* (E. Cooke, ed.) (Oxford: Hart Publishing, 2005) vol. III at 91.

Trusts without separation of legal and equitable title

It is possible for a person to hold an asset subject to a fiduciary duty, and even as a trustee, without any separation of legal and equitable title to the asset.

The administration of estates

When property comes to an executor under a will for the purpose of carrying out the functions and duties of administering the estate of a deceased person, the property comes to him '*in full ownership, without distinction between legal and equitable interests*'.[128] It follows that residuary legatees, who may or may not receive something from the deceased's estate after payment of specific gifts from the estate and payment of debts and tax owed by the estate, do not have a beneficial interest in the assets in the executor's hands during the course of administration. Nevertheless, although the whole property belongs, in theory, to the executor, he does not hold it for his own benefit: he holds it subject to a fiduciary duty to distribute it in accordance with the will. In a sense, then, he is a trustee subject to:

> trusts to preserve the assets, to deal properly with them, and to apply them in a due course of administration for the benefit of those interested according to that course, creditors, the death duty authorities, legatees of various sorts, and the residuary beneficiaries.[129]

The same principle applies as well to administrators of intestate estates as it does to executors of wills.[130]

Discretionary trusts

In a discretionary trust, which is a trust in which the trustees are required to exercise a discretion to appoint beneficiaries from a given class and to determine the size of the beneficiaries' respective entitlements, the beneficiaries' interest in the income is more than a mere speculative hope (a '*spes*'), but it is not a beneficial proprietary interest until the trustees actually exercise discretion in the beneficiaries' favour.[131] So a discretionary trust is somewhat analogous to the trust binding an executor or an administrator of an estate, in that it binds the property in the trustees' hands, but without immediately conferring equitable title on the ultimate beneficiaries of the distribution. A discretionary trust can therefore be regarded as a trust in which legal and equitable titles are separate, in the sense that the trustee is legally, but not beneficially, entitled, but without being separate in such a way that it is possible to identify the true beneficial owner prior to the trustees exercising their discretion in her favour.

Beneficial joint tenancy of land

The beneficial joint tenancy of land is a theoretically and socially significant form of trust under which two or more persons jointly own land at law and in equity, with

---

[128] *Commissioner of Stamp Duties (Queensland) v. Livingston* [1965] AC 694, PC, *per* Viscount Radcliffe at 707. See, further, Chapter 2.

[129] Ibid. Followed in *Marshall (Inspector of Taxes) v. Kerr* [1995] 1 AC 148, HL.

[130] *Eastbourne Mutual Building Society v. Hastings Corporation* [1965] 1 All ER 779.

[131] *Gartside v. IRC* [1968] AC 553, HL.

identical interests and no notion of separate individual shares. Under this arrangement, which is common when a husband and wife acquire land as a matrimonial home, the ownership of each 'beneficial joint tenant' is so joined to the ownership of the other that neither is able to dispose of a share of the property by their will when they die. Instead, the last surviving joint tenant becomes the sole absolute owner of the land by 'right of survivorship'. Statute provides that there is a trust whenever land is held under a beneficial joint tenancy, despite the total absence of any separation of ownership, because each joint tenant has the option of severing his or her equitable share of the asset in their lifetime simply by giving the appropriate form of notice to the other joint tenants.[132] Once severed, a share can be left by will.

Trusts in civil jurisdictions

Civil jurisdictions, which base their law upon the model of the Roman civil law code, have little difficulty with the idea of a trust of property, provided that it does not involve the distinction, quite alien to the Civilian mind, between legal and equitable title:[133]

> *Dans le trust, le droit de propriété est éclaté suivant une division inconnue des systèmes civilistes.*[134]

So, for example, our close neighbours, the Scots, have a Civilian system of law and they have a form of trust, but in the Scottish trust, the beneficiary's right is purely personal against the trustee. The Scottish solution to the problem of insolvency is to treat the beneficiary's property as a 'special patrimony' in the hands of the trustee, so it does not become available to the trustee's creditors in the event of his insolvency.[135] As the Scottish example shows, the tendency of Civil jurisdictions is to employ distinct laws to fulfil different functions, each of which is performed automatically by the English trust.[136] Germany provides another example. The German idea of holding property faithfully for another (*Treuhänderschaft*)[137] belongs to a quite different branch of law to

---

[132] Law of Property Act 1925, s. 36(1), (2).

[133] See D. Hayton, 'When is a trust not a trust?' (1992) 1 J Int Planning 3. The European Court of Justice has held that a beneficiary's interest under a trust is not a 'real' right: *Webb v. Webb* [1994] ECR I-1717.

[134] 'In the trust, the right to property is split in a manner unknown to Civil systems of law'. J.-P. Béraudo, *Les Trusts Anglo-Saxons et Le Droit Français* (Paris: LGDA, 1992) at 8, para. 18. As of 19 February 2007, France has at last admitted a form of trust into its Civil Code, albeit one that does not contain the defining feature of the English trust, i.e. division of the property right. The new law 'de la fiducie' is inserted as 'titre XIV' in book III of the Code Civil (LOI n° 2007–211 du instituant la fiducie). See also F. H. Lawson, *A Common Lawyer Looks at the Civil Law* (Ann Arbor: University of Michigan Law School, 1953) at 201. Cited in George L. Gretton, 'Trusts without equity' (2000) 49 ICLQ 599.

[135] W. A. Wilson and A. G. M. Duncan, *Trusts, Trustees and Executors*, 2nd edn (Edinburgh: W. Green & Sons, 1995) paras 1-42 to 1-51; *Sharp v. Thompson*, 1995 SLT 837, 857; cf. at 867–8. A. Honoré, 'Obstacles to the reception of trust law? The examples of South Africa and Scotland' in A. M. Rabello (ed.), *Aequitas, and Equity: Equity in Civil Law and Mixed Jurisdictions* (Jerusalem: Hebrew University of Jerusalem, Sacher Institute, 1997) 793 at 812.

[136] See, generally, M. Lupoi, *Trusts: A Comparative Study* (Cambridge: Cambridge University Press, 2000).

[137] For an historical account, see Oliver Wendell Holmes, 'Early English equity' (1885) 1 LQR 162 and R. H. Helmholz and R. Zimmerman (eds), *Itinera Fiduciae: Trust and Treuhand in Historical Perspective* (Berlin: Duncker & Humblot, 1998).

the German idea of special property set aside for a particular purpose (*Sondervermögen*). There are some Civilian devices that might be said to be true hybrids of property and obligation—the Swiss *substitution fideicommissaire* is a candidate[138]—but there is none that involves a genuine split in ownership of the subject matter of the obligation. The result has been a recognition in certain Civil jurisdictions that the commercial utility of the English trust has given common law systems a commercial advantage over their Civilian counterparts.[139] Ironically, it is in Italy—source of the original Civil law—that the need for a form of trust has been most keenly appreciated. One result is a growing body of Italian scholarship on trusts that has sought to express the English idea in Civilian terms.[140] The benefit to English scholars is a perceptive and critical insight into ideas that we thought we understood: 'What knows he of English trusts that only English trusts knows' is the new version of an old motto.

Bailment

It is arguable that, in the idea of 'bailment',[141] the English common law developed its own version of the trust without equity being involved at all. It is notable that bailment was itself conceived using arguments and authorities adopted from the Civil law.[142] Bailment and trust are compared in the next chapter.

The paradox of property and obligation

> [A] trust is a matter which is difficult to define, but which essentially imposes an obligation to deal with property in a particular way on behalf of another person.[143]

Richard Nolan argues that beneficiaries have a right to require performance from their trustees and a distinct type of right to prevent interference by third parties.[144] Paul Matthews has observed that, if the beneficiary's personal rights against the trustee had remained purely personal, the law of trusts might today lie firmly within the law of obligations.[145] Whatever theory we settle on, it is clear that the trust is a hybrid of property and obligations. The result is paradoxical: what began as a human relationship of trust established in connection with certain property, usually land, has become, in effect, a

---

[138] A. Dyer and H. van Loon, 'Report on trusts and analogous institutions', in *Actes et Documents of 15th Session of Hague Conference on Trusts*, vol. II, para. 177.

[139] See, for example, G. Ll. H. Griffiths and M. Ganado, 'The Malta Trusts project: the genesis of a new trusts act in a civil law jurisdiction' in *Contemporary Perspectives on Property, Equity and Trust Law* (M. Dixon and G. Ll. H. Griffiths, eds) (Oxford: Oxford University Press, 2007) 203–17.

[140] See M. Lupoi, *Trusts: A Comparative Study* (Cambridge: Cambridge University Press, 2000).

[141] See Chapter 2.

[142] *Coggs v. Bernard* (1703) 2 Lord Raym 909, although there is some evidence that it has earlier, purely English, origins. *Williams v. Lloyd* (1628) W Jones 179; cf. Blackburn J in *Taylor v. Caldwell* (1863) B & S 826.

[143] *Staden v. Jones* [2008] EWCA Civ 936, *per* Arden LJ at para. [25].

[144] R. C. Nolan, 'Equitable property' (2006) 122 LQR 232.

[145] P. Matthews, 'The new trust: obligations without rights?', in *Trends in Contemporary Trust Law* (A. J. Oakley, ed.) (Oxford: Clarendon Press, 1996) at 1.

propertized form of relationship. Today, '*the trust … is the same as the land*'.[146] James Penner reaches a similar conclusion:

> The trustee is not a person with whom [the beneficiaries] have any personal relationship of any substance—he is the personification of the trust agreement, and it is that which really settles how the gift is to work. He is like a human instrument.[147]

The frequent lack of any meaningful personal relationship between trustee and beneficiary produces another paradox: that the trust relationship becomes a relationship of mistrust instead of trust, social trust having been replaced by trust mediated through the terms of the trust and the general law. No theory can perfectly encapsulate and explain the long and complex history of the trust and any theory designed to control its future development should strive to appreciate, rather than to resolve, the paradox of property and obligation which gives the trust its theoretical and practical dynamism.

The way to understand the trust is not to force it into the preconceived categories of 'obligation' and 'property' that are much cherished in the codes of Civil lawyers,[148] but to accept that it is something of a law unto itself. In short, to understand the trust, one must appreciate that it does not make perfect sense. After all, the true value of the trust, like the true value of a case-based common law system of law, is to be found, not in conformity to logical absolutes, but in flexibility and functional utility: '[T]*he life of the law has not been logic; it has been experience.*'[149]

Perspectives

As we progress through the remaining chapters of this book, it will be useful to bear in mind that laws and legal decisions can be viewed from a number of different perspectives, each of which provides a unique critical insight into the subject matter of our study. Four perspectives that are always worth bearing in mind are precedent, principle, policy, and pragmatism. When a judge is presented with a legal problem, the judge is bound to look first to statutory law and judicial precedent for a solution, but, if it appears to the judge (rightly or wrongly) that there is no clear solution in precedent, the judge should, in theory, seek to produce a solution that is consistent with principles derived from precedent. Maxims, such as 'equity follows the law',[150] are one species of principle, but other principles may commend themselves to judges even though they have not acquired the status of a maxim. It is important to appreciate, however, that

---

[146] Lord Mansfield in *Burgess v. Wheale* (1759) 1 123 W Bl at 162.

[147] *The Idea of Property in Law* (Oxford: Clarendon Press, 1997) at 125.

[148] Gretton, op. cit., tries to sidestep the problem by attempting to place the trust within the civil law of persons, arguing that '[t]he trust itself is not a person. A special patrimony never is. But a special patrimony operates very like a person, as an autonomous, quasi-personal, fund' ((2000) 49 ICLQ 599 at 614).

[149] Oliver Wendell Holmes, *The Common Law* (Boston: Little, Brown & Co, 1923), quoted by Lord MacMillan in *Read v. J. Lyons & Co Ltd* [1947] AC 156, HL.

[150] The list of major equitable maxims is considered in depth in Chapter 16.

judges do not reach their decisions in a logical vacuum: judges are very often acutely aware of the impact that their decisions might have upon the wider community or society at large. They are therefore sensitive to what we might call 'policy considerations', or considerations based on the public interest. One such policy is the need to maintain certainty in dealings with property rights;[151] another is the need to maintain certainty in commercial transactions; yet another is the policy underlying the Insolvency Acts (the statutes that determine how the claims of various interested persons and groups should be balanced fairly in the event of a party's insolvency).

Policies often conflict and, as with principles, there is no easy way to determine when one policy should take priority over another. The express trust has always had to tread carefully between the policy that a beneficial owner of property should be permitted to use and dispose of his or her property as he or she thinks fit, and the policy that imperative conditions attached to dispositions (sometimes from beyond the grave) must be obeyed even to the diminution of a beneficial owner's freedom.[152] In short, the freedoms of the present owner of property must be balanced against the like freedoms of past owners of the same property. Trusts, express and non-express, have also had to tread carefully between the policy that the trustee should be under an obligation to hold the trust property for the benefit of the beneficiaries and the policy that the trustees' personal creditors should be entitled to enforce their legitimate claims against any assets in the trustees' hands. Last, but by no means least, above all considerations of principle and policy—and sometimes even above precedent—judges are concerned to achieve a solution that works in practice and which will not bring the entire judicial process into disrepute. The judicial process is nothing if not pragmatic. As Lord Goff of Chieveley has observed:

> It is a truism that, in deciding a question of law in any particular case, the courts are much influenced by considerations of practical justice, and especially by the results which would flow from the recognition of a particular claim on the facts of the case before the court.[153]

Precedent, principle, policy, and pragmatism are blended subtly in the mind of the judge. Nevertheless, the task of students in this, as indeed in any area of law, is to attempt to discern the true basis for decisions and to distil, from the subtle blend, the fractions of precedent, principles, policy, and pragmatism in the purest form they can. It is the task of the textbook writer to help in this distillation process, to which end, the reader will hopefully see that a special attempt has been made throughout this book to bring all four perspectives to bear upon the subject. We will discover that decisions that seem

---

[151] See Chapter 8 on the institutional nature of constructive trusts.

[152] R. Cotterrell, 'Trusting in law: legal and moral concepts of trust' (1993) CLP 75.

[153] *Westdeutsche Landesbank Girozentrale v. Islington LBC* [1996] 2 WLR 802 at 810G. His Lordship has made the same observation extra-judicially: Sir Robert Goff, 'Judge, jurist and legislature' [1987] Denning LJ 79 at 80. See, generally, R. Cotterrell, *The Politics of Jurisprudence* (London: Butterworths, 1989); P. S. Atiyah, *Pragmatism and Theory in English Law, The Hamlyn Lectures* (London, 1987); P. S. Atiyah, *From Principles to Pragmatism: Changes in the Function of the Judicial Process and the Law* (Oxford: Oxford University Press, 1978).

to be unprecedented and to make no principled sense can sometimes make sense from the perspective of policy, or as an attempt to find a pragmatic workable solution to a novel problem.

Further reading

In addition to the following print sources, the Online Resource Centre accompanying this book contains web links to further reading as well as guide answers to assessment questions relevant to this chapter.

BAKER, J. H., 'The Court of Chancery and Equity' in *An Introduction to English Legal History*, 4th edn (London: Butterworths, 2002), ch. 6.

BURROWS, A. S., *Fusing Common Law and Equity: Remedies, Restitution and Reform—Hochelaga Lectures 2001* (Hong Kong: Sweet & Maxwell Asia, 2002).

DICKENS, *Bleak House* (1852–53).

DOUPE, M. and SALTER, M., 'Concealing the past? Questioning textbook interpretations of the history of equity and trusts' (2000) 22 Liverpool L R 253.

DUGGAN, A. J., 'Is equity efficient?' (1997) 113 LQR 601.

GOODHART, SIR WILLIAM, QC, 'Trust law for the twenty-first century' (1996) 10(2) TLI 38.

GRETTON, G. L., 'Trusts without equity' (2000) 49 ICLQ 599.

HALLIWELL, M., *Equity and Good Conscience in a Contemporary Context*, 2nd edn (London: Old Bailey, 2004).

HARDING, M., 'Manifesting trust' (2009) 29(2) Oxford Journal of Legal Studies 245.

HAYTON, D., 'Whither trusts in the twenty-first century? Part 1' (2000) 2 PCB 94.

HAYTON, D., 'Whither trusts in the twenty-first century? Part 2' (2000) 3 PCB 163.

HAYTON, D., 'Whither trusts in the twenty-first century? Part 3' (2000) 4 PCB 244.

HOLDSWORTH, W. S., 'Relation of the equity administered by the common law judges to the equity administered by the Chancellor' (1916) 26 Yale LJ 1.

HOLMES, O. W., 'Early English equity' (1885) 1 LQR 162.

KLINCK, D., *Conscience, Equity and the Court of Chancery in Early Modern England* (London: Ashgate, 2010).

KLINCK, D.,'Lord Nottingham and the Conscience of Equity' (2006) 67 Journal of the History of Ideas 123–47.

LUPOI, M., 'Trust and Confidence' (2009) 125 LQR 253–87.

MAITLAND, F. W., 'Uses and trusts' in *Equity: A Course of Lectures* (revd by J. BRUNYATE) (Cambridge: Cambridge University Press, 1936) 23–42.

MARTIN, J., 'Fusion, fallacy and confusion: a comparative study' [1994] Conv 13.

MATTHEWS, P., 'The new trust: obligations without rights?' in *Trends in Contemporary Trust Law* (Oxford: Clarendon Press, 1996).

MATTHEWS, P., 'The French fiducie: and now for something completely different'? (2007) 21(1) TLI 17–21.

MILLETT, SIR PETER, 'Equity—the road ahead' (1995) 9(2) TLI 35.

POUND, R., 'The decadence of equity' (1905) 5 Columbia LR 20.

REID, K., 'Patrimony not equity: the trust in Scotland' (2000) 8 Eur Rev Priv Law 427.

TUDSBERY, F., 'Equity and the common law' (1913) 29 LQR 154.

VINOGRADOFF, SIR PAUL, 'Reason and conscience in sixteenth century jurisprudence' (1908) 96 LQR 373.

WATKIN, T. G., 'Changing concepts of ownership in English law during the nineteenth and twentieth centuries: the changing idea of beneficial ownership under the English trust' in *Contemporary Perspectives on Property, Equity and Trust Law* (M. Dixon and G. L. H. Griffiths, eds) (Oxford: Oxford University Press, 2007).

WATT, G., *Equity Stirring: The Story of Justice Beyond Law* (Oxford: Hart Publishing, 2009).

WORTHINGTON, S., *Equity* (Oxford: Clarendon Press, 2003).

YNTEMA, H. E., 'Equity in the civil law and the common law' (1967) 15 Am J Comp L 60.

2

Trusts in context

This is the second of two chapters designed to provide a general introduction to trusts and equity. In the first chapter, we identified the theoretical and historical foundations of our subject, and we acquired certain critical perspectives that will be useful in helping us to discern when a judicial decision is influenced by precedent, principle, policy, or pragmatism. In this chapter, we will position trusts in their contemporary social, economic, legal, and international context.

In the first part of this chapter, we will identify the significance of trusts to the world outside the lawyer's office. We will see that trusts play a significant social and economic role in the lives of ordinary people. Most of us live in homes that are co-owned and therefore subject to a trust, and we contribute to pensions that are held in trust and leave our property on express or statutory trusts when we die. Pension funds, life assurance funds, and residential buildings represent around 60 per cent of all wealth in the country.[1] The rich use trusts to plan their estates so as to avoid tax; the poor benefit from charitable trusts,[2] a trustee in bankruptcy holds the estate of a bankrupt. Trusts are used to hold funds for the benefit of persons affected by tragedies such as Hillsborough[3] and Aberfan.[4] The premises and assets of the clubs and associations to which we belong will often be held on trust for the benefit of the members. Wherever property is co-owned, and especially where it is held by the few for the benefit of the many, one can expect to find a trust. We will also see that the trust plays a significant and diverse role in commerce, from its usefulness as a vehicle for collective investment, to its ability to shield mail-order customers from the insolvency of the companies with which they deal. All this before we have even begun to consider the range of trust-like, or 'fiduciary', relationships that permeate our lives from cradle to grave: the doctor who delivered us into this world was a fiduciary to his patients; the priest who may solemnize our delivery from this world is in a fiduciary position to his parishioners. The company directors, solicitors, and estate agents who give meaning to the intervening period are fiduciaries to their companies and clients. The whole world is a trust—but, of course, this author is biased.

---

[1] Office of National Statistics, *Social Trends* (1999). [2] And not just the poor. See Chapter 7.
[3] 15 April 1989, Hillsborough Stadium, Sheffield. [4] 21 October 1966, Aberfan, Wales.

In the second part of this chapter, we will return to the lawyer's office, with the aim of identifying how the trust corresponds to, and coexists with, other legal ideas such as contract, debt, powers, gift, agency, bailment, and corporation. In the third part of the chapter, we will examine the international and comparative dimension of the trust.

There is, however, a question implicit in the title to this chapter that must be addressed before we progress further. The title refers to 'trusts' in the plural: this raises the question of whether we have a single law of trusts or several distinct laws dealing with different types of trust. The question is, of course, an academic one to which there is no easy answer, but there is an important point to it: the more integrated the law of trusts is, the more justified we will be in applying rules and principles developed in connection with trust A to a case involving trust B. As we progress through this chapter and future chapters, we will see that there is, in fact, a remarkable consistency in the fundamentals of the trust concept across the many contexts in which it operates, but that there are certain contexts, such as the pensions context and the charity context, in which, in a number of significant respects, the relevant trust appears to have fragmented from the general body of trusts law.

The social and economic significance of the trust

The private trust is one of many institutions—such as the family, the church, and the private partnership—that lie between, or 'mediate', the individual and the state. The trust operates in such significant spheres as home, employment, and commerce. These are spheres in which contract has traditionally been the predominant legal model for understanding non-legal and extralegal social relationships, but the idea of trust is frequently more apposite, as philosophers,[5] socio-economic theorists,[6] and legal commentators[7] have observed. Contract has also been the predominant model for understanding the relationship between citizens and state, but we will see towards the end of this section that the relationship between state and citizens has sometimes been conceived in terms of trust—albeit 'trust in the higher sense', as opposed to trust in the technical, legal, justiciable sense, as developed in Chancery. Until then, our concern in this section is to identify how trusts (in the technical sense) operate in the spheres of employment and commerce. The significant role played by the trust in the context of home ownership is considered in detail in Chapter 8.

---

[5] For example, A. Baier, 'Trust and anti-trust' (1986) 96 Ethics 231; T. Govier, 'Distrust as a practical problem' (1992) 23(1) J Social Philosophy 52.

[6] F. Fukuyama, *Trust, The Social Virtues and the Creation of Prosperity* (New York: Macmillan, 1995); P. Sztompka, *Trust: A Sociological Theory* (Cambridge: Cambridge University Press, 2000); M. Schluter and D. Lee, *The R Factor* (London: Hodder & Stoughton, 1993).

[7] 'Distributive liberty: a relational model of freedom, coercion, and property law' (1994) 107 Harvard LR 859, an unattributed note; G. Watt, 'Relational theory and the trust concept' [1994] Nott LJ 56.

Employment

Employment law is governed, for the most part, by contract and statute. At first sight, property and trusts do not appear to play a significant role. Employment is no doubt a great asset, probably the most valuable many of us will ever possess (and not only in financial terms), but employment is not an item of property. Employment lacks proprietary characteristics: an employee's employment is not binding on any person other than his employer; neither is employment transferable by an employee to another employee. There may be a case for extending the constitutional protection enjoyed by proprietary rights to employment rights and to the welfare rights of the unemployed,[8] but that is a different matter. Nevertheless, despite the predominantly contractual and statutory basis of employment, trusts perform crucial employment-related functions by way of providing pension benefits, trade union benefits, employee share-ownership schemes,[9] benevolent funds,[10] and recreational facilities.[11] Furthermore, an employee is sometimes subject to a fiduciary ('trust-like') duty not to act in conflict with the interests of his employer.[12]

Pensions

The majority of people who read this book will, sooner or later, pay money into a pension scheme. If it is an occupational pension scheme, their employer will also pay money into the fund, which will then, in the typical case, be held on trust for present and future pensioners by a body of trustees comprising representatives of the employer and representatives of the employees. Trusts are a useful vehicle for pension provision, because they allow the managerial control (including investment)[13] of large funds to be concentrated in the hands of a few trustees, while conferring a proprietary interest in the fund on every member of the scheme, giving each member a degree of security in the event of their employer becoming insolvent or being taken over by another company. The fact that members of the pension scheme have a proprietary interest in the fund means, in addition, that they are entitled to leave an interest in the fund to a nominated beneficiary when they die.

The trust also brings with it the advantage of subjecting the pension fund manager to strict fiduciary obligations.[14] These are considered in detail in Chapter 10. When the trustees breach their trust obligations, especially when they do so fraudulently, the consequences can be devastating for the members of the pension scheme. It is at such times that the concentration in a few hands of powers and discretions over such large funds looks anything but advantageous. The misappropriation of occupational pension funds lay at the root of the fraudulent plots perpetrated by the late Robert Maxwell that came

---

[8] C. Reich, 'The new property' (1964) 73 Yale LJ 733. See, also, by the same author: 'Individual rights and social welfare: the emerging legal issues' (1965) 74 Yale LJ 1245; 'Beyond the new property: an ecological view of due process' (1990) 56 Brooklyn LR 731. Reich adopted the term 'new property' from R. J. Lynn, 'Legal and economic implications of the emergence of quasi-public wealth' (1956) 65 Yale LJ 786.

[9] Known by an array of acronyms of the sort so beloved by the business community, including such fabulous creatures as the QUEST and the AESOP.

[10] See Chapter 5.   [11] See Chapter 3.   [12] See Chapter 10.   [13] See Chapter 12.

[14] See, generally, D. Pollard, 'Review and disclosure of decisions by pension trustees' (1997) 11(2) TLI 42.

to light after his mysterious death on, or around, 'Guy Fawkes night' 1991.[15] As the auto-cratic head of a number of national and international publishing concerns, including the *Daily Mirror* newspaper, Maxwell had been able to misappropriate pension funds held in trust by his companies for their employees. The scandal led to the Goode Report of the Pension Law Review Committee[16] and, in turn, to the Pensions Act 1995. The 1995 Act requires that the board of trustees must now contain at least two member-nominated trustees (if the scheme comprises 100 or more members) and otherwise at least one member-nominated trustee, and in any event that member-nominated trustees shall constitute at least one third of the board.[17] The Act also requires, if the trustee is a corporation, that the board of directors must now contain at least two member-nominated directors (if the scheme comprises 100 or more members) and otherwise at least one member-nominated director, and in any event that member-nominated directors shall constitute at least one third of the board.[18]

The fact that pension trusts operate in the employment context means that they have a special social significance, but also that they have a special legal significance, the trust itself being overlaid by the contractual rules of the scheme and numerous statutory rules designed to protect the scheme members. Almost 20 years ago, Sir Robert Megarry VC accepted that the general law of trusts is subordinated to the provisions of the pension scheme, but suggested that, beyond that, '*the trusts of pension funds are subject to the same rules as other trusts*'.[19] Since then, there have been decisions in the pensions context on such matters as the exercise of trustees' discretions,[20] the destina-tion of surplus funds,[21] and the rules against perpetuity,[22] which suggest that pension trusts are subject to quite different rules to those that govern express trusts generally. This raises the question whether the law of trusts that governs pension funds is now fundamentally different to the general law of trusts.[23] Hence, less than 10 years after Robert Megarry VC's statement on the subject, Browne-Wilkinson VC suggested that:

> Pension schemes are of quite a different nature to traditional trusts. The traditional trust is one under which the settlor, by way of bounty, transfers property to trustees to be adminis-tered for the beneficiaries as objects of his bounty ... Pension benefits are part of the consid-eration which an employee receives in return for the rendering of his services.[24]

Taxation

There is nothing in life more certain than death and taxes, and trusts can be used to plan for both. Ever since the days of its predecessor, the medieval 'use', the trust has been

---

[15] *Bishopsgate Investment Management Ltd (in liq) v. Maxwell* [1993] Ch 1, CA.

[16] Chaired by Professor Roy Goode, September 1993. See D. A. Chatterton, 'The trust concept in relation to occupational pension schemes—has the Goode Report got it right?' (1993) 7(4) TLI 91.

[17] Section 16(6).   [18] Section 18(6).   [19] *Cowan v. Scargill* [1985] Ch 270 at 290F.

[20] See Chapter 11.   [21] See Chapter 5.   [22] See Chapter 6.

[23] G. Moffat, 'Pension funds: a fragmentation of trust law' (1993) 56(4) MLR 471.

[24] *Imperial Group Pension Trust Ltd v. Imperial Tobacco Ltd* [1991] 1 WLR 589 at 597. See also *Mettoy Pension Trustees Ltd v. Evans* [1991] 2 All ER 513 *per* Warner J at 537.

employed to separate beneficial enjoyment of an asset (originally land) from formal title to the asset in order to escape taxes charged on benefits, and duties charged on formal ownership. It is not the purpose of this book to engage in a detailed analysis of tax law—it would become out of date at the next Budget if it was—but it is important to be aware of the general relationship between trusts and taxation.

The first point to note is that, if an owner of property wishes to settle it on trust to avoid tax, HM Revenue and Customs is very astute to spot any attempt by the settlor to reserve a beneficial interest for himself and any attempt to reserve control (by means, for example, of a power to revoke, vary, or regulate the trusts) might also be construed as a taxable reservation of benefit.[25]

The second point to note is the distinction between tax avoidance and tax evasion. It is a somewhat fine distinction and one that is blurred at the margins. Broadly speaking, tax evasion is criminal financial planning carried out to avoid the payment of a tax that has already fallen due, whereas tax avoidance is legitimate financial estate planning carried out to prevent a tax from falling due in the first place. In fact, the courts frequently exercise their statutory power to approve schemes for the variation of beneficial interests under trusts even where the purpose of the schemes is the avoidance of tax.[26] However, whereas it is perfectly permissible to arrange one's affairs so as to reduce one's tax burden,[27] any entirely sham or artificial steps in the arrangement of one's affairs will be ignored so as to enable HM Revenue and Customs to tax the transaction according to its true nature.[28] There are even statutory anti-avoidance provisions designed to address particular tax 'loopholes'.[29] Nevertheless, HM Revenue and Customs and the English courts can do little about trusts, such as 'non-resident' or 'offshore' trusts,[30] over which they have no jurisdiction.

Lord Walker has observed that 'in the private client world trusts are mostly established by and for wealthy families for whom taxes (whether on capital, capital gains or income) are a constant preoccupation'.[31] He warned that considerations of tax avoidance might be 'driving out consideration of other relevant matters', thereby endangering the faith of those who still regard family trusts as 'potentially beneficial to society as a whole'.[32] This danger, he notes, is 'particularly true of off-shore trusts'.[33]

We will see in Chapter 7 that charitable trusts are already wholly, or partially, exempt from most taxes.[34]

---

[25] Known as a 'gift with reservation' (Finance Act 1986, s. 102(1)(a) and s. 102(1)(b)). See *Inland Revenue Commissioners v. Eversden* [2002] EWHC 1360 (Ch); [2002] STC 1109, High Court; *Lyon v. Revenue and Customs Commissioners* [2007] STI 1816 Special Commissioners, 26 June 2007.

[26] See Chapter 9.   [27] See examples in the next section.

[28] *Ramsay v. IRC* [1982] AC 300, HL.

[29] See, for example, Income and Corporation Taxes Act 1988 (ICTA), Part XV.

[30] Also called 'non-resident' trusts. See later.

[31] *Futter v. HMRC Commissioners; Pitt v. HMRC Commissioners* [2013] UKSC 26, UK Supreme Court, para. [55].

[32] Ibid.   [33] Note 31 at para. [66].   [34] See Chapter 7.

Trusts and equity in commerce

In 1995, Lord Nicholls of Birkenhead observed that '[t]*he proper role of equity in commercial transactions is a topical question*'.[35] It is by no means a new question, of course, but, during the past two decades, there has been a discernible shift in judicial attitudes to the intervention of equity into commerce and commercial law. While the flexibility of equity was, at one time, regarded as an unwelcome trespasser[36] into a sphere in which common lawyers insisted that the legal consequences of transactions should be certain and predictable, the '*intervention of equity in commercial transactions . . . can no longer be withstood*'.[37] None of this should be taken to mean that the old Court of Chancery was unacquainted with commercial matters: on the contrary, as early as the fifteenth century, tort and commercial cases featured as prominently in Chancery as property disputes.[38] The old Court of Chancery was also responsible for breathing commercial vitality into concepts such as the mortgage, which had become something of a dead letter at common law. Nevertheless, equity's discretion to remedy individual unconscionability was regarded by common law lawyers as something that ought to be resisted, because it tended to undermine the important public interest in certainty in commercial transactions. Even the trust, which is a very well-established equitable institution (and one whose formation is rarely attributed to judicial discretion) received a cold reception from common law lawyers keen to restrain equity in the early years after the passing of the Judicature Acts. The following comment of Bramwell LJ was typical:

> Now I do not desire to find fault with the various intricacies and doctrines concerned with trusts, but I should be very sorry to see them introduced into commercial transactions, and an agent in a commercial case turned into a trustee with all the troubles that attend that relation.[39]

Nowadays, it is accepted that equitable 'creatures', such as express trusts, constructive trusts, and fiduciary duties, may be used or imposed in order to reflect more accurately the substantive intentions of the parties to a commercial deal.[40] Nevertheless, it is still the case that caution must be exercised before introducing into commerce equitable doctrines that were developed in the context of the family or land ownership.[41] The doctrine of notice is a case in point. The doctrine provides, in brief, that a good faith purchaser from a trustee of legal title to land will take free of the trust if he had no actual notice that the vendor was a trustee and would not have discovered the trust by making the sort of searches that a prudent purchaser would normally make.[42] No doubt the

---

[35] *Royal Brunei Airlines v. Tan* [1995] 2 AC 378 at 381.

[36] Atkin LJ criticized the introduction of equitable principles into commercial sale of goods transactions as a migration '*into territory where they are trespassers*': *Re Wait* [1927] 1 Ch 606 at 635.

[37] Sir Peter Millett, 'Equity—the road ahead' (1995) 9(2) TLI 35 at 36.

[38] J. H. Baker, *An Introduction to English Legal History* (London: Butterworths, 1990) at 120.

[39] *New Zealand & Australian Land Co v. Watson* (1881) 7 QBD 374 at 382.

[40] See discussion of the *Quistclose* trust later.

[41] Such caution was exercised in *Yeoman's Row Management Ltd v. Cobbe* [2008] UKHL 55; [2008] 1 WLR 1752, discussed in Chapter 8.

[42] For a fuller account of the doctrine of notice in the context of land law, see M. P. Thompson, *Modern Land Law*, 2nd edn (Oxford: Oxford University Press, 2003) ch. 3.

doctrine of notice is appropriate to the transfer of assets such as land and ships, title to which can be investigated and traced, but it may be less appropriate where a commercial party has received ordinary goods or money in the usual course of his business:

> In dealing with estates in land title is everything, and it can be leisurely investigated; in commercial transactions possession is everything and there is no time to investigate title; and if we were to extend the doctrine of constructive notice to commercial transactions we should be doing infinite mischief and paralyzing the trade of the country.[43]

We will return to consider the significance of the doctrine of notice in commerce in Chapter 15.

Trusts and equity in insolvency

When a person (human or corporate) becomes insolvent, any property to which he is beneficially entitled will be divided amongst his creditors according to a strict statutory order of priority,[44] subject to human bankrupts being entitled to retain certain highly personal and essential assets.[45] Because commerce brings with it the risk of insolvency, it often makes good sense for one party to a commercial transaction to guard against the insolvency of the other party. How can this be achieved? Suppose A wishes to sell a quantity of wood to B, possibly the oldest and most basic commercial transaction of them all. If A delivers the wood in return for B's personal promise to pay for it, A will have acquired a mere personal right (right *in personam*) against B. The right is only as good as B's promise to repay. A could have gone a step further and taken security over the wood, but this would still leave A with a mere personal right against B, albeit one which allows A to insist that the wood be sold in order to yield the payment due to A. The problem with a mere personal right against B is that it is a right against B personally and not a right in the wood itself. B is the beneficial owner of the wood and in the event of his insolvency all of B's assets, including the wood, will be made available to satisfy his creditors according to the strict statutory order of priority. It is true that A will take priority over unsecured creditors if A secured his personal right to repayment against the wood, but there may be other secured creditors who take priority over A.

A's best hope of escaping B's insolvency relatively unscathed is to recover the wood itself. To do this, A should ensure that B does not become beneficial owner of the wood until A receives payment. There are basically two methods of making sure that B does not become beneficial owner of the wood. The first is for A expressly to retain both legal title and beneficial ownership to the goods by means of a 'retention of title' clause. The second, which is our concern here, is to transfer legal title to B, but for A to retain beneficial ownership of the wood under a trust. The best method for creating a trust is to create one expressly; indeed, there is nothing (apart from B's unwillingness to agree)

---

[43] *Manchester Trust v. Furness* [1895] 2 QB 539, *per* Lindley LJ at 545, followed in *Eagle Trust v. SBC Securities* [1991] BCLC 438, *per* Vinelott J at 458 and approved in *Polly Peck International plc v. Asil Nadir* [1992] 4 All ER 769, *per* Scott LJ at 782A, CA.
[44] Insolvency Act 1986.   [45] Ibid. s. 283.

to prevent A from creating a trust by the express terms of the contract between the parties. A trust may even be *implied* into a commercial contract, but only in an exceptional case.[46]

Incidentally, if B had paid money to A in advance of delivery of the wood, there would be nothing (apart from A's unwillingness to contract) to prevent B expressly providing that the purchase monies should be held on trust for B pending delivery of the wood. B might also consider making payment in return for an immediate grant of title to the wood. If A agreed, A could simply execute a deed granting legal title in the wood to B; from that point, A would no longer be beneficial owner of the wood (beneficial title is presumed to pass with legal title) and B would be protected in the event of A becoming insolvent prior to actual physical delivery of the wood.

Asset protection trusts

No party to a commercial transaction is more at risk in the event of the other party's insolvency than the one who delivers goods on credit or lends money. It follows that no party will be more keen to take steps to protect his proprietary interest in the goods or money transferred:

> He who lends money to a trading company neither wishes nor expects it to become insolvent. Its prosperous trading is the best assurance of the return of his money with interest. But against an evil day he wants the best security the company can give him consistently with its ability to trade meanwhile.[47]

The usual method of protecting a lender's right to recover monies loaned to a company is to secure the loan against the company's assets, by way of a mortgage debenture secured on the company's land, a fixed charge over other fixed assets, or a floating charge over the company's general assets, such as stock-in-trade. If the borrower defaults on repayments of the loan, the lender is able to enforce its security. If necessary, this will involve selling the assets on which the loan was secured and discharging the loan from the proceeds of sale.

An alternative method of protecting the lender is for the lender to retain his proprietary interest in the loan monies until the transaction is fulfilled. This can be achieved by transferring the loan monies on trust to fulfil a particular specified purpose, such as the acquisition of machines to act as security for the loan.[48] By retaining his proprietary interest in the loan monies until the express purpose of the loan has been fulfilled, the lender is protected in the event of the borrower becoming insolvent before that date. If the machines are acquired, the trust will have been fulfilled and the transaction will proceed as a normal loan secured on the machines, but if the machines are not acquired, and cannot be acquired, the borrower will be a trustee of a trust that cannot be fulfilled. The trustee will therefore be obliged to return the loan monies to the lender

---

[46] See, for example, the *Quistclose* trust (discussed later in this chapter, and in Chapter 5).

[47] *Re New Bullas Trading Ltd* [1994] BCC 36, *per* Nourse LJ at 37E.

[48] See *Re EVTR* [1987] BCLC 646, discussed in Chapter 5.

under a resulting trust (literally a trust that 'jumps back').[49] The best way to create an asset protection trust of this sort is to transfer the loan monies expressly 'on trust' for the specified purpose. However, an express trust can be created without using the word 'trust', so the mere expression of an imperative specified purpose for the loan may suffice—as it did in the leading case of *Barclays Bank v. Quistclose Investments Ltd.*[50]

We will consider *Quistclose* trusts in Chapter 5, but an example of a *Quistclose* trust that will serve here to illustrate their commercial utility is that which arose on the facts of *Carreras Rothmans Ltd v. Freeman Mathews Treasure Ltd.*[51] CR Ltd, a cigarette manufacturer, had for many years employed FMT Ltd to advertise its products, for which service FMT received an annual fee. The annual fee was paid on a monthly basis. FMT fell into financial difficulties and was unable to meet its own monthly debts to third-party agents. Fearing that it would lose the custom of CR, FMT set up a special account into which CR would henceforth make its monthly payments and out of which FMT would finance advertising on CR's behalf. However, FMT went into a creditor's voluntary liquidation and the special account was frozen. CR was obliged thereafter to pay FMT's agents directly in order to maintain the advertising campaign. CR brought an action against FMT and its liquidators, claiming a declaration that the balance of monies in the special account had been held by FMT on trust to pay for CR's advertising and that, the trust having failed, the monies should now be held by the liquidators on resulting trust for CR. CR was successful. It was held that the monies in the special account had been held by FMT for a specific commercial purpose and not for its own benefit, so the monies were therefore held by the liquidator on trust for CR and would not be available to FMT's general creditors.

Governmental trust

We now turn to consider a range of situations involving what Megarry VC referred to in *Tito v. Waddell (No. 2)*[52] as 'trust in the higher sense'.[53] In that case, his Lordship held that, when a trust is created in which the trustee is referred to by his public office rather than by his personal name, it should be presumed that the settlor intended to create a governmental obligation, rather than a private trust of the ordinary sort that is justiciable in court.[54] One such case, *Kinloch v. Secretary of State for India*,[55] concerned the terms of a Royal Warrant by which Queen Victoria had granted certain spoils of war to the '*Secretary of State for India in Council for the time being*' expressly '*in trust*' for specified members of her armed forces. The plaintiff claimed that the Secretary of State should be made to distribute the property to the beneficiaries identified in the Royal Warrant. Lord O'Hagan dismissed the claim, because there had been no transfer of the 'booty' from the Crown to independent trustees, merely a transfer from the

---

[49] See Chapter 5.   [50] [1970] AC 567.   [51] [1985] 1 Ch 207.   [52] [1977] Ch 106.
[53] Ibid. at 238b. See, generally, R. Hardin, 'Do we want trust in government?' in M. Warren (ed.), *Democracy and Trust* (Cambridge: Cambridge University Press, 1999) at 22–41.
[54] Ibid. at 221.   [55] (1882) 7 LR App Cas 619, HL.

Queen to one of her servants. Only the defendant, as agent of the Queen, could actually divest the Crown of the property. This he had not done and a court of equity would not require him to do so. The *Quistclose* trusts considered in the previous section demonstrated that an express trust can be created without using the word 'trust' and *Kinloch v. Secretary of State for India* demonstrates that the word 'trust' can be used without creating an express trust. In fact, Lord O'Hagan observed that there is 'no magic in the word "trust"',[56] but, as trust lawyers, we cannot agree with that.

Tito v. Waddell (No. 2) concerned the unfortunate plight of some five hundred Banaban inhabitants of Ocean Island, a coral island located just south of the equator in the Western Pacific. Phosphate was discovered on the island in 1900 and the Pacific Islands Company moved in to extract it through mining operations. In 1920, the British Phosphate Commissioners, an unincorporated body established by the governments of the United Kingdom, Australia, and New Zealand, acquired these operations. In due course, it leased additional land from the Banabans for mining purposes and the lease, as well as correspondence and a declaration by the resident Commissioner, assured the Banabans that royalties from the mining operation would be held 'on trust' by the resident commissioner for the Banaban community generally. A subsequent ordinance omitted the word 'trust' but still provided, *inter alia*, that the resident Commissioner would hold royalties from the phosphate for the benefit of the Banabans. In the course of his very lengthy judgment, Megarry VC concluded that the fiduciary claims of the Banabans failed, because any obligation that the Crown owed towards the Banabans was not justiciable in the courts: it was a governmental obligation or *'trust in the higher sense'*.[57]

In one exceptional case, the House of Lords held that the former Greater London Council owed a fiduciary duty to ratepayers *'analogous to that of a trustee'*. Their Lordships held that it had breached its fiduciary duty by failing fairly to balance the interests of ratepayers with those of transport users when it decided to increase rates in order to reduce the price of travel by bus and tube.[58] However, another House of Lords decision handed down the following year confirmed the *Tito v. Waddell* approach:

> if a public duty is breached, there are the remedies of judicial review, declaration, injunction and recovery of money if wrongly demanded and paid. There is no remedy in breach of trust or equitable account...The duty imposed on the possessor of a statutory power for public purposes is not accurately described as fiduciary because there is no beneficiary in the equitable sense.[59]

---

[56] Ibid. at 630.

[57] [1977] Ch 106 at 238B.

[58] *Bromley LBC v. Greater London Council* [1983] 1 AC 768 at 841F–842A, 853D–E.

[59] *Swain v. The Law Society* [1983] AC 598, *per* Lord Brightman at 618, approving *The Skinners' Co v. The Irish Society* (1845) 12 Cl & F 425, HL. The Court of Appeal in *Williams v. Central Bank of Nigeria* [2013] EWCA Civ 785 confirmed that a document executed by the president of Nigeria in his public capacity could not support a claim based on a private trust.

In contrast to the approach taken in *Tito v. Waddell*, it has been accepted in other jurisdictions, notably Canada, that, in circumstances similar to those in *Tito v. Waddell* the government will owe native inhabitants trust-like ('fiduciary') duties that are justiciable in court in much the same way as the duties owed by an ordinary trustee of a private trust.[60]

The trust in the context of laws

In this section, we will compare the trust to other legal concepts. In doing so, it should be borne in mind that the trust is not only a legal *idea*, it is also a practical *instrumentality*. It can be compared and contrasted with other legal ideas at a purely theoretical level, or on the basis of practical function and utility. The Anglo-Saxon trust is in competition with other legal ideas and instrumentalities; and not only domestically, but also internationally. Langbein thinks of the trust as '*a competitor, locked in a sort of Darwinian struggle against other modes of business organization and finance, in particular the corporation, but also the partnership and the various techniques of secured finance*'.[61] It is a struggle in which the trust frequently prevails. Langbein identifies four broad reasons for the success of the trust. We have already considered two in this chapter: namely, the protection of beneficial interests in the event of the trustee's insolvency and assistance in tax planning. The third is the regime of fiduciary obligations, which is the subject of Chapter 10 of this book. The fourth is the '*trust's flexibility of design in matters of governance and in the structuring of beneficial interests*'.[62] These particular advantages of the trust combine to create an institution of practically unlimited functional flexibility. One scholar of comparative law has even suggested that it is not possible to '*identify the function of the trust because there is no such function. The trust is functionally protean*'.[63] Another has observed that trusts:

> are like those extraordinary drugs curing, at the same time, toothache, sprained ankles, and baldness, sold by peddlers on the Paris Boulevards: they solve equally well family troubles, business difficulties, religious and charitable problems. What amazes the sceptical civilian is that they really do solve them![64]

In the following sections, we will compare and contrast the trust with other legal ideas and instrumentalities, keeping in mind the sometimes cooperative, sometimes competitive, nature of their coexistence.

---

[60] Note the following decisions of the Supreme Court of Canada: *Guerin v. The Queen* (1984) 2 SCR 335; *Sparrow v. The Queen* (1990) 1 SCR 1075; *R. v. Badger* (1996) I SCR 771; *Delgamuukw v. British Columbia* (1997) 3 SCR 1010.

[61] J. H. Langbein, 'The secret life of the trust: the trust as an instrument of commerce' (1997) 107 Yale LJ 165 at 179.   [62] Ibid.

[63] G. L. Gretton, 'Trusts without equity' (2000) 49 ICLQ 599.

[64] P. Lepaulle, 'Civil law substitutes for trusts' (1927) 36 Yale LJ at 1126.

Corporation

The corporation bears a close resemblance to the trust in so far as they both may involve the management of assets and wealth by a few for the benefit of many.[65] In fact, the modern business corporation has been described as a direct descendent of the trust[66] and, if one goes even further back, one discovers that the deed of settlement trust, on which the modern company is based, first came to prominence as a successor to the very earliest form of trading corporation. After speculative trade in early forms of company stock brought about the burst of the South Sea Bubble in 1720, the creation of unchartered trading companies was prohibited and collective investment for business purposes was only possible through chartered corporations. '*An unincorporated group could not hold property, but property could be held on trust for it*',[67] so joint-stock companies came to be established by deed of settlement trusts.[68] To some extent, the company and trust still offer alternative legal routes to the discharge of identical functions: for example, a charity can be established by trust or company. However, for all of their functional similarities, there are fundamental differences between the corporation and the trust. The differences fall into three broad categories: legal personality, ownership of property, and personal obligations.

Legal personality

A corporation has a separate legal personality, which means that it is treated as a distinct person for purposes of law:[69] it is sued and sues in its own name. A trust, in contrast, has no legal personality apart from that of the trustees. A trust is sued and sues in the capacity of the trustees, although many other jurisdictions, the USA for example, permit trustees to sue and be sued in the name of the trust. To confuse matters, some companies are given the name 'trust'. Thus an 'investment trust' is not, in fact, a trust, but a company that buys and holds assets, such as shares in other companies, by way of investment for the benefit of its shareholders. The so-called National Health Service (NHS) Trust is also a corporation,[70] although the Secretary of State may provide for the appointment of trustees in the true sense to hold property on trust for the purposes of the NHS Trust. This is called for largely because trustees are required to administer certain charitable trusts that were established for the promotion of public health care before the creation of the NHS.

On the subject of legal personality, brief mention should be made of the 'private foundation'. This is a tax-planning instrument, popular in jurisdictions such as Panama

---

[65] F. W. Maitland, 'Trust and corporation' in *Collected Papers*, vol. III (Cambridge: Cambridge University Press, 1911). Reproduced in *Selected Essays* (H. D. Hazeltine, G. T. Lapsley, and P. H. Winfield, eds) (Cambridge: Cambridge University Press, 1936).

[66] D. R. Marsh, *Corporate Trustees* (London: Europa Publications, 1952).

[67] C. A. Cooke, *Corporation, Trust and Company* (Manchester: Manchester University Press, 1950) at 86.

[68] A. B. DuBois, *The English Business Company after the Bubble Act 1720–1800* (New York: Octagon Books, 1971).   [69] *Saloman v. Saloman & Co* [1897] AC 22, HL.

[70] See R. T. Bartlett, 'When is a "trust" not a trust? The National Health Service Trust' [1996] Conv 186.

and Liechtenstein, which performs some of the functions of a trust, but by means of separate legal personality.[71]

Ownership of property

A trustee is the legal owner and manager of trust property, which he holds on trust for the beneficiaries as beneficial owners of the trust property in equity. Neither trustee nor beneficiary is an absolute owner of anything; both are 'limited' owners. At first sight, the relationship between a corporation and its shareholders has a structural and functional resemblance to the trust, in that the corporation owns various assets, such as business premises and stock-in-trade, which are employed for the benefit of its shareholders and not for its own benefit per se. However, the crucial distinction is that a corporation is the absolute owner of its business premises and stock-in-trade, and the shareholders have no equitable or other proprietary interest in those assets.[72] Rather, the shareholders are absolute owners of quite different assets: shares in the corporation. So whereas a trustee and beneficiary share ownership of the trust property at law and in equity, a corporation and its shareholders share nothing: each is an absolute owner of a distinct asset. Of course, none of this means that a corporation cannot be made a corporate trustee of its assets for certain beneficiaries, just as it is possible for shares in a corporation to be held by a shareholder as a trustee rather than as absolute owner, but it does mean that corporations are not trustees for their shareholders.

Personal obligations

It is tempting to assume that a director is a trustee to the shareholders of his company. As a matter of social responsibility or 'corporate governance', he may be a trustee to them in some 'higher', non-justiciable sense,[73] but as a matter of law, he is presumed not to be a trustee to the shareholders.[74] (Of course, in a special case, the facts might show that a director has become a trustee for a particular shareholder or group of shareholders.)[75] A director, especially a managing director, will have a degree of control of trust property to the extent that he constitutes the guiding mind of the company, but he does not hold title to any corporate property in his capacity as director and therefore cannot be a trustee as such. Despite this, it is certainly true that directors owe a fiduciary, that is 'trust like', duty to their corporation.[76] It follows that, if they misappropriate corporate property to their own use they will become constructive trustees of that property for the benefit of the corporation[77] and if they take personal advantage of a business

---

[71] There are suggestions for further reading on this topic at the end of this chapter.

[72] *J. J. Harrison (Properties) Ltd v. Harrison* [2002] 1 BCLC 162, CA.

[73] A. A. Berle, 'For whom corporate managers are trustees' (1932) 45 Harv LR 1365.

[74] L. S. Sealy, 'The director as trustee' (1967) CLJ 83.

[75] See, for example, *Shaker v. Al-Bedrawi* [2002] 4 All ER 835, CA.

[76] *Report of the Jenkins Committee* (1962), Cmnd. 1749 at para. 89. See also D. D. Prentice, 'Directors, creditors, and Shareholders' in *Commercial Aspects of Trusts and Fiduciary Obligations* (E. McKendrick, ed.) (Oxford: Clarendon Press, 1992) at 73; R. Barrett, 'Director's duties to creditors' [1977] MLR 226; *Bairstow v. Queens Moat Houses plc* [2001] 2 BCLC 531, CA; *J. J. Harrison (Properties) Ltd v. Harrison* [2002] 1 BCLC 162, CA.

[77] *Selangor United Rubber Estates Ltd v. Cradock* [1965] Ch 896; *Clark v. Cutland* [2004] 1 WLR 783, CA.

opportunity 'belonging' to the company, they will be accountable just as if they were trustees of property.[78] Furthermore, a director of an insolvent company owes a duty of good faith to the corporation's creditors.[79]

It is especially tempting to imagine that the director of a corporate trustee must be a trustee directly to the beneficiaries of the trust, but it was established long ago that, although a director owes a fiduciary duty to the corporate trustee and the corporate trustee is trustee to the beneficiaries of the trust, the director is not a trustee directly to the beneficiaries of the trust.[80] If, however, a director makes an unauthorized profit from his fiduciary position to the trust, he may be liable, in the same way as any other agent of the trust,[81] to account directly to the trust beneficiaries and, if he knowingly receives trust property in breach of trust or dishonestly assists in a breach of trust, he will be personally liable to the trust beneficiaries.[82]

Contract

The aim of this section is twofold: first, to distinguish the legal idea of 'trust' from the legal idea of 'contract' and, second, to identify some circumstances in which a single practical arrangement or transaction may give rise to both a trust and a contract.

Theoretical comparison of contract and trust

> Whilst recognising that the same transaction may involve both legal relationships, contracts and trusts are in essence two distinct legal concepts.[83]

We noted, in Chapter 1, that some legal commentators consider the trust to be a special form of contract for the benefit of a third party. At a superficial level, that is a plausible description of trusts created when a living settlor transfers property to trustees expressly on trust, but it does not explain those trusts that only come into effect when the settlor (testator) dies, because it is not possible for the trustees to enter into a contract with a dead person. Nor is the contractarian analysis competent to explain non-express trusts, such as resulting[84] and constructive[85] trusts, and Langbein, the leading exponent of the contractarian analysis, does not even attempt to bring such trusts within his theory.[86] Another criticism of the 'contractarian' analysis of trusts is that it attaches insufficient

---

[78] *Foster Bryant Surveying Ltd v. Bryant* [2007] EWCA Civ 200; approving *CMS Dolphin Ltd v. Simonet* [2001] 2 BCLC 704.

[79] The duty was not codified by the Companies Act 2006, but exists in case law. See *West Mercia Safetywear Ltd [in Liquidation] v. Dodd* [1988] BCLC 250. See, generally, A. Keay, 'The duty of directors to take account of creditors' interests: has it any role to play?' [2002] (July) JBL 379.

[80] *Bath v. Standard Land Co Ltd* [1911] 1 Ch 618; *Hogg Robinson Trustees Ltd v. J. Alsford Pensions Trustees Ltd* [1997] PLR 99.

[81] See *Boardman v. Phipps* [1967] 2 AC 46, and Chapter 10.

[82] See Chapter 15.

[83] *Clarence House Ltd v. National Westminster Bank plc* [2009] 1 WLR 1651, *per* Judge Hodge QC at para. [18].   [84] See Chapter 5.

[85] See Chapter 8.   [86] See Chapter 1.

weight to the theoretical distinction between actually transferring assets to someone by gift or trust and a mere contractual agreement or promise to transfer assets. As a general rule, a contract to transfer assets does not alter the beneficial ownership of the assets: it merely places a personal obligation on the person making the promise to fulfil it. The one exception to this rule is, as we will see,[87] the specifically performable contract.

Even though trusts are not contracts for third parties, it used to be the case that a person could only claim the benefit of a contract to which he was not a party if he could demonstrate that one of the contracting parties had entered the contract as his trustee.[88] Since the enactment of the Contracts (Rights of Third Parties) Act 1999, this is no longer necessary. Subject to the provisions of that Act, a person who is not a party to a contract may enforce a term of the contract in his own right if (a) the contract expressly provides that he may, or (b) the term purports to confer a benefit on him.[89]

At this point, it is worth making brief mention of the restrictive covenant. This is a concept that has been developed almost exclusively in relation to freehold land law, but the underlying principle has wider implications for the relationship between property and contract, and the relationship between equity and law. A covenant is a promise made in a deed and the common law rule of privity of contract provides that the burden of the promise will only be enforced against the person who made it. This means that, as far as the common law is concerned, a purchaser of freehold land can purchase land at a low price by promising in the purchase deed that he will not build on it, only to sell the land to a stranger at a great profit, knowing full well that the stranger, not being subject to the covenant, will be at liberty to build on the land. In 1848, Lord Chancellor Cottenham adjudged that *'nothing could be more inequitable'* than this state of affairs and therefore held that equity would enforce a freehold covenant against persons who had not been a party to it.[90] However, it is not the function of equity to undermine the common law rules, so Lord Cottenham limited the equitable enforcement of freehold covenants to covenants that put the stranger to no financial or other expense (so-called 'restrictive' covenants), and only then if the stranger had notice[91] of the restrictive covenant before he acquired the burdened land. This reasoning has been applied outside the context of land law. Thus in *Lord Strathcona Steamship Co Ltd v. Dominion Coal Co Ltd*,[92] which involved the sale of a ship subject to an existing obligation to carry a third party's cargo,[93] the Privy Council held that Lord Chancellor Cottenham's reasoning is:

> still part of English equity jurisprudence, and an injunction can still be granted thereunder to compel, as in a court of conscience, one who obtains a conveyance or grant sub conditione from violating the condition of his purchase to the prejudice of the original contractor. Honesty forbids this; and a Court of equity will grant an injunction against it.[94]

---

[87] In Chapter 16.   [88] *Beswick v. Beswick* [1968] AC 58, HL; *Harmer v. Armstrong* [1934] Ch 65 at 86.

[89] Section 1(1). The Act is considered further in Chapter 4.

[90] *Tulk v. Moxhay* (1848) [1943–60] All ER Rep 90.

[91] In the case of freehold restrictive covenants entered into after 1925, notice can only be supplied by registering the restrictive covenant.   [92] [1926] AC 108.

[93] Called a 'charter party'.   [94] [1926] AC 108, *per* Lord Shaw at 120.

Practical coexistence of contract and trust

A trust or fiduciary duty may be created by the express terms of a contract, in which case, the terms of the trust, and the nature and extent of the fiduciary duty, will be determined first and foremost by the contractual terms as expressed. We will consider the express creation of trusts in the next chapter, but here our principal concern is to identify the circumstances in which a contractual arrangement may give rise to a trust or fiduciary duty even though the parties have made no express reference to the creation of such a trust or fiduciary duty.

The core principle is that a fiduciary duty 'cannot be prayed in aid to enlarge the scope of contractual duties'[95] and that it is 'not legitimate to import into the contract the idea of a trust when the parties have given no indication that such was their intention.'[96] In short: 'Chancery mends no man's bargain.'[97] Of course, it is perfectly permissible to imply or infer a trust or fiduciary duty in order to *give effect* to the intentions of the contracting parties, but the challenge is to identify when this will be appropriate. The House of Lords have engaged this challenge in two important cases. They are discussed briefly in the next section and considered at length in Chapter 5.

The first case is *Barclays Bank v. Quistclose Investments Ltd*,[98] which was touched upon earlier in this chapter under the heading 'Asset protection trusts'. Although there is usually a great deal of reluctance to allow commercial parties to establish trusts to make up for the shortcomings of their contractual arrangements, Lord Wilberforce stated, in the *Quistclose* case, that '[t]*here is surely no difficulty in recognising the co-existence in one transaction of legal and equitable rights and remedies*.'[99] It will be recalled that the case concerned a loan of money for a specified purpose. The arrangement was, at one level, a straightforward contract, but the borrower became insolvent before the loan monies could be applied towards the specified purpose. The House of Lords held that the imperative nature of the specified purpose made the borrower a trustee of the loan monies, which it would therefore be obliged to hold for the lender under a trust.[100]

The second House of Lords decision, *Westdeutsche Landesbank Girozentrale v. Islington LBC*,[101] is another that exemplifies how much difficulty can arise when one attempts to identify the coexistence in a single transaction of both contract and trust. The substantial question in that case was whether or not, when money has been paid under a contract that turns out to have been ultra vires (and therefore void *ab initio*), beneficial ownership of the money is retained by the payer so as to make the payee, as possessor and therefore legal owner of the money, a trustee of the benefit for the payer. A clause could have been incorporated into the contract to provide a straightforward answer to that question, but in the absence of such a clause, it fell to be determined whether it would be appropriate to use a trust to compensate for the imperfections of

---

[95] *Clark Boyce v. Mouat* [1994] 1 AC 428, *per* Lord Jauncey of Tullichettle at 437g–h; *Hageman v. Holmes* [2009] EWHC 50 (Ch).   [96] *Re Schebsman, decd.* [1944] Ch 83, *per* Lord Greene MR at 89.
[97] *Maynard v. Moseley* (1676) Swanst 651, *per* Lord Nottingham at 655.   [98] [1970] AC 567.
[99] Ibid. at 582.   [100] There is much debate about the nature of this trust. See Chapter 5.
[101] [1996] AC 669.

the contract. It was decided, for complex reasons that we will consider in Chapter 5, that it would *not* be appropriate. However, a revealing section of Lord Browne-Wilkinson's speech suggests that, despite the very sophisticated arguments placed before their Lordships, the decision was, to some extent (perhaps to a great extent), reached because of traditional judicial reluctance to allow trusts to be used to enlarge the scope of contractual duties:

> wise judges have often warned against the wholesale importation into commercial law of equitable principles inconsistent with the certainty and speed which are essential requirements for the orderly conduct of business affairs.[102]

One conclusion that can certainly be reached, on the question of the relationship between contract and trust, is that the court will be especially reluctant to imply a trust into a contract under which one of the contracting parties is a society of lawyers that should be expected to have made any intention to create a trust utterly express and crystal clear.[103] This conclusion begs the question whether it can ever be appropriate, in the absence of overriding policy reasons (such as those that were seemingly at play in the *Quistclose* case),[104] to imply a trust into a contract drafted with legal advice. The answer to that question ought probably to be 'no', especially when it is borne in mind that judicial reluctance to supplement contracts with trusts extends to private individuals who have acted without legal advice. In *Lloyds Bank plc v. Carrick*,[105] for example, a man contracted to sell a long lease of a maisonette to his sister-in-law. The sister-in-law paid the purchase price, took possession, and spent money improving the property, but no formal deed was ever completed to transfer legal title to her. She had an 'estate contract', but she neglected to protect it by registration as required by the law. Consequently, when her brother-in-law later mortgaged the lease to a bank, the bank took free of her estate contract. Having lost her estate contract, the sister-in-law then claimed, as an alternative to the estate contract, to have an interest in the land under a trust arising because she had paid the full purchase price to her brother-in-law.[106] That claim failed on the ground that the express contract between the parties left no room for the implication of any intention to create a trust. The claimant would have been better off if the contract had been void, for lack of formality or for some other reason, because the court acknowledged that, in such a circumstance, there would have been scope to imply an intention that she should acquire an interest under a trust.[107]

Debt

A debt has been defined as '*a monetary obligation owed by one person to another which is an item of value because it can be transferred to a third party*'.[108] At first sight, this

---

[102] [1996] AC 669 at 704. See also *Barnes v. Addy* (1874) 9 LR Ch App 244 at 251, 255; *Scandinavian Trading Tanker Co. A.B. v. Flota Petrolera Ecuatoriana* [1983] 2 AC 694 at 703–4.

[103] *Swain v. The Law Society* [1983] AC 598, HL at 621.   [104] See Chapter 5.

[105] [1996] 2 FLR 600.   [106] See Chapter 8 on the informal creation of trusts of land.

[107] As occurred in *Yaxley v. Gotts* [2000] Ch 162, CA.

[108] M. Bridge, *Personal Property*, 2nd edn (London: Blackstone Press, 1996) at 4.

suggests that a trustee is a debtor and that the trust beneficiary owns a debt. There are, however, crucial differences between 'trust' and 'debt'. The essence of the distinction is to be found by contrasting 'owning' with 'owing': a trustee may be the absolute owner of his personal private property, but he is the owner of the trust property only in a limited, formal sense. One consequence of this is that, if a trustee becomes insolvent, his private property is made available to satisfy the claims of his creditors, from his milkman to his mortgagee, but the trust property is owned in equity by the trust beneficiaries and it is they, not the trustee's general creditors, who are entitled to it. If the trustee merely owed the beneficiaries a personal debt, the beneficiaries would have no better claim to money in the trustee's hands than any of the trustee's personal creditors.

Despite this essential difference between trust and debt (and indeed *because* of it), it is clear from the *Quistclose* case[109] that contracts of loan, which have as their primary purpose the creation of a personal debt at common law, can sometimes be interpreted as giving rise to a trust if the primary purpose is defeated by the insolvency of the intended debtor. Hence Lord Wilberforce held that:

> when money is advanced, the lender acquires an equitable right to see that it is applied for the primary designated purpose...when the purpose has been carried out (i.e., the debt paid) the lender has his remedy against the borrower in debt: if the primary purpose cannot be carried out, the question arises if a secondary purpose (i.e., repayment to the lender) has been agreed, expressly or by implication; if it has, the remedies of equity may be invoked to give effect to it, if it has not (and the money is intended to fall within the general fund of the debtor's assets) then there is the appropriate remedy for recovery of a loan. I can appreciate no reason why the flexible interplay of law and equity cannot let in these practical arrangements.[110]

Since that case, it has frequently been confirmed that a transaction might '*bear a dual character*' of debt and trust.[111] Of course, this makes it more important than ever to be able to distinguish the character of debt from the character of trust. On that, *Jacob's Law of Trusts in Australia* provides useful guidance:

> The answer to the question whether a debt or a trust was created in any particular case depends upon the intention of the parties...If the payee was entitled to use the money as his own, being under an obligation merely to repay the same amount of money at a future time, then he is merely a debtor.[112]

One everyday transaction in which the parties intend to create a debt rather than a trust is a simple deposit of money into a bank account. In more unusual transactions it may not be so straightforward to identify the parties' intentions. The deposit of a prisoner's

---

[109] *Barclays Bank Ltd v. Quistclose Investments Ltd* [1970] AC 567, HL. Followed in *Twinsectia Ltd v. Yardley* [2002] AC 164, HL.   [110] Ibid. at 582.

[111] *Re Australian Elizabethan Theatre Trust* (1991) 102 ALR 681, *per* Meagher J at 693; *AG for Hong Kong v. Reid* [1994] 1 AC 324, *per* Lord Templeman at 331E–F.

[112] 6th edn (R. P. Meagher and W. M. C. Gummow, eds) *Jacob's Law of Trusts in Australia* (Sydney: Butterworths, 1997) at 13.

money with the prison governor is an example: the governor holds the prisoner's money as a banker—that is, in debt, rather than on trust.[113]

Agency

Agency bears some resemblance to a trust inasmuch as the agent will often have some degree of managerial control over his principal's property and an agent will usually owe a fiduciary or 'trust-like' duty of loyalty to his principal, comprising such obligations as the obligation not to compete with his principal or to make unauthorized gains by reason of his agency.[114] Sir Peter Millett, as he then was, has observed extra-judicially that there is no single test for determining whether an agent is a mere agent or a trustee. The answer depends on all of the circumstances of the particular case and, in particular, upon the parties' express or inferred intentions:

> the usual approach is to consider whether it is appropriate to superimpose a trust relationship onto the commercial relationship which exists between the parties; or whether it was contemplated that the agent should be free to treat the money as his own, in which case no trust relationship is created.[115]

In the case of *Paragon Finance plc v. D. B. Thakerar & Co (a firm)*,[116] his Lordship confirmed that an agent who has the right to mix his principal's money with his own and use it as part of his cash flow, and who merely has a duty to account to his principal annually, cannot be a trustee. A trustee is obliged to keep the trust property separate from his own, to use it for the exclusive benefit of the beneficiary, and to account to the beneficiary on demand. In *HMRC v. Annabel's (Berkeley Square) Ltd*,[117] a 'troncmaster' who used a dedicated bank account to hold tips paid to staff at an exclusive London nightclub was held to be a trustee of the tips.

Note, however, that the retention of monies in a separate account is not in itself proof of a trust. In *Re Multi Guarantee Co Ltd*,[118] MG (an insurer of domestic appliances) retained customers' premiums in a special account. MG agreed to transfer the premiums to the retailer who had collected them and the retailer agreed to indemnify MG in respect of any insurance claims. However, MG became insolvent before the terms of the indemnity had been agreed. The claim, that MG had held the premiums in the special account on trust for the retailer, failed. Nourse LJ could not conceive that the managing director of MG would have divested his company '*of all possible beneficial interest in the monies*' until he knew the terms of the indemnity.[119]

It should be noted that a person who holds another's money or property as stakeholder is not an agent as such and is not a fiduciary. A simple case of stakeholding would arise if X and Y were to bet against each other on a horse and deposit £20 each

---

[113] *Duggan v. Governor of Full Sutton Prison* [2004] 2 All ER 966, CA.   [114] See Chapter 10.
[115] Sir Peter Millett, 'Bribes and secret commissions' [1993] RLR 7 at 23.   [116] [1999] 1 All ER 400.
[117] (2008) ICR 1076.   [118] [1987] BCLC 257.   [119] Ibid. at 266f–h.

with Z, with instructions to pay the entire £40 to the winner of the bet. The relationship between stakeholder and depositors is simply contractual.[120]

Tort

A trust beneficiary is entitled to bring an action in equity against her trustee for breach of trust and against any third party who wrongfully assists in a breach of trust or wrongfully receives trust property. In Chapter 13, we will consider how the trustees' duty of care compares to the duty of care in tort and, in Chapter 15, we will consider how the equitable liability of third parties compares to tortious liability. Our present concern is what happens when a third party, such as an agent to the trust, breaches a common law tortious or contractual duty owed to the trust. The beneficiary must usually rely upon the trustee to bring a claim on her behalf, because the trustee's entitlement is at common law,[121] but there are three major exceptions to this rule.

The first is that the beneficiary can be subrogated to the trustee's common law right of action, standing, as it were, in the trustee's common law shoes, in any case in which the trustee unreasonably refuses to pursue a claim (or has disqualified himself from bringing the claim) at law:

> a beneficiary has no cause of action against a third party save in special circumstances which embrace a failure, excusable or inexcusable, by the trustees in the performance of the duty owed by the trustees to the beneficiary to protect the trust estate or to protect the interests of the beneficiary in the trust estate.[122]

The second is founded on the assumption that the trustees' contractual and tortious rights against agents acting for the trust cannot be rights that the trustees hold for their own benefit. The trustees' rights against trust agents therefore become part of the trust property and, as such, may be enforced by the beneficiaries in a suitable case '*if the trustees are unable or unwilling to do so*'.[123] This somewhat indirect, crooked route to bringing a common law contractual or tortious action against a trust agent has been referred to as a 'dog-leg' claim.[124]

---

[120] *Gribbon v. Lutton* [2002] QB 902, CA at 911, 915. See also *Potters v. Loppert* [1973] Ch 399 at 406 and *Hastingwood Property Ltd v. Saunders Bearman Anselm* [1991] Ch 114 at 123.

[121] '[T]he beneficiary has no personal right to sue, and is suing on behalf of the estate, or more accurately, the trustee' (*per* Lord Collins SCJ in *Roberts v. Gill & Co* [2010] UKSC 22; [2010] 2 WLR 1227 at para. [62]).

[122] *Hayim v. Citibank* [1987] AC 730, *per* Lord Templeman at 748, PC. Followed in *Parker-Tweedale v. Dunbar Bank plc* [1991] Ch 12, CA at 19. If a company is legal owner of fuel pipes and depots which it holds on trust for an oil company, economic losses caused by a depot fire can be recovered by the beneficiary oil company (*Colour Quest Ltd v. Total Downstream UK Plc* [2010] EWCA Civ 180; [2010] 3 All ER 793 (CA (Civ Div)) at para. [132]); in such a case, the beneficial owner can join the legal owner in the proceedings, so it does not matter that the beneficial owner was not himself in possession of the pipes and depots (applying *Chappell v. Somers & Blake* [2003] EWHC 1644 (Ch), [2004] Ch. 19).

[123] *Royal Brunei Airlines v. Tan* [1995] 2 AC 378, *per* Lord Nicholls of Birkenhead at 391.

[124] *Hogg Robinson Trustees Ltd v. J. Alsford Pensions Trustees Ltd* [1997] PLR 99, *per* Lindsay J at 117–19.

The third applies to cases in which a third party voluntarily assumes a direct common law duty of care to a beneficiary under a trust. In such a case, breach of the duty will enable the beneficiary to bring a direct claim against the third party in the common law tort of negligence in respect of any economic loss caused. The leading authority in this category is the decision of the House of Lords in *White v. Jones*.[125] Their Lordships awarded damages against a solicitor who had negligently failed to amend a will in favour of certain beneficiaries. Although the solicitor's only contractual obligation had been to the testator, it was held that the solicitor had voluntarily assumed a duty of care to the intended beneficiaries. It has since been confirmed that a duty of care of this sort is limited to cases in which the solicitor was aware of the benefit the testator intended to confer and the person or class of persons upon whom he intended to confer it.[126]

Restitution

Restitution is a free-standing remedy, relatively new to English law, which effects the reversal of an unjust enrichment made by a defendant at the claimant's expense.[127] In one case, for example, the purchaser of a car mistakenly transferred with a valuable personalized number plate was held liable to account in restitution for the value of the number plate, because he knew of the mistake at the time of the purchase and had therefore been unjustly enriched at the vendor's expense.[128] Restitution can also be said to encompass traditional remedies which allow a claimant to recover unjust enrichment made by a defendant through the commission of a wrong, such as the order made against a fiduciary to account for unauthorized profits.[129] Restitution can even be said to encompass traditional actions for the recovery of misapplied trust property,[130] although that view has been criticized by those who (wrongly, in this author's view) prefer to analyse traditional rights for the recovery of property in terms of the reversal of unjust enrichment.[131] At one time, the status of 'restitution' in English law was nothing higher than that of a remedy associated with a miscellany of causes of action, including the account for gains made in breach of fiduciary duty and the return of consideration paid under a void or frustrated contract. Its status in Civilian systems of law—notably, the German system—has always been superior. Even US law, which is a common law system like our own, has long recognized an independent cause of action for the reversal of unjust enrichment.[132] For many years, it seemed that English law had 'missed a trick'. However,

---

[125] [1995] 2 AC 207.

[126] *Gibbons v. Nelsons (a firm)*, *The Times*, 21 April 2000; [2000] PNLR 734.

[127] A. Burrows, *The Law of Restitution*, 2nd edn (London: Butterworths, 2002) at 1.

[128] *Cressman v. Coys of Kensington* [2004] EWCA Civ 47; [2004] All ER (D) 69 (Feb), CA; although it appears that a car registration cannot be classified as property (*Goel v. Pick* [2006] EWHC 833 (Ch)).

[129] See Chapter 10.

[130] G. Virgo, *The Principles of the Law of Restitution* (Oxford: Oxford University Press, 1999); *Foskett v. McKeown* [2001] 1 AC 102; see Chapter 14.

[131] A. Burrows, 'Proprietary restitution: unmasking unjust enrichment' (2001) 117 LQR 412.

[132] W. A. Seavey and A. W. Scott, *Restatement of Restitution* (St Paul: American Law Institute, 1937).

over the past 30 years or so, there have been concerted efforts by certain scholars and judges to address this omission. At the vanguard of the project were Professor Gareth Jones and Lord Goff, whose textbook *The Law of Restitution*[133] was first published in 1966 and is still the most comprehensive attempt to draw together into one place the diverse routes to restitution recognized in English law. The project was then enjoined by Professor Peter Birks, whose textbook on the subject makes a bold case for establishing a substantive law of restitution on a par with existing conceptual categories of English law such as property, contract, and tort.[134] The number of textbooks and casebooks now devoted to the subject of restitution, and, more significantly, the increased volume of references to restitution in the law reports, suggest that the project has been a success. There is insufficient space here to engage in anything like an adequate rehearsal of the strengths and weaknesses of the restitution school of thought, not least because of the sheer volume of literature devoted to the subject and the diversity of views within 'the school', but one or two critical perspectives might be borne in mind.

The first is to question the assumed elemental quality of such ideas as 'unjust' and 'enrichment'. Enrichment is not too problematic, although it begs the question whether a defendant is enriched to the full extent of his receipts or only to the extent to which a receipt has conferred a net gain or profit on him. Far more difficult is the 'unjust' nature of enrichment. The notion of 'unjust' enrichment assumes a distinction between 'just' and 'unjust' enrichment—but how is that distinction established? Property law and contract law provide comprehensive institutional means for identifying when an enrichment is legitimate. They inform us that an enrichment is legitimate when it arises from a recognized consensual transaction engaged in according to the general law of property or contract, and, crucially, they inform us that a legitimate enrichment will not become illegitimate unless, and until, it is impeached on grounds of public policy or impeached by equity on grounds of unconscionability. We have seen that, properly understood, equity does not act on a whim, but according to principles and doctrines developed over many centuries to provide a sophisticated check on the exercise of broad judicial discretion. As Lord Greene MR observed in *Re Diplock*:[135]

> if the claim in equity exists it must be shown to have an ancestry founded in history and in the practice and precedents of the courts administering equity jurisdiction. It is not sufficient that because we may think that the 'justice' of the present case requires it, we should invent such a jurisdiction for the first time.[136]

It is not suggested that the rather antiquated term 'unconscionability' cannot be improved upon, but it is still useful shorthand to describe an oppressive abuse of legal rights or powers. Restitution is portrayed as a bold new scientific approach to English law, but it seems, at times, to mistake elements for compounds. Take property rights,

---

[133] 6th edn (London: Sweet & Maxwell, 2002). See also G. Jones, 'Unjust enrichment and the fiduciary's duty of loyalty' (1968) 84 LQR 477.

[134] P. B. H. Birks, *An Introduction to the Law of Restitution* (Oxford: Clarendon Press, 1985) (revd edn 1989).

[135] [1948] 1 Ch 465.   [136] Ibid. at 481–2.

for example: Professor Birks argued that property rights are a secondary construct and that the legal world should be anatomized into more basic elements, such as enrichment and consent.[137] No doubt property rights are an artificial construct, but public policy has decided that they should be treated in law as if they were an elemental fact, indeed a more basic elemental fact than 'enrichment'. It must be acknowledged that, in the world of law, constructs are sometimes more real than mere factual evidence. Consider the example of the corporation: its legal personality is legally constructed—some would say 'artificial'—but in the world of law there is no person more real than the corporation; the corporate person is wholly law.

It cannot be denied that restitution is a conceptual experiment on a grand scale and that it is beginning to yield results, but the equitable experiment has already yielded much that is useful and has not yet run its course. It follows that the integration of equitable and restitutionary principles is destined to remain '*the greatest challenge in the law of restitution*'.[138]

The second critical perspective is that restitution is concerned with a fairly limited range of remedial concerns. It is not, for example, concerned with compensation for loss. What is more, its concern seems to be largely *inter partes*; it is concerned with injustice between the particular defendant and the particular claimant. That is all very well, but it is arguable that, as a consequence, it attaches insufficient significance to wider public interests, such as the public interest in the integrity of the institution of property law and the public interest in holding fiduciaries to strict exemplary standards of behaviour. The prophylactic, as opposed to the remedial, function of restitution is relatively underdeveloped.

Despite these reservations, and others,[139] arguments based on a substantive law of restitution will doubtless continue to have a greater instinctive appeal to English lawyers than its Civilian origins might, at first, suggest. The adversarial nature of the English legal system, and the fact that inconsistent causes of action can be pleaded in the alternative, means that claimants will always be willing to accommodate a new weapon in their arsenal and, if the weapon works in practice, it will be employed again. The irony is that the development of restitution as a free-standing remedy to reverse unjust enrichment is driven by academics intent upon creating a system of obligations and remedies with the logical coherence of a European civil code, but that the greatest hope for its success lies with the willingness of practitioners to add restitutionary claims to their usual claims in equity and common law, in accordance with the peculiar common law rule that mutually inconsistent causes may be pleaded in the alternative in the same action.

---

[137] P. Birks, 'Receipt' in *Breach of Trust* (P. Birks and A. Pretto, eds) (Oxford: Hart Publishing, 2002) 213 at 220.

[138] J. Beatson, *The Use and Abuse of Unjust Enrichment: Essays on the Law of Restitution* (Oxford: Clarendon Press, 1991) at 245.

[139] The 'unjust enrichment' school of restitution has some implacable opponents. See, for example, S. Hedley, 'Unjust enrichment' [1995] CLJ 578.

The possibility of pleading restitution for unjust enrichment as a free-standing claim was opened up by the decision of the House of Lords in *Lipkin Gorman (a firm) v. Karpnale Ltd.*[140] The claimant firm of solicitors claimed restitution of an unjust enrichment as one of its grounds of appeal to the House of Lords. A partner in the claimant firm of solicitors had used monies from the firm's client account in order to gamble at the 'Playboy' casino (run by the first defendant, Karpnale Ltd). The House of Lords decided that the casino had to pay back the monies it had received, on the ground that it had been unjustly enriched by them. However, the casino was not required to account for the full value of all sums received. It had paid out winnings to the fraudulent solicitor and had therefore changed its position in good faith, so the casino was only obliged to account to the firm for sums received less winnings it had paid out to the fraudulent partner.

According to Professor Birks, '[t]*heir Lordships [*in *Lipkin] looked forward to the day in which there might be a synthesis of common law and equity relating to restitution of misapplied funds*.'[141] Certainly, the majority approved the speech of Lord Goff (the co-author, with Professor Gareth Jones, of *The Law of Restitution*). His Lordship, having accepted that the solicitors' claim was founded upon the unjust enrichment of the club and that the club was entitled to defend that claim to the extent that it had changed its position in good faith, said:

> the recognition of change of position as a defence should be doubly beneficial. It will enable a more generous approach to be taken to the recognition of the right to restitution, in the knowledge that the defence is, in appropriate cases, available.[142]

Since then, there has been the significant decision of the House of Lords in *Westdeutsche Landesbank Girozentrale v. Islington LBC*.[143] The *ratio* of the case concerns nothing more than the type of interest that should be awarded on a judgment,[144] but the case became something of a judicial battleground between restitution and orthodox trust law. In *Westdeutsche*, Lord Browne-Wilkinson commented that '*the search for a perceived need to strengthen the remedies of a plaintiff claiming in restitution involves, to my mind, a distortion of trust principles*.'[145] We will consider *Westdeutsche* at length in Chapter 5, but if Lord Browne-Wilkinson is correct in his assessment of the potential impact of restitution, the end result will be deeply ironic. An idea of restitution imported from the jurisdictions of mainland Continental Europe will have undermined the English institution of the trust just as those jurisdictions are showing themselves most receptive to the English trust.[146] Maitland once described the trust as 'the greatest and most distinctive achievement performed by Englishmen in the field of jurisprudence'.[147] Whether the English trust is a cause for national pride we may doubt (some of the things at

---

[140] [1991] 2 AC 548.   [141] *Civil Wrongs: A New World*, The Butterworth Lectures (1990–91) 55 at 56.
[142] [1991] 2 AC 548 at 581.   [143] [1996] AC 669.
[144] See Chapter 13 for consideration of interest charged on judgments.
[145] [1996] AC 669 at 709, but see P. Birks, 'Trusts raised to reverse unjust enrichment: The *Westdeutsche Case*' [1996] 4 RLR 3, esp. at 20.   [146] See the section on 'Trusts in civil jurisdictions' in Chapter 1.
[147] F. W. Maitland, 'The unincorporate body' in *Collected Papers of Frederich William Maitland* (H. A. L. Fisher, ed.) (Cambridge: Cambridge University Press, 1911) vol. III at 272.

which it is 'greatest' are things that the general public may regard as no good thing at all—tax avoidance by the rich for one), but it is at least a 'distinctive achievement'. It is also distinctively flexible, as Maitland also observed,[148] and it would be a shame to jeopardize that.

Powers of appointment

When an asset is given to a trustee 'on trust', he is obliged to hold it for the designated object (beneficiary or purpose). The trust obligation is imperative and, if necessary, the court will order the trustee to discharge his trust. This is in stark contrast to the situation in which an asset is given to a trustee or some other person with a 'power' to appoint an object: the holder of such a power is not obliged to exercise the power at all and a court will not compel its exercise.[149] If, however, such a power is conferred on him in his fiduciary capacity, he is obliged, from time to time, to consider whether or not to exercise it and the court may direct him so to consider.[150] If the trustee actually exercises the power, he, like any other holder of a power, must ensure that he distributes within the range of the power, and in accordance with its terms and not capriciously. However, in addition to being satisfied that it is appropriate to appoint an individual object of the power, when the holder of a power of appointment holds it as a trustee, he must also make such a survey of the range of objects or possible beneficiaries as will enable him to carry out his fiduciary duty to make a proper distribution.[151]

The wording of the power must be clear. A power, like a trust, will be void if it is conceptually uncertain or administratively unworkable.[152] If one is ever in doubt as to whether a disposition has created a trust or a power of appointment, the basic rule is that the matter should be determined in accordance with the intention of the settlor, having regard to the effect that the disposition would have as a trust or a power.[153] The presence of a 'gift over' in default of appointment is good evidence that the donee was not intended to be a trustee. Take, for example, a gift of a crate of champagne 'to A to hold for B, with a gift over to C of any bottles of champagne that have not been given to B by the end of 2005'. A holds a power to distribute the bottles and the fact that C is entitled to the gift in default of appointment demonstrates that A is not subject to any

---

[148] 'Of all the exploits of Equity the largest and the most important is the invention and development of the Trust. It is an "institute" of great elasticity and generality; as elastic, as general as contract': F. W. Maitland, 'Uses and Trusts' in *Equity: A Course of Lectures* (revd. by J. Brunyate) (Cambridge: Cambridge University Press, 1936).

[149] But see the special case of a fiduciary power in the hands of a pension fund trustee, where the court itself will exercise the power if the trustees are unable to do so: *Mettoy Pension Trustees v. Evans* [1990] 1 WLR 1587. See, generally, G. W. Thomas, *Powers* (London: Sweet & Maxwell, 1998).

[150] See *Re Abrahams' Will Trusts* [1969] 1 Ch 463, *per* Cross J at 474; *Re Manisty's Settlement* [1974] Ch 17, *per* Templeman J at 24; *Re Hay's Settlement Trusts* [1982] 1 WLR 202, *per* Sir Robert Megarry VC at 210.

[151] *McPhail v. Doulton, Re Baden (No. 1)* [1971] AC 424, *per* Lord Wilberforce at 449, 457; *Re Hay's Settlement Trusts* [1982] 1 WLR 202.

[152] *Re Hay's Settlement Trusts* [1982] 1 WLR 202, *per* Sir Robert Megarry VC at 211H–212A. For the meaning of 'administratively unworkable', see Chapter 3.   [153] *Re Combe* [1925] Ch 210.

obligation or trust to give the champagne to B. It would, however, be a 'fraud on the power' for the holder of the power (A) wrongfully to prejudice the rights of any person (such as C) entitled in default of appointment, by, say, colluding with the primary object (B) to make an appointment in favour of B in exchange for A taking a share.[154]

Despite the seeming simplicity of the 'power of appointment', the law on the subject is bedevilled by technical, terminological distinctions. A 'mere' or 'bare' power of appointment becomes a 'fiduciary power' if it is conferred on a trustee or fiduciary,[155] unless the holder of the power is the only potential object of the power, in which case it makes no sense to describe the holder as a fiduciary for himself.[156] If a trustee is bound to make a distribution, but with a discretion as to the manner of the distribution, the power is then known as a 'trust power'—something that is actually more trust than power, because of the imperative obligation to make a distribution. This so-called 'trust power' is more often referred to as a 'discretionary trust'.[157]

Powers of appointment can be further classified into one of three categories according to the range of potential objects of the power: general powers, special powers, and intermediate or hybrid powers.[158] A general power can be exercised in favour of anyone at all. A special power can be exercised in favour of anyone falling within a defined class of objects. An intermediate or hybrid power can be exercised in favour of anyone at all, except persons expressly excluded by their membership of a defined class. An example of an intermediate power of appointment would be a donation 'to A to be distributed amongst such persons, apart from employees of X Co, as A in his absolute discretion thinks fit'.[159]

Powers can be arranged still further into a threefold classification according to the extent to which the holder of the power has a personal interest in the manner of its exercise: powers collateral, powers in gross, and powers appendant or appurtenant.[160] The holder of a collateral power has no interest in the subject assets. The holder of a power in gross has an interest in the subject assets, but an interest that will be unaffected regardless of how the power is exercised (the simplest example being the person who has a beneficial interest in an asset for the duration of her lifetime, but who has a power to appoint the person who should take the benefit after her death).[161] The holder of the third kind of power has an interest in the property that is capable of being affected by its exercise, which is why it is said to be 'appendant or appurtenant'.

The power to appoint objects is just one type of power that might be conferred on a trustee. Typically, a trustee will have powers to determine whether to distribute trust capital[162] and income[163] to the beneficiaries before the beneficiaries are, strictly

---

[154] *Re Mills* [1930] 1 Ch 654 and *Re Greaves* [1954] Ch 434.
[155] *Re Somes* [1896] 1 Ch 250, *per* Chitty J at 255.   [156] *Re Mills* [1930] 1 Ch 654.
[157] See Chapter 3.
[158] *Re Hay's Settlement Trusts* [1982] 1 WLR 202, *per* Sir Robert Megarry VC at 208–10.
[159] For another example, see *Re Manisty's Settlement* [1974] Ch 17.
[160] *Re D'Angibau* (1880) 15 Ch D 228, *per* Jessel MR at 232–3.
[161] See the facts of *Re Suffert's* [1961] Ch 1 (Chapter 9).
[162] The power of advancement (see Chapter 9).   [163] The power of maintenance (see Chapter 9).

speaking, entitled to it, and powers to manage and invest the trust property in the meantime.[164] Powers of the former type are said to be 'dispositive' and powers of the latter type are said to be 'administrative'.

Charge

The most familiar form of charge is a charge by way of legal mortgage of land. A charge is a form of burden with which an asset is encumbered until such time as the burden is discharged. In the case of a mortgage, the charge is discharged by paying off the debt secured on the land. The essential difference between a charge and a trust is that the owner of a charge owns a quite different asset to the assets upon which his charge is secured, whereas a trustee and a beneficiary own the same asset in different ways. We return to this distinction towards the end of the book, when we consider, in the context of tracing, the difference between a claim to an equitable interest *in* an asset held by a defendant and a claim to an equitable charge[165] *over* an asset held by the defendant.

Bailment

Bailment describes a disparate range of processes by which a person (the bailor) transfers possession of goods to another person (the bailee), usually for a specific purpose and always with a power to use them, but without the bailee acquiring legal title to them.[166] Bailment is usually contractual, but may be gratuitous. Examples of bailment include possession of a car taken on hire from a car hire company,[167] possession of goods for the purpose of delivery, and possession of goods deposited with a pawnbroker as security for money borrowed.[168] A bailee's possession is '*nine-tenths of the law*' and it will '*defeat any equitable or other interest short of a legal title*',[169] but a bailee lacks the final 'tenth', namely actual legal title to the goods. A bailment therefore rebuts the usual prima facie assumption that physical possession of moveable goods is evidence of the possessor's legal title to those goods.

Although a bailment is, in theory, quite distinct from an outright transfer of legal title, such as occurs when property is transferred to a trustee, in practice a simple bailment of goods delivered by the bailor to the bailee to keep for the use of the bailor is not easily distinguishable from a trust. The reason for this is twofold: first, as regards

---

[164] See Chapter 12. [165] Called a 'lien'.

[166] See, generally, *Palmer on Bailment*, 2nd edn (London: Sweet & Maxwell, 1991). See, also, G. P. McMeel, 'The redundancy of bailment' (2003) Lloyd's Maritime and Commercial Law Quarterly 169. For an argument that bailment should be codified, see G. S. McBain, 'Modernising and codifying the law of bailment' (2008) Journal of Business Law 1.

[167] *Karflex Ltd v. Poole* [1933] 2 KB 251. Contrast *Ashby v. Tolhurst* [1937] 2 KB 242, CA, in which a car left in a car park created a mere licence.

[168] This type of bailment is said to involve a 'pledge' of the goods. See R. Goode, *Commercial Law*, 2nd edn (London: Penguin, 1995) at 643.

[169] *C. N. Marine Inc. v. Stena Line A/B and Regie Voor Maritiem Transport (The Stena Nautica) (No. 2)* [1982] 2 Lloyd's Rep 336, *per* Lord Denning MR at 347 CA.

property, the transfer of physical possession of goods is prima facie evidence that the transferee has acquired legal title to the goods; second, as regards obligation, the bailor 'entrusts' the bailee with his property in the everyday (but not the Chancery) sense of the word 'trust'. In the classic case *Coggs v. Bernard*,[170] Holt CJ described the bailment as '*an obligation which is upon persons in cases of trust*'.[171] Even Blackstone referred to the bailment as '*a delivery of goods in trust upon a contract expressed or implied, that the trust shall be faithfully executed on the part of the bailee*'.[172]

If a bailee sells the goods and if this is unauthorized by the terms of the bailment, the buyer gets no title, even if he acts in good faith and has no notice of the existence of the bailment. This is because a bailee has no title, legal or equitable, to sell, so a purchaser from him gets neither legal nor equitable title.[173] If, on the other hand, a trustee sells goods in breach of trust, a bona fide purchaser for value without notice of the trust not only obtains legal title from the trustee, but takes it free of the equitable title of the trust beneficiaries.

Administration of estates

The estate of a deceased person passes into the hands of his personal representatives (executors or administrators). The personal representative holds the estate in a fiduciary capacity, but, in order to administer the estate, the personal representative must be treated as being the absolute owner of the deceased's property, so a person entitled under the unadministered estate of a deceased person does not have a beneficial interest in the estate until the estate has been administered.[174] The reason for this is simple: it is possible that the deceased's liabilities may exceed his assets. In such a case, there will be no assets in which any beneficial interest can be established. However, once the estate has been administered, the personal representative becomes a trustee of the assets. In summary, we can say that the personal representative of a deceased person is an absolute owner for the purpose of administration and a trustee for the purpose of distribution. The only right of a person entitled under the unadministered estate of a deceased person is to see that the estate is duly administered.[175]

Crime

A court of equity is not a court of punishment,[176] but equity's traditional concern for matters of conscience has led to some interesting points of overlap with the criminal

---

[170] (1703) 3 Ld Raym 909.

[171] Ibid. at 913. But a bailee is not a fiduciary: *Re Goldcorp Exchange* [1995] 1 AC 74 at 84.

[172] *Commentaries on the Laws of England* (1765–69) vol. II at 451.

[173] Although, in certain commercial contexts, the Factors Act 1889, ss. 2, 8, and 9, and the Sale of Goods Act 1979, ss. 21–26 validate dispositions by an apparent owner of goods.

[174] *Marshall v. Kerr* [1995] 1 AC 148, HL. *Commissioners for Stamp Duty (Queensland) v. Livingston* [1965] AC 694, PC.   [175] *Re Leigh's Will Trusts* [1970] Ch 277, *per* Buckley J at 281.

[176] *Vyse v. Foster* (1872) 8 LR Ch App 309 at 333. It is arguable that courts should be able to award punitive damages in response to equitable wrongs (A. Burrows, 'We do this at common law but that in equity' (2002) 22(1) OJLS 1).

law. One example is the courts' refusal to give effect to trusts established for criminal or other illegal purposes;[177] another is the so-called 'forfeiture rule', which prevents a killer and a killer's successors in title from retaining property inherited from the killer's victim.[178] Unfortunately, the forfeiture rule will prevent the killer's innocent children from inheriting under the victim's intestacy, with the result that the estate may pass to some more remote relative of the victim in ways that the victim would never have intended. This seems unfair, so the Law Commission recommended that where a potential heir is disqualified under the 'forfeiture rule', the estate should be distributed on the assumption (somewhat unlikely in reality) that the killer had predeceased the victim.[179] Incidentally, when a person lacks capacity to consent to life-saving medical treatment, there is nothing to prevent their attorney[180] refusing consent and taking a benefit under the will.

If the criminal law has influenced the law of trusts, so the influence has also occurred in reverse. The criminal courts acknowledge equitable notions of conscience and fiduciary obligation to the extent of treating breach of trust as an aggravating factor in cases of theft. In *R v. Clark*,[181] the sentencing guidelines in relation to theft by employees and professional persons were updated. The defendant in that case had been a bursar of the Royal Academy and treasurer of his local church, who had stolen money entrusted to him and spent it on himself with some extravagance. The Court of Appeal suggested a tariff of prison sentences variable according to the amounts stolen. The tariff ranges from a prison term of no more than 21 months, if the sum stolen was less than £17,500, to 10 years or more, if the sum stolen is greater than £1m. It was held that sentences might run consecutively if the theft occurred on a number of occasions, or if the sums involved were exceptionally large, or if, as in the instant case, there was more than one group of victims. A guilty plea will attract the appropriate discount.

International trusts

In this section we are concerned with trusts established in, or exported to, other jurisdictions so as to avoid UK tax. We will then consider trusts established across more than one jurisdiction for the purpose of asset protection and, finally, we will consider the extent to which foreign jurisdictions recognize the trust concept.

Non-resident trusts

The next time you walk down a street in one of London's prestigious residential areas, consider, for a moment, that any of the houses you pass might be owned and rented out

---

[177] See Chapter 6.   [178] *Re Sigsworth* [1935] Ch 89.

[179] *The Forfeiture Rule and the Law of Succession*, Law Commission Report (Law Commission No. 295), 27 July 2005. This reform has now been enacted by the Estates of Deceased Persons (Forfeiture Rule and Law of Succession) Act 2011, which came into force in February 2012.

[180] By a 'Lasting Power of Attorney' under the Mental Capacity Act 2005.

[181] *The Times*, 4 December 1997.

by a Panamanian company. The shares in that company might be wholly owned by a trust, the trustee of which (a one-trust corporation registered in the Cayman Islands) holds the shares on discretionary trusts for certain beneficiaries. The settlor may have given the trustee some guidance by a non-binding letter of wishes as to how it should exercise its discretion.[182] He may even have appointed a trusted friend or acquaintance to supervise the trustee from time to time to ensure that the trust is being administered and the income distributed in accordance with his wishes. He has granted this friend, or 'protector', the power to replace the trustee. The trustee is well remunerated for its services, and is motivated to exercise its discretion so as not to displease the settlor and risk removal; after all, there will always be another corporation willing to act as trustee. It will come as no surprise, therefore, if the trustee exercises its discretion in such a way that the income finds its way to members of the settlor's close family and even, sometimes, to the settlor himself. Surely he will declare to HM Revenue and Customs whatever income he receives from the non-resident ('offshore') trust, but he will not pay income tax on the rental income from the house in London, or on any of the other London houses owned by 'his' Panamanian company. As long as the income is held on discretionary trusts, the settlor has no firm entitlement to it and will not be taxed on it.[183] He must also be careful to avoid any appearance of control over the trust assets, because a court will ignore the appointment of sham trustees.[184]

This, as they say in the movies, is intended to bear no resemblance to the facts of any real case, but it illustrates the convoluted accounting trail that can be achieved by a combination of non-resident trusts and offshore companies. The scheme could be made even more convoluted by introducing a parent offshore trust corporation into the structure. The parent offshore trust corporation might hold all of the shares in the existing offshore corporation on trusts, not for a beneficiary, but solely for the purpose of holding shares in the existing offshore corporation and enabling the existing offshore corporation to act as trustee of the trust of the shares in the Panamanian company.[185] The detail of the particular scheme is not important for our purposes. A global industry of trusts and estate planners exists to provide wealthy individuals with schemes or 'products' such as these, and, as the laws of host jurisdictions change and tax laws change, so the details of the particular schemes change. The precise scheme outlined

---

[182] A binding letter of wishes is less legitimate because it can be used to 'prevail over a sham part of a trust instrument' (D. Hayton, 'Irreducible core content of trusteeship' in *Trends in Contemporary Trust Law* (A. J. Oakley, ed.) (Oxford: Clarendon Press, 1996) 47 at 53, n. 35. It may be that beneficiaries have no right to see the letter of wishes (*Re Rabbaiotti's 1989 Settlement* [2000] WTLR 953 Jersey Royal Court; *Hartigan Nominees Pty Ltd v. Rydge* (1992) 29 NSWLR 405).

[183] *Gartside v. IRC* [1968] AC 553, HL; *IRC v. Schroder* [1983] STC 480.

[184] *Re Marriage of Goodwin* (1990) 101 FLR 386; *Rahman v. Chase Bank (CI) Trust Co Ltd* (1991) JLR 103; *Midland Bank v. Wyatt* [1995] 1 FLR 696; *Turner v. Turner* [1983] 2 All ER 745.

[185] Professor Matthews suggests this possibility, but contemplates that a trust purely for the purpose of holding company shares might be struck down as a sham. Most trustees hold shares as an incident of providing for beneficiaries, rather than as an end in itself: 'The new trust: obligations without rights?' in *Trends in Contemporary Trust Law* (A. J. Oakley, ed.) (Oxford: Clarendon Press, 1996) 1 at 20.

earlier may already be out of date by the time this book is read, but some version of it will be flourishing.

The great advantage of complex international corporate trust structures lies not so much in their theoretical legal complexity, but in their practical legal complexity. They work because interested parties lose the will to untangle a knot that may have strands on every continent.[186] Of course, this is why structures such as these commend themselves not only to the 'legitimate' tax avoider, but also to rogues ranging from the wealthy businessperson seeking to hide assets from their creditors in the event of insolvency (or their spouse in the event of divorce), to the drug dealer and terrorist who uses such schemes to hide funds from investigative agencies.[187] According to one estimate, as much as one tenth of global proceeds from the illegal sale of drugs is laundered in the Caribbean alone.[188]

When is a trust non-resident?

The significance of the question, 'When is a trust non-resident?', varies according to the type of tax that one is concerned to avoid.[189] Residence is an important consideration in relation to capital gains tax and income tax; it is less important in relation to inheritance tax and stamp duty.

For capital gains tax purposes, trustees are treated as a single and continuing body of persons, and that body is treated as non-resident in the UK if the general administration of the trust is ordinarily carried on outside the UK and if the trustees or a majority of them are not resident, or not ordinarily resident, in the UK.[190] If trust assets, including bank accounts, are located abroad, and if decision making and trust administration are carried out offshore, and if correspondence emanates from offshore, this is all good evidence that the general administration of the trust is ordinarily carried on outside the UK. When determining whether a majority of the trustees are non-resident, it should be borne in mind that many professional trustees resident in the UK, such as trust corporations and solicitors, may be deemed non-resident for capital gains tax purposes if the settlor was not resident, ordinarily resident, or domiciled in the UK when the settlement was set up.[191]

Trustees are treated as being non-resident for income tax purposes if they are all non-resident. They are also treated as non-resident if *some* of the trustees are non-resident

---

[186] D. McNair, 'Risk assessment in multi-jurisdictional asset protection structures' (1996) 2(1) *Trusts and Trustees and International Asset Management* 15.

[187] J. Fisher and J. Bewsey, 'Laundering the proceeds of fiscal crime' (2000) 15(1) JIBL 11 at 20. For a critique of the use of 'letters of wishes' and 'protectors' and the abuse of basic trust principles in offshore trusts see J. Wadham (ed.), *Willoughby's Misplaced Trust*, 2nd edn (Saffron Walden: Gostick Hall Publications, 2002).

[188] D. Farah, 'Russian crime finds haven in the Caribbean', *Washington Post Foreign Service*, October 1996, at A15.

[189] See, generally, P. Soares, *Non-Resident Trusts*, 6th edn (London: Sweet & Maxwell, 2001); R. Venables, *Non-Resident Trusts*, 8th edn (London: Key Haven Publications, 2000).

[190] TCGA 1992, s. 69(1).   [191] Ibid. s. 69(2).

and the settlor or testator was not resident, ordinarily resident, or domiciled in the UK when the trust came into effect, or at any other time at which he settled assets on the trust.[192]

Exporting trusts

The scenario set out at the start of this section involved a sophisticated corporate trust structure that was designed from the outset to operate offshore. A different possibility is to export an existing UK trust to a foreign jurisdiction. This involves the wholesale removal of the administration of a trust abroad and will often involve the retirement of UK resident trustees in favour of non-resident trustees. If there is a benefit to the beneficiaries in exporting the trust—for example, smoother administration—without any outweighing disadvantages, the court will generally give its approval. Thus in *Re Seale's Marriage Settlement*,[193] the court approved an application to export a trust to Canada. The beneficiaries under the original UK settlement had emigrated to Canada a number of years before the date on which their application was heard. They had taken Canadian citizenship and intended to live there permanently. Exporting the trust produced significant saving in administration costs.

Benefit

Whether the export of a trust is beneficial to the beneficiaries is not solely a question of finance. In *Re Weston's Settlements*, the Court of Appeal refused to approve an arrangement that would have been financially most advantageous to the beneficiaries. The applicant, the father of the Weston family, applied for an order approving an arrangement under which the trust would be exported to Jersey from England with a view to saving £163,000 in capital gains tax. The family had been resident in Jersey for only three months and it was unlikely that they would remain there after the trust had been exported. Crucially, Lord Denning did not deny that tax avoidance could, in other circumstances, be a legitimate reason for exporting a trust:

> the exodus of this family to Jersey is done to avoid British taxation. Having made great wealth here, they want to quit without paying the taxes and duties which are imposed on those who stay. So be it. If it really be for the benefit of the children, let it be done.[194]

In declining to approve the export in this case, Lord Denning MR emphasized the moral and social benefits of being brought up in England, which, in his judgment, outweighed the financial benefits of tax avoidance:

> There are many things in life more worthwhile than money. One of these things is to be brought up in this our England which is still 'the envy of less happier lands'.[195]

---

[192] Finance Act 1989, s. 110.   [193] [1961] 3 WLR 262.   [194] [1969] 1 Ch 223 at 246.
[195] Ibid. at 245. The reference to the '*envy of less happier lands*' is a quotation from the famous '*scept'red isle*' soliloquy in Shakespeare's *Richard II* (II.i).

The suggestion that Jersey is a less happy land than England is somewhat surprising and it seems that the real basis for his Lordship's decision was to prevent disruption to the young beneficiaries:

> Are they to be wanderers over the face of the earth, moving from this country to that, according to where they can best avoid tax? I cannot believe that to be right. Children are like trees: they grow stronger with firm roots.[196]

Accordingly, in *Re Windeatt's WT*,[197] the court approved an application to export a trust to Jersey made by a family who, having lived in Jersey for 19 years, were clearly settled there.

Non-resident trustees

In *Re Whitehead's WT*,[198] Pennycuick VC held that except in '*exceptional circumstances*', it is not '*proper*' to appoint non-resident trustees of an English trust. He added that:

> The most obvious exceptional circumstances are those in which the beneficiaries have settled permanently in some country outside the United Kingdom and what is proposed to be done is to appoint new trustees in that country.[199]

Nearly two decades later, it was suggested, in *Richard v. Mackay*, that '*the language of Sir John Pennycuick…is too restrictive for the circumstances of the present day*'.[200] In that case, the trustees had decided that the export of part of a trust fund to Bermuda would be for the benefit of the beneficiaries, and they sought a declaration of the court's approval. Approving the export, Millett J held that the court may be more generous when asked to approve an arrangement that the trustees, having exercised their own discretion, had seen fit to approve, than the court might be if it had been asked to exercise an original discretion of its own. In the latter situation, the applicants would have to make out a positive case to show that the scheme was beneficial to the beneficiaries.

There is certainly an argument for saying that general trusts law should not be reformed so as to provide an automatic power to appoint non-resident trustees or to export the administration or proper law of the trust. As William Goodhart, who advanced this argument, points out: '*It is not the function of a Trustee Act to assist tax avoidance*'.[201]

Capital gains tax 'trap'

Exporting a trust is not the attractive option it once was.[202] Capital gains tax savings of the sort anticipated by the applicant in *Re Weston* have been wiped out by an export charge introduced by section 80 of the Taxation of Chargeable Gains Act 1992. If, after 18 March 1991, trustees become non-resident, there is a deemed disposal and

---

[196] [1969] 1 Ch 223 at 246.   [197] [1969] 1 WLR 693.   [198] [1971] 1 WLR 833.
[199] [1971] 1 WLR 833 at 837B.   [200] Unreported, 14 March 1987, *per* Millett J.
[201] 'Trust law for the twenty-first century' in *Trends in Contemporary Trust Law* (A. J. Oakley, ed.) (Oxford: Clarendon Press, 1996) 257 at 269, n. 56.
[202] See the observations made in *Cooper v. Billingham*; *Fisher v. Edwards* [2001] EWCA Civ 1041, CA.

reacquisition by the trustees at the full market value of the settled assets. Suppose UK resident trustees acquire shares for £100,000 that are valued at £500,000 when the trustees later retire in favour of non-resident trustees: the UK-resident trustees will be liable to pay tax on a deemed gain of £400,000.

The protector

The character of the 'protector' appeared in the hypothetical scenario with which we began our discussion of non-resident trusts. There is no statutory definition of his function, although it has been considered judicially.[203] His function is to supervise non-resident trustees on behalf of the settlor, especially in connection with such matters as investment of the fund and distribution of the estate.[204] He usually has power to change the outer parameters of trust business without having day-to-day control. Thus he might have power to replace and appoint trustees, and to appoint his own successor and to alter the governing law. However, he sometimes has a veto over the exercise of trustees' dispositive and administrative discretions. The problem if his powers are too extensive is that the protector might be treated as a trustee for tax purposes,[205] although this risk will not be so great if the protector is resident offshore.[206] The protector is normally subject to a fiduciary duty with regard to the exercise of any power that could adversely affect the beneficiaries.[207] It is also arguable that a protector voluntarily assumes responsibility to the beneficiaries and may therefore be liable to them in the tort of negligence.[208]

International asset protection trusts

Tax avoidance is not the only purpose for which an offshore trust or offshore corporate trust arrangement may prove useful. Another is to protect corporate[209] and individual assets in times of war and political upheaval in the domestic host jurisdiction. In such circumstances, there is little point in securing the leisurely exportation of assets; what is required is an emergency escape mechanism. Trusts, sometimes in combination with corporations, have proved useful for the task.[210] The trust has certain advantages over

---

[203] *Jurgen von Knieriem v. Bermuda Trust Co Ltd and Grosvenor Trust Co Ltd* [1994] SCB 154.

[204] D. W. M. Waters, 'The protector: new wine in old bottles?' in *Trends in Contemporary Trust Law* (A. J. Oakley, ed.) (Oxford: Clarendon Press, 1996) 63 at 119. See, further, A. Duckworth, 'Protectors: fish or fowl?' Parts I and II [1995] PCB 103, 245; P. Matthews, 'Protectors: two cases, twenty questions' (1995) 9(4) Tru L I 108 and T. H. Tey, 'Trust enforcer' (2009) Tru L I 151.

[205] Waters ibid. at p. 64.   [206] See 'The office of protector' (1995) 1(4) TTIAM 12, J. Conder.

[207] *IRC v. Schroder* [1983] STC 480; D. Hayton, 'Irreducible core content of trusteeship' in *Trends in Contemporary Trust Law* (A. J. Oakley, ed.) (Oxford: Clarendon Press, 1996) 47 at 54.

[208] See the section on 'Tort' in this chapter.

[209] See Mann, 'The confiscation of corporations, corporate rights and corporate assets and the conflict of laws' (1962) 11 ICLQ 471 at 499–502.

[210] See J. Schoenblum, 'The adaptation of the asset protection trust for use by the multinational corporation: the American perspective' in *Commercial Aspects of Trusts and Fiduciary Obligations* (E. McKendrick, ed.) (Oxford: Clarendon Press, 1992) at 217; in the same volume (at 195): H. Wiggin, 'Asset protection for multinational corporations'.

the corporation: trusts are more private (there is no public register of trusts); they are not subject to the same complex and intrusive legislation that dominates corporate law; perhaps most importantly of all, the governing law of a trust is a matter of the settlor's choice, whereas a corporation is governed by the law of its domicile.

To protect an individual's assets, a trust might be created containing a 'flee clause', which defines certain trigger events in response to which the administration and assets of the trust will be exported forthwith, or a person with the power to export the trust may be appointed to keep a watchful eye on the stability of the host jurisdiction. Where the assets of multinational corporations are concerned, an even more sophisticated mechanism is called for. The most significant precedent is the US Philips trust.[211] It was created by the Dutch electronics manufacturer NV Philips Gloeilampenfabriken on 25 August 1939, in anticipation of the imminent Nazi invasion of the Netherlands. Its purpose was to transfer the company's USA-based operations to a US trust.[212] Although the Philips trust was employed to protect assets internationally, the trust itself was hardly international. All of the trustees were resident and all of the assets were situate in the USA. Schoenblum suggests that the '*theoretically safest structure for the asset protection trust is one in which the assets, the trustee, and the designated governing law are all in a single, stable jurisdiction*'.[213] That may be true, but the practical benefit of basing the trustees, the trust fund, the settlor, and the governing law in different jurisdictions is that assets may be protected by the simple fact that potential adverse claimants may lose the will to litigate in the face of such legal, procedural, and evidential complexity.[214]

International recognition of trusts

In common law jurisdictions based on the English model, there is usually little difficulty as a matter of private international law in recognizing a foreign trust of the English design, thus English-type trusts are recognized in Australia, Canada, and the USA.[215] Civil law jurisdictions, on the other hand, are generally incapable of recognizing the English form of trust for the purposes of private international law unless they have ratified the 1985 Hague Convention on the Law Applicable to Trusts and on their Recognition.[216] It is important to be clear that it is not the purpose of the Convention to incorporate the English idea of the trust into foreign jurisdictions: the Convention does not require that the ratifying state must adopt the laws of the jurisdiction in which the

---

[211] Schoenblum, ibid. at 262.

[212] Schoenblum notes (at 263) that Philips set up a second, similar, trust in the UK later in 1939.

[213] Ibid. at 227.

[214] D. McNair, 'Risk assessment in multi-jurisdictional asset protection structures' (1996) 2(1) *Trusts and Trustees and International Asset Management* 15.

[215] See, generally, D. Hayton, 'International recognition of trusts' in *International Trusts* (J. Glasson, ed.) (London: Jordan Publishing, updated in loose leaf to 2001); D. Hayton, *Modern International Developments in Trust Law* (The Hague, London: Kluwer Law International, 1999).

[216] Which came into effect on 1 January 1992. The Convention was incorporated into English law by the Recognition of Trusts Act 1987. See, generally, J. Harris, *The Hague Trusts Convention* (Oxford: Hart Publishing, 2002).

trust was created; it merely empowers the recognizing state to know a trust when it sees one. Thus the Convention is concerned with trusts created by wills, but it is not concerned with the will itself or with national laws governing testamentary disposition; the Convention is concerned with the rocket, but not the rocket launcher, as David Hayton has described it.[217] The usual rule of private international law, that disputes concerning the transfer and acquisition of title to property should be determined by the laws of the country in which the assets are situated (the *lex situs*), is unaffected by the Convention. The priority of domestic laws of bankruptcy and succession (*lex successionis*) is likewise preserved,[218] so that, if a settlor dies leaving assets in a civil jurisdiction, his trust will not be recognized to the extent that it purports to oust the fixed entitlement of any 'heir' recognized under the civil jurisdiction's 'forced heirship' rules.[219] There is, however, scope in a rare case for a trustee to refuse to transfer assets in accordance with the *lex situs*, if he can show that he is prohibited by the mandatory international law of another jurisdiction from making the transfer.[220] The Convention will not be applied in manifest conflict with the public (including fiscal) policy of any ratifying state.[221]

The Hague Convention is not concerned with trusts that are not created expressly, but it provides a broad conceptual description of expressly created trusts. It is therefore an appropriate place to conclude our introduction to trusts and equity:

> For the purposes of this Convention the term 'trust' refers to the legal relationship created— *inter vivos* or on death—by a person, the settlor, when assets have been placed under the control of a trustee for the benefit of a beneficiary or for a specified purpose. A trust has the following characteristics—*a* the assets constitute a separate fund and are not part of the trustee's estate; *b* title to the trust assets stands in the name of the trustee or in the name of another person on behalf of the trustee;[222] *c* the trustee has the power and the duty, in respect of which he is accountable, to manage, employ or dispose of the assets in accordance with the terms of the trust and the special duties imposed upon him by law. The reservation by the settlor of certain rights and powers, and the fact that the trustee may himself have rights as a beneficiary, are not necessarily inconsistent with the existence of a trust.[223]

---

[217] Hayton, 'International recognition of trusts' in *International Trusts* (J. Glasson, ed.) (London: Jordan Publishing, updated in loose leaf to 2001). But for a contrary view, see J. Harris, ibid.

[218] See A. E. von Overbeck's *Explanatory Report on the Convention*, at para. 150 (cited in *International Trusts* (J. Glasson, ed.) (London: Jordan Publishing, updated in loose leaf to 2001) part C).

[219] For example, the French *réserve héréditaire*, the Italian *legitima portio*, and the German *Pflichtteil* (D. Hayton, 'International recognition of trusts' in *International Trusts* (J. Glasson, ed.) (London: Jordan Publishing, updated in loose leaf to 2001) at C1.21). For a criticism of forced heirship rules, from the perspective of an English trusts practitioner, see A. Duckworth, 'An offshore view of forced heirship: global conflict and its planning implications', Parts I–III [1995] PCB 270, 334, 408.

[220] Art. 16, para. 2 of the Convention. This exception was excluded under a power conferred by Art. 16, para. 3 when the Convention was incorporated into English law. See D. Hayton, 'International recognition of trusts' (ibid.) at C1.24–25.   [221] Arts 18 and 19.

[222] A so-called 'nominee'.

[223] Convention on the Law Applicable to Trusts and on their Recognition, The Hague, 1 July 1985.

Further reading

In addition to the following print sources, the Online Resource Centre accompanying this book contains web links to further reading as well as guide answers to assessment questions relevant to this chapter.

True trust or not true trust?

BARTLETT, R. T., 'When is a "trust" not a trust? The National Health Service Trust' (1996) Conv 186.

HAYTON, D., 'When is a trust not a trust?' (1992) 1 J Int P 3.

HAYTON, D., 'Pension trusts and traditional trusts: drastically different species of trusts' (2005) 18 Conv 229.

MOFFAT, G., 'Pension funds: a fragmentation of trust law?' (1993) 56(4) MLR 471.

SEALY, L. S., 'The director as trustee' (1967) CLJ 83.

WARBURTON J., 'Charitable trusts: unique?' (1999) Conv 20.

Restitution

BIRKS, P. B. H., *An Introduction to the Law of Restitution* (Oxford: Oxford University Press, 1985) (revd edn, 1989).

BIRKS, P. B. H., 'The English recognition of unjust enrichment' [1991] LMCLQ 473.

BURROWS, A. S., *The Law of Restitution*, 3rd edn (Oxford: Oxford University Press, 2010).

VIRGO G., *The Principles of the Law of Restitution*, 2nd edn (Oxford: Oxford University Press, 2006).

Contract

ATIYAH, P. S., (S. A. Smith, ed.), *Introduction to the Law of Contract*, 6th edn (Oxford: Clarendon Press, 2006).

BEALE, H. (ed.), *Chitty on Contracts*, 30th edn (London: Sweet and Maxwell, 2008).

BEATSON, J. (ed.), *Anson's Law of Contract*, 29th edn (Oxford: Oxford University Press, 2010).

LANGBEIN, J. H., 'The contractarian basis of the law of trusts' (1995) 105 Yale LJ 625.

Tort

CANE, P., *Tort Law and Economic Interests*, 2nd edn (Oxford: Clarendon Press, 1996).

Non-resident trusts

SOARES, P., *Non-Resident Trusts*, 6th edn (London: Sweet & Maxwell, 2001).

VENABLES, R., *Non Resident Trusts*, 9th edn (London: Key Haven Publications, 2009).

Comparative law of trusts

HARRIS, D., 'Chinese trusts: sweet or sour' (2004) 93(4) PCB 204.

GOLDSWORTHY, J., (ed.) *Private Foundations: A World Review* (2006) 12(5) Trusts and Trustees (special issue).

GRAZIADEI, M., MATTEI, U. and SMITH, L. (eds), *Commercial Trusts In European Private Law* (Cambridge: Cambridge University Press, 2005).

LUPOI, M., 'The shapeless trust' (1995) 1(3) T&T 15.

LUPOI, M., *Trusts: A Comparative Study* (S. Dix tr.) (Cambridge: Cambridge University Press, 2000).

LUPOI, M., O'HAGAN, P., 'Foundations and trusts' (2009) 23(2) Tru LI 80.

PANICO, P., *International Trust Laws* (Oxford: Oxford University Press, 2010).

PART II

Creation and Recognition of Trusts

3

Trusts created expressly

A gratuitous disposition of property in favour of another usually takes the form of an absolute gift. Holidays and anniversaries would not be the same were it otherwise. One could, however, choose to make a conditional gift or to make a gift subject to a charge. An example of the former would be a gift of a house to Grace 'on condition that she allows Viv to live there rent-free for life, and in default to Robert'.[1] An example of the latter would be a gift of a house to Peter 'subject to Peter paying £10,000 to Charles'.[2] Another possibility is to make a gift on trust. A simple example of an expressly created trust would be a transfer of property 'to Terry on trust for Ben'. A trust in this form constitutes Terry a trustee of the property for the beneficiary, Ben. Terry would become the legal owner of the property and Ben would become the equitable, or beneficial, owner. Of course, not every express trust is created gratuitously; it is quite possible that the settlor in our example was under a contractual obligation to create the trust for Ben.

When a settlor creates a trust, he is free to define the obligations of the trustees and the entitlement of the beneficiaries as he thinks fit, subject only to limitations imposed for reasons of public policy.[3] If he desires that the trustees should be bound to care for part only of the trust fund, he may so provide.[4] If he intends that the trustees should speculate recklessly with the fund with a view to doubling it or losing it all within a two-year period, he may so provide and '*no beneficiary can complain if the money is lost*'.[5]

The great freedom of property owners to dispose of their property as they choose can be a source of great uncertainty. Even when a disposition is made in writing, it is not always clear that a trust has been created, and even when it is clear that a trust has been created, the terms of the trust may be uncertain. Sometimes, it will fall to the courts to adjudicate between litigating parties with competing interpretations of the terms of a disposition; at other times, the trustees merely require guidance in a particular matter, so the court will make an '*order for directions*'.[6] Where the question to be resolved is the very fundamental one—'was the disposition intended to take effect by way of express

---

[1] See Re *Barlow's Will Trusts* [1979] 1 WLR 278.

[2] *Merchant Taylor's Co v. AG* (1871) LR 6 Ch App 512 at 515.   [3] See Chapters 6 and 7.

[4] *Hayim v. Citibank* [1987] AC 730.

[5] David Hayton identifies this possibility in 'Irreducible core content of trusteeship' in *Trends in Contemporary Trust Law* (A. J. Oakley, ed.) (Oxford: Clarendon Press, 1996) 47 at 57.

[6] CPR 1998, Part 64, r. 64, and Practice Direction 64.

trust or absolute gift?'—courts will hold that an absolute gift had been intended unless it is certain, from the context and the expressions used, that the person making the disposition had intended to create a trust.[7] Indeed, the very fact that it has been necessary to call upon the court to interpret a disposition arguably raises a presumption that the disposition is insufficiently certain to give rise to a trust.[8] If it is clear that a trust had been intended and the question that arises is therefore of a secondary nature—for example, 'Who is entitled to the benefit of this trust and in what proportions?'—courts will then endeavour, as far as they are able, to interpret the settlor's or testator's words and conduct so as to give effect to the trust. The courts apply the rule of construction *certum est quod certum reddi potest*, which translated means 'that is certain which can be made certain'. As Lord Langdale MR observed of the testamentary trust in *Knight v. Knight*:[9]

> In the construction and execution of wills, it is undoubtedly the duty of this court to give effect to the intention of the testator whenever it can be ascertained.[10]

The three certainties

It was in *Knight v. Knight* that Lord Langdale MR identified '*three certainties*' that have to be satisfied before a court will acknowledge that a settlor or testator has created a private express trust: certainty of *intention* to create a trust; certainty as to the *subject* (property) of the trust; certainty as to the *object* (beneficiaries or purposes) of the trust. According to his Lordship, there will be no difficulty in the application of these three certainties '*in simple cases*', but

> in the infinite variety of expressions which are employed . . . there is often the greatest difficulty in determining, whether the act desired or recommended is an act which the testator intended to be executed as a trust, or which the court ought to deem fit to be, or capable of being enforced as such.[11]

It is to this '*infinite variety of expressions*' that we now turn our attention.

Certainty of intention

The requirement of certainty of intention is designed to protect transferors and transferees of property. It protects transferors by ensuring that their property is applied only in accordance with their expressed intentions and it protects transferees by ensuring that they are burdened with trust obligations only when it ought to have been clear to them that they were to take the property as trustees. There will be no express trust

---

[7] *Lassence v. Tierney* [1849] 1 Mac & G 551; *Hancock v. Watson* [1902] AC 14. *Hancock* confirmed that an absolute gift is still effective even where trusts, expressed to take effect after the gift, have failed for some reason such as lack of issue or perpetuity.

[8] *Knight v. Knight* (1840) 3 Beav 148, *per* Lord Langdale MR, referring to the judgment of Lord Eldon in *Wright v. Atkyns* (1823) Turn & Russ 143.   [9] (1840) 3 Beav 148.

[10] Ibid. at 172.   [11] Ibid. at 172–3.

unless the original owner certainly intended to create one, but neither will there be an express trust if the intention to create one was expressed with insufficient certainty to bind the conscience of the recipient.

The fundamental question boils down to this: is the transferee of certain property entitled to use the property beneficially, or is he conscience-bound to hold his legal title to the property and exercise his powers as legal owner for the benefit of someone else? There will be a trust in the latter case, but not in the former. As Professor Waters has observed:

> The old-time property lawyer's sole distinction between those who may act selfishly and those who must act selflessly remains as valid as it ever was when we are inferring the intent of the donor of assets.[12]

Intention is a question of substance

There is no need to employ technical legal language in order to create a trust:—'*a trust can be created without using the words "trust" or "confidence" or the like*'.[13] However, if a settlor omits to use the word 'trust',

> he must do something which is equivalent to it, and use expressions which have that meaning, for, however anxious the court may be to carry out a man's intentions, it is not at liberty to construe words otherwise than according to their proper meaning.[14]

If, on the other hand, a person disposing of property does use the word 'trust', it is still possible (albeit unlikely) that he does not intend to create a justiciable private trust. We have seen that this is a possibility in the political context, where 'trust' might refer to that 'higher' form of trust to which agencies of state are subject.[15] There are even occasions when a disposition accompanied by the word 'trust' is not intended to impose an obligation of any sort upon the recipient. Suppose a doting grandparent were to hand money to a grandchild with the words 'I trust you will get yourself a nice jumper.' Clearly, it is not intended that the grandchild should hold the money for the benefit of someone else. Possibly the grandchild has a moral obligation to buy a jumper, but that is not enforceable in court.[16]

Precatory words

There will be no trust if the donor of property (such as the grandparent in our previous example) *appeals* to the donee to apply it in a particular way instead of *obliging* the donee to apply it in a particular way. Hence there will be no trust if a disposition takes any of the following forms: 'I give my property to B *hoping* that B will look after my niece'; 'I give my property to X *desiring* that X should allow Y an annuity of £25';[17]

---

[12] D. W. M. Waters, 'The protector: new wine in old bottles?' in *Trends in Contemporary Trust Law* (A. J. Oakley, ed.) (Oxford: Clarendon Press, 1996) 63 at 103.

[13] *Re Kayford Ltd* [1975] 1 WLR 279, *per* Megarry J at 282; *Staden v. Jones* [2008] EWCA Civ 936.

[14] *Richards v. Delbridge* LR 18 Eq 11, *per* Sir George Jessel MR at 14.

[15] See Chapter 2.   [16] See *Re Diggles* (1888) 39 Ch D 253.   [17] *Re Diggles* (1888) 39 Ch D 253.

'I leave all my real and personal property to my widow *feeling confident* that she will act justly to our children in dividing the same when no longer required by her';[18] 'I leave my estate to X *requesting* that X will leave what remains of it on her death to Y'.[19] The words in italics are 'precatory words', that is to say, words of prayer or petition, from the Latin *precari* meaning 'to beg'. At one time, such words routinely gave rise to trusts, but in 1840, counsel in *Knight v. Knight* observed that the practice of finding trusts based on precatory words had frequently been disapproved; by the time of the Judicature Acts 1873–75, the practice had all but come to an end.

The case of *Re Diggles*,[20] decided in 1888, is typical of the modern approach to precatory words. The testatrix left all her real and personal property to her daughter, expressing her 'desire' that her daughter should pay an annuity of £25 to a named relative and 'allow' that relative to use whatever household furniture her daughter did not need. For a number of years, the annuity was paid, but it was eventually discontinued. Thereafter, the annuitant applied to court, claiming that the daughter had become a trustee by the wording of the will and was therefore obliged to pay the annuity. The Court of Appeal held that there was no trust imposed upon the daughter requiring her to pay the annuity to her relative. The expression of the testatrix's 'desire' was held to be precatory and, construing the will as a whole, it could not be said that she had intended to create a trust of the annuity. Bowen LJ noted that the daughter had merely a '*moral duty to pay reasonable attention to the wishes of the testatrix*'.[21]

Formal dispositions

When a person disposes of property by means of a formal document such as a will, the court endeavours to ascertain his intention '*from the words he has used … in the light of such knowledge of relevant facts as … he must have had*'.[22] In short, the words used will be given their natural meaning according to the context in which they appear.[23] '*[O]ne reads the document within the four corners of the document itself, and taking account of such surrounding circumstances as are admissible*'.[24] Although the intention to create a trust must be substantial, the courts are reluctant to look behind the words used in the documents that evidence the intention. Thus in the Australian case *Byrnes v. Kendle*,[25] the defendant tried to deny that he had intended to create a trust even though he had signed an Acknowledgment of Trust declaring that he held one undivided half interest in land as tenant in common upon trust for the claimant. The trial judge held that even if the defendant might not have fully understood what he was creating, the terms of the Acknowledgement were clear and they established a sufficient objective certainty of intention to create a trust, whatever the defendant's subjective intent might have been. Extraneous evidence as to the meaning of words, such as opinions written by barristers

---

[18] *Mussoorie Bank Ltd v. Raynor* (1882) LR 7 App Cas 321, PC.   [19] *Re Johnson* [1939] 2 All ER 458.
[20] (1888) 39 Ch D 253.   [21] Ibid. at 257.   [22] *Re Osoba* [1979] 1 WLR 247, *per* Goff LJ at 251E.
[23] If a court concludes that a deed does not reflect the settlor's true intentions, it might order the deed to be rectified. See, for example, *Re Joseph Eagle 1989 Settlement* (2000) 1 WTLR 137.
[24] *Rafferty v. Philp* [2011] EWHC 709 at para.[41].   [25] [2011] HCA 26, High Court of Australia.

and correspondence with the settlor in the course of preparing the trust deed, will not be admitted.[26] Nor will the court have regard to similar transactions previously carried out by the same testator or settlor as evidence of his intention in the instant case.[27] Courts are even reluctant to take into account the construction that other courts have placed on similar words in the past:[28]

> if you come to the conclusion that no trust is intended, you say so, although previous judges have said the contrary on some wills more or less similar to the one which you have to construe.[29]

If, however, a disposition is made in terms that reproduce *exactly* the peculiar wording of a disposition considered in a previously reported case, the court may infer that the person making the present disposition intended to achieve the same result as that achieved in the earlier case. *Re Steele's Will Trusts*[30] illustrates this point. The testatrix left an heirloom to her son, to be held by him for his eldest son, and so on '*as far as the rules of law and equity will permit*', and with the request that the son should '*do all in his power by his will or otherwise to give effect to this my wish*'. The phrasing of the gift exactly reproduced the wording of a disposition considered in an earlier case.[31] It was therefore held that the testatrix had made clear her intention to achieve the same outcome as that achieved in the earlier case, namely a trust.

Without the benefit of such an exact precedent, the construction of formal dispositions falls to be decided on a case-by-case basis. It is sometimes hard to determine whether a gift or a trust was intended, as the following examples show.

In *Lambe v. Eames*,[32] the testator left his entire estate to his widow '*to be at her disposal in any way she may think best, for the benefit of herself and her family*'. It was held that these words had not created a trust in favour of 'her family'. Nor was there a trust when, in another case, a testator provided by his will that all his property real and personal should pass to his wife '*in full confidence that she would do what was right*' as to the disposal thereof between his children, either in her lifetime or by will after her death.[33] The lack of detailed directions in both cases created uncertainty, which indicated that neither testator had intended to subject his widow to a binding trust.[34]

Comiskey v. Bowring-Hanbury[35] is a contrasting case in which the testator's very detailed directions were held to demonstrate a clear intention to create an express trust. The disposition was in the following terms:

> I give bequeath and devise to my very dear wife Ellen Hanbury the whole of my real and personal estate and property absolutely in full confidence that she will make such use of it as I should have made myself and that at her death she will devise it to such one or more of

---

[26] *Rabin v. Gerson* [1986] 1 WLR 526.
[27] *Murless v. Franklin* (1818) 1 Swanst 13, followed in *Shephard v. Cartwright* [1955] AC 431.
[28] *Lambe v. Eames* (1871) LR 6 Ch App 597, CA.
[29] *Re Hamilton* (1895) 2 Ch 370, *per* Lindley LJ at 373.   [30] [1948] Ch 603.
[31] *Shelley v. Shelley* (1868) LR 6 Eq 540.   [32] (1871) LR 6 Ch App 597.
[33] *Re Adams and the Kensington Vestry* (1884) LR 27 Ch D 394, CA.
[34] *Re Williams* [1897] 2 Ch 12 is another case of this type.   [35] [1905] AC 84, HL.

my nieces as she may think fit and in default of any disposition by her thereof by her will or
testament I hereby direct that all my estate and property acquired by her under this my will
shall at her death be equally divided among the surviving said nieces.

The initial part of the disposition (the gift 'absolutely in full confidence') might have created an absolute gift had it appeared on its own. (The word 'confidence' is particularly
apt to create uncertainty, because it can describe the two quite opposite states of putting faith in others and having faith in oneself.) However, the direction that the nieces
should, in any event, acquire an interest demonstrated that the testator had intended to
subject his widow to a binding trust.

A pragmatic approach to the construction of intention

Consider the contrasting outcomes of *Re The Trusts of the Abbott Fund*[36] and *Re Andrew's
Trust*,[37] first-instance decisions decided only a few years apart. In the former case, a
doctor had collected £500 from various subscribers for 'the maintenance and support'
of two elderly, deaf sisters, but they died leaving a surplus of £367 in the fund. The question was whether the gift had been to the old ladies by way of absolute gift or subject to
a trust requiring that the monies be used for no other purpose than their 'maintenance
and support'. In the second case, a fund was set up to finance the education of certain
children, but when the children had grown up and their education had been completed,
there remained a surplus of monies in the fund. Again, the question was whether the
donations had been made on trust for no other purpose than the children's education
or whether they had been by way of absolute gift to the children.

  The facts of the cases are substantially the same and it is hard to believe that the
donors to the two funds differed very much in their intentions at the time of making
their donations. Nevertheless, it was held, in the first case, that the surplus should be
held on a resulting trust for the donors to the fund in proportion to their contributions
thereto, but, in the second case, that the surplus should be divided equally between the
children. It is hard to see any justification for the different decisions in these two cases
apart from the pragmatic one, namely that the donees in *Re Abbott Fund* had died by
the time the court came to consider the nature of the donation, whereas the donees in
Re Andrew's were still alive at the date of the judgment. In *Re Andrew's*, Kekewich J distinguished *Re Abbott Fund* on that very basis: '*I am dealing with different facts, including
the fact that the children are still alive.*'[38]

  In *Re Osoba*,[39] Goff LJ stated that both *Re Abbott Fund* and *Re Andrew's* '*may well have
been right on their particular facts*'.[40] *Re Osoba* was something of a factual hybrid of the
earlier two cases. The testator had made a bequest to his widow for her '*maintenance*'
and to his daughter for her '*training... up to University grade*'. Shortly after the widow's
death, the daughter completed her university education. The testator's son claimed a
share of the surplus that had not been used for the daughter's education. He failed. It

---

[36] [1900] 2 Ch 326.   [37] [1905] 2 Ch 48.   [38] Ibid. at 52.
[39] [1979] 2 All ER 393, CA.   [40] Ibid. at 251D–E.

was held that the gift had been an absolute gift to the wife and daughter equally, the expression of the purposes for which the gift was to be used being merely an indication of the testator's motive for making it. It should also be borne in mind that the words 'up to University grade' might have been nothing more than an attempt by the testator to give helpful guidance to the trustees as to the timing of the final disposition of capital in favour of the wife and daughter. As Turner LJ stated in *Oddie v. Brown*,[41] words *'which in other cases might import condition or contingency'* may be used merely for the purpose *'of conveying the necessary directions to the trustees'*.[42] A letter of wishes outside the will would have been a less formal, and therefore more appropriate, means of communicating such guidance.

Informal dealings

Where a disposition does not appear in a formal document, extra significance is attached to the context in which words are expressed. *Jones v. Lock*[43] is a case in point. In 1863, Jones, an ironmonger, had returned home to Wales from conducting some business in Birmingham. He was in the kitchen of his house with his wife, their baby son, and the baby's nurse, when the nurse remarked that he had returned with no present for his nine-month-old son.

Jones responded: 'Oh, I gave him a pair of boots, and now I will give him a handsome present.' He then produced a cheque in the sum of £900 made payable to himself, said, 'Look you here, I give this to baby; it is for himself,' and placed the cheque in the baby's hand.

His wife said, 'Don't let him tear it,' which is understandable given that today one would need around £60,000 to match the purchasing power of £900 in 1863.

We are told that Jones's response was: 'Never mind if he does; it is his own, and he may do what he likes with it.' He then took the cheque saying: 'I am going to put it away for him.'

Jones died six days later and the cheque was found among his possessions. At first instance, Stuart VC held this to be a valid declaration of trust by the father for the baby, but the Court of Appeal held that there had been neither a valid gift nor a valid declaration of trust in favour of the infant. Lord Cranworth LC thought *'it would be of very dangerous example if loose conversations of this sort, in important transactions of this kind, should have the effect of declarations of trust'*.[44] The fact that Mr Jones had met with his solicitor to discuss his intention to settle the money on the baby changed nothing.[45]

The dangers to which the Lord Chancellor alludes did not deter the Court of Appeal in *Paul v. Constance*[46] from holding, on the basis of equally casual statements, that a trust had been declared of money in a bank account. A woman called Paul and a man called Constance had lived together for many years, but when Mr Constance died

---

[41] (1859) 4 De G & J 179.   [42] Ibid. at 194.
[43] (1865) LR 1 Ch App 25.   [44] Ibid. at 29.
[45] Compare the broadly similar facts in *Pennington v. Waine* [2002] 1 WLR 2075, CA, where the outcome was very different (see Chapter 4).   [46] [1977] 1 WLR 527.

intestate, his estranged wife became the administrator of his estate, including the balance of a bank account held in Mr Constance's sole name. Mrs Paul claimed to be entitled to money in the bank account. She claimed that Mr Constance had assured her on more than one occasion, when referring to the money in the bank account, that 'this money is as much yours as mine'. Scarman LJ was particularly impressed by the context in which the words were uttered:

> When one bears in mind the unsophisticated character of Mr Constance and his relationship with the plaintiff during the last few years of his life...the words that he did use...convey clearly a present declaration that the existing fund was as much the plaintiff's as his own.[47]

The fact that the deceased had expressed his intentions on more than one occasion was essential to establishing the seriousness of his desire to create a trust (a one-off statement might have been dismissed as a 'loose conversation' of the *Jones v. Lock* variety), but it had the adverse effect of rendering uncertain the date at which the express trust came into being. The date of trust creation can be of crucial importance. If, for example, the first statement had occurred in one tax year and the second statement had occurred in the next tax year, there would be uncertainty as to who should be treated as owner for tax purposes. The court's decision to find an express trust on these facts was a pragmatic one. If it had dismissed the claim, Mrs Paul would have been left with nothing, and the estranged wife of Mr Constance would have received a windfall at Mrs Paul's expense.

Commercial contexts

Commerce brings with it the risk of insolvency and insolvency brings with it the virtual certainty that there will be insufficient funds to satisfy, in full, the legitimate claims of creditors against the personal estate of the insolvent party. It follows that claimants in commercial contexts may be anxious to establish that they have proprietary rights under trusts, especially where the defendant is already insolvent. In some cases, they will seek to establish interests under constructive trusts or resulting trusts, but here we are concerned with attempts to establish express trusts.

The claimants in *Re Kayford Ltd (in liquidation)*[48] were successful. They were customers of a mail-order company, each of whom had paid the full price or a deposit prior to receipt of their goods. When the company fell into financial trouble, its accountants advised it to set up a 'customers' trust deposit account' to hold customers' monies until delivery of their goods. The intention was to protect the customers in the event of the company becoming insolvent. The company accepted this advice, but continued to pay customers' monies into one of its existing, dormant accounts for a further month before eventually renaming that account the 'customers' trust deposit account'. Soon afterwards, the company went into voluntary liquidation and the liquidator asked the court whether the balance of monies in the special account belonged to the customers or to the company's general creditors.

---

[47] [1977] 1 WLR 527 at 532B–C.   [48] [1975] 1 WLR 279.

It was held that the customers were entitled to the monies in the account. The intention to create a trust was held to have been manifestly clear, despite the failure to use a separate nominated 'trust' account from the outset.[49] Megarry J held that:

> In cases concerning the public...it is an entirely proper and honourable thing for a company to do what this company did...namely, to start to pay the money into a trust account as soon as there begin to be doubts as to the company's ability to fulfil its obligations to deliver the goods or provide the services.[50]

As a result of *Re Kayford*, it would appear to make good sense, whenever payment is made in advance of delivery or the rendering of services, to make payments expressly 'on trust' for the provision of those goods or services, but it is doubtful that even equity lawyers do this in practice.[51] In *Re Kayford*, Megarry J was impressed that the trust had been set up to protect members of the general public; it is clear from his judgment that the protection achieved for the Kayford customers can also be achieved for beneficiaries who are not drawn from the general public. In the course of his judgment, his Lordship referred with approval to an earlier case in which a company invited its shareholders to subscribe to an issue of capital on the understanding that, if certain conditions were not fulfilled, their application monies would be refunded and, in the meantime, they would be retained in a separate account.[52] The company was held to be a trustee of the application monies for the subscribers. In another case, deposits paid by tenants to a property management company were recovered under a trust when the management company became insolvent.[53] The deposits had been held in a separate account for the express purpose of meeting tenants' liabilities in the event of damage being caused to the rented premises.

In *Re Kayford*, Megarry J suggested that different principles might apply to an attempt by trade creditors to establish trusts in insolvency, but since then, even trade creditors have had some notable successes.

Re Lewis's of Leicester Ltd[54] concerned an insolvent company that had traded as a department store in which floor space had been licensed to concessionaires on a 'shop within a shop' basis. These traders sold their own goods on Lewis's premises, but paid their takings into Lewis's tills, some of which were paid into a separate bank account in Lewis's name. A key question was whether the monies in the separate bank account had been held on trust for the concessionaires or whether the concessionaires should be treated as normal trade creditors. Robert Walker J held that the concessionaires were entitled to recover their monies under a trust, but that Lewis's (and hence Lewis's general creditors) had been entitled to assert its own beneficial claim to the fund to the extent of its entitlement to commission on the gross till receipts. His Lordship observed

---

[49] Note, however, that the retention of monies in a separate account is not in itself proof of a trust. See *Re Multi Guarantee Co Ltd* [1987] BCLC 257, in Chapter 2.   [50] [1975] 1 WLR 279 at 282F–G.

[51] An observation made by Pumfrey J in *OT Computers Ltd (in administration) v. First National Tricity Finance Ltd* [2003] EWHC 1010 (Ch) at para. 16.

[52] *Re Nanwa Gold Mines Ltd* [1955] 1 WLR 1080, Ch D.

[53] *Re Chelsea Cloisters Ltd (in liquidation)* (1980) 41 P & CR 98.   [54] [1995] 1 BCLC 514.

that *'the trust is a very versatile medium which can be and is used for a wide variety of commercial arrangements'.*[55]

Not every attempt to establish an express 'asset protection' trust in a commercial context has succeeded. *Mac-Jordan Construction Ltd v. Brookmount Erostin Ltd*[56] is a case in point.[57] BE was a property development company and MJC was a construction company, which BE had contracted to carry out certain building works. The contract provided that BE should make interim payments to MJC, but that BE should retain 3 per cent of each interim payment in a retention fund. The contract further provided that BE would hold the retained monies as a trustee for MJC. BE retained the monies, which came to more than £100,000, but failed to keep them in a separate fund. BE's bankers had taken a floating charge over all BE's assets and, when BE fell into financial difficulties, the bank appointed an administrative receiver under the charge. MJC claimed that the retained monies were held on trust for it, whereas the bank argued that the monies were subject to their charge. The Court of Appeal held that the retention fund had not, in fact, been set up, despite the contractual agreement that it should be. There was therefore no fund that could be identified as being fixed with a trust in favour of MJC.

In *Re Farepak Foods and Gifts Ltd (in administration)*,[58] the attempted asset protection was only partially successful. Farepak became insolvent just before Christmas 2006, creating anxiety to thousands of customers that, in turn, prompted widespread coverage in the national media.[59] In the three days leading up to the administration, the directors had sought to set up a trust of monies received by the customers' account in that period, but the deed mistakenly failed to identify the correct customer account. The judge held that the mistake could be remedied by rectification, but that monies received earlier in the year could not be subject to a trust in favour of customers, because there was no obligation on Farepak to keep those monies in a separate customers' account.

Certainty of subject

As long as the subject matter of a trust is capable of being located, mere evidential uncertainty as to its location will not cause the trust to fail. This follows from the principle *certum est quod certum reddi potest*—'that is certain which can be made certain'. Thus if a man leaves his wedding ring to his wife to hold on trust for his son, it is not fatal to the trust that the ring is not found among his personal effects when he dies. On the other hand, a trust may fail if there are evidential difficulties in *identifying* the subject matter, so a trust of 'my special pair of cufflinks' will fail if no evidence can be adduced to identify the particular set of cufflinks that the settlor had in mind.

A trust of 'the bulk of my jewellery' will fail on grounds of 'conceptual' or 'linguistic' uncertainty, because the language that the settlor has employed is incapable of being understood and applied with any certainty. How is a court to establish how much

---

[55] Ibid. at 522A.   [56] [1992] BCLC 350.

[57] *Re Multi Guarantee Co Ltd* (see 'Agency' in Chapter 2) is another.   [58] [2006] EWHC 3272 (Ch).

[59] The BBC website called it the 'Nightmare before Christmas'.

jewellery constitutes 'the bulk'? The very concept is uncertain. The settlor might have had in mind bulk by weight or by number of pieces or by value.[60] On the other hand, a trust purporting to grant a 'reasonable' income to a beneficiary will be valid, because the court is constantly involved in making objective assessments of what is 'reasonable'.[61]

Conceptual uncertainty may be fatal to an entire trust or merely to a particular power conferred on the trustees. An example of the latter is provided by *Re Kolb's Will Trusts*,[62] in which the testator purported to grant his trustees a power to invest in 'blue chip' securities. The court held that the 'blue chip' status of securities was not capable of being assessed objectively. ('Blue chip' is nothing more than a loose description of stocks and shares that demonstrate prolonged secure and profitable performance.)

Even if the trust property and the trust beneficiaries are ascertained or ascertainable, the trust will fail if there is no means of ascertaining which part of the subject matter is to go to which of the beneficiaries. So if a testator leaves two houses on trust for his two daughters, directing that the youngest should have the house remaining after the eldest had chosen hers, the trust in favour of the youngest daughter will fail if the eldest daughter dies before making her choice.[63] In such a case, although the trust fails due to uncertainty of subject matter, the property itself is certain and will be held by the trustee under a resulting trust for the testator's estate.[64] In any case, where the property itself is uncertain—as in the case of a trust of 'the bulk of my jewellery' or 'my favourite pen'—there will be no trust at all, because there cannot be a resulting trust of unascertainable assets.

Trusts of a homogeneous mass

If a mass of property comprises a number of substantially distinct but apparently identical, parts—such as a flock of sheep, a barrel of apples, a stack of gold ingots,[65] or a cellar of wine of particular vintage from a certain chateau[66]—a trust of the constituent parts will fail for uncertainty unless the relevant parts are specifically identified.[67] There is no difficulty with a trust of the whole mass, or of a certain percentage or fixed proportion (for example, one quarter) of the whole,[68] but if I declare that two sheep from my flock are held by me on trust for you, I must refine my description beyond the word 'sheep' in order to enable my trustees to identify with certainty *which* two sheep are subject to the trust.[69] Were it otherwise, my trustees would be obliged to care for the whole flock, simply to ensure that they had cared for the relevant two.

A flock of sheep might be described as an apparently homogeneous mass, because the constituent parts, although practically indistinguishable, are substantially different. A truly homogeneous mass, such as 'money in a bank account', within which each

---

[60] A gift of the 'bulk' of a testator's residuary estate failed in *Palmer v. Simmonds* (1854) 2 Drew 221.
[61] *Re Golay* [1965] 1 WLR 969, *per* Ungoed-Thomas J at 972B.   [62] [1962] Ch 531.
[63] *Boyce v. Boyce* (1849) 16 Sim 476.   [64] On 'resulting trusts', see Chapter 5.
[65] In *Re Goldcorp Exchange (in receivership)* [1995] 1 AC 74 (see later), the gold bullion held by the company for its customers had not been turned into identifiable ingots.
[66] *Re London Wine Co (Shippers) Ltd* (1975) [1986] PCC 121.   [67] Ibid. *per* Oliver J at 152.
[68] Ibid. at 137.   [69] *Re London Wine Co (Shippers) Ltd* (1975) [1986] PCC 121 at 137.

constituent part of the blended fund is substantially identical, does not raise the same difficulty. As de Montesquieu observed:

> Money is a sign which represents the value of all merchandizes … The Athenians, not having the use of metals, made use of oxen, and the Romans of sheep: but one ox is not the same as another ox, in the manner that one piece of metal may be the same as another.[70]

So an express trust of £1,000 is valid even if the settlor fails to identify which of the banknotes in his possession are subject to the trust. According to the Court of Appeal in *Hunter v. Moss*,[71] the same is true of shares in a company, provided that all of the shares are of the same type.

The facts of *Hunter v. Moss* were that the defendant and claimant had a conversation, during which the defendant declared himself to be a trustee for the claimant of 5 per cent of the issued share capital of Moss Electrical Co Ltd. The total issued share capital comprised 1,000 shares, so if the trust was valid, the defendant would be trustee of 50 shares for the claimant. The Court of Appeal held that the requirement of certainty of subject matter did not require segregation of 50 shares from the total body of shares, because the shares held by the defendant were indistinguishable from each other and therefore any 50 shares were as capable as any others of satisfying the trust. According to this reasoning, the trust would have been held valid if the defendant had expressly declared himself trustee of '50 shares' as opposed to the '5 per cent' he actually declared. Despite this indulgence, the essential rule remains that a trust cannot attach to part of a shared fund unless both the fund and the claimed share can be identified with certainty.[72]

However, even identical shares may exhibit substantial differences according to the number of shares held. Suppose, for example, that a settlor declared a trust of 50 of his shares in X Co. and then immediately sold his controlling shareholding of 1,000 shares in X Co. at a great profit, retaining only 50 shares. Because the 50 retained shares will confer no control of the company and will therefore be worth relatively little, the beneficiary of the trust will be inclined to argue that her 50 shares were sold as part of the valuable block of 1,000 and to claim the sale proceeds from the trustee, whereas the settlor is likely to argue that the retained shares are subject to the trust. It is disputes of this nature that the requirement of certainty of subject is designed to avoid, so a harsh critic might argue that *Hunter v. Moss* was wrongly decided. However, in defence of the decision, it is submitted that the trust in that case was quite rightly binding on the conscience of the settlor, because he had the power to segregate, and therefore to ascertain, the particular 50 shares he had in mind, even though he did not, in fact, segregate them. This argument is by analogy to the rule that a trustee of an express trust is not permitted to escape his trust by mixing trust property with his own. If a trustee is not permitted

---

[70] C. de Secondat, Baron de Montesquieu, *The Spirit of Laws*, 1748, Book 22(ii).

[71] [1994] 1 WLR 452, affirming the decision of Mr Colin Rimer QC sitting as deputy High Court judge in the Chancery Division ([1993] 1 WLR 934).

[72] *Lehman Brothers International (Europe) (In Administration) v. Lehman Brothers Finance SA and others* [2010] EWHC 2914 (Ch) at 243.

to escape his trust by creating a homogeneous mass, it should follow that a person who declares himself to be a trustee of 50 shares within a homogeneous mass should not be permitted to deny the trust when it lies within his power to segregate the particular 50 shares subject to the trust.[73]

An express trust of a homogeneous mass may fail for lack of certainty of subject even when there is no doubt that a trust was expressly intended. In *Re London Wine Co. (Shippers) Ltd*,[74] the company, a wine merchant, conducted its business on the understanding that wine would be held on trust for its customers until the moment it was delivered to them. The company's publicity even described its customers as 'beneficial owners' of any wine ordered and described the company as having nothing more than an unpaid vendor's lien (a form of charge) over the wine from the date of each order until the receipt of payment. The very existence of the lien confirmed that, from the date of each order, the vendor was no longer to be regarded as the beneficial owner of the purchased wine, because the purpose of the 'unpaid vendor's lien' is to authorize the vendor to retain possession of goods in which beneficial ownership has already passed to the purchaser until the vendor is paid. Nevertheless, despite the company's expressed intention to create trusts, the trusts failed, because it was not the company's policy physically to segregate the subject matter of each order from its general stock.

In *Hunter v. Moss*, the judge at first instance distinguished *Re London Wine* on the basis that the principles applicable to trusts of a homogeneous mass of intangible property (such as shares) are different to those applicable to trusts of tangible property (such as wine). It was suggested that only in the case of tangibles might '*ostensibly similar or identical assets . . . in fact have characteristics which distinguish them from other assets in the class*'.[75] That distinction, upheld on appeal, was followed in *Re Harvard Securities Ltd (in liquidation)*,[76] in which the court held that it was possible to have a valid equitable assignment of unappropriated shares, but not of unappropriated chattels. The problem with the *Hunter v. Moss* distinction between trusts of tangible and intangible property is that it suggests a distinction in equity that has no counterpart in the common law of sale of goods. We know from cases such as *Barclays Bank v. Quistclose*[77] that a trust may be employed as a secondary device to give effect to a valid contract that has, for some reason, been frustrated, but *Hunter v. Moss* suggests the quite different (and undesirable) possibility that a valid trust might be declared of unallocated intangible property when a contract for the sale of such property could never have been specifically enforceable.[78] Another problem with the distinction between tangible and intangible property suggested in *Hunter v. Moss* is that it assumes that apparently identical intangible property

---

[73] Similar reasoning appears in *Re Diplock* [1948] Cn 465, CA, *per* Lord Greene MR at 552.

[74] [1986] PCC 121.

[75] [1993] 1 WLR 934, *per* Mr Colin Rimer QC (sitting as deputy High Court judge) at 940, affirmed [1994] 1 WLR 452, CA.   [76] [1997] 2 BCLC 369.

[77] [1970] AC 567, HL.

[78] Sale of Goods Act 1979, s. 52. See S. Worthington, 'Sorting out ownership interests in a bulk: gifts, sales and trusts' (1999) J Bus Law 1 at 8. Worthington notes one case in which the award of an injunction effectively created an exception to the rule: *Sky Petroleum Ltd v. VIP Petroleum Ltd* [1974] 1 WLR 576.

is necessarily substantially identical. This, as we observed earlier, will not be the case when the voting powers attached to different sized blocks of ordinary shares are taken into account.

When the Privy Council heard the case of *Re Goldcorp Exchange Ltd (in receivership)*,[79] it did so shortly before the Court of Appeal decided *Hunter v. Moss*,[80] so the Privy Council applied *Re London Wine* free of the caution expressed about that case in *Hunter v. Moss*. Goldcorp Exchange Ltd was a company dealing in gold and other precious metals. It had become insolvent and its receivers had applied to the High Court of New Zealand for directions in relation to the disposal of the company's remaining stock of gold bullion.[81] Although the company had been in the business of selling gold, its practice had been to give its customers a certificate of ownership rather than the metal. The company retained the actual gold in bullion form. The customers were nevertheless in no doubt that they were acquiring interests in actual gold and not merely in a 'gilt-edged security'. A standard form of certificate read as follows:

> This is to certify that [name] is the registered holder of [quantity] fine gold. The above metal is stored and insured free of charge by Goldcorp Exchange Ltd on a non-allocated basis. Delivery may be taken upon seven days' notice and payment of delivery charges. The owner shall be entitled to the collection of the bullion, or funds from the sale of bullion, only upon presentation of this certificate.

Their Lordships, emphasizing the primacy of the contractual agreement between the parties, held that no property in any bullion passed to the customers under the contracts, because a vendor of unascertained generic goods is permitted to deliver *any* goods in satisfaction of a contract as long as they answer the contractual description.[82] No customer could have acquired a proprietary interest in the bullion until the very gold to which they were entitled had been ascertained. Furthermore, it was held that the company was not estopped from denying the title of those customers to whom it had given an express assurance of secure title to bullion.[83] Their Lordships reasoned that an estoppel could not be established in relation to an unappropriated part of a homogeneous mass unless the mass itself was fixed and capable of being identified with certainty when the express assurance was given. In this case, Goldcorp's bullion reserves were changing constantly, so estoppel was not possible. Customers' claims to be entitled under trusts declared in their favour likewise failed due to uncertainty of subject matter. Because there was no fixed bulk out of which trusts could have been declared, the only alternative would have been to recognize trusts floating over the company's entire stock-in-trade. Their Lordships could not accept that the company would have intended to create trusts over its entire stock of gold (sold and unsold), the consequence

---

[79] [1995] 1 AC 74.

[80] Although the opinion of the Privy Council was not delivered until 25 May 1994, the case was actually heard in November 1993, a month before *Hunter v. Moss*.

[81] Under the New Zealand Companies Act 1955, s. 345(1).

[82] Lord Blackburn, *Treatise on The Effect of the Contract of Sale*, 1st edn (1845) at 122–3.

[83] For discussion of the concept of proprietary estoppel, see Chapter 8.

of which would have been to prevent any dealing with the gold otherwise than by delivery to its customers. No express trust would have been intended in such circumstances and no other trust should be inferred:

> it is possible without misuse of language to say that the customers put faith in the company, and that their trust has not been repaid. But the vocabulary is misleading; high expectations do not necessarily lead to equitable remedies.[84]

Having refused to *infer* that a trust had been intended, their Lordships also refused to *impose* a 'remedial constructive trust' [85] to achieve justice between the parties after the event:

> The company's stock of bullion had no connection with the claimants' purchases, and to enable the claimants to reach out and not only abstract it from the assets available to the body of creditors as a whole, but also to afford a priority over a secured creditor, would give them an adventitious benefit devoid of...foundation in logic and justice.[86]

The Privy Council accepted that where *specific* goods are sold, the vendor may agree to retain physical possession on behalf of the purchaser after the sale has been completed, thereby effecting '*constructive delivery and redelivery of possession, so as to transform the vendor into a bailee or pledgee without the goods actually changing hands*',[87] but on the facts of *Re Goldcorp*, the goods were generic, not specific. It would have been otherwise if the gold bullion had been held in the form of ingots impressed or labelled with specific serial numbers, because then customers could have protected themselves by the simple expedient of purchasing ingots by number.[88]

Shortly after the decision in *Re Goldcorp Exchange*, Parliament enacted the Sale of Goods (Amendment) Act 1995 '*to amend the law relating to the sale of unascertained goods forming part of an identified bulk and the sale of undivided shares in goods*'.[89] Although the Act is specifically concerned with contracts for the sale of goods, its underlying purpose is to render subject matter certain that would otherwise be uncertain. It follows that courts might look to the logic of the Act as an objective basis for establishing certainty of subject matter in trusts of the *Re Goldcorp* and *Re London Wine* variety. The Act deals with contracts for the sale of goods under which the goods are not identified individually, but are identified as parts of a homogeneous mass or 'bulk': for example, a contract to buy '20 bottles of Krug 1979 from the 100 bottles now in your cellar'. Subsection 1(3) of the Act inserts a new section[90] into the Sale of Goods Act 1979. The section provides that, unless the parties otherwise agree, a contract for the sale of a specified quantity of unascertained goods in an identified bulk transfers property in an undivided share of the bulk to the buyer, as long as the buyer has paid the price for some, or all, of the goods. The buyer therefore becomes a co-owner of the bulk under

---

[84] [1995] 1 AC 74 at 98.   [85] See Chapter 8.   [86] [1995] 1 AC 74 at 99.

[87] Ibid. at 92, citing *Dublin City Distillery Ltd v. Doherty* [1914] AC 823, HL(I), *per* Lord Atkinson at 844. For the concepts of 'bailment' and 'pledge', see Chapter 2.

[88] Note that the disputed casks held in the warehouse in the *Dublin City Distillery* case (ibid. at 825) were individually numbered.   [89] This is the long title to the Act.

[90] Section 20A.

a tenancy in common with the other co-owners, her share being proportionate to the quantity of goods paid for and due to her. One consequence of the 1995 amendments is that, where (continuing the earlier example) bottles of Krug 1979 have been removed from the cellar until there are only 20 left, it is possible, at that moment, to identify those 20 bottles as the subject of the contract. There is no obvious reason why the same logic should not be applied in an appropriate case to validate a trust declared of assets within a homogeneous mass.

Gifts of residue

Something may be conceptually certain even when it is evidentially unquantifiable: thus we all know what is meant by the concept 'forever', even though we cannot measure it. Another concept that may be practically unquantifiable, but is always conceptually certain, is 'everything'. If A leaves 'everything' to B when he dies, we know for certain that B is entitled to everything in A's estate, even though it might be impracticable to quantify the exact contents of A's estate. It follows that a gift of the residue of a deceased's estate is certain, because it is a gift of 'everything' that remains after specific gifts have been made. So if I leave my car to my brother, my piano to my sister, and 'everything else' to my wife, the subject matter of the residue is certain and the gift to my wife will be valid. It even appears that a valid trust can be declared of the residue (in the sense of 'everything that remains') of the assets of a settlor while he is still alive. In *T. Choithram International SA v. Pagarani*,[91] the Privy Council upheld an *inter vivos* trust of the entire estate of a living settlor. Mr Pagarani executed a trust deed on his deathbed in order to establish a foundation to be an umbrella organization for a number of charities he had established during his life. Immediately after signing the deed, he stated that all of his wealth belonged henceforth to the foundation. Perhaps the imminence of the settlor's death persuaded the Privy Council that a fund which was at present uncertain would shortly be made certain.

A valid gift of residue should be contrasted with gifts of the sort considered in *Sprange v. Barnard*.[92] A testatrix left a legacy to her husband 'for his sole use', but went on to provide that 'at his death the remaining part of what is left that he does not want for his own wants and use' should go to X. X claimed to have an ascertainable interest in the legacy, and even requested that the court should impound the legacy and order an annual assessment of the sum wanted by the husband for his own use. That claim was rejected. The court held that the residue of the legacy was, in practice, incapable of being ascertained, so the husband was subject to no trust.

Certainty of object

A trust can be created even if the settlor fails to identify the object (the beneficiary or purpose) of the trust. If a person receives certain property from a settlor knowing that

---

[91] [2001] 1 WLR 1.   [92] (1789) 2 Bro CC 585, following *Wynne v. Hawkins* (1782) 1 Bro CC 179.

he receives it as a trustee, but not knowing (and having no reasonable means of ascertaining) for whose benefit he is to hold it, a trust has been created under which the settlor himself is presumed to be the beneficiary. The recipient is said to hold the property on 'resulting trust' for the settlor.[93] If, however, the settlor intended, as he generally will, that the trust property should be held for the benefit of *other* persons, it is incumbent upon him to furnish the trustee with some means of ascertaining who they are. The reason is simple: with the exception of trusts for public (charitable) purposes [94] and a few anomalous trusts for purely private purposes,[95] an owner cannot dispose of the benefit of his property in favour of 'nobody'. Either he makes a disposition to 'somebody' (this could be a human being or an 'artificial' person such as a corporation) or he makes no disposition at all.[96]

Fixed trusts

Under a fixed trust, such as 'to Bobby for life and Brendan in remainder', or 'for Barbara and Bill in shares of two-thirds and one-third respectively' or 'for my nephews in equal shares', the trustee has no say in the choice of beneficiaries and each beneficiary's share is fixed. It follows that, in order for trustees to effect a division of the trust fund, they need to know exactly how many beneficiaries there are in total. In other words, a fixed trust will fail for uncertainty of object unless a 'fixed list' of beneficiaries can be drawn up. If it is not possible to ascertain the number of beneficiaries, the trustees will not know how much of the fund to give to any particular beneficiary and, because an overpayment will be a breach of trust, the trust will be unworkable. In such a case, the trust property will return to the settlor under a resulting trust.

Nevertheless, provided that the number of beneficiaries in the class is *ascertainable*, the trust will be valid and workable even if the exact number of beneficiaries has not yet been ascertained. A trust 'to divide the fund equally between my nephews' will fall into this category, because the number of the settlor's nephews can be ascertained even if it is not yet known. But what if there is a long-lost nephew of whom the trustees have no knowledge? The answer is that the trustees are permitted to distribute the trust fund without regard to any claim of which they have no notice.[97] However, the trustees can only be said to lack notice if they still have no notice despite placing advertisements in the *London Gazette* and in papers in the locality of any land subject to the trust.[98] The advertisements are required to declare the trustees' intention to distribute the fund and they must specify a period, of not less than two months, within which interested parties must furnish the trustees with particulars of claims.

It is also important to realize that a fixed trust does not fail for uncertainty merely because known beneficiaries cannot be located. If a beneficiary is 'missing', the court can make an order, called a '*Benjamin* order', permitting the trustees to distribute her share amongst the

---

[93] See Chapter 5.   [94] See Chapter 7.   [95] See nn. 166–181.
[96] This, the so-called 'beneficiary principle', is considered later in this chapter.
[97] Trustee Act 1925, s. 27(2).   [98] Trustee Act 1925, s. 27(1).

other beneficiaries on the assumption that the missing beneficiary no longer qualifies for an interest under the trust.[99] However, a *Benjamin* order '*does not vary or destroy beneficial interests. It merely enables trust property to be distributed in accordance with the practical probabilities*',[100] so if the missing beneficiary eventually reappears, she will be entitled to assert her right to her share.[101] For this reason, courts will generally require as a condition of making a *Benjamin* order that the beneficiaries receiving the 'windfall' give security,[102] or an undertaking,[103] to refund the windfall if the need arises. If the 'missing' beneficiary eventually reappears, she will still be able to rely upon the security or undertaking. If there is no security or undertaking, she might be able to trace the value of her share into the hands of those who received the windfall at her expense and recover it from them.[104]

Any trustee making a distribution without the protection of a *Benjamin* order should take out insurance against the risk that missing beneficiaries might reappear after distribution of the fund. 'Missing beneficiary' insurance protects the trustee, but it also protects the missing beneficiary in a way that a *Benjamin* order does not. Insurance will frequently be cheaper than an application to court, which might make it the only viable alternative where the trust fund is small.[105] Having said that, a small trust will only be able to afford to purchase basic cover, which will leave the trustees exposed to personal liability for any erroneous distribution, albeit subject to the possibility of relief.[106]

Certainty of object is just as much a consideration where express trusts are created in commercial contexts. In *OT Computers Ltd (in administration) v. First National Tricity Finance Ltd*,[107] a fixed trust for 'urgent suppliers' failed because the description did not identify the objects with sufficient certainty.

Discretionary trusts

A discretionary trust may be set up for the benefit of an individual beneficiary if it is undesirable for tax and other financial planning reasons for the beneficiary to have immediate beneficial enjoyment of an entire fund,[108] but a discretionary trust is usually employed for the benefit of a *class* of beneficiaries. Under a discretionary trust, the duty of the trustees is '*to select from among a class of beneficiaries those who are to receive, and the proportions in which they are to receive, income or capital of the trust property*'.[109]

---

[99] *Re Benjamin* [1902] 1 Ch 723.
[100] *Re Green's Will Trusts* [1985] 3 All ER 455, Nourse J, Ch D noted at 49 MLR 258. See, also, *Re MF Global UK Ltd (In Special Administration)* [2013] EWHC 1655 (Ch); [2013] WTLR 1239.
[101] *Re Evans (decd)* [1999] 2 All ER 777, Ch D.   [102] *Dowley v. Winfield* (1844) 14 Sim 277.
[103] *Bullas v. Public Trustee* [1981] 1 NSWLR 641.
[104] Section 27(2)(a) does not permit tracing into the hands of a purchaser, but it otherwise preserves the usual rights of following and tracing that are available to beneficiaries (see Chapter 14). Trustees should take out insurance to cover any beneficiaries they know about. If they have actual notice of the existence of beneficiaries and forget about them, section 27 will not absolve the trustees. (*AON Pension Trustees Ltd v. MCP Pension Trustees Ltd* [2010] EWCA Civ 377; [2011] 3 WLR 455.)
[105] *Re Evans (decd)* [1999] 2 All ER 777, Ch D.   [106] See Chapter 13.
[107] [2003] EWHC 1010 (Ch), Pumfrey J.
[108] As where damages for serious personal injury are designed to last a lifetime, e.g., *Lindsay v. Wood* [2006] EWHC 2895 (QB).   [109] *Mettoy v. Evans* [1990] 1 WLR 1587, *per* Warner J at 1614E–F.

Each potential object of a discretionary trust has the right '*to be considered as a potential recipient of benefit by the trustees and a right to have his interest protected by a court of equity*'.[110] Although such a right is not a vested beneficial interest and therefore cannot be taxed, it is more than a mere *spes* (specious hope).[111]

At one time, the 'fixed list' test for certainty of object, which applies to determine whether the objects of a fixed trust are sufficiently certain, also applied to discretionary trusts. It might seem odd that it should ever have been thought necessary to determine the precise number of potential beneficiaries of a discretionary trust when the whole point of such a trust is that the settlor probably did not intend that every potential beneficiary should take an interest and almost certainly did not intend that each should receive an equal share.[112] So the question arises: what was the reasoning behind the former rule that a discretionary trust must fail unless every beneficiary could be listed? The answer is that the rule was a response to the fact that a trust must be discharged and that, if no trustee could be found to discharge it, it might fall to be carried out by the courts. Courts are unable to exercise a private discretion relating to the division and distribution of the trust property,[113] so the court would have no option but to divide the fund equally between all potential beneficiaries just as if the discretionary trust were, in fact, a fixed trust.[114] In practice, the likelihood of a court being called upon to discharge a discretionary trust is very remote, but it is nevertheless a theoretical possibility.

Adoption of the individual ascertainability test

The 'individual ascertainability test' was developed outside the law of trusts; it was developed in relation to *powers of appointment*.[115] The test provides that the objects of a power will be sufficiently certain if it can be said with certainty of any individual claimant, as and when she presents herself, that she does or does not fall within the class of potential objects.[116] Suppose I were to give £2,000 to the president of the student law society with a power to distribute it as she thinks fit amongst my present and former trusts students, and, in default, to give the balance of the fund to the student law society. Any one of my trusts students can apply to be considered for a grant. It may be that it is not possible to produce a fixed list of every student who has been taught trusts by me, because the university records do not go back far enough, but the power of appointment is nevertheless valid, because the *concept* of 'my trusts student' is clear enough for me to be able to say for certain of any applicant that she is or is not one of my trusts students. If a certain applicant (sometimes called a 'postulant' in this context) cannot

---

[110] *Gartside v. IRC* [1968] AC 553, *per* Lord Wilberforce at 617.   [111] Ibid. at 618.

[112] As Lord Wilberforce said in *McPhail v. Doulton* [1971] AC 424 at 451A–B: '*Equal division is surely the last thing the settlor ever intended.*'

[113] So-called 'dispositive discretions'. Actually, there are ancient precedents for the judicial exercise of dispositive discretions, a number of which are recited in *Kemp v. Kemp* (1801) 5 Ves Jr 849, but, as Sir Richard Arden MR observed in that case, those authorities are no longer followed.

[114] *IRC v. Broadway Cottages Trust* [1955] Ch 20, CA.

[115] See Chapter 2 ('Powers of Appointment').

[116] *Re Gestener's Settlement* [1953] Ch 672; as followed in *Re Gulbenkian's Settlement* [1970] AC 508 at 523, HL.

produce evidence of her eligibility, the power will not be exercised in her favour, but such evidential difficulties do not alter the fact that the power is itself valid, because the criteria for eligibility are certain and they can be applied to each individual postulant on a case-by-case basis.

The reason why the test for certainty of objects has traditionally been more relaxed in the case of powers of appointment than in the case of trusts is because of the theoretical possibility that the court might be called upon to exercise a trust. A trust is an imperative obligation, so it must be carried out. If there is no trustee able to carry it out, it might in theory fall to the court to carry it out. In that event, the only fair way for the court to proceed, as we noted earlier, would be to make an equal division according to a fixed list of all eligible beneficiaries. Distribution under a power of appointment is not imperative and so it will not fall to be carried out by the court and so it does not depend for its validity on the availability of a fixed list of every potential object. The only circumstance in which a court will compel the holder of a power to exercise it is where it was initially exercised capriciously or in favour of objects outside the permitted range, or where, because of a conflict of fiduciary duties, the power cannot be exercised without the guidance of the court.[117]

The reason why the fixed list test for certainty of object no longer applies to discretionary trusts is because the courts have now adopted the more relaxed 'individual ascertainability test' from the law relating to powers of appointment. At first, the courts introduced the more relaxed test by the back door, by artificially construing discretionary trusts to be powers, but in *McPhail v. Doulton*,[118] Lord Wilberforce let the new test in by the front door.[119] In doing so, his Lordship stressed the close similarity between powers and discretionary trusts, even referring to the latter as '*trust powers*':[120]

> Differences there certainly are between trust (trust powers) and powers, but as regards validity, should they be so great as that in one case complete, or practically complete, ascertainment is needed, but not in the other? Such distinction as there is would seem to lie in the extent of the survey which the trustee is required to carry out: if he has to distribute the whole of a fund's income, he must necessarily make a wider and more systematic survey than if his duty is expressed in terms of a power to make grants...the danger lies in overstating what the trustee requires to know or to inquire into before he can properly execute his trust. The difference may be one of degree rather than of principle: in the well-known words of Sir George Farwell, *Farwell on Powers*, 3rd ed. (1916), p. 10, trusts and powers are often blended, and the mixture may vary in its ingredients.[121]

Two of Lord Wilberforce's fellow Law Lords concurred with his analysis,[122] but two did not,[123] and so Lord Wilberforce carried the day by a bare majority. Lord Hodson's

---

[117] In *Mettoy Pension Trustees v. Evans* [1990] 1 WLR 1587 it was held (at 1617D) that the court may intervene to require the exercise of a so-called 'fiduciary power' (a power held by a trustee or other person in a fiduciary capacity).   [118] *Sub nom. Re Baden's Deed Trusts (No. 1)* [1971] AC 424, HL.

[119] [1971] AC 424 at 456C.

[120] *IRC v. Broadway Cottages Trust* [1955] Ch 20, CA was overruled in this regard, but remains authority for the requirement of a fixed list in cases of fixed trust.

[121] [1971] AC 424 at 449F–H. Quoting *Farwell on Powers*, 3rd edn (London: Stevens & Sons, 1916).

[122] Viscount Dilhorne and Lord Reid.   [123] Lord Hodson and Lord Guest.

dissenting speech was powerfully argued and had the support of contemporary House of Lords authority:

> To adopt [Lord Wilberforce's] solution is, I think, to do the very thing which the court cannot do. As was pointed out by my noble and learned friend Lord Upjohn in the *Gulbenkian* case [1970] A.C. 508, 524:
>
> 'The trustees have a duty to select the donees of the donor's bounty from among the class designated by the donor; he has not entrusted them with any power to select the donees merely from among claimants who are within the class, for that is constituting a narrower class and the donor has given them no power to do this.'[124]

Lord Hodson's analysis is theoretically rigorous, but Lord Wilberforce's approach can be seen as the triumph of pragmatism over theory. Certainly, it would seem a practical absurdity if a grant of '£10,000 to my wife to be distributed amongst my cousins *if* she should think fit' were valid and a grant of '£10,000 to my wife to be distributed amongst my cousins *as* she should think fit' were invalid on the ground that the objects are uncertain.[125] And the distinction between discretionary trusts and powers of appointment looks even more technical in the case of a non-exhaustive discretionary trust,[126] for there the trustees are under no obligation to apply the entire trust income in any given year but instead have the power to accumulate the income on a temporary basis.

One has to admire Lord Wiberforce for his grasp of the rhetorical arts of persuasion. In *McPhail v. Doulton* his Lordship employed a winning metaphor to suggest that the difference between a trust and a power is one of 'delicate shading' and he persuaded enough of his fellow Law Lords to accept that a 'trust' might be regarded as a species of 'power'. And yet, this is the same Lord Wilberforce, who a year earlier, in *Barclays Bank v. Quistclose*,[127] purported to transform a 'power' (which is how Lord Millett described the reality of the mechanism in that case) into a 'trust'. Trusts and powers are in theory quite different things—the former being *obligatory*, the latter being *optional*—so his Lordship achieved, within the space of a year, the judicial equivalent of turning lead into gold . . . and turning it back again!

Application of the individual ascertainability test

The fund in *McPhail v. Doulton* comprised shares in a company controlled by Mr Baden. The deed recited that:

> The trustees shall apply the net income . . . in making at their absolute discretion grants to or for the benefit of any officers and employees or ex officers or ex-employees of the company or to any relatives or dependants of any such persons in such amounts at such times and on such conditions (if any) as they think fit.

After the House of Lords decided to adopt the individual ascertainability test, the Baden deed was referred to the Chancery Division of the High Court for a judge to determine,

---

[124] Lord Hodson at 443.

[125] Professor Scott regarded this possibility as the '*height of technicality*' (*Scott on Trusts* (1939) vol. 1 at 613).

[126] The trust in *Gartside v. IRC* [1968] AC 553, HL, was of this sort.

[127] Considered in depth in Chapters 2 and 5.

in *Re Baden's Deed Trusts (No. 2)*,[128] whether the deed, and in particular the gift to 'relatives', passed the new 'individual ascertainability' test of certainty. The judge, Brightman J, was guided by Lord Wilberforce's speech in *McPhail v. Doulton*, which contained important guidance as to the various types of uncertainty.

First, there is 'linguistic or semantic uncertainty', which is also called *conceptual uncertainty*. This causes discretionary trusts to fail. An example of a conceptually uncertain class of beneficiaries would be 'friends', because it is impossible to say of every potential individual claimant that she is or is not a 'friend'.[129] As Cicero said, '*everyone has an idea how many goats and sheep he owns, but nobody can say how many friends he possesses*'.[130] Some will certainly be friends by any definition; some will certainly not be friends; many will satisfy some definitions and not others. Thus the very concept of 'friend' is inadequate to establish with certainty the range of potential beneficiaries. If the range of potential beneficiaries cannot be estimated (if the 'field cannot be surveyed', to paraphrase Lord Wilberforce), the trustees will not know whether they should distribute the fund in small parcels or distribute more generously. In short, a discretionary trust for friends fails because uncertainty of object prevents a fair distribution and therefore prevents the proper discharge of the trustees' duty of impartiality.

Second, there is *evidential uncertainty*, which is the practical difficulty of ascertaining the existence or whereabouts of beneficiaries. *Evidential uncertainty* will not cause a power or discretionary trust to fail. In fact, the evidence of experts with special knowledge of the meaning of a particular class description, such as the description 'Jewish', may be admitted to assist the court to determine whether the description is objectively certain. Thus in *Re Tuck's Settlement Trusts*,[131] which concerned a conditional gift rather than a discretionary trust, the beneficiary of the gift was required to be of the Jewish faith, and married and living with an 'approved wife', and any dispute of fact was to be determined by the Chief Rabbi. The court accepted that the Chief Rabbi was competent to resolve any uncertainty on the question of 'Jewish faith' and 'approved wife'. In *Re Tepper's Will Trusts*,[132] which concerned a gift subject to a condition subsequent, Scott J even took the bold step of admitting evidence of the testator's own practice as a Jew in order to render certain what the testator had meant by the term 'Jewish'.[133] Despite judicial generosity on the question of evidential uncertainty, no amount of expert evidence will be able to overcome fundamental conceptual uncertainty. Not even those who know us best—in fact, not even we ourselves—are able to say for certain who are and who are not our 'friends'.

Third, but not strictly speaking a case of uncertainty, is the case in which the meaning of the words is clear, but the description of the beneficiaries is so hopelessly wide as not to form anything like a class, with the result that the trust is 'administratively

---

[128] [1972] Ch 607.
[129] Browne-Willkinson J in *Re Barlow's Will Trusts* [1979] 1 WLR 278 at 282C–F.
[130] '*...amicos quot haberet, non posse dicere*': Cicero, *De Amicitia* ('On Friendship').   [131] [1978] Ch 49.
[132] [1987] 1 All ER 970.
[133] Following *Clayton v. Ramsden* [1943] AC 320.

unworkable'. Lord Wilberforce suggested the example of a trust to benefit '*all the residents of greater London*'. A further example is a trust 'for the benefit of any or all or some of the inhabitants of the county of West Yorkshire'.[134]

Brightman J held that the reference to 'relatives' in the Baden deed identified the potential objects with sufficient certainty for the discretionary trust to be carried out. His Lordship reasoned that 'relatives' can be defined as persons who trace descent from a common ancestor. When Brightman J's judgment[135] was appealed, the Court of Appeal upheld it.[136] Sachs LJ and Megaw LJ agreed with Brightman J's conclusion that the term 'relative' was conceptually certain if taken to mean '*descendants from a common ancestor*'. Sachs LJ acknowledged that the class of potential beneficiaries might be so large as to be administratively unworkable if all descendants from a common ancestor were deemed to be relatives (the class could indeed include everyone on earth), but suggested that, in practice, family trees rarely stretch back very far, so the apparent problem of 'administrative unworkability' does not, in fact, arise.[137]

A literal reading of Lord Wilberforce's test would appear to hold that trustees must be able to say for certain of any potential claimant that she does *or does not* qualify to be considered as a beneficiary. Such a reading would have the effect of reintroducing the 'fixed list' test by the back door, so Megaw LJ opted for a more pragmatic construction:

> the test is satisfied if, as regards at least a substantial number of objects, it can be said with certainty that they fall within the trust; even though, as regards a substantial number of other persons, if they ever for some fanciful reason fell to be considered, the answer would have to be, not 'they are outside the trust', but 'it is not proven whether they are in or out'.[138]

Sachs LJ agreed with Megaw LJ's opinion that it would be wrong to place too great an emphasis on the words 'or is not' appearing in Lord Wilberforce's test, but Megaw LJ was alone amongst their Lordships in acknowledging that a distribution may be valid even though potentially substantial numbers of applicants with otherwise meritorious claims might fail simply because it is impossible to say for certain whether they are or are not 'relatives'.

Stamp LJ did not agree with Megaw LJ and Sachs LJ that Brightman J's definition of 'relatives' ('*descendants from a common ancestor*') was sufficient to ascertain the potential range of beneficiaries of the Baden trust. Stamp LJ held, instead, that the relatives of a dead person should be identified with their '*legal next-of-kin*',[139] and that relatives of a living person should be taken to mean '*nearest blood relations*'.[140] Sachs LJ and Megaw LJ took the view that such narrow definitions would only be necessary to give effect to a *fixed* trust for 'relatives'. It appears that Stamp LJ's motive for preferring the narrower definition of relatives for discretionary trusts was to compel the trustees to carry out a more accurate survey of the range of potential beneficiaries, but it is hard to see what practical difference the narrower definition would make. The narrower and wider

[134] *R. v. District Auditor, Ex p West Yorkshire Metropolitan County Council* [1986] RVR 24.
[135] [1972] Ch 607.   [136] [1973] Ch 9.   [137] Ibid. at 22B.   [138] Ibid. at 24.
[139] Ibid. at 29B.   [140] Ibid. at 21A.

definitions both lead to potentially very large classes, so the trustees will be aware, no matter which definition of 'relatives' is adopted, that they are to refrain from making an overgenerous award to any individual applicant. In any case, certainty at the first stage, the stage of surveying the range of potential objects, is surely not as important as certainty at the second stage, the stage at which the merits of individual applicants fall to be considered. Any improvements in certainty yielded by Stamp LJ's narrower definition of relatives at the survey stage would surely have very little impact on the actual distribution of the fund, because '*nearest blood relations*' still lets in a good deal of uncertainty at the crucial second stage of making appointments.

In all three judgments in the Court of Appeal, as there was in Lord Wilberforce's speech in the House of Lords, there is express or implicit acceptance that the validity of a discretionary trust does not depend upon conceptual perfection. In fact, it is arguable that the work begun by their Lordships in the *McPhail v. Doulton* cases will not be complete until the day the courts acknowledge that a discretionary trust is valid even when its objects cannot be perfectly ascertained, provided it is certain that there are *some* objects and that the trust is administratively workable. Whether that work would be work to the good is another question. One might conclude that the *McPhail v. Doulton* cases have already been generous enough when one considers that discretionary trusts are a highly favoured device for the avoidance of tax.[141]

A discretionary trust for friends distinguished from individual gifts to friends

A discretionary trust calls, by its very nature, for the fair *division* and allocation of assets, or a fund of assets, in favour of certain members of a class. It should therefore be contrasted with a gift of an *entire* asset to any candidate who can establish that she qualifies for it. Thus if a testator made a gift in his will of one painting each 'to any of my friends who apply for it', the gift will be valid because the executor can safely give a painting to anybody who can establish that he or she is a 'friend' of the testator. It does not matter that it is impossible to reach objective agreement upon the definition of 'friend', because the terms of the donation do not require the trustees to survey the entire class of 'my friends' and allocate the paintings fairly amongst the class.[142]

To emphasize the somewhat subtle difference between a series of individual gifts to friends and a discretionary trust for friends, imagine that you have been left a small cellar of wine by a will. The cellar comprises ten cases of red wine and ten cases of white. You are required to give a case of red wine to any of the settlor's friends who might come forward and to make a fair distribution of the white wine amongst the testator's friends, as you think fit. The first claimant to present himself is Fred. He attended the same school as the testator and had kept in touch ever since. He always sent birthday cards and presents to the testator, a gesture that the testator had always reciprocated. You will give Fred a case of red wine, because he is certainly eligible for one. However,

---

[141] On taxation generally see Chapter 2.
[142] *Re Barlow's Will Trusts* [1979] 1 WLR 278, following *Re Allen* [1953] Ch 810 and distinguishing *Re Gulbenkian's Settlement Trusts*. See also *Re Coates, decd* [1955] Ch 495.

you cannot know how many eligible friends might come forward, so you cannot know for certain how much white wine it is fair to give to Fred. Perhaps he should receive a case, perhaps only a bottle. Accordingly, the gifts of red wine will be valid, but the discretionary trust of white wine will fail due to uncertainty of object.

Interrelation of the three certainties

Failure by the donor of property to provide the donee with the means to ascertain the subject matter and object of the donation is persuasive evidence that the donor did not intend to create a trust.[143] Sir Arthur Hobhouse put it this way:

> uncertainty in the subject of the gift has a reflex action upon the previous words, and throws doubt upon the intention of the testator, and seems to shew that he could not possibly have intended his words of confidence, hope, or whatever they may be,—his appeal to the conscience of the first taker,—to be imperative words.[144]

Consider the disposition in *Lambe v. Eames*,[145] which, as you will recall, was a gift by a testator to his widow of his entire estate 'to be at her disposal in any way she may think best, for the benefit of herself and her family'. If the testator had intended this disposition to take effect as a trust, he would surely have identified the class of beneficiaries with greater certainty than the word 'family' can provide and he would surely have identified with precision a specific part of the estate to which the widow herself would be beneficially entitled.

Capacity to create a trust

Even if it appears that the owner of an asset intended to create a trust of the asset, the trust will not be held against him if he lacked legal capacity to create it. According to the *Oxford English Dictionary*, capacity means, in this context, '*legal competency or qualification*'. Two common reasons for lack of legal capacity are poor mental health and minority (infancy). These are considered next. However, even so-called 'artificial' persons, such as corporations, might also lack capacity if the legal documentation according to which they are constituted restricts or excludes their powers. Thus the 'objects clause' in the memorandum of a limited liability company might expressly or impliedly exclude the company's power to act as a trustee.

Medical evidence as to the mental state of property owners may raise a presumption that they lack the mental capacity necessary to make valid dispositions of their property. Unless it is rebutted by other evidence, this presumption renders a purported disposition ineffective to transfer the beneficial interests in the property.[146] The Court of

---

[143] *Knight v. Knight* (1840) 3 Beav 148 ER, *per* Lord Langdale MR at 174 citing *Morice v. Bishop of Durham* (1804) 9 Ves 399. [144] In *The Mussoorie Bank Ltd v. Raynor* (1882) LR 7 App Cas 321 at 331. [145] (1871) LR 6 Ch App 597. [146] *Simpson v. Simpson* [1992] 1 FLR 601.

Protection is authorized to deal with the property of a person judged to be incapacitated in this way.[147] Dealings can be varied by a nominated judge in certain circumstances.[148]

Any person who has not yet attained 18 years of age (known as the age of majority) is a minor (infant) for legal purposes. A settlement of *any* property made by an infant by instrument on, or since, 1 January 1970, although not void *ab initio*, is nevertheless voidable if repudiated within a reasonable time of the infant having attained majority.[149]

Trusts established for private purposes: the beneficiary principle

Trusts for purposes beneficial to the public are known as trusts for 'charitable' purposes; they are considered in Chapter 7. Here, we are concerned with trusts established for private purposes. Such trusts are generally void for lack of a beneficiary.[150] As learned judges have said: '*a gift on trust must have a* cestui que trust',[151] and '[t]*here must be somebody, in whose favour the Court can decree performance*'.[152] This is the so-called 'beneficiary principle'.[153] Viscount Simmonds expressed it thus:

> A gift can be made to persons (including a corporation) but it cannot be made to a purpose or to an object; so, also, a trust may be created for the benefit of persons as cestuis que trustent, but not for a purpose or object unless the purpose or object be charitable. For a purpose or object cannot sue, but, if it be charitable, the Attorney-General can sue to enforce it.[154]

So far, in the course of this chapter, we have seen that judicial interpretation of proprietary dispositions is dominated by respect for the intentions of the donor or settlor. We might call that the 'benefactor principle'. The 'beneficiary principle' is a major qualification to the 'benefactor principle', for it requires that a non-charitable disposition by a benefactor must always be made by way of outright gift to a donee or on trust for ascertainable beneficiaries.

The underlying aim of the beneficiary principle is to ensure that somebody owns the trust property in equity at all times—that is, to ensure that the benefit of property is transferred effectively from settlor to beneficiary. The benefit might not, in fact, be transferred if there is no beneficiary sufficiently interested in the trust to enforce it against the trustees, so the overt aim of the beneficiary principle is to seek to ensure that there is someone able and willing to enforce the trust. The beneficiary principle also satisfies fundamental policy concerns. The first is that property should always

---

[147] Mental Capacity Act 2005.

[148] Ibid. s. 96(3). The Lord Chancellor also had this power before the Constitutional Reform Act 2005 removed it.   [149] Family Law Reform Act 1969, s. 1.

[150] A useful list of cases in which courts have held purpose trusts to be valid appears in P. Baxendale-Walker, *Purpose Trusts* (London: Butterworths, 1999).   [151] *Re Wood* [1949] Ch 498, *per* Harman J at 501.

[152] *Morice v. Bishop of Durham* (1804) 9 Ves 399, *per* Sir William Grant MR at 405, CA.

[153] *Re Denley's Trust Deed* [1969] 1 Ch 373, *per* Goff J at 383C–D.

[154] *Leahy v. AG for New South Wales* [1959] AC 457, *per* Viscount Simonds at 478.

have an owner so that it is capable of participating in, and contributing to, the national economy. The second is that the fiduciary office of trustee should not be brought into disrepute by the creation of a trusteeship under which there is no effective obligation on the trustee to discharge his trust. The first policy reflects the ownership dimension of the trust and the second reflects the obligation dimension.

Trusts established purely for private purposes are void, because they offend the 'beneficiary principle', but many would, in any event, fail for other reasons. Some would fail for infringing the rule against inalienability of capital,[155] because the pursuit of a purpose usually requires the production of income, which, in turn, requires that at least part of the trust capital, as the means of income production, must remain unsold. (There is no infringement of the rule against inalienability of capital if there is an express requirement to apply the capital within the perpetuity period.) Other trusts for private purposes would fail for vagueness. According to Roxburgh J in *Re Astor's ST*, '*purposes must be so defined that, if the trustees surrendered their discretion, the court could carry out the purposes declared*', and not merely '*a selection of them arrived at by eliminating those which are too uncertain to be carried out*'.[156] In that case, a trust of substantially all of the issued shares of The Observer Ltd (the newspaper company) failed. The trust had been established for purposes including the '*maintenance... of good understanding... between nations*'. The bequest in *Morice v. Bishop of Durham*[157] for 'objects of benevolence and liberality' would also have failed for vagueness had it not already failed for infringing the beneficiary principle. Finally, many trusts for purely private purposes would fail simply because they are capricious.

Capricious purposes

[T]he League was founded by an American millionaire, Ezekiah Hopkins, who was very peculiar in his ways. He was himself red-headed, and he had a great sympathy for all red-headed men; so, when he died, it was found that he had left his enormous fortune in the hands of trustees, with instructions to apply the interest to the providing of easy berths to men whose hair is of that colour.

Sir Arthur Conan Doyle, 'The red-headed league' in *The Adventures of Sherlock Holmes* (London: G. Newnes Ltd, 1892)

Any trust for public[158] or private purposes will fail if it is capricious,[159] including trusts for 'red-headed men'. A curious example is the trust in *Brown v. Burdett*,[160] which was for the purpose of blocking up the windows and doors of a house for 20 years.

---

[155] An example is the attempt to establish a church tennis club in *Re St Andrew's (Cheam) Lawn Tennis Club Trust (sub nom Philippe v. Cameron)* [2012] EWHC 1040 (Ch); [2012] 3 All ER 746. It failed because it represented 'an attempt to achieve the legally impossible: a perpetual trust for a non-charitable purpose' (*per* Arnold J at para. [45]). On perpetuities and the rule against inalienability of capital see Chapter 6.

[156] [1952] Ch 534 at 548.   [157] (1804) 9 Ves 399.

[158] That is, charitable. See Chapter 7.

[159] Whimsical, playful, or unpredictable, from the Latin *caper*, meaning 'goat'.

[160] (1882) 21 Ch D 667.

Capriciousness is often raised as an objection to trusts for the erection of tombs and monuments. In the Scottish case *M'Caig v. University of Glasgow*,[161] the court refused to recognize a trust to erect various monuments to the memory of John Stuart McCaig, a wealthy Scottish banker. Lord Kyllachy stated that it

> ought to be unlawful, to dedicate...the whole income of a large estate...to objects of no utility...which have no other purpose or use than that of perpetuating at great cost, and in an absurd manner, the idiosyncrasies of an eccentric testator.[162]

Of course, nothing could prevent McCaig from pursuing similar purposes during his lifetime as long as he pursued them directly and not by means of any trust, and, between 1897 and his death in 1902, he did indeed manage to part-build a replica of the Roman Colosseum on the hill above Oban harbour. Known as 'McCaig's Folly', it still stands there today.

Certain trusts of the income from the residuary estate of George Bernard Shaw were established for the purpose of ascertaining, amongst other things, the number of persons currently using the 26-letter English alphabet and how much effort could be saved by replacing it with a 40-letter phonetic 'British Alphabet'.[163] The trusts failed because they were for purely private, rather than charitable, purposes and therefore infringed the beneficiary principle, but it is arguable that they should, in any event, have failed for capriciousness.[164]

In the USA, the beneficiary principle is not applied as strictly as it is in England and Wales. In the USA, when property is transferred upon an invalid *trust* for pure private purposes, the transferee is deemed to have a valid *power* '*to apply the property to the designated purpose*'. However, even though the beneficiary principle is relaxed in the USA, a pure purpose trust will still be invalid if the transferee is authorized to apply the property beyond the perpetuity period or if the purpose is capricious.[165]

An exception to the rule against private purpose trusts

We know that trusts for public purposes are valid if the purposes are exclusively charitable, but that trusts for private purposes are void for infringing the beneficiary principle. The following private non-charitable purposes are, however, exceptions to the rule against private purpose trusts: the erection or maintenance of tombs, graves, or monuments;[166] the care and maintenance of specific animals, such as a horse;[167] the saying

---

[161] [1907] SC 231.   [162] Ibid. at 242.   [163] *Re Shaw* [1957] 1 WLR 729.

[164] In the event, a threatened appeal from the court's decision was compromised when certain of Shaw's residuary legatees undertook to fund a prize for the best translation into his 40-letter alphabet of Shaw's play *Androcles and the Lion* (see the Foreword by the Public Trustee C. R. Sopwith to *The Shaw Alphabet Edition of Androcles and the Lion* (London: Penguin, 1962)).

[165] American Law Institute, *Restatement* (Third) *of the Law of Trusts* (St Paul, MN: American Law Institute, 2003) §§46–7.

[166] Subject to the rule against inalienability of capital (see Chapter 6). *Mussett v. Bingle* [1876] WN 170 concerned a bequest of £300 to erect a monument and a bequest of £200 for its upkeep. The latter bequest failed because capital would have to be rendered inalienable in order to provide income in perpetuity. The upkeep of tombs and monuments that form part of the fabric of a church is charitable and therefore not subject to the rule against inalienability (*Re Hooper* [1932] 1 Ch 38).

[167] *Re Dean* (1889) 41 Ch D 552. A trust for the care and maintenance of animals generally is capable of being charitable (*Re Wedgwood* [1915] 1 Ch 113).

of Roman Catholic masses in private;[168] and finally fox hunting.[169] The ban on hunting wild mammals with dogs that was introduced by the Hunting Act 2004 does not render the last category obsolete, because hunting is exempt from the statutory prohibition in certain circumstances, one of which is stalking and flushing out vermin to be shot.[170]

It is important to realize that these anomalous private purpose trusts have no basis in logic or principle;[171] they were admitted in the past as *'concessions to human weakness or sentiment'*[172] and the courts have refused to admit any further exceptions.[173] Not only are they illogical, they are practically speaking unenforceable. Nobody is beneficially entitled under such trusts, so nobody has the right to enforce them in court; hence they are known as trusts of imperfect obligation.[174] The trustees are under no obligation to apply the trust fund for the purposes stated. All that is required of them is an undertaking not to apply the fund for *other* purposes. This undertaking is procured by a court order known as a *'Pettingall order'*.[175] The *Pettingall* order grants *locus standi* to interested parties (such as the persons who will be entitled to the fund when the horse dies) to come to court if the trustees apply the fund for purposes other than those stated.

It is arguable that non-obligatory trusts are not trusts at all. There is, as Megarry VC has observed, *'a certain awkwardness in describing as a trust a relationship which is not enforceable by the courts'*.[176] It may be more accurate to regard 'trusts' of imperfect obligation as mere powers held by trustees.[177] This would permit the neat conclusion that there are no 'true' exceptions to the principle that a private express trust must have an ascertainable beneficiary. A non-obligatory trust will certainly resemble a power if it makes express provision for what should occur in the event of the trust remaining unfulfilled during the perpetuity period. So an eccentric testatrix might leave her house to her neighbour 'on trust' to allow the testatrix's cat to spend the rest of its life in the house and expressly provide that, in default of the trust being discharged, the house should pass to the residuary beneficiaries of the testatrix's estate.[178] Although in form

---

[168] A trust for the saying of masses in public may be charitable (*Re Hetherington* [1989] 2 All ER 129) and if there is a general gift for the saying of masses, raising the possibility that the masses might be said in public or private, the gift will be construed as a charitable gift to be carried out only by the saying of masses in public (*Re White* [1893] 2 Ch 41, 52–3; *Re Banfield* [1968] 1 WLR 846). For an interesting discussion of the legal history of masses, see *Bourne v. Keane* [1919] AC 815.   [169] *Re Thompson* [1934] Ch 342.

[170] Hunting Act 2004, Sch. 1, para. 1(1).

[171] In *Re Endacott* [1960] Ch 232, Harman LJ described them as *'occasions when Homer has nodded'* (echoing the lament of Horace in his treatise on the art of poetry: *indignor quandoque bonus dormitat Homerus*—'I am aggrieved when sometimes even the excellent Homer falls asleep').

[172] Sir Arthur Underhill, *Underhill's Law of Trusts and Trustees*, 10th edn (London: Butterworths, 1950) at 97; *Re Astor's Settlement Trusts* [1952] Ch 534.   [173] *Re Endacott* [1960] Ch 232 at 246.

[174] *Tito v. Waddell (No. 2)* [1977] Ch 106.

[175] *Pettingall v. Pettingall* (1842) 11 LJ Ch 176, 177 concerned a gift for 'a favourite black mare'.

[176] (1842) 11 LJ Ch 176 at 216E–F.

[177] P. Matthews, 'The new trust: obligations without rights?' in *Trends in Contemporary Trust Law* (A. J. Oakley, ed.) (Oxford: Clarendon Press, 1996) 1 at 8.

[178] For an example along these lines, see the item that appeared under the headline 'The aristocat' in the *Daily Mail* on 14 September 2002. 'Tinker' was apparently left a £350,000 house and *'£100,000 to keep him in sardines and cream for life'*. The *Daily Mirror* subsequently reported that Tinker was *'moved to a secret safe house after a series of death threats'* (9 February 2005).

a trust, it would be difficult to argue that this arrangement is not in substance a power. It has even been suggested that a trust of imperfect obligation will be invalid unless it appears in a will which makes clear that any part of the fund not expended on the designated purpose will fall into the residue of the deceased's estate,[179] but that suggestion is not convincing. After all, there is no reason why the residue itself should not be the subject matter of a trust of imperfect obligation.[180] A more likely reason for the invalidity of a trust of imperfect obligation is 'capriciousness' or perpetuity.[181] It should be borne in mind that, although trusts of imperfect obligation are exempt from the beneficiary principle, they remain subject to the rules against capriciousness and perpetuity.

Circumventing the rule against private purpose trusts

If one wishes to donate money to achieve some private purpose, how should one go about it? Although one cannot create a trust for private purposes, there are other options. Probably the most straightforward device for promoting non-charitable purposes is to create a company with objects corresponding to the intended purposes.[182] There are, however, a number of other possibilities.

One possibility is to establish, or to find, an unincorporated association with purposes matching one's own and to donate money to it. The donation will usually be construed as an absolute gift to the present members of the association,[183] but subject to the members being contractually obliged (according to the constitution and rules of the association) to apply the funds for the purposes of the association. However, this device will only succeed if the members are free to agree between themselves to wind up the association and take away their respective beneficial shares in the association's funds.[184]

Another possibility is to make a gift to a charity determinable in favour of another charity upon the happening of an event connected to the desired purpose. This also works to enable a trust of imperfect obligation to be carried out in perpetuity. So if, for example, one's intended purpose is to maintain the legibility of a gravestone in perpetuity, one should make a gift to a charity that will determine in the event of the gravestone becoming illegible.[185] The gift will then pass to a second named charity. As long as the desired purpose is not unlawful, this device will not only fulfil the intended purpose, but also enable the purpose to be carried out in perpetuity, because capital devoted to charitable purposes is not subject to the rule against inalienability.[186] It is essential that

---

[179] *Re Thompson* [1934] Ch 342 at 344; *Re Astor's ST* [1952] Ch 534 at 546.

[180] Parker & Mellows, *The Modern Law of Trusts*, 6th edn (London: Sweet & Maxwell, 1994) at 117.

[181] See Chapter 6.

[182] For the detail of that method, the reader will need to consult a specialist text on company law such as *Gower's Principles of Modern Company Law* (Paul L. Davies, ed.) 7th edn (London: Sweet & Maxwell, 2003).

[183] *Re Recher's* [1972] Ch 526. See 'Donations to unincorporated associations'.

[184] *Re Grant's WT* [1980] 1 WLR 360. See 'Donations to unincorporated associations'.

[185] *Re Tyler* [1891] 3 Ch 252. Local authorities are usually paid to take on the task of maintaining graves under the Parish Councils and Burial Authorities (Miscellaneous Provisions) Act 1970, s. 1(3).

[186] See Chapter 6.

the gift to the first charity is expressed to be *determinable* upon failure of the desired purpose, rather than *conditional* upon its fulfilment. If fulfilment of the private purposes is expressed to be a condition of the gift, the arrangement will be construed as a void attempt to create an imperative trust for private purposes. If the gift is merely determinable in the event of the expressed purposes being unfulfilled, the arrangement creates nothing more than an incentive for fulfilling the private purpose.[187]

Another device, which also depends for its success on creating an incentive, is to transfer funds to trustees:

> on trust during the perpetuity period to pay out of the income to such of a large class of persons as spend money out of their own resources on the like objects sums equal to 110 per cent of such sums as they spend, until the income for a particular period be exhausted, the capital at the end of the perpetuity period to go to charity.[188]

Relaxation of the rule in 'offshore' jurisdictions

The trust is a balancing act between the rights of a settlor to determine how his property should be dealt with and the beneficiaries' rights of self-determination. In England, the rule is that there must be beneficiaries and that the beneficiaries have the right to terminate the trust if they are competent, agree to do so, and are together absolutely entitled.[189] The English approach, therefore, displays great deference to the proprietary entitlement of the beneficiaries.[190] This may reflect, albeit in an indirect and unarticulated way, one of the oldest ideas in the English law of property—that entitlement to deal with property should prima facie lie with the possessor. However, not every jurisdiction shares the English perspective on the trust. We noted earlier that the USA does not follow the rule in *Saunders v. Vautier*, but instead places greater emphasis on giving effect to the settlor's intentions. It would be a fairly natural extension of this approach for the US legislature to allow the creation of trusts purely for private purposes—that is, trusts without any identifiable beneficiary—provided that such a trust did not infringe the rules against perpetuity. The STAR trust established in the Cayman Islands by the Special Trusts (Alternative Regime) Law 1997 goes even further.[191] The STAR trust is not subject to the rules against perpetuity at all. Furthermore, the trust not only permits trusts for the advancement of non-charitable purposes, but also provides that the only persons who may enforce the trust are persons expressly nominated for that purpose by the trust instrument. By separating enforcement from beneficial ownership and in several other respects,[192] the STAR trust resembles the English idea of the charitable

---

[187] *Re Dalziel* [1943] Ch 277.

[188] P. Matthews, 'The new trust: obligations without rights?' in *Trends in Contemporary Trust Law* (A. J. Oakley, ed.) (Oxford: Clarendon Press, 1996) 1 at 18.   [189] *Saunders v. Vautier* (1841) 10 LJ Ch 354.

[190] See, generally, D. J. Hayton, 'Developing the obligation characteristic of the trust' (2001) 117 LQR at 96–108.

[191] The 1997 Law has been consolidated in the Trust Law (2001 Revision).

[192] STAR trusts do not fail for perpetuity or uncertainty of object and they can be varied according to a cy-près jurisdiction (see Chapter 7).

trust.[193] However, whereas charitable trusts must, broadly speaking, be beneficial to the public to attract privileged legal status and tax exemptions, the concern must be that the purposes advanced by the STAR trust and other non-resident private purpose trusts will not always be beneficial to the public, and, in some cases, may be positively detrimental.[194] In any case, if the public does not benefit, then someone else must: there will be a person behind the purpose. One thing is for sure: where there is a trust asset, sooner or later an answer must be provided to the question, 'Who owns it?'[195]

Trusts for private purposes, but with identifiable beneficiaries

Whether a trust is for persons or purely for private purposes comes down to the construction of the instrument in which it appears. Very often, a trust that, on one level, appears to be for a particular purpose—for example, '*to build a swimming pool* for my employees to swim in'—ought, in fact, to be construed as a trust for particular persons—that is, 'to build a swimming pool *for my employees* to swim in'. *Re Bowes*[196] provides a straightforward example. The testator in that case had made a bequest of £5,000 'upon trust to expend the same in planting trees for shelter on the Wemergill estate'. The estate owners, objecting that it would not be to the best advantage of the estate to spend the fund on planting trees, argued that the words of the bequest had created a power, not a trust. North J disagreed, but he held that the trust was not void as a trust purely for private purposes. It was a trust '*for the benefit of the estate, and the persons who, for the time being, are entitled to the estate*'.[197] The expressed purpose of planting trees was not intended to be imperative; it was merely intended to indicate the testator's motive for creating a trust for the benefit of the estate owners.

The fact that the estate owners (the tenant for life and tenant in tail in remainder) were between them able to bring the trust to an end under the rule in *Saunders v. Vautier* was a significant factor in North J's conclusion that the expressed purposes would not be binding on the beneficiaries. It is not a decisive factor, however, because a trust established for private purposes has been upheld even when the ascertainable beneficiaries of the purposes are infants and, as such, are unable to bring the trust to an end under the rule in *Saunders v. Vautier*.[198]

It was stated in *Re Denley's Trust Deed* that, if a trust '*though expressed as a purpose, is directly for the benefit of an individual or individuals... it is in general outside the mischief of the beneficiary principle*'.[199] The brief facts of *Re Denley's* are that land was

---

[193] See A. Duckworth, 'The new frontier of purpose trusts' (2000) *Papers of the International Academy of Estate and Trust Law* 199 and A. Duckworth, 'STAR wars, the colony strikes back' (1998) 12 TLI 16.

[194] See Chapter 2 'Non-resident trusts'.

[195] A point made by Professor Matthews under the heading '*Cui Bono?*' in his paper 'The new trust: obligations without rights?' in *Trends in Contemporary Trust Law* (A. J. Oakley, ed.) (Oxford: Clarendon Press, 1996) 1 at 31. For an argument that the UK should legislate to permit pure purpose trusts see M. Pawlowski and J. Summers, 'Private Purpose Trusts—a reform proposal' (2007) Conv 440.

[196] [1896] 1 Ch 507.   [197] Ibid. at 511.   [198] *Re Lipinski* [1976] 1 Ch 235.

[199] [1969] 1 Ch 373.

settled on trustees *for use as a sports club* 'primarily' for the benefit of the employees of a company and 'secondarily' for the benefit of such other persons, if any, as the trustees might allow. Goff J held that, on account of their connection to a private company, the potential beneficiaries did not constitute a sufficient section of the public for the trust to qualify as charitable. On the other hand, because there were ascertainable beneficiaries, it was not a trust purely for private purposes, and so it did not fall foul of the beneficiary principle. Despite this, the trust would still have failed for inalienability of capital were it not for the fact that the instrument had expressly required the money to be applied towards the designated purposes within the perpetuity period or not at all. Likewise, in *Leahy v. AG for New South Wales*,[200] a decision of the Privy Council that was followed in *Re Denley's*, a trust for orders of nuns and monks would have failed for inalienability of capital had it not been saved by a particular New South Wales statute which construed purposes of a not exclusively charitable nature as if they were exclusively charitable.

The decision in *Re Denley* confirms that a trust is valid provided that the capital will vest in ascertainable beneficiaries within the perpetuity period. Of course this means that all the beneficiaries, if they are competent adults, could agree to bring the trust to an end and thereby defeat the testator's expressed intention. But surely that risk is the price that a settlor *ought* to pay if he wishes to pass the entire beneficial ownership of certain assets while at the same time purporting to determine the purposes to which they will be applied. If the settlor wants to retain secure control over future use of settled assets, he will find that the Inland Revenue considers him to be still the beneficial owner of the assets and liable to be taxed accordingly.

Donations to unincorporated associations

In this section, we are concerned with gifts to unincorporated, non-profit, non-charitable associations, or, to put it in everyday language, gifts to 'clubs and societies'. Whereas a gift to an incorporated company or other person is straightforward, a gift to an unincorporated association is problematic, because the association has no separate legal personality. An unincorporated association is merely an association of individuals. There are statutes governing incorporated companies,[201] profit-orientated unincorporated associations,[202] and charitable associations,[203] but, with a few exceptions,[204] there is no statutory scheme for unincorporated, non-profit, non-charitable associations. It is therefore hard to know how to construe a donation made to a club or society.[205]

A donation is usually construed to have been an absolute gift to the present members of the association. A gift of four crates of champagne to 'The Warwick String Quartet'

---

[200] [1959] 2 WLR 722, PC.   [201] Companies Act 1985.   [202] Partnership Act 1890.
[203] Charities Act 1993.
[204] For example, the Trade Union and Labour Relations (Consolidation) Act 1992, the Friendly Societies Act 1992, and the Literary and Scientific Institutions Act 1854.
[205] P. Matthews, 'Gifts to unincorporated associations' [1995] Conv 302.

might be construed as a gift to the members as joint tenants, enabling each member to sever his or her share and claim a crate whether or not he or she continues to be a member.[206] In relation to severable donations of this type, '*the association is used in effect as a convenient label or definition of the class which it is intended to take*'.[207] Of course, there would be a tenancy in common instead of a joint tenancy if the donation were itself accompanied by words of severance, as would be the case if a donation were made 'to the members of the Warwick String Quartet *in equal shares*'.

It is, however, most unusual for a donation by way of absolute gift to present members of an association to be construed in such a way as to allow the individual members to remove their shares. Usually a donation to an unincorporated association is construed to be an absolute gift to the present members, but subject to a requirement that they hold the donation subject to:

> their respective contractual rights and liabilities towards one another as members of the association. In such a case a member cannot sever his share. It will accrue to the other members on his death or resignation, even though such members include persons who became members after the gift took effect.[208]

Although a donation will usually be construed as an absolute gift to the present members of the association, it may be clear that the members were not intended to take absolutely, but on trust. The use of the word 'trust' is good evidence of such an intention, but a trust may exist even if the benefactor omits to use the word 'trust'. There will be a trust when it is clear that the present members were not intended to take absolutely. Conversely, the fact that a donation is made to 'trustees' of an association will not always mean that the donation was made on trust.[209] If a donation is construed to be a trust, it will usually be construed as a trust for present and future members. The donation will not, of course, be construed as a trust purely for the private purposes of the association, because the very nature of a club or society suggests that there are identifiable human beneficiaries.

Exceptionally, a donation on trust to an unincorporated association will be held to have created a trust for the benefit of present members only. One such exceptional case was *Re Turkington*,[210] the exceptional feature of that case being that every member of the association was both a trustee and a beneficiary, with the result that the members were together able to bring the trust to an end under the rule in *Saunders v. Vautier*. It follows that, because infants cannot take advantage of *Saunders v. Vautier*, a donation

---

[206] *Neville Estates v. Madden* [1962] Ch 832, *per* Cross J at 849.

[207] *Re Grant's WT* [1980] 1 WLR 360, *per* Vinelott J at 365G.

[208] *Neville Estates v. Madden* [1962] Ch 832, *per* Cross J at 849; followed in *Re Recher's WT* [1972] 3 All ER 401. The rules of an association set out the terms of the contract between an individual member and the remaining members *collectively*, so unless the rules expressly permit, one individual member cannot sue another individual member under the rules (*Anderton & Rowland (a firm) v. Rowland, The Times*, 5 November 1999).

[209] In *Re Recher's* [1972] Ch 526, Brightman J held, at 537–8, that the donation was an absolute gift to the members, subject to their contractual obligations *inter se*, even though the land had been given to 'honorary trustees' to be held 'on trust'.   [210] [1937] 4 All ER 501.

to an association with infant members should not be construed as a trust for the benefit of present members only.[211]

In one case, a donation to an association was held to have created neither an absolute gift nor a trust, but a mandate, binding upon the officer of the association who received it, to apply the donation towards the donor's intended purposes.[212] Such an arrangement is not a true mode of disposing of property at all. It is merely a personal arrangement, akin to agency; hence it can only operate where the donation is made *inter vivos*.

It is also possible for a donation to be construed as conferring a mere power on the members of the association to apply the gift towards the purposes of the association, but such a construction will only be appropriate where the donor expressly provides for other persons to take the gift (by way of 'gift over') in default of the power being exercised.

The list of possible constructions that might be placed upon a donation to an unincorporated association is not yet closed. In each case, the words used by the donor must be read so as to put the most sensible construction on them. Professor Paul Matthews has suggested two other possibilities that have not yet come before the courts in any reported case.[213] The first is a donation made:

> on trust for the purposes of the association until such time as the members for the time being agree to take it themselves (or until the perpetuity period expires, whichever is sooner), whereupon on trust for the then members.[214]

The second is a donation:

> to trustees on trust for such of the current members of the association as permit the same to be used according to the rules of the association, determinable on their ceasing so to permit.[215]

Donations fail if capital is rendered inalienable in perpetuity

Where a donation is construed to have been made *on trust* for present and future members, the trust will fail for infringing the rule against inalienability of capital unless the trust is expressly limited to take effect within the perpetuity period:[216]

> if a gift is made to individuals, whether under their own names or in the name of their society, and the conclusion is reached that they are not intended to take beneficially, then they take as trustees. If so, it must be ascertained who are the beneficiaries. If at the death of the testator the class of beneficiaries is fixed and ascertained or ascertainable within the limit of the rule against perpetuities, all is well. If it is not so fixed and not so ascertainable the trust must fail.[217]

---

[211] But see *Re Lipinski* [1976] 1 Ch 235, later.

[212] *Conservative and Unionist Central Office v. Burrell* [1982] 1 WLR 522. It was held in this case that members of the Conservative Party were not liable to corporation tax because members of local constituency associations were not linked to Parliamentary members of the Party by contractual links of the sort that would render the Party an unincorporated association within s. 526(5) of the Income and Corporation Taxes Act 1970. [213] P. Matthews, 'Gifts to unincorporated associations' [1995] Conv 302.

[214] [1995] Conv 302 at 306. [215] Ibid. at 307. [216] See Chapter 6.

[217] *Re Leahy* [1959] AC 457, *per* Viscount Simonds at 484, PC, followed in *Re Denley's Trust Deed* [1969] 1 Ch 373.

By ensuring that the entire class of beneficiaries is ascertainable within the perpetuity period, the rule against inalienability of capital ensures that the beneficiaries (assuming that they are all adult and competent) can together agree to bring the trust to an end and then apply the capital as they wish.

Even an *absolute gift* to present members will be void for infringing the rule against inalienability of capital if the rules according to which the funds of the association are held do not permit the members to bring the association to an end and divide the fund between them. In *Re Grant's WT*,[218] Grant made a bequest to the Chertsey and Walton Constituency Labour Party, an unincorporated association subject to rules laid down by the national executive committee of the Labour Party and the national annual party conference. Vinelott J held that the gift could not take effect as a gift to the current members of the new constituency party subject to their contractual rights and duties *inter se*, because the members were not free under the rules of their association to dispose of the property in any way they thought fit. On the contrary, the rules made it plain that the decisions of the members of the local party were subject to the control of the national Labour Party. Hence the gift offended the rule against inalienability of capital. If the local branch, according to its own rules, had been able to secede from the national organization and dissolve itself, the gift would have been valid.[219] Even where there is no rule *providing* for dissolution, the court will be inclined to accept that the members can dissolve the association by unanimous consent,[220] the crucial requirement being that there is no rule *preventing* dissolution.

A pragmatic approach to the construction of donations

In the light of the many alternative ways of construing a donation to an unincorporated association, does the reader believe that there is any basis on which the following testamentary disposition could have been effective?

> I give and devise the rest residue and remainder of my estate real and personal whatsoever and wheresoever unto my trustees upon trust...to hold...one half thereof for the Hull Judeans (Maccabi) Association in memory of my late wife to be used solely in the work of constructing the new buildings for the association and/or improvements to the said buildings.[221]

A crucial factor to be borne in mind is that the principal aim of the Hull Judeans (Maccabi) Association was '*to promote the interest, and the active participation of Anglo-Jewish youth of both sexes, in amateur sports, in all forms of cultural, and in non-political, communal activities*'. In other words, many, if not all, of the ultimate beneficiaries of the association's purposes were infants.

---

[218] [1980] 1 WLR 360.
[219] *News Group Newspapers Ltd v. SOGAT 1982* [1986] ICR 716, CA, concerned a local branch of a trade union.   [220] *Universe Tankships Inc. of Monrovia v. ITWF* [1983] 1 AC 366, HL.
[221] *Re Lipinski* [1976] 1 Ch 235 at 239A.

Oliver J held that, although the donation was not valid as a gift for charitable purposes, neither was it void for promoting purely private purposes, despite being expressed to be 'solely' for the erection and maintenance of buildings in memory of the testator's wife. There *were* identifiable human beneficiaries. In fact, Oliver J discovered three alternative bases for holding the disposition to be a valid donation to the association: first, because it was a gift to the present members of the association, subject to the association's rules;[222] second, because it was a trust for present and future beneficiaries;[223] third, because it was a trust for the present members only and the present members were therefore able to vest the capital in themselves according to the rule in *Saunders v. Vautier*.[224] However, not one of these reasons is completely convincing. First, the majority of the members of the association (Anglo-Jewish 'youth') would be precluded by their infancy from taking an absolute gift of that part of the residuary estate that comprised land. Second, a trust for present and future members must be limited to take effect within the perpetuity period, which this trust was not. Third, the infancy of the members precluded reliance on the rule in *Saunders v. Vautier*. Thus Oliver J demonstrated the triumph of judicial pragmatism over the many theoretical obstacles that lay between the testator's words and the testator's underlying intent.

What is most remarkable about Oliver J's approach is that he was willing to hold that the donation had created an absolute gift or, *in the alternative*, a trust.[225] Usually, a court will at least choose between the two on account of the fundamental theoretical differences between them. Indeed, many important cases revolve, as we have seen, around that very choice. Nevertheless, even in cases in which the judge wrestles with the choice between construing a disposition to be a trust or an absolute gift, one can frequently detect a bias in favour of the pragmatic over the theoretical approach. This is entirely to be expected, of course, because whilst, in theory, the character of a disposition is determined from the very outset on the basis of the donor's expressions of intent, in practice, the court may not be called upon to construe the donor's wishes until many years after he uttered or wrote those expressions of intent. Consequently, the court does not determine the nature of a donation in a logical vacuum, but with the full benefit of hindsight. The court knows far better at the date of judgment what will be the consequences of declaring the donation to be either a trust or an absolute gift than the donor could have known when he made the donation in the first place.

Property as the essence of unincorporated associations

The reason why unincorporated associations present such a challenge to the law of donations is because the system of property law cannot accept that a donor has divested himself of the beneficial interest in his property unless he has divested it in favour of

---

[222] *Re Recher's* [1972] Ch 526.   [223] *Re Denley's Trust Deed* [1969] 1 Ch 373.
[224] *Re Turkington* [1937] 4 All ER 501.
[225] His Lordship's judgment ends with the overtly pragmatic assumption that '*all roads lead to the same conclusion*': [1976] 1 Ch 235 at 250.

another legal person. The same reasoning underlies the beneficiary principle, as we observed earlier, and it also informs the creation of resulting trusts, as we will consider in Chapter 5. We are therefore required, because an unincorporated association is said to have no legal personality of its own, to construe donations to associations to be, in one form or another, donations to the individual members of the association. If we were not so constrained, we might prefer to identify some unincorporated associations with the property of the association rather than with its members. Members of the cricket club come and go, but the clubhouse and pitch remain. As Professor S. J. Stoljar observed:

> legal personality requires something to be either a person or not a person, the unincorporated body must end up as a non-person; and hence, for example, the traditional, but very false, statement that an unincorporated society does not exist in law. Legal personality further tends to overemphasise the external as against the internal aspect of a group. Not that the external point is unimportant, since it is through its legal relations with third parties that a group's corporate qualities are put to the test. The crucial point rather is that these external relations do not result from the group being a 'person' (however 'personal' it may look where it is both liable and suable in its own right); the external relations completely depend on the group's internal structure and, in particular, upon the existence of a committable common fund; for without such a common fund the members may act as joint debtors or joint tortfeasors, but they cannot act specifically as group.[226]

The dissolution of unincorporated associations

To conclude this section, it is worth noting that there are four situations in which an unincorporated association or fund should be regarded as having been dissolved or terminated: (1) in accordance with the association's rules; (2) by agreement of all persons interested; (3) by order of the court in the exercise of its inherent jurisdiction; (4) when the substratum, upon which the association or fund was founded, has gone, so that the association or fund no longer has any effective purpose.[227] These categories were confirmed by Sir Robert Megarry VC in *Re GKN Bolts and Nuts Sports and Social Club*,[228] where he added that clubs do not dissolve through mere inactivity unless the only reasonable inference is that the club had ceased to exist: '*The question is whether, put together, the facts carry sufficient conviction that the society is at an end and not merely dormant.*' [229] In *Re GKN Bolts and Nuts Sports and Social Club* itself, it was held that the club had ceased to exist, but only by virtue of the positive resolution of the members to sell the club's sports ground. Sir Robert Megarry VC's approach was essentially a pragmatic one. He observed that,

---

[226] *Groups and Entities: An Inquiry into Corporate Theory* (Canberra: Australian National University Press, 1973) at 189.

[227] *Re William Denby & Sons Ltd Sick and Benevolent Fund* [1971] 2 All ER 1196.

[228] *Re GKN Bolts and Nuts Sports and Social Club* [1982] 1 WLR 774.

[229] Ibid. at 780. In *Keene v. Wellcom London Ltd* [2014] EWHC 134 (Ch), 27 years activity did not amount to dissolution.

in club cases, there are many obscurities and uncertainties, and some difficulty in the law. In such cases, the court usually has to take a broad sword to the problems, and eschew an unduly meticulous examination of the rules and regulations.[230]

The same pragmatic approach was adopted in *Re Horley Town Football Club*,[231] when the trustees of the Club sought directions of the court as to whether they held club assets for 'temporary members' and 'associate members', as well as full members. It was held that beneficial ownership was held on bare trust for full members only, because they could either unanimously, or at an annual general meeting, call for the assets to be transferred to them. The destination of assets on dissolution is considered further in Chapter 5.[232]

Last thoughts on the construction of dispositions

The basic rule for construing formal instruments of disposition, such as trust deeds and wills, is to give effect to the straightforward meaning of the words used. However, we noted at the start of the chapter that courts take a generous approach to the construction of instruments, so that, when it is clear that a benefactor intended to create a gift or a trust, the courts will construe the instrument so far as reasonably possible in order to give effect to his intention. We have called this the 'benefactor principle'. We also noted that the courts tend to construe the intentions of the benefactor on a case-by-case basis and that precedent is rarely decisive in determining the meaning of the words used in a particular case. We have noted particular examples, such as the cases of *Re Andrew's Trust* and *Re Lipinski*, where the decisions of the courts were very hard to reconcile with earlier judgments and in which the judges appear to have taken the pragmatic decision to make the dispositions work as the benefactor would probably have intended, despite the fact that the benefactor had not made his intentions entirely clear.

It seems appropriate, therefore, to end this chapter with the case of *Re Last*.[233] As far as strict legal doctrine is concerned, this is a case in which *Last* is most certainly *least*, but as an exercise in judicial pragmatism, the case is unparalleled. The testatrix, L, had left all her property to her brother, directing that upon his death 'anything that is left' should pass to her late husband's grandchildren. Accordingly, when L's brother died intestate, the grandchildren applied to court claiming the residue of L's estate. The Treasury Solicitor responded that L had made an absolute gift of her property to her brother and that the Crown was therefore entitled to the residue as *bona vacantia*.[234] Karminski J held that, on a proper construction of the will, L's brother had been entitled to a mere equitable life interest in the property and that the grandchildren would therefore be entitled to equal shares of the residue of L's estate. Despite this, one suspects that,

---

[230] Ibid. at 776.   [231] [2006] EWHC 2386, Ch D.
[232] See, also, *Hanchett-Stamford v. HM Attorney General* [2008] EWHC 330 (Ch).
[233] [1958] 1 All ER 316.   [234] 'Ownerless property'.

if L had applied to court during his lifetime for a declaration that the property was his absolutely, the court would have made the declaration as asked.

Contrary to the rule that an absolute gift should be presumed unless there is evidence of a certain intention to create a trust, Karminski J stated that he had been impressed by the absence of words indicating the absolute nature of the gift to L's brother. In other words, his Lordship presumed a trust in the absence of a certain intention to create a gift. Then, having so casually overcome the absence of any certain intention to create a trust, the judge gave equally short shrift to the requirement of certainty of subject matter. A trust of 'whatever may be left' had failed in the leading case of *Sprange v. Barnard*,[235] but not here. This was a pragmatic judgment. The will was construed in the only way guaranteed to prevent L's property from becoming ownerless and passing to the Crown as *bona vacantia*, which would have been the last thing L would have wanted. The judge can be criticized for riding roughshod over the usual rules of trust creation that we have examined in this chapter, but he did, at least, adhere unstintingly to the golden principle of loyalty to the benefactor's underlying dispositive intentions.

Further reading

In addition to the following print sources, the Online Resource Centre accompanying this book contains web links to further reading as well as guide answers to assessment questions relevant to this chapter.

BAXENDALE-WALKER, P., *Purpose Trusts for Commercial and Private Use*, 1st edn (London: Butterworths, 1999).

GARDNER, S., 'A detail in the construction of gifts to unincorporated associations' [1998] Conv 8.

HARDCASTLE, I. M., 'Administrative unworkability: a reassessment of an abiding problem' [1990] Conv 24.

HARGREAVES, P., 'Charitable, purpose and hybrid trusts: a jersey perspective' (2002) 1 PCB 30.

KESSLER, J. and SARTIN, L., *Drafting Trusts and Will Trusts: A Modern Approach*, 10th revd edn (London: Sweet & Maxwell, 2010).

MATTHEWS, P., 'Gifts to unincorporated associations' [1995] Conv 302.

SANDERS, C., *Declaration of Trusts: A Draftsman's Handbook*, 4th edn (London: Sweet & Maxwell, 2009).

SMART, P. ST J., 'Holding property for non-charitable purposes: mandates, conditions and estoppels' [1987] Conv 415.

STOLJAR, S. J., *Groups and Entities: An Inquiry into Corporate Theory* (Sydney: Australian University Press, 1973).

WORTHINGTON, S., 'Sorting out ownership interests in a bulk: gifts, sales and trusts' (1999) J Bus Law 1.

---

[235] (1789) 2 Bro CC 585, ER, Rolls (discussed earlier in this chapter).

4

Effective disposition of benefit: constitution of trusts

The aim of this chapter is to identify the reasons why a trust must be completely constituted in order to be valid and to identify the steps that must be taken in order to constitute a trust. Constitution is important, because the beneficiaries of an incompletely constituted trust have no rights in the trust property and therefore have no standing to enforce the trust in court. They are said to be 'mere volunteers' and, as such, equity will not assist them.

If I give you something or promise to give you something, but you neither give, nor promise to give, anything in return, I am said to have made my disposition or promise 'voluntarily' and you are said to be a 'volunteer'. In other words, a volunteer is a donee or promisee who does not give any 'legal consideration' in return for a disposition or promise made in his or her favour. All is well for the volunteer if an effective disposition is actually made, but what happens if an attempted disposition fails, or if a promise to make a disposition is not fulfilled? Suppose, for example, that I were to telephone you on your birthday to say 'I will send you a present tomorrow'. If I decide not to fulfil my promise to send the present tomorrow, I cannot be compelled to send it. At law, a volunteer cannot enforce a voluntary gift or a voluntary promise made in their favour and, following the law, equity 'will not assist a volunteer' and 'will not perfect an imperfected gift'. (If equity were to assist volunteers, it would undermine the common law doctrine of consideration that underpins contract law.) For a gift to be 'perfect', the donor must actually complete the disposition of the subject matter in favour of the intended donee or execute a formal 'deed of gift'.

Similar rules apply to the effective disposition of benefits 'on trust' as apply to dispositions by outright gift. If I purport or promise to create a trust of £10,000 in favour of a volunteer, the trust will not be enforceable (it will not be 'completely constituted') until I make an effective transfer of the £10,000 to the intended trustees or declare myself to be trustee of the £10,000. Because equity will not assist a volunteer, it will not enforce an incompletely constituted trust. If I actually transfer the £10,000 to the trustees or actually declare myself to be the trustee, the trust will then be completely constituted and the volunteer will become a beneficiary of the trust. The moment that a volunteer becomes a beneficiary of a completely constituted trust, the volunteer no longer requires the assistance of equity; the beneficiary is from that moment *entitled* in equity to enforce her beneficial interest against the trustees.

Reasons behind the requirement of constitution

Only when a trust is completely constituted is the trustee bound by it, the beneficiary entitled under it, and the settlor deprived of the subject matter of it—but *why* must a trust be completely constituted in order to be enforceable? Why is it not sufficient merely to establish that the settlor *intended* to make a trust? There are, in fact, a number of reasons for the requirement that a trust be properly constituted.

The first reason is that it provides an important test of the seriousness of a donor's or settlor's intent. A person who makes a perfect gift, or a completely constituted trust, thereby makes an irrevocable disposition of his beneficial interest in the subject matter of the gift or trust,[1] except to the extent that he names himself as one of the beneficiaries. It is one thing to promise to make a gift or trust, but quite another thing actually to make it. The requirement of proper constitution ensures that gifts and trusts are not binding on the donor or settlor until he has taken tangible steps to dispose of his beneficial interest. For a gift, there must be an actual transfer of the subject matter to the donee, or a formally executed deed of gift in her favour. For a trust, there must be an actual transfer of the subject matter to the trustees, or an express declaration by the owner that he will henceforth hold the subject matter on trust for the beneficiaries. In the absence of such clear evidence of the donor's intention to dispose of his beneficial interest, neither law nor equity has any business enforcing voluntary dispositions.

A second reason for the rules on the constitution of trusts is that they prevent the casual imposition of obligations on trustees. Unless the trust assets are properly transferred to the trustees, they will be under no obligation to fulfil the terms of the trust. This is just as well, because constitution ensures, third, that trustees actually have the power to fulfil their trust obligations. Until the legal title is formally transferred to them, they have no legal power to deal with the trust property in any way—whether by way of sale, or mortgage, or lease—and, crucially, they will have no power to invest the trust property or, ultimately, to distribute it to the beneficiaries.

There is, it is submitted, a fourth justification for the rules on the perfection of gifts and the constitution of trusts. It is based on a common-sense view of the economics and fairness of gift-making. Voluntary gifts and trusts are economically inefficient and inherently unfair, because the beneficiary of the gift or trust is getting something for nothing. The economic cost and unfairness cannot be justified on the basis of the donor's intention alone, because intention can be mistakenly inferred. Intention must be joined by action. If the donor intends to transfer his assets by gift or on trust, then the disposition ought not to be binding until he has done all that he can to carry out the transfer. The courts have no business completing an inherently uneconomical and unfair transaction, hence the maxim that equity will not lend its active *assistance* to a volunteer. It is somewhat different when a benefactor declares himself to be a trustee

---

[1] *Re Bowden* [1936] Ch 71.

of his property for the benefit of a volunteer. There is nothing that the court can do to assist him in making that declaration; in theory, the court cannot put words into his mouth. In such a case, the role of the court is simply to construe the benefactor's intention from the words used. We have seen that the courts will not hold that an owner has declared himself a trustee of his own property unless his intention to create a trust has been expressed in very clear terms.[2]

In addition to these points, we will observe in future chapters that the creation of trusts may be objected to on several grounds of public policy, so the requirement of complete constitution can be justified for reasons of public policy because, along with the requirement of certainty, it acts as a barrier to casual trust creation.

Modes of constitution of trusts

A valid will automatically constitutes any trust incorporated within it and the trust takes effect upon the death of the testator. *Inter vivos* trusts, on the other hand, must comply with one of the two modes of constitution upon which we touched earlier. The first is a declaration by the owner of property that he henceforth holds the property on trust for someone else. This mode of trust creation is referred to as 'declaration of self as trustee'. The second is where an absolute owner transfers the trust assets to a trustee, or trustees, for the benefit of designated beneficiaries. This mode of trust creation is referred to as 'a trust by transfer to trustees'.

The two modes of trust creation are mutually exclusive, because a settlor cannot intend to create a trust by transfer to trustees and, at the same time, intend to declare himself to be the trustee of the property with immediate effect. Thus, if an intended transfer to trustees is ineffective for any reason, the court will not 'rescue' the trust by pretending that the unsuccessful settlor had, all along, intended to declare himself to be the trustee.[3] It is incumbent upon the person attempting to create a trust to complete either one of the two modes of constitution; the courts will not assist. The courts' attitude in this regard should be contrasted with the attitude taken in cases such as *Barclays Bank v. Quistclose*,[4] in which the court is happy to spell out an intention to create a trust, despite a primary intention to create a contract. However, there have been signs, as we shall shortly see, that the courts' traditionally strict refusal to spell out a declaration of trust from a failed transfer might be relaxing.

Mode I: declaration of self as trustee

The simplest mode of constituting a trust is for the absolute owner of certain property orally to declare himself to be the trustee of that property for a certain beneficiary. Such

---

[2] See *Jones v. Lock* (1865) LR 1 Ch App 25, discussed later.
[3] *Milroy v. Lord* (1862) 4 De G F & J 264.
[4] [1970] AC 567, HL. See Chapter 2 and Chapter 5.

a declaration has the effect of transferring the beneficial interest in the property to the beneficiary, while the legal title remains with the original owner as trustee. Such a declaration is effective to create a trust even when, at the date of the declaration, a nominee, such as a bank, is the formal holder of the owner's legal title.

Because it is so simple to dispose of a beneficial interest in this way, the court will require very clear evidence that an owner had intended to constitute himself a trustee of his own property. You should recall the facts of *Jones v. Lock* [5] from Chapter 3: the case in which Jones produced a cheque in the sum of £900 payable to himself, said 'Look you here, I give this to baby; it is for himself,' and placed the cheque in the baby's hand. He then took the cheque saying: 'I am going to put it away for him.' It was held that there had been no effective gift by transfer and Lord Cranworth LC firmly rejected counsel's alternative argument, that the father had constituted himself a trustee of the £900. His Lordship held that a failed gift cannot be construed to be a valid declaration of trust. The crucial principle is that an owner must not be deprived of his property unless, by making a valid gift or trust, he has demonstrated the seriousness of his intention to dispose of the benefit of his property. As his Lordship said: *'the testator would have been very much surprised if he had been told that he had parted with the £900, and could no longer dispose of it.'* [6] Despite the relaxed theoretical position that an oral *'declaration of trust of personalty may be perfectly valid even where voluntary',* [7] the practical implication of the decision in *Jones v. Lock* is that a trust is unlikely to be enforced against a person in Mr Jones's position unless he actually says something equivalent to 'I am trustee' or confirms the declaration by signed writing.[8]

Mode II: transfer to trustees

In the case of a transfer to trustees, the transferor is required to establish that he has *'done everything which, according to the nature of the property comprised in the settlement, was necessary to be done in order to transfer the property'.*[9] To be more precise, the transferor must have done everything *within his power* [10] to transfer the property by the method generally employed for transferring legal title to property of that type.[11] So a transfer of registered land is binding if the deed of transfer is completed in the proper form and delivered to the transferee, together with the transferor's land certificate.[12] The transferor could have done more, by personally registering the transferee as the new proprietor of the legal title,[13] but the transfer is effective, because it is general practice

---

[5] (1865) LR 1 Ch App 25. See Chapter 3.   [6] Ibid. at 29.   [7] Ibid. *per* Lord Cranworth LC at 28.
[8] This is a *requirement* whenever a trust is declared of land (Law of Property Act 1925, s. 53(1), (6)).
[9] *Milroy v. Lord* (1862) 4 De G F & J 264, *per* Turner LJ at 274.
[10] *Re Rose* [1952] Ch 499.
[11] *Mascall v. Mascall* (1985) 50 P & CR 119.
[12] (1985) 50 P & CR 119.
[13] Land Registration Act 1925, s. 19.

for the transferee to apply for registration.[14] As long as the transferor has transferred everything that the transferee needs to perfect his title, the transfer is effective.

The decision of the Court of Appeal in *Re Rose*[15] is the leading authority for this point. The case concerned an absolute gift to transferees, but the principle in the case applies equally where the transfer is made on trust. Mr Rose executed formal transfers of company shares on 30 March 1943 and delivered the transfers to the company with his share certificates, but the company did not register them until 30 June. Mr Rose died four years after the execution of the transfers, whereupon the Inland Revenue claimed estate duty (the precursor to inheritance tax) on the ground that the transfers had not been completed before 10 April 1943, which was the relevant date for tax purposes. The Revenue's claim was unsuccessful. The Court of Appeal held that the deceased had done everything in his power to transfer his legal and beneficial interest to the transferees in March. The actual registration of the transfers was outside of his control. Although Mr Rose had retained formal legal title in the shares until the date of registration, he had been unable to assert any beneficial interest in the shares between the date of transfer and the date of registration, the benefit of the shares having already passed to the transferees.

The necessary consequence of Mr Rose having passed the beneficial interest whilst retaining legal title was that he became a trustee during the period between the date of transfer and the date of registration.[16] However, the Court of Appeal in no way decided that Mr Rose had constituted himself a trustee by choice and so cannot be accused of having improperly 'rescued' a failed 'trust by transfer' by finding a valid 'declaration of self as trustee'. There was no artificial ascription to Mr Rose of an *intention* to create a trust. Mr Rose's temporary trusteeship between the date of transfer and the date of registration was, in fact, an entirely accidental and unforeseen incident of the company's failure to register the transferees as owners of the shares. The temporary 'trusteeship' was also entirely passive. Mr Rose had no powers: not even a bare trustee's usual power to transfer the trust property to the beneficiaries. His only obligation between the date of transfer and the date of registration was to take no improper advantage of the form of trusteeship, say by borrowing money against it or retaining a dividend declared on the shares.

Since legal title to the shares in *Re Rose* did not pass to the transferees until registration, it must therefore have been in equity that the court recognized the beneficial interest to have changed hands at the moment of transfer. At first sight, this appears to offend the maxims 'equity does not assist a volunteer' and 'equity does not perfect an imperfect gift', but, in *Re Rose*, the assistance given by the court was not of the active sort contemplated by the maxims. If a volunteer donee '*needs to get an order from a court of equity in order to complete his title, he will not get it*',[17] but that was not the situation in

---

[14] This practice has been compulsory since the Land Registration Act 2002, s. 6(1), (3), (4) has been in force.

[15] *Re Rose, Rose v. IRC* [1952] Ch 499. This case approved the authority of *Re Rose, Midland Bank v. Rose* [1949] Ch 78, but the cases are otherwise unrelated. To add further confusion, Jenkins J appeared in the earlier case and also, by this time as Jenkins LJ, in the later case.   [16] Ibid. at 513.

[17] *Mascall v. Mascall* (1985) 50 P & CR 119, *per* Browne-Wilkinson LJ at 126, CA.

Re Rose. In March, the donee had received everything he needed to perfect his legal title without assistance from the court.

If *Re Rose* demonstrates that courts will try to give effect to an intended transfer whenever they can do so without actually making an order to assist the volunteer transferee, the decision of the Privy Council in *T. Choithram International SA v. Pagarani*[18] illustrates just how generous the courts can be when there is a judicial desire that the transfer should succeed. Mr Pagarani was a successful businessman who had been diagnosed as having terminal cancer. He executed a trust deed at his bedside in order to establish a foundation to be an umbrella organization for a number of charities that he had established during his life. Immediately after signing the deed, he stated that all of his wealth would henceforth belong to the foundation. Mr Pagarani was a trustee of the foundation and the other trustees signed the deed on the same day, or soon after. Not long afterwards, the directors of four companies controlled by Mr Pagarani passed resolutions confirming that the trustees of the foundation would henceforth be the holders of the companies' shares and assets. After Mr Pagarani's death, the companies registered the trustees of the foundation as shareholders. Members of Mr Pagarani's family brought the present action. They claimed that the donation to the foundation had been ineffective, because Mr Pagarani had failed to transfer the shares before his death. The Privy Council disagreed, stating that, '[a]*lthough equity will not aid a volunteer, it will not strive officiously to defeat a gift*'.[19] Their Lordships held that the words 'I give everything to the foundation' could have meant only one thing in the context of the case—namely, 'I give to the trustees of the foundation'—because the foundation had no identity apart from its trustees. The fact that Mr Pagarani was one of the trustees of the foundation was held to be sufficient to overcome his failure to vest the property in the remaining trustees by formal transfer. It was held that, from the moment of his declaration, it would have been unconscionable for him to assert continuing beneficial ownership in the property and to deny that the subject matter of the donation belonged beneficially to the foundation. In short, this was not a case in which an intention to create a trust had been spelled out of a failed gift; rather, this was a case in which a constructive trust had been imposed on the donor to prevent him asserting an ongoing interest in the property in denial of the transfer. The claim brought by members of Mr Pagarani's family failed, because they could not acquire better title to Mr Pagarani's property than he himself had had at the moment of his death.

The English Court of Appeal has approved the decision in *Choithram*. It did so in the difficult case of *Pennington v. Waine*.[20] Mr Pennington was a partner in a firm of auditors that acted for a private limited company in which Mrs Ada Crampton held shares. She told Mr Pennington that she wished to transfer 400 of her shares to her nephew, Harold, and later signed a share transfer form to that effect, which she gave to Mr Pennington.

---

[18] [2001] 1 WLR 1. Noted J. Hopkins (2001) 60(3) CLJ 483.
[19] Ibid. *Per* Lord Browne-Wilkinson at 11.   [20] [2002] 1 WLR 2075.

He placed the form on file and took no further action prior to Ada's death, except to write to Harold enclosing a form for Harold to sign his consent to become a director of the company. The letter also informed Harold that Mr Pennington's firm had been instructed to arrange for the transfer of the 400 shares and that Harold need take no further action. Ada also informed Harold directly of her intention to transfer shares to him and of her desire that he should become a director of the company. However, when Ada died, her will made no disposition of the shares in favour of Harold, so the question arose as to whether she had made an effective disposition during her life. At first instance, the court noted that there was no evidence that the gift had been intended to take effect in the future [21] or subject to any condition precedent. Accordingly, the court could have held the gift to be ineffective, but instead it held that the gift had been effective immediately the share transfer forms had been executed, even though the forms were never delivered to Harold or to the company.

The Court of Appeal upheld that judgment and, in doing so, it demonstrated even greater generosity than that which the courts had shown in *Re Rose* and *Choithram*. The decision in *Pennington* was more generous than that of *Re Rose*, because, in *Re Rose*, there had actually been a transfer to the donee and all that remained to be done was to register the donee at the company, a step over which the donor had no control. The decision in *Pennington* was more generous than that in *Choithram*, because, in *Choithram*, it was at least arguable, if one agrees with the Privy Council, that there had been a transfer from Mr Pagarani in his capacity as donor to Mr Pagarani in his capacity as trustee of the donee foundation; in *Pennington*, the donor had merely passed the share transfer form to her own agent, which is like passing it from one's left hand to one's right hand (there is no true *transfer*). It is hard to see how she could be said to have disposed outright of her beneficial interest in the shares when it remained open to her to revoke her instructions to the agent.

So on what basis was the Court of Appeal able to conclude that Ada Crampton had divested herself entirely of her interest in the 400 shares before her death? Their Lordships' judgments provide two main answers to that question.[22] Clarke LJ held that the execution of the stock transfer form could take effect as a valid equitable assignment without the need for actual delivery of the stock transfer forms or the share certificates, provided that the execution of the stock transfer forms were intended to take

---

[21] The form had not been signed in escrow. A document executed 'in escrow' will take effect in the future, usually upon the happening of a particular event such as payment. See, for example, *Security Trust Co v. Royal Bank of Canada* [1976] AC 503, PC, in which a conveyance and mortgage were held in escrow pending payment.

[22] In addition to her major line of analysis, discussed next, Arden LJ made brief reference to two alternative justifications for their Lordships' conclusion that the gift in this case had been effective during Ada's lifetime. The first was to apply the principle that a court should take a benevolent construction in order to give effect to the donor's clear intentions. This, of course, depends upon a benevolent view of the court's ability to second-guess the donor's intentions, despite her failure to take irrevocable steps towards giving effect to them. The second, which her Ladyship described as being an application of the first, was that '*Ada and, through her, Mr Pennington became agents for Harold*'.

immediate effect. If his Lordship is right on that point, then, from the moment at which the forms were transferred, Ada had actually done everything within her power that was required in order to divest herself of her beneficial interest in the shares. However, it is surely doubtful that a donor should be construed to have transferred beneficial ownership, whilst retaining legal ownership, in the absence of a clear intention to become a trustee of the transferred assets. Arden LJ suggested an even more radical solution. Her Ladyship took the view that it would be unconscionable for Ada to resile from the transfer that she had embarked upon. Arden LJ described 'unconscionability' as a 'policy consideration' that operates in favour of holding that a transfer has been perfected. Whilst it may be broadly accurate to say that unconscionability promotes fundamental policy concerns, such as the prevention of the abuse of legal rights and powers, unconscionability should not be resorted to as if it were itself a policy consideration. On the contrary, it is, as we observed in Chapter 1, an equitable doctrine that operates *in personam* to restrain *particular* instances of abuse of legal rights and powers. Furthermore, even if 'unconscionability' were a policy consideration, it should not lead inexorably to the conclusion that an intended disposition should be binding on the conscience of the donor or settlor. The policy, if it were such, of preventing a donor from unconscionably denying that a disposition has taken place ought generally to be outweighed by the 'policy' that the court will not take active steps to remove assets from an owner when that owner has omitted to carry out the actions normally required to transfer assets of that type.

However that may be, it is notable that Arden LJ's actual decision in the case seems to owe more to the orthodox *in personam* view of unconscionability than to any policy-based analysis of the concept, in so far as her Ladyship identified a number of specific facts that, in her judgment, would have made it unconscionable for the particular donor in this case to have denied the donee's beneficial interest in the 400 shares. Those facts were as follows:

1. Ada made the donation of her own free will.
2. She signed the share transfer form and delivered it to Mr Pennington to secure registration.
3. She told Harold about the gift.
4. Mr Pennington told Harold that he need take no further action to perfect the gift.
5. Harold signed a form by which he agreed to become a director without limit of time, which he could not do without shares in the company.

If the first three facts, taken together or individually, were sufficient to bind Ada's conscience, it would surely never be safe for a competent person voluntarily to promise to make a gift, and still less to instruct their agent to take steps preliminary to making a gift. We must conclude, it is submitted, that the first three facts could have had no impact on Ada's conscience. That brings us to facts (4) and (5). Fact (4) was no doubt a representation, but was it a representation upon which Harold had relied to his detriment so that Ada's conscience must be affected? That is doubtful. There was nothing that Harold could have done to perfect the gift in his favour, so his omission to do that which he could not have done can hardly be regarded as detrimental reliance. What then of fact (5)? Here, at last, is a candidate: by accepting the directorship, it is certainly arguable that Harold acted to his detriment in reliance on an expectation that he would acquire some shares in the company.

However, even if there had been a representation plus detrimental reliance thereon, this would normally be said to raise an estoppel binding on the conscience of the representor—but their Lordships made no reference to estoppel, preferring instead to base their decision on the more general notion of unconscionability. That, it is respectfully submitted, will not suffice where a concept as vague as 'unconscionability' is being applied in relation to something as dependent upon certainty as the transfer of beneficial ownership. The court should have said what unconscionability means in this context[23] and why unconscionabilty arose on the facts of the present case. Despite this concern, Schiemann LJ agreed with Arden LJ's reasoning without discussion and Clarke LJ agreed that:

> if unconscionability is the test...it would have been unconscionable of Ada, as at the time of her death (if not earlier), to assert that the beneficial interest in the 400 shares had not passed to Harold.[24]

Courts have not always felt able to exercise such generosity as was demonstrated in *Re Rose, Choithram*, and *Pennington. Re Fry, deceased*[25] is a case in point. Like *Re Rose*, it involved a wartime transfer of shares in an English company, but in *Re Fry*, the transferor (Mr Fry) was resident outside the 'sterling' jurisdiction (he was resident in the USA). As a result of wartime restrictions, the English company was prohibited from registering the transfer without Treasury consent.[26] The forms necessary to obtain consent were sent to the transferor to sign, which he duly did, and he returned them to the company. Unfortunately, the transferor died before consent was obtained from the Treasury and the transfer was therefore held to have been ineffective. Although the transferor had done everything within his power to dispose of the shares, the transferee was in no position to complete the transfer; he still required the consent of the Treasury. In coming to the conclusion that the transfer was ineffective, the court noted that the transferor could have frustrated the transfer, even after sending the forms to the Treasury, by simply refusing to respond to questions that the Treasury might have raised between receipt of the forms and granting its consent.

The decision of the Court of Appeal in *Kaye v. Zeital*[27] was more orthodox. It followed the approach laid down in *Milroy v. Lord*, holding that an intended transfer of

---

[23] See Chapter 1.

[24] [2002] 1 WLR 2075 at 2094A–B, 2105G. It is interesting to note that, in the event, the transfer to Harold was ineffective due to a breach of the company's articles (*Brian Hurst v. Crampton Bros (Coopers) Ltd* [2002] 2 P & CR D 21).

[25] [1946] Ch 312, Ch D.

[26] Defence (Finance) Regulations 1940, reg. 3A(1), (4) (Statutory Rules and Orders 1940, No. 1254).

[27] [2010] EWCA Civ 159; [2010] 2 BCLC 1.

the beneficial interest in company shares failed because the transferor had not done the actions necessary to effect such a transfer. He had not declared himself a trustee of the beneficial interest, neither had he assigned it in writing by way of gift or trust. *Kaye v. Zeital* was followed in *Curtis v. Pulbrook*.[28] In *Curtis*, Briggs J acknowledged that *Pennington v. Waine* had identified three ways to perfect apparently imperfect donations: 'The first is where the donor has done everything necessary to enable the donee to enforce a beneficial claim without further assistance from the donor ... The second is where some detrimental reliance by the donee upon an apparent although ineffective gift may so bind the conscience of the donor to justify the imposition of a constructive trust ... The third is where by a benevolent construction an effective gift or implied declaration of trust may be teased out of the words used.'[29]

Despite the very benevolent construction adopted in *Choithram* and *Pennington*, it is doubtless still true that a settlor should at least *try* to do everything in his power necessary to transfer property of the type intended to be subject to the trust.[30] Accordingly, in the following sections, we will identify how the prerequisites for transfer vary according to the type of trust asset.

Transfer of land

Subject to certain exceptions,[31] legal title to land will only pass where it is transferred by deed.[32] The deed must be signed, witnessed, delivered, and apparent on its face that it is a deed.[33] In *Richards v. Delbridge*,[34] the tenant of business premises purported to make a gift of a lease to his infant grandson by indorsing the following signed memorandum on it: 'This deed and all thereto belonging I give to Edward Bennetto Richards from this time forth, with all the stock-in-trade.' He then delivered the deed to Richards' mother to hold for her son. He made no reference to the gift in his will, so, upon his death, the question arose whether the lease and business had passed to Richards either by *inter vivos* gift or by trust. If they had not, they would pass to other persons under the will. Sir George Jessel MR held that the transfer had been legally ineffective for lack of a deed and refused to hold, in the alternative, that the tenant had declared himself to be a trustee:

> It is true he need not use the words, 'I declare myself a trustee' but he must do something which is equivalent to it, and use expressions which have that meaning; for, however anxious the court may be to carry out a man's intention, it is not at liberty to construe words otherwise than according to their proper meaning.[35]

---

[28] [2011] EWHC 167 (Ch); [2011] 1 BCLC 638.   [29] Ibid. at para. [43].

[30] See *Milroy v. Lord* (1862) 4 De GF & J 264 at 274 and *Re Rose* [1952] Ch 499 at 511.

[31] Including '*assents by a personal representative*', '*conveyances taking effect by operation of law*' (including conveyances in satisfaction of a proprietary estoppel: see *Pascoe v. Turner* [1979] 1 WLR 431, in Chapter 8), '*leases taking effect in possession for a term not exceeding three years ... at the best rent which can be reasonably obtained without taking a fine*', and certain '*disclaimers*' and '*surrenders*' (Law of Property Act 1925, ss. 52(2), 54).   [32] LPA 1925, s. 52(1).

[33] Law of Property (Miscellaneous Provisions) Act 1989, s. 1. Thus the old rule that a deed must be signed, *sealed*, and delivered is replaced by a new rule that the deed must be signed, *seen*, and delivered (taking *seen* to mean both 'witnessed' and 'apparent').   [34] (1874) LR 18 Eq 11.

[35] Ibid. at 14.

Where legal title to land is registered, it is not finally transferred until the transferee is registered as the new proprietor.[36] Nevertheless, once the transferee has received the deed of transfer together with the transferor's land certificate, the transferee has everything he needs to register his title and the transferor has no power to stop him.[37] Accordingly, if the transfer had been made on trust, the trust will be completely constituted and binding upon the transferor at the moment he delivers the documents.

Transfer of company shares

According to Holdsworth, it was not until the seventeenth century that moveable property acquired the '*permanent character of land*', because it was then that accumulations of capital were first invested in the form of transferable stock.[38] Land and shares in companies are still the most valuable forms of property that most people will ever own, and the transfer of legal title to shares is subject to safeguards similar to those that apply to registered land. In the case of shares in private companies, the transferor must execute a stock transfer form and deliver it to the transferee with the share certificate, at which point the transfer is binding on the transferor and legal title will not vest in the transferee until the company actually registers him as the new shareholder,[39] although, since the introduction of the CREST system on the London Stock Exchange in 1996, a great deal of share dealing takes place electronically.[40]

Shares in *public* companies must be transferred via the stock exchange.

Transfer of ordinary chattels

Chattels are moveable items of personal property, including such things as jewellery, books, furniture, and cattle (from which the term is derived). To transfer legal title in a chattel, there must be physical delivery prior to, contemporaneous with, or subsequent to the words of gift. Alternatively, legal title to a chattel can be transferred by a properly executed deed of gift or trust.

In *Re Cole*,[41] a man bought a house in London while his wife and family were living elsewhere. When the time came to show his wife around the house, she was especially impressed by a particular silk carpet and a certain card table. At the end of the tour, her husband announced that the house and its contents were all hers. Some 16 years later, the husband was declared bankrupt and the following year his wife sold the moveable contents of the house. An action was brought by the trustee in bankruptcy to recover the proceeds of sale from the wife.

It was held that, words of gift being insufficient to perfect a gift of chattels, the wife would have to prove some act of delivery or change of possession such as would

---

[36] Land Registration Act 1925, s. 19(1) (freehold); s. 22(1) (leasehold).

[37] *Mascall v. Mascall* (1985) 50 P & CR 119.

[38] W. S. Holdsworth, *An Historical Introduction to the Land Law* (Oxford: Clarendon Press, 1927) at 145.

[39] Stock Transfer Act 1963, s. 1; Companies Act 2006, s. 771 and Part 21. See *Milroy v. Lord* (1862) 4 De GF & J 264 and *Re Rose* [1952] Ch 499. But see *Pennington v. Waine* (earlier).

[40] Part 21 of the Companies Act 2006 further facilitates this.   [41] [1964] 1 Ch 175, CA.

demonstrate unequivocally that the husband intended to transfer title to her. In the absence of evidence of such an act, legal title to the chattels remained with the husband and vested in his trustee in bankruptcy. The Court of Appeal rejected a novel argument submitted by R. E. Megarry QC that it is enough for the transferee to be brought to the chattels, rather than the chattels to the transferee. Harman LJ did accept, however, that, if the chattels are numerous or bulky, there may be 'symbolical delivery'. He gave the example of a case involving a church organ, 'where the donor put his hand upon it in the presence of the donee and accompanied his gesture with words of gift'.[42] In some circumstances, even symbolic physical delivery of the chattel may not be needed. In *Jaffa v. The Taylor Gallery*,[43] a trust of a painting had been declared in a document (not a deed), of which the trustees each had a copy. The trust was held to have been validly constituted even though the painting had not been physically transferred to the trustees. The judge held that it would be absurd to insist on physical transfer when 'one trustee was in Northern Ireland' and 'another in England'.

Transfer of a legal 'chose in action'

A chose ('thing') in action is a personal right of one person against another that can be sold, given away, subjected to a trust, etc., as if it were property. Common examples include a company share, a patent and contractual rights and obligations including debts:

> The scope of the trusts recognized in equity is unlimited. There can be a trust of a chattel or of a chose in action, or of a right or obligation under an ordinary legal contract, just as much as a trust of land.[44]

Indeed, the scope of trusts is so 'unlimited' that even when rights under a contract are non-assignable according to the terms of the contract, the very benefit of *being a party to the contract* may be held on trust.[45] According to established principles, a trustee will hold any benefit arising from his trusteeship—including the benefit of being a contracting party (such as renewals of the contract) on trust for the beneficiaries.[46]

Most choses in action are capable of being assigned, but it is worth noting that an assignment of a chose in action will fail if the underlying purpose of the transaction is to allow the assignee to finance the litigation of the assignor's action (the action to which the 'chose' relates). As a general rule, the law does not permit the 'maintenance' of another person's litigation.[47]

Statute will sometimes prescribe the appropriate method of assignment for specific forms of chose in action. Thus the Bills of Exchange Act 1882 provides that an unconditional order in writing requiring one person to pay money to another must be endorsed

---

[42] Ibid. at 187.   [43] *The Times*, 21 March 1990.

[44] *Lord Strathcona Steamship Co. Ltd v. Dominion Coal Co. Ltd* [1926] AC 108, *per* Lord Shaw at 124.

[45] *Don King Productions Inc. v. Warren* [2000] Ch 291, CA (affirming Lightman J [1999] 3 WLR 276 at 279). The chose in action in that case was the benefit of being a party to a contract to promote boxing. See also *Pathirana v. Pathirana* [1967] 1 AC 233, PC, and *Thompson's Trustee in Bankruptcy v. Heaton* [1974] 1 WLR 605.   [46] *Don King Productions Inc. v. Warren*, ibid. at 317.

[47] See *Trendtex Trading Corporation v. Suisse* [1982] AC 679, CA.

in favour of the transferee[48] and the Copyright Act 1956 requires that a copyright must be assigned in writing. In the absence of specific statutory provision, the general statutory and non-statutory rules laid out in the following sections will apply.

Legal assignment of a chose in action

Legal title to a debt or other legal chose in action may be assigned in writing, but for the assignment to be effective at law it must be 'absolute',[49] which means that the *entire* chose in action must be assigned [50] and that the assignment cannot be by way of mere security for a loan made by the assignee to the assignor.[51] The assignment is not fully effective until the date on which express notice of the assignment is given to the debtor, or other person from whom the assignor would have been entitled to claim such debt or thing in action.[52] If the assignor fails to give written notice to the debtor, the assignees (the trustees) can perfect their legal title to the chose in action by giving written notice of the assignment to the debtor.[53]

Equitable assignment of a chose in action

If either or both of the requirements for assignment at law, namely 'absolute assignment' of the whole debt and 'writing under the hand of the assignor', is not complied with, the assignment will be effective *in equity* if the assignment is made for legal consideration. Consideration brings equity into play because of the burden it places on the conscience of the assignor. If such an assignment is *not* made for consideration, the Australian position is that it is not effective in equity,[54] but there are old English authorities to the contrary.[55] The English authorities hold that an assignor who intends to make an *immediate* assignment of an existing debt or chose in action is deemed to have declared himself a trustee of it for the benefit of the assignee. These older English authorities were raised in argument by counsel in *Jones v. Lock*.[56] One might have expected Lord Cranworth to dismiss them in the light of the decision in *Milroy v. Lord* which, only three years previously, had held that a declaration of trust should not be spelled out of a failed transfer; in fact, his Lordship cast no doubt on the older cases and it is arguable that they remain law.[57] However, for the avoidance of doubt, any person wishing to assign only *part* of a legal debt or chose in action should clearly and unequivocally declare himself to be a trustee of that part for the benefit of the assignee, or else contract with the debtor to renew the debt on the basis of the desired apportionment between assignor and the assignee.

---

[48] Section 31.   [49] Law of Property Act 1925, s. 136(1).

[50] *Foster v. Baker* [1910] 2 KB 636, CA.   [51] *Durham Bros v. Robertson* [1898] 1 QB 765.

[52] Law of Property Act 1925, s. 136(1).

[53] H. Beale (ed.), *Chitty on Contract*, 28th edn (London: Sweet & Maxwell, 1999) at 200–16; *Van Lynn Developments Ltd v. Pelias Construction Co Ltd* [1969] 1 QB 607 at 615.

[54] *Olsson v. Dyson* (1969) 120 CLR 365.

[55] For example, *Ex p Pye* (1811) 18 Ves Jr 140; *Kekewich v. Manning* (1851) 1 De G M & G 176.

[56] Note 5.   [57] *Palmer v. Carey* [1926] AC 703, PC.

Once a legal chose of action has been transferred in equity, it will thereafter be an equitable chose in action, which means that, in future, it can only be assigned in writing.[58] There is no rule that the equitable assignment of a chose in action is ineffective without giving notice to the debtor (or other person subject to the chose in action), but, by giving notice to the debtor, the assignee acquires priority over obligations that the debtor might subsequently incur.[59] This is the so-called rule in *Dearle v. Hall*:[60]

> The rule is based upon the inequity of allowing an assignee, who has taken no steps (by giving notice to the trustees to whom inquiry might be made) to protect subsequent assignees against the possibility of fraud on the part of the assignor, from setting up his prior assignment against those who have been deceived.[61]

The case of *Re McArdle*[62] demonstrates that the courts will not spell out a valid equitable assignment from a failed contract. A testator left his residuary estate upon trust for his widow for life, with the remainder to his five children in equal shares. During the lifetime of the widow, one of the children, Monty, carried out improvements to a farm forming part of the testator's residuary estate. The testator's other children then signed a document in these terms:

> To Monty...in consideration of your carrying out certain alterations and improvements to the...Farm...at present occupied by you, we the beneficiaries under the will of William Edward McArdle hereby agree that the executors...shall repay to you from the said estate when so distributed the sum of £488 in settlement of the amount spent on such improvements.

When the widow died, the other children refused to accede to Monty's claim to the £488. The Court of Appeal held that transfer of the relevant part of the residuary estate would only be effective if Monty (in fact, Monty's widow by this time) could establish that the signed document had been a binding contract or a valid transfer of an equitable interest. The court held that it was neither. The works of improvement had been completed before the execution of the document, so that the consideration for the contract was entirely in the past, thus rendering the contract legally unenforceable. However, the document had been in form and intent a contract, so the court refused to construe it as a valid equitable assignment. Lord Evershed MR regretted that the other children had been able '*to evade the obligation which they imposed on themselves in 1945*', but that, he said, '*is a matter for their conscience and not for this court*'.[63] Jenkins LJ added that, in the absence of consideration or a perfected transfer, the donor of an imperfect gift (each of the 'other children' in this case) '*has a* locus poenitentiae *and can change his mind at any time*', thus '*no question of conscience enters into the matter*'.[64] This approach provides

---

[58] Law of Property Act 1925, s. 53(1)(c). See Chapter 6.
[59] *Raiffeisen Zentrabank Osterreich AG v. Five Star Trading LLC* [2001] QB 825, CA.
[60] (1828) 3 Russ 1.
[61] *United Bank of Kuwait plc v. Sahib* [1997] Ch 107, *per* Chadwick J at 119 (approved at 132, CA).
[62] [1951] 1 Ch 669.   [63] [1951] 1 Ch 669 at 676.
[64] Ibid. at 677. *Locus poenitentiae* means 'place (i.e. opportunity) to repent'.

a stark contrast to the expansive approach to 'unconscionability' taken by the Court of Appeal in the case of *Pennington v. Waine*, considered earlier.[65]

'Future' or 'after-acquired' property

Normally, a transferor already owns property before purporting to transfer it to another, but is it possible to transfer property that one has not yet acquired? On its face, such a transfer is nonsensical and, at common law, '*it cannot take effect as an actual transfer, but can be effective at most as a promise or contract to transfer*'.[66] Equity, on the other hand, looks to the substance of a purported transfer of property that has not yet been acquired. It sees as done that which ought to be done and will order specific performance of the transfer in favour of any person who has given valuable consideration.[67] The transfer will be effective in equity to pass the beneficial interest the moment the transferor acquires the subject matter of the transfer.[68]

Examples of 'future' property include future income,[69] royalties from books that have not yet been sold,[70] copyright in songs that have not yet been written,[71] and an heir's expectation of a legacy.[72] A covenant to transfer the *entirety* of one's after-acquired property may not be enforceable.[73]

The rationale for equity's recognition of a purported present assignment for valuable consideration of future property was explained by Buckley J in *Re Ellenborough*:[74]

> An assignment for value binds the conscience of the assignor. A Court of Equity as against him will compel him to do that which *ex hypothesi* he has not yet effectually done.[75]

It follows that a different rationale is required to govern the case of a transferor who does not purport to make a present transfer at all, but merely promises that he will transfer the property *when, in the future, he acquires it*. The law reports are full of cases of this sort. Usually, the promise is made in a deed and is therefore known as a 'covenant'.

Covenants to settle after-acquired property

Most reported cases of covenants to transfer after-acquired property concern marriage settlements of the sort that were especially popular in nineteenth-century England. The parties to a typical marriage settlement were the man and woman engaged to be married, and the intended trustees of the settlement. The terms of a standard marriage settlement would provide that the trust property should be held for the wife for her life, then for her husband for his life, and then for their children. If the husband predeceased his wife, the property would pass directly to their children on the wife's death and, if

---

[65] See earlier.

[66] P. S. Atiyah, *Introduction to the Law of Contract* (Oxford: Clarendon Press, 1961) at 192–3.

[67] *Re Brooks' Settlement Trusts* [1939] Ch 993, *per* Farwell J; following *Lovett v. Lovett* [1898] 1 Ch 82 and *Re Ellenborough* [1903] 1 Ch 697. *Raiffeisen Zentralbank Osterreich AG v. Five Star Trading LLC* [2001] QB 825, CA.   [68] *Collyer v. Isaacs* (1881) 19 Ch D 342, *per* Jessel MR at 351.

[69] *Re Gillott's Settlement* [1934] Ch 97.   [70] *Re Trytel* (1952) 2 TLR 32.

[71] *Performing Rights Society v. London Theatre of Varieties* [1924] AC 1, HL.

[72] *Hobson v. Trevor* (1723) 2 Peere Wms 191.   [73] *Re Turcan* (1888) 40 Ch D 5, CA.

[74] [1903] 1 Ch 697.   [75] Ibid. at 700.

there were no children of the marriage, the property would pass to the wife's next of kin. The original trust property was typically given by the woman's parents to the trustees of the settlement to be held according to its terms.

The original purpose of marriage settlements was to make secure financial provision for a wife and her children in the days before a married woman could hold property absolutely in her own right. There is not much call for marriage settlements nowadays, but the reasoning in the older cases is as useful as ever for illustrating the interplay of law and equity.

The marriage settlement may sound like a standard trust, but the distinctive feature of a marriage settlement was that, in a typical case, the woman would covenant to transfer her after-acquired property to the trustees of the marriage settlement to be held according to its terms.[76] In theory, the trustees could enforce such a covenant against her the moment she acquired the 'after-acquired property', because the trustees would have been parties to the trust deed and, as such, would be deemed to have given nominal legal consideration for the promise.[77] However, because enforcement of the covenant by the trustees would completely constitute the trust of after-acquired property, thereby vesting interests in beneficiaries who may possibly be mere volunteers, the courts do not permit trustees to enforce such covenants unless the beneficiaries have themselves given consideration. If the trustees were allowed to enforce the trust, the beneficiaries would obtain indirectly that which, as volunteers, they would have been unable to obtain directly.

If the trustees cannot enforce the covenant in favour of volunteer beneficiaries, the question naturally arises: who *can* enforce the covenant? The answer is that any beneficiary who has given consideration for the covenant, and who is therefore not a volunteer, may enforce it without any question of having to resort to the assistance of the trustees. This is because equity considers the covenantor's conscience to be burdened by the consideration received from the non-volunteer beneficiaries. In the traditional marriage covenant, the covenantor's husband can enforce the covenant, because a spouse is said to give 'marriage consideration' by the very act of marriage.[78] The issue of the marriage can also enforce such a covenant, for by a deliberate legal 'fiction'[79] the issue of the marriage are also said to fall within the 'marriage consideration'. 'Issue' obviously includes immediate children of the marriage and it can also include grandchildren,[80] but children of a previous relationship do not come within the marriage consideration unless their interests are 'interwoven' with those of the children of the marriage,[81] as would be

---

[76] Until 1907, a husband could make this covenant on his wife's behalf and without her confirmation under a *jus mariti* preserved by the Married Women's Property Act 1882, s. 19. The husband's *jus mariti* was finally removed by the Law Reform (Married Women's and Tortfeasors) Act 1935, s. 2.

[77] Gratuitous promises made in deeds were binding long before English law recognized the binding nature of contracts by exchange of promises: P. S. Atiyah, *Introduction to the Law of Contract* (Oxford: Clarendon Press, 1961) at 22–3.

[78] Marriage consideration has been described as '*the most valuable consideration imaginable*' (*AG v. Jacobs Smith* [1895] 2 QB 341, *per* Kay LJ at 354, CA).   [79] *Re Cook's ST* [1965] Ch 902, *per* Buckley J at 916B.

[80] *Macdonald v. Scott* [1893] AC 642, HL (SC).   [81] *AG v. Jacobs Smith* [1895] 2 QB 341, CA.

the case, for example, if stepbrothers or sisters had been brought up together from an early age. It should be noted that marriage consideration, like all forms of consideration, is ineffective if it was given in the past in exchange for a present promise. For a settlement to be made in consideration of marriage, it must be made before the marriage takes place; although one exception may be if the marriage settlement is made after the marriage, but in accordance with a premarital (antenuptial) agreement to make it.[82]

An intended volunteer beneficiary who was a party to the deed containing the covenant is a 'party to the covenant' and may take action on the covenant at common law, even though he has given no consideration.[83] The deed supplements the lack of consideration at common law. Equity, on the other hand, does not consider the covenantor's conscience to be burdened by the claims of a person who, being merely a party to the deed, has given only nominal consideration to the covenantor. The upshot is that the intended volunteer beneficiary will be able to take action on the covenant, but he will be restricted to the common law remedy of damages for breach of the covenant.[84] Equity will not grant an order for specific performance of the covenant, so the covenantor will not be required to settle her after-acquired property on the trustees *in specie*. The claimant will also be required to bring his claim within the limitation period set down for the common law action.[85]

If a covenant is enforced by a person who has provided valuable or marriage consideration, or by trustees on their behalf,[86] equity will require the covenantor's after-acquired property to be transferred to the trustees of the marriage settlement, at which point the trust of the after-acquired property will be completely constituted. At the moment the trust is completely constituted even *volunteer* beneficiaries under the trust will be entitled to claim their interests under it, even though they themselves had been unable to enforce the covenant.[87] Thus, if intended beneficiaries who are children of the marriage (and are therefore within the marriage consideration) enforce the covenant for their own benefit, intended beneficiaries who had not given consideration (such as relations who lie outside the marriage consideration)[88] will become fully fledged beneficiaries as a by-product of the children's action.

Following the logic of the previous point, one might suppose that volunteer beneficiaries would become fully fledged beneficiaries as a by-product of action taken by *trustees* to enforce the covenant on their behalf. That, however, as we noted earlier, is not what happens. Even though trustees, as parties to the deed, are deemed to have given notional consideration and therefore have the legal power to enforce the covenant, the courts insist that trustees should not exercise that power unless the intended

---

[82] *AG v. Jacobs Smith* [1895] 2 QB 341, CA.   [83] *Cannon v. Hartley* [1949] 1 Ch 213.

[84] Ibid. at 217. Damages for breach of covenant will be fixed at a level calculated to compensate for the loss of the anticipated interest under the trust (*Re Cavendish-Browne's Settlement Trusts* [1916] WN 341).

[85] A covenant is a 'specialty' within the Limitation Act 1980, s. 8, breach of which is subject to a 12-year limitation period. For limitation, generally, see Chapter 13.   [86] *Pullan v. Koe* [1913] 1 Ch 9.

[87] *Paul v. Paul* (1882) 20 Ch D 742; *Re D'Angibau* (1880) 15 Ch D 228.

[88] *Re Plumtree* [1910] 1 Ch 609.

beneficiaries have given real consideration.[89] It is deemed inappropriate that volunteers should acquire by indirect means that which they could not have acquired directly. An inventive volunteer might argue that, although the trustees have the legal power of enforcement, the benefit of the power must belong to the intended beneficiaries of the trust. On that basis, the volunteer, as one of the intended beneficiaries, might claim to be able to compel the trustee to enforce the covenant. Older decisions, such as *Fletcher v. Fletcher*,[90] allowed this argument, but later courts were surely correct to deny volunteers the possibility of compelling trustees in this way. What is harder to understand, however, is why modern courts took the additional step of depriving the trustees of the right to enforce the covenant of their own volition[91] and even went so far as to state that trustees should not even sue for damages for breach of the covenant.[92] There is no equitable ground for restraining the trustees' exercise of their legal power; certainly it could hardly be described as 'unconscionable' for a trustee to exercise it, so the suspicion arises that there may be policy reasons why trustees are so restrained. Simon Gardner may have been correct when he suggested that the reluctance of modern courts to assist in the enforcement of marriage covenants to settle after-acquired property can be attributed to judicial recognition of women's increasing autonomy in property ownership, as well as to the promotion of unfettered participation of property in the free market.[93]

The Contracts (Rights of Third Parties) Act 1999

According to the Contracts (Rights of Third Parties) Act 1999, a person who is not a party to a contract may enforce a term of the contract in his own right if (a) the contract expressly provides that he may; or (b) the contractual term purports to confer a benefit on him,[94] although (b) will not apply if on a proper construction of the contract it appears that the parties did not intend the term to be enforceable by the third party.[95] As a result of the Act, mere volunteers, who previously would have been unable to enforce covenants to settle after-acquired property for their benefit, will be able to enforce post-1999 Act[96] covenants in their own right,[97] provided (as will always be the case with beneficiaries) that they are expressly identified in the covenant by name, as a member of a class, or as answering a particular description.[98] It does not matter that at the date of the covenant the beneficiaries were yet to be born.[99]

The Act provides that, for the purpose of exercising his right to enforce a term of the contract, there shall be available to the third party (the volunteer beneficiary) any remedy that would have been available to him in an action for breach of contract if he

---

[89] *Re Cook's Settlement Trusts* [1965] 1 Ch 902.   [90] (1844) 4 Hare 67.

[91] *Re Pryce* [1917] 1 Ch 234.   [92] *Re Kay's Settlement* [1939] Ch 329.

[93] *An Introduction to the Law of Trusts* (Oxford: Clarendon Press, 1990) at 70.   [94] Section 1(1).

[95] Section 1(2).

[96] The Act applies to contracts entered into on or after 11 May 2000—or 11 November 1999 in the case of contracts in which it had been expressly provided that the Act should apply.

[97] The issue of having to rely upon trustees to enforce the covenant (*Re Pryce* [1917] 1 Ch 234) does not arise.

[98] Section 1(3).   [99] Ibid.

had been a party to the contract, and that the rules relating to damages, injunctions, specific performance, and other relief shall apply accordingly.[100] It follows from this that the Act does not put the third-party beneficiary in a better position than the other parties to the contract. Accordingly, if the covenant had been 'voluntary' (not made for valuable or marriage consideration), the volunteer beneficiary will be restricted to the remedies available to other parties to the covenant—namely, common law damages for non-performance. The equitable remedy of specific performance will not be available, just as, prior to the Act, it had been unavailable to parties to voluntary covenants.[101]

The rule in *Strong v. Bird*

Strong v. Bird[102] illustrates how facts can sometimes combine fortuitously to perfect what would otherwise have been an imperfect gift. Bird had borrowed £1,100 from his stepmother, with whom he shared his house. She paid him a quarterly rent, so it was agreed that he would repay the loan by reducing her rent by £100 per instalment. The deduction was made on two consecutive quarter-days, but, on the third quarter-day, the stepmother insisted upon paying her full rent without deduction. She continued to make full payments of rent on every quarter-day up until her death four years later, whereupon Bird was appointed to be the sole executor of his stepmother's estate. The stepmother's next of kin, Strong, alleged that Bird ought to repay the £900 balance of the loan, but Sir George Jessell MR held that no debt was owed to the stepmother's estate, because the testatrix had made her debtor her executor and had thereby released the debt at law. To succeed under the rule in *Strong v. Bird*, there must be: (1) evidence of the donor's intention to make an immediate *inter vivos* gift (if the gift were testamentary, it would fail for lack of formality);[103] and (2) evidence that the intention to make the gift continued throughout the entire period up until the donor's death.

Of course, this is not a case of equity assisting a volunteer:

> equity will not aid the donee, but on the other hand if the donee gets the legal title to the property vested in him he no longer wants the assistance of equity and is entitled to rely on his legal title as against the donor or persons claiming through him.[104]

Furthermore, for the rule to apply, the donor must not have treated the property as his own during that period, for example, by giving part of it away to someone other than the claimant.[105] *Re Stewart*[106] confirms that the rule is not restricted to the release of a debt: it can apply to a regular gift. It can also apply if the intended donee is not a sole executor, but one of many. Nor is the rule restricted to cases in which the donee is an executor.[107]

---

[100] Section 1(5).   [101] *Cannon v. Hartley* [1949] 1 Ch 213.   [102] (1874) LR 18 Eq 315.
[103] See Chapter 6.   [104] *Re James* [1935] 1 Ch 449, *per* Farwell J at 451.
[105] *Re Gonin, decd* [1979] Ch 16.   [106] [1908] 2 Ch 251.   [107] *Re James* [1935] 1 Ch 449.

However, according to Walton J in *Re Gonin*, the application of the rule to benefit an administrator (or administratrix) goes too far, because the appointment of an administrator is '*not an act of the deceased but of the law*' and '*it is often a matter of pure chance which of many persons equally entitled to a grant of letters of administration finally takes them out*'.[108]

Day v. Royal College of Music[109] illustrates the application of the rule. It concerned a dispute between the adult children of the composer Sir Malcolm Arnold and his former carer, Mr Day. The dispute related to manuscript musical scores which had been deposited with the Royal College since the 1980s. Mr Day claimed that he had become owner of the manuscripts through a 1998 document executed by Sir Malcolm which recorded a gift in Mr Day's favour. However, Mr Day conceded that he never had physical possession of the manuscripts and that the 1998 document had not been executed as a deed. The Court of Appeal upheld the judge's decision that the Rule in *Strong v. Bird* operated to perfect the formal imperfections of the gift when, upon Sir Malcolm's death, Mr Day became an executor under Sir Malcolm's will.

The fortuitous constitution of trusts

The rule in *Strong v. Bird* permits the fortuitous, even accidental, perfection of imperfect gifts. In theory, therefore, it might be possible, on parallel facts, fully to constitute an incompletely constituted trust. Cast your mind back to the 'double character' of the rule in *Strong v. Bird* as set out in *Re Stewart*. On the first line of reasoning—that the vesting of the property in the executor at the testator's death completes the imperfect gift made in the lifetime—there would appear to be no reason, in principle, why the rule should not be effective to transfer legal title to trustees. On the second line of reasoning—that the intention of the testator to give the beneficial interest to the executor is sufficient to defeat the equity of beneficiaries under the will—there should likewise be no difficulty in applying the rule to give effect to an *inter vivos* declaration of trust. The equities of the beneficiaries under that trust would take priority over the equitable claims of the beneficiaries under the will, because the first equity in time will prevail where the equities are equal.[110]

In *Re Ralli's Will Trusts*,[111] the testator, Ralli, left his residuary estate to trustees on trust for his wife for life, with remainder to his daughters H and I. Later, by a separate marriage settlement, H covenanted that, when she came into possession of her share under Ralli's will, she would settle her share on trustees for the benefit of her own children and, ultimately, for the children of I. A clause of H's marriage settlement declared that all property within the terms of the covenant should be subject to the terms of the trusts pending assignment to the trustees. In the event, H died childless. Some time later, I's husband, who had been a party to, and was nominated to be a trustee of, H's

---

[108] [1979] Ch 16 at 35A–B.   [109] [2013] EWCA Civ 191; [2013] WLR(D) 112, Court of Appeal.
[110] See Chapter 16 on maxims of equity.   [111] [1964] Ch 288.

marriage settlement, was appointed to be a trustee under Ralli's will trust. He therefore asked the court whether he had the power to hold H's share of her father's residuary estate on the trusts of the marriage settlement. He claimed that he did have the power, which was hardly surprising given that his own children stood to benefit under the trusts of H's marriage settlement. H's personal representatives disagreed. They claimed that H's interest under Ralli's will trust should be held by I's husband for the benefit of the persons entitled to the residue of H's estate under H's will.

The court held that I's husband was free to hold H's share of Ralli's estate on the trusts of the marriage settlement. Those trusts had become completely constituted the moment legal title to the property had, quite fortuitously, vested in I's husband in his capacity as trustee of Ralli's will trusts. If it had been necessary to enforce performance of the covenant, equity would not have done so at the request of the beneficiaries under the settlement, because they were mere volunteers, but, in the present case, there had been no need to invoke the assistance of equity to enforce performance of the covenant. On the contrary, it had been for the defendants to invoke equity to show that it would be '*unconscientious*'[112] for I's husband to exercise his legal power to hold the property on the trusts of the marriage settlement. This they had failed to do. As with the rule in *Strong v. Bird*, the state of the defendant's ownership took priority over the obligations inherent in his office:

> the circumstance that the plaintiff holds the fund because he was appointed a trustee of the will is irrelevant. He is at law the owner of the fund and the means by which he became so have no effect on the quality of his legal ownership.[113]

We might think that the 'quality' of his legal ownership is not really the point. We might think that equitable (beneficial) ownership is the real issue, and that in equity the 'circumstances' under which legal title comes to be held is never irrelevant. However that may be, Buckley J was, in fact, prepared to dispose of the case on the straight-forward assumption that H's remainder interest under Ralli's will had been vested, not after-acquired, property at the date of execution of the marriage settlement. On that view, by executing the marriage settlement, H would have done everything in her power to divest herself of her remainder interest under Ralli's will, so the execution of the marriage settlement would have been a declaration of trust immediately binding upon H pending transfer of her interest to the trustees of the settlement. This 'immediate' binding effect supplies the clearest point of distinction between *Re Ralli's Will Trusts* and *Re Brooks' Settlement Trusts*.[114] In the latter case, a person with a contingent interest under a trust purported to divest himself of that interest by voluntary settlement. The settlement was held to be not binding on him because his share was not yet his to give at the time of the purported voluntary settlement. His interest was at that time still contingent or specious because it would only pass to him in default of appointment to another.

---

[112] Ibid. *per* Buckley J at 302.   [113] Ibid. at 301.   [114] [1939] Ch 993.

Although the constitution of incompletely constituted trusts in a case such as *Re Ralli's* parallels closely the perfection of imperfect gifts by the rule in *Strong v. Bird*, it would be putting it too high to say that *Re Ralli's* was an *application* of the rule in *Strong v. Bird*. The '*Strong v. Bird* case' *Re James*,[115] was referred to by way of illustration in *Re Ralli's*, but the rule in *Strong v. Bird* was not mentioned directly. No reported case has overtly applied the rule in *Strong v. Bird* to trusts.

Gifts made in contemplation of death

The law takes a generous approach to gifts made in contemplation of death. In the case of soldiers and mariners on active military service, it is even possible to make an informal 'nuncupative will' by simply making an oral declaration in the presence of a witness. The law does not go as far as that in the case of ordinary citizens,[116] but, in certain circumstances, an imperfect gift will be perfected if it is made in contemplation of the donor's death.

The doctrine of *donationes mortis causa* (gifts made in contemplation of death) is often cited as an exception to the maxim 'equity will not assist a volunteer' to perfect an imperfect gift. There is support for this view in the many judgments that suggest the doctrine is effective in English law by means of an implied or constructive trust.[117] In truth, however, the doctrine was imported virtually without alteration from Roman law.[118] Analysis of the doctrine in terms of common law and equity, although necessary to the integrity of English jurisprudence, is inevitably strained and imprecise. A *donatio mortis causa* will never fit comfortably into English law: for one thing, it is neither an *inter vivos* gift nor a testamentary gift, but something in between. The subject matter of the gift must be delivered before the donor's death, but the gift takes effect when the donor dies and not before. In English law, the doctrine is formulated as follows:

> For an effectual *donatio mortis causa* three things must combine: first, the gift or donation must have been in contemplation, though not necessarily in expectation of death; secondly, there must have been delivery to the donee of the subject matter of the gift; and thirdly, the gift must be made under such circumstances as to show that the thing is to revert to the donor in case he should recover.[119]

---

[115] [1935] Ch 449. In *Re Gonin* [1979] Ch 16, Walton J cast doubt on the correctness of the decision in *Re James* [1935] 1 Ch 449.

[116] For the statutory formalities governing testamentary dispositions, see Chapter 6.

[117] See, for example, *Sen v. Headley* [1991] Ch 425, *per* Nourse LJ at 440C, CA.

[118] Henry de Bracton, *De legibus et consuetudinibus Angliae*, Book 2, folio 60. Justinian's Digest recites that '[i]t is permissible to make a gift mortis causa not only on grounds of weak health, but also on grounds of impending danger of death' (Citation 39.6.3–6) and that 'a gift mortis causa differs considerably from the true and absolute sort of gift which proceeds in such a way that it can in no circumstances be revoked' (Citation 39.6.35.2).

[119] *Cain v. Moon* [1896] 2 QB 283, *per* Lord Russell of Killowen CJ at 286.

The third requirement is, in essence, a requirement that the gift should be conditional—that is, on terms that, if the donor does not die he will be entitled to resume '*complete dominion... of the subject matter of the gift*'.[120]

The two major distinctions between the English formulation and the Roman formulation are, first, that delivery of the subject matter of the gift is always essential to a valid *donatio mortis causa* in English law, and, second, that there has never been a requirement in English law that *donationes mortis causa* be witnessed.[121] The definitive Roman statement of the doctrine appears in *Justinian's Digest*,[122] in which, in addition to the basic statement of the doctrine, there appears the following jurisprudential commentary:

> A gift mortis causa differs considerably from the true and absolute sort of gift which proceeds in such a way that it can in no circumstances be revoked. In that sort of case, of course, the donor wishes the recipient rather than himself to have the property. But the person who makes a gift mortis causa is thinking of himself and, loving life, prefers to receive rather than to give. This is why it is commonly said: 'He wishes himself rather than the recipient to have the property, but, that said, wishes the recipient rather than the heir to have it.'[123]

The English authorities

In *Wilkes v. Allington*,[124] a widow granted a mortgage over her interest in a farm. After her death, the mortgagee passed the deeds to the farm, except the mortgage deed, to the widow's executors (who happened to be the mortgagee's nieces). When it later emerged that the mortgagee was dying of an incurable disease, he passed the mortgage deed to his nieces in a sealed envelope. Some short time later, the mortgagee died of pneumonia. His executors, claiming that the mortgage was a subsisting security enforceable against the nieces, brought the present action. Lord Tomlin held that the mortgage could not be enforced. The otherwise imperfect gift of the mortgage to the nieces was made perfect by a valid *donatio mortis causa*, because it was clear that the gift was only to become binding on the donor's death (an intention could be implied that the property should be returned to him if he recovered). It did not matter that the donor died from a different disorder from that which had caused him to make the gift in contemplation of death.

In a later case, it was held that the doctrine could apply to gifts of land other than mortgages,[125] a point that had previously been in doubt. The facts were, briefly, that Mrs Sen, who had lived with a man for several years in a house owned by him, was given a set of keys as he lay on his deathbed. The keys unlocked a box containing the deeds to the man's house.

---

[120] *Re Lillingston* [1952] 2 All ER 184, *per* Wynn-Parry J at 187.

[121] A. Borkowski discusses these and other distinctions in *Deathbed Gifts: The Law of* Donatio Mortis Causa (Oxford: Blackstone Press, 1999) at 22–3.

[122] The Byzantine Roman Emperor Justinian (527–65 AD) oversaw the codification of Roman Law into the *Corpus Juris Civilis*, the major part of which was named in his honour.

[123] Citation 39.6.35.2. Cited in A. Borkowski, *Deathbed Gifts: The Law of* Donatio Mortis Causa (Oxford: Blackstone Press, 1999).

[124] [1931] 2 Ch 104, Ch D.   [125] *Sen v. Headley* [1991] Ch 425.

As he passed the keys to her, the dying man stated that the house was to be hers. It was held that passing possession of the deeds was sufficient to effect the *donatio*, because there had been '*a parting with dominion over the essential* indicia *of title*'.[126] (The notion of 'dominion', like the doctrine itself, is imported directly from Roman Law.) In holding that the doctrine was applicable to land, Nourse LJ said:

> Let it be agreed that the doctrine is anomalous, anomalies do not justify anomalous exceptions…to make a distinction in the case of land would be to make just such an exception. A donatio mortis causa of land is neither more nor less anomalous than any other. Every such gift is a circumvention of the Wills Act 1837.[127]

In another rare case of *donatio mortis causa* of land, it was confirmed that, whereas the delivery of title deeds will fail to pass dominion if the donor reserves a power to deal with the land in a manner incompatible with the gift, the mere fact that the donor continues to use the property is not incompatible with the gift, as the gift is not intended to take effect until the donor's death.[128] Whether *donatio mortis causa* is applicable to registered land, since the Land Registration Act 2002 abolished the land certificate, is debatable.[129]

The same reasoning must surely apply to a *donatio mortis causa* of shares. There had been some doubt that the doctrine could apply to company shares,[130] but, if the share certificates (being 'the essential indicia or evidence of title') are transferred, there seems to be no good reason why the doctrine should not apply in such a case.[131]

The fact that the Court of Appeal in *Sen v. Headley* decided to take an expansive approach to *donatio mortis causa*, on the basis that '*anomalies do not justify anomalous exceptions*', sidesteps the question of whether or not the continued existence of the anomaly can be justified. It is an answer to that question to say that, for all its conceptual difficulties, the doctrine addresses the real practical problem of deathbed dispositions and therefore fulfils a '*deep felt need of mankind*'.[132]

Concluding remarks

We concluded the previous chapter with the observation that courts take a pragmatic approach to the creation of trusts. We noted that, when asked to determine whether a trust or an absolute gift had been intended, judges do not approach the question in a logical vacuum and do not always produce the result demanded by strict theory. Judges reach their judgments in the light of all of the facts, some of which may not have been foreseen by the settlor, with the aim of producing an outcome in conformity with the settlor's underlying intentions. In this chapter, we have considered the question of constitution, which,

---

[126] Ibid. at 438A.   [127] Ibid. at 440.

[128] *Re Bogusz (Deceased) (sub nom. Vallee v. Birchwood)* [2013] EWHC 1449 (Ch); [2013] 2 P & CR DG 15. Should the court have been troubled that the donee did not make a will when he had the chance?

[129] N. Roberts, 'Donationes mortis causa in a dematerialised world' (2013) 2 Conv 113–28.

[130] *Re Weston* [1902] 1 Ch 680.   [131] *Staniland v. Willott* [1852] 3 Mac & G 664.

[132] J. H. Baker, 'Land as a *donatio mortis causa*' (1993) 109 LQR 19 at 19 (a note on *Sen v. Headley* [1991] Ch 425).

in essence, is the question of whether the settlor has done enough to transfer the trust property to the trustees, or to constitute himself a trustee. The constitution of a trust is not merely a matter of intention; it is a question of action or transaction, especially if the trust was intended to take effect by transfer of trust property to trustees. For this reason, the traditional approach of the courts to questions of constitution has tended to be less flexible or 'creative' than their approach to the issue of certainty of intention. There are exceptions in which the courts have taken a very generous and pragmatic approach to reach the conclusion that a trust has been completely constituted. In *Re Rose*, it will be recalled that a gift was said to have been completed before legal title had actually been transferred to the transferee. However, the fact that legal title had been registered in the names of the transferees by the time the matter came to be considered by the court may have been a significant factor in persuading the court to act pragmatically in holding that the gift had been perfected before registration. *Re Rose* was not a case in which the volunteer claimant actually required the active assistance of the court to complete the gift. The courts have also taken a generous approach to cases such as *Strong v. Bird* and *Re Ralli's*, in which legal title was successfully transferred by accident or good fortune, but in these, again, the courts' active assistance was not required to complete the gift or constitute the trust.

There has, however, been a sea change in the law relating to the constitution of trusts. It is difficult, if not impossible, to accept that the successful constitution of the trusts in *Choithram* and *Pennington* could have been achieved without the active assistance of the Judicial Committee of the Privy Council and the Court of Appeal, respectively. The settlor in each case had taken some active steps to demonstrate a serious intention to constitute a trust, but neither had done everything within their power actually to transfer legal title in the relevant property to the intended trustees. In fact, in both cases, the settlors had died before they could carry out the necessary formal transfers to the intended trustees. Leaving aside exceptional cases such as criminal confiscation and compulsory purchase, it is a fundamental principle of justice—not to mention a pillar of property law—that an owner of property cannot be deprived of the ownership of his property unless he disposes of it by a legally recognized mode of disposition. Even if an owner takes serious steps to dispose of his property, he has the right to change his mind right up until the moment at which he actually transfers everything that the transferee needs to perfect his title. The courts in *Choithram* and *Pennington* seem to have been content to assume that the transferors, had they lived, would not have changed their minds about making the transfer. The courts could not admit that they were assisting settlors to do that which the settlors had themselves failed to do, so, in both cases, the courts employed a different technique to ensure the successful constitution of the trusts. That technique was to hold that the settlors had so conducted themselves that they had bound their consciences to complete the dispositions which they had embarked upon (but had failed to complete) during their lifetimes. This burden of conscience became, in turn, a burden on the settlor's personal representatives. At the risk of sounding flippant, it would appear that the lesson for property owners is simple: do not take serious steps towards disposing of your property unless you are sure that you will not change your mind and, if you might wish to change your mind, try not to die in the meantime.

Further reading

In addition to the following print sources, the Online Resource Centre accompanying this book contains web links to further reading as well as guide answers to assessment questions relevant to this chapter.

BAKER, J. H., 'Land as a *donatio mortis causa*' (1993) 109 LQR 19.

BARTON, J. L., 'Trusts and covenants' (1975) 91 LQR 236.

BORKOWSKI, A., *Deathbed Gifts: The Law of* Donatio Mortis Causa (Oxford: Blackstone Press, 1999).

BORKOWSKI, A., and DU PLESSIS, P., *Textbook on Roman Law*, 4th edn (Oxford: Oxford University Press, 2010).

GARTON, J., 'The role of the trust mechanism in the rule in *Re Rose*' [2003] Conv 364.

HOPKINS, J., 'Constitution of trusts: a novel point' (2001) 60(3) CLJ 483.

JACONELLI, J., 'Problems in the rule in *Strong v. Bird*' (2006) Conv 432.

RICKETT, C., 'Completely constituting an *inter vivos* trust: property rules' [2001] Conv 515.

ROBERTS, N., '*Donationes mortis causa* in a dematerialised world' (2013) 2 Conv 113–28.

TJIO, H. and YEO, T. M., '*Re Rose* revisited: the shorn lamb's equity' [2002] LMCLQ 296.

5

Ineffective disposition of benefit: resulting trusts

In the previous two chapters, we considered the creation and complete constitution of a trust in circumstances in which the settlor expressly intended to create the trust. In this chapter, we will examine a type of trust that arises in the absence of any express intention to create it.

If B, the beneficial owner of an asset, transfers the asset to A in circumstances where A neither gives nor promises anything in return, and where there is no evidence of any intention on B's part to make a gift or trust of the property, one cannot tell to whom the benefit of the asset belongs. (Crucially, it will never be *presumed* that B intended to make a gift in favour of A unless there is a special relationship between B and A.)[1] The beneficial ownership of the asset cannot be left in this uncertain state, so it is said to be held by A for B under a resulting trust. This legal response to transfers of undefined intent is of very long standing. Thus, in 1530, St German commented that:

> If a man seised of land make a feoffment thereof, and it appeareth not to what use the feoffment was made, nor it is not upon any bargain or other recompence, then it shall be taken to the use of the feoffor, except the contrary can be proved.[2]

The word 'resulting' is derived from *saltare*, the Latin verb 'to jump'.[3] This gives the impression that a resulting trust is descriptive of the process by which benefits 'jump back' to a transferor. In fact, the key to understanding the resulting trust is to appreciate that the benefit 'jumps back' because the apparent disposition had actually been ineffective, in other words that the benefit jumps back because it had never really left. As Plowman J once said:

> a man does not cease to own property simply by saying 'I don't want it.' If he tries to give it away the question must always be, has he succeeded in doing so or not?[4]

---

[1] See 'presumption of advancement', later.

[2] Christopher St German, *Dialogue in English between a Doctor of Divinity and a Student in the Laws of England etc* (London: Treverys, 1530). Cited in W. Swadling, 'A new role for resulting trusts?' (1996) 16 Legal Studies 133.

[3] Hence *somersaults* and a balletic *saut*.

[4] *Vandervell v. IRC* [1966] Ch 261 at 275. This view was confirmed by Lord Upjohn on appeal in the same case [1967] 2 AC 291 at 314 and by Lord Millett in *Air Jamaica Ltd v. Charlton* [1999] 1 WLR 1399, PC.

A simple example of a resulting trust is where someone pays money into the bank account of a company that no longer exists.[5] The money cannot belong to the company. If no other recipient is entitled to the money under a contract or such like, this leaves two possibilities. Either the money belongs to nobody, in which case it will pass to the Crown as '*bona vacantia*' ('ownerless assets'), or it will return to the original owner under a resulting trust. Judges know that the former outcome is the last that any donor would intend, so the latter outcome is preferred—not only on the basis of the donor's intention, but because as a matter of policy private property should be kept in private ownership where possible. One way to imagine the mechanism of the resulting trust is to picture the benefit of the asset as a bouncy ball that is thrown to a person who does not exist. The law is most reluctant for the benefit to be deemed ownerless, so the court erects a notional barrier to prevent the wealth from passing into Crown ownership. The bouncy ball of benefit having missed the intended donee, it hits the barrier raised to prevent *bona vacantia* and bounces straight back to the person who put the benefit in to begin with. On the other hand, where it is clear that the donor intends to retain no interest in the asset whatsoever (an example would be throwing a coin in the fountain in the town square) he or she will be deemed to have launched the ball so high and out-of-sight that if it is not caught it will clear the barrier and pass to the Crown.

The established factual categories of resulting trust

In *Westdeutsche Landesbank Girozentrale v. Islington LBC*,[6] Lord Browne-Wilkinson confirmed that all resulting trusts are capable of being placed in one of two categories according to the factual circumstances in which they arise.

The first category covers cases in which B makes a voluntary payment to A or pays (wholly or in part) for the purchase of property that is vested either in A alone or in the joint names of A and B. (It is important to note that the 'family home' is an exception to the usual rules.)[7] In such cases, there is a presumption that B did not intend to make a gift to A. Lord Browne-Wilkinson stressed that '*this is only a presumption, which presumption is easily rebutted either by the counter-presumption of advancement*[8] *or by direct evidence of A's intention to make an outright transfer*'.[9] The second category covers cases in which B transfers the property on express trusts, but the trusts declared do

---

[5] See the facts of the unreported case *Omojole v. HSBC Bank Plc* (1 October 2012).

[6] [1996] AC 669. See Chapter 2. The case involved an attempt by a German bank to recover money paid to a London Council under a contract the council had no authority to make.

[7] This category of resulting trust goes back at least as far as *Bird v. Blosse* (1683) 2 Vent 361, but as a result of the decision of the House of Lords in *Stack v. Dowden* [2007] UKHL 17; [2007] 2 WLR 831 and the related decision of the UK Supreme Court in *Jones v. Kernott* [2011] UKSC 53; [2011] 3 WLR 1121 (discussed in detail in Chapter 8), there is no longer a presumption of resulting trust when a 'family home' is transferred into cohabitants' joint names.

[8] See later.

[9] [1996] AC 669 at 708. It has long been acknowledged that a resulting trust is rebuttable by contrary evidence (see *Graham v. Graham* (1791) 1 Ves Jun 272, 275–6).

not exhaust the entirety of the beneficial interest.[10] In both situations, B becomes the beneficiary of the resulting trust when it arises.

We will encounter resulting trusts of both types as we proceed through this chapter. Resulting trusts in the first category, which are sometimes called 'purchase money resulting trusts', are particularly relevant where the asset purchased is land. Special issues concerning resulting trusts of land are considered in Chapter 8, including the fact that the presumption of resulting trust no longer applies where 'romantic' cohabitants contribute unequally to the purchase of land in joint names.[11] Purchase money resulting trusts are also relevant to the purchase of property other than land.[12] An interesting contemporary example is provided by the purchase of a winning lottery ticket. In *Abrahams v. Trustee in Bankruptcy of Abrahams*,[13] a wife paid £1 each week into a National Lottery syndicate in the name of her husband, from whom she had separated. The syndicate won. The court held that the right to winnings had the character of a property right and that this right, although in the husband's name, was presumed to be the wife's under a resulting trust because she had contributed the winning £1.

The theory behind resulting trusts

The proper theoretical basis for the resulting trust is a matter of some debate. It is usually said that whereas an express trust gives effect to a settlor's expressed intention, a resulting trust gives effect to a settlor's (or donor's) *presumed* intention in circumstances that were not anticipated by his expressed intentions. There are, however, cases in which a resulting trust has been said to arise automatically by operation of law even though the settlor or donor patently had no intention that it should.[14] It is this author's opinion that, at the level of theory, all resulting trusts are of one type. It is submitted that all resulting trusts arise as an automatic consequence of a transferor's failure effectively to dispose of beneficial ownership in the asset purportedly transferred. The integrity of property law and the inviolability of proprietary rights automatically raise a presumption that a beneficial owner intends to retain his beneficial ownership unless he transfers it effectively in a manner that is recognized by property law.[15] The presumption will, of course, be rebutted by the transferor's contrary intention wherever, on the evidence, that contrary intention is expressed or must be implied. A presumed intention cannot prevail over an actual intention.[16] Thus if B lends money to A, who agrees to repay the money by

---

[10] See *Vandervell v. IRC* [1967] 2 AC 291.

[11] *Stack v. Dowden* [2007] UKHL 17; [2007] 2 WLR 831.

[12] *Dyer v. Dyer* (1788) 2 Cox Eq Cas 92.

[13] [1999] BPIR 637.

[14] See *Vandervell v. IRC* [1967] 2 AC 291.

[15] For example, *Prest v. Petrodel* [2013] UKSC 34. Here Lord Sumption advised (at para. [52]) that where cohabitees reside in a home held in the name of a company controlled by one of them, judges should suspect that the cohabitee who controls the company intends to retain beneficial ownership of the land.

[16] *Muschinski v. Dodds* (1985) 160 CLR 583, *per* Deane J at 612.

instalments with interest, B has intentionally bargained for a mere contractual, personal right to recover his money from A. That contractual intention to create a loan rebuts the presumption that B intended to recover the money under a resulting trust.

A resulting trust will arise not only where a transferor fails to make clear that a transfer is made by way of gift or trust, but also when a purported gift or trust fails to dispose effectively of the entire benefit of the subject matter. Thus there will be a resulting trust if certain property is transferred to trustees on trust to distribute the property among persons whose identity is incapable of being ascertained. As Russell LJ stated in *Hodgson v. Marks*:

> If an attempted express trust fails, that seems to me just the occasion for implication of a resulting trust, whether the failure be due to uncertainty, or perpetuity, or lack of form.[17]

A resulting trust may even arise when an express trust is successful if the trust is fulfilled leaving a surplus of funds. The settlor is presumed to have retained a beneficial interest in any surplus funds that might remain after the trust objects have been fulfilled, although this presumption is rebutted by facts that clearly indicate that the settlor had no intention ever to see the property again. Thus a payment of 'loose change' into a collection box for a good cause will not be returnable to the donor. The surplus—always assuming that the collection was at no time for exclusively 'charitable' purposes—will pass to the Crown as ownerless property (*bona vacantia*).[18] However, a payment by cheque, for example, of £10,000 to an officer of the good cause will be returnable under a resulting trust.

Mistaken payments

A mistaken transfer of money raises a particularly difficult issue. Suppose that B paid off a £100 debt to A, but, some time later, B transferred another £100 to A in the mistaken belief that the debt was still due. There is authority to suggest that a mistaken payment of this sort affects A's conscience so as to make A a trustee for B under a 'constructive' trust, because A's conscience is affected by the receipt of B's property,[19] but the authority is at first instance and it has not enjoyed a great deal of academic support. Some commentators have argued that there should be no trust in such a case;[20] others have argued that a mistaken payment gives rise to a new proprietary right in favour of the transferor under a resulting trust.[21] There is certainly an arguable case for a resulting trust, in so far as the second payment is not any orthodox legal transfer and is therefore

---

[17] *Hodgson v. Marks* [1971] 1 Ch 892, *per* Russell LJ at 933C–D, CA.
[18] *Re West Sussex Constabulary's Widows, Children and Benevolent (1930) Fund Trusts* [1971] Ch 1. If the collection is for a disaster fund, it will be charitable and Charities Act 1993, s. 14 (as amended by the Charities Act 2006) provides that, in most situations, surplus monies donated to collecting boxes, raffles, entertainments, and other gifts made by donors 'unknown or disclaiming' may be applied cy-près without having to obtain the donors' consent.
[19] *Chase Manhattan Bank v. Israel-British Bank* [1981] Ch 105.
[20] P. Millett, 'Restitution and constructive trusts' (1998) 114 LQR 399 at 412–13 and Swadling (see n. 2).
[21] R. Chambers, *Resulting Trusts* (Oxford: Clarendon Press, 1997) 129.

ineffective to dispose of B's beneficial interest, with the consequence that A ought to hold the £100 on resulting trust for B in accordance with B's presumed intention to recover. There is, however, a powerful objection to the resulting trust analysis of these facts—namely, that B's evident (albeit mistaken) intention to pay off a debt leaves no room to presume any intention on B's part to recover the payment under a resulting trust.[22] A similar argument, as we shall shortly see, persuaded the House of Lords in *Westdeutsche Landesbank Girozentrale v. Islington LBC*[23] to decline to find any resulting trust arising from a contractual payment made under a mistake of law. The House of Lords held that money paid under an ultra vires contract was held by the recipient subject to a mere personal obligation to return it.

Mistakes, by their nature, do not admit of perfect theoretical solutions, but even if we were to work out a solution to the question of whether there should be a proprietary or personal remedial response to mistaken payments, we would no doubt find the courts willing to throw the spanner of policy into the works. However compelling might be the theoretical case for a proprietary remedy to recover a mistaken payment under a resulting or constructive trust, the courts will be reluctant to infer such trusts into a commercial transaction. As Lord Browne-Wilkinson stated in *Westdeutsche Landesbank Girozentrale v. Islington LBC*:[24]

> wise judges have often warned against the wholesale importation into commercial law of equitable principles inconsistent with the certainty and speed which are essential requirements for the orderly conduct of business affairs.[25]

One reason for judicial reluctance to infer a trust into a commercial transaction is the proprietary nature of the trust and the consequent prejudice to the trustee's innocent third party creditors. Another is that courts are unwilling to infer a trust into a commercial transaction where the parties ought to have anticipated the possibility that the type of mistake in question might occur. Thus one justification for the decision not to find a resulting trust in *Westdeutsche* is that the commercial parties in that case had the benefit of top-class legal advice and therefore ought to have entered an express term in their contract to deal with the reasonably foreseeable possibility that the contract might, for some reason, prove to be ultra vires the authority of the defendant council. In other cases, such as that of our simple mistaken double payment, it may be that a court would conclude that the mistake was not reasonably foreseeable and the court might therefore be less resistant to a trust solution.

However, before we too readily concede that there cannot be a resulting trust of a mistaken contractual payment, let us consider if there may yet be an argument in its favour. Chambers argues that a resulting trust will arise, because the transferor lacked any positive intention to confer a benefit, but against this is the prevailing view that

---

[22] See the papers by Millett and Swadling mentioned earlier.
[23] [1996] AC 669.
[24] Ibid.
[25] Ibid. at 704G. See also *Barnes v. Addy* (1874) LR 9 Ch App 244 at 251, 255; *Scandinavian Trading Tanker Co AB v. Flota Petrolera Ecuatoriana* [1983] 2 AC 694 at 703–4.

there will be no resulting trust if the transferor intended (albeit mistakenly) to fulfil some other positive intention, contractual or otherwise. The arguments on both sides turn upon the state of B's intentions, but it can be argued that a resulting trust should arise, independently of the state of B's intentions, by looking at the matter from A's perspective—not in terms of A's conscience, as was advocated in *Chase Manhattan*, but on the basis that A, having failed to take the property by any valid contract or proprietary transfer, cannot be the absolute owner of it, and, in the absence of any other obligation, must be obliged to return the property to the transferee under a resulting trust. A is really just like a lucky 'finder' who has come into possession of property that does not belong to him. It is submitted, in short, that a resulting trust should arise not only in the absence of the transferor's contrary intention, but also in the absence of the transferee's contrary entitlement.

The transferee's knowledge of the relevant facts

It is perfectly appropriate to impose a resulting trust on surplus benefits in the hands of a transferee where the original transfer was expressly 'on trust', because the transferee will have been in no doubt that he received as a trustee and was therefore obliged to keep the transferred property separate from his own. The question is whether it is ever appropriate to impose a resulting trust on a transferee who was not aware of the facts that are alleged to have given rise to the resulting trust. There are two main schools of thought. Bearing in mind what was said in the previous section on mistaken payments, the reader will see that this author favours the first school of thought.

The first school of thought maintains that a resulting trust arises automatically when a transferee, who is not entitled to the benefit of the transferred assets, holds them for no ascertainable object and subject to no identifiable obligation. In such circumstances, the benefit of the assets must belong to the transferor under a resulting trust, or belong to nobody and pass to the Crown as *bona vacantia*. Private property will only be declared ownerless as a last resort, so the resulting trust solution will be adopted unless it is necessary to conclude from the facts that the transferor has abandoned the benefit or irrevocably disclaimed his entire beneficial interest in the transferred assets. According to this school of thought, the resulting trust is an automatic incident of the splitting of legal and equitable title to the assets. In short, the trust arises as an incident of property law and the obligation on the transferee's conscience (the obligation to transfer back under a resulting trust) arises because a trust has been created.

The second school of thought maintains that a person can never become a trustee until he knows, or ought to know, of the facts that give rise to the trust, because, until such time, his conscience must be unaffected. According to this school of thought, the resulting trust arises because there is a burden on the trustee's conscience and not, as the first school of thought would have it, the other way around. The principal authority for the second school is the speech of Lord Browne-Wilkinson in *Westdeutsche Landesbank Girozentrale*:

> Since the equitable jurisdiction to enforce trusts depends upon the conscience of the holder of the legal interest being affected, he cannot be a trustee of the property if and so long as he is ignorant of the facts alleged to affect his conscience.[26]

It is respectfully submitted that Lord Browne-Wilkinson attached too little weight to the great volume of authorities in which, in all manner of factual contexts, trusts have arisen despite the trustee's ignorance of facts affecting his conscience. Our system of property law conceives of two distinct forms of ownership: ownership at law and ownership in equity. When absolute ownership of an asset is divided into legal title and equitable property, and the two forms of ownership are vested in different persons, a trust arises.[27]

Lord Browne-Wilkinson acknowledges that resulting trusts have been held to arise in '*cases where property has been put into the name of X without X's knowledge but in circumstances where no gift to X was intended*'.[28] His Lordship seeks to explain such cases away on the basis that:

> by the time action was brought, X or his successors in title have become aware of the facts which gave rise to a resulting trust; his conscience was affected as from the time of such discovery and thereafter he held on a resulting trust under which the property was recovered from him.[29]

The problem with this explanation is that it leaves the beneficial interest floating in the air until such time as the transferee's conscience is 'affected'. In any case, it assumes that knowledge of the transferor's claim to the assets is the same as knowledge of the transferor's right to the assets. Clearly, it is not: the transferee may dispute the transferor's claim to the benefit of the assets; he cannot deny that he has knowledge of the facts that *allegedly* give rise to the trust, but why should his conscience be bound by a mere allegation?[30]

Of course, if the first school of thought is correct, there is one inconvenient (but not insuperable) difficulty. It is that an entirely innocent transferee might become a trustee despite his being unaware of the facts giving rise to the trust. From this, it follows that the transferee might inadvertently commit a technical breach of trust by applying the trust property for his own benefit. However, even if the recipient is a trustee as a matter of property law, there is no reason why, as a matter of obligation, the recipient should be held liable to account as a trustee until such time as he was aware, or ought to have been aware, of the obligation to restore it.[31]

---

[26] [1996] AC 669 at 705.

[27] See Millett, 'Restitution and constructive trusts' (1998) 114 LQR 399 at 403–4.

[28] [1996] AC 669 at 705. The cases to which his Lordship referred include *Birch v. Blagrave* (1755) 1 Amb 264; *Childers v. Childers* (1857) 1 De G & J 482; *Re Muller* [1953] NZLR 879; and *Re Vinogradoff* [1935] WN 68. In the latter case, a lady placed £800 worth of stock into the joint names of herself and her granddaughter, who was then only four years old.   [29] [1996] AC 669 at 705H.

[30] See *Carl Zeiss v. Herbert Smith* [1969] 2 Ch 276, CA. See Chapter 15.

[31] For a similar argument, see Chambers, op. cit. at 212.

Is the resulting trust a remedy to reverse unjust enrichment?

This 'third' school of thought is a variation on the first school, in that it acknowledges that a trust arises whenever a transferee receives another's property, regardless of the transferee's state of knowledge. Supporters of this school maintain that the transfer of property to a transferee who was not intended to take beneficially results in the unjust enrichment of the transferee and that the role of the resulting trust is to reverse this unjust enrichment.[32] According to Robert Chambers '[a]*ll resulting trusts effect restitution of what would otherwise be the unjust enrichment of the recipient*'.[33] Chambers' related assertion that '[t]*he resulting trust is not merely the passive preservation of the provider's pre-existing property interest, but is one of equity's active responses to non-voluntary transfer*'[34] is unproblematic for supporters of the first school of thought outlined in the previous section. This supporter of the first school would not accept that the resulting trust is active in the sense that it aims to reverse unjust enrichment per se, but would accept that it is active in the sense that it aims to avoid the least desirable of all possible outcomes (and the one outcome we can be sure the transferor never intended): the passing of unallocated proprietary benefits to the Crown as *bona vacantia*.

In this vein, Harman J once described the resulting trust as '*the* last resort *to which the law has recourse when the draftsman has made a blunder or failed to dispose of that which he has set out to dispose of*.[35] Elsewhere, his Lordship stated that the resulting trust:

> does not, in my judgment, rest on any evidence of the state of mind of the settlor, for in the vast majority of cases no doubt he does not expect to see his money back; he has created a trust which, as far as he can see, will absorb the whole of it. The resulting trust arises where that expectation is, for some unforeseen reason, cheated of fruition, and is an inference of law based on after-knowledge of the event.[36]

The pragmatic nature of the transferor's presumed intention to create a resulting trust has also been acknowledged in the House of Lords in the important case of *Vandervell v. IRC*:[37]

> In reality the so-called presumption of a resulting trust is nothing more than a long stop to provide the answer when the relevant facts and circumstances fail to yield a solution.[38]

The problem with the claim that a resulting trust is active in the sense that it aims to reverse unjust enrichment per se is that it only makes sense to describe that enrichment as 'unjust' if it has already been acknowledged that the transferee holds the benefit under a resulting trust for the transferor. It is the trust that arises as an automatic

---

[32] See Chambers, ibid.; P. Birks, *Restitution and Resulting Trusts in Equity: Contemporary Legal Developments* (S. Goldstein, ed.) (Jerusalem: Hebrew University of Jerusalem, 1992) at 335; P. Birks, 'No consideration: restitution after void contracts' (1993) 23 WALR 195. For a critical response to Birks' argument, see W. J. Swadling, 'A new role for resulting trusts?' (1996) 16 Legal Studies 133. See also Swadling, 'Restitution for no consideration' [1994] RLR 73 and Swadling, 'Explaining Resulting Trusts' (2008) 124 LQR 72.

[33] Ibid. at 220.   [34] Ibid.

[35] *Re Cochrane's Settlement Trusts* [1955] 1 All ER 222 (emphasis added).

[36] *Re Gillingham Bus Disaster Fund* [1958] Ch 300 at 310.   [37] [1967] 2 AC 291.

[38] Ibid. *per* Lord Upjohn at 313D.

incident of the transferor's ongoing beneficial interest that renders 'unjust' the apparent or claimed beneficial ownership of the transferee.

Very often, the language of unjust enrichment is simply out of place. Suppose, for example, that B had transferred property to A on trust for C 'for so long as C shall live', but had failed to direct for whom the property should be held on C's death. The resulting trust that arises in favour of B when C dies is, in no sense, a response to the possibility that A will be personally unjustly enriched. A is fully aware that he has taken the property on trust and, if he is unaware that B retains an interest in the property entitling him to retake possession when C dies, A should seek the directions of the court. At no point will A appear, or claim, to own the property beneficially—so he will never be enriched—and if he does claim the property beneficially, he will have breached his trust and will have to account to B. It is artificial, and takes insufficient account of the nature of the office of trustee, to suggest that, when a trustee accounts to trust beneficiaries he is merely acting in a negative way to prevent his own unjust enrichment, rather than acting in a positive way to discharge his trust in accordance with the best interests of the beneficiaries. Supporters of the restitution school acknowledge that:

> The sanctity of property and its immunity to discretionary 'adjustment' is deeply rooted in legal thought. It is dictated by respect for the individual and individual preferences and by the fear of prejudicing third parties.[39]

But the fear remains that certainty of proprietary title will be undermined if the current focus of the law of trusts, which aims to give effect to beneficiaries' proprietary rights, is refocused on the reversal of unjust enrichment.

The *Vandervell* affair

In 1958, Mr Vandervell (V), instructed his bank to transfer to the Royal College of Surgeons ('the college') 100,000 shares in a company controlled by him. It was intended that the college should keep the shares for a limited period only and should relinquish them after receiving £150,000 in dividends. To ensure that the college did not keep the shares forever, the college granted an option in favour of a trustee company set up by V. The terms of the option provided that, in the event of the trustee company paying £5,000, the college should transfer the shares to the trustee company. By 1961, the college had received over £150,000 in dividends from the shares, so the trustee company exercised the option to repurchase the shares for £5,000. However, although it was clear that the trustee company now held the shares on trust, it was not clear for whose benefit the shares were held. The Inland Revenue claimed that V had retained beneficial ownership of the option (and hence the shares) between 1958 and 1961, and should be taxed on dividends declared on the shares in that time. It argued, *inter alia*, that V, in directing the bank to transfer the shares to the college, had purported to dispose of his

---

[39] P. Birks, 'Proprietary rights as remedies' in *Frontiers of Liability* (P. Birks, ed.) (Oxford: Clarendon Press, 1999) 214 at 223.

equitable interest in the shares, but had failed to do so because the disposition had not been made in writing.[40]

The House of Lords rejected that argument, but held in favour of the Revenue on other grounds: a bare majority of their Lordships held that the option had been held by the trustee company upon unspecified trusts and that, accordingly, V had failed to dispose of the benefit of the option. It followed that the trustee company held the benefit of the option, and hence the shares, under a resulting trust for V, who was therefore liable to pay tax on the dividends declared on the shares.[41] Lord Wilberforce held that a resulting trust had arisen as an automatic consequence of Mr Vandervell's ineffective attempt to dispose of his beneficial interest in the shares and that there was no need to attribute the creation of the trust to Mr Vandervell's presumed underlying intentions:

> There is no need, or room, as I see it, to invoke a presumption. The conclusion, on the facts found, is simply that the option was vested in the trustee company as a trustee on trusts, not defined at the time, possibly to be defined later. But the equitable, or beneficial interest, cannot remain in the air: the consequence in law must be that it remains in the settlor. Mr. Vandervell...had, as the direct result of the option and of the failure to place the beneficial interest in it securely away from him, not divested himself absolutely of the shares which it controlled.[42]

In 1965, in response to the Revenue's action, V executed a deed under which he transferred to the trustee company all or any right, title, or interest that he *might* have in the option, to be held by it on trust for his children according to the terms of an existing children's settlement. In 1967, V died and his executors brought an action against the trustee company, claiming that V had owned the shares for the period between 1961 (when the option was exercised) and 1965 (when V executed the deed transferring the entirety of his equitable interest).[43] The trustee company claimed that the shares should be treated as belonging to the children's settlement. (In a preliminary action, the executors had tried to join the Revenue as second defendants to their action against the trustee company, but the trustee company objected and the executors were unsuccessful,[44] so the executors' appeal against the Revenue's assessment was stood over pending their action against the trustee company.)

Having decided that the trustee company had taken the option on trust, Megarry J asked: '*Was the option held on a resulting trust or other trust for [V], or was it held on the trusts of the children's settlement?*'[45] His Lordship concluded that a resulting trust in favour of V had arisen automatically:

> I cannot see how an intention not to get the shares back can negative a resulting trust if in the event he made no effective disposition of his beneficial interest in them and the operation of equity brought them back to him in ways never considered by him. Whatever may be the position under a presumed resulting trust, I do not see how the donor's intention not to have the beneficial interest can prevail where the resulting trust is automatic.[46]

---

[40] Law of Property Act 1925, s. 53(1)(c). See, further, the discussion of this statutory section in relation to the *Vandervell* case in Chapter 6.   [41] *Vandervell v. IRC* [1967] 2 AC 291.

[42] [1967] 2 AC 291 at 329B.   [43] *Re Vandervell's Trusts (No. 2)* [1974] Ch 269.

[44] *Re Vandervell's Trusts* [1971] AC 912, HL.   [45] *Re Vandervell's Trusts (No. 2)* [1974] Ch 269 at 288B.

[46] Ibid. at 298G.

Megarry J's reasoning, which follows very closely the reasoning advanced by Lord Wilberforce in *Vandervell v. IRC*,[47] exemplifies what was referred to earlier as the 'first school of thought' on resulting trusts, in that it contemplates that a resulting trust may arise as an automatic consequence of undisposed-of proprietary benefits. Megarry J's judgment was, however, reversed by the Court of Appeal, where their Lordships seemed to disagree more with the result than with the reasoning in the court below.[48] Their Lordships held that, after the exercise of the option in 1961, the trustee company had held the shares on the trusts of the children's settlement. Lord Denning MR reasoned that it had been the (unexpressed) intention of V and the trustee company that the shares should be held for the benefit of the children's settlement—a conclusion reinforced by the fact that the £5,000 used to exercise the option had been taken from the existing fund of the children's settlement. From this, it followed that, after the exercise of the option, the shares did not form part of V's estate and his estate could not be taxed on the shares for the period 1961 to 1965. Lord Denning MR stated that, when the option was exercised, the 'gap in the beneficial ownership' came to an end. According to his Lordship, the resulting trust under which the shares had previously been held for the benefit of V ceased to exist upon the exercise of the option and the registration of the shares in the name of the trustee company.

The Court of Appeal was very generous to V and, arguably, generous to a fault. There was certainly evidence that the trustee company believed that it was acquiring the shares on behalf of the children's settlement, but V's intention was the all-important one and V did not appreciate, until 1965, that he might still have a beneficial interest in the shares.

The approach taken by Megarry J at first instance would have led to a less satisfactory outcome from V's point of view, but his Lordship did, at least, hold that the benefit should be held for V under a resulting trust. Other judges might have declared the shares to be *bona vacantia*. Thus, in *Westdeutsche Landesbank Girozentrale v. Islington LBC*,[49] Lord Browne-Wilkinson cast doubt on Megarry J's suggestion that a resulting trust of a surplus operates automatically: '*If the settlor has expressly, or by necessary implication, abandoned any beneficial interest in the trust property, there is in my view no resulting trust.*'[50]

With respect to Lord Browne-Wilkinson, it must surely be a very rare case in which it is 'necessary' to imply that an owner has simply abandoned his beneficial interest in his property. If Mr Vandervell had cast gold coins into the ocean from his yacht, that would look like abandonment; likewise, if he had dropped the coins into a collection box anonymously—but he did nothing of the sort. He gave property subject to strict directions and it is reasonable to presume that, in relation to any property surplus to those directions, he would have preferred to recover it himself than see it pass to the Crown. Megarry J's analysis recognizes that V still owned his property precisely because he had neither disposed of it effectively nor abandoned it outright.

---

[47] [1967] 2 AC 291, HL. [48] *Re Vandervell's Trusts (No. 2)* [1974] Ch 269. [49] [1996] AC 669.
[50] Ibid. at 708D.

Rebutting the presumption of a resulting trust

We know that, when property is transferred and there is no evidence of the transferor's reason for making the transfer, he is presumed to have intended to recover it under a resulting trust, but we also know that the presumption of a resulting trust is easily rebutted by evidence that the transferor intended the transfer to take effect in some other way.[51] It may be that the transferor intended an outright gift, or that he intended to transfer the property by way of loan[52] or some other contractual arrangement.[53] Even evidence of a particular relationship between the transferor and transferee may be sufficient to rebut the presumption of a resulting trust. In the following sections, we will take a closer look at some of the circumstances that rebut the presumption of a resulting trust.

Evidence of an intention to make a gift

The usual situation, as we know, is that, in the absence of evidence of the transferor's intentions, a voluntary transfer is presumed to give rise to a resulting trust. *Re Vinogradoff*[54] is a typical case. Mrs V placed £800 worth of stock into the joint names of herself and her granddaughter, and, when Mrs V died, it was held that Mrs V's estate was entitled to the benefit of the stock under a resulting trust. Nevertheless, when quite similar facts came to be considered in *Fowkes v. Pascoe*,[55] the Court of Appeal held that the presumption of a resulting trust had been rebutted by evidence that a gift had been intended. Mrs B had purchased certain stock in the joint names of herself and P, the son of her daughter-in-law. On the same day, she purchased more of the same stock in the joint names of herself and a lady companion. Mrs B's will left the residue of her estate to her daughter-in-law for life, thereafter to P and his sister equally. Mellish LJ could think of no other reason, unless it was to make a gift, why Mrs B, who already owned £5,000 worth of the stock in her own name, should invest £250 in the joint names of herself and P on the same day as investing £250 in the joint names of herself and her companion.

Evidence raising the presumption of advancement

Where a voluntary conveyance is made by a man in favour of his wife or fiancée or to his child or any person to whom he stands *in loco parentis* (and, to a lesser extent, if a

---

[51] Swadling n. 2.

[52] *Re Diplock* [1948] 1 Ch 465, *per* Lord Greene MR at 519; *Vajpeyi v. Yusaf* [2003] All ER (D) 128 (Sep) (approved judgment).

[53] So, for example, if a sole depositor opens a bank account in joint names the agreement with the bank will generally make it clear that the account holders are jointly entitled to the benefit of the monies in the account, thereby rebutting the presumption of a resulting trust in favour of the depositor (*Aroso v. Coutts & Co* [2002] 1 All ER (Comm) 241). [54] [1935] WN 68.

[55] (1875) LR 10 Ch App 343.

conveyance is made by a mother in favour of her child),[56] there is a presumption that the transferor intended to make a gift for the advancement of the transferee. This so-called 'presumption of advancement' rebuts the presumption that the transferor intended to recover the benefit of the transferred property under a resulting trust. However, the presumption of advancement can itself be rebutted if there is evidence that the transferor did not intend to make a gift. Thus in *McGrath v. Wallis*,[57] when a father bought a house subject to a mortgage and placed both the house and the mortgage in the name of the son, Nourse LJ held that the presumption of advancement had been rebutted by evidence that the father merely intended to make provision until his unemployed son could afford to purchase a house on his own.[58] Likewise, in *Lavelle v. Lavelle*,[59] the presumption of advancement from father to daughter was rebutted by evidence that the transfer of land into the daughter's name had been made with the intention of avoiding inheritance tax. If, on the other hand, the transfer had been made to evade tax or in order to carry out any other illegal purpose, the father would have been unable to rely on evidence of the true purpose of the transaction and the presumption of advancement would have stood. Thus a husband who purchased a lease in his wife's name for the illegal purpose of defrauding his creditors was unable to recover it from her,[60] and a father suffered the same fate when he transferred a freehold to his daughter for the same illegal purpose.[61]

The presumption of advancement, which is based on the assumed financial dependence of wives and children upon the husband and father of the family, is now less appropriate than it used to be to dispositions within families and it is relatively easily rebutted by evidence that the transferor did not, in fact, intend to make a gift to the wife or child. When s. 199 of the Equality Act 2010 becomes law, the presumption will be abolished; this is because the presumption is discriminatory insofar as it applies to husbands and fathers but not to wives and mothers. However, s. 199 does not affect past transactions, with the result that existing discrimination is confirmed and will continue.[62]

In *Pettitt v. Pettitt*,[63] the House of Lords expressed some doubt that the 'presumption of advancement' as between husband and wife still survives, and observed that, even if it does survive, it will seldom play a decisive part in disputes between living spouses.[64] Arguably, the presumption is incompatible with the anti-discrimination provisions in the European Convention on Human Rights.[65]

---

[56] See *Bennett v. Bennett* (1879) 10 Ch D 474, CA.   [57] [1995] 2 FLR 114, CA.

[58] See also *Sekhon v. Alissa* [1989] 2 FLR 94.

[59] [2004] EWCA Civ 223, CA; followed in *Kyriakides v. Pippas* [2004] EWHC 646.

[60] *Gascoigne v. Gascoigne* [1918] 1 KB 223.

[61] *Collier v. Collier* [2002] BPIR 1057. The effect of illegality on trusts is considered further in Chapter 6.

[62] J Glister, 'Section 199 of the Equality Act 2010: how not to abolish the presumption of advancement' (2010) 73(5) MLR 807.   [63] [1970] AC 777, confirmed in *Gissing v. Gissing* [1971] AC 886.

[64] *Pettitt v. Pettitt* [1970] AC 777, *per* Lord Diplock at 824A–D.

[65] Which is binding on English courts according to the Human Rights Act 1998. (See, further, G. Andrews, 'The Presumption of advancement: equity, equality and human rights' (2007) Conv 340).

Resulting trusts of surplus benefits

A resulting trust will arise in favour of a transferor if the property transferred proves to be more than sufficient to satisfy in full the claims of all persons with a beneficial interest in it, or if a beneficiary disclaims their beneficial interest in it.[66] In short, there will be a resulting trust of any 'surplus' benefits in the property. So if B transfers assets to A 'on trust for the use and benefit of C, so long as C shall live', when C dies, there will be a resulting trust in favour of A of any remaining benefits.[67] Of course, if the assets were 'wasting' or 'comestible'—such as a case of wine—and have been entirely exhausted during C's lifetime, there will be no surplus and no resulting trust. A relevant surplus may be of capital[68] or income.[69]

The destination of surplus donations

Sometimes, courts decide that an apparent surplus is not really a surplus at all. Consider the example of a donation to a fund 'for the education of the children of the Revd Jones'. If the donation is construed to have been made on trust for the sole purpose of educating the children, they will be unable to keep any surplus when their formal education is complete, but if the donation is construed to have been an absolute gift to the children, merely 'motivated' by the desire to educate them, the children will be able to do whatever they like with the donation when their formal education is complete.[70] In the latter circumstance, it appears that the children are acquiring the surplus; in substance, however, there never was a surplus. The benefit of the donation had always belonged to the children as a result of the donor's absolute gift. Likewise, if a donation is made to an unincorporated association, any apparent surplus remaining after the dissolution of the association will not be a true surplus if the donation had been made by way of absolute gift to the members for the time being.[71] In theory, any 'surplus' remaining after the dissolution of the association always belonged to the present members beneficially and, at the date of dissolution, the present members were entitled to depart with a share of it, subject to the association's rules.[72]

In *Cunnack v. Edwards*,[73] members paid subscriptions to an association on the basis of a contract that obliged the association to provide annuities for the widows of deceased members. The last member died in 1879 and the last widow died in 1892, the association having then a surplus of £1,250. It was held that the widows, not the members, were

---

[66] *Re Guinness's Settlement* [1966] 1 WLR 1355.

[67] Subject to the rules against perpetuities. Law Commission Report No. 251: *The Law of Trusts: The Rules Against Perpetuities and Excessive Accumulations*, 11 February 1998, recommends that the rule against perpetuities should continue to apply to '*an estate or interest which arises under a resulting trust on the determination of a determinable interest*' (para. 11.2(1)(b)).   [68] *Re The Trusts of the Abbott Fund* [1900] 2 Ch 326.

[69] *Re Wragg* [1954] 1 WLR 922.   [70] *Re Andrew's Trust* [1905] 2 Ch 48.

[71] See Chapter 3.   [72] See Chapter 3.   [73] [1986] 2 Ch 679.

the beneficiaries of the society's funds and, accordingly, the personal representatives of the deceased members were unable to make a direct claim to the benefit of the surplus. Neither could the members' estates claim the surplus under a resulting trust, because the members had already received everything that they had bargained for under their contract with each other.[74] A. L. Smith LJ held that:

> as the member paid his money to the society, so he divested himself of all interest in this money for ever, with this one reservation, that if the member left a widow she was to be provided for during her widowhood.[75]

Because the donation did not belong to the members' estates either directly or under a resulting trust, and because no other identifiable persons could claim to be beneficial owners of the surplus, there was no option but for the surplus to pass to the Crown as *bona vacantia*.

The *bona vacantia* solution may be undesirable from the donor's point of view, but it at least has the merit of finality. There have, however, been cases in which courts have chosen to leave surplus assets in a state of limbo rather than declare them to be *bona vacantia*. One such case is *Re Gillingham Bus Disaster Fund*.[76] In 1951, a bus careered into a column of Royal Marine cadets who were marching along a road near Chatham, Kent. Twenty-four were killed and others were injured and the Gillingham Bus Disaster fund was set up for the purpose of meeting funeral expenses, caring for the disabled, and for other related purposes. It was decided that the surplus should be held on resulting trust for the donors. Harman J held that:

> where money is held on trust and the trusts declared do not exhaust the fund it will revert to the donor or settlor under what is called a resulting trust. The reasoning behind this is that the settlor or donor did not part with his money absolutely out and out, but only *sub modo* to the intent that his wishes, as declared by the declaration of trust, should be carried into effect. When, therefore, this has been done, any surplus still belongs to him.[77]

With some invention, the court might have construed the donations to have been out-and-out gifts to the disabled survivors, but then the questions would have been asked: 'Why were they not out-and-out gifts to the parents of the deceased?' and 'How could they be out-and-out gifts when there was an imperative intention to pay funeral expenses and to care for the disabled?' So the court declined to go that way. The donations were clearly not contractual in any sense (the donee had given nothing in return for the donation) so the only remaining conclusion was that the donations had been given for a particular purpose and, that purpose having been fulfilled, the benefit of any surplus belonged to the donors under a resulting trust.

Harman J was unimpressed by the Crown's submission that the resulting trust solution should be avoided due to the impracticalities of identifying anonymous donors. His Lordship reasoned that, if the resulting trust solution is appropriate to donations

---

[74] See, also, *Braithwaite v. AG* [1909] 1 Ch 510.   [75] [1896] 2 Ch 679, *per* A. L. Smith LJ at 683.
[76] [1958] 1 Ch 300.   [77] Ibid. at 310.

from known persons, it must likewise be appropriate to donations made anonymously. If the anonymous donors could not be found, the surplus should be held on the court's account, but by no means should it pass to the Crown as *bona vacantia*:

> It will be merely money held on a trust for which no beneficiary can be found. Such cases are common, and where it is known that there are beneficiaries, the fact that they cannot be ascertained does not entitle the Treasury Solicitor to come in and claim. The trustees must pay the money into court like any other trustee who cannot find his beneficiary. I conclude, therefore, that there must be an inquiry for the subscribers to this fund.[78]

If it were possible to imagine any outcome worse than *bona vacantia*, then this would surely be it. *Bona vacantia* might be the death of private property, but consigning property to the court's account is to consign it to a fate worse than death, because it will be condemned to languish there, subject to an expensive and probably fruitless scheme to identify the numerous anonymous donors to the fund. The public interest in certainty of proprietary title will have been maintained, but at the expense of the public interest in free alienability of wealth.

The undesirable outcome in *Re Gillingham* was decisively rejected by Goff J in *Re West Sussex Constabulary's Widows, Children and Benevolent (1930) Fund Trusts*.[79]

Disapproving Harman J's decision to impute to the anonymous donors in the *Gillingham* case an intention to create a resulting trust, Goff J stated that '*equity will not impute an intention which it considers would be absurd on the face of it*'.[80] It is important to appreciate that Harman J's reasoning was, for the most part, perfectly sound, but his Lordship's judgment could have been immeasurably improved by one refinement— namely, to recognize that the donor's presumed intention to recover his donation under a resulting trust is rebutted by evidence (including his anonymity and the small size of his donation) that he actually intended to make an outright disposition of the donation, regardless of its ultimate destination. The fund in *Re West Sussex* had been established to provide for widows and orphans of deceased members of the West Sussex constabulary, but when the constabulary amalgamated with other forces in 1968, it was not clear how the fund should be distributed. The sources of the fund were as follows:

1. members' subscriptions;
2. receipts from entertainments, raffles, and sweepstakes;
3. collecting boxes;
4. donations and legacies.

Goff J held that surplus of sources (1), (2), and (3) would pass to the Crown as *bona vacantia*, but surplus of source (4) would be held on resulting trusts for the donors. His Lordship reasoned that the members had received everything they had bargained for in return for the surplus of sources (1) and (2). Furthermore, source (2) did not comprise

---

[78] [1958] 1 All ER 37 at 314.   [79] [1971] Ch 1.
[80] Ibid. at 14B–C. See, also, *Re Welsh Hospital (Netley) Fund* [1921] 1 Ch 655.

direct donations to the fund, but merely donations of net profits after payment out of prizes and so on. Regarding source (3), his Lordship held, in contrast to Harman J in the *Gillingham* case, that anonymous donors to collecting boxes intend to part with their monies outright.[81]

Goff J was equally pragmatic when it came to quantifying how much of the surplus should be declared *bona vacantia* and how much should be held on resulting trust: he held that equity would '*cut the Gordian knot*' by dividing the surplus in proportion to the sources from which it had arisen. However, in *Re Bucks Constabulary Widows' and Orphans' Fund Friendly Society*,[82] Walton J suggested an even more pragmatic solution to the problem of surplus funds on the dissolution of an unincorporated association— namely, that, regardless of the source of the surplus, a term should be implied into the contractual rules by which the members are bound together to the effect that any surplus should be divided equally between existing members at the date of dissolution. His Lordship suggested that if there is only one—or, perhaps, depending on the type of association, only a very few—existing member(s) of the association at the date of dissolution, there will be no association at all and the surplus funds will pass to the Crown as *bona vacantia*.[83] More recently, it has been held that even the sole-surviving member of an association should take the association's assets (in part to avoid a possible breach of Art. 1 of Protocol 1 of the European Convention on Human Rights and Fundamental Freedoms 1950, which guarantees the peaceful enjoyment of possessions).[84]

The doctrine of acceleration

Where an express trust establishes successive interests in a fund, as in a traditional settlement trust 'for X for life and Y in remainder', the failure, for perpetuity or any other reason, of X's beneficial interest in the income of the fund will not always produce a resulting trust of the income for the benefit of the settlor. The doctrine of acceleration provides that, in such a case, the benefit of the income should pass to Y. However, the doctrine will only apply if Y's interest is merely postponed by X's interest; it will not apply if Y's interest is also contingent upon some other event. So it would not apply to a trust 'for X for life and Y in remainder provided that Y is a qualified lawyer'.[85] In fact, the doctrine will only prevent a resulting trust to the settlor if it can be presumed that the settlor intended the income to be accelerated to Y. For this reason, it may be especially hard to make out a case for acceleration if Y is some quite remote friend or relation whom the settlor probably intended should receive nothing greater than a remainder interest in capital. It has also been suggested that an intention to accelerate may be harder to establish where the settlement was made *inter vivos*, because, in such a case, it can be presumed that the settlor intended to receive surplus income under a resulting trust.[86]

---

[81] [1971] Ch 1 at 13.   [82] [1979] 1 WLR 936.   [83] Ibid. at 943–4.
[84] *Hanchett-Stamford v. HM Attorney-General* [2008] EWHC 330 (Ch). The law governing the distribution of the association's funds on dissolution was considered in Chapter 3.
[85] *Re Scott (decd); Widows v. Friends of the Clergy Corporation* [1975] 1 WLR 1260.
[86] *Re Flower's Settlement Trusts* [1957] 1 All ER 462, *per* Jenkins LJ at 465.

The *Quistclose* trust

We have encountered the *Quistclose* trust in previous chapters, where we saw that it is
a useful illustration of the way in which courts handle the relationship between common law and equity, and, in particular, the interaction between contract (or debt) and
trust. The case is worth revisiting here because it is frequently cited as an example of a
resulting trust. The facts were that Quistclose Investments Ltd (Q), a finance company,
made a loan to Rolls Razor Ltd (RR) for the express purpose of paying a dividend that
RR had declared in favour of its shareholders. The loan monies were placed in a separate
account at Barclays Bank. Q knew that RR was teetering near the brink of insolvency
when the loan was made and, in the event, RR became insolvent before the dividend
could be paid. When it came to distributing RR's funds to those entitled on its insolvency, Barclays Bank—which happened also to be the principal secured creditor of
RR—naturally assumed that its claims would take priority over Q's unsecured claim for
damages under the loan contract. Q argued, however, that it had retained a proprietary
interest in the loan monies. This argument, if correct, would mean that the loan monies
had never belonged beneficially to RR and would not be available to satisfy the personal
claims of RR's creditors, whether secured or unsecured.

A majority of the House of Lords decided in favour of Q.[87] Lord Wilberforce held
that the arrangement between Q and RR was basically contractual, but that, alongside
the contractual arrangement, there was a primary trust in favour of the shareholders
in whose favour the dividend had been declared and a secondary trust in favour of Q,
which had arisen when the first trust became impossible to perform. His Lordship held
that Barclays Bank had notice of the primary and secondary trusts (and was therefore
bound by them) by virtue of a covering letter which accompanied the payment of the
loan monies into RR's account with Barclays Bank.

Despite the intervention of the House of Lords and, in large part, because of it, academic controversy regarding the nature of the *Quistclose* device is still ongoing. It was
said of Jarndyce and Jarndyce (the fictional case at the centre of Dickens's *Bleak House*)
that '*no two Chancery lawyers can talk about it for five minutes, without coming to a total
disagreement as to all the premises*'; the same thing can be said of the *Quistclose* trust.[88]

The main candidates to be recognized as the 'correct' theoretical analysis of the
Quistclose-type trust are as follows.

1. The secondary trust is a resulting trust arising because the primary express trust was
   incapable of being fulfilled.[89]

---

[87] *Barclays Bank Ltd v. Quistclose Investments Ltd* [1970] AC 567.

[88] For an overview of competing analyses, see C. Rickett, 'Different views on the scope of the *Quistclose* analysis' (1991) 107 LQR 608. A whole book has been devoted to the debate (see W. Swadling (ed.), *The* Quistclose
Trust: Critical Essays (Oxford: Hart Publishing, 2004), which is reviewed by this author at [2004] Conv 418).

[89] This is the analysis favoured by Lord Wilberforce in the *Quistclose* case itself.

2. The primary and secondary trusts are in fact two limbs of a single express trust.[90]

3. The *Quistclose* trust is an illusory trust under which the beneficial interest remains in the lender throughout, with the borrower taking the money subject to a power (sometimes a duty) to apply it towards the lender's designated purpose, in accordance with a mandate that the lender can revoke if his purpose is frustrated.[91]

In addition to, or as an alternative to, these analytical candidates, it can also be argued that the recognition of the *Quistclose*-type trust—and certainly that in *Quistclose* itself—is explicable on policy grounds, because it protects lenders who advance money to companies on the brink of insolvency. In the following sections, we will consider the strengths and weaknesses of some of the leading analyses of the *Quistclose* trust, but, before we do so, it is worth bearing in mind that it may be impossible perfectly to align the *Quistclose* trust with any orthodox category of trust. Ultimately, the *Quistclose* trust is a special commercial arrangement that is limited to a narrow range of special fact situations. Its appeal is practical in that it enables the borrower to have recourse to the lender's money for a particular purpose without entrenching on the lender's property rights more than necessary to enable the purpose to be achieved.[92] The *Quistclose* trust continues to be employed because, for whatever reason, it continues to work.

The resulting trust explanation for *Quistclose*

The difficulty with the argument that the primary trust was 'express' and the secondary trust was 'resulting' involves the identity of the type of primary express trust and the reason why it failed. The express trust would have been void as a private purpose trust if it existed for the sole purpose of paying the dividend. Clearly, the express trust could only be valid if, in addition to the expressed purpose, there was an identifiable beneficiary. At one level, the obvious candidate beneficiaries are the shareholders, because they are the persons intended to receive the money, but the insolvency of RR would not have prevented a primary express trust for the shareholders from being carried out. To put it another way, if the shareholders had had a vested beneficial interest by virtue of the primary express trust, the subsequent insolvency of RR would not have prevented them from enforcing the primary trust in their favour.[93]

---

[90] This argument is advanced by W. Swadling, 'A new role for resulting trusts' (1996) 16 Legal Studies 133.

[91] Sir P. Millett, 'The *Quistclose* trust: who can enforce it?' (1985) 101 LQR 269. Approved in *General Communications Ltd v. Development Finance Corpn of New Zealand Ltd* [1990] 3 NZLR 406 (by the New Zealand Court of Appeal) and by Lord Millett himself in *Twinsectra Ltd v. Yardley* [2002] 2 AC 164, HL, with whom Lord Hutton agreed.

[92] *Twinsectra*, ibid. at 187. Given the strongly pragmatic flavour of the *Quistclose* trust, we may doubt Lord Millett's suggestion (in *Twinsectra*) that it can be explained by 'orthodox' trust law. Compare Lord Millett's more pragmatic approach (in his Lordship's foreword to W. Swadling (ed.), *The* Quistclose *Trust: Critical Essays* (Oxford: Hart Publishing, 2004)).

[93] P. Millett, 'The *Quistclose* trust: who can enforce it?' (1985) 101 LQR 269 at 275–6. See also W. Goodhart and G. H. Jones, 'The infiltration of equitable doctrine into English commercial law' (1980) 43 MLR 489 at 494; F. Oditah, 'Assets and the treatment of claims in insolvency' (1992) 108 LQR 459 at 475.

Another possibility is that Q intended to benefit RR. However, it would be odd for a commercial lender to enter into a valuable loan transaction for the benefit of the other party: the natural presumption in a commercial transaction entered into at arm's length is that the party who created the trust intended it to be for their own benefit, unless there is a clear intention to benefit some other person. This presents a problem if one believes that resulting trusts necessarily describe the 'jumping back' of entirely disposed-of benefits, but it presents less difficulty if one accepts the view that resulting trusts are more accurately understood as arising from the transferor's omission to dispose entirely of his beneficial interest in the first place.

Robert Chambers argues that the secondary trust in *Quistclose* is a resulting trust under which the entire beneficial ownership is transferred to the borrower while the lender retains some other beneficial interest in the monies transferred:

> [t]he borrower receives the entire beneficial ownership of the money, subject only to the lender's right to prevent it being used for any other purpose [and] upon failure of that purpose, there is a resulting trust in favour of the lender, which arises because the lender did not intend the borrower to keep the beneficial ownership of the money for any other purpose.[94]

This description is reminiscent of the image of the angler with which we commenced this chapter: the transferor transfers the entire beneficial ownership of the money, but the transferor is still linked to the money by a thread. According to Chambers, that thread (in the *Quistclose* case) is the transferor's interest in seeing how the money is transferred. If the fish do not bite as intended—that is, if the loaned monies are not paid to the shareholders—the transferor will reel back the 'bait'. A potential problem with Chambers' analysis is that it concedes that the lender does not retain an ownership interest in the loaned monies, but only some equitable interest that is less than ownership, in which case, the usual inference is that the lender will have no proprietary right to recover its monies in the event of the borrower becoming insolvent before paying the loan. However, this problem can be overcome by recognizing that the lender's retained 'beneficial' interest in the money, whilst not an ownership interest *in* the money, may be some species of proprietary interest *over* the money.[95] If the shareholders are not paid, the beneficial ownership is reeled in again. If the money passes, the bait is swallowed and the trust comes to an end; the transaction takes effect thereafter as an ordinary loan.

Lord Millett has suggested that it would sit well with Chambers' general thesis to regard the *Quistclose* trust as a '*resulting trust for the transferor with a mandate to the transferee to apply the money for the stated purpose*'.[96] However, an alternative resulting trust analysis of the *Quistclose* trust is, it is submitted, to regard Q as having transferred beneficial ownership of the loaned monies to RR for the sole purpose of 'paying the shareholders *provided RR is still solvent*', the words emphasized being necessarily implied into the

---

[94] Op. cit. at 68.

[95] But see *Twinsectra Ltd v. Yardley* [2002] 2 AC 164, HL, at 190–1, approving L. Ho and P. St. J. Smart (see 'Further reading' at the end of this chapter). See, also, W. Swadling, 'Orthodoxy' in W. Swadling (ed.), *The Quistclose Trust: Critical Essays* (Oxford: Hart Publishing, 2004) for an argument that it would be unorthodox to afford proprietary status to a mere equitable right of restraint.   [96] *Twinsectra*, ibid. at 190.

primary trust to make commercial sense of the transaction. The moment it became impossible to fulfil the purpose as intended, the loaned money could not belong to RR, because its ownership was from the outset conditional upon paying the shareholders; neither could the loaned monies belong to the shareholders, because, by then, it was too late to transfer it to them. The only remaining possibilities were to declare the money ownerless or to return it to the lender. Because it can be presumed that the *last thing* the lender would have intended is that the money should be declared ownerless and pass to the Crown as *bona vacantia*, the court will automatically return the money to the lender under a resulting trust arising in accordance with his presumed intention: not that he should recover it, but that it should not pass to the Crown.

The express trust explanation for *Quistclose*

It is hard to account for Q's success unless Q, in fact, retained a beneficial interest in the loaned monies throughout the sequence of events, so the real issue is the basis on which Q retained that beneficial interest. A fairly strong case has been made for the resulting trust on the basis that the lender retained a beneficial interest over the monies throughout the transaction, or can be presumed to have intended to recover the monies in the event of his primary expressed purpose not being carried out. However, the problem with the resulting trust analysis is twofold. First, a resulting trust normally arises when the primary expressed purpose is incapable of being carried out and, in *Quistclose*, the expressed purpose 'to pay the shareholders' was still capable of being carried out. That problem is fairly easily overcome, as we have already observed, by inferring that the true expressed intention was 'to pay the shareholders *provided* RR is still solvent'. The second problem is, as we also observed earlier, that the primary expressed purpose 'to pay a dividend' will be a void trust for a purely private purpose unless construed to be for the benefit of an identifiable beneficiary. In other words, the identification of the beneficiary is not a secondary stage that comes after the express trust, but a limb of the express trust that is a fundamental prerequisite to the validity of the express trust. On this view, Lord Wilberforce's primary and secondary trusts are, in fact, merely primary and secondary limbs of the same express trust for an identifiable beneficiary.[97] Lord Wilberforce said himself that '*the intention to create a secondary trust for the benefit of the lender ... is clear*'.[98] A leading Australian judge and commentator on equity has held that the arrangement in *Quistclose* was '*indicative of an express trust with two limbs rather than an express trust in favour of the shareholders and a resulting trust in favour of Quistclose*'.[99] The significance of this analysis, as William Swadling has argued,[100] is that it takes the *Quistclose* trust outside of the realm of restitution, because, quoting Birks, '*express trusts never create restitutionary beneficial interests*'.[101] The analysis is therefore

---

[97] An argument advanced by Swadling, op. cit. (n. 2).   [98] [1970] AC 567 at 582.
[99] *Re Australian Elizabethan Theatre Trust* (1991) 102 ALR 681, *per* Gummow J at 691.
[100] Op. cit., n. 2.
[101] P. Birks, *An Introduction to the Law of Restitution* (Oxford: Oxford University Press, 1985; revd edn 1989) 55.

in direct competition with Robert Chambers' assertion that all resulting trusts, including the *Quistclose* trust, are restitutionary. There is, though, a clear problem with the express trust analysis: at no stage did Q actually express its intention to retain or recover its wealth upon failure of its primary expressed intention to lend monies to pay the dividend.

The revocable power explanation for *Quistclose*

A settlor cannot revoke an express trust after it has been fully constituted,[102] but *Quistclose* had the right to recover its monies in the event of the loan being misapplied. In the light of this, and other observations, Sir Peter Millett (as he then was), has argued extra-judicially that the primary trust in *Quistclose* was not a true trust at all, but an '*illusory trust*'.[103] The argument is that, apart from where the transferor (Q) has a private interest of its own—separate and distinct from any interest of the transferee (RR)—in seeing that the loaned sums are applied for the stated purpose, the purpose of arrangements such as those in *Quistclose* would be fulfilled if they were treated '*as leaving the beneficial interest in the fund in* [Q] *throughout, but subject to a power in* [RR], *revocable by* [Q] *at any time, to apply the fund for the stated purpose*'.[104]

A close variant of Lord Millett's analysis has now been approved by the House of Lords in *Twinsectra v. Yardley*, as noted earlier. Lord Hoffmann (with whom Lords Slynn and Hutton agreed) accepted that the transferee holds the money on trust for the transferor subject to a power to apply it in accordance with the contract between them, and Lord Millett (with whom Lord Hutton agreed) held that:

> the borrower is treated as holding the money on a resulting trust for the lender but with power (or in some cases a duty) to carry out the lender's revocable mandate, and [if] the lender's object in giving the mandate is frustrated, he is entitled to revoke the mandate and demand the return of money which never ceased to be his beneficially.[105]

One problem with the *Twinsectra* analysis is that it blurs the crucial conceptual distinction between power and duty, as expressed in the legal ideas of the power and the trust.[106] This distinction can be a fine one in practice, as we saw in the context of discretionary trusts,[107] but it is so fundamental a theoretical distinction that it should, so far as possible, be kept distinct in the cases.

In summary, then, we can say that the resulting trust is genuine, but that the so-called primary 'trust' is illusory, because the obligation on the borrower is not a positive

---

[102] Unless, of course, the trust instrument provides, or the court orders otherwise.

[103] Sir P. Millett, 'The *Quistclose* trust: who can enforce it?' (1985) 101 LQR 269.

[104] Ibid. at 275–6. Surprisingly, Lord Millett has described this complex, inventive analysis as 'orthodox' trust law (*Twinsectra Ltd v. Yardley* [2002] 2 AC 164, HL, at 187). His Lordship has also defended his *Twinsectra* analysis extra-judicially: 'The Quistclose trust: a reply' (2011) 17(1) Trusts & Trustees 7–16.

[105] [2002] AC 164 at 192.

[106] P. Birks, 'Retrieving tied money' in W. Swadling (ed.), *The* Quistclose *Trust: Critical Essays* (Oxford: Hart Publishing, 2004) 121 at 128.

[107] See Chapter 3.

obligation to apply the money for the designated purpose, but merely a negative obligation to refrain from applying it for any other purpose.[108] Ultimately, the dogmatic question 'Is the *Quistclose* trust a form of express, implied, constructive or resulting trust?'
demands a pragmatic answer:

> it may be any of them... From a commercial point of view... the trust is simply a mecha-
> nism... The commercial need for such a mechanism is obvious.[109]

A policy explanation for the *Quistclose* trust

One might wonder whether any policy could be more compelling than the
well-established policy of protecting the priority of secured creditors such as Barclays
Bank in *Quistclose*, but there is one policy that might be: the desire to protect lenders
who make emergency loans with the purpose of 'saving' corporations on the brink of
insolvency.

The fact is that *Quistclose* trusts frequently provide an injection of capital designed to
rescue a company in financial difficulties.[110] A rescued company is a rescued trader and
a rescued employer; a failed company very often results in unemployment with all the
social ills that entails. (It is notable that the authorities relied upon by Lord Wilberforce
in support of the *Quistclose* trust concerned money loaned for the purpose of staving
off the borrower's insolvency.)[111]

Yet despite the 'political' desirability of the *Quistclose* trusts, the irony is that, if the
loan in *Quistclose* itself had actually been applied to pay the dividend to the shareholders, the lender would, at that point, have lost its priority over other creditors even
though the loan had not at that time been repaid. Thus the *Quistclose* trust provides,
at best, only a short-term form of security. It is perhaps this 'short-termism' that, more
than any other feature, explains judicial willingness to recognize '*Quistclose* trusts',
despite the conceptual difficulties that they raise for orthodox trust law.

We might be persuaded that the *Quistclose* trust is defensible where it promotes
the public interest in saving a failing company, but we might doubt that the *Quistclose*
trust should be employed to protect purely private contractual interests. A case in the
latter category is *Cooper v. PRG Powerhouse*,[112] where the departing managing director of a company paid money to the company on the understanding that it would be
paid onwards to allow him to complete the private purchase of his company car. The
company went insolvent before the money was paid. A *Quistclose* trust was held in

---

[108] *Re Margaretta Ltd; Freeman v. HM Commissioners of Customs and Excise* [2005] BCC 506; [2005] EWHC
582 (Ch), Ch D (Companies Ct). This interesting case concerned a company that owed VAT. Money to pay the
VAT was advanced to an accountancy firm, which misappropriated it. The company was made insolvent as a
result, but because the accountant had received the money for the purpose of paying VAT, HM Customs and
Excise was able to recover the VAT under a *Quistclose* trust.

[109] Lord Millett, from his Lordship's foreword to W. Swadling (ed.), *The* Quistclose *Trust: Critical Essays*
(Oxford: Hart Publishing, 2004), reviewed G. Watt [2004] Conv 418.

[110] J. Ulph, 'Equitable proprietary rights in insolvency: the ebbing tide?' [1996] JBL 482 at 495.

[111] Swadling n. 2.   [112] [2008] EWHC 498.

the director's favour, but one surely has to question whether the former director of an insolvent company should be able to use a trust to get a good deal on a company car in priority to the company's general creditors.[113] *Mundy v. Brown*[114] is more easily justified. In this case, an accountant to an insolvent company recovered his fees by virtue of a *Quistclose* trust, but he was a truly independent party.

Are judges too indulgent of *Quistclose* claims?

In *Quistclose*, it is clear that the contract of loan had been frustrated by the insolvency of RR and it is equally clear that, if the dividend had been paid to the shareholders prior to the insolvency, RR would thereby have performed its side of the contract—leaving Q with nothing but its contractual remedy in damages. Suppose, however, that B (a lender) had transferred monies to A (a borrowing company in financial difficulties) 'for the sole purpose of buying new equipment', and A *had paid* C for the equipment, but had gone into receivership before taking delivery of the equipment. Clearly, A has done more to perform the contract than the borrower in *Quistclose*, but has the purpose of the loan still failed? These were the facts of *Re EVTR*,[115] and the decision of the Court of Appeal was that the sole purpose of the contract, 'to purchase equipment', had failed. As Dillon LJ put it: '*I do not see why the final whistle should be blown at half time*.' Accordingly, when A's receivers recovered part of the purchase price from C, they were obliged to hold it on trust for B. Dillon and Bingham LJJ agreed that the trust was a resulting trust. Of course, it could be argued to the contrary that a trust for 'buying' new equipment is complete when the contract is made and does not depend upon actual receipt of the goods. If you purchase an item on 'eBay' or such like and the seller becomes insolvent before sending you the item, you can hardly deny that you did buy it. *Re EVTR* is yet another example of judges using clever rhetoric (in this case the metaphor of the full-time whistle) to persuade us to accept an unorthodox but practical outcome.

Despite judicial indulgence, *Quistclose* claims do not always succeed. Merely to show that money is transferred for a specific purpose will not suffice,[116] and whereas it will be material to show that a fund was required to be kept segregated for a specific purpose, it has not yet been conclusively determined whether the factors of 'segregation' and 'specific purpose', taken together, are essential (or indeed sufficient) to found a *Quistclose* trust.[117] A duty to keep the fund segregated or separately identifiable (if only on the account book) is of the essence of any trust,[118] but arguably the stipulation of an

---

[113] A similarly questionable case, where a *Quistclose* trust was upheld almost as if it were a resulting trust of first resort is *Wise v. Jimenez* 11 October 2013 (Chancery Division, unreported).

[114] [2011] EWHC 377 (Ch).   [115] [1987] BCLC 646.

[116] *Tuthill v. Equine FX Ltd* [2013] EWHC 1207 Queen's Bench Division (Commercial Court).

[117] See, for example, *Eleftheriou v. Costi* [2013] EWHC 2168 (Ch); *Patel v. Mirza* [2013] EWHC 1892 (Ch).

[118] In *Gabriel v. Little & Ors* [2013] EWCA Civ 1513, money was loaned to a company in the belief that it would be used to develop property, but without any express restriction to a 'sole' or 'exclusive' purpose. The claim of a *Quistclose* trust failed. The Court of Appeal approved Lord Millett in *Twinsectra v. Yardley* (at para. [73]) who had said that there would be no *Quistclose* trust where the loaned monies were 'at the free disposal of the borrower'.

exclusive purpose is not the only circumstance which can negate the transferee's intention to part with beneficial ownership.[119]

Pension fund surpluses

While a 'defined benefit'[120] pension scheme is on foot, there is no way to know for sure whether the fund will be sufficient to satisfy in full the pension entitlements of all present and future pensioners. The most that can be done is to make actuarial estimates from time to time as to the likely future performance of the fund according to the best available statistical information. In the late 1980s, after several years of stock market growth and increases in the value of real estate, many pension funds were greatly in surplus.[121] Today, after several years of declining performance on the stock markets, pension surpluses are looking increasingly to be a thing of the past. Nowadays, many pension funds are notionally in deficit.

Although pension surpluses may be a thing of the past, the question of who should be entitled to them is still pertinent to the relationship between pensions and trusts, and, correspondingly, the relationship between contract and trusts.[122]

The employer and the employee will both claim to recover the pension surplus under a resulting trust. However, neither party can claim to be in the usual situation of the transferor who voluntarily makes a gift or sets up an express trust for another's benefit. Their contributions to the fund were not made voluntarily, but under the terms of contract made between them,[123] and therefore their entitlement to any surplus will turn, in large part, upon the terms of the trust deed and the contract (the pension 'plan' or 'scheme') by which the trust deed is established:

> Where a trust deed is silent as to the destination of a surplus the law will supply a resulting trust in favour of the provider of the funds in question.[124]

If the trust deed expressly provides that any surplus should be applied in such and such a way, this will normally be conclusive. In fact, as was stated in *Davis v. Richards and Wallington Industries Ltd*:[125]

> a resulting trust will be excluded not only by an express provision but also if its exclusion is to be implied. If the intention of a contributor that a resulting trust should not apply is the proper conclusion, it would not be right, in my opinion, for the law to contradict that intention.[126]

---

[119] *Challinor v. Juliet Bellis & Co* [2013] EWHC 347 (Ch).

[120] A pension scheme that fixes the final pension entitlement rather than giving the pensioner a proportionate share of the whole fund.

[121] The pension fund in *Mettoy Pension Trustees Ltd v. Evans* [1990] 1 WLR 1587 was in surplus to the order of £9m in 1988. The surplus in *Davis v. Richards and Wallington Industries Ltd* [1990] 1 WLR 1511 had reached £3m by 1986.

[122] See, generally, R. Ellison, 'Pension fund surpluses' (1991) TLI 60; R. Nobles, 'Who owns a pension surplus?' (1990) 19 ILJ 204.

[123] *Kerr v. British Leyland (Staff) Trustees Ltd*, unreported, 26 March 1986; EWCA Civ Transcript No. 286 of 1986, *per* Fox LJ: '*the employees . . . have purchased their rights as part of their terms of employment*'.

[124] *Jones v. Williams*, unreported, 15 March 1988, Knox J.   [125] [1990] 1 WLR 1511.

[126] Ibid. *per* Scott J at 1541 H.

Scott J went to great lengths in *Davis* to justify the employer's entitlement to the surplus, but he dismissed the employees' claim on the ground that a resulting trust would have infringed a statutory limit on the amount of benefits that the employees were entitled to receive from the pension scheme. Accordingly, that part of the surplus representing employees' contributions was declared *bona vacantia*. However, the essence of a resulting trust, in this author's opinion, is that in the interests of public policy judges will assume that the last thing any transferor intends is that their wealth should pass to the Crown as *bona vacantia*. A pension surplus is quite unlike the surplus arising where anonymous donors have paid different amounts of petty cash into a collection box for some deserving cause. Employees do not intend to part with their contributions outright (least of all to the Crown), so the presumption that the employees should recover any surplus under a resulting trust (whether or not they expressly intended that outcome) should stand. The *Davis* employees might fare better today as a result of *Air Jamaica Ltd v. Charlton*,[127] in which the Privy Council went to great lengths to preserve the members' interests in the fund. The pension scheme of employees of Air Jamaica was discontinued in 1994, when the company was privatized. Defined benefits were paid out under the terms of the scheme, but there remained a surplus of $400m. The claimants, who were members of the discontinued pension scheme, claimed to be entitled to the surplus. Section 13.3(ii) of the rules of the scheme provided that, in the event of discontinuance of the scheme:

> any balance of the fund shall be applied to provide additional benefits for members and after their death for their widows or their designated beneficiaries in such equitable and non-discriminatory manner as the trustees may determine in accordance with the advice of an actuary.

Clause 4 of the trust deed provided that: '*No moneys which at any time have been contributed by the company under the terms hereof shall in any circumstances be repayable to the company.*' Despite these terms (and because of them), the company purported to amend the pension plan so as to acquire the surplus itself and had to be restrained by means of an interlocutory junction from implementing its intended amendments. When the matter eventually came before the Privy Council, the amendments were disallowed on three grounds: first, that the power to amend the plan was void for perpetuity; second, that the amendments had been made in bad faith;[128] third, that they infringed Clause 4 of the trust deed. However, the company argued that, even if it could not recover under the terms of the original or amended scheme, it ought to be permitted to recover its contributions by a resulting trust operating outside the scheme. To make matters worse for the claimants, their claims were resisted not only by the company, but also by the Attorney General. The Attorney General argued on behalf of the Crown that the surplus had become *bona*

---

[127] [1999] 1 WLR 1399, PC.

[128] Having been made with no regard for the interests of the members of the scheme (see *Imperial Group Pension Trust Ltd v. Imperial Tobacco Ltd* [1991] 1 WLR 589).

vacantia. The Crown argued that the employees' claim must fail because the pension trust was void for perpetuity and that the employer's claim must fail because of Clause 4.[129]

The opinion of the Privy Council, delivered by Lord Millett, reaffirms the 'first school of thought' on resulting trusts and its applicability to pension surpluses:

> Prima facie the surplus is held on a resulting trust for those who provided it. This sometimes creates a problem of some perplexity. In the present case, however, it does not. Contributions were payable by the members with matching contributions by the company. In the absence of any evidence that this is not what happened in practice, the surplus must be treated as provided as to one half by the company and as to one half by the members
>
> …in *Vandervell v. Inland Revenue Commissioners* [1967] 2 AC 291 …The House of Lords affirmed the principle that a resulting trust is not defeated by evidence that the transferor intended to part with the beneficial interest if he has not in fact succeeded in doing so…Lord Upjohn [1967] 2 AC 291, 314.
>
> Consequently their Lordships think that clauses of this kind in a pension scheme should generally be construed as forbidding the repayment of contributions under the terms of the scheme, and not as a pre-emptive but misguided attempt to rebut a resulting trust which would arise *dehors* [130] the scheme.[131]

His Lordship confirmed that the scheme, including Clause 4, had been an ineffective attempt by the company to dispose of the entirety of its beneficial interest in the fund. The consequence was that it was entitled to recover half the surplus under a resulting trust; the members were also entitled to recover the half representing their contributions. The Crown's argument on perpetuity failed, for reasons we will consider in Chapter 6.

Further reading

In addition to the following print sources, the Online Resource Centre accompanying this book contains web links to further reading as well as guide answers to assessment questions relevant to this chapter.

BIRKS, P. B. H., 'Restitution and Resulting Trusts' in *Equity: Contemporary Legal Developments* (S. Goldstein, ed.) (Jerusalem: Hebrew University of Jerusalem, 1992).

BIRKS, P. B. H., 'Trusts raised to reverse unjust enrichment: the *Westdeutsche* case' [1996] RLR 3.

BURROWS, A. S., 'Swaps and the friction between common law and equity' [1995] RLR 15.

CHAMBERS, R., *Resulting Trusts* (Oxford: Clarendon Press, 1997).

ELLISON, R., 'Pension fund surpluses' (1991) TLI 60.

---

[129] As it happened, the government owed money to the newly privatized company under the privatization agreement, so the court allowed the company to take the surplus in return for an undertaking from the government that it would pay an equivalent sum to the plaintiffs if they succeeded.

[130] 'Outside'.

[131] *Air Jamaica Ltd v. Charlton* [1999] 1 WLR 1399, PC, at 1412.

GLISTER, J., 'Section 199 of the Equality Act 2010: How Not to Abolish the Presumption of Advancement' (2010) 73(5) MLR 807.

HUDSON, A., *Swaps, Restitution and Trusts*, 1st edn (London: Sweet & Maxwell, 1999).

ING, N. D. *Bona Vacantia*, 2nd edn (London: Butterworths, 2000).

LUSINA HO, L. and SMART, P. ST J., 'Reinterpreting the *Quistclose* trust: a critique of Chambers' analysis' (2001) 21 OJLS 267.

NOBLES, R., 'Who owns a pension surplus?' (1990) 19 ILJ 204.

SWADLING, W., 'A new role for resulting trusts?' (1996) 16 Legal Studies 133.

SWADLING, W., 'Explaining resulting trusts' (2008) 124 LQR 72.

6

Formality, perpetuity, and illegality: trust creation and public policy I

It is somewhat surprising that any state permits its citizens to create private trusts. The essence of a trust is that the apparent owner of trust property, the person with all the forms and powers of ownership, is not the true owner. A trust therefore creates an illusion in ownership that has the potential to prejudice trade creditors in the event of the trustee's insolvency and to deceive the state's tax collection agencies. A private limited company produces a similar illusion, but whereas a private company must be registered and submit annual accounts, the trustees of a private trust are subject to no such public scrutiny and accountability. There are, however, other safeguards in place that are designed to prevent the undesirable creation and operation of trusts. Amongst the most significant is the requirement that the disposition of equitable interests under trusts must be *made* in writing and the requirement that the creation of trusts of land must be *evidenced* in writing. These formality requirements seek to prevent fraud and the avoidance, or evasion, of tax. There are also rules in place to prohibit trusts which aim at such illegal outcomes as racial discrimination, restraint of marriage, and the avoidance of statutory schemes governing the priorities of creditors' claims in insolvency.

Other rules address the danger, which is inherent in the way a trust separates formal ownership from beneficial ownership, that the trust property might never return to the state of being owned absolutely. For as long as property remains subject to a trust, it will be unable to participate in the marketplace with complete freedom and its ability to contribute to the national 'commonwealth' will, accordingly, be diminished. The rule against remoteness of vesting, which is one of the rules against perpetuity, addresses this concern by ensuring that all of the interests under a trust vest in beneficiaries (that is, 'vest in interest')[1] before the end of the 'perpetuity period'. When all of the interests under a trust have vested in interest, the beneficiaries may agree, if they are all competent adults, to bring the trust to an end.[2] Calculating the perpetuity period can be complex, but, as a rule of thumb, it is worth bearing in mind that the perpetuity period will

---

[1] See Chapter 1.   [2] Under the rule in *Saunders v. Vautier* (1841) LJ 10 Ch 354. See Chapter 1.

rarely exceed 100 years. Another rule against perpetuity, the rule against inalienability of capital, addresses the equally undesirable possibility that trust capital may be tied up indefinitely. An expressly created trust is, in a sense, a delayed gift[3]—and the function of the rule against inalienability is to set limits on the period of 'delay'. Trust property dedicated to the advancement of charitable purposes is exempt from this rule. A third rule against perpetuity sets a limit on the period for which it is permissible to accumulate income instead of spending it.

Formality

Formality requirements must not be confused with the requirements of trust constitution that were considered in Chapter 4. It is true that a trust in which the settlor is not intended to be a trustee will be fully constituted only when the legal title to the trust property has been formally transferred to the intended trustees, but such formality requirements have nothing to do with trust creation as such—they apply equally to transfers of legal title whether made on trust or by way of absolute gift. The formality requirements we are concerned with here are those that govern the documents in which the intention to create a trust is expressed, and those that govern the transfer of equitable interests under existing trusts. These formality requirements are laid down in the Law of Property Act 1925 and the Wills Act 1837. They aim to promote certainty in dealings with wealth and thereby to reduce the opportunity for fraud. It is therefore consistent with the aim of the Acts for the statutory formality requirements to be bypassed, or exceptions admitted, in the interest of preventing fraud. In particular, the courts will not allow the formality statutes to be used as instruments of fraud.

Constructive, implied, and resulting trusts

According to the Law of Property Act 1925, constructive, implied, and resulting trusts are created, and operate, without formality.[4] This makes them particularly useful for giving effect to informal agreements between home-sharers in relation to ownership of their land and for giving effect to 'secret' arrangements. Co-ownership trusts are considered in Chapter 8 and the important topic of 'secret trusts' is considered later in this chapter. It is a moot point whether 'implied trust' is merely a collective term for constructive trusts and resulting trusts, or whether it is a separate category that is distinct from constructive and resulting trusts. At present, it is hard to conceive of a non-express trust that could not be categorized as either a resulting or a constructive trust, but, increasingly, the conceptual boundaries between constructive trusts and resulting trusts are being rigidly defined by the courts; if this trend continues, there

---

[3] F. H. Lawson and B. Rudden, *The Law of Property*, 2nd edn (Oxford: Clarendon Press, 1982) at 55.
[4] Section 53(2).

will inevitably be a need for a residual category, such as 'implied trusts', to cater for non-express trusts that do not fit easily within the mainstream categories of 'constructive' and 'resulting' trusts.

Inter vivos transactions

With *inter vivos* transactions, we are concerned with formality requirements in relation to the creation of trusts that are intended to take effect during the lifetime of the settlor and the disposition of interests under trusts during the lifetime of the person making the disposition.

The creation of express trusts

The basic rule is that express trusts may be created *inter vivos* without formality. Hence there is nothing to prevent a settlor from declaring orally, 'See this gold pen of mine, I henceforth hold it on trust for the benefit of my sister.' Assuming the context showed that the settlor had intended to create legal relations, these words would be sufficient to move the beneficial (equitable) ownership of the pen from the settlor to his sister. On account of a few words, the settlor would have become a trustee of the pen for his sister, and the settlor would no longer be entitled to the use and enjoyment of the pen even though he may have kept the pen in his physical possession throughout the entire transaction. The sister could, at any time, demand that the pen be transferred into her possession.

An *inter vivos* express trust of *land* can also be created without formality, but it is unenforceable in court unless evidenced in writing.[5] In other words, it will only be enforceable against the settlor if he created it in writing or made a written memorandum of the trust sometime after its creation.

The disposition of interests under trusts

After a trust has been declared (created), any disposition of an equitable interest under the trust must be made in writing to be effective and the written disposition must be signed by the person making the disposition, or by his agent lawfully authorized in writing or by will.[6]

The document, or 'instrument', by which the equitable interest is disposed is subject to a documentary tax called stamp duty, which is charged 'according to the value of' (*ad valorem*) the equitable interest disposed. It is hardly surprising, therefore, that the law reports record many attempts to dispose of equitable interests without documentary formality, so as to avoid stamp duty. One such case is *Grey v. Inland Revenue Commissioners*.[7] The settlor, H, settled six trusts in favour of his grandchildren between 1949 and 1950. On 1 February 1955, he transferred 18,000 £1 shares to the trustees, and,

---

[5] Law of Property Act 1925, s. 53(1)(b). But see Chapter 8.   [6] Law of Property Act 1925, s. 53(1)(c).
[7] [1960] AC 1, HL.

on 18 February, he orally and irrevocably directed that the shares should be held on the trusts of the six settlements: 3,000 shares to each settlement. On 25 March, the trustees, including Grey, made written declarations of trust in accordance with H's directions. The Inland Revenue assessed these declarations to *ad valorem* stamp duty, but the trustees argued that the entire value of the shares had already passed on 18 February and that the documents of 25 March were merely formal confirmation of that transfer.

Their Lordships held that H's attempt to dispose of his equitable interest in the shares by the oral direction of 18 February had been ineffective, because it had not been made in writing as required by s. 53(1)(c) of the Law of Property Act 1925. The later formal declarations of 25 March were the effective disposition of H's equitable interest in the shares and, because those declarations constituted 'instruments' for the purposes of the Stamp Act 1891, they had rightly been assessed to *ad valorem* stamp duty.

Oughtred v. IRC[8] is a similar case. In this case, 200,000 shares in a private company were held upon trust for Mrs Oughtred for life, thereafter for her son absolutely. Mrs Oughtred also owned 72,700 shares outright. In order to avoid estate duty payable on the 72,700 shares on Mrs Oughtred's death, the parties agreed orally to exchange their interests. Mrs Oughtred promised to transfer the 72,700 shares to her son and he, in turn, promised to transfer his remainder interest in the 200,000 shares to Mrs Oughtred. Two documents of transfer were executed at a later date. The first document recorded the transfer of legal title in the 200,000 shares from the trustees to Mrs Oughtred in consideration of the sum of 10 shillings. The second document recorded the transfer of Mrs Oughtred's 72,700 shares to her son's nominees, again for a consideration of 10 shillings.

The Inland Revenue argued that the document recording the transfer of the legal title in the 200,000 shares was a 'conveyance on sale' within the Stamp Act 1891[9] and therefore attracted *ad valorem* stamp duty on the consideration (the 72,700 shares) given by Mrs Oughtred. Mrs Oughtred's counter-argument was that her son's equitable interest in the 200,000 shares had been fully transferred to her by the earlier oral agreement, so that no value had passed to her under the later formal document of transfer, with the result that no stamp duty was payable.

Mrs Oughtred's argument ran along the following lines: the shares are shares in a *private* company and are therefore unique (because it might not be possible to buy equivalent replacement shares on the open market). It follows that common law damages will be inadequate to remedy a breach by either party of the oral agreement to transfer their interest in the shares. Equity will therefore grant specific performance of the oral agreement almost as a matter of routine,[10] provided that the claimant comes to equity 'with clean hands'.[11] Equity regards a specifically *performable* agreement as having been *already performed* the moment the agreement is made, in accordance with the maxim 'equity sees as done that which *ought to be* done',[12] so equity will regard beneficial ownership of the shares as having been transferred the moment the parties entered the specifically performable agreement to transfer them. Therefore, from the

---

[8] [1960] AC 206.   [9] Section 54.   [10] Even though the remedy is in theory, discretionary.
[11] See Chapter 16 on equitable maxims.   [12] Ibid.

date of the oral agreement, the son should no longer be regarded as the beneficial owner of the remainder interest in the 200,000 shares and Mrs Oughtred should no longer be regarded as being absolutely entitled to the 72,700 shares. On the contrary, each party should be considered conscience-bound to hold their original beneficial interests on constructive trust for the other. A constructive trust is valid without formal confirmation[13] and, without writing, there is no written 'instrument' subject to stamp duty.

Despite the ingenuity of the preceding line of argument, the House of Lords held that, even if a constructive trust had been created in accordance with Mrs Oughtred's reasoning, the parties had intended the later formal document to be part of the transaction and it should be assessed to *ad valorem* stamp duty. Their Lordships considered the agreement to exchange interests in the shares to be analogous to a simple case of a contract for sale of land. Land, like private company shares, is considered to be unique and a constructive trust is said to arise as soon as parties to the sale of land contractually agree to the sale, but the formal deed that completes the formal transfer of legal title to the land has always been treated as stampable *ad valorem*.

Lord Radcliffe, who had delivered the leading speech in *Grey v. IRC*, dissented. His Lordship considered the subsequent written transfer by the son to be nothing more than a transfer of the bare legal title to Mrs Oughtred. In his Lordship's opinion, it did not transfer any equitable interest at all and should not have been assessed to *ad valorem* stamp duty. His Lordship argued that Mrs Oughtred had not needed to call for the subsequent written instrument of transfer; she could simply have called upon the trustees to transfer their bare legal title to the 200,000 shares to her.

Lord Radcliffe's dissenting opinion was later put to the test in *Neville v. Wilson*.[14] Neville carried on business through N Ltd. Shortly before Neville's death, N Ltd acquired all of the issued share capital in U Ltd, 120 shares being held by nominees of N Ltd and the remainder by N Ltd as registered owner. In 1969, N Ltd was *informally* liquidated by shareholder agreement; its liabilities were discharged and its assets were divided between its shareholders. N Ltd was later struck off the register and formally dissolved. Some years later, after profitable business and after U Ltd's assets had been reduced to cash, Neville's children (who had been shareholders in N Ltd) commenced proceedings against ex-shareholders in N Ltd to determine, *inter alia*, the beneficial ownership of the 120 shares in U Ltd held by nominees.

Applying Mrs Oughtred's argument, it was held that the informal 1969 agreement had made the shareholders in N Ltd implied or constructive trustees for each other of the assets of N Ltd, the equitable interest of each shareholder under the constructive trust being of a size proportionate to his shareholding in N Ltd. In short, it was held that N Ltd's equitable interest in the 120 U Ltd shares had been disposed of successfully in favour of N Ltd's shareholders without any formality. It was held that the formality requirement laid down by s. 53(1)(c) of the Law of Property Act 1925 had no application, because constructive trusts are exempted from the effect of that section of the Act.[15] Lord Radcliffe had been correct: Mrs Oughtred's argument would probably have

---

[13] Law of Property Act 1925, s. 53(2).

[14] [1996] 3 WLR 460. Noted Watt [1997] Nott LJ 86.   [15] Law of Property Act 1925, s. 53(2).

worked if she and her son had allowed their agreement to remain entirely informal. Their mistake had been to confirm their agreement in formal documentation, so as to make the transaction appear broadly analogous to a typical conveyance of land (under which the initial contract is later confirmed by a deed). Of course, the Inland Revenue was not a party to the litigation in *Neville*. When the Inland Revenue resists an attempt to avoid the s. 53(1) (c) requirement, the reported cases suggest that it usually succeeds.

What is a 'disposition' for the purposes of s. 53(1)(c)?

The transfer by a beneficiary of her interest under a trust to some other person and a direction by a beneficiary to her trustee henceforth to hold her equitable interest on trust for some other person are both clear examples of a 'disposition' for the purposes of s. 53(1)(c). But what if Brenda (a beneficiary) declares that she henceforth holds her equitable interest on trust for someone else? It was judicially accepted long ago that an equitable interest might be held on trust,[16] but it is difficult to know whether Brenda's declaration is a 'disposition' for the purposes of s. 53(1)(c) and so required to be made in writing, or a declaration of trust (a so-called 'sub-trust')[17] that is able to take effect without any need for formal writing. There are statements in *Grey v. IRC* that suggest that Brenda's declaration will cause her to fall out of the picture completely, so as to make her trustee the trustee of the intended beneficiary of her sub-trust.[18] The transaction would therefore be an outright disposition.

In theory the answer is simple: if Brenda's declaration merely transfers a subsisting equitable interest, it will be a 'disposition', but if it creates an entirely novel equitable interest, it will be a 'declaration of trust'. In practice, however, the answer is far from straightforward.[19] Whether or not a transaction is a 'declaration' or a 'disposition' depends upon the facts of each case. If the beneficiary, having made the declaration, has no ongoing duties in relation to the equitable property, it would be nonsensical to describe the beneficiary as being a trustee of it. In such a case, the equitable interest, although expressly held on trust, has, in fact, been disposed of outright.[20]

Miscellaneous cases falling outside s. 53(1)(c) include the following:

1. The case of a beneficiary of a bare trust who transfers her equitable interest to X, but at the same time directs her bare trustee to transfer legal title to X. Section 53(1)(c) is only concerned with dispositions of equitable interests made independently of the disposition of legal title.[21]

---

[16] *Gilbert v. Overton* (1864) 2 H & M 110 at 116; *Re Chrimes* [1917] 1 Ch 30; *Re Bostock's Settlement* [1921] 2 Ch 469 at 480–1.
[17] An established concept in US trusts law (see W. Fratcher, *Scott on Trusts*, 4th edn (Boston: Little, Brown & Co, 1987) § 83).   [18] [1958] Ch 375 at 382.
[19] See, generally, B. Green, '*Grey, Oughtred* and *Vandervell*: a contextual reappraisal' (1984) 47 MLR 385 at 395–9.   [20] *Grainge v. Wilberforce* (1889) 5 TLR 436.
[21] *Vandervell v. IRC* [1967] 1 All ER 1, HL. In *Vandervell*, a bank held legal title to shares owned beneficially by Mr V. When he directed the bank to transfer legal title to a charity it was held that he intended his benefit to pass simultaneously. Contrast *Prest v. Petrodel* [2013] UKSC 34 where A, having held legal title for the benefit of B, transferred it to C. It was held that B retained the benefit, because he had not intended to confer a benefit on C (*per* Lord Sumption at para. [49].)

2. The case of a person who disclaims a beneficial interest to which she is entitled under a trust. Disclaimer does not operate by way of disposition, but by way of avoidance, so it does not have to comply with s. 53(1)(c).[22]

3. Disposition of interests as part of an arrangement to vary beneficial interests under a trust in accordance with the Variation of Trusts Act 1958.[23]

Testamentary transactions: mutual wills and secret trusts

Any trust or disposition coming into effect upon the death of the person setting up the trust or making the disposition is said to be 'testamentary'. The basic policy of the law is to support the 'testamentary freedom' of property owners to dispose of their estates as they like when they die, but a testamentary disposition will be invalid unless it complies with the formalities laid down by the Wills Act 1837.[24] The Act provides that no will shall be valid unless it is in writing and signed by the testator (or by some other person in his presence and by his direction) and it appears that the testator intended by his signature to give effect to the will, and the signature is made or acknowledged by the testator in the presence of two or more witnesses present at the same time, and each witness either attests and signs the will, or acknowledges his signature, in the presence of the testator (but not necessarily in the presence of any other witness).[25]

In the following two sections, we consider mutual wills and secret trusts and their relationship to the Wills Act.

Mutual wills

The typical case of mutual wills occurs when a husband and wife enter into a binding agreement, intended to be irrevocable by either party acting unilaterally, that they will both draft their wills in a particular way so as to ensure that, on the death of the first to die, the surviving spouse will receive the property of the deceased. Frequently, the wills also provide that, on the death of the last surviving spouse, certain other named persons (often their children) will receive some, or all, of the deceased's property. The surviving spouse may receive a life interest in the property,[26] or an absolute interest,[27] according to whether the particular facts of the case show, respectively, that there was, or was not, to be a gift over to other persons on his or her death. Of course, the device is not restricted to spouses or even to unmarried couples. Several people could, in theory, create mutual wills with one another. It is not even required that the parties leave everything (or anything) to each other; the only requirement is that the wills be executed in a mutual form.

The traditional justification for equity's recognition of the agreement on which mutual wills are based is the prevention of fraud.[28] It would be a fraud for the surviving

[22] *Re Paradise Motor Co Ltd* [1968] 2 All ER 625, CA.   [23] See Chapter 9.
[24] 7 Will 4 & 1 Vict. c.26.   [25] Section 9, as amended by the Administration of Justice Act 1982, s. 17.
[26] *Re Green* [1951] Ch 148.   [27] *Dufour v. Pereira* (1769) Dick 419.   [28] Ibid. at 421.

party to renege on the agreement, the deceased party having already performed their part of it. Therefore, from the date of the death of the first party to die, the survivor is obliged in equity to exercise his or her testamentary rights of disposition in accordance with his or her side of the mutual agreement. Of course, nothing can actually be done to prevent the survivor from creating a different *form* of will,[29] but, when the survivor dies, his personal representatives must hold the estate according to the form of the mutual wills.[30] It is said that the surviving spouse is bound in equity under a constructive trust to dispose of property in accordance with the agreement to create mutual wills. Crucially, the trust does not arise under the wills, but '*out of the agreement between the two testators not to revoke their wills*'.[31] However, the person who seeks to enforce a mutual will is not a party to the contract that created the mutuality of the wills. She claims under a trust; she does not seek specific performance of a contract.[32]

In *Re Dale*,[33] a husband and wife agreed that they would both draw up wills leaving their estates to their son and daughter equally. On his death, the husband left his estate in accordance with the agreement. The wife, however, later drew up a new will, leaving the vast majority of the estate to her son, whom she also named as her executor. It was held that the husband and wife had entered into a binding agreement to create mutual wills, and that the son must hold his mother's estate on trust for himself and his sister equally. The most novel aspect of this decision was the acceptance that mutual wills could be created by persons not named as beneficiaries under the wills, but the judgment of Morritt J also confirms the contractual basis of mutual wills:

> There is no doubt that for the doctrine to apply there must be a contract at law. It is apparent from all the cases...that it is necessary to establish an agreement to make and not revoke mutual wills, some understanding or arrangement being insufficient...it is necessary to find consideration sufficient to support a contract at law...It is to be assumed that the first testator and the second testator had agreed to make and not to revoke the mutual wills in question. The performance of that promise by the execution of the will by the first testator is in my judgment sufficient consideration by itself.[34]

It is interesting that a mere 'understanding or arrangement' between home-sharers as to their respective entitlements to the land is a sufficient basis for establishing a constructive trust between them,[35] whereas, according to Morritt J, a mere 'understanding or

---

[29] A will, by its very nature, can always be revoked as a matter of form (*Vynior's Case* (1610) 8 Rep 82a). In a sense, the form is inherently dishonest, because it says *last* will and testament, even though it is accepted that a new one may be made sooner or later.

[30] '[T]*he doctrine of mutual wills...is a doctrine which, if applicable, entitles the beneficiaries named in a testator's revoked will to compel the executors named in his last will to administer his estate in accordance with the terms of the revoked will rather than with those of his last one*' (*Birch v. Curtis* [2002] 29 EG 139 (CS), *per* Rimer J at [58]).

[31] *The Thomas and Agnes Carvel Foundation v. Carvel* [2007] EWHC 1314 (Ch), *per* Lewison J at [27].

[32] *Olins v. Walters* [2008] EWCA Civ 782; [2009] 2 WLR 1, CA. (Noted Luxton (2009) Conv. 498. Reflecting on the devastation that the litigation brought upon the family, Professor Luxton observes that '[i]t was nearly 40 years ago that Robert Burgess, writing in the pages of this journal, concluded that he would "avoid mutual wills like the plague"' and asks '[i]s it not time that practitioners heeded his advice?').   [33] [1994] Ch 31.

[34] Ibid. at 38.   [35] See *Lloyds Bank v. Rosset*, Chapter 8.

arrangement' is an insufficient basis for establishing a constructive trust to give effect to mutual wills. Even the action of executing identical wills will not be conclusive evidence of mutuality: there must be an actual agreement to that effect.[36] It should go without saying that the contract creating mutual wills does not need to be in writing, even if the estate includes land. The statutory requirement of formality for a contract to transfer land does not apply in cases of proprietary estoppel or constructive trust.[37] This is a recognition that equity will not allow statutory formality to be used as an instrument of fraud.

Indeed, it might be said that the whole rationale for mutual wills is that equity will not permit a formality statute to be used as an instrument of fraud. The *locus classicus* of this principle is the case of *Rochefoucauld v. Boustead*,[38] a case in which s. 7 of the Statute of Frauds,[39] the precursor to the Law of Property Act 1925, s. 53(1), was considered. In *Rochefoucauld*, Lindley LJ held that:

> the Statute of Frauds does not prevent proof of a fraud; and it is a fraud on the part of a person to whom land is conveyed as a trustee, and who knows it was so conveyed, to deny the trust and claim the land himself. Consequently, notwithstanding the statute, it is competent for a person claiming land conveyed to another to prove by parol [oral] evidence that it was so conveyed upon trust for the claimant.[40]

For consideration of other candidate rationales for mutual wills, including the possibility that they take effect by means of a 'floating' or 'suspensory' trust, and the possibility that they operate by raising a proprietary estoppel which is satisfied by constructive trust, see later.[41]

Secret trusts

Throughout its history, the secret trust has probably been of most use to the man wishing to make provision for his mistress or illegitimate children after his death. If he made such provision in the usual way, he would have to comply with the formalities laid down by the Wills Act 1837 and there would therefore be a written record revealing facts he might have preferred to remain secret. Perhaps sympathetic to the gentleman's dilemma, perhaps mindful of the risk that provision might not otherwise be made for mistresses and illegitimate children,[42] the judges of the Chancery Division allowed him (sometimes reluctantly)[43] to create a secret trust. Secret trusts work despite a lack of testamentary formality, because they operate *dehors*[44] the will; as one judge has said: '*[t]he*

---

[36] *Re Oldham* [1925] Ch 75.   [37] Law of Property Miscellaneous Provisions Act 1989, s. 2(5).

[38] [1897] 1 Ch 196, CA.

[39] 29 Car. 2, c. 3 (1677). The drafting of the Statute of Frauds has been attributed to Lord Nottingham (see Chapter 1).   [40] [1897] 1 Ch 196, CA, at 206.

[41] In the section headed 'The "floating" or "suspensory" trust theory'.

[42] Before the Inheritance (Provision for Family and Dependants) Act 1975. (Legitimacy is defined by the Legitimacy Act 1976, as amended.)

[43] Lord Nottingham objected to the potential of secret trusts to disinherit lawful heirs (J. H. Baker and S. F. C. Milsom, *Sources of English Legal History* (London: Butterworths, 1986) at 244–8).

[44] 'Outside' (tr. French).

whole theory of the formation of a secret trust is that the Wills Act has nothing to do with the matter.[45]

Certain incidental advantages flow from the fact that secret trusts are not subject to the Wills Act, including that, contrary to the usual rule,[46] a party may witness the will and still take a benefit under the secret trust.

Secret trusts are of two sorts: fully secret and half-secret.

Fully secret trusts

A fully secret trust is created where X *formally* leaves property to Y by his will in circumstances under which Y is *informally* made aware by X, during X's lifetime, that Y is to hold some, or all, of the property as trustee for the benefit of Z. The facts and the terms of the trust must be communicated to, and accepted by, Y before X dies, so it can be said that X has relied on Y.[47] On the face of the will, Y will appear to be the absolute beneficial owner of the property, but a constructive trust is imposed upon Y to prevent him from unconscionably denying Z's rights.[48] The precise date of the informal agreement, whether before or after the will was made, is unimportant, but it is essential that the precise objects of the trust were communicated to the trustee and that the trustee expressly or impliedly accepted the trust during the settlor's lifetime.[49]

In *Re Boyes*,[50] the secret trust failed, because its object was uncertain. B made a gift to his executor by his will, having previously instructed the executor to hold the gift on trust for other persons. Although the executor accepted that instruction during B's lifetime, the names of the 'other persons' were not communicated to the executor and were not ascertained until letters were discovered after B's death. The secret trust would have been valid if, before he died, B had placed a sealed envelope containing detailed instructions into the executor's hand. That would have constituted constructive notice of the trusts to the executor and the executor would be deemed to have accepted the trusts as detailed in the letter. As Lord Wright put it: *'a ship which sails under sealed orders, is sailing under orders though the exact terms are not ascertained by the captain until later.'*[51] It is, however, required that the trustee was aware that the envelope contained the terms of a trust and that he accepted the envelope on that basis. Acceptance can be by words or silent acquiescence.[52]

Secret trusts are not recognized lightly. The beneficiary claiming under the secret trust must prove that what the testator formally provided by his will is not what he actually intended to provide, but judicial opinion is divided on the question of the appropriate standard of proof. When a court is called upon to rectify a will on the ground that it does not accurately reflect the testator's intentions, the claimant will have to satisfy a high standard of proof,[53] and it has been suggested that a similarly high standard

---

[45] *Re Young* [1951] Ch 344, *per* Danckwerts J at 350.   [46] Wills Act 1837, s. 15.

[47] *Wallgrave v. Tebbs* (1855) 2 K & J 313.   [48] *McCormick v. Grogan* (1869) LR 4 HL 82.

[49] *Ottaway v. Norman* [1972] Ch 698.   [50] (1884) LR 26 Ch D 531.

[51] *Re Keen* [1937] Ch 236 at 242.

[52] *Moss v. Cooper* (1861) 1 J H 352; *Ottaway v. Norman* [1972] Ch 698.

[53] *Joscelyne v. Nissen* [1970] 2 QB 86, CA.

of proof should be required of a person claiming to be entitled under a secret trust.[54] However, unless it is alleged that the secret trustee has acted fraudulently, the ordinary civil standard of proof 'on the balance of probabilities' should suffice.[55] In circumstances under which X leaves property to co-owners intending that they should hold it under a secret trust, the trust must be communicated and accepted by every co-owner—unless the co-owners are equitable joint tenants, in which case acceptance by one counts as acceptance by all.[56]

Half-secret trusts

A half-secret trust arises where X *formally* leaves property by his will to Y *expressly* 'on trust' for another, but in circumstances under which Y is only *informally* made aware of the identity of that other. X must communicate the trust to Y, and Y must accept, before the will is executed. Accordingly, the crucial distinction between a half-secret and a fully secret trust is that, in the case of a half-secret trust, it will be clear on the face of the will that Y is *not* the beneficial owner of the property. Despite this important formal distinction, Viscount Sumner[57] has stated that, in substance, there is no relevant distinction between fully secret and half-secret trusts, because the 'fraud' to be prevented is the same in both cases:

> In both cases the testator's wishes are incompletely expressed in his will. Why should equity, over a mere matter of words, give effect to them in one case and frustrate them in the other?[58]

However, it is submitted that the distinction between the two types of secret trust is more than a 'mere matter of words'. For one thing, the risk of fraud is surely much greater in the case of a fully secret trust, under which the trustee appears to be entitled to the property absolutely. In fact, on closer examination, it appears that the two types of secret trust rest on entirely different conceptual foundations. Whereas a fully secret trust has nothing to do with the Wills Act and can be created before or after the will, a half-secret trust is effective only when it precedes the execution of the will and can be regarded as having been incorporated into the will. If the will makes reference to a trust that has not yet been declared, the trust cannot take effect as a half-secret trust. It will be construed to be a void attempt to dispose of the estate by a non-testamentary instrument.[59]

Blackwell v. Blackwell[60] is a classic instance of a valid half-secret trust. The testator left a legacy of £12,000 to five persons by a codicil to his will and directed them to apply the income 'for the purposes indicated by me to them', with power to apply two-thirds of the capital 'to such person or persons indicated by me to them'. The identities of the beneficiaries of the trusts (a mistress and her illegitimate son) were orally communicated to the intended trustees, with detailed instructions being given to one of them. The

---

[54] Brightman J in *Ottaway v. Norman* [1972] Ch 698 at 712.
[55] *Re Snowden* [1979] Ch 528, *per* Sir Robert Megarry VC at 536.   [56] *Re Stead* [1900] 1 Ch 237.
[57] *Blackwell v. Blackwell* [1929] AC 318, HL.   [58] Ibid. at 337.
[59] *Re Bateman's WT* [1970] 3 All ER 817, *per* Pennycuik VC at 820E–F.   [60] [1929] AC 318, HL.

testator's widow challenged the validity of the half-secret trust and claimed the £12,000 for herself. Because the intended trustees accepted the trusts before the execution of the codicil, the House of Lords held that evidence of the oral arrangement was admissible and established a valid half-secret trust in favour of the mistress and illegitimate son.

The fact that the secret trust precedes the execution of a will does not, however, guarantee that the trust will be a valid half-secret trust. The terms of the trust must be so consistent with the later will that the court can deem the trust to have been incorporated into it. In *Re Keen*,[61] the testator, K, handed a sealed envelope to E. E was aware that the envelope contained the name of a woman to whom K had not been married, although he did not actually open it until after K's death. At a later date, K executed his will. If the will had left property to E 'subject to trusts of which he is already aware', or simply 'subject to trusts', E would have been bound by a half-secret trust. However, the only reference in the will to informal testamentary dispositions was to dispositions that might be made *after* the execution of the will. According to the usual rules of documentary construction, by expressly providing that the will should be read subject to *future* informal dispositions, it had to be presumed that the testator did not want his will to be read subject to dispositions made in the *past*. On account of that single clause, the court was unable to hold that the earlier trust had been incorporated into the later will. That was so, even though the clause itself was, for all other purposes, void, because it purported to allow the will to be amended without a formal codicil.[62]

Contemporary analogies to secret trusts

Secret trusts are not only useful in their own right; they provide a useful analogy and precedent for anyone attempting to find a way around testamentary formalities. Thus, in *Gold v. Hill*,[63] an attempt to validate the nomination of a beneficiary under a life insurance policy was argued by analogy to secret trusts. It was argued successfully that, because the proceeds of a life insurance policy never form part of the deceased's estate during his lifetime, the beneficiary of the policy takes under the policy rather than under the estate of the deceased, so the beneficiary does not receive by a testamentary disposition at all. The Wills Act, as in the case of a secret trust, has nothing to do with the matter. A similar case is *Re Danish Bacon Co Ltd Staff Pension Fund Trusts*,[64] in which an employee of the Danish Bacon Co Ltd nominated his wife, by signed writing, to receive his pension entitlement in the event of his death. The nomination was held not to be a testamentary instrument.

Mutual wills and secret trusts: proprietary estoppel giving rise to constructive trust?

In cases of mutual wills and secret trusts, the essential facts are the same: an informal agreement is reached between two people under which it is understood that, when one party dies, the surviving party will be obliged, as the legal owner of certain property,

---

[61] [1937] Ch 236.   [62] Wills Act 1837.   [63] [1999] 1 FLR 54.   [64] [1971] 1 WLR 248.

to hold his legal title and exercise his legal powers in accordance with the terms of the informal agreement. In the case of mutual wills, the agreement must be fully contractual in order to bind the survivor's conscience, because the burden on the conscience of the survivor must be substantial before he will be deprived of a legal owner's usual entitlement to freedom of testamentary disposition. In the case of a secret trust, the agreement need not be fully contractual: a mere understanding between the testator and the secret trustee will suffice. In every case of secret trust (fully- or half-secret) equity will be interested in upholding the undertaking made by the secret trustee. Equity is interested not because of the arrangement between the testator and the secret trustee alone, but also because the testator, to the extent that he trusts in the secret trustee, foregoes his freedom to trust someone else (and, in the case of a half-secret trust, foregoes his freedom to change his will). It is this detrimental reliance upon the arrangement which makes it unconscionable for the secret trustee to renege on his undertaking and calls for equity's intervention.

There is an equitable doctrine that seems to fit well with the essential facts underlying mutual wills and secret trusts: that doctrine is proprietary estoppel. As Mr Edward Nugee QC observed when sitting as a judge of the Chancery Division:

> The rights to which proprietary estoppel gives rise, and the machinery by which effect is given to them, are similar in many respects to those involved in cases of secret trusts, mutual wills and other comparable cases in which property is vested in B on the faith of an understanding that it will be dealt with in a particular manner.[65]

To paraphrase his Lordship in the same case, the doctrine of proprietary estoppel provides that, where one person has acted to his detriment in the belief, knowingly encouraged by another person, that the former will acquire a right in or over the latter's property, the latter cannot insist on his strict legal rights if to do so would be inconsistent with the belief of the former. In the case of mutual wills, the first party to die acts to his detriment, because, by executing his will in the agreed form, he forgoes his general freedom of testamentary disposition. In the case of a secret trust, the testator acts to his detriment by transferring his property to the trustee. In both types of case, the deceased believes that he has acquired, by virtue of his informal understanding with the survivor, a right to determine how the survivor will use certain property to which the survivor is legally entitled—and in both types of case, it would be unconscionable for the survivor to act in denial of that right.

There are, however, fault lines in the proprietary estoppel analysis of mutual wills and secret trusts. One, which was noted by Robert Walker LJ in *Gillett v. Holt*,[66] is the fact that mutual wills and secret trusts usually operate for the benefit of a third party, whereas proprietary estoppel is usually concerned with the equitable disposal of an arrangement affecting the two primary parties: the representor and the representee.

---

[65] *Re Basham, decd* [1986] 1 WLR 1498, *per* Mr Edward Nugee QC at 1504A–B. See also *Re Pearson Fund Trusts*, unreported, 21 October 1977, *per* Slade J at 52 (official transcript).

[66] [2001] Ch 210. The case is considered at length in Chapter 8.

Another potential fault line noted by Robert Walker LJ in *Gillett v. Holt* is the fact that a mutual will depends upon a contractual agreement whereas proprietary estoppel does not. In any case, proprietary estoppel is not a remedy in itself, but merely a cause of action leading to an ultimate remedy—often a constructive trust.[67] In the case of a secret trust or mutual will, it makes sense to ignore the estoppel stage (if there is one) and to simply acknowledge the constructive trust. As Nourse J stated in a case concerning mutual wills:

> The principle of all these cases is that a court of equity will not permit a person to whom property is transferred by way of gift, but on the faith of an agreement or clear understanding that it is to be dealt with in a particular way for the benefit of a third person, to deal with that property inconsistently with that agreement or understanding. If he attempts to do so after having received the benefit of the gift equity will intervene by imposing a constructive trust on the property which is the subject matter of the agreement or understanding.[68]

The 'floating' or 'suspensory' trust theory

The 'floating' or 'suspensory' trust theory of mutual wills and secret trusts can be traced back to *Birmingham v. Renfrew*,[69] an early Australian case on mutual wills. In that case, Dixon J observed that the surviving party to a mutual wills agreement cannot make '*gifts and settlements* inter vivos...*calculated to defeat the intention of the compact*'.[70] His Lordship took the view that there must be a trust binding on the property in the survivor's hands during the survivor's lifetime, hence the opinion of the learned authors of *Lewin on Trusts*:

> Mutual wills (if established) take effect by way of a 'floating trust' which becomes irrevocable following the death of the first testator and crystallises on the death of the second.[71]

This idea of the 'floating' or 'suspensory' trust is not limited to cases of mutual wills. In *Ottaway v. Norman*,[72] Brightman J was 'content to assume' that the 'suspensory trust' might give effect to a secret trust in cases in which the trust was not intended to bind on the death of the testator, but on the death of the secret trustee:

> where property is given to [A] on the understanding that [A] will dispose by his will of such assets, if any, as he may have at his command at his death in favour of [B], a valid trust is created in favour of [B] which is in suspense during the lifetime of [A] but attaches to the estate of [A] at the moment of [A]'s death.[73]

The 'suspensory trust' was invented to explain mutual wills, and it has been used to explain those rare secret trusts under which the trust is not intended to bind immediately upon the death of the person who set it up, but it explains very little else and there is no great weight of precedent to support the existence of such a trust. It is submitted

---

[67] See Chapter 8.   [68] *Re Cleaver, decd* [1981] 1 WLR 939, *per* Nourse J at 947.
[69] (1936) 57 CLR 666.   [70] Ibid. at 689.
[71] 17th edn (J. Mowbray et al., eds) (London: Sweet & Maxwell, 2000) at 10–28 referring to *Re Goodchild* [1996] 1 WLR 694 at 702, *per* Carnwath J (affirmed on appeal: [1997] 1 WLR 1216).
[72] [1972] Ch 698.   [73] Ibid. at 713–14.

that it introduces too much certainty with regard to the subject matter of the trust. In the case of mutual wills, a suspensory trust analysis does not indicate how much of the survivor's property is covered by the 'suspensory' trust. The survivor's estate at the date of the death of the other testator is presumably within the trust, but what about its traceable proceeds and exchange products, and what about after-acquired property? The suspensory trust theory is not really an analytical explanation of the operation of mutual wills and secret trusts, but merely an attempt to describe it, and therefore the orthodox maxim ('equity will not permit a statute to be used as an instrument of fraud') and the language of unconscionability and constructive trust may be preferred.

Perpetuity

The law will recognize absolute ownership in perpetuity. Thus the legal estate of fee simple absolute in possession of land will, in theory, last forever. The law recognizes absolute ownership in perpetuity, because property that is owned absolutely can participate freely in the national economy. The absolute owner of property can sell it in order to realize its capital value and, if it is retained and produces income, he is free to spend the income or accumulate it as he pleases. In contrast, the law is most reluctant to recognize any transaction or disposition that might prevent property from vesting in an absolute owner until a remote future date, or which might otherwise postpone for too long the power of a legal owner of property to apply capital and income as he thinks fit. These concerns are reflected in a number of rules against perpetuities: the rule against remoteness of vesting, the rule against inalienability of capital, and the rule against accumulation of income.

The rule against remoteness of vesting

Before we turn to the technicalities, we should pause to consider why we have this rule at all. Nowadays, the explanation generally given is an economic one: we have the rule to ensure that wealth cannot be suspended in trust—that is, kept out of absolute ownership—for too long. If that is the truth, it is nevertheless not the whole truth: the origins of the rule seem to lie, not only in economic reasoning, but also in the religious belief that perpetual gifts trench on God's prerogative to provide future well-being.[74]

---

[74] The modern rule against remoteness of vesting has its source in principles laid down by Heneage Finch, Lord Nottingham LC, in *The Duke of Norfolk's Case* (1681) 3 Chan Cas 1. (See A. W. B. Simpson, *An Introduction to the History of the Land Law*, 1979, at pp. 211, 212). Lord Nottingham relied, in that case, upon two earlier authorities, the principal one being *Pells v. Browne* (1620) Cro Jac 590, in which Dodridge J stated (at 221): '*quant Deus dedit terras filiis hominis, & si homes poient faire continuance de terre in lour families for ever, ceo fuit a preventer le providence de Dieu*' (which roughly translates 'because God gives land to the children of men, if men were able to keep land in their families forever it would deny the Providence of God'). (I am grateful to my colleague John Snape for bringing *Pells v. Browne* to my attention.)

When it is certain that a beneficiary of an express trust is entitled to a beneficial inter-est under the trust, her interest is said to have 'vested in interest'. So, in a traditional trust of the sort 'for A for life and B in remainder', the interests of A and B are said to 'vest in interest' the moment the trust is created, because it is known from that moment that A and B are certainly entitled to a beneficial interest under the trust. If it is not certain that A and B will acquire a beneficial interest under the trust, perhaps because the trust is 'for A for life *if* A is a barrister, and to B in remainder *if* B is married', the interests of A and B are not 'vested'; they are 'contingent'. The problem with contingent gifts to A and B under a trust is that the interests of A and B will only 'vest in interest' when, and if, the contingencies are met and, because we cannot be sure that the contingencies will be met, we cannot be sure when, if ever, the interests of A and B will vest. There is therefore a risk that their interests will not vest until after the end of the perpetuity period. This is a problem, because public policy requires that property settled on trust must not remain in suspense indefinitely. It is in the public interest that the ownership of private property should be ascertained and resolved within a reasonable time. The rule against remoteness of vesting therefore provides that a gift will be void if it might vest beyond 'the perpetuity period'. Regrettably for the student, there are three ways of calculating this period. We will see at the end of this section that the Perpetuities and Accumulations Act 2009 provides a practical way for trustees to overcome technical problems of perpetuity, but that the statute as a whole has temporarily added to, rather than removed, the conceptual complexity of the rule.

The first method of calculation is the most straightforward. According to the Perpetuities and Accumulations Act 1964,[75] if the instrument by which a disposition is made specifies a perpetuity period of not more than 80 years, there is no need to look any further. One simply applies the rule against remoteness of vesting, as set out in the Act, on the basis of the period specified in the instrument.

Matters become more complicated if no perpetuity period is specified in the instru-ment by which the disposition is made. One must then calculate the perpetuity period according to the common law rule of remoteness of vesting. This provides that, if an interest is disposed of in favour of X subject to a 'contingency' (a requirement that may or may not be met), it will be void for perpetuity from the date of the disposi-tion unless the contingency will certainly be met, if it will be met at all, not later than *21 years after the death of all 'lives in being'*.[76] 'Lives in being' are persons who, at the 'effective date of the disposition' are alive or in their mother's womb[77]—assuming that the latter are subsequently born.[78] (An *inter vivos* deed of gift or trust is effective at the date of its execution; a testamentary gift or trust is effective at the date of the donor's death.) However, the only relevant 'lives in being' are those persons who are expressly or impliedly referred to in the instrument by which the disposition is made. So the

---

[75] Section 1(1).
[76] See J. C. Gray, *The Rule Against Perpetuities*, 4th edn (Boston: Little Brown & Co, 1942) para. 201.
[77] Referred to in the cases as a life in being *'en ventre sa mere'* (French) or *'in ventre matris'* (Latin).
[78] *Re Wilmer's Trusts* [1903] 2 Ch 411.

lives in being at the date of execution of an *inter vivos* trust in favour of 'such of my grandchildren as qualify as lawyers' include the grandchildren, the settlor, and any of the settlor's children, but no others. Lives in being can be expressly appointed who have no connection with the settlor or the intended beneficiary of the disposition, hence it would be perfectly valid for a settlor expressly to provide that the perpetuity period will end '21 years after the death of all living lineal descendants of Queen Elizabeth II'.[79] However, a trust in which the lives in being are specified to be 'all persons who shall be living at my death' will fail for uncertainty.[80] There was even a failed attempt in one Irish case to use animals as measuring lives.[81]

The third method of calculating the perpetuity period will only be resorted to if a disposition is void under the common law rule. The third method, set out in the Perpetuities and Accumulations Act 1964, s. 3, provides that the perpetuity period ends 21 years after the death of all 'statutory lives' in being. The basic point to grasp is that 'statutory lives' are more numerous than common law lives in being. They include, for example, not only the person in whose favour a gift is made, but the parents and grandparents of every such person. The Act states that some categories of statutory lives should be disregarded if they cannot practicably be ascertained,[82] but, unfortunately, the Act fails to identify which lives should be disregarded and in what circumstances. The Act can also be criticized because it states that the donee of a power is a life in being for the purpose of determining the validity of the power,[83] but it fails to state whether the donee is a life in being for the purpose of determining the validity of a disposition made by exercising the power. The law governing remoteness of vesting has just become a little more complicated, albeit with the promise of simplicity in the longer term. This is as a result of the Perpetuities and Accumulations Act 2009, which came into force on 6 April 2010. The reforms introduced by the 2009 Act are outlined later, just before we move on to the topic of illegality.

The strictness of the common law rule

According to the common law rule against remoteness of vesting, a disposition subject to a contingency (a condition which might not be met) will be void for perpetuity if there is the slightest possibility that the contingency might be met, if it is met at all, outside the perpetuity period. The rule is said to be concerned with possibilities, not probabilities. Thus it permits the assumption that a 60-year-old woman might bear a child[84] (probably in recognition of the possibility of divine providence,[85] rather than in anticipation of recent advances in fertility science). The court in *Re Gaite's WT*[86]

---

[79] In *Re Villar* [1929] 1 Ch 243, the testator directed that capital left in trust by his will should not vest until '20 years from the day of the death of the last survivor of all the lineal descendants of Her Late Majesty Queen Victoria who shall be living at the time of my death'. In *Wyndham v. Egremont* [2009] EWHC 2076 (Ch) a royal lives clause originally executed on 20 May 1940 specified '20 years from the death of the last survivor of the issue, whether children or more remote, of His late Majesty King George V living on 20 May 1940'.

[80] In *Re Moore* [1901] 1 Ch 936.   [81] *Re Kelly* [1932] IR 255.   [82] Section 3(4)(a).

[83] Section 3(5)(b)(v).   [84] *Re Dawson* (1888) LR 39 Ch D 155.

[85] The Bible recounts how Abraham's wife, Sarah, gave birth at the age of 90 (Genesis 17:17).

[86] [1949] 1 All ER 459.

was apparently prepared to apply the common law rule on the assumption that a five-year-old girl was physically capable of giving birth, but, because a child of that age could not give birth to children within a legal marriage,[87] it was held that the possibility should not be taken into account when applying a legal rule.

Class gifts

Gifts and trusts are often made in favour of a class: for example 'nephews' or 'employees'. A 'class' for this purpose comprises persons who

> come within a certain category or description defined by a general or collective formula, and who, if they take at all, are to take one divisible subject in certain proportionate shares.[88]

Unfortunately, according to the basic common law rule against remoteness of vesting, a contingent gift or trust in favour of a class will be void unless *all* potential members of the class are certain to satisfy the contingency within the perpetuity period. In practice, this can produce harsh results. Thus, if today a settlor disposes of £1,000 on trust for all of his nieces who qualify as barristers, the disposition will fail and none of the nieces will take any benefit under it—even if today he has three living nieces and one of those is already a barrister. This is because every one of the lives in being (the three nieces and the settlor) *might* die tomorrow, in which event the 21 years of the perpetuity period will start to run. Yet, assuming the settlor is survived by a fertile brother or sister, a fourth niece may be born a year from now. This fourth niece is not certain to qualify as a barrister before the end of the perpetuity period—indeed, only a precocious student could—so the gift to her must fail for perpetuity and, because it was a class gift, the gift to the entire class will fail.[89] This does not seem fair to the three nieces who are already alive. Why should they lose out because of the remote possibility, first, that they will all three of them suddenly die and, second, that a fourth niece will be born who will qualify as a barrister in record time?

In *Andrews v. Partington*,[90] the court took pity on beneficiaries in a comparable predicament to our three nieces. It was held that where there is a gift to a class each member of the class who at the date of the gift has already satisfied the contingency (each member who has qualified as a barrister in our example) is entitled to take her share of it at once. The class is closed at the date of the gift to include only those members of the class ('nieces') who are then alive and any members of the closed class who later satisfy the contingency will be entitled to take their share. If they die without having satisfied the contingency, their share will be divided equally between the surviving members of the closed class, being those members of the class who have already satisfied the contingency and those who still might satisfy the contingency.

If members of the class are alive at the effective date of the gift but none has at that time met the contingency, the rule in *Andrews v. Partington* permits the trustees to wait to see if any beneficiary satisfies the contingency within the perpetuity period. The first

---

[87] Marriage Act 1929.   [88] *Pearks v. Moseley* (1880) LR 5 App Cas 714 *per* Lord Selborne LC at 723.
[89] This was also the problem in *Re Dawson* (1888) LR 39 Ch D 155.
[90] (1791) 3 Bro CC 401. See, generally, H. C. Morris (1954) 70 LQR 61.

to do so may take her share at that time.[91] The size of her share is again worked out by closing the class of potential beneficiaries to include only those persons who answer the class description ('niece') at the date at which the first member of the class satisfies the contingency (qualifies as a barrister). Any person answering the class description who is born after the class has closed and any person who cannot possibly satisfy the contingency within the perpetuity period will be excluded from taking any part of the fund.[92]

The rule in *Andrews v. Partington* is merely a convenient rule of construction. It can therefore be displaced by an express intention to exclude it.[93] In *Re Tom's Settlement*,[94] an express provision that the class should close on a particular date was held to have excluded the rule in *Andrews v. Partington*.

Total failure to satisfy the contingency

It should not be forgotten that the common law rule only applies to contingent dispositions, and that a disposition will be ineffective, quite apart from any issue of perpetuity, if the intended beneficiary is simply unable to meet the contingency. Thus a gift 'to Sarah if she qualifies as a medical doctor before the age of 30' will fail if she reaches the age of 30 and has not yet qualified.

The Perpetuities and Accumulations Act 1964

The 1964 Act applies a statutory rule against remoteness of vesting to dispositions coming into effect after 15 July 1964. The statutory rule is more generous than the common law rule and ought therefore to have rendered the common law rule otiose, but the common law rule must still be applied first. Only if a disposition is void for remoteness of vesting according to the common law rule can the statutory rule be applied to save it. The most significant aspect of the statutory rule against remoteness of vesting is that it presumes a disposition to be valid until there is no possibility of it vesting within the perpetuity period, whereas the common law rule declares a disposition to be void from the outset if there is any possibility that it might vest outside the perpetuity period. The statute operates a 'wait and see' approach.[95] One very important consequence of the statutory presumption in favour of validity is that trustees are permitted during the 'wait and see' period to apply income and capital in favour of a beneficiary (in the exercise of their powers of maintenance and advancement, respectively),[96] and such applications will stand even if it is later established that the beneficiary will not be able to satisfy the contingency before the end of the perpetuity period. The 'wait and see' perpetuity period ends 21 years after the death of the last surviving statutory life in being,[97] unless the number of statutory lives is so large as to render it impracticable to ascertain the date of the death of the survivor.[98] If there are no statutory lives in being, the period is a bare 21 years, as is the case at common law when there are no lives in being.

---

[91] *Re Clifford's Settlement Trusts* [1981] 1 Ch 63.
[92] *Hawkins on Wills* (C. P. Sanger, ed.), 3rd edn (London: Sweet & Maxwell, 1925) at 96.
[93] Law Commission Report No. 251, para. 5.26.   [94] [1987] 1 WLR 1021.   [95] Section 3.
[96] See Chapter 9.   [97] See earlier.   [98] Section 3(4).

Class-closing rules under the Act

Under the 1964 Act, class-closing provisions operate in combination with the 'wait and see' principle so as to exclude from the closed class of potential beneficiaries only such persons as will certainly fail to satisfy the contingency within the perpetuity period. In other words, the trustees are permitted to wait until the end of the perpetuity period to see which members of the class have, by that time, satisfied the contingency[99] (with or without the benefit of age reduction);[100] all such members will take their shares. However, the class will be closed to exclude any members of the class who have not yet been born and any members who have failed, or certainly will fail, to satisfy the contingency by the end of the perpetuity period.

Fertility presumptions

The 1964 Act not only presumes validity until such time as the disposition is certain to vest outside the perpetuity period, it also introduces common-sense presumptions as to fertility. It is presumed that a male of 14 years or over can become a father, but that a younger male cannot; it is presumed that a female can give birth at the age of 12 years or over, but not under that age or over the age of 55.[101] These presumptions also apply to the potential of a person to have a child by adoption, legitimation, or other means.[102] In the case of a living person, medical evidence may be admitted to show that he or she will or will not be able to have a child at the time in question.[103] Of course, developments in reproductive science might one day require the basic presumptions to be revised or removed entirely.

Age reduction

The trustees are permitted to wait and see whether any beneficiaries will attain the contingent age before the end of the perpetuity period. As soon as it is apparent that a beneficiary will not be able to attain the contingent age within the perpetuity period, the contingent age will be reduced as regards that beneficiary *to whatever extent is necessary* to ensure that her interest may vest within the perpetuity period.[104] So, in the case of a trust for grandchildren upon their reaching the age of 30, any grandchild who is still only aged 25 at the end of the perpetuity period will only be required to attain the age of 25, and likewise any grandchild who is then aged 22 will only be required to attain the age of 22. However, any grandchild who is below the age of 21 at the end of the perpetuity period will get nothing, because, even under the Act, the contingent age will not be reduced below the age of 21. A slightly different rule applies to contingent gifts made before the Perpetuities and Accumulations Act 1964 came into force on 15 July 1964.[105]

The problem of the unascertained spouse

The identity of a surviving spouse can never be conclusively ascertained until the death of the other spouse. This uncertainty would render several dispositions void for

---

[99] Section 4(4).   [100] See later.   [101] Section 2(1)(a).   [102] Section 2(4).
[103] Section 2(1)(b).   [104] Section 4(1).   [105] Law of Property Act 1925, s. 163.

remoteness of vesting, were it not for a special rule which ensures that a gift will never fail for perpetuity on account of an unascertained spouse. Consider a testamentary gift 'to Larry for life, with remainder to any wife of Larry who may survive him for life, with remainder to such of his brothers living at the death of that wife'. It is possible that, at the effective date of the gift (the date of the testator's death), the person who is destined to be Larry's widow has not yet been conceived, so the common law rule against remoteness of vesting will be applied on the assumption that the future widow is not a life in being. The lives in being will therefore be Larry and any of his brothers alive at the testator's death, and the perpetuity period will end 21 years after the death of the last of them. The gift to the widow cannot be void for remoteness, because her interest will vest on Larry's death and it will therefore vest, if it vests at all, within the perpetuity period. However, the difficulty comes in relation to the gift to the brothers. Their interests will not vest until the widow dies, but it cannot be said for certain that the widow will die within the perpetuity period. In relation to the brothers who are lives in being there is no real problem, because if they take an interest at all, they *must* take it within the perpetuity period. The real problem arises in relation to brothers who may come into existence after the testator's death. It follows from the fact that such later-born brothers will not be lives in being and the fact that the widow might die outside the perpetuity period that the interests of those brothers might not vest until after the end of the perpetuity period. The gift to such later-born brothers would therefore be void for remoteness were it not for s. 5 of the 1964 Act, which provides that no disposition will be void for remoteness of vesting if it is void merely because it is limited by reference to the time of death of a surviving spouse.

The rule against inalienability of capital

With the exception of trusts for charitable purposes, a trust will be void for perpetuity if it renders capital inalienable for a period longer than the perpetuity period. In other words, '*a non-charitable trust is void unless from the outset it is certain that the rule in* Saunders v. Vautier *must be capable of being applied to it by the end of the perpetuity period*'.[106] The perpetuity period for the rule against inalienability of capital is the same as for the common law rule against remoteness of vesting, namely lives in being plus 21 years.[107] The statutory 80-year period may be adopted in the case of a trust for beneficiaries,[108] but many trusts in which capital is rendered inalienable are trusts purely for private purposes, such as trusts for the upkeep of monuments.[109]

The essential reason for the rule against inalienability of capital is a reason of public policy: capital that is owned absolutely can participate freely in the economy, but capital that is set aside on trust to be held solely for the production of income cannot

---

[106] P. Matthews, 'The new trust: obligations without rights?' in *Trends in Contemporary Trust Law* (A. J. Oakley, ed.) (Oxford: Clarendon Press, 1996) at 11.   [107] *Re Howard, The Times*, 30 October 1908.
[108] The 1964 Act, s. 15(4). Matthews earlier, at 12.   [109] See Chapter 3.

participate so freely. Of course, it participates to some extent, because trustees now have very wide powers of investment.[110]

The rule against excessive accumulation of income

The accumulation of income is something more than the mere retention of income for administrative purposes: it is the process of adding income to capital, thereby '*increasing the estate in favour of those entitled to capital and against the interests of those entitled to income*'.[111] The rule against excessive accumulations has a colourful history, traceable back to *Thellusson v. Woodford*.[112] Thellusson had the bright idea of directing his trustees to accumulate income on a large fund for the duration of the lives of his sons, grandsons, and great-grandsons living at the time of his death. On the death of the last survivor, Thullusson's direction was that the fund should be divided between the three eldest living male descendants of his three sons. If there were no such descendants, the property was to pass to the Crown. In the event, the accumulation lasted for 70 years, but it could conceivably have gone on even longer. Nevertheless, Thellusson's direction was perfectly valid as the law then stood and the House of Lords upheld it.

There was an outcry against Thellusson's will. A contemporary magazine suggested that, if the accumulation continued for 120 years, the fund would reach £140m.[113] On appeal to the House of Lords, counsel for Thellusson's widow described the will as:

> morally vicious ... politically injurious ... and by the time, when the accumulation shall end, it will have created a fund, the revenue of which will be greater than the civil list; and will therefore give its possessor the means of disturbing the whole economy of the country.[114]

In the event, the expenses of the lawsuit contributed in large part to the final value of the fund being not much greater than the value originally settled on trust. Nevertheless, the panic over the will led to the enactment of the Accumulations Act 1800.[115] This Act was eventually repealed and replaced by s. 164 of the Law of Property Act 1925, which we will examine shortly. Now, as a result of s. 13 of the Perpetuities and Accumulations Act 2009, there is no restriction on accumulations under non-charitable trusts created on or after 6 April 2010 (the commencement date of the Act), so for the purpose of such trusts ss. 162–166 of the 1925 Act have been repealed. Statutory restrictions will, however, still apply to trusts taking effect before the commencement date of the 2009 Act, and so at the time of writing the next section of this chapter still applies to most trusts. According to s. 14 of the 2009 Act, charitable trusts remain a special case. For charities,

---

[110] See Chapter 12.   [111] *Re the Earl of Berkeley* [1968] Ch 744, *per* Harman LJ at 772.
[112] (1798) 4 Ves Jun 227.
[113] Compare D. Adams, *The Hitchhiker's Guide to the Galaxy* (Pan Macmillan, 1979), which informs us that to dine at '*The Restaurant at the End of the Universe*' all one has to do is '*deposit one penny in a savings account in your own era, and when you arrive at the End of Time the operation of compound interest means that the fabulous cost of your meal has been paid for*'.   [114] (1805) 11 Ves 112 at 114.
[115] The so-called 'Thellusson Act' (see P. Polden, 'Panic or prudence? The Thelluson Act 1800 and trusts for accumulation' (1994) 45 NILQ 13).

the statutory period is a period of 21 years starting with the first day on which the trust directs or empowers the trustees to accumulate income. If, under such a trust, the duty or power would last beyond the end of the statutory period, it ceases to have effect at the end of that period unless sub-s. 5 applies. Subsection 5 applies 'if the instrument provides for the duty or power to cease to have effect (a) on the death of the settlor, or (b) on the death of one of the settlors, determined by name or by the order of their deaths'. If a duty or power ceases to have effect under s. 14, the income to which the duty or power would have applied will instead pass 'to the person who would have been entitled to it if there had been no duty or power to accumulate', or 'be applied for the purposes for which it would have had to be applied if there had been no such duty or power'.

Statutory limits on accumulation of income

According to s. 164 of the Law of Property Act 1925, as amended by the Perpetuities and Accumulations Act 1964,[116] no person[117] may settle or dispose of any property in such manner that the income thereof shall be accumulated for a period longer than '*one of the following*' (the disposition will be construed to determine which of the following periods was most likely intended):[118]

   (i) the lifetime of the settlor; or

   (ii) a term of 21 years from the death of the settlor or testator; or

   (iii) the duration of the respective minorities of any beneficiaries with a present interest in the income directed to be accumulated; or

   (iv) the period of 21 years from the date of the making of the disposition;[119] or

   (v) the duration of the respective minorities of any person or persons living or *en ventre sa mere* at the death of the settlor or testator; or

   (vi) the duration of the minority or minorities of any person in being at the date of making an *inter vivos* disposition.[120]

Any other directions to accumulate (except those within s. 165, next) shall be void and the income on the property directed to be accumulated shall go to the person or persons who would have been entitled to it if the direction to accumulate had not been made.

Section 165 of the Law of Property Act 1925 provides, *inter alia*, that when accumulations of surplus income are made during the minority of a beneficiary under any statutory power[121] or under the general law, the period for which such accumulations are made is not to be taken into account in determining compliance with the periods set out in s. 164.

---

[116] Section 13.

[117] Section 164 does not apply to dispositions made by corporate persons (*Re Dodwell & Co Ltd Trust* [1979] Ch 301).   [118] *Re Watt's Will Trusts* [1936] 2 All ER 1555.

[119] Added by the 1964 Act, s. 13, and applicable to directions made after 15 July 1964.   [120] Ibid.

[121] For example, under the Trustee Act 1925, s. 31(2), see Chapter 9.

Charities and the rules against perpetuity

The rule against remoteness of vesting applies to charities so far as it requires that a disposition must vest in charity within the perpetuity period. However, once property has been devoted to charitable purposes, a gift over to another charity will be valid even if the gift over vests after the end of the perpetuity period. The rule against inalienability of capital has no application to capital devoted to exclusively charitable purposes.[122] The rule against excessive accumulations applies to charities, but, in practice, charities avoid the restrictions of the statutory rule by making extensive use of the administrative power that every trustee has to retain income on a temporary basis when it is in surfeit, in order to cover needs arising at leaner times; this so-called 'administrative retention' is not accumulation per se, because the income is never treated as capital.[123]

Perpetuities and Accumulations Act 2009

According to s. 12 of the Act, the trustees of *any trust created at any time* can execute an irrevocable deed to adopt a perpetuity period of 100 years if the trust specifies a perpetuity period by reference to lives in being and if the trustees express (in their deed) their belief 'that it is difficult or not reasonably practicable for them to ascertain whether the lives have ended'. Apart from trusts falling within s. 12, the 2009 Act applies to all trusts taking effect on or after 6 April 2010, but not to any trusts effective before that date. The principal changes introduced by the 2009 Act can be summarized as follows:

1. The rule against perpetuities is restricted in its application to successive estates and interests in property and to powers of appointment, thereby restoring it to its original function. It ceases to apply to rights over property such as options, rights of pre-emption, and future easements. The rule will no longer apply to occupational pension schemes, personal pension schemes, and public service pension schemes.[124]

2. There is a single perpetuity period of 125 years and the principle of 'wait and see' applies to this period (which will apply regardless of any express provision to the contrary).

3. As detailed earlier, statutory restrictions on accumulations are repealed except in relation to charitable trusts (to which special considerations apply).[125]

The Law Commission did not propose any reform of the rule against inalienability of capital, preferring that reform of that rule should take place as part of a more comprehensive reform of the law relating to purpose trusts.

The good news of the Perpetuities and Accumulations Act 2009 is that all new trusts are subject to the simple 125-year period specified in the Act. The bad news is that for the time

---

[122] See *Re Tyler* [1891] 3 Ch 252 CA, considered in Chapter 3.
[123] See *Re Earl of Berkeley* [1968] Ch 744, CA, at 772E–F, *per* Harman LJ.
[124] Sections 2(4), 20(4). Witness the perpetuity problem that arose in relation to the pension fund in *Air Jamaica v. Charlton*, Chapter 5.   [125] Section 14.

being we have three rules of remoteness of vesting running concurrently (common law, 1964 Act, and 2009 Act), an outcome that the Law Commission acknowledges to be the price of reform.[126] It has been argued that the price is too high and that the best thing would be to abolish the rule altogether.[127]

Illegality

It is inconceivable that a court would ever recognize a trust established to advance a criminal purpose or a trust 'for the benefit of X on condition that X commits a crime', but, in certain circumstances, courts will even refuse to recognize a trust created for purposes falling short of 'criminal'. Thus a trust that prejudices the settlor's creditors, or which discourages a beneficiary from marrying, is illegal on grounds of public policy. Furthermore, in certain, quite limited, circumstances, courts will refuse to recognize trusts arising informally according to the usual rules of property law if the transactions from which they arise are 'tainted' with illegality. As we come to examine the range of circumstances in which express and non-express trusts will be void for illegality, we will see that the courts' concern is both to prevent the illegality per se, where possible, and also to avoid any impression that the law, through its system of property law and the courts, has indirectly assisted in the illegality.

Trusts contrary to the policy of insolvency law

When a trustee becomes insolvent, there is, in theory, no competition between the trustee's personal creditors and the beneficiaries of his trust: his personal creditors are interested in making a claim against the trustee's property, whereas the beneficiaries are only interested in recovering their own property from the trustee. In practice, however, competition between creditors and beneficiaries frequently arises precisely because the beneficiaries claim that assets in the possession of the insolvent trustee are assets of the trust, whereas the creditors claim that the assets are owned absolutely by the insolvent trustee and should therefore be available to satisfy his personal debts.[128] Nevertheless, it is because there is, *in theory*, no basic competition between trust beneficiaries and the creditors of an insolvent trustee that trusts are not automatically considered to be contrary to the policy of insolvency law.

The policy of insolvency law is essentially twofold. On the one hand, it is to bring the liability of an insolvent debtor to his creditors to an end, with a view to encouraging commerce: who would take on the risks of commerce if bankruptcy could never be

---

[126] Law Commission Report No. 251, *The Law of Trusts: The Rules against Perpetuities and Excessive Accumulations, 1998*, para. 1.20.

[127] See T. P. Gallanis 'The rule against perpetuities and the Law Commission's flawed philosophy' (2000) 59 CLJ 284.

[128] Trust Law Committee Consultation Paper: *Rights of Creditors Against Trustees and Trust Funds* (1997) (see D. Hayton, 'Rights of creditors against trustees and trust funds' (1997) 11 TLI 58 and 'Creditors' rights against trustees and trust funds' (1999) 6 Tru & ELJ 4–6).

discharged?[129] Finality of indebtedness also brings with it finality to civil dispute, which mirrors the concerns of statutes of limitation and the doctrine of laches.[130] The second is to ensure, so far as possible, that the debtor meets his personal liability to his creditors. The Insolvency Act 1986 gives effect to these policies by means of a statutory scheme for the distribution of the estate of an insolvent party amongst his creditors,[131] and any trust designed to evade the statutory scheme of distribution or otherwise undermine the policy of fairness between creditors and debtors will be *voidable*.[132] As Sir George Jessell MR stated in *Re Butterworth*:[133]

> a man is not entitled to go into a hazardous business, and immediately before doing so settle all his property voluntarily, the object being this: 'If I succeed in business, I make a fortune for myself. If I fail, I leave my creditors unpaid. They will bear the loss.'[134]

Butterworth, who was a baker, had tried to have his cake and eat it. Just prior to embarking upon new trade as a grocer, he had settled his assets on trust for his wife and children just in case his new business venture was unsuccessful. The settlement was voluntary: in other words, his wife and children gave nothing by way of legal consideration for it. In the event, Butterworth's grocery business failed, as he feared it might. The Master of the Rolls held that the settlement was void at common law as an illegal attempt to put property beyond the reach of creditors, but he and his fellow judges in the Court of Appeal agreed that Butterworth had, in fact, been technically bankrupt at the date of the settlement because he would have been unable to pay off all of his existing debts without recourse to the subject matter of the settlement. That being the case, the settlement was set aside on the straightforward basis that it infringed the Bankruptcy Act 1869. Statutory measures designed to prevent the employment of uses and trusts for the purpose of prejudicing creditors can, in fact, be found as far back as 1377.[135]

Today, a voluntary declaration of trust or any other 'transaction at an undervalue' will be voidable, whether or not the settlor was insolvent, if a substantial purpose of entering the transaction was to prejudice his creditors.[136] The 'purpose' of the transaction is all important, thus the transfer of the matrimonial home by a husband to his wife did not defraud his creditors where the facts showed that he intended the transaction to persuade his wife not to divorce him.[137] The court may, if it thinks fit, make an order restoring the position to what it was prior to the transaction and protecting the interests of victims of the transaction.[138] When a person is declared bankrupt, the trustee in

---

[129] A debtor is insolvent when it is unable to pay all of its debts as they fall due.   [130] See Chapter 13.

[131] The detail lies outside the scope of this book. See, generally, R. M. Goode, *Principles of Corporate Insolvency Law*, 2nd edn (London: Sweet & Maxwell, 1997).

[132] *British Eagle International Airlines Ltd v. Compagnie Nationale Air France* [1975] 1 WLR 758, HL.

[133] (1882) LR 19 Ch D 588.   [134] Ibid. at 598, applying *Mackay v. Douglas* (1872) LR 14 Eq 106.

[135] 50 Ed. 3, c.6.

[136] Insolvency Act 1986, s. 423(1)(a); *National Bank of Kuwait v. Menzies* [1994] 2 BCLC 306, CA; *IRC v. Hashmi* [2002] 2 BCLC 489, CA; *Beckenham MC Ltd v. Centralex Ltd* [2004] EWHC 1287 (Ch), (Transcript). See, generally, R. Parry (with H. Anderson), *Transaction Avoidance in Insolvencies* (Oxford: Oxford University Press, 2001).   [137] *Rubin v. Dweck* [2012] BPIR 854.

[138] Section 423(2); *Midland Bank plc v. Wyatt* [1997] 1 BCLC 242.

bankruptcy will seek to rescind transactions, where possible, whenever they prejudice the bankrupt's creditors. Two dubious species of transaction are 'preferences' (that is, intentional attempts by the bankrupt to prefer certain creditors ahead of others, intent being presumed where the preferred creditor is a person, such as a spouse, who has a particular connection to the bankrupt)[139] and 'transfers at an undervalue' (that is, the transfer of an asset for nothing or for substantially less than its market value or in consideration of entering into a marriage or civil partnership).[140] A preference (not being a transaction at an undervalue) is voidable if entered into within six months prior to bankruptcy.[141] Within two years prior to bankruptcy a transaction is voidable if it was a 'preference' conferred on a connected person (such as a spouse) or if it was a 'transfer at an undervalue'.[142] Beyond two years prior to bankruptcy, but still within five years prior to bankruptcy, a transfer at an undervalue is only voidable if the bankrupt person was already bankrupt at the date of the transaction, or if the transaction was a cause of their bankruptcy, or if the transaction was entered into with a non-employee associate (for example, a business partner) of the bankrupt.[143]

Before we conclude this section, it should be noted that, although some express private trusts are a threat to the policy of insolvency law, other trusts positively promote it as part of the very machinery of insolvency law. Thus, when a person is declared bankrupt, legal title to his property vests in a trustee in bankruptcy who holds the bankrupt's estate, apart from the bankrupt's basic necessities and assets personal to the bankrupt,[144] under a statutory trust for the benefit of the bankrupt's creditors.

Protective trusts

It has been said that protective trusts demonstrate '*the furthest extent to which English law will permit property to be denied to creditors*'.[145] Under a protective trust, the settlor grants the principal beneficiary a life interest in the trust fund that will end if a specified 'determining event' occurs. The standard determining event is the commission by the principal beneficiary of any transaction, such as 'an act of bankruptcy', that would require the trustees to pay the trust income to the principal beneficiary's trustee in bankruptcy, or any person other than the principal beneficiary. When a determining event occurs the protective trust requires the trustees thereafter to hold the fund on a discretionary trust to distribute the income at their discretion among the members of a specified class of beneficiaries. The principal beneficiary will very often be named as a member of that specified class, but because she will now have no vested entitlement to the trust income, it will not form part of her estate and her creditors will be unable to claim it from her. Of course, when she is eventually discharged from her bankruptcy, there will be nothing to deter the trustees from choosing to pay income to her at that time. The net result is that protective trusts protect the principal beneficiary from the

---

[139] Insolvency Act 1986, s. 340.   [140] Ibid. s. 339.   [141] Ibid. s. 341(2).   [142] Ibid.

[143] Ibid.

[144] Insolvency Act 1986, ss. 306, 436; *Ord v. Upton* [2000] Ch 352, CA. (Noted G. Watt (1999) 8(2) Nott LJ 89.)

[145] E. H. Burn, *Maudsley & Burn's Trusts and Trustees*, 5th edn (London: Butterworths, 1996) at 170.

consequences of her own folly or misfortune, and protect the trust fund from the claims of her creditors and other third parties. For this reason, protective trusts are subject to certain strict limits.

First, a life interest that is limited to take effect *until* bankruptcy will be valid, but a *condition* purporting to forfeit the life interest of the principal beneficiary in the event of her bankruptcy will be void.[146] The thinking behind this distinction is that a forfeiture for breach of a condition brings the life interest to a premature end, which smacks of a fraud on the creditors, whereas the termination of a determinable interest brings the life interest to an end at its natural time: it was never intended to last beyond a determining event. However, given that a life interest should, by definition, last 'for life', this theoretical distinction is a fine one, to say the least. The distinction is further blurred by the habitual use of the term 'forfeiture' to describe the termination of a life interest upon the occurrence of a determining event.[147] If it is true that the life interest has come to a natural end, why say it has been 'forfeited'? The term 'forfeiture' seems especially out of place when one considers that the person who suffers the 'forfeiture' is usually the person who gains most from the protective trust.

Second, a life interest conferred on the *settlor* and limited to take effect until the *settlor's* bankruptcy is void as an attempt to undermine the policy of insolvency law and will not bind the settlor's trustee in bankruptcy.[148]

Third, when a settlor creates a protective trust, its terms will be presumed to be those set out in s. 33 of the Trustee Act 1925 unless the instrument creating the trust makes express contrary provision.[149] Section 33 provides that the trust in favour of the principal beneficiary, whether for life or for a shorter specified period, will determine if an event occurs which would deprive the principal beneficiary of the right to receive the income from the fund. It further provides that, upon the determination of the principal trust, a discretionary trust will spring up for the benefit of the principal beneficiary and any spouse, child, and remoter issue (such as grandchildren) of the principal beneficiary. The section expressly provides that the trustees will not be '*liable to account for the exercise of such discretion*', so there is nothing to prevent them from paying all of the income to the principal beneficiary. However, if they were to bind themselves irrevocably to a policy of paying all of the income to the principal beneficiary throughout the remaining lifetime of the trust, they would be personally liable for having abdicated their discretion in breach of trust.[150]

Determining events

The principal beneficiary of a protective trust must be careful how she acts, for it is not only financial imprudence that may bring about the determination of her life interest.

---

[146] *Re Leach* [1912] 2 Ch 422.   [147] See, for example, *Gibbon v. Mitchell* [1990] 1 WLR 1304.
[148] *Re Burroughs-Fowler* [1916] 2 Ch 251.   [149] *Re Balfour's Settlement* [1938] 3 All ER 259.
[150] *Re Pauling's Settlement Trusts* [1964] Ch 303, CA.

In *Re Baring's Settlement Trusts*,[151] Mrs Baring had a protected life interest under a family settlement, but, when she absconded abroad with the children of the family and ignored a court order to return them to England, her husband obtained a further court order against her property. In the instant case, Morton J held that the court order against Mrs Baring's property had deprived her of her interest in the income (thereby determining her life interest under the protective trust), because the settlor of the protective trust had intended that her life interest should determine if ever Mrs Baring was no longer in a position to deal freely with the income from her life interest.

In *Gibbon v. Mitchell*,[152] Mr Gibbon had a life interest under a protective trust. On the advice of his accountants and solicitors, he executed a deed purporting to surrender his life interest in favour of his children. However, when it later became apparent that the true effect of the surrender had been to determine his life interest, so that it was no longer within his right to transfer it to his children, he applied to have the deed of surrender set aside. Millett J granted the application under the court's equitable jurisdiction to relieve against the consequences of mistake. The fiasco could have been avoided if at the outset Mr Gibbon had applied to court under the Variation of Trusts Act 1958 to have the trust varied in favour of his children.[153]

Asset protection trusts

It is not permitted to create a trust to protect one's own assets in the event of one's own insolvency, but it is permitted to employ a trust to protect another person's assets against the event of one's own insolvency[154] and to employ a trust to protect one's own assets against the event of another person's insolvency.[155] Legitimate assets protection trusts were considered earlier in this book.[156]

Abuse of a trust to conceal true ownership

The scope of this principle is debatable, because every trust has the effect of concealing true—that is, 'beneficial'—ownership. The maxim 'equity looks to substance and not form' is normally applied in order to recognize the existence of a trust behind formal legal title, but when equity looks to substance in this context, the result is to deny the existence of a trust for which there is no bona fide reason and the *form* of which has been used to conceal the true ownership position. Such unjustified concealment has been held to be '*an abuse of the forms of trust for the purpose of creating a reputation of ownership*'.[157] The difficulty of knowing where to draw the line as between an abuse and a legitimate use of the trust's inherent capacity for 'concealment' probably explains why HM Revenue and Customs has not made more use of this principle. Courts in the Family Division of the High Court have been willing to strike down trusts, especially

---

[151] [1940] Ch 737. [152] [1990] 3 All ER 338. [153] Section 1(1)(d). See Chapter 9.
[154] See *Re Kayford Ltd*, Chapter 3.
[155] See *Barclays Bank Ltd v. Quistclose Investments Ltd*, Chapters 2 and 5.
[156] Chapter 2. [157] *Great Western Rly Co v. Turner* (1872) LR 8 Ch App 149 at 154.

those established outside England and Wales, as 'shams' in order to treat the fund as wealth available for distribution between spouses on divorce. In one recent case, the judge sounded a note of caution against this trend, stressing that a purported trust must be scrutinized by the light of the governing law of property in the relevant jurisdiction.[158]

Trusts in restraint of marriage

'*Conditions in restraint of marriage are odious... They are contrary to sound policy*',[159] but conditions in restraint of marriage to a particular person or class of persons—such as marriage to Juliet Capulet, or to a Roman Catholic,[160] or to a 'Scotchman'[161]—are enforceable, although today they may fall foul of laws against discrimination.[162] A condition in restraint of marriage must be distinguished from trusts that create beneficial interests limited in time *until* marriage. It is contrary to public policy for a trust to provide that a beneficiary will forfeit his or her interest if he or she marries, but it is not contrary to public policy to confer the benefit of a trust on a person only for so long as he or she remains unmarried. In the days when the vast majority of women were financially dependent upon the wealth of fathers and husbands, a trust making provision for a woman until her marriage was not likely to be construed to have been an illegal attempt to discourage her from marrying.[163]

A condition in restraint of the *remarriage* of a beneficiary[164] is valid and, consistent with this, conditions that might encourage divorce or separation of husband and wife are void. Thus, in *Re Johnson's Wills Trust*,[165] a clause was declared void which provided that the beneficiary would receive more income from the fund if she split up from her husband. It had not been the testator's intention to promote divorce, but to make greater provision in the event of breakdown of the marriage. The judge held, nevertheless, that the clause might operate as an incentive to divorce or separation and must therefore be declared void. Any clause which might encourage the separation of a parent from their child is also void.[166]

Trusts void on grounds of discrimination

The basic presumption of the law is that an absolute owner is permitted to dispose of his property as he likes, but it is not always clear where the line should be drawn between legitimate private choice and illegal discrimination. Lord Wilberforce attempted to draw the line when he noted, in *Blathwayt v. Cawley*, that:

---

[158] *A v A and St George Trustees Ltd* [2007] EWHC 99 (Fam).
[159] *Per* Lord Mansfield in *Long v. Dennis* (1767) 4 Burr 2052 at 2055. See, generally, O. Browder, 'Conditions and limitations in restraint of marriage' (1941) 39 Mich LR 1288.
[160] *Duggan v. Kelly* (1848) 10 I Eq R 473; actually, the term 'papist' was used.
[161] *Perrin v. Lyon* (1807) 9 East 170.   [162] Discussed in the next section.
[163] See *Re Hewett* [1918] 1 Ch 458; *Re Elliott* [1918] 1 IR 41; *Re Lovell* [1920] 1 Ch 122; *Morley v. Rennoldson* (1843) 2 Hare 570.   [164] *Jordan v. Holkham* (1753) Amb 209.
[165] [1967] Ch 387.
[166] *Re Boulter* [1922] 1 Ch 75; *Borwick v. Borwick* [1933] Ch 657.

Discrimination is not the same thing as choice: it operates over a larger and less personal area, and neither by express provision nor by implication has private selection yet become a matter of public policy.[167]

The question whether a trust provision amounts to illegal discrimination is particularly problematic in the context of religious discrimination, which was Lord Wilberforce's immediate concern in *Blathwayt v. Cawley*. In that case, a clause of a testator's will provided that, in the event that one of the beneficiaries under his will should 'be or become a Roman Catholic...the estate hereby limited to him shall cease and determine and be utterly void'. It later transpired that a life tenant had indeed become a Roman Catholic. The judge at first instance held that his estate should be forfeit, a judgment that was ultimately upheld in the House of Lords. Lord Cross had this to say in relation to religious discrimination:

> it is true that it is widely thought nowadays that it is wrong for a government to treat some of its citizens less favourably than others because of differences in their religious beliefs; but it does not follow from that that it is against public policy for an adherent of one religion to distinguish in disposing of his property between adherents of his faith and those of another. So to hold would amount to saying that although it is in order for a man to have a mild preference for one religion as opposed to another it is disreputable for him to be convinced of the importance of holding true religious beliefs and of the fact that his religious beliefs are the true ones.[168]

Lord Cross's analysis seems to assume that religious affiliation or persuasion is a matter of personal choice, and that the choice to confer wealth on one religion over another is merely an extension of that choice. There is no doubt some merit in that argument, but there are also dangers. For one thing, some forms of religious affiliation—Judaism, for example—can only very loosely be said to be a matter of choice. For another, the conclusion that religious choice or discrimination is a good thing ought logically to lead to the conclusion that a trust condition that restricts the beneficiary's choice is a bad thing. Thus the decision in *Blathwayt* should be contrasted with the decision in the Canadian case of *Re Murley*,[169] in which a clause in a will making a son's inheritance conditional upon his remaining within an orthodox Christian denomination was struck down as being contrary to public policy.

Even if it could safely be concluded that a particular private selection were discriminatory,[170] there would remain the further vexed question of whether the court ought, in principle, to strike it out. In other words, the question arises to what extent a person

---

[167] [1976] AC 397, *per* Lord Wilberforce at 426C.   [168] Ibid. at 429–30.

[169] [1995] Newfoundland and Prince Edward Island Reports 271. The Canadian courts seem to take a bolder approach than the English courts. In another Canadian case, a charitable trust for scholars of the 'white race' was varied to remove the racist condition (see Chapter 7).

[170] The trust in *Re Gwyon* [1930] 1 Ch 255, which established a foundation to provide trousers to boys between the ages of 10 and 15 in a certain district, but which excluded any 'black boy' from benefiting, would nowadays be considered odious. Typical of the time, the judge made no adverse comment on the racist restriction in his judgment.

should be permitted to dispose of his property subject to restrictions and conditions that the general public, or significant sections of it, might consider to be odious or morally reprehensible. The kernel of the question is the extent to which private property is truly private. It might be thought that the European Convention on Human Rights (ECHR) would herald a solution to the dilemma between private dispositive choice and public discrimination, but, if anything, it compounds it. The Convention sets out a number of basic human rights and requires that public bodies[171] shall secure those rights 'without discrimination on any ground'.[172] However, one of the rights protected by the Convention is the citizen's right to the peaceful enjoyment of his possessions.[173] So if a trust were established for certain beneficiaries on condition that they abstain from joining a particular religious movement, and a court were to strike out the limitation, it would be a moot point whether the court had thereby acted consistent with the Convention or in conflict with it. It could even be argued, although it would be a harsh argument, that a volunteer beneficiary of a donor's bounty has the choice to take the gift subject to any conditions attached to it or to decline to take the gift at all—after all, the volunteer did not pay for the gift. A similar, and equally harsh, argument, based on a literal reading of the ECHR, would hold that the volunteer beneficiary who receives private property subject to certain conditions is free peacefully to enjoy her possessions in accordance with Art. 1 of Protocol 1, but that at the moment she breaches the conditions she no longer has possessions to which the right to peaceful enjoyment can attach. Against this, one would question how enjoyment of one's possessions could ever be truly peaceful if they were liable to be lost the moment one decided to change religion or marry someone of another faith.[174]

Charitable trusts present special difficulties in this context: to declare a charitable trust to be entirely void on grounds of discrimination might have the effect of denying funding to an otherwise worthy cause. The courts and Charity Commissioners therefore try, wherever possible, to give effect to the general charitable intention underlying a disposition, whilst removing any illegal or offensive discriminatory provision.[175]

Illegality and the presumption of resulting trust

This section continues to consider some of the themes and issues from the previous section, and, in particular, the question of the extent to which a person should be permitted to enjoy the usual rights of property ownership when their enjoyment is, in some way, tainted by illegality. In Chapter 5, we observed that, when an absolute owner

---

[171] Human Rights Act 1998, s. 8. The courts and Charity Commission are 'public bodies'.
[172] Article 14.   [173] Article 1 of the First Protocol.
[174] 'Conditions on testamentary gifts as a device of control' 36 (1936) Columbia LR 439 (an anonymous note); S. Grattan, 'Testamentary conditions in restraint of religion' in *Modern Studies in Property Law: Property 2000* (E. Cooke, ed.) (Oxford: Hart Publishing, 2001) vol. I at 257; (in the same volume) G. Watt, 'The frontiers of forfeiture: property rights and wrongs', 113 at 118, 125.
[175] See cy-près, Chapter 7.

of property attempts, but fails, to transfer the benefit of his property to another, the undisposed-of benefit will be held by the transferee on resulting trust for the transferor. The resulting trust arises because the very last thing the transferor would have intended is that the property should be declared ownerless and pass to the Crown as *bona vacantia*. He is presumed to have intended to retain or recover the benefit of his property in the event of failure to transfer the benefit as originally intended. The question that concerns us now is whether a transferor should still be permitted to benefit from a resulting trust under which the original transfer had been made in order to advance some illegal purpose.

This very question arose for consideration in *Tinsley v. Milligan*.[176] Tinsley and Milligan were two women who had purchased a house on the understanding that they would be joint beneficial owners, but they agreed that legal title should be vested in Tinsley's sole name. This was to enable them to defraud the Department of Social Security of certain welfare benefits. Subsequently, the relationship between Tinsley and Milligan broke down, and Tinsley left the premises. She then brought proceedings against Milligan claiming possession, and asserting sole legal and beneficial ownership. Milligan counterclaimed for an order for sale and for a declaration that Tinsley had held the property on trust for the two of them in equal shares. The judge held for Milligan, and Tinsley's appeals were dismissed in turn by a bare majority of the Court of Appeal and a bare majority of the House of Lords. At every stage, the case was argued on the assumption that Milligan's interest had arisen under a resulting trust of the sort that arises when two parties provide purchase money to buy a property that is conveyed into the name of one of them alone.[177] The equally plausible possibility that the defendant might actually be entitled under a constructive trust was never advanced.

Lord Browne-Wilkinson was with the majority in the House of Lords and Lord Goff was with the minority, so Lord Browne-Wilkinson agreed with the result in the Court of Appeal, whereas Lord Goff did not. Nevertheless, both their Lordships agreed that the majority in the Court of Appeal had been wrong to dispose of the case by asking whether the public conscience would be offended if the defendant succeeded in establishing an interest under a trust. Their Lordships agreed that a 'public conscience' test would require judges to exercise a broad, policy-based discretion that is inappropriate to the determination of property rights.[178] As to the correct approach to cases such as the present, both of their Lordships were again broadly in agreement that it would be wrong for courts to intervene in any active way to assist a litigant, such as the defendant, who had been party to a joint illegal venture. The basic principle, they agreed, was that parties should be left to their strict entitlement without any additional benefits that the

---

[176] [1994] 1 AC 340, HL.

[177] A so-called 'purchase money' resulting trust. See Chapter 5 and Chapter 8.

[178] For arguments that the public conscience test or some version of it would be an improvement on the present doctrinaire, and somewhat confused, state of the law, see J. E. Martin, 'Fraudulent transferors and the public conscience' [1992] Conv 153 and H. Davies, 'Presumptions and illegality' in A. J. Oakley (ed.), *Trends in Contemporary Trust Law* (Oxford: Clarendon Press, 1996) 33 at 36.

exercise of judicial discretion might bestow. The point on which their Lordships disagreed was that of their opinion as to which rights should be left undisturbed.

Lord Goff was of the opinion that *legal* entitlement should be left undisturbed— following Lord Chancellor Eldon's long-standing exhortation to 'let the estate lie where it falls'.[179] Applying that approach to the facts of *Tinsley v. Milligan* would have confirmed Tinsley's legal title unencumbered by the equitable interest claimed by Milligan. For Lord Goff, the defendant's claim to be entitled in equity ought to be denied, because she had not come to equity with clean hands; in contrast, Lord Browne-Wilkinson stressed that a transaction might have proprietary consequences in equity without the need to establish clean hands. His Lordship reasoned that the arrangement between the parties in *Tinsley v. Milligan* was of this sort: the defendant had acquired an interest under a resulting trust on the basis of legal presumptions that applied generally; the defendant had no particular need to rely on the court's assistance to establish her interest under the trust and she should therefore be allowed to take that to which she would have been entitled as against the claimant under the general law of property, quite regardless of the illegality of their joint design. Lord Browne-Wilkinson, together with the majority of their Lordships, applied the so-called '*Bowmaker* rule',[180] which provides that a party to a transaction tainted by illegality is entitled to that which the law would bestow on her in a similar case not tainted by illegality, provided that she, at no stage, pleads or relies upon the fact of her illegality.

It is submitted that the reasoning of Lord Browne-Wilkinson and the majority in *Tinsley* was basically correct, because it affirms the integrity of the system of property law by recognizing the substantial parity of legal and equitable rights. It is arguable, though, that, in *Tinsley*, Lord Browne-Wilkinson relied upon an automatic form of resulting trust of precisely the sort upon which he later cast doubt in the case of *Westdeutsche Landesbank Girozentrale*.[181]

The problem with Lord Goff's approach is that it borders on forfeiture: it is one thing to deny a person a property right because she has breached an agreement between the parties, such as an equitable estate contract; it is quite another thing to deny a person a proprietary right when the wrong has no relevance to the fair allocation of property rights *as between the parties*. Ever since the Dark Ages, the law has been reluctant to deprive persons of property in response to such 'independent' wrongs and has done so only in extreme cases, such as homicide, smuggling, and drugs offences. Even in such cases, the forfeiture has generally been limited to the fruits, or tools, of the offence.[182] Thus the principle, based in public policy,[183] that no court should lend its aid to a cause of action arising out of an illegal venture—as expressed in the maxim *ex turpi causa*

---

[179] *Muckleston v. Brown* (1801) 6 Ves 52 at 69; see *Sajan Singh v. Sardara Ali* [1960] AC 167, PC.

[180] See *Bowmakers Ltd v. Barnet Instruments Ltd* [1945] KB 65 at 65; *Barrett v. Barrett* [2008] EWHC 1061 (Ch); [2008] BPIR 817.   [181] [1996] AC 669. See Chapter 5.

[182] M. Levi, 'Taking the profit out of crime: the UK experience' (1997) 5(3) Eur J Crim, Cr L Cr J 228; G. Watt, 'The frontiers of forfeiture: property rights and wrongs' in *Modern Studies in Property Law: Property 2000* (E. Cooke, ed.) (Oxford: Hart Publishing, 2001) vol. I at 113.

[183] *Holman v. Johnson* (1775) 1 Cowp 341.

non oritur actio—should only exceptionally be applied to deny an otherwise legitimate proprietary claim:

> There are many cases which show that, when two persons agree together in a conspiracy to effect a fraudulent or illegal purpose—and one of them transfers property to the other in pursuance of the conspiracy—then, so soon as the contract is executed and the fraudulent or illegal purpose is achieved, the property (be it absolute or special) which has been transferred by the one to the other remains vested in the transferee, notwithstanding its illegal origin...the transferee, having got the property, can assert his title to it against all the world, not because he has any merit of his own, but because there is no one who can assert a better title to it. The court does not confiscate the property because of the illegality—it has no power to do so.[184]

Tinsley v. Milligan was followed in *Lowson v. Coombes*.[185] In *Lowson*, a married man bought a house with his mistress, but conveyed it into her sole name in order to prevent his wife from claiming his share of the house in matrimonial proceedings. The court declared that he was entitled under a resulting trust to a half-share of the house, because he had not needed to rely upon his illegal motive in order to establish his equitable interest. A husband who places property in the sole name of his wife in order to defraud his creditors may not be so fortunate, because, in such a case, the 'presumption of a resulting trust' may be displaced by the 'presumption of advancement'.[186] This occurred in *Tinker v. Tinker*,[187] in which a husband placed his house in his wife's sole name with a view to putting it beyond the reach of his trade creditors. The Divisional Court held that he had made a perfectly legal absolute gift to his wife. Had the husband and wife still been together, that result might have been ideal, but, unfortunately for the husband, he and his wife had separated and, as a result, the husband lost his beneficial interest in the house. To prove that he had not intended to make a gift to his wife (to rebut the presumption of advancement), the husband would have been obliged to rely upon evidence of his illegal plan to defraud his creditors; this he was not permitted to do. The father in *Collier v. Collier*[188] suffered the same fate as the husband in *Tinker* and for the same reason. The father had granted his daughter a lease with an option to purchase the freehold. She exercised that option and sought to take possession of the freehold from her father. The judge held that, although the daughter knew that she had not received the property by way of gift, but on trust, the trust was unenforceable because it had been established for the illegal purpose of defrauding the father's creditors.

Tinker demonstrates that the so-called 'reliance principle'—the principle that illegality is only relevant if it is relied upon in evidence—can sometimes have an arbitrary and unfair impact upon different parties. Property law automatically grants rights to wives in circumstances in which the same rights would be denied to husbands, with the result that husbands may be forced, in an attempt to establish a right, to refer to evidence that wives in the same circumstances would have no need to raise. The Law Commission recommended that the 'reliance principle' should be abolished and replaced with a broad judicial discretion to decide on a case-by-case basis whether illegality should displace the

---

[184] *Sajan Singh v. Sardara Ali* [1960] AC 167 at 176, PC.   [185] [1999] 3 WLR 720.
[186] See Chapter 5.   [187] [1970] P 136.   [188] [2002] BPIR 1057.

application of general trust principles,[189] but in March 2012 the government declared that it intends not to adopt the Law Commission's proposed reforms and the Commission's website now admits that it no longer considers the proposals to be 'sufficient'.

The abolition of the presumption of advancement by s. 199 of the Equality Act 2010 will improve matters.[190] It is unfairness inherent in that presumption, rather than any flaw in the reliance principle itself, which produces cases like *Tinker*.

Having said that, it might be argued that the reliance principle is too generous to the wrongdoer when it allows the wrongdoer to rely upon evidence of his own illegal design where no part of that design actually came to fruition.[191] The rationale for the exception is that it encourages wrongdoers to repent of their illegal plans before carrying them out. This is the so-called principle of *locus poenitentiae*. According to Millett LJ (as he then was) in *Tribe v. Tribe*:[192]

> if the policy which underlies the primary rule is to discourage fraud, the policy which underlies the exception must be taken to be to encourage withdrawal from a proposed fraud before it is implemented, an end which is no less desirable.[193]

It is said that *locus poenitentiae* will not be available to assist a claimant whose illegal purpose is frustrated by factors unrelated to his own conduct.[194] Thus in *Patel v. Mirza* the claimant failed to recover monies paid to a broker under a transaction that was declared criminal on account of 'insider dealing'.[195] Nevertheless, the problem with the *locus poenitentiae* exception is that it comes to the aid of those who attempt illegality, but do not succeed, and those who have no intention of repenting from their illegal design, but find that they no longer have any need to carry it through. *Tribe v. Tribe* was itself a case falling in the latter category.[196] A father transferred shares in 'his' company to his son for a sham consideration at a time when the company was threatened with insolvency. If the company had actually become insolvent, the transfer by the father would have been an illegal attempt to defraud the company's creditors. However, in the event, the company did not become insolvent and the father was permitted to recover the shares under a resulting trust. This was despite the fact that the father had to rely upon evidence of his own illegal design in order to rebut the 'presumption of advancement' that he had made an absolute gift to his son. It is not sufficient for a claimant in the father's position merely to 'hint' that he had been involved in an illegal transaction; he must '*plead . . . and prove . . . a proper ground for rebutting the presumption*'.[197] Thus if

> a defendant means to say that he claims to hold property given to him for an immoral purpose . . . he must say so in plain terms, and must clearly put forward his own scoundrelism if he means to reap the benefit of it.[198]

---

[189] *Illegal Transactions: The Effect of Illegality on Contracts and Trusts*, Law Commission Consultation Paper No. 154, January 1999.   [190] See Chapter 5.

[191] Although the opportunity to repent of a transaction is lost if the other party acts to their detriment in reliance on it (*Q v. Q* [2008] EWHC 1874 (Fam). Noted Pawlowski (2009) Conv 145).

[192] [1995] 3 WLR 913, CA.   [193] Ibid. at 937E.

[194] *Bigos v. Bousted* [1951] 1 All ER 92.   [195] [2013] EWHC 1892 (Ch) (this case is pending appeal).

[196] Another is *Rowan v. Dann* (1991) 64 P & CR 202.

[197] R. E. Megarry (1962) 78 LQR 171 (a note) cited in J. E. Martin 'Fraudulent transferors and the public conscience' [1992] Conv 153.   [198] *Haigh v. Kaye* (1871–2) LR 7 Ch App 469 at 473.

Tribe v. Tribe illustrates how difficult it is in these cases to maintain public, symbolic justice—the idea that wrongdoers should not be permitted to take advantage of property law for their own illegal ends—without creating injustice *inter partes*. In *Tribe v. Tribe*, justice would have been ill served by leaving the property in the hands of a son who was fully aware both of his father's intention one day to recover the shares and of the illegality of his father's design.

Further reading

In addition to the following print sources, the Online Resource Centre accompanying this book contains web links to further reading as well as guide answers to assessment questions relevant to this chapter.

BAKER, P. V., (1958) 74 LQR 180 (untitled note on *Grey v. IRC* [1960] AC 1, HL).

BOUGHEN, G., 'Mutual wills' [1951] Conv 28.

BROWDER, O., 'Conditions and limitations in restraint of marriage' (1941) 39 Mich LR 1288.

ENONCHONG, N., 'Title claims and illegal transactions' (1995) 111 LQR 135.

GLISTER, J., 'The Presumption of Advancement' in C Mitchell (ed), *Constructive and Resulting Trusts* (Oxford: Hart Publishing, 2010) 289.

GRATTAN, S., 'Mutual wills and remarriage' [1997] Conv 153.

GRATTAN, S. and CONWAY, H., 'Testamentary conditions in restraint of religion in the twenty-first century: an Anglo-Canadian perspective' (2005) 50 McGill LJ 511.

GREEN, B., '*Grey*, *Oughtred* and *Vandervell*: a contextual reappraisal' (1984) 47 MLR 385.

LINCAID, D., 'The tangled web: the relationship between a secret trust and the will' [2000] Conv 420.

MEE, J., 'Half-secret trusts in England and Ireland' [1992] Conv 202.

NORRIS, A. and LEGGE, H., 'Contract and conscience: the decline of the mutual will' (1998) 6 PCB 332.

PARRY, R., AYLIFFE J. and SHIVJI, S., (with ANDERSON, H. and TROWER, W.), *Transaction Avoidance in Insolvencies* 2nd edn (Oxford: Oxford University Press, 2011).

QUINT, F., 'The Perpetuities and Accumulations Bill: Clarity or Confusion?" [2009] PCB 126.

RICKETT, C., 'Mutual wills and the law of restitution' (1989) 105 LQR 534.

SAMET, I., 'Repentance, Withdrawal and Luck' in C. Mitchell (ed.), *Constructive and Resulting Trusts* (Oxford: Hart Publishing, 2010) 335.

7

Charity: trust creation
and public policy II

This is the second of two chapters focusing upon particular ways in which the creation of trusts is influenced by special considerations of public policy. In the first of these chapters, we examined formality and perpetuity rules, which are policy-based, predominantly statutory, restrictions on property owners' freedom of disposition. We also identified circumstances in which the usual rules of property law, including the law of trusts, are displaced on account of the illegal nature of a transaction or disposition. In this chapter, we will be looking at charity, which, in a sense, is the direct opposite of illegality: illegality is detrimental to the public; charity is beneficial to the public. Illegality will sometimes render an interest or transaction void or unenforceable that the law of trusts and gifts would generally consider to be valid. Charity, on the other hand, will render a purpose trust valid that the law of trusts would generally consider to be void.

Given that charity and illegality are, in this sense, opposites, we should not be surprised that the law in both contexts occasionally seems to advance identical notions of the 'public interest'—thus a trust tending to discourage membership of the armed forces is void for illegality,[1] whereas a trust to promote the well-being of members of the armed forces is charitable. Yet, despite examples such as this, it is hard to discern across the two contexts any clear consensus as to what is and what is not beneficial to the public. In fact, it is hard to imagine any concept less susceptible to precise definition and more amenable to abuse than 'public benefit', and yet this is, as we will see, the founding concept upon which the entire law of charity is built.

Having considered the creation of charitable trusts, this chapter will conclude by considering their variation in accordance with the 'cy-près' doctrine (a topic that should be considered alongside Chapter 9, in which we consider 'the flexibility of benefit' in private trusts). The term 'cy-près' derives from the French for 'as near as' and, in simple terms, the doctrine provides that, in any case in which assets are dedicated to charitable purposes that are, or become, incapable of being properly fulfilled, or are fulfilled leaving surplus funds, the benefit of the assets will be applied to advance charitable purposes approximating those originally intended.

---

[1] *Re Beard* [1908] 1 Ch 383.

Charitable trusts

At the start of every new topic, it is useful to pause to reflect. When it comes to a chapter on charity, it is more important than ever. Charity is a big idea; it has the potential to be the greatest of ideas. The word is, after all, a direct descendant of the Latin word '*caritas*', meaning 'love'. Unfortunately, the law has not lived up to the potential of the word. As Lord Macnaghten once stated:

> Of all the words in the English language bearing a popular as well as a legal signification I am not sure that there is one which more unmistakably has a technical meaning in the strictest sense of term, that is a meaning clear and distinct, peculiar to the law as understood and administered in this country, and not depending upon or coterminous with the popular or vulgar use of the word.[2]

Without decrying the humanitarian work of the armed forces, the point is born out by the fact that a non-profit trust to supply provisions to the British Army will almost certainly be charitable, whereas a trust to campaign for unilateral nuclear disarmament will certainly not be. The words 'charity' and 'charitable' are:

> technical words in English law and must be so construed unless it can be seen from the wording of the will as a whole that they are used in some other than their technical sense.[3]

In an appeal against a decision of the Commissioners for Her Majesty's Revenue & Customs, the Special Commissioner praised the appellants for their 'selfless generosity' in making payments to support their local amateur football club, but held that those payments had not been payments to charity and were not tax exempt.[4] We should not be surprised that, in law, the word 'charity' is a good deal removed from love, but, in life, the connection is apparently still strong. The UK public has supported a number of high-profile charitable fund-raising initiatives over the years, including Live Aid in 1985 and Comic Relief's 'Red Nose Day', which has run every year since then.[5] If that gives cause for self-satisfaction, it might surprise us to discover that we still lag far behind our US friends when it comes to charitable giving.[6]

Charitable trusts are, in many respects, fundamentally different from private trusts,[7] with the result that it is often unhelpful to apply principles derived from the law of private trusts to the law of charitable trusts, and vice versa.[8] One commentator has even suggested that it is purely an '*historical accident that the Court of Chancery hijacked the*

---

[2] *Commissioners for Special Purpose of the Income Tax v. Pemsel* [1891] AC 531 at 581–2.

[3] *Chichester Diocesan Fund and Board of Finance v. Simpson* [1944] AC 341 *per* Lord Porter at 363.

[4] *Simpson (Trustee of the East Berkshire Sports Foundation) v. The Commissioners for Her Majesty's Revenue & Customs*, 19 January 2009; [2009] STC(SCD) 226.

[5] According to the Charity Commission there are currently around 250,000 registered charities in England and Wales, having a combined income of more than £53 billion and combined investments exceeding £77 billion.

[6] Sir Philip Christopher Ondaatje, OC, CBE, 'Giving it all away', *New Statesman*, 15 January 2007. Sir Philip is a noted philanthropist (an entire new wing of the National Portrait Gallery was been named after his family).

[7] *Gaudiya Mission v. Brahmachary* [1997] 4 All ER 957, *per* Mummery LJ at 963.

[8] J. Warburton, 'Charitable trusts:—unique' (1999) Conv 20.

charitable gift and squeezed it (with some difficulty) into the pre-existing framework of the trust.[9] Certainly, many charities nowadays prefer to advance their objects as companies limited by guarantee rather than to pursue their purposes as trusts.[10] Nevertheless, it is useful to study charitable trusts, because they exemplify the great flexibility and utility of the trust concept, and they demonstrate a unique relationship between private property and the public interest. Even if charitable trusts were not a useful thing to study, they would be a worthy object for scholarship, if only because of the fascinating insights that the cases provide into the diversity of human social life: from the relief of poverty to advancement of the arts; from religion to sport.

Before proceeding further in this chapter, the reader is alerted to the fact that the Charities Act 2011 received royal assent on 14 December 2011 and came into effect on 14 March 2012. The 2011 Act is a consolidating statute which brings the Charities Acts 1993 and 2006 and the Recreational Charities Act 1958 under one new title without changing the substance of the law in any significant way. Given the recent date of this change and in the interests of cross-referencing between this text and reported case law, references to corresponding parts of repealed statutes are sometimes retained in parenthesis where reference is made to the 2011 Act.

The special status of charitable trusts

Charitable trusts are exempt from many of the usual rules governing the creation and operation of private trusts. They are, however, subject to a regulatory scheme to which private trusts are not subject. So, for example, charity trustees are required to register the charity,[11] to keep accounts in a form appropriate to the size of the charity,[12] and to prepare an annual report.[13] Charitable trusts are also treated a good deal more favourably than private trusts for the purposes of tax law, as we shall shortly see.

The exclusivity requirement

To qualify for special treatment, a trust must be exclusively charitable both with regard to its stated purposes and in the practical pursuit of those purposes. Section 1(1)(a) of the Charities Act 2011 retains this rule by stating that a body or trust is a charity if it is established for charitable purposes '*only*'. Whether trust purposes are exclusively charitable is a question of construction. It has been held that:

> [i]n construing trust deeds the intention of which is to set up a charitable trust . . . where it can be claimed that there is ambiguity, a benignant construction should be given if possible.[14]

---

[9] P. Matthews, 'The new trust: obligations without rights?' in *Trends in Contemporary Trust Law* (A. J. Oakley, ed.) (Oxford: Clarendon Press, 1996) 1 at 4–5.

[10] Law Commission, *Charities: A Framework for the Future* (1989) Cm. 694 at 3.

[11] Charities Act 2011, Part 4 (Charities Act 1993, s. 3), subject to certain exceptions.

[12] Charities Ac 2011, Part 8 (Charities Act 1993, ss. 41–4).

[13] Charities Act 2011, Part 8, Chapter 4 (Charities Act 1993, s. 45).

[14] *IRC v. McMullen* [1981] AC 1, *per* Lord Hailsham of St Marylebone at 14. See also *Weir v. Crum-Brown* [1908] AC 162, *per* Lord Loreburn at 167: '*there is no better rule than that a benignant construction will be placed upon charitable bequests*'.

Thus a trust for 'charitable *and* benevolent' objects is exclusively charitable,[15] even though the term 'benevolent' has an uncertain meaning in law. A trust for 'charitable *or* benevolent' objects, on the other hand, is not exclusively charitable and will therefore fail for uncertainty.[16] A trust provision effective before 16 December 1952 that could properly be construed as being for exclusively charitable purposes, but which could nevertheless be used for non-charitable purposes, will be considered valid *to the extent* that it authorizes the use of trust property for charitable purposes.[17] A trust will also be valid if the wording of the trust permits the severance of the charitable objects from any non-charitable objects.[18]

A charity is permitted to pursue non-charitable purposes that are merely ancillary to, incidental to, or *de minimis* in comparison with, its charitable purposes. Thus, in *Re Coxen*,[19] the testator gave the residue of his estate—some £200,000—to the Court of Aldermen of the City of London upon trust: to spend £100 towards an annual dinner for the aldermen upon their meeting together on trust business; to pay one guinea to each alderman attending the whole of a committee meeting in connection with the trust; to apply the remainder for the benefit of certain medical charities. It was held that all of the trusts were valid charitable trusts, because the provisions in favour of the aldermen personally were made to ensure the better administration of the main charitable trusts. It was held, in any event, that even if those provisions had not been charitable per se, the sums involved were so insignificant in comparison with that part of the fund devoted to the medical charities that the provisions for the benefit of the aldermen personally could be seen as merely ancillary to the principal trust and would take effect on that basis. A charity is permitted to charge for its services as long as it is not in the business of making commercial profits.[20] A commercial venture run for the primary purpose of making profits is not charitable, even though it may well be highly beneficial to the community.[21]

If a trust established for a certain class of people does not specify any purpose, the courts may construe it to be for purely charitable purposes. This occurred in *Re Harding*,[22] where Lewison J held that a trust 'for the black community of Hackney, Haringey, Islington and Tower Hamlets' was held to be charitable. The judge was content for the precise purposes to which the money should be applied to be determined by a charitable scheme settled on by the trustees. (Incidentally, the limitation in favour of the 'black community' was struck out as being in breach of s. 34(1) of the Race Relations Act 1976.)

---

[15] *Re Best* [1904] 2 Ch 354.

[16] *Chichester Diocesan Fund and Board of Finance (Incorporated) v. Simpson* [1944] 2 All ER 60, HL. *Morice v. Bishop of Durham* [1803–13] All ER Rep 451, CA, *per* Sir William Grant MR.

[17] Charitable Trusts (Validation) Act 1954, s. 1(2).   [18] *Salusbury v. Denton* (1857) 3 K & J 529.

[19] [1948] Ch 747.

[20] *Scottish Burial Reform and Cremation Society Ltd v. Glasgow Corporation* [1968] AC 138, HL; *IRC v. Falkirk Temperance Café Trust*, 1927 SC 261. Lord Wilberforce reached the same conclusion in relation to a private hospital in *Re Resch's Will Trusts* [1969] 1 AC 514.   [21] Goodman Committee (1976) at para. 27.

[22] [2008] Ch 235.

Special status in trust law

We have already seen that a benignant construction is applied to charitable bequests; in fact, it has been held that a trust which is certainly dedicated to charitable purposes will be valid even if its terms are otherwise vague or uncertain.[23] Charitable trusts are also exempt from the beneficiary principle, because the beneficiary of a charitable trust is the public at large, or a section of it, so it falls to the Charity Commissioners to ensure that the trustees discharge their trust.[24] Charities are also exempt from the rule against inalienability of capital: it is permissible to render trust capital inalienable in perpetuity provided that the trust income is dedicated to charitable purposes and is actually applied to charitable purposes within the perpetuity period. Of course, the fact that there are no beneficiaries and that trust capital may be rendered inalienable are essentially two sides of the same coin, because only competent adult beneficiaries can agree to bring a trust to an end under the rule in *Saunders v. Vautier*. Charitable trusts are different from private trusts not only in their creation and operation, but also in the manner of their termination. If a charitable trust fails, the fund will not return to the settlor under a resulting trust and it will not pass to the Crown as *bona vacantia*; it will be applied cy-près by the court or the Charity Commissioners to charitable purposes as near as possible in kind to the charitable purposes specified by the settlor. We will consider the cy-près doctrine in more depth later in this chapter.

Special status for tax

Charities are exempt from income tax and corporation tax on income from land, investments, and certain other sources.[25] Charities are also exempt from capital gains tax on gains applied exclusively for charitable purposes;[26] donors to charities are exempt from capital gains tax[27] and inheritance tax[28] on their donation, and, since 6 April 2000, can claim income tax on most donations (called 'gift aid' donations) of any value.[29] Charities can reclaim income tax on 'gift aid' payments. Transfers by charities are exempt from stamp duty.[30] Charities have to pay a maximum of 20 per cent of their non-domestic rates, but may be required to pay less, at the discretion of the local authority.[31]

The various tax benefits of charitable status have prompted the suggestion that a cost–benefit calculation should be carried out before charitable status is granted.[32] If such an

---

[23] *Chichester Diocesan Fund and Board of Finance v. Simpson* [1944] AC 341, *per* Viscount Simon LC at 348.

[24] Although they are not public institutions, charities are subject to the constitutional *protection* of the Crown as *parens patriae* (acting through the Attorney General), to the *supervision* of the Charity Commissioners, and to judicial *control*.

[25] Income and Corporation Taxes Act 1988, s. 505. For general information about the tax position of charities or reliefs for charitable giving, see HM Revenue and Custom's website (www.hmrc.gov.uk).

[26] Taxation of Chargeable Gains Act 1992, s. 256.

[27] Ibid. s. 257, as amended by Finance Act 1995, s. 72(5).

[28] Inheritance Tax Act 1984, ss. 23, 76, as amended by Finance Act 1998, s. 143(2)(a), (4)(c).

[29] Finance Act 1990, s. 25(1) and (2), as amended by Finance (No. 2) Act 2005, s. 11(1), subject to the Gift Aid Regulations (Donations to Charity by Individuals (Appropriate Declarations) Regulations (SI 2000, No. 2074)).

[30] If made after 22 March 1982: Finance Act 1982, s. 129, as amended by Finance Act 1999, Sch. 14, para. 7.

[31] Local Government Finance Act 1988, ss. 43, 47.

[32] Lord Cross in *Dingle v. Turner* [1972] AC 601.

approach were adopted, a purpose would only be regarded as charitable if it conferred a public benefit sufficiently great to justify fiscal immunity, but if such a process were to occur, it might be '*constitutionally inappropriate for the judges and Charity Commissioners to carry it out*'.[33] In any event, it would undoubtedly be a calculation of great complexity. Lord Cross has held that '*in deciding that such and such a trust is a charitable trust the court is endowing it with a substantial annual subsidy at the expense of the taxpayer*',[34] but it cannot be assumed that gains made by charities due to fiscal immunity are as great as the losses suffered by HM Revenue and Customs as a result of that privilege. To use the economists' term, it is not a 'zero-sum game'. The fiscal privilege of charitable status may itself influence the size and frequency of donations made to a charity, thus the calculation is an impracticably complex one even before an attempt has been made to quantify the benefit to the public of such charitable purposes as research into a cure for cancer, education in the arts, and the advancement of religion. The cost–benefit debate is currently a hot political topic for independent fee-charging schools.[35]

Charitable purposes

The definition of charitable purposes in the Charities Act 2011, s.1 (Charities Act 2006, s.1) is rather circular: 'charity' means '*an institution which is established for charitable purposes only*' and is '*subject to the control of the High Court in the exercise of its jurisdiction with respect to charities*'. The definition provides that a purpose is charitable if it satisfies two criteria: that it comes under one of the 'heads' of charity listed in the statute and that it is for the public benefit.[36]

The long list of 'heads', or categories, of charitable purpose which are now set down in statute are, despite their open-endedness, more useful than the list which was previously relied upon. Before the Charities Act 2006, 'charitable purposes' were those that the Preamble to the Charitable Uses Act 1601—the so-called 'Statute of Elizabeth'[37]— enumerated, or which 'by analogies' were deemed 'within its spirit and intendment'.[38] Although charitable purposes were recognized before 1601, the Preamble to the statute contains a list of charitable purposes '*so varied and comprehensive that it became the practice of the court* [of Chancery] *to refer to it as a sort of index or chart*'.[39] It includes:

> Relief of aged, impotent and poor People...the Maintenance of sick and maimed Soldiers and Mariners, Schools of Learning, Free Schools, and Scholars in Universities...the Repair of Bridges, Ports, Havens, Causeways, Churches, Sea-Banks and Highways,...the

---

[33] S. Gardner, *An Introduction to the Law of Trusts* (Oxford: Clarendon Press, 1990) at 105.

[34] *Dingle v. Turner* [1972] AC 601 at 624F. His Lordship approved the suggestion of the *Radcliffe Commission on Taxation* (1955) Cmd. 9474 that a distinction should be drawn between charities that merely confer a public benefit sufficient to deserve recognition as a charity in law and those that confer a public benefit sufficient to attract fiscal privileges.   [35] See later.

[36] Charities Act 2011, s. 2(1) (Charities Act 2006, s. 2(1)).   [37] 43 Eliz. 1, c.4.

[38] Sir William Grant MR, *Morice v. Bishop of Durham* (1804) 9 Ves 399 at 405.

[39] *Income Tax Commissioners v. Pemsel* [1891] AC 531, *per* Lord Macnaghten at 581.

Education and Preferment of Orphans,...Relief, Stock or Maintenance for Houses of Correction,...the Marriages of Poor Maids...Supportation, Aid and Help of young Tradesmen, Handicraftsmen and Persons decayed,...the Relief or Redemption of Prisoners or Captives, and for Aid or Ease of any poor Inhabitants concerning...setting out of Soldiers and other Taxes.[40]

Charitable purposes and the public benefit—introduction

We can hypothezise that the purposes that the law regards as charitable are, or are analogous to, purposes that might otherwise fall to be met out of public funds.[41] It rather confirms this that the Charity Commission has stated that charity funds should not be applied to replace assistance that is already being provided by the state.[42] The authorities rarely acknowledge that the legal concept of 'charitable purpose' is shorthand for 'saves public money', but, in essence, that is what it appears to mean. It is certainly difficult to make systematic sense of the legal definition of public benefit.[43] The proper interpretation of 'public benefit' ought, one might think, have been left to the courts, but s. 4 of the 2006 Act mandated the Charity Commission for England and Wales to issue (and, from time to time revise) guidance as to the meaning of public benefit '*after such public and other consultation as it considers appropriate*'. The trustees of a charity must have regard to any such guidance when exercising any powers or duties to which the guidance is relevant.[44]

According to the Charity Commission's 2013 official guidance on public benefit,[45] for a purpose to be 'for the public benefit' it must generally satisfy both the 'benefit' and 'public' aspects. The exception is if the purpose is to relieve or prevent poverty, where different rules apply.[46] The Commission explains that in order to satisfy the 'benefit aspect' of public benefit, the purpose must be 'beneficial' and 'any detriment or harm that results from the purpose must not outweigh the benefit'. To satisfy the 'public aspect' of public benefit, the purpose must 'benefit the public in general, or a sufficient section of the public' and 'not give rise to more than incidental personal benefit'. The Commission acknowledges that the 'benefit' and 'public' aspects can overlap, and warns that where a charity has more than one purpose, the public benefit of one purpose 'cannot be used to offset any lack of public benefit in another'. To satisfy the 'beneficial'

---

[40] Recited in Mortmain and Charitable Uses Act 1888, s. 13(2).

[41] Subject to what is said later about trusts for the advancement of religion.

[42] Charity Commission Leaflet CC4, August 2001, para. 17.

[43] But see Jonathan Garton, *Public Benefit in Charity Law* (Oxford: Oxford University Press, 2013) who argues that it is possible to identify four discrete elements within the assessment of public benefit. In broad terms: the public benefit inherent in the categories ('heads') of charity; the extent to which individual would-be charities can demonstrate sufficient direct and tangible benefit; the extent to which those benefits are open to a sufficient section of the community; and, the restriction of private benefits to those that are merely incidental.

[44] Section 4(6).

[45] The Charity Commission, *Public benefit: the public benefit requirement (PB1)* (London: Crown Copyright, 2013) (available free online).   [46] See later.

requirement of the 'benefit aspect', the beneficial aspect must be identifiable and 'capable of being proved by evidence where necessary' and 'not based on personal views'. The Commission gives the example of emergency aid in response to natural disaster as one where the beneficial element is objectively self-evident and will not need to be proved. The artistic merit of paintings or the health benefits of a therapy, for example, are not objectively self-evident in that sense. Objective evidence of the detrimental effects of a purpose can outweigh its beneficial aspect, but where the benefit is clearly strong it will take especially strong evidence of detriment to outweigh it. In short, there seems to be a presumption in favour of supporting benefits in the face of possible detriment.

Under the 'public aspect' of public benefit, the requirement of benefit to the public in general is self-explanatory (it would include, for example, the benefit of protecting an endangered species), but the alternative requirement of benefiting 'a sufficient section of the public' (also called a 'public class' of people) requires more explanation. People in a certain area or belonging to a certain community will generally be a 'public class' of people. More controversially, so are charities to benefit people defined by reference to a 'protected characteristic' under the Equality Act 2010. Thus a 'public class' may be identified by age, disability, sex, sexual orientation, gender reassignment, marriage and civil partnership, pregnancy and maternity, race or nationality (but not skin colour), religion or belief, 'provided the restriction of benefits to people having that characteristic is justified in relation to the purpose'. The question of what is and is not 'justified' promises to be hotly disputed in future cases. Instinctively one senses that minority groups require more charitable assistance than majority groups, but majority groups will clearly find it easier to prove that they are a 'sufficient section of the public'. Having said that, instinct can be misleading. The fact is that minority size may not be a sound indicator of charitable need. For example, the people who enact, enforce, and administer the laws of the land are a minority group, but a very powerful one. A particular profession (such as lawyers) may constitute a 'public class' as might a group connected by employment status (for example, 'the unemployed'), but generally speaking a 'public class' cannot comprise persons connected to each other by family relationship, employment by a particular employer, or through membership of an unincorporated association (for example a club or social society). Would a trust for the UK legal profession be charitable, given that all solicitors and barristers are members of the Law Society or one of the Inns of Court? The big exception to the limitation based on particular relationship is trusts for the relief or prevention of poverty.[47] Correspondingly, a trust that excludes the poor from benefiting will not be for a 'sufficient section of the public'. Other trusts that will not be for a 'sufficient section of the public' will be determined on a case-by-case basis, but according to the Commission's guidance they will include the following: 'a purpose which is confined to a closed religious organisation'; 'a purpose where all the

---

[47] *Attorney General v. Charity Commission* Upper Tribunal (Tax And Chancery Chamber) FTC/84/2011 (20 February 2012) paras [22], [35]. Applying *R (on the application of Independent Schools Council) v. Charity Commission for England and Wales* [2011] UKUT 421 (TCC); [2012] 2 WLR 100.

potential beneficiaries (now and in the future) are named, such as an individual or individuals or a fixed group of individuals'; 'a purpose where the number of people who can benefit (now and in the future) is numerically negligible (unless the purpose is for the relief, and in some cases the prevention, of poverty)'; 'a purpose which defines who can benefit in a manner which, when related to the purpose, is "capricious" (eg wholly irrelevant, irrational or without good reason)'; 'a purpose which benefits members of a mutual benefit society'; '(unless the purpose is for the relief, and in some cases the prevention, of poverty) a purpose which exists for the benefit of an organisation's members only unless: a sufficient section of the public can access those benefits by becoming members and the membership is a suitable way of carrying out the charity's purpose for the public benefit'.

Finally, a charitable purpose may only confer personal benefits if these are 'incidental' to carrying out the purpose.[48] This sounds uncontroversial in theory, but in practice one of the great controversies of charity law is that people employed by charities, especially at the executive level of large charities, frequently receive very large personal remuneration from the charities they manage.

The heads of charity

The absence of any comprehensive statutory definition of the concepts 'charity' and 'charitable'[49] has required the courts and Charity Commissioners to develop the concepts, within certain broad guidelines, on a case-by-case basis. According to Lord Simonds, 'the law of charity . . . has been built up not logically but empirically'.[50] The result is a vast body of case law, built upon a fairly meagre skeleton of principle. The law of charities is encyclopaedic and there are, indeed, several textbooks devoted solely to its study.[51] This is not the place for another encyclopaedia on charitable trusts, so the approach adopted here is to identify the kernel of the law of charitable trusts as it relates to the main heads of charity.

In *Commissioners for Special Purpose of the Income Tax v. Pemsel*,[52] Lord Macnaghten suggested that every charitable purpose can be classified under one of four heads: trusts for the relief of poverty; trusts for the advancement of education; trusts for the advancement of religion; trusts for other purposes beneficial to the community not falling under any of the preceding heads.[53] This classification has been very influential on judges and

---

[48] The Charity Commision, *Public benefit: the public benefit requirement (PB1)* (London: Crown Copyright, 2013) part 6.

[49] The Charities Act 1993 merely defined a charity as an institution established 'for charitable purposes' (s. 96(1)) and charitable purposes as purposes that are *exclusively charitable according to the law of England and Wales*' (s. 97(1)).   [50] *Gilmour v. Coats* [1949] AC 426 at 449.

[51] L. A. Sheridan, *Keeton & Sheridan's The Modern Law of Charities*, 4th edn (Chichester: Barry Rose, 1992); P. Luxton, *The Law of Charities* (Oxford: Oxford University Press, 2001); *Tudor on Charities* (J. Warburton and D. Morris, eds) 8th edn (London: Sweet & Maxwell, 1997).   [52] [1891] AC 531.

[53] Lord Macnaghten's classification was adopted from Sir Samuel Romilly's argument in *Morice v. Bishop of Durham* (1805) 10 Ves 522.

Charity Commissioners ever since, and has exerted a greater influence on modern decisions than the Preamble to the 1601 Act.[54] However, the Charities Act 2006 extended the 'heads' of charity to a 'baker's dozen'—that is, 12 substantive categories,[55] plus a 13th residual category comprising '*other existing charitable purposes or analogous charitable purposes*'.[56]

The 12 substantive heads of charity under the Charities Act 2011, s. 3(1) (Charities Act 2006, s. 2(2)) are as follows:

- '*prevention or relief of poverty*';[57]
- '*advancement of education*';[58]
- '*advancement of religion*';[59]
- '*advancement of health or the saving of lives*';[60]
- '*advancement of citizenship or community development*';[61]
- '*advancement of arts, culture, heritage or science*';[62]
- '*advancement of amateur sport*';[63]
- '*promotion of human rights, conflict resolution or reconciliation or the promotion of religious or racial harmony or equality and diversity*';[64]
- '*advancement of environmental protection or improvement*';[65]
- '*relief of those in need, by reason of youth, age, ill-health, disability, financial hardship or other disadvantage*';[66]
- '*advancement of animal welfare*';[67]
- '*promotion of the efficiency of the armed forces of the Crown or of the efficiency of the police, fire and rescue services or the ambulance services*'.[68]

The Charity Commission website contains a useful *Commentary on the Descriptions of Charitable Purposes in the Charities Act 2006.*[69] (References to '*The* Charity

---

[54] *Scottish Burial Reform and Cremation Society Ltd v. Glasgow Corporation* [1968] AC 138, HL.
[55] Charities Act 2011, s. 3(1)(a)–(l) (Charities Act 2006, s. 2(2)(a)–(l)).
[56] Charities Act 2011, s. 3(1)(m) (Charities Act 2006, s. 2(2)(m)).
[57] Charities Act 2011, s. 3(1)(a) (Charities Act 2006, s. 2(2)(a)).
[58] Charities Act 2011, s. 3(1)(b) (Charities Act 2006, s. 2(2)(b)).
[59] Charities Act 2011, s. 3(1)(c) (Charities Act 2006, s. 2(2)(c)).
[60] Charities Act 2011, s. 3(1)(d) (Charities Act 2006, s. 2(2)(d)).
[61] Charities Act 2011, s. 3(1)(e) (Charities Act 2006, s. 2(2)(e)).
[62] Charities Act 2011, s. 3(1)(f) (Charities Act 2006, s. 2(2)(f)).
[63] Charities Act 2011, s. 3(1)(g) (Charities Act 2006, s. 2(2)(g)).
[64] Charities Act 2011, s. 3(1)(h) (Charities Act 2006, s. 2(2)(h)).
[65] Charities Act 2011, s. 3(1)(i) (Charities Act 2006, s. 2(2)(i)).
[66] Charities Act 2011, s. 3(1)(j) (Charities Act 2006, s. 2(2)(j)).
[67] Charities Act 2011, s. 3(1)(k) (Charities Act 2006, s. 2(2)(k)).
[68] Charities Act 2011, s. 3(1)(l) (Charities Act 2006, s. 2(2)(l)).
[69] The commentary is periodically updated (see www.charity-commission.gov.uk).

Commission *Commentary'* throughout the remainder of this chapter are references to that document.)

Of Lord Macnaghten's original heads of charity, the prevention or relief of poverty and the advancement of education are essentially unchanged, but the advancement of religion now includes a religion that involves belief in more than one god [70] and a religion that does not involve belief in a god.[71] The 13 new and revised heads are considered in detail in the following sections.

The first head: the prevention or relief of poverty

Charitable benefits under this head are restricted to '*people who can fairly be said to be, according to current standards, "poor persons"*',[72] although the Charity Commission notes that the 'prevention' of poverty includes '*preventing persons who are not poor from becoming poor*'.[73] The attitude of the courts has been that the destitute are always poor, but that the poor are not always destitute: '*there are degrees of poverty less acute than abject poverty or destitution, but poverty nevertheless*'.[74] According to the Charity Commission, '*anyone who cannot afford the normal things in life which most people take for granted would probably qualify for help*'.[75] (The Institute for Fiscal Studies measures poverty in terms of the number of people whose household income is below 60 per cent of that earned by those in the middle of the national income distribution.)[76] In *Re Coulthurst*,[77] it was held that a person in poverty is one who has to '"*go short*" *in the ordinary acceptation of that term, due regard being had to their status in life, and so forth*'.[78] The law student's idea of 'going short' may be some way removed from what passes for poverty amongst qualified practising lawyers, but it is not inconceivable that a valid charitable trust could be established to relieve the poverty of 'lawyers who have fallen on hard times' or 'legal aid and pro bono lawyers in special financial need'. Provided that the trustees have the power to prevent the materially affluent from taking a benefit under the trust, it cannot be assumed that a trust for the relief of poor professional persons, or even a trust for impoverished members of the 'upper' classes,[79] will not be a valid charitable trust. There is even a reported case in which a valid charitable trust was established for members of one of London's exclusive gentleman's clubs who 'have fallen on evil days'.[80] Neither can it be presumed that a trust established for the benefit of the so-called 'working classes' will be a valid charitable trust for the relief of the poor; there are many very affluent members of the working classes.[81] Some words do,

---

[70] Charities Act 2011, s. 3(2)(a)(i).   [71] Charities Act 2011, s. 3(2)(a)(ii).

[72] *Dingle v. Turner* [1972] AC 601, *per* Lord Cross at 617D, HL.

[73] *The Prevention or Relief of Poverty for the Public Benefit* (December 2008).

[74] *Re Gardom* [1914] 1 Ch 662 at 668.   [75] Charity Commission leaflet CC4, August 2001, para. 3.

[76] 'Poverty and Inequality in the UK: 2011' (IFS Commentary C118).   [77] [1951] Ch 622, CA.

[78] Ibid. *per* Evershed MR at 666.

[79] In *Re Gardom* [1914] 1 Ch 662 a trust for 'ladies of limited means' was held to be charitable, as was a trust for 'distressed gentlefolk' in *Re Young* [1951] Ch 344.   [80] *Re Young* [1955] 1 WLR 1269.

[81] *Per* Lord Wrenbury in *Re Sutton* [1901] 2 Ch 640, 646; *Re Sanders' Will Trusts* [1954] Ch 265; *Re Niyazi's Will Trusts* [1978] 1 WLR 910.

however, imply poverty. Thus a trust to build 'hostels' for working men was held to be a valid charitable trust[82] for the relief of poverty, whereas a trust to provide 'dwellings' for working class families was not.[83] The Charity Commission has stated that 'the issue is whether people lack the basic things in life, rather than why they lack them',[84] so there is no possibility of returning to the invidious distinction, favoured by some Victorians, between 'deserving' and 'undeserving' poor.

What *is* required, because a charity must be exclusively charitable, is that the trustees will have power to deny benefits to the financially well-off. In *Re Gwyon*,[85] the testator directed that the residue of his estate should be applied by his executor to establish the 'Gwyon's Boys Clothing Foundation': a foundation to provide 'knickers' (a sort of trouser) for boys aged between 10 and 15 in a certain district. The boys could replace their old pair for a new pair, provided that the words 'Gwyon's Present' were still legible on the waistband of the old pair. The claim that the gift was a valid charitable trust for the relief of poverty failed. None of the conditions of the gift necessarily imported poverty. Eve J noted that the trustees would have no power to refuse a boy his gift on the ground merely that the boy was materially affluent.

The public benefit requirement under the first head

We have seen that the Charities Act 2006 removed any presumption that charitable purposes are for the public benefit. This change even applies to trusts for the relief of poverty.[86] However, it is not necessary to demonstrate the 'sufficient section of the public' element of public benefit in the case of trusts for the relief (and in some cases for the prevention) of poverty.[87] A trust to relieve the poverty of an identified individual or individuals will not be charitable, but a trust to relieve the poverty of a class of private persons will be, unless the class is so small and closed that it becomes in essence a trust for certain identifiable individuals.[88] In *Re Coulthurst*, a trust for the benefit of widows and orphaned children of deceased officers and deceased ex-officers of a particular bank was held to be a valid charitable trust, despite the fact that the potential beneficiaries were all connected to a single private employer. It is even permitted to establish valid charitable trusts exclusively for the benefit of one's own poor relations.[89] In *Re Segelman*,[90] a trust for the 'poor and needy' of a class comprising, at the time of the hearing, a mere 26 people related to the testator, a multimillionaire, was held to be a valid charitable trust. Chadwick J held that, although this case very nearly infringed the rule that relief should not be restricted to named individuals, it was saved by the

---

[82] *Re Niyazi's Will Trusts* [1978] 1 WLR 910.   [83] *Re Sanders' Will Trusts* [1954] Ch 265.

[84] Charity Commission leaflet CC4, August 2001.   [85] [1930] 1 Ch 255.

[86] See, generally, The Charity Commission, *The Prevention or Relief of Poverty for the Public Benefit* (December 2008) accessible online at www.charity-commission.gov.uk.

[87] *Attorney General v. Charity Commission* Upper Tribunal (Tax And Chancery Chamber) FTC/84/2011 (20 February 2012).

[88] *Dingle v. Turner* [1972] AC 601, HL. See, now, The Charity Commision, *Public benefit: the public benefit requirement (PB1)* (London: Crown Copyright, 2013) Annex A.

[89] *Re Scarisbrick* [1951] Ch 622; *Re Cohen* [1973] 1 All ER 889.   [90] [1996] 2 WLR 173.

inclusion of after-born issue of the 26 identified beneficiaries within the class of potential beneficiaries, thereby raising the possibility of quite substantial numbers of additional beneficiaries who might themselves be, or become, poor.

The second head: the advancement of education

According to Buckley LJ in *Incorporated Council of Law Reporting for England and Wales v. AG*, 'the second head should be regarded as extending to the improvement of a useful branch of human knowledge and its public dissemination'.[91] On that basis, law reporting was held to be charitable—doubtless to the delight of law students and legal scholars everywhere. However, a trust for the mere increase of knowledge is not charitable. In *Re Shaw*,[92] it was held that knowledge must be combined with teaching or education. *Re Shaw* concerned, amongst other things, a failed attempt by the writer George Bernard Shaw to establish a trust to determine how much effort might be saved by replacing the 26-letter English alphabet with a new 40-letter phonetic 'British alphabet'. Harman J held that this was not a valid charitable (public) trust for the advancement of education, but a trust for the advancement of purely private purposes. In another case with literary connections, in which the object of the trust was the heretical one of searching for evidence for Francis Bacon's authorship of plays commonly attributed to William Shakespeare, the trust was held to be charitable.[93] The judge accepted that expert evidence was almost unanimously against the Baconian claim, but noted that 'heretics are not necessarily wrong'.[94] His Lordship also held that a trust for the advancement of education is a valid charitable trust, even though it might advance the education of none but the researchers themselves.[95]

Sport

The only reference to education in the Preamble to the Statute of Elizabeth 1601 was to schools, scholars, and universities. Sport is nowhere mentioned, but it is now accepted that sport is charitable in an educational context. 'The Englishman', it has been said, 'never enjoys himself except for a noble purpose. He does not play cricket because it is a good game, but because it makes good citizens'.[96] Thus, in *Re Dupree's Trusts*,[97] Vaisey J was persuaded to recognize the charitable status of a gift for the promotion of an annual chess tournament, because chess is more than a mere game—it encourages foresight, concentration, memory, and ingenuity—and the trustees included the chairman of the Portsmouth Education Committee and the headmaster of Portsmouth Grammar School. The FA Youth Trust, created by the Football Association in 1972 in response to England's failure to retain the World Cup in 1970, was also held to be charitable, because its purpose was not merely to organize the playing of sport, but to promote physical education.[98] The possibility that the FA Youth Trust might be charitable under

---

[91] [1972] Ch 73 at 102.   [92] [1957] 1 WLR 729.   [93] *Re Hopkins* [1965] Ch 669.
[94] Ibid. at 677.   [95] Ibid. at 680.
[96] Plush J in *R. v. Leather* (a fictional case in A. P. Herbert, *Uncommon Law* (London: Methuen, 1942) at 195).
[97] [1944] 2 All ER 443.
[98] *IRC v. McMullen* [1981] AC 1, HL.

the Recreational Charities Act 1958 was left open.[99] The Charities Act 2011 provides that amateur sport should be recognized as charitable even when it does not appear in an educational context.[100]

The public benefit requirement under the second head

Trusts for the advancement of education must confer an identifiable benefit on the general public or upon a sufficient section of the public.[101] An educational trust established for the benefit of a numerically negligible class of persons or persons distinguishable from other members of the public by reason of their relationship to a particular individual will not be charitable. This is in stark contrast with the relief of poverty, where we saw that a trust for 'my poor relations' or 'poor employees' can be a perfectly valid charitable trust. In *Oppenheim v. Tobacco Securities Trust Co. Ltd*,[102] a trust for 'the education of children of employees or former employees of the British-American Tobacco Co. Ltd' was refused charitable status because, although the employees referred to numbered over 110,000, they were all identified by their personal 'nexus' to the employer company. In his dissenting speech, Lord MacDermott argued that the number of potential beneficiaries represented a sufficient section of the public,[103] but it is surely correct that tax-free benefits should not be conferred on the employees of one company unless they are also conferred on the employees of its competitors.

By extension of the *Oppenheim* principle, a trust established for the education of members of the general public will not be charitable if the settlor directs the trustees to prefer the employees of a particular company or members of his own family,[104] but if the settlor merely expresses his 'wish' that the trustees should prefer the employees of a particular company or members of his own family, the trust will be presumed charitable.[105] In the latter case, charitable status will only be withdrawn if the trustees actually prefer the employees of the settlor's company when they come to distribute the trust income.[106] In fact, even when a preference is not expressed, charitable status will be withdrawn if a preference is exercised in practice.[107]

Charities that charge high fees (a category that includes many private schools) must demonstrate that there is sufficient opportunity for people who cannot afford the fees to benefit in a material way that is related to the charity's aims.[108] The Upper Tribunal Tax and Chancery Chamber has considered the law governing fee-charging schools and

---

[99] For the Recreational Charities Act 1958, see later.

[100] See 'The seventh head'.

[101] See, generally, The Charity Commission, *The Advancement of Education for the Public Benefit* (December 2008) and *Analysis of the law underpinning the Advancement of Education for the Public Benefit*, both accessible online at www.charity-commission.gov.uk.   [102] [1951] AC 297, HL.

[103] An argument approved by Lord Cross of Chelsea in *Dingle v. Turner* [1972] 1 All ER 878.

[104] *Caffoor v. Commissioners of Income Tax* [1961] AC 584, PC.

[105] *Re Koettgen* [1954] 1 All ER 581.

[106] *IRC v. Educational Grants Association Ltd* [1967] 1 Ch 123, *per* Pennycuick J (confirmed on appeal, [1967] 1 Ch 993).   [107] Ibid. at 139, 144.

[108] Charity Commission, *Public Benefit and Fee-Charging* (December 2008).

concluded that the 2006 Act (now the 2011 Act) 'makes little, if any, difference to the legal position of the independent schools sector', but that it does 'bring into focus what it is that the pre-existing law already required'.[109]

The Upper Tribunal confirmed that 'a trust which excludes the poor from benefit cannot be a charity' and therefore concluded that a school which operates *solely* for the benefit of fee-paying students is not sufficiently for the public benefit even though it undoubtedly operates for the public benefit in the general sense of advancing the overall level of education in the population at large. Taking a distinctly laissez-faire approach to an issue which the tribunal suggested ought to be resolved by politicians rather than judges, the tribunal held that it should lie within the trustees' discretion to determine what level of provision (above the minimum necessary to secure charitable status) should be made for the poor to access the educational benefits arising from a fee-charging school.[110]

The third head: the advancement of religion

This head of charity is alone in having no analogy in the Preamble to the 1601 Act and it is practically unique amongst the four heads in advancing a purpose that is unlikely to attract state funding.

What is a 'religion' for the purposes of charitable status?

This is obviously too large a question to be fully addressed here.[111] We can say, however, that English law has traditionally approached the question from two more or less opposite starting positions. At one starting position, there are the major established religions—including Christianity, Judaism, Islam, Hinduism, and Buddhism—all of which, with the exception of certain branches of Buddhism, involve the worship of God, gods, or some transcendental being. At the other starting position, there are humanist ethical societies[112] and other avowedly non-religious belief systems. In very broad terms, a belief system is more likely to be recognized as religious the more closely it resembles the major religions and less likely to be recognized as religious if it resembles humanist societies.[113] The US approach, in contrast, has been to regard non-religious belief systems as equivalent to religious belief systems and to treat both as equally deserving of legal recognition.

---

[109] *The Independent Schools Council v. The Charity Commission for England and Wales* [2011] UKUT 421 (TCC) at para. [88].

[110] Ibid. at para. [220].

[111] The problem of defining 'religion' is one that extends beyond the law of charity. See, for example, the recent finding that in the employment context philosophical beliefs concerning 'climate change' deserve the same protection against illegal discrimination as religious beliefs (Tim Nicholson, 'Judge rules activist's beliefs on climate change akin to religion', *The Guardian*, 3 November 2009).

[112] See *Re South Place Ethical Society, sub nom. Barralet v. AG* [1980] 1 WLR 1565.

[113] This tends to create a bias against the legal recognition of new religious movements. See P. Edge, 'The legal challenges of paganism and other diffuse faiths' (1996) 1 J Civ Lib 216–29, 226; G. Watt, 'Giving unto Caesar: rationality, reciprocity and legal recognition of religion' in *Current Legal Issues: Law and Religion* (R. O'Dair and A. Lewis, eds) (Oxford: Oxford University Press, 2001) at 45–64.

Traditionally, the English courts have accepted that non-religious belief systems may hold a place in the lives of humanist adherents that is, in many respects, parallel to the place held by religious belief systems in religious adherents, but have concluded (by arguably inaccurate geometric reasoning) that *'parallels never meet'*.[114] According to the Charities Act 2011, the charity law meaning of 'religion' should now be taken to include not only monotheism and polytheism, but even some atheistic or, more properly, 'non-deistic', religions. Inclusion of 'non-deistic' religions brings the UK definition of religion more closely (but not exactly) in line with the US definition described earlier. The Charity Commission notes that the courts have identified a number of characteristics which indicate religious belief, the first of which is:

> belief in a god (or gods) or goddess (or goddesses), or supreme being, or divine or transcendental being or entity or spiritual principle, which is the object or focus of the religion (referred to throughout this guidance as 'supreme being or entity')[115]

The Charity Commission's summary makes clear that non-deistic religions such as Buddhism will qualify (most Buddhists consider the Buddha to be an enlightened human rather than a deity). Other requirements in the Charity Commission's summary are *'a relationship between the believer and the supreme being or entity by showing worship of, reverence for or veneration of the supreme being or entity'*; *'a degree of cogency, cohesion, seriousness and importance'* and *'an identifiable positive, beneficial, moral or ethical framework'*. Applying these criteria, the Charity Commission decided in 2010 that 'The Druid Network' should be registered as an unincorporated association that exists for the purpose of advancing religion for the public benefit.[116] According to its adherents, modern Druidry is principally concerned with 'the spiritual interaction between an individual and the spirits of nature, including those of landscape and ancestry, together with the continuities of spiritual, literary and cultural heritage'. What isn't clear is where the line should be drawn (if indeed a line should be drawn), especially if one takes account of 'literary and cultural heritage'. Is Shakespearism a religion? It has a revered book (William Shakespeare's *Complete Works*), Stratford-upon-Avon is a focal point for international pilgrimage, and the rituals of the religion are performed daily in dedicated temples around the globe (including *the* 'Globe Theatre' itself). Dominic Dromgoole, the artistic director of the Globe Theatre, professes the faith in *Will & Me: How Shakespeare Took Over My Life* (Penguin, 2006): *'Stratford was electrifying... we went to his tomb and liked it so much we went back twice more... I was a Catholic in Rome, a Moslem in Mecca.'* A religion of Shakespearism is not too far-fetched, bearing in mind that the 'Church of Scientology' bases its teachings on the works of a pulp science-fiction author[117] and

---

[114] See *Barralet v. AG* [1980] 1 WLR 1565 at 1571H.

[115] Charity Commission, *PB4: The Advancement of Religion for the Public Benefit* (2008) section C2.

[116] Decision of the Charity Commission, 21 September 2010.

[117] L. Ron Hubbard. The title of the source book of Scientology, Hubbard's *Dianetics: The Modern Science of Mental Health*, reveals that it has not always conceived of itself as a religion. In 1999, the Charity Commission rejected Scientology's claim to be a religion, but the UK Supreme Court has since recognized it to be a religion in a non-charity context (see *R (Hodkin and anor) v Registrar General of Births, Deaths and Marriages* [2013] UKSC 77; [2014] 2 WLR 23).

has been recognized as a religion in some jurisdictions (although not in the UK).[118] Given the wide definition of religion under the Charities Act 2011, it may be harder in the future to resist the religious claims of groups such as the Scientologists. Ancestor worship, on the other hand, will presumably, as before, fail to attract charitable status. It would be stretching the label 'Supreme Being' too far to attach it to ordinary human ancestors.[119]

Judicial 'neutrality' between religions

According to George Bernard Shaw, who, as we noted earlier, failed in his own attempt to create a trust for the advancement of education, '*there is only one religion, though there are a hundred versions of it*'.[120] Absent the cynicism, the courts have taken a similarly liberal approach to the recognition of religion. According to Cross J in *Neville Estates v. Madden*,[121] '*As between different religions the law stands neutral, but it assumes that any religion is at least likely to be better than none*'.[122] In the context of recognizing charitable status, whether or not 'any' religion is better than 'none' is completely irrelevant unless 'better' means better for the public, and this is clearly what Cross J had in mind: '*the court is, I think, entitled to assume that some benefit accrues to the public from the attendance at places of worship of persons who live in this world and mix with their fellow citizens*'.[123]

The courts and the Charity Commission are correct to disclaim any competence to judge between the validity of religious claims.[124] For example, in *Khaira v. Shergill*,[125] the Court of Appeal declined to adjudicate on the claim that one of the parties was a 'holy' person according to the Sikh religion. The question of whether a group or practice is religious or not is one that has rarely been debated to the credit of the courts. In *Thornton v. Howe*,[126] a gift of land to assist in the promotion and publication of the 'sacred writings of the late Joanna Southcote' was held to be charitable even though that 'foolish ignorant woman' claimed to be with child by the Holy Spirit. The Master of the Rolls represented his judgment to be a paradigm of enlightened liberality:

> the Court of Chancery makes no distinction between one religion and another...[or] one sect and another...[unless] the tenets of a particular sect inculcate doctrines adverse to the very foundations of all religions and...subversive of all morality.[127]

In fact, despite his liberal words, his Lordship's judgment had the effect of causing the gift to fail. In 1862, a charitable gifts of land were void under the Statute of Mortmain,[128]

---

[118] Charity Commission, *Decision of the Charity Commissioners for England and Wales: Application for Registration as a Charity by the Church of Scientology* (England and Wales) 17 November 1999.
[119] *Yeap Cheah Neo v. Ong Chen Neo* (1875) LR 6 PC 381.
[120] *Plays Pleasant and Unpleasant*, vol. II (Chicago: Herbert S. Stone, 1898).   [121] [1962] Ch 832.
[122] Ibid. at 853.   [123] Ibid.
[124] See S. Fish, 'Mission impossible: settling the just bounds between Church and State' (1997) 97 Columbia LR 2255; G. Watt, 'Giving unto Caesar: rationality, reciprocity and legal recognition of religion' in *Current Legal Issues: Law and Religion* (R. O'Dair and A. Lewis, eds) (Oxford: Oxford University Press, 2001) at 45–64.
[125] [2012] EWCA Civ 983.   [126] [1862] 31 Beav 14; compare *Re Watson* [1973] 1 WLR 1472.
[127] *Per* Romilly MR, ibid. at 19.   [128] Act 9 Geo. 2.

so, by holding this gift to be charitable, the Master of the Rolls ensured that the land would pass to the testator's heir.

In the Australian case *Church of the New Faith v. Commisioner for Pay-Roll Tax (Vic)*,[129] which concerned the tax-exempt status of the Church of Scientology,[130] Murphy J presented his judgment in similarly liberal terms: '*Any body which claims to be religious, and offers a way to find meaning and purpose in life, is religious.*'[131] However, once again, the appearance of the judgment does not reflect the underlying reality of the judge's reasoning and motives. The late Murphy J was a confirmed, even militant, atheist and, seen in that light, his judgment appears less like liberality and more like condescension. Reading his judgment, one might presume he was of the view that all religions are equally valid. In fact, like George Bernard Shaw before him, the judge believed that all religions are equally invalid and for *that* reason should be treated equally in law.[132]

It is a nice question whether sincerity matters, or should matter, when it comes to legal recognition of religion. Thousands of respondents to the 2001 official census of the UK population listed 'Jedi' as their religion. Would a trust established to promote the Jedi faith attract charitable status? And what of a trust to set up 'the Free Church of Country Sports' (an article in *The Daily Telegraph* reported plans by a group of hunting enthusiasts to defend fox hunting as part of this 'religion').[133] Established procedures seem to be more important than sincerity. Thus the Equality Act 2010 acknowledges that charities may limit public access to benefits by requiring would-be members 'to make a statement which asserts or implies membership or acceptance of a religion or belief',[134] provided the charity 'first imposed such a requirement before 18 May 2005' and 'has not ceased since that date to impose such a requirement'.[135]

Proselytization

Proselytization is the practice of converting, or seeking to convert, a person from one religion to another. In keeping with the courts' professed neutrality between religions, it must follow that proselytization, even though it is undoubtedly a religious purpose, is not a charitable one.[136] It would, after all, be somewhat self-defeating to grant fiscal immunity to a group seeking to convert Muslims to Christianity and, at the same time, to grant fiscal immunity to a corresponding group whose purpose is to convert Christians to Islam. The Charity Commission's website distinguishes sensitive and appropriate

---

[129] (1983) 49 ALR 65, High Court of Australia.

[130] See, generally, Charity Commission, *Decision of the Charity Commissioners for England and Wales: Application for Registration as a Charity by the Church of Scientology* (England and Wales) 17 November 1999.

[131] (1983) 49 ALR 65 at 86.

[132] For an argument that religion should not attract charitable status see P. Edge, 'Charitable status for the advancement of religion: an abolitionist's view' (1995–6) 3 CL&PR 29–35.

[133] D. Foggo 'Hunt enthusiasts call faithful to Free Church of Country Sports', *The Daily Telegraph*, 23 May 2004.

[134] Equality Act 2010, s. 193(5). At the time of writing this provision is not yet in force.

[135] Equality Act 2010, s. 193(6). At the time of writing this provision is not yet in force.

[136] *Commissioners for Special Purpose of the Income Tax v. Pemsel* [1891] AC 531, *per* Lord Bramwell at 565.

'proselytization' from inappropriate 'proselytization' (such as brainwashing), but it fails to record any adequate distinction between the perfectly valid charitable purpose of evangelism from the (in secular terms) 'self-defeating' purpose of proselytization.

The public benefit requirement under the third head

When the available evidence demonstrates that a particular religion or religious practice is actually detrimental to the public, or confers no tangible benefit on the public (perhaps because its adherents live in a convent and have no interaction with the outside world),[137] that religion or religious practice will not be recognized as charitable—at any rate, as long as charitable status enjoys fiscal immunity. Even if we assume that no court or other agency of state is competent to judge between religions, it cannot be denied that state agents are competent to discriminate, albeit according to their own limited terms of reference, between those activities and purposes that are beneficial to the public and those that are detrimental; this, after all, is the very business of state.

The fourth head: the advancement of health or the saving of lives

The advancement of health includes the prevention or relief of sickness, disease, or human suffering. A gift for the purposes of a hospital is prima facie a good charitable gift under this head, but the presumption could be rebutted if evidence showed that the hospital was carried on commercially for the benefit of private individuals. In *Re Resch's Will Trusts*,[138] the testator left his residuary estate (then valued around AUS $8m) to trustees upon trust to pay two-thirds of the income 'to the Sisters of Charity for a period of 200 years so long as they shall conduct the St Vincent's Private Hospital'. The hospital did not seek to make a commercial profit, but its charges for treatment, while not necessarily excluding the poor, were not low. The Privy Council held that it was a valid charitable trust for purposes beneficial to the community. The requisite public benefit had been satisfied, because evidence showed that the public needed accommodation and treatment of the type provided by the hospital. The Charity Commission[139] has confirmed that charity trustees can make gifts or loans to hospitals provided that '*the trustees are satisfied that the hospital concerned is one attended primarily by sick people from the charity's area of benefit, and that they will benefit directly from the gifts*'; trustees can make grants to local doctors' surgeries for the purchase of necessary equipment if it cannot be acquired using the practice's funds, provided that the funds will be used to benefit patients. Other purposes falling under this head include charities that provide 'complementary' or 'alternative' medical treatment or health-related services such as

---

[137] In *Gilmour v. Coats* [1949] AC 426 a Carmelite priory was denied charitable status because its members lived in cloistered seclusion from the outside world. *Gilmour v. Coats* was distinguished in *Neville Estates Ltd v. Madden* [1962] Ch 832, in which the Catford Synagogue was recognized to be charitable because its members '*spend their lives in the world*'. Cross J held that the court is '*entitled to assume that some benefit accrues to the public from the attendance at places of worship of persons who live in this world and mix with their fellow citizens*' (at 853).   [138] [1969] 1 AC 514.

[139] Booklet CC6, *Charities for the Relief of Sickness*, March 2000.

research and hospital radio and even (according to the Charity Commission website) self-defence classes.

The fifth head: the advancement of citizenship or community development

Having effectively defined religion out of existence, the Charities Act 2011 (Charities Act 2006 as was) appears, at first sight, to fill the vacuum with a new secular cult of 'citizenship'.[140] It hardly seems to matter that individual and 'community' notions of citizenship vary according to individual beliefs and the nature of communities, and still less that, in the UK, we are technically not citizens at all, but subjects of the Crown. But perhaps the labels 'citizenship' and 'community development' are merely 'spin'. The Act itself equates those lofty ambitions with modest and appealing aims such as *'rural or urban regeneration'*,[141] and *'the promotion of civic responsibility, volunteering, the voluntary sector or the effectiveness or efficiency of charities'*. The *Commentary* cites the example of Scout and Guide groups. Another example is the promotion of so-called 'community capacity building'.[142] It is an ugly label, but it turns out to be an attractive, albeit vague, idea. 'Community capacity building' addresses social disadvantage in particular communities (usually, but not necessarily, economic disadvantage). It is broad enough to encompass the provision of IT skills training to a community of well-to-do old people in England, as well as the provision of IT skills training to a poor village in Africa.

The sixth head: the advancement of arts, culture, heritage, or science

There is no reference to the arts in the Preamble of 1601, even though Shakespeare was then at the height of his powers, but the promotion of the arts is now an established charitable purpose for the advancement of education, even if it takes place outside of schools and universities. According to Lord Greene MR, *'the education of artistic taste is one of the most important things in the development of a civilised human being'*.[143] However, the cases suggest that it is only charitable to promote artistic taste if it is *good* taste, whatever that might be. In *Re Delius*,[144] the widow of Frederick Delius, the composer, left her residuary estate to trustees upon trust to apply the income therefrom

> for or towards the advancement...of the musical works of my late husband under conditions in which the making of profit is not the object to be attained...by means of the recording upon the gramophone or other instrument for the mechanical reproduction of music of those works...the publication and issue of a uniform edition of the whole body of the works...and...the performance in public of the works.

In the course of holding this to be a valid charitable purpose, Roxburgh J stated that *'it must be charitable to promote music of a particular composer, presupposing...that the composer is one whose music is worth appreciating'*.[145] One might have thought that

---

[140] On the religious quality of 'citizenship', see, generally, S. Critchley, 'The catechism of the citizen: politics, law and religion in, after, with and against Rousseau', (2007) 1(1) *Law and Humanities* 79.

[141] See Charity Commission, 'Promotion of urban and rural regeneration', *Review of the Register* RR2.

[142] This concept is considered in the Charity Commission document *Review of the Register* RR5.

[143] *Royal Choral Society v. IRC* [1943] 2 All ER 101 at 104.   [144] [1957] 1 Ch 299.   [145] Ibid. at 307.

matters of taste would be non-justiciable, in accordance with the maxim *de gustibus non est disputandum*,[146] but judges have been prepared to admit expert evidence to help determine whether or not artwork has any educational value. The leading case is *Re Pinion*,[147] which, appropriately enough, turned on a matter of opinion. The testator had left his freehold studio, together with his paintings and some antique furniture, silver, china and so forth, to be offered to the National Trust to be kept together as a collection. The income from his residuary estate was left to be used for the maintenance of the collection. In the event that the National Trust might decline the gift, his executors were directed to keep the collection as a museum. Harman LJ agreed with the judge at first instance that '*there is an accepted canon of taste on which the court must rely, for it has itself no judicial knowledge of such matters*', but this did not prevent his Lordship from disagreeing with the judge (who had found some slight merit in the collection) in apparently opinionated terms: 'I can conceive of no useful object to be served in foisting on the public this mass of junk.'

A charitable trust such as the *Delius* trust is bound to enhance the composer's reputation, but this private benefit is no reason to deny charitable status. The trust would have failed, however, had there been a possibility that the residuary legatee could have profited personally from the trusts to any significant degree.

The seventh head: the advancement of amateur sport

The word 'sport' is derived from the word 'disport', which is itself derived from the french *porter*, meaning 'to carry'. Sport is that which carries us away—that which acts as a diversion from work. The reader may be tempted to set up a charitable sports club for watching football on television—it is a diversion from work, so why not?—but it should be noted that sport under the 'seventh head' must promote health by involving physical or mental skill or exertion. Less energetic sports, such as chess, may also be charitable, if (like chess) they are educational.[148] The Charity Commission has recognized the charitable status of an amateur bridge club on the basis of the mental health benefits that are engendered by the card game.[149]

Since the enactment of the Charities Act 2006, a registered sports club established for charitable purposes is treated as not being so established and is therefore not a charity, but a club for the time being registered under Schedule 18 to the Finance Act 2002 (a 'community amateur sports club') enjoys some special tax relief whether or not it is a charity. To be a charity, the sport must be '*capable of improving physical health and fitness*' and the club must have an '*open membership*', which means that '*access to the club's facilities must be genuinely available to anyone who wishes to take advantage of them*'.[150]

---

[146] In matters of taste, there can be no dispute.   [147] *Re Pinion* [1964] 1 All ER 890.

[148] *Re Dupree's Deed Trusts* [1945] Ch 16.

[149] *Hitchen Bridge Club* Charity Commission Decision, 28 February 2011. But it was subsequently ruled that bridge is not a sport for tax purposes (*English Bridge Union Ltd v. Revenue and Customs Commissioners* [2014] UKFTT 181).

[150] Charity Commission, 'Charitable status and sport', *Review of the Register* RR11.

The eighth head: the promotion of human rights, conflict resolution or reconciliation, or the promotion of religious or racial harmony, or equality and diversity

This set of aims is laudable, but does it look more like a political manifesto than a charitable category? Purposes under this head will surely run the risk of infringing the general prohibition on political charities.[151] According to the Charity Commission website, examples of charitable purposes falling under this head include: 'promotion of human rights, at home or abroad, such as relieving victims of human rights abuse, raising awareness of human rights issues, securing the enforcement of human rights law'; 'promotion of restorative justice and other forms of conflict resolution or reconciliation'; 'resolution of national or international conflicts'; 'mediation'; 'promoting good relations between persons of different racial groups'; 'promoting equality and diversity by the elimination of discrimination on the grounds of age, sex or sexual orientation'; and 'enabling people of one faith to understand the religious beliefs of others'.[152]

How can such purposes not be political? The Charity Commission's answer is not wholly convincing:

> Charities are able to engage in political campaigning in order to further their charitable purposes. Charity law draws a distinction between political purposes and political activities. An organisation which has purposes which include the promotion of human rights by seeking a change in the law, or a shift in government policy, or a reversal of a government decision has (at least in part) political purposes and cannot be a charity. However, the trustees of a charity may nonetheless use political means without jeopardising charitable status. What is important for charitable status is that political means should not be the dominant method by which the organisation will pursue its apparently charitable objects.[153]

Quite apart from the political nature of the purposes, it is also clear that such aims as the 'promotion of equality' and 'the promotion of religious harmony' will produce new conflicts requiring resolution. Some questions of public benefit have proved very controversial. According to The Equality Act 2010 s.193(7), which is not in force at the time of writing, it is not a contravention of the Act to restrict to persons of one sex participation in an activity which is carried on for the purpose of promoting or supporting a charity. However, restriction according to sexual orientation is another thing. In *Catholic Care v. Charity Commission*,[154] Briggs J held that '[a]n organisation which proposes to fulfil a purpose for the public benefit will only qualify as a charity if, taking into account any dis-benefit arising from its *modus operandi*, its activities nonetheless yield a net public benefit... Thus, a charity which proposed to apply differential treatment on grounds of sexual orientation otherwise than as a proportionate means of achieving a legitimate aim might thereby fail to achieve charitable status...'.[155] On

---

[151] See the heading 'Political purposes'.

[152] See, further, Charity Commission, 'The promotion of human rights', *Review of the Register* RR12.

[153] Ibid. at [33].

[154] [2010] EWHC 520 (Ch); [2010] 4 All ER 1041, First-Tier Tribunal (Charity) General Regulatory Chamber.   [155] Ibid. at para. [97].

appeal from this decision, the Upper Tribunal held that the charity in this case had not demonstrated such clear net benefits that exceptional discrimination could be justified. It was acknowledged that '[t]he fact that same sex couples could seek to have access to adoption services offered elsewhere tended to reduce somewhat the immediate detrimental effect on them, but it did not remove the harm that would be caused to them through feeling that discrimination on grounds of sexual orientation was practised at some point in the adoption system'.[156] The decision of the Upper Tribunal shows how hard it is to balance the problem of systemic discrimination on grounds of sexual orientation against the problem of systemic discrimination on grounds of religion. Part of the Upper Tribunal's decision was to reject, as too speculative, the Catholic adoption agency's argument that potential donors might be put off if charity were required to place children with homosexual couples.

The ninth head: the advancement of environmental protection or improvement

This is another laudable purpose but, again, one which is potentially highly political and liable to irritate the government. There are also problems of definition. If woodland is replaced by a thousand new homes equipped with solar panels, charities such as the Woodland Trust will no doubt object, but charities promoting solar power might approve.

The tenth head: the relief of those in need, by reason of youth, age, ill health, disability, financial hardship, or other disadvantage

A trust under this head will not be charitable if it *excludes* the poor. After all, we would not expect a trust for the relief of aged millionaires to be charitable. On the other hand, an incidental financial benefit might be permitted. *Joseph Rowntree Memorial Trust Housing Association Ltd v. AG*[157] concerned a charitable housing association that desired to build individual dwellings for sale to elderly people on long leases in consideration of a capital payment. On the tenant's death, the lease would be assigned to the tenant's spouse or a family member, provided that that person was also elderly. Failing such an assignment, the lease would revert to the association, which would pay to the tenant's estate 70 per cent of the then current market value of the lease. The Charity Commissioners objected to the scheme on the grounds, *inter alia*, that it operated by way of contract, benefited private individuals rather than a charitable class, and could produce a financial profit for those individuals. The court held that the scheme was a valid charitable scheme for the relief of the aged, notwithstanding the objections of the Charity Commissioners. Also falling under this head, according to the Charity Commission website, are such purposes as 'children's care homes'; 'apprenticing'; senior citizens' 'drop-in centres'; 'the relief of disability'; and the 'provision of housing'.

---

[156] *Catholic Care (Diocese of Leeds) v. Charity Commission (on appeal to the Upper Tribunal)* CA/2010/0007 (26 April 2011).   [157] [1983] 2 WLR 284.

The eleventh head: the advancement of animal welfare

A trust 'for my faithful hound, Fido' will not be charitable, although it might be a valid trust of imperfect obligation,[158] but a trust established for the well-being of animals generally may be charitable. Examples include a trust to establish a home for lost dogs[159] and a trust 'for animal welfare'.[160] It is said that such trusts tend to

> promote and encourage kindness towards [animals], and to ameliorate the condition of the brute creation, and thus to stimulate humane and generous sentiments in man towards the lower animals, and by this means to promote feelings of humanity and thus elevate the human race.[161]

The focus of the charitable status of animal welfare is on the benefits it provides to humans and the improvement it engenders in humanity. Accordingly, an animal 'sanctuary' run by anti-vivisectionists and opponents of blood sports failed to attract charitable status, because the animals would be free to molest each other,[162] whereas a trust to promote humane ways of slaughtering animals was held to be a valid charitable trust for animal welfare.[163] In any event, anti-vivisection charities are liable to clash with the courts' general refusal to recognize charities established for the political purpose of changing the law of the land.[164] This was the outcome in *National Anti-Vivisection Society v. IRC*.[165] In *Hanchett-Stamford v. HM Attorney General*,[166] the court confirmed that the express recognition of the advancement of animal welfare in the Charities Act 2006 did not change the rule that withholds charitable status from political aims such as changing the law (in this case, the organization had been established to seek an outright ban on performing animals).

The twelfth head: the promotion of the efficiency of the armed forces of the Crown, or of the efficiency of the police, fire, and rescue services, or the ambulance services

We noted, at the very start of this chapter, that a trust to promote the well-being of members of the armed forces is charitable; indeed, this purpose has a very long history of charitable status. The Statute of Elizabeth 1601 refers to '*the Maintenance of sick and maimed Soldiers and Mariners*' and the '*setting out of Soldiers*'. The fact that it is mentioned twice lends strong support to our working hypothesis that charitable purposes are typically those of which the government approves and upon which the government would be prepared to expend its own funds. Charities currently registered for the improvement of the serving armed forces include the Army Air Corps Fund, the Army Physical Training Corps Association, the Army Rugby Union Trust, and the Army Rifle Association. 'Fire and rescue services' means services provided by fire and rescue authorities under Part 2 of the Fire and Rescue Services Act 2004, so 'private'

---

[158] See Chapter 3.   [159] *Re Douglas* (1887) LR 35 Ch D 472.   [160] *Re Wedgwood* [1915] 1 Ch 113.
[161] Ibid. *per* Swinfen-Eady LJ, at 122.   [162] *Re Grove-Grady* [1929] 1 Ch 557, CA.
[163] *Re Wedgwood* [1915] 1 Ch 113.   [164] Considered under the heading 'Political purposes'.
[165] Ibid.   [166] [2008] EWHC 330 (Ch).

rescue services such as the Royal National Lifeboat Institute (RNLI) and the wide range
of mountain rescue services are not included under this head; they are analogous to this
head and will fall under the next—residual—head of charity.

The thirteenth (residual) head: other existing charitable purposes or analogous charitable purposes

One cannot predict the new charitable purposes that will be added to this residual category, but we might be surprised if a purpose is added that is one on which the government would not consider spending its own (*the public's* own) money.

The theory that novel charitable purposes are purposes that a modern government
might see as being its own responsibility is borne out by a number of purposes that were
admitted into the residual head (then the fourth head) before the Charities Act 2006.
Examples include the purpose of providing cremation services[167] and '*retraining and
assistance to the unemployed*'.[168] The Charity Commission *Commentary* on the 2006 Act
also identifies the following examples of purposes within the residual head:

> '*Provision of facilities under the Recreational Charities Act 1958*';169

> '*The provision of public works and services and the provision of public amenities (such
> as the repair of bridges, ports, havens, causeways and highways, the provision of
> water and lighting, etc)*';

> '*The promotion of certain patriotic purposes, such as war memorials*';

> '*The social relief, resettlement and rehabilitation of persons under a disability or depri-
> vation (including disaster funds)*'.

Certain examples lend especially strong support to the thesis that charitable purposes
have little to do with altruistic love and more to do with governmental concerns regarding the generation of national wealth:

> '[t]*he promotion of industry and commerce*';

> '[t]*he promotion of agriculture and horticulture*';

> '[t]*he preservation of public order*';

> '[p]*romoting the sound administration and development of the law*';

> '[t]*he promotion of ethical standards of conduct and compliance with the law in the
> public and private sectors*';

> '[t]*he rehabilitation of ex-offenders and the prevention of crime*'.

Two purposes in the list ('*promotion of mental or moral improvement*' and '*promotion
of the moral or spiritual welfare or improvement of the community*') give the court and

---

[167] *Scottish Burial Reform and Cremation Society Ltd v. Glasgow Corporation* [1968] AC 138, HL.
[168] *IRC v. Oldham Training and Enterprise Council* [1996] STC 1218. See Charity Commission, 'Charities for
the relief of unemployment', *Review of the Register* RR3.
[169] See 'Recreational charities'.

Commission an arguably unwarranted power to pass judgment on matters of private morality.

Before the Charities Act 2006, a purpose beneficial to the community only fell within the final, residual head if it was within the 'spirit and intendment' of the Preamble to the Statute of Elizabeth 1601. It is not clear whether this transcendent consideration is relevant to the law after the Charities Act 2006. In any event, Lord Wilberforce stated many years ago that reference to the 'spirit and intendment' of the Preamble is not of practical significance, but is merely carried out *'for reassurance'*.[170] Russell LJ described the 'spirit and intendment' requirement as:

> a line of retreat … in case [the courts] are faced with a purpose (e.g. a political purpose) which could not have been within the contemplation of the Statute even if the then legislators had been endowed with the gift of foresight into the circumstances of later centuries.[171]

The public benefit requirement under the residual head

In *IRC v. Baddeley*,[172] land was conveyed for the benefit of the Stratford Newtown Methodist Mission, for 'persons resident in the County Boroughs of West Ham and Leyton' who, in the opinion of the trustees, were, or were likely to become, 'members of the Methodist Church and of insufficient means otherwise to enjoy the advantages provided by [the donation]'. The donation was held not to satisfy the requirement of public benefit because it purported to operate for the benefit of a class within a class. We know from the Charity Commission's 2013 guidance on public benefit (discussed earlier in this chapter) that a charity must be established for a 'sufficient section of the public'. It remains to be seen whether the courts' traditional concern to ensure that public benefit under the residual head should not be restricted to a class-within-a-class will continue to be regarded as a factor bearing on the question whether the section of the public is 'sufficient'.

Recreational charities

The Charities Act 2011, s. 5 (repealing and replacing the Recreational Charities Act 1958) recognizes the provision of facilities for recreation or other leisure-time occupation to be charitable if the facilities are provided in the interests of social welfare.[173]

This requirement can be satisfied by either or both of the following two routes:

Route one requires the provision of facilities for persons in need due to youth, age, infirmity or disability, poverty, or social and economic circumstances,[174] with the object of improving the conditions of life for the persons for whom the facilities are primarily intended.[175]

---

[170] *Re Resch's Will Trusts* [1969] 1 AC 514, PC.   [171] *Council of Law Reporting v. AG* [1972] Ch 73 at 88.
[172] [1955] AC 572.
[173] Charities Act 2011, s. 5(1). See, generally, Charity Commission, 'The Recreational Charities Act 1958', *Review of the Register* RR4.   [174] Charities Act 2011, s. 5(3)(b)(i).
[175] Charities Act 2011, s. 5(3)(a).

Route two requires the provision of facilities available to members of the public at large or to male,[176] or to female, members of the public at large,[177] with the object of improving the conditions of life for the persons for whom the facilities are primarily intended.[178] When a testator left the residue of his estate 'to the town council of North Berwick for the use in connection with the sports centre in North Berwick or some similar purpose in connection with sport', his bequest was held to be charitable under this route even though the intended beneficiaries were not in a position of social disadvantage and did not suffer from any particular deprivation.[179]

Political purposes

When the National Anti-Vivisection Society claimed to be exempt from income tax as '*a body of persons established for charitable purposes only*',[180] it failed, because a prime objective of the society was to secure the repeal of the Cruelty to Animals Act 1876 and to see it replaced by an absolute prohibition on vivisection. Courts cannot recognize a political purpose such as this to be charitable; the function of the courts is to implement the will of Parliament, to influence the will of Parliament perhaps, but never to oppose it or to support those who oppose it. Generally speaking, it is for the legislature, not the courts, to determine whether a reform of the law will be for the public benefit.[181] It was for this reason that, in 1998, the RSPCA was forced to drop its political support for 'animal rights'.[182] It was also for this reason that a university project to educate the public 'in the subject of militarism and disarmament' was denied charitable status; the Court of Appeal held that the project was, in fact, a project to advance the political cause of '*demilitarisation*'.[183]

Charitable status will also be denied to trusts set up for the purpose of exerting political pressure on *foreign* legislatures.[184] Such trusts are presumed to be detrimental to the public interest, because they might sour diplomatic relations with foreign states. For this reason, student unions are not permitted to use their charitable funds to campaign for an end to war in Iraq,[185] or similar. It should be noted, however, that, whereas a trust for political *purposes* is not charitable, it is permissible for a charitable trust to fund political *activities* ancillary to, and reasonably expected to advance, its charitable

---

[176] Section 5(2) of the Charities Act 2006 (since consolidated in Charities Act 2011) amended the 1958 Act so that facilities made available to men only are now to be regarded as charitable on the same basis as facilities made available to the public as a whole or to women only, bringing the Act into line with the European Convention on Human Rights.   [177] Charities Act 2011, s. 5(3)(b)(ii).

[178] Charities Act 2011, s. 5(3)(a).   [179] *Re Guild* [1992] 2 AC 310.

[180] *National Anti-Vivisection Society v. IRC* [1948] AC 31, HL.

[181] *Bowman v. Secular Society Ltd* [1917] AC 406, *per* Lord Parker at 442.

[182] *The Daily Telegraph*, 7 February 1998.

[183] *Southwood v. AG* [2000] WL 877698; *The Times*, 18 July, CA. Dr Southwood is the author of *Disarming Military Industries: Turning an Outbreak of Peace into an Enduring Legacy* (London: Macmillan, 1991).

[184] *McGovern v. AG* [1981] 3 All ER 493 (Amnesty International).

[185] *Webb v. O'Doherty*, *The Times*, 11 February 1991, *per* Hoffmann J. See, generally, *AG v. Ross* [1986] 1 WLR 252, *per* Scott J.

purposes.[186] So a student union is permitted to finance a debate on war in Iraq as part
of its general charitable purpose of advancing education; and an organization (English
PEN, a branch of International PEN) that promotes peace and human rights through
the power of literature and free speech has been granted charitable status[187] even though
(according to its website) 25 per cent of its funds are devoted to campaigns, including
the reform of English libel law on the basis that it 'has a profoundly negative impact on
freedom of expression, both in the UK and around the world'.

Administration of charitable trusts

The role of the courts in deciding whether or not a body is charitable was, in large part,
transferred to the Charity Commission by the Charities Act 1993. The court remains
the forum of ultimate appeal and the court's jurisdiction to establish a scheme for the
administration of a charity (matters such as the appointment of trustees, extending
powers of investment, etc.) is concurrent with that of the Charity Commission.[188]

The Charity Commission

As a result of the Charities Act 2006 (as now consolidated in the Charities Act 2011), the
Commission has been incorporated with an expanded board drawn from a wider section of society. The Charity Commission will still supervise the compulsory registration
and administration of most charitable trusts, and will still have the power to institute ad
hoc inquiries with regard to any charity.[189]

    When required to determine whether or not a particular purpose is or is not charita-
ble, the Commission's general approach is 'to favour charity':[190]

> We see it as our responsibility to ensure that novel applications for charitable status are
> treated as flexibly as possible within the fundamental principles of the existing legal frame-
> work. Just as it is important to ensure that the register accurately reflects the established
> legal definition and principles of charity, equally it is essential that the concept of charity:
>
> 1. keeps pace with social change;
> 2. responds to new circumstances and challenges;
> 3. reflects public concerns and opinions; and
> 4. is intelligible to the general public.[191]

---

[186] *Political Activities and Campaigning by Charities* (Charity Commission Leaflet CC9, September 1999) section 3, paras. 9–14. See, more recently, the 2008 publication *Charity Commission: Speaking Out: Guidance on
campaigning and political activity by charities* (CC9).
[187] Charity Commissioners, *English PEN's Application for Registration as a Charity* 21 July 2008 [2008]
WTLR 1799.
[188] Charities Act 2011, ss. 69–72 (Charities Act 1993, s. 17).
[189] Charities Act 2011, Part 5 (Charities Act 1993, s. 8).
[190] *Annual Report of the Charity Commissioners 1985*, para. 27.
[191] *Annual Report of the Charity Commissioners 1995*, para. 88.

Charities Act 2011 Part 2 defines more precisely the objectives, functions, and duties of the Charity Commission. Its objectives are as follows:

- its *'public confidence objective is to increase public trust and confidence in charities'*;
- its *'public benefit objective is to promote awareness and understanding of the operation of the public benefit requirement'*;
- its *'compliance objective is to promote compliance by charity trustees with their legal obligations in exercising control and management of the administration of their charities'*;
- its *'charitable resources objective is to promote the effective use of charitable resources'*;
- ts *'accountability objective is to enhance the accountability of charities to donors, beneficiaries and the general public'*.

The Commission's general functions include:

- determining whether institutions are or are not charities;
- encouraging and facilitating the better administration of charities;
- identifying and investigating apparent misconduct or mismanagement in the administration of charities, and taking remedial or protective action in connection with misconduct or mismanagement therein;
- determining whether public collections certificates should be issued, and remain in force, in respect of public charitable collections;
- obtaining, evaluating and disseminating information in connection with the performance of any of the Commission's functions or meeting any of its objectives (including the maintenance of an accurate and up-to-date register of charities);
- giving information or advice, or making proposals, to any Minister of the Crown on matters relating to any of the Commission's functions or meeting any of its objectives.

The Commission's general duties require it to act, so far as is reasonably practicable, in a way that is compatible with its objectives and which it considers most appropriate for the purpose of meeting those objectives, and so as to encourage all forms of charitable giving and voluntary participation in charity work.

Cy-près

When a private trust fails or is prematurely fulfilled, the surplus trust property usually returns to the settlor or testator under a resulting trust, but when assets have been dedicated to a charitable purpose that cannot be carried out or is prematurely fulfilled, any surplus will usually be applied to advance charitable purposes 'as near as'[192] possible in

---

[192] French: *cy-près*.

type to those originally intended. Property can only be applied cy-près at the direction of the Chancery Division, the High Court, or the Charity Commissioners, the trustees having a duty to make an application to the appropriate forum wherever circumstances deem it necessary.[193] Leaving aside exempt charities, such as universities and the church commissioners,[194] the Charities Act 2011 (consolidating the Charities Act 1993) provides that the Charity Commissioners may not exercise their general jurisdiction to order a cy-près scheme[195] except on the application of the charity[196] or the Attorney General.[197] If the trust income from all sources does not exceed £500 in any year, the Commissioners may exercise their jurisdiction on the application of any one or more of the charity trustees, any person interested in the charity, or any two or more inhabitants of the area of a local charity.[198] In any case in which the Commissioners are satisfied that the charity trustees have unreasonably refused or neglected to apply for a scheme, and the Commissioners have given the charity trustees an opportunity to make representations to them, the Commissioners may proceed as if an application for a scheme had been made by the charity, although the Commissioners have no power under this subsection to alter the purposes of a charity unless 40 years have elapsed from the date of its foundation.[199]

Different considerations apply to the operation of cy-près according to whether the gift fails *ab initio* (from the outset) or at some later date.

Initial failure

An example of failure *ab initio* without general charitable intent occurred in *Kings v. Bultitude*.[200] When the last surviving priest of a church denomination died, the church was deemed to have 'died' with her. She left her residuary estate to the church, but because cy-près did not apply the residue was distributed on the basis of intestacy and other effects passed to the Attorney General. Where a donation fails from the outset, it will only be applied cy-près if the donor had a so-called 'general' or 'paramount' charitable intent (with the exception of donations made to a public charitable collection).[201] This means that, if a donation cannot be applied to the donor's specified charitable purpose, but the donor intended to make the donation to charity in any event, the donation will be applied cy-près. If, on the other hand, it was a prerequisite to the donor's willingness to part with the subject matter of the gift that the donation should be applied to advance the particular charitable purpose specified by him and, in the event,

---

[193] Charities Act 2011, ss. 61–2 (Charities Act 1993, s. 13(5)).
[194] Charities Act 2011, Sch. 3 (Charities Act 1993, s. 3(5)(a) and Sch. 2).
[195] Charities Act 2011, s. 69 (Charities Act 1993, s. 16(1)).
[196] Charities Act 2011, s. 70(2)(a) (Charities Act 1993, s. 16(4)(a)).
[197] Charities Act 2011, s. 70(2)(c) (Charities Act 1993, s. 16(4)(c)).
[198] Charities Act 2011, s. 70(3) (Charities Act 1993, s. 16(5)).
[199] Charities Act 2011, s. 70(5) (Charities Act 1993, s. 16(6)).
[200] [2010] EWHC 1795 (Ch).
[201] Charities Act 2011, s. 15 (Charities Act 1993, s. 14), discussed later.

the donation cannot be so applied, the donation will not be applied cy-près, but will, instead, return to the donor under a resulting trust. If the donor is dead, the donation will pass under a resulting trust to the beneficiaries of the donor's residuary estate—which no doubt explains why it is this class of beneficiaries who most often dispute any suggestion that the donor had a 'general' or 'paramount' charitable intent. If the donor cannot be identified, the donation will pass *bona vacantia*.

What constitutes initial 'failure'

Prior to the Charities Act 1960, the official position was that a trust would only be deemed to have failed if it was 'impossible' or 'impracticable' to carry out the charitable purposes. This meant that many trusts went unreformed even though amendment by application of a cy-près scheme would have been beneficial.[202] There were, of course, some notable instances of the strict rule being relaxed. One such was *Re Dominion Students' Hall Trust*.[203] In that case, a charitable foundation established to promote cultural interface between nations of the British Commonwealth was applied cy-près on the same trusts, but with a clause of its constitution removed that had restricted residence of the hall to students of European origin.

The most straightforward case of initial failure through 'impossibility' is where a donation is made to a charitable institution that no longer exists. A donation to an unincorporated institution might survive the dissolution of the association if the donation can be construed to be a trust for the charitable purposes of the association,[204] but a donation made to a corporation to advance charitable purposes will inevitably fail if the corporation ceases to exist,[205] unless the donation to the corporation can be construed to be merely a way of expressing an intention to further the charitable purposes of the corporation.[206]

The very fact that a donation is made to a *specific* institution means that it will rarely be accompanied by a *general* charitable intent, so if such a donation fails, it will not be applied cy-près. If the donor successfully identifies '*some particular specified institution or purpose as the object of his bounty*',[207] it will be very hard to show that the testator had a general charitable intent: '*The specific displaces the general*'.[208] If, on the other hand, the testator demonstrates a charitable intention, but is unsuccessful in his attempt to identify '*some particular specified institution or purpose as the object of his bounty*',[209] in such a case, '*the absence of the specific leaves the general undisturbed*'.[210]

In *Re Rymer*,[211] a charitable legacy of £5,000 'to the rector for the time being of St Thomas' Seminary for the education of priests in the diocese of Westminster' was held to have failed, because the seminary no longer existed at the date of the testator's death, but, because the testator had intended to make a gift to the particular seminary, the

---

[202] Nathan Committee, *Report of the Committee on the Law and Practice relating to Charitable Trusts* (HMSO, London, Cmd. 8710, 1952) para. 104.   [203] [1947] Ch 183.

[204] *Re Lucas* [1948] 2 All ER 22.   [205] *Re Vernon's Will Trusts* [1972] Ch 300 at 303.

[206] *Re Finger's WT* [1972] 1 Ch 286.   [207] Megarry VC in *Re Spence* [1979] Ch 483.

[208] Ibid. at 493B.   [209] Ibid. at 493B.   [210] Ibid. at 493C.   [211] [1895] 1 Ch 19.

gift was not applied cy-près: there was no evidence of a general charitable intention to educate priests in the diocese of Westminster. *Re Wilson*[212] was a similar case. The testator left money to pay the salary of a schoolmaster to teach at a specified school according to a syllabus of the testator's design, but, in the event, the school was never built. It was held that there was an initial failure, but that the doctrine of cy-près would not apply to save the gift, because the fine details of the testator's gift were not consistent with a general charitable intent. These cases should be contrasted with cases in which the intended donee institution had never existed at all. In *Re Harwood*,[213] a testatrix left £300 to the Peace Society of Belfast, but there had never been any such institution. The gift of £300 was applied cy-près on the ground that the testatrix's specific intention was meaningless, so it could be concluded that she had a general charitable intention to benefit any society connected with Belfast that existed for the promotion of peace. Incidentally, the testatrix had also left £200 to the Wisbech Peace Society, Cambridge, a real institution that had ceased to exist before the date of her death; that gift failed because the identification of a *specific* institution was evidence that the testatrix lacked a *general* charitable intention.

Instances of initial failure through 'impracticability' would include, for example, a charitable donation to pay for the erection of a building for which the donation is insufficiently large, or for which planning permission cannot be obtained, or for which no suitable site can be found.[214]

Section 13 of the Charities Act 1960 expanded the list of circumstances in which a donation may be held to have suffered an initial failure. That list was subsequently consolidated into s. 13 of the Charities Act 1993, which has since been consolidated in the Charities Act 2011. Before proceeding to examine that list, it is absolutely crucial to note that Charities Act 2011, s. 62 (Charities Act 1993, s. 13) does not affect the need to show a general or paramount charitable intent before the doctrine of cy-près will apply in cases of initial failure.[215] The following is the current list of circumstances in which a charitable gift will be deemed to have failed *ab initio*, so as to allow the gift to be applied cy-près.

1. Impossibility—this includes situations in which the original purposes have been fulfilled, in whole or in part, as far as they possibly may be,[216] and situations in which the original purposes cannot be carried out or cannot be carried out in accordance with the '*spirit of the gift*'.[217] The reference to the spirit of the gift suggests, at first sight, that there is greater fidelity to the settlor's intentions in this context than in the context of variation of private trusts, but that may be misleading. Prior to the Charities Act 1960, a finding of initial failure on the basis of 'impossibility' was frequently caused by the specific nature of the donor's intentions, which, being incompatible

---

[212] [1913] 1 Ch 314. [213] [1936] Ch 285. [214] *Re Weir Hospital* [1910] 2 Ch 124.
[215] Charities Act 2011, s. 62(1) (Charities Act 1993, s. 13(2)); *Varsani v. Jesani* [1999] Ch 219, CA.
[216] Charities Act 2011, s. 62(1)(a)(i) (Charities Act 1993, s. 13(1)(a)(i)).
[217] Charities Act 2011, s. 62(1)(a)(ii) (Charities Act 1993, s. 13(1)(a)(ii)).

with a finding of general charitable intent, meant that the trust property would result to the donor, or to his residuary estate if he were deceased. After the Charities Act 1960, if a donation fails because it cannot be applied in accordance with the 'spirit of the gift', it may be more likely that failure will be accompanied by a finding of general charitable intent, with the consequence that the donation will be applied cy-près. However, against this, the courts have identified their role to be to apply the provisions of s. 62 of the 2011 Act (s. 13 of the 1993 Act) 'to the circumstances of each case without any predilection either to making or to refusing to make a scheme altering the original purposes of the charity'.[218] The Charity Commissioners have likewise stated their intention to adopt 'a flexible and imaginative approach, consistent with due regard to the donor's wishes'.[219] This may mean that property is applied cy-près to purposes that are quite different to the original purposes, if all near-variants of the original purposes are already adequately catered for.[220] The Charities Act 2011 contains a provision that substitutes the phrase 'appropriate considerations' for the phrase 'spirit of the gift' which had appeared in s. 13 of the 1993 Act. The 'appropriate considerations' are defined in the 2011 Act as the spirit of the gift concerned and (significantly) 'the social and economic circumstances prevailing at the time of the proposed alteration of the original purposes'.[221]

2. Surplus property—this covers situations in which fulfilment of the original purposes does not fully exhaust the donated property.[222]

3. Common investment—this covers situations in which the donation can be more effectively employed in conjunction with other property applicable for similar purposes, rather than alone.[223] This is considered further in the section on amalgamation, later.

4. Unsuitability or impracticality to the beneficiaries or the area—this covers situations in which the original purposes were laid down by reference to a class of persons, or to an area, which has, for some reason, ceased to be suitable or practical,[224] regard being had to the spirit of the gift. In Peggs v. Lamb,[225] the Charity Commissioners advised the trustees of certain charities established for Freemen and Widows of Freemen in the Borough of Huntingdon to seek the court's directions as to whether the annual trust income of more than £500,000 should be applied cy-près in favour of all inhabitants of the borough, because a sharp decline in the number of eligible beneficiaries meant that each beneficiary received a huge annuity from the fund. Morritt J held that the trust income should be applied cy-près.[226]

---

[218] Varsani v. Jesani [1999] Ch 219, CA, per Morritt LJ at 235.

[219] Government White Paper, Charities: A Framework for the Future (1989) Cm. 694, para. 6.18.

[220] Annual Report of the Charity Commissioners 1989, para. 73. See, generally, J. Warburton, The Spirit of the Gift (1995–96) 3(1) CL&PR 1–10.   [221] Charities Act 2011, s. 62(2)(b).

[222] Charities Act 2011, s. 62(1)(b) (Charities Act 1993, s. 13(1)(b)).

[223] Charities Act 2011, s. 62(1)(c) (Charities Act 1993, s. 13(1)(c)).

[224] Charities Act 2011, s. 62(1)(d) (Charities Act 1993, s. 13(1)(d)).   [225] [1994] Ch 172.

[226] For a broadly similar case, see Re Lepton's Charity [1972] Ch 276.

5. Ineffectiveness—this covers situations in which the original purposes have been adequately provided for, in whole or in part, by other means.[227] According to the Charity Commissioners, cy-près schemes in this category have been used where charities for the repair of roads and bridges have been rendered obsolete by the activities of local councils.[228] Substitute general purposes for the benefit of local communities include the promotion of the arts, the provision of seats and shelters, the preservation of old buildings, and the improvement of local amenities. It is notable that the Charities Act 2011 Part 15 authorizes local authorities to keep a record of local charities and to review the coordination of the activities of local authorities and local charities. Also included within the fifth category of failure are situations in which the original purposes have, for some reason, ceased to be charitable in law, as being, for example, useless or harmful to the community,[229] and situations in which the original purposes have ceased in some other way to provide a suitable and effective method of using the property available by virtue of the gift, regard being had to appropriate considerations including the spirit of the gift.[230]

Since the enactment of the Human Rights Act 1998, which requires English courts to interpret and develop English law consistent with the European Convention on Human Rights,[231] it is arguable that trusts should be deemed to have failed under the fifth category if they infringe Art. 14 of the Convention. That Article requires public bodies not to discriminate on grounds of colour, gender, religion, and so forth, when seeking to apply the protection of the Convention. This might mean that the courts and Charity Commissioners should treat any discriminatory trust as having failed *ab initio*. The problem, of course, is how to achieve that consistent with the donor's intention to dispose of his private property in the manner of his choosing. Prima facie the donor's private choice does not amount to public discrimination.[232] The Ontario Court of Appeal overcame the problem in *Re Canada Trust Co and Ontario Human Rights Commission*.[233] The trust in that case had been established in 1916 by a Canadian entrepreneur to provide educational scholarships to any 'British Subject of the White Race and of the Christian Religion in its Protestant Form'.[234] The judge at first instance held that the trust was valid,[235] but all three judges on appeal held that the trust failed *ab initio*, because society had changed since the establishment of the trust and particularly since World War II, as evidenced by the 1928 Universal Declaration of Human Rights, the Canadian Bill of Rights, and so on, with the result that even private discrimination of this sort should no longer be tolerated by the courts.

[227] Charities Act 2011, s. 62(1)(e)(i) (Charities Act 1993, s.13(1)(e)(i)).
[228] Annual Report 1970, para. 43.
[229] Charities Act 2011, s. 62(1)(e)(ii) (Charities Act 1993, s.13(1)(e)(ii)).
[230] Charities Act 2011, s. 62(1)(e)(iii) (Charities Act 1993, s.13(1)(e)(iii)).
[231] The European Convention for the Protection of Human Rights and Fundamental Freedoms, Rome, 1950.
[232] *Blathwayt v. Baron Cawley* [1976] AC 397.   [233] (1990) 69 DLR (4th) 321.
[234] See B. Ziff, *Unforseen Legacies: Reuben Wells Leonard and the Leonard Foundation Trust* (Toronto: University of Toronto Press, 2000) at 176.
[235] 42 DLR (4th) 263, *per* McKeown J.

In fact, long before the Human Rights Act 1998 came into force, English courts showed creativity in their approach to discriminatory trusts. We have already considered *Re Dominion Students' Hall Trust*;[236] *Re Lysaght*[237] was a similar case. A testatrix had settled the net residue of her estate on the Royal College of Surgeons as trustee for the charitable purposes of the college, but conditions attaching to the gift excluded women, Jews, and Roman Catholics from partaking of any studentship funded by the gift. The college threatened to disclaim the trusteeship unless the offensive conditions were removed from the gift.[238] The court held that the refusal of the college had caused the trust to fail and that the donation could only be saved by applying it cy-près on identical terms, but with the discriminatory conditions removed. To that end, the court held, somewhat imaginatively, that the testatrix had demonstrated a *general* charitable intention to benefit the college. The reality, of course, is that the court quite deliberately bypassed the letter, and probably the spirit, of the donation. The unspoken rule seems to be that malevolent spirits do not count.

To conclude this section, it should be noted that a mere accidental misdescription of a charitable object will not cause the donation to fail, provided that it is still possible to identify the intended object.[239]

Amalgamation

In *Re Faraker*,[240] a testatrix left £200 to 'Mrs Bailey's Charity, Rotherhithe'. That charity had been founded in 1756 for the benefit of poor widows of Rotherhithe, but, in 1905, the Charity Commission amalgamated it with other local charities to create a consolidated charity for the relief of poverty in the area of Rotherhithe. The Court of Appeal held that the amalgamated charity was entitled to the £200. However, there had been no initial failure and this was not a case for the application of the doctrine of cy-près. The amalgamated charities were entitled to receive the legacy because the original charity continued to exist in a slightly modified form. Even though the amalgamated charity made no specific reference to the relief of widows, Farwell LJ refused to accept the argument advanced by the testatrix's residuary beneficiaries that the Charity Commissioners had destroyed the original charity, causing the legacy to fail. His Lordship held that they

> cannot take an existing charity and destroy it; they are obliged to administer it ... no alteration of the machinery can destroy the charitable trust for the benefit of which the machinery is provided.[241]

What is not clear, however, is whether the trustees of the amalgamated charity were still required to apply the £200 for the benefit of poor widows. Note that the constitution of a modern charity will often grant the trustees the power to amalgamate the charity with other charities with similar purposes.[242] Note, also, that, even after amalgamation,

---

[236] [1947] Ch 183.   [237] [1966] 1 Ch 191.
[238] No apparent objection was made to the sexual discrimination.   [239] *Re Spence* [1979] Ch 483.
[240] [1912] 2 Ch 488.   [241] Ibid. at 495.
[242] For the amalgamation of Charitable Incorporated Organisations see Charities Act 2011, ss. 235–9.

it may be wise to leave the basic administration of the original charity intact to avoid problems of the sort that arose in *Re Faraker*.[243]

Subsequent failure and funds surplus to fulfilment

A forward-thinking donor to some charitable object might expressly provide for a gift over to a non-charitable object in the event of failure of his primary charitable donation. In the usual case, however, once property has been dedicated to charitable purposes, it remains charitable in perpetuity.[244] This means that, in cases in which a charitable trust donation is initially successful, but subsequently 'fails', the donation will be applied cy-près without having to prove that the donor had a paramount, general charitable intent.[245] It also means that there is no requirement to prove that the charitable donation has failed in the sense that it has become impossible or impracticable to perform. In cases of subsequent failure, cy-près can be used simply to keep the objects of the trust up-to-date and most effective. Genuine cases of subsequent failure, in which the trust needs to be saved, tend to be dealt with by the courts, because only they are competent to deal with this especially complex and contentious issue; cases in which a trust is merely updated tend to be dealt with by the Charity Commissioners, whose jurisdiction is equivalent to the court's for this purpose.[246] In the latter type of case, cy-près performs a broadly similar function in relation to public trusts to that performed by the Variation of Trusts Act 1958 in relation to private trusts.[247] Of course, the theoretical bases for the two jurisdictions are quite different: the former is concerned with the quite abstract idea of how public wealth should be most efficiently allocated; the latter is based on the consent of the beneficiaries of private property.

In *National Anti-Vivisection Society v. IRC*, Lord Simonds stated obiter that the concept of what is charitable may change from age to age, and that a trust that was once held to be charitable might one day cease to be so, in which case the trust fund should be applied cy-près.[248] The crucial point to grasp is that, in cases of subsequent impossibility, the property can be applied cy-près without the need to show a general or paramount charitable intention.

In *Re King*,[249] the testatrix left the residue of her estate to provide for the erection of a stained glass window in a parish church to the memory of the testatrix and her relations. This was held to be a valid charitable trust of the whole fund, so that any surplus remaining after the erection of the stained glass window should be applied cy-près, with the consent of the Attorney General, towards the provision of a further stained glass window or windows in the same church. Romer J stated:

> in the case of a legacy to a charitable institution that exists at the death of the testator, but ceases to exist after his death and before the legacy is paid over, the legacy is applied *cy-près*, even in the absence of a general charitable intention.[250]

---

[243] [1912] 2 Ch 488.   [244] *Re Slevin* [1891] 2 Ch 236.
[245] Ibid.   [246] Charities Act 2011, s. 69 (Charities Act 1993, s. 16).
[247] See Chapter 9.   [248] [1948] AC 31 at 74.   [249] [1923] 1 Ch 243.
[250] [1923] 1 Ch 243 at 246. Referring to *Re Slevin* [1891] 2 Ch 236.

Surplus from public collections

Charities Act 2011, ss. 63–6 (Charities Act 1993, s. 14), provides that surplus monies donated to collecting boxes, raffles, entertainments, and other gifts made by donors *'unknown or disclaiming'* may be applied cy-près without having to obtain the donors' consent. As regards other donations, the trustees must advertise and take steps to find the donors and, if they are found, return the donation to them or obtain in writing a waiver of the donors' claims to the donation. However, this advertising and inquiry process can be dispensed with by order of the court where it appears to the court either that it would be *'unreasonable, having regard to the amounts likely to be returned to the donors, to incur expense with a view to returning the property'*[251] or that it would be *'unreasonable, having regard to the nature, circumstances and amounts of the gifts, and to the lapse of time since the gifts were made, for the donors to expect the property to be returned'.*[252] The Charities Act 2006 extended this power of the court to the Charity Commission. The Act also inserted a (very poorly drafted) s. 14A after s. 14 of the Charities Act 1993. The essential import of the new s. 14A (now consolidated as Charities Act 2011, s. 65) is that, if a donation for a specific charitable purpose is solicited from the donor with the assurance that it will be applied cy-près if that specific purpose fails, the donor can declare, at the time he makes the donation, that he would like to be offered the return of his donation. The section sets out the steps that the trustees are required to take to inform the donor that the specific purpose has failed and the steps that the donor must then take to secure the return of his donation. A further clause of the 1993 Act inserted a new s. 14B (now consolidated as Charities Act 2011, s. 67), which provides that where property is applicable cy-près, the court or the Commission may make a scheme providing for the property to be applied as appropriate in the light of the spirit of the original gift, the desirability of securing that the property is applied for charitable purposes which are close to the original purposes, and the need for the benefiting charity to have purposes which are suitable and effective in the light of current social and economic circumstances.

The hybrid nature of charitable property

Our study of cy-près indicates that charity is a hybrid of private and public property; it is not fully private, because no private persons will ever have the power to bring the trust to an end and claim the assets beneficially, but neither is it fully public, because, when determining what should happen to the trust fund in the event of failure of the charitable purposes, consideration is still given to the settlor's intentions.

---

[251] Charities Act 2011, s. 64(2)(a) (Charities Act 1993, s. 4(4)(a)).
[252] Charities Act 2011, s. 64(2)(b) (Charities Act 1993, s. 4(4)(b)).

Further reading

In addition to the following print sources, the Online Resource Centre accompanying this book contains web links to further reading as well as guide answers to assessment questions relevant to this chapter.

CHARITY COMMISSION, *Decision of the Charity Commissioners for England & Wales: Application for Registration as a Charity by the Church of Scientology* (England and Wales), 17 November 1999.

CHESTERMAN, M., 'Foundations of charity law in the new welfare state' [1999] 62(3) MLR 333.

DUNN, A. and RILEY, C. A., 'Supporting the not-for-profit sector: the government's review of charitable and social enterprise' (2004) 67(4) MLR 632.

EDGE, P., 'Charitable status for the advancement of religion: an abolitionist's view' (1995–96) 3 CL&PR 29–35.

EDWARDES, J., 'Twelve heads are better than four' (2004) 154 New LJ 1076.

JACONELLI, J., 'Adjudicating on charitable status – a reconsideration of the elements' (2013) 2 Conv 96–112.

JONES G., *History of the Law of Charity, 1532–1827 (Cambridge Studies in English Legal History)* (Cambridge: Cambridge University Press, 2008).

LAW COMMISSION FOR ENGLAND AND WALES, *Charities: A Framework for the Future* (1989) Cm 694.

LUXTON, P., EVANS N., and SMITH J., *The Law of Charities* 2nd edn (Oxford: Oxford University Press, 2012).

LUXTON, P., EVANS N., and SMITH J., 'Public benefit and charities: the impact of the Charities Act 2006 on independent schools and private hospitals' in *Contemporary Perspectives on Property, Equity and Trust Law* (M. DIXON and G. L. H. GRIFFITHS, eds) (Oxford: Oxford University Press, 2007) 181–202.

NATIONAL COUNCIL FOR VOLUNTARY ORGANISATIONS, *For the Public Benefit? A Consultation Document on Charity Law Reform* (2001).

QUINT, F., 'Recent developments in the cy pres principle' (2009) 11(2) Charity Law and Practice Review 49–57.

QUINT, F. (and SPRING, T.), 'Religion, charity law and human rights' (1999) 5(3) Charity Law and Practice Review 153.

RAHMATIAN, A., 'The continued relevance of the "poor relations" and the "poor employees" cases under the Charities Act 2006' (2009) 73(1) Conv 12–20.

WARBURTON, J., 'Charitable trusts: unique' (1999) Conv 20.

WARBURTON, J. and MORRIS, D. (eds), *Tudor on Charities*, 8th edn (London: Sweet & Maxwell, 1997).

WATT, G., 'Giving unto Caesar: rationality, reciprocity and legal recognition of religion' in *Current Legal Issues: Law and Religion* (R. O'Dair and A. Lewis, eds) (Oxford: Oxford University Press, 2001) at 45.

8

Constructive trusts and informal trusts of land

A constructive trust, is in some respects, the polar opposite of an express trust: an express trust gives effect to an owner's intention to transfer a beneficial interest in his property, whereas a constructive trust may be imposed directly contrary to the owner's intentions.[1] A constructive trust arises by operation of law where the facts are such that it would be unconscionable for an owner to deny that another person has acquired a beneficial interest in his property.

Another respect in which a constructive trust is the polar opposite of an express trust concerns the relationship between the creation of the trust and the burden on the trustee's conscience. In the case of an express trust, the fact that property has vested in the trustee 'on trust' gives rise to the burden on the trustee's conscience; in the case of a constructive trust, the process operates in reverse: the fact that the trustee's conscience is affected gives rise to the trust. As Professor Scott put it, a party '*is not compelled to convey the property because he is a constructive trustee; it is because he can be compelled to convey it that he is a constructive trustee*',[2] and Sir Robert Megarry VC has stated in a similar vein that:

> In determining whether a constructive trust has been created, the fundamental question is whether the conscience of the recipient is bound in such a way as to justify equity in imposing a trust on him.[3]

One of the most significant distinctions between express trusts and constructive trusts is that an express trust of land is unenforceable unless it is evidenced in writing, whereas a constructive trust of land is created and operates without formality.[4] In the context of cohabitation of land, this has produced a situation in which courts routinely recognize express arrangements between cohabitees as arrangements giving rise to constructive trusts rather than regarding them as express trusts, for to regard them as express trusts

---

[1] Lord Browne-Wilkinson in *Westdeutsche Landesbank Girozentrale v. Islington LBC* [1996] AC 669 at 705D. For a striking illustration, see *Grant v. Edwards* [1986] Ch 638.

[2] A. W. Scott, *The Law of Trusts*, 3rd edn (Boston: Little Brown & Co, 1967) vol. 5 at 3413.

[3] *Re Montagu's Settlement Trusts* [1987] Ch 264 at 277.

[4] Law of Property Act 1925, s. 53(2).

would be to render them ineffective due to informality. Although they are, in many respects, opposites, express and constructive trusts, by their very nature as trusts, do have a number of significant features in common. The most fundamental is the presence of ascertainable property in which a beneficiary has a proprietary interest which the trustee is personally bound to respect. There is, however, one anomalous case—that of a person who dishonestly assists in a breach of trust—in which the wrongdoer is said to be personally liable in equity as if he were a constructive trustee, even though he might never have held ascertainable trust property. This situation, which is not a true case of constructive trust, is considered in depth in Chapter 15.

The first half of this chapter is devoted to the nature, operation, and variety of constructive trusts. The second half focuses on one special category of constructive trusts: informal trusts of land. We will see that resulting trusts and the doctrine of proprietary estoppel also play a significant part in the regulation of informal dealings in land.

The nature of constructive trusts

From the preceding introduction, it should be clear that the distinguishing feature of the constructive trust is that it is not created expressly; indeed, constructive trusts and resulting trusts can be classified together as the two major categories of non-express trust. Another category is the implied trust, which seems to be a residual category designed to catch trusts that are neither express, nor resulting, nor constructive.[5]

The suggestion that resulting trusts and constructive trusts are not expressly created trusts requires some elaboration. When we considered resulting trusts in Chapter 5, we observed that many of the situations in which resulting trusts arise concern express trusts that are fulfilled, or fail, leaving surplus funds. In such cases, the trust is expressly created (the trustee took the property 'on trust'), so when we say that the resulting trust is a non-express trust, we really mean that, although some sort of trust was expressly created, a resulting trust was not. Similar reasoning applies to constructive trusts arising when an attempt to create an express trust fails due to lack of proper formality or for some other technical reason.

The most likely reason for an express trust to fail 'on a technicality' is because the trust is a testamentary trust or a trust of land that does not fulfil the statutory formalities. Constructive and resulting trusts provide a way of by-passing these formalities. The use of constructive trusts to avoid testamentary formalities in the case of secret trusts and mutual wills was considered in Chapter 6. In the second half of this chapter we will focus on *inter vivos* trusts of land, under which we will see that s. 53(2) of the Law of Property Act 1925 exempts the creation and operation of 'resulting, constructive

---

[5] See the discussion in Chapter 6.

and implied' trusts from the usual requirement that the creation of an express trust of land must be evidenced in writing.[6]

Apart from constructive trusts created to prevent unconscionable reliance upon failure of formality, constructive trusts arise in a wide range of situations in which the parties never intended to create a trust. So, for example, constructive trusts have been imposed, rightly or wrongly, upon agents who receive bribes and secret commissions, and upon persons who have property transferred to them by mistake. In every case of constructive trust, the aim is to prevent the trustee from unconscionably asserting his own title to the trust property in denial of another person's legitimate claim to beneficial ownership.[7]

The institutional nature of the constructive trust

Although a constructive trust '*is the concept employed by a court of equity to prevent a person from relying on his legal rights where it would be unconscionable for him to do so*',[8] it is important to appreciate that, in English law, a constructive trust is not a freestanding remedy for wrongdoing. As Dillon LJ stated in *Springette v. Defoe*:[9] 'The court does not as yet sit, as under a palm tree, to exercise a general discretion to do what the man in the street, on a general overview of the case, might regard as fair.'[10]

The English constructive trust is said to be institutional, not remedial. Of course, in one sense, all constructive trusts are remedial, in so far as they remedy the parties' failure to put their affairs on the proper footing of express trusts or express contracts, but some constructive trusts are more remedial than others, as the following sections demonstrate.

The institutional constructive trust

According to Lord Browne-Wilkinson in *Westdeutsche Landesbank Girozentrale v. Islington LBC*:

> Under an institutional constructive trust, the trust arises by operation of law as from the date of the circumstances which give rise to it: the function of the court is merely to declare that such trust has arisen in the past. The consequences that flow from such trust having arisen (including the possibly unfair consequences to third parties who in the interim have received the trust property) are also determined by rules of law, not under a discretion.[11]

---

[6] It should also be noted that '*the creation or operation of resulting, implied or constructive trusts*' is exempt from the requirement of writing in relation to *contracts* for the sale of land (Law of Property (Miscellaneous Provisions) Act 1989, s. 2(5)).

[7] *Paragon Finance plc v. DB. Thakerar & Co* [1999] 1 All ER 400, *per* Millett LJ at 409; see also *Bannister v. Bannister* [1948] 2 All ER 133.

[8] *Re Basham, decd* [1986] 1 WLR 1498, Ch D, *per* Edward Nugee QC (sitting as a High Court judge) at 1504A–B.

[9] [1992] 2 FLR 388, CA.　　　[10] Ibid. at 393.

[11] *Westdeutsche Landesbank Girozentrale v. Islington LBC* [1996] AC 669, HL, *per* Lord Browne-Wilkinson at 714G approving *Metall und Rohstoff AG v. Donaldson Lufkin & Jenrette Inc.* [1990] 1 QB 391 at 478–80 (in *Metall*, it was opined, at 479H, that there might be circumstances in which the court would impose a remedial constructive trust). In *Westdeutsche*, Lord Browne-Wilkinson said that a remedial constructive trust might be appropriate in cases in which a defendant knowingly retains property of which the plaintiff has been unjustly deprived. (716G). Against this, see 'Knowing Receipt', in Chapter 15 .

This means that an institutional constructive trust will ordinarily be declared only in response to a particular type of unconscionable behaviour—namely, the unconscionable assertion of proprietary entitlement, or the unconscionable exercise of the rights and benefits that accompany proprietary entitlement, *in circumstances that deny another person's existing proprietary entitlement.*

If my next-door neighbour deliberately throws stones into my garden causing £500 worth of damage, the court will not award me a £500 beneficial share in my neighbour's land under a constructive trust. It is wrong of my neighbour to throw stones and he may be liable to pay damages at common law for trespass, but he is not acting unconscionably, because he is not abusing a legal right to throw stones into my garden—clearly, he has no such right. If, on the other hand, my neighbour were to invite me to make a small contribution to the cost of building twin garages on his land, with the promise that I would be entitled to the exclusive use of one of the garages for so long as I remain his neighbour, he would be acting unconscionably if, after I have paid my contribution, he were to exercise his legal right to prevent me entering his land. The court will impose a constructive trust to prevent my neighbour from unconscionably denying my interest in the garage. It is worth noting that, as an alternative to a constructive trust, I could seek a resulting trust on these facts, but a resulting trust would only give me back the same proportion of the current value of the garage as the proportion I contributed to the initial value of the garage. An interest under a constructive trust is established *and quantified* to whatever extent is necessary to address the unconscionability of the legal owner, so an interest under a constructive trust has the potential to give me a more valuable interest in the garage than a resulting trust would give.

It is crucial to be aware that the same facts will often give rise to both a resulting and a constructive trust, in which event the claimant will obviously seek whichever trust is likely to be most beneficial. When we come to consider informal trusts of land, we will see that a constructive trust is often more beneficial than a resulting trust, because it prevents the trustee from denying the beneficiary's legitimate expectations, whereas a resulting trust merely returns the beneficiary's contribution, including any increase in its value.

The remedial constructive trust

In contrast with an institutional constructive trust, a remedial constructive trust does not 'arise directly from the transaction between the individual claimants'; instead, it is 'created by the court as a measure of justice after the event'.[12] The extent to which such a trust operates retrospectively to the prejudice of third parties would also lie in the discretion of the court.[13] The broad discretion associated with the remedial constructive trust is for some its major strength and for others its major weakness. US jurists tended to see the positive benefits of a remedial constructive trust. It has been said that

---

[12] *Re Goldcorp Exchange Ltd (in receivership)* [1995] 1 AC 74, *per* Lord Mustill at 99.
[13] *Westdeutsche*, n. 1, *per* Lord Goff of Chieveley at 714.

a constructive trust '*is the formula through which the conscience of equity finds expression*',[14] and that it is '*a fiction imposed as an equitable device for achieving justice*'.[15]

English jurists, on the other hand, have tended on the whole to take a more negative view:[16]

> It is unlikely that the remedial constructive trust…will gain acceptance in England or Australia. It is a counsel of despair which too readily concedes the impossibility of propounding a general rationale for the availability of a proprietary remedy.[17]

Even if there is no English authority binding against the remedial constructive trust, '*an English Court will be very slow indeed to adopt the US and Canadian model*'.[18]

Re Sharpe (a bankrupt) was one of Browne-Wilkinson J's earliest judgments. Mr Sharpe, his wife, and his aunt were living together in a maisonette purchased by Sharpe for £17,000. The aunt had provided £12,000 of the purchase price, having been assured by Sharpe and his wife that they would look after her. She also paid more than £2,000 for decorations and fittings for the property, and paid £9,000 in an unsuccessful attempt to stave off Sharpe's bankruptcy. When the trustee in bankruptcy contracted to sell the maisonette, the aunt claimed to have an interest in the premises under a resulting or constructive trust. It was held that she had intended to make a loan, which left no room for a resulting trust in her favour. It might have been thought that an intention to create a loan would likewise have left no room for a constructive trust, but Browne-Wilkinson J felt constrained by authority [19] to hold that the aunt's irrevocable 'contractual licence'[20] to remain in the maisonette was sufficient to bind not only Sharpe's conscience, but also the conscience of the trustee in bankruptcy, so as to make the trustee in bankruptcy a constructive trustee of the maisonette for the aunt. His Lordship did not rule out the possibility of a remedial constructive trust, but the essence of his judgment was to support the orthodox institutional constructive trust:

> Even if it be right to say that the courts can impose a constructive trust as a remedy in certain cases—which to my mind is a novel concept in English law—in order to provide a remedy the court must first find a right which has been infringed…it cannot be that the interest in property arises for the first time when the court declares it to exist.[21]

His Lordship was expressing a common objection to the 'discovery' of constructive trusts in commercial arrangements—namely, that they are not easily predicted by the parties to such transactions, with the result that the proprietary advantage conferred by

---

[14] *Beatty v. Guggenheim Exploration Co.* (1919) 225 NY 380, *per* Judge Cardozo at 386.

[15] *Healy v. Commissioner of Internal Revenue* (1953) 345 US 278, US Supreme Court, *per* Vinson CJ at 282.

[16] A notable exception is Professor Donovan Waters. See D. W. M. Waters, *Constructive Trusts* (London: The Athlone Press, 1964) ch. 1, and especially his conclusion at 73.

[17] Sir Peter Millett, 'Remedies: the error in *Lister v. Stubbs*' in P. Birks (ed.), *The Frontiers of Liability* (Oxford: Oxford University Press, 1994) vol. I, 51 at 52.

[18] *London Allied Holdings Ltd v. Lee* [2007] EWHC 2061 (Ch), *per* Etherton J at [274].

[19] Notably *Binions v. Evans* [1972] Ch 359.

[20] A licence is a personal permission.

[21] *Re Sharpe (a bankrupt)* [1980] 1 WLR 219, *per* Browne-Wilkinson J at 225H.

the constructive trust may be unfairly prejudicial to the constructive trustee's general creditors in the event of the constructive trustee becoming insolvent.[22] The question is whether it would be fairer to third parties if the proprietary consequences of recognizing a constructive trust were 'managed' by giving courts a broad remedial discretion to recognize or refuse to recognize such trusts, rather than to persist with the present approach which, in theory, denies the courts any jurisdiction to control proprietary consequences in the interests of justice. The basic tendency of the law has always been against allowing judges to create and determine proprietary rights at their discretion, and there are strong public policy and 'human rights' justifications for continuing with that approach. Nevertheless, Lord Browne-Wilkinson accepted in *Westdeutsche*[23] that a remedial constructive trust might help to avoid prejudice to third parties in individual cases, because it can be *'tailored to the circumstances of the particular case'.*[24] His Lordship did not go so far as to approve the remedial constructive trust, suggesting instead that the question of whether English law should adopt it would have to be decided in a future case when the point was directly in issue.

If the House of Lords were to approve and adopt the remedial constructive trust, it would mark a dramatic departure from legal orthodoxy. Certainly, it does not appear that such a reform is imminent. Barely two years after Lord Browne-Wilkinson had raised hope for the remedial constructive trust, the Court of Appeal removed any such hope, at least in the cases where insolvency has already occurred:

> The insolvency road is blocked off to remedial constructive trusts, at least when judge driven in a vehicle of discretion . . . To a trust lawyer and, even more so to an insolvency lawyer, the prospect of a court imposing such a trust is inconceivable.[25]

Supporters of the remedial constructive trust might not be ready to raise the white flag of surrender, but they will surely admit that its potential is restricted to cases outside the insolvency context, and, very probably, restricted to cases for restitution for wrongs such as torts and breach of contractual duties. It will not extend to restitution for unjust enrichment, as discussed next.

The restitutionary remedial constructive trust

The constructive trust in the USA has long been a remedy designed to prevent the trustee from being unjustly enriched:[26]

> The court does not give relief because a constructive trust has been created; but the court gives relief because otherwise the defendant would be unjustly enriched; and because the court gives this relief it declares that the defendant is chargeable as a constructive trustee.[27]

---

[22] A. J. Oakley, 'Proprietary claims and their priority in insolvency' [1995] CLJ 377 at 381. See, generally, A. J. Oakley, *Constructive Trusts*, 3rd edn (London: Sweet & Maxwell, 1997) and E. Sherwin, 'Constructive trusts in bankruptcy' (1989) U Ill LR 297 at 335.   [23] See n. 1.

[24] Ibid. at 716.

[25] *Re Polly Peck International plc (No. 2)* [1998] 3 All ER 812, *per* Mummery LJ at 827f. See also, Nourse LJ at 831d. But see C. Rickett and R. Grantham, 'Toward a more constructive classification of trustees' [1999] LMCLQ III at 117.   [26] *Chase Manhattan Bank v. Israel-British Bank* [1981] Ch 105.

[27] A. W. Scott, 'Constructive trusts' (1955) 71 LQR 39 at 41.

When English courts recognize a constructive trust as a response to unjust enrich-ment, such recognition is never purely remedial in the retrospective sense; rather, it is designed to recognize the claimant's pre-existing proprietary entitlement. To the extent that it is concerned to reverse unjust enrichment, it is restricted to cases in which the enrichment of the defendant was at the plaintiff's financial expense (so-called 'subtrac-tive unjust enrichment'). In *Halifax Building Society v. Thomas*,[28] a mortgagee claimed to be entitled to the surplus proceeds of sale of the mortgagor's property even after full repayment of its loan. The claim was brought on the basis of a constructive trust arising because the mortgage loan had been obtained by fraud. The Court of Appeal rejected the mortgagee's claim, because the fraudulent borrower had not been unjustly enriched *at the mortgagee's expense*.

The suggestion that English law should adopt a remedial constructive trust similar to the US restitutionary model has many distinguished critics. Amongst them is Sir Nicolas Browne-Wilkinson, who has stated extra-judicially that '*there are great dangers in seeking to turn equity into one comprehensive law of unjust enrichment based on some sweeping fundamental concept*'.[29]

The operation of constructive trusts

In later chapters, we will consider the extensive rules that govern express trusts. We will see that, in the absence of a comprehensive trust instrument, the general law provides extensive and detailed guidance as to the demands of the 'office' of an express trustee, one of the most significant demands being the requirement that the trust fund be properly invested. The obligations of a constructive trustee are quite different from those of an express trustee.[30] In fact, the basic duty of a constructive trustee is negative: it is simply to refrain from enjoying and employing for his own benefit property that belongs in equity to the beneficiary of the constructive trust. There is a positive dimension to the obligations of a constructive trus-tee, but it is generally limited to the duty to account to the beneficiary of the constructive trust to the extent of that beneficiary's equitable ownership. So, for example, if land held on constructive trust is rented out, the constructive trustee is obliged to account to the ben-eficiary for a share of the rent in proportion to the size of the beneficiary's equitable share in the land and, when the land is sold, the constructive trustee is obliged to account to the beneficiary for the appropriate share of the capital proceeds of sale.

Occasionally, constructive trusteeship will be governed by more detailed terms. If a constructive trust is imposed to prevent an owner from denying that he holds his

---

[28] [1995] 4 All ER 673.
[29] 'Constructive trusts and unjust enrichment' (1996) 10(4) TLI 98–101, first published as the *Presidential Address to the Holdsworth Club* (Holdsworth Club, University of Birmingham, 1991).
[30] '*It is a mistake to suppose that in every situation in which a constructive trust arises the legal owner is nec-essarily subject to all the fiduciary obligations and disabilities of an express trustee*' (per Millett J in *Lonrho plc v. Fayed (No. 2)* [1992] 1 WLR 1 at 12).

property subject to a contractual obligation, the terms of the contract will *ipso facto* become 'the terms' of the trust.[31] And if a constructive trust is imposed upon a person who takes property with notice that the property is subject to express trusts, the terms of the constructive trust are presumed to follow the terms of the express trust.

Categories of constructive trust

Sir Robert Megarry once opined that ' *"Constructive" is, of course, an unhappy word in the law… "Constructive" seems to mean "It isn't, but has to be treated as if it were", and the less of this there is in the law, the better'.*[32] The problem is that there are few alternative words to choose from. If a judge decides that a trust should be recognized—i.e. that in order to restrain or prevent the unconscionability of the legal owner of an asset, the owner ought to be subject to a binding obligation to exercise their legal rights and powers for the benefit of another (in such a way as to respect the proprietary entitlement of that other)—there is a limited range of trust 'labels' that can be applied to the trust in hand. If the strict rules for establishing an express trust do not fit the case and if the narrow mechanical requirements for a resulting trust do not fit the case, the case is liable, in default, to be called a constructive trust. The label 'implied trust' lies in reserve, but has so far not proved popular with the judges. At some point in every study of constructive trusts it therefore becomes necessary to catalogue the somewhat disorganized collection of trusts that, rightly or wrongly, bear the name 'constructive'. The following catalogue is not intended to be exhaustive and, although the constructive trusts are arranged in descending order according to their broad similarity to express trusts (constructive trusts most similar to express trusts appearing first), any such conceptual ordering of the catalogue is necessarily approximate and based to a large extent upon the author's personal impression of the cases.

1. Express trusts or gifts lacking formality

We have encountered examples of trusts in this category in earlier chapters. It includes the case of the person who receives legal title to land as a trustee in the absence of any formal declaration of trust and relies upon the lack of formality to claim absolute ownership of the land.[33] Secret trusts are also included in this category.[34]

---

[31] '[T]*he extent and nature of the fiduciary duties owed in any particular case fall to be determined by reference to any underlying contractual relationship between the parties*' (*per* Lord Browne-Wilkinson in *Henderson v. Merrett Syndicates Ltd* [1995] 2 AC 145, HL at 206); followed in *John Youngs Insurance Services Ltd v. Aviva Insurance Service UK Ltd* [2011] EWHC 1515 (TCC).

[32] 'Historical development' in *Fiduciary Duties (Special Lectures of the Law Society of Upper Canada 1990)* (Ontario: De Boo, 1991) 1 at 5.   [33] *Rochefoucauld v. Boustead* [1897] 1 Ch 196, CA.

[34] See Chapter 6.

We might reluctantly include in this category the constructive trust that is said to arise when an express gift is made in favour of a trust foundation, by a trustee of the foundation, but without the formal transfer necessary fully to constitute the gift.[35] Similar, and no less dubious, inclusions in this category are *donationes mortis causa*, because these are said to take effect by means of an implied or constructive trust.[36]

2. Trustees *de son tort*

A person who has not been properly appointed a trustee of an express trust, but who nevertheless takes it upon himself to intermeddle with the business of the trust, or to act as if he were a trustee, is said to be a constructive trustee; in fact, he is accountable 'as a trustee *de son tort*' on substantially the same principles as an express trustee of the trust in which he has interfered.[37]

3. Trusts of property acquired with notice of express trust

A person who receives property with notice that it is subject to an express trust[38] will hold it on trust for the beneficiaries of the express trust. In essence, 'notice' is knowledge of the trust that has been acquired, or would have been acquired, by making reasonable inquiries appropriate to receipt of that type of property. Where the property is land, the doctrine of notice is subject to technical rules (including the possibility of notice through registration) that lie outside the scope of this book.[39] A purchaser of property who has notice that it is trust property can, however, take free of the beneficiaries' interests in the trust property if he 'overreaches' their beneficial interests.[40] Overreaching will occur if the purchaser purchases the property from trustees who are acting within the scope of a legitimate power to sell it and if all of the trustees sign the receipt for the purchase monies.[41]

---

[35] *T. Choithram International SA v. Pagarani* [2001] 1 WLR 1. See Chapter 4.

[36] *Sen v. Headley* [1991] Ch 425, CA, *per* Nourse LJ at 440C. See Chapter 6.

[37] *Bishopsgate Investment Management Ltd (in liquidation) v. Maxwell* [1993] Ch 1, CA, *per* Dillon LJ at 38. See Chapter 15 for further detail on trustees *de son tort*.

[38] But note the concern expressed by Sir Robert Megarry VC in *Re Montagu's Settlement Trusts* [1987] Ch 264 at 278: '*I do not see why one of the touchstones for determining the burdens on property should be the same as that for deciding whether to impose a personal obligation on a man. The cold calculus of constructive and imputed notice does not seem to me to be an appropriate instrument for deciding whether a man's conscience is sufficiently affected for it to be right to bind him by the obligations of a constructive trustee.*'

[39] For further detail, the reader should consult a specialist text on land law.

[40] See, generally, C. Harpum, 'Overreaching, trustees' powers and the reform of the 1925 legislation' [1990] CLJ 277 and D. Fox, 'Overreaching' in *Breach of Trust* (P. Birks and A. Pretto, eds) (Oxford: Hart Publishing, 2002) at 95.

[41] In the case of land, overreaching not only requires the receipt of all the trustees; there must also be at least two trustees or a trust corporation (Law of Property Act 1925, s. 2(2)). However, provided that this requirement is met, the purchaser is protected by statute even if the sale by the trustees was unauthorized (Law of Property Act 1925, s. 27(1)).

The recipient of property who receives it with notice that it is subject to an express trust may not know the exact identity of the true beneficiary of the express trust, or even the terms of the express trust, but he is still a trustee. The question is, what kind of trustee? Certainly, the recipient does not become a trustee of the express trust as such, because a special procedure must be followed for a person to be appointed trustee of an express trust.[42] The answer is that he becomes a constructive trustee.[43] Penner has suggested that he is a *'constructive trustee of an express trust interest'*.[44] Professor Lionel Smith, whilst acknowledging that Penner's may be the best description currently available,[45] has looked behind the description to try to explain the rather mysterious process by which property subject to an express trust becomes subject to a constructive trust in the hands of a recipient with notice. His explanation is that it is a version of the same mysterious process that occurred historically when the trust was first recognized in English law. To begin with, the trust conferred a mere personal right on the trust beneficiary enforceable against the trustee with regard to the use of the thing: a so-called *jus in personam ad rem*—that is, a right against the person (the trustee), with regard to a thing (the trust property). When the trustee transferred the property to a third party, the question arose whether the third party also came under a personal obligation to the beneficiary. There was reluctance to impose a positive trust obligation on the third party, but the courts were willing to impose a negative obligation on the recipient not to interfere with the beneficiary's right against the trustee. Having acknowledged that the beneficiary's negative right (to prevent interference with his rights against the trustee) was binding on anyone in the world who received the property with knowledge (later, 'notice') of the beneficiary's right, the next step was, for convenience, to recognize that the beneficiary's right was no longer simply a right against people with regard to a thing (a *jus in personam ad rem*), but a right in the thing itself (a right *in rem*). So, argues Smith, when, today, a recipient acquires property with notice of an express trust, or (which is often the same thing) knowledge that the property has been transferred in breach of trust, the recipient comes under a duty not to interfere with the express trust. This duty of non-interference could, like the duty not to interfere in another person's contract, have remained a purely personal duty conferring mere personal rights on the beneficiary, but the fact that it is a duty of non-interference *with property* (a *jus in personam ad rem*) means that, following the historical model, it is convenient to recognize the beneficiary as having a proprietary right in the property in the hands of the recipient. Because the recipient has a duty to hold the property not for his own benefit but for the benefit of the beneficiary, the recipient is therefore a trustee and, for want of a better term, we call him a 'constructive trustee'.

---

[42] See Chapter 11.   [43] *Re Montagu's Settlement Trusts* [1987] Ch 264.

[44] J. E. Penner, *The Law of Trusts*, 2nd edn (London: Butterworths, 2000) 120, para. 5.4.

[45] 'Transfers' in *Breach of Trust* (P. Birks and A. Pretto, eds) (Oxford: Hart Publishing, 2002) 111 at 138.

4. Trusts arising from a contract to transfer property

The most obvious candidate for inclusion in this category is the constructive trust that arises under a specifically enforceable contract for the sale of unique property, such as shares in a private company or land. We have already considered this form of constructive trust at various points in the book. In *Lysaght v. Edwards*, a case concerning land, it was held that '*the vendor is a constructive trustee for the purchaser of the estate from the moment the contract is entered into*'.[46] However, it is a peculiar type of trust, because the vendor is entitled to remain in possession of the land until the sale is actually completed, or at least for as long as he remains unpaid.

We can also include mutual wills within this category, because it has been held that only a fully contractual agreement to create mutual wills is sufficient to burden the conscience of the parties.[47]

5. Trusts that fulfil an assurance that has been relied on

When the owner of certain property (A) assures another person (B) that B has acquired, or will acquire, an interest in or over A's property and B relies on that assurance to her detriment, A will be stopped ('estopped') from denying that B has acquired whatever interest was the subject of the assurance and the detrimental reliance thereon. This proprietary estoppel arises in equity to prevent A from unconscionably asserting his strict legal rights. However, it has a positive aspect too, in that it must be fulfilled by some award of an interest in favour of B. The nature of the award lies in the discretion of the court and frequently, especially where the interest claimed is an interest in land, the remedy awarded is a constructive trust.[48]

6. Trusts under a joint venture to acquire property: the '*Pallant v. Morgan*' equity

We know that equity will impose a constructive trust on a person who receives property with notice that it is already subject to an express trust,[49] but equity will also require a defendant to disgorge any property that the defendant acquired on his own account when he should have acquired it, if at all, for the claimant.[50] This equity is known as the *Pallant v. Morgan*[51] equity after a case in which the parties agreed that one would refrain from bidding at an auction of two lots of land on the understanding that the other would bid for both lots and (if successful) would sell one of them to the non-bidding party. The bidding party won the auction and was required to hold the lots on trust for both parties pending fulfilment of his promise.

---

[46] (1876) LR 2 Ch D 499 at 506–10.   [47] See Chapter 6.
[48] See 'Proprietary estoppel', later.   [49] See section 3.
[50] *Lonrho plc v. Fayed (No. 2)* [1992] 1 WLR 1, *per* Millett J at 9–10.   [51] [1952] 2 All ER 951.

Today, the leading application of the *Pallant v. Morgan* equity is the decision of the Court of Appeal in *Banner Homes Group plc v. Luff Developments Ltd (No. 1)*.[52] Luff agreed *in principle* with Banner that they would create a new joint venture company in order to purchase a commercial site. They agreed to take equal shares in the new company. On that understanding, Luff purchased S Ltd (a new company) for use in the joint venture. Luff subsequently began to have doubts about the proposed joint venture and started looking for a new partner. It did not tell Banner, fearing that Banner might put in an independent bid for the commercial site. Banner continued to act on the footing that the joint venture would proceed, always anticipating that Banner and Luff would enter into a formal agreement setting out the terms of the joint venture. S Ltd eventually acquired the site with funds provided by Luff and only then did Luff inform Banner that the proposed joint venture would not be going ahead. Banner contended, *inter alia*, that it was entitled to half of the shares in S Ltd under a constructive trust. The judge at first instance rejected this contention, holding that equity could not transform an agreement, which was implicitly qualified by the right of either side to withdraw, into a binding arrangement.

The Court of Appeal overturned that judgment. It was held that the *Pallant v. Morgan* equity arose, because it would have been inequitable to allow Luff to claim outright a site that it had acquired in furtherance of a pre-acquisition understanding, albeit non-contractual, that the site would be held for the joint benefit of Luff and Banner. The court would have held otherwise if Luff had informed Banner soon enough to avoid advantage to Luff and to avoid detriment to Banner. Their Lordships held that, in many cases, the advantage or detriment would be found, as in this case, in the undertaking of the non-purchasing party not to make an independent bid for the site. Their Lordships did stress, however, that it was not necessary that there should be both an advantage and a detriment; either would do. The advantage to Luff in the instant case was not merely the knowledge that Banner would not make an independent bid, but the comfort of knowing that Banner would support Luff in acquiring a site that Luff had originally been wary of purchasing at its sole risk.

A controversial aspect of the decision in *Banner v. Luff* is that Luff's 'conscience' was bound by Banner's *detrimental* reliance without evidence that Banner *would probably* have made an independent bid in the absence of the agreement with Luff. It seems that Luff's knowledge that Banner *might possibly* make a bid was sufficient to bind Luff's conscience. Another controversial aspect was the decision to dispose of the facts on the basis of the so-called *Pallant v. Morgan* equity when, to the extent that the case was based on Banner's detrimental reliance, the facts appear to be amenable to a straightforward proprietary estoppel analysis.[53] Accordingly, it has been argued that the *Pallant v. Morgan* equity should be restricted to cases not already adequately covered by proprietary estoppel—that is, to cases in which the defendant makes a gain, but the claimant suffers no detrimental reliance.[54] One problem with this approach is that parties

---

[52] [2000] Ch 372.   [53] See N. Hopkins, 'The *Pallant v. Morgan* "equity"?' (2002) 66 Conv 35.
[54] Ibid. at 46–8.

acquiring property according to the terms of a joint venture would have no guarantee that the terms of the venture would be enforced as agreed, but instead would be subject to the court's discretion to remedy the estoppel as it sees fit.[55] It has even been argued that the *Pallant v. Morgan* equity should not be recognized at all, especially when one considers that it operates in commercial transactions to confer proprietary rights under a constructive trust on a claimant who has suffered no loss of a pre-existing proprietary right and that it imposes a constructive trust on a defendant who owed the claimant no pre-existing fiduciary or other equitable duty.[56] In its defence, however, it seems to allocate the disputed property in an appropriate way to take account of the risks taken by the parties: if the property does badly, the purchaser will look to his partner to share the loss, so it is only right that the latter should be permitted to look to the purchaser for a share of the gain if the property does well.

It remains to be seen if the *Pallant v. Morgan* equity will be applied to joint ventures to acquire a shared home, which is an area normally governed (as we will see later in this chapter) by a combination of resulting trusts, constructive trusts, and proprietary estoppel, but it has already been applied where an engaged couple (both of them barristers) acquired a flat as a commercial investment on the understanding (as the judge found) that it would be for the woman's sole benefit. Each of them had contributed half the deposit (both claiming that their half was a direct contribution to the purchase and that the other's half was contributed by way of loan).[57] The main dispute related to ownership of certain assets, including a flat in the name of the man (Mr Jones). Mann J held that the woman (Miss Cox) should be recognized as the absolute beneficial owner of the flat, because there was a clear arrangement before the acquisition that Mr Jones would hold as trustee and not beneficially, and that, in the absence of their prior arrangement, there would have been no purchase at all. Crucially, his Lordship held that Miss Cox had suffered a detriment '*in that she did not pursue her own attempts to acquire the property herself in her sole name*', even allowing for the fact that '*it was not conclusively proved that those attempts would have been successful*'.[58]

The prevailing judicial opinion is that the *Pallant v. Morgan* equity arises on the same basis as a common intention constructive trust[59] and therefore will not arise unless the defendant's conscience is affected by knowledge that a binding agreement was intended.[60] The equity depends upon an intention that the claimant would acquire a proprietary interest in the disputed assets, but it is not necessary that the nature of the intended proprietary interest should be specified precisely in advance.[61]

---

[55] B. McFarlane, 'Constructive trusts arising on a receipt of property *sub conditione*' (2004) 120 LQR 667 at 689.   [56] N. Hopkins, 'The *Pallant v. Morgan* "Equity"?' (2002) 66 Conv 35 at 49.

[57] *Cox v. Jones* [2004] EWHC 1486 (Ch).   [58] Ibid. at para. 46.

[59] *Crossco No 4 Unlimited v. Jolan Ltd* [2011] EWCA Civ 1619. So-called 'common intention' constructive trusts are those arising from some shared understanding between the parties. They are important in the case of informal trusts of a shared home (see the section on 'Informal trusts of land').

[60] *Herbert v. Doyle* [2010] EWCA Civ 1095.

[61] *Kearns Brothers Ltd v. Hova Developments Ltd* [2012] EWHC 2968 (Ch).

7. Trusts of property acquired 'subject to' personal rights

Suppose that A acquires property from V, but acquires it expressly 'subject to' a right over the property (such as a contractual licence to occupy or use it), which V had personally conferred on B. The question arises whether B's personal right against V is binding on A. The answer is that B's interest will only bind A if it would be unconscionable for A to deny B's interest.[62] A classic case in which A was bound is the case of *Binions v. Evans*.[63] The facts of *Binions v. Evans* epitomize 'bad conscience' in the moral, as well as the equitable, sense. Mr and Mrs Evans had, for many years, lived rent-free in a cottage owned by Mr Evans's employer. After Mr Evans's death, his employers made a written agreement with Mrs Evans, under which she had licence to stay in the cottage for the rest of her life. In return, Mrs Evans agreed to keep the cottage and garden in good condition as long as she lived there, and not to part with possession of the cottage in favour of any third party. Some years later, Binions bought the legal title to the cottage, the employers having inserted a special clause in the contract of sale in order to protect Mrs Evans. Binions paid a reduced price because of that clause, but, less than a year later, Binions issued a notice to quit on Mrs Evans and sought to repossess the cottage. The judge dismissed Binions' outrageous attempt to evict the 79-year-old Mrs Evans. Unashamed, Binions appealed, but with no prospect of success—because the case fell to be heard by Lord Denning MR, a judge famed for the ingenious manner in which he frequently overcame the strict letter of the law in the pursuit of what he believed to be just. His Lordship held that Binions had taken the cottage subject to Mrs Evans's contractual right to reside in it for the rest of her life:[64] Binions therefore held the cottage on a constructive trust for Mrs Evans for her life.[65]

A quite different case in which B's *mere personal right* will bind a third party, A, under a constructive trust is the case of a trustee in bankruptcy (A) having possession of property and money belonging to the bankrupt (B) personally. Examples include damages for pain and suffering awarded in favour of the bankrupt in an action for personal injury,[66] the bankrupt's private correspondence,[67] and a tribunal claim under the Race Relations Act 1976.[68]

8. Trusts of mistaken payments

Chase Manhattan Bank NA v. Israel-British Bank (London) Ltd[69] is a classic case of mistaken payment, in which the claimant needed to establish a proprietary right in order to

---

[62] *Lyus v. Prowsa Developments Ltd* [1982] 1 WLR 1044, *per* Dillon J at 1051; *Ashburn Anstalt v. Arnold* [1989] Ch 1, CA, at 25–6.

[63] [1972] Ch 359. Others include *Lyus v. Prowsa Developments Ltd* [1982] 1 WLR 1044; *Peffer v. Rigg* [1977] 1 WLR 285.   [64] [1972] Ch 359 at 368–9.

[65] Ibid. at 368A. See also *Swiss Bank Corporation v. Lloyds Bank Ltd* [1979] Ch 548, *per* Browne-Wilkinson J at 571; *Lord Strathcona Steamship Co Ltd v. Dominion Coal Co Ltd* [1926] AC 108 at 125.

[66] *Ord v. Upton* [2000] 2 WLR 755 (noted G. Watt (1999) 8(2) Nott LJ 89).

[67] *Haig v. Aitken* [2001] 2 Ch 110.   [68] *Khan v. Trident Safeguards Ltd* [2004] EWCA Civ 624.

[69] [1981] Ch 105.

recover its money from the estate of an insolvent defendant. The claimant had intended to make a payment of US$2m to the defendant bank, but made the payment twice by mistake. Goulding J held that the claimant could trace the overpaid $2m into the hands of the defendant bank and that the defendant was a constructive trustee of the mistaken payment for B, because B retained '*an equitable property in it*'.[70] The better view, it is submitted, is that a mistaken payment of this sort should give rise to a resulting trust, if it is to give rise to any trust at all.[71]

9. Trusts of unauthorized fiduciary gains

A fiduciary's personal obligation to account to his principal obviously correlates to some right held by the principal, but what is not always clear is whether the principal's right is a mere personal right to enforce the fiduciary duty to account or a proprietary right, under a constructive trust, in the gain itself. Clearly, this is a question with an important policy dimension, because the answer will have significant implications for the fiduciary's personal creditors in the event of the fiduciary becoming insolvent. (If the principal has a proprietary right in the unauthorized gain, the gain will not be available to the fiduciaries' personal creditors, whereas if the principal merely has a personal right to claim the unauthorized gain, he will not have priority ahead of the personal claims of the fiduciary's general creditors.)

In *Keech v. Sandford*,[72] a trustee renewed a lease for himself after the landlord had made it clear that he was not prepared to offer the renewal to the current tenant, who happened to be the infant beneficiary of the trust. Lord Chancellor King decided that the trustee held the renewed lease on constructive trust for the infant beneficiary. The decision was based on the policy of deterring fiduciaries from placing themselves in positions of actual, or potential, conflict with the interests of their principals. The decision that the defendant in *Keech v. Sandford* was a constructive trustee is defensible, because he had been an express trustee of the old lease and ought clearly to have remained a trustee of some sort in relation to the new lease. (Lord Chancellor King decided that he was a constructive trustee, but a case can be made for saying that he remained an express trustee of the new lease on the same terms according to which the old lease had been held.) However, when there is no express trust to begin with, it is hard to see how the policy of deterring fiduciaries is better served by giving their principals constructive trust interests in unauthorized gains, as opposed to mere personal claims to recover unauthorized gains.

Professor Birks argued that a principal ought to be able to claim a constructive trust interest in unauthorized gains made by his fiduciary only when, as in *Keech v. Sandford*, the principal can prove some '*proprietary base*' to his claim.[73] In other words, the

---

[70] [1918] Ch 105 at 119.
[71] See Chapter 5. But for the possibility that a constructive trust might be based on unconscionable retention of a mistaken payment, see *Papamichael v. NatWest Bank plc* [2003] All ER (D) 204.
[72] (1726) Sel Cas Ch 61.
[73] 'Establishing a proprietary base' [1995] Restitution LR 83.

claimant must have had a relevant and connected interest in property in the fiduciary's hands before the unauthorized gain was made. Cases subsequent to *Keech v. Sandford* have sometimes held fiduciaries to be constructive trustees of gains that were not derived from any trust *property*, but were merely derived from the fiduciary's *position* of trust. Sometimes such decisions may be justified because, for instance, the wrongful fiduciary has appropriated an opportunity for proprietary gain that would have been available to the principal. An example in this category is *Cook v. Deeks*.[74] Three directors of a company, who obtained a contract in their own names to the exclusion of the company, were held to be constructive trustees of their unauthorized gains even though the opportunity to enter the contract had come to them in their fiduciary capacity and not because of any company property held by them in that capacity.

Keech v. Sandford was applied by the House of Lords in *Boardman v. Phipps*,[75] but it is notable that one of the strong dissenting speeches in that case, that of Lord Upjohn, sought to distinguish *Keech v. Sandford* from the facts of *Boardman v. Phipps* on the very ground that *Keech v. Sandford* involved a beneficiary with an existing interest in the lease and that *Boardman v. Phipps* involved a claimant with no such pre-existing interest. In *Boardman v. Phipps*, the House of Lords held a solicitor to account as a constructive trustee to the beneficiaries of an express trust for shares he had purchased, without the full authority of all of the trust beneficiaries, in the course of acting as solicitor to the trust.[76] A bare majority (three out of five) of their Lordships upheld the conclusion reached by Wilberforce J at first instance (and affirmed by the Court of Appeal) that the solicitor held the shares as a constructive trustee, but, of that bare majority, Lord Guest was alone in expressly stating that the solicitor was a constructive trustee of the shares.[77] Professor Birks may have gone too far when he argued that the judgment in *Boardman v. Phipps* was, in reality, a judgment in favour of a mere personal duty account, because, as Professor Burrows has pointed out, '*the plaintiffs would have been entitled to proprietary remedies, affording priority, had the defendants been insolvent*',[78] but Professor Birks was surely right, it is submitted, to the extent that he argued that the case *should* have been disposed of as one involving a mere personal fiduciary duty to account and not a constructive trust.[79]

10. Trusts of wrongful fiduciary gains

Lister & Co v. Stubbs[80] concerned a classic corrupt transaction. Stubbs was employed by the claimant to purchase materials to be used by the claimants in their business as silk spinners. One of the suppliers paid large bribes to Stubbs in order to procure his principal's trade. He then invested the bribes in land and other investments. The claimants sought to establish a proprietary interest in the bribes as a basis for claiming an

---

[74] [1916] 1 AC 554.   [75] [1967] 2 AC 46.   [76] The facts are more fully set out in Chapter 10.
[77] [1967] 2 AC 46 at 117.   [78] *The Law of Restitution* (London: Butterworths, 1993) at 413.
[79] 'Establishing a proprietary base' [1995] Restitution LR 83.   [80] (1890) LR 45 Ch D 1, CA.

injunction to prevent Stubbs from disposing of the various investments prior to trial. They failed. The Court of Appeal held unanimously that Stubbs had been under a mere personal obligation to account to his principal for the bribes. Lindley LJ was adamant that the contrary argument (that Stubbs was a trustee for his principal) was based on an unsound confusion of *'ownership with obligation'.*[81]

The decision in *Lister & Co v. Stubbs* proved controversial,[82] but it was followed and applied in many subsequent cases,[83] including a decision of the House of Lords.[84] *Lister & Co v. Stubbs* was, however, expressly disapproved by the Privy Council in the *AG for Hong Kong v. Reid.* Mr Reid was a senior public prosecutor in Hong Kong who accepted large sums of money, in return for which he obstructed the prosecution of certain criminals. He invested the bribes in land and other investments, including a number of properties in New Zealand, and the Crown sought to claim beneficial ownership of the various tainted investments on the basis that Mr Reid had held the bribes on constructive trust. The salient part of Lord Templeman's analysis in *AG General for Hong Kong v. Reid* is where his Lordship states that:[85]

> The decision in *Lister & Co. v. Stubbs* is not consistent with the principles that a fiduciary must not be allowed to benefit from his own breach of duty, that the fiduciary should account for the bribe as soon as he receives it *and that equity regards as done that which ought to be done.* From these principles it would appear to follow that the bribe and the property from time to time representing the bribe are held on a constructive trust for the person injured.

However, the question of what *ought to be done* in the interests of the fiduciary's principal must surely be answered by taking into account that which policy suggests *ought not to be done* as regards the interests of third parties in the event of the fiduciary's insolvency. As Professor Harris has asked: *'Why should the principal take a windfall in priority to those to whom the fiduciary owes purchased obligations?'*[86]

We should therefore welcome the recent decision of the Court of Appeal in *Sinclair Investments (UK) Ltd v. Versailles Trade Finance Ltd (In Administration),*[87] which reaffirms that *Reid* does not alter the long line of English decisions establishing that the beneficiary of a fiduciary's duties cannot claim a proprietary interest in wrongful gains, but is only entitled to an equitable account. One established exception (where a

---

[81] Ibid. at 15.

[82] See, for example, Sir Peter Millett, 'Remedies: the error in *Lister v. Stubbs'* in P. Birks (ed.), *The Frontiers of Liability* (Oxford: Oxford University Press, 1994) vol. I, 51 at 56; Goff and Jones, *The Law of Restitution*, 2nd edn (1978) 509–10. But in defence of the decision, see Goode, 'The right to trace and its impact in commercial transactions' (1976) 92 LQR 534–6.

[83] See, for example, *AG's Reference (No. 1 of 1985)* [1986] 1 QB 491 at 503G–H and *Powell v. MacRae* [1977] Crim LR 571.   [84] *Reading v. AG* [1951] AC 507, HL.

[85] [1994] 1 AC 324, 336.

[86] Professor J. W. Harris, *Property and Justice* (Oxford: Clarendon Press, 1996) at 338.

[87] [2011] EWCA Civ 347. Followed in *FHR European Ventures LLP v. Mankarious* [2013] EWCA Civ 17, but contrast the Australian position, where the reasoning in *Reid* is still preferred (see, for example, *Grimaldi v. Chameleon Mining NL (No. 2)* [2012] FCAFC 6).

constructive trust *will* be imposed on a bribe or other wrongful gain in the fiduciary's control) is where the asset or money wrongfully gained was or had been beneficially the property of the beneficiary or the trustee. It was on this basis that a constructive trust was imposed on the facts of *Daraydan Holdings Ltd v. Solland Interiors Ltd.*[88] The facts of that case were that the claimant principal had a prior proprietary interest in the bribe claimed from his dishonest fiduciary (a director of the principal company), because the price paid by the claimant to a third party under a contract had been artificially inflated by the defendant fiduciary to allow the third party to pay a bribe to the defendant. The facts of *Sinclair Investments*, in which the principal (the claimant company) failed to obtain a constructive trust in wrongful gains made by one of its directors, were subtly but significantly different, for the director had made the gains from selling shares in *another* company at an artificially inflated value. Expressly disapproving *Reid*, Lord Neuberger MR held that 'a bribe paid to a fiduciary could not possibly be said to be an asset which the fiduciary was under a duty to take for the beneficiary'.[89] His Lordship pointed to 'a fundamental distinction between (i) a fiduciary enriching himself by depriving a Claimant of an asset and (ii) a fiduciary enriching himself by doing a wrong to the Claimant'.[90] *Sinclair*, in which the wrongful gain came from monies not already belonging to the principal, was a case in category (ii) and therefore no constructive trust arose. In most cases a bribe would also fall in category (ii).

This is a rational development of legal doctrine in this area, but it must be acknowledged that the Court of Appeal's decision makes it more difficult to deprive a wrongful fiduciary of a bribe,[91] and (because the wrongful gain will not be treated as property) it also makes it more difficult to trace the wrongful gain into the hands of strangers and recover it from them (see Chapter 14).

Lord Templeman in *Reid* was clearly concerned to provide an equitable justification for the principal's proprietary interest in the bribe.[92] His Lordship's judgment was apparently driven by a wider 'political' concern to eradicate bribery, as his Lordship stated at the start of his judgment: '*Bribery is an evil practice which threatens the foundations of any civilised society. In particular bribery of policemen and prosecutors brings the administration of justice into disrepute.*'[93] Indeed, it is a criminal offence for a person in a 'position of trust' to give or receive a bribe.[94] Lord Millett, Sir Peter Millett as he then was, argued extra-judicially that the fundamental question in a case of bribery is one of

---

[88] [2004] EWHC 622 (Ch).

[89] [2011] EWCA Civ 347 at para. [80] (the decision in *Sinclair v. Versailles* was followed in *Page v. Hewetts Solicitors* [2011] EWHC 2449 (Ch).   [90] [2011] EWCA Civ 347 at para. [80].

[91] For criticism of the decision see D. Hayton, 'Proprietary liability for secret profits' (2011) 127 LQR 487. For support for the decision see, for example, G. Virgo, 'Profits obtained in breach of fiduciary duty: personal or proprietary claim?' (2011) 70(3) CLJ 502.

[92] Bribery is a criminal offence (Bribery Act 2010), but here we are concerned with civil claims relating to bribery. In this context, a payment by X will be considered to be a bribe where it is paid secretly to the agent of a person with whom X is dealing (*Bank of Ireland v. Jaffery* [2012] EWHC 1377 (Ch)), although it has been said that a gift can sometimes be too small to count as a bribe or incentive to conflict (*Fiona Trust & Holding Corp v. Privalov* [2010] EWHC 3199).   [93] *AG for Hong Kong v. Reid* [1994] 1 AC 324 at 330.

[94] Bribery Act 2010, s. 3(5).

policy. His Lordship identifies the relevant policy to be well settled. It is the policy that a fiduciary should by no means retain any part of any unauthorized gain.[95] According to his Lordship, this policy requires that a false fiduciary be stripped of the beneficial ownership of unauthorized gains the moment they are made. So on his Lordship's argument, *Reid* is preferable to *Sinclair* as a matter of policy even if *Sinclair* is preferable to *Reid* as a matter of legal principle.

Informal trusts of land

English law does not presume 'community of ownership' of land even when two adults have lived together in a stable relationship for a long period of time. Even as between husband and wife, there is no presumption of communal ownership of the matrimonial home. If one 'newly-wed' moves into a home held solely in the name of the other 'newly-wed', the married couple may regard the house as jointly theirs, but the law does not consider the newcomer to have acquired any interest in the house by the mere fact of marriage. If the couple divorce or are judicially separated, the court has very wide powers under the Matrimonial Causes Act 1973[96] to allocate the property of the parties to the marriage as it thinks fit, provided that certain specified matters are taken into account,[97] but even this might not lead to a straightforward declaration that the matrimonial home is owned equally by husband and wife.[98] Cohabitees who are neither married nor in a civil partnership represent an increasingly large proportion of all cohabiting couples.[99] In their case, the court has no discretion equivalent to that conferred by the Matrimonial Causes Act 1973 (it has been suggested it should),[100] so, on the breakdown of a stable relationship of that sort, ownership of the shared home is determined in accordance with the general law of property and trusts.[101]

If married or unmarried cohabitees want the legal understanding of their ownership to reflect their particular expectations, rather than the general law, it is incumbent upon them to take steps to formalize their ownership position. The best way to do this is for the party or parties with legal title to the land to declare an express trust of the land, making clear who is to have a beneficial interest in it and, if it is not to be held jointly, declaring in what shares it is to be held. Courts have repeatedly urged conveyancers to

---

[95] Sir Peter Millett, 'Remedies: the error in *Lister v. Stubbs*' in P. Birks (ed.), *The Frontiers of Liability* (Oxford: Oxford University Press, 1994) vol. I, 51 at 56–7.

[96] Sections 22A and 23A, as amended by the Family Law Act 1996.

[97] The welfare of children is the paramount consideration. The Matrimonial Causes Act 1973, s. 25(1) lists a number of other significant factors.

[98] In these respects, the parties to a civil partnership are subject to the same legal regime as a married couple.

[99] According to the Office of National Statistics, see C. Shaw and J. Haskey, 'New estimates and projections of the population cohabiting in England and Wales' (1999) 95 Population Trends, ONS; J. Haskey, 'Cohabitation in Great Britain: past, present and future trends—and attitudes' (2001) 103 Population Trends 4, ONS.

[100] The Law Society, *Cohabitation: The Case for Clear Law*, July 2002.

[101] In *Hammond v. Mitchell* [1991] 1 WLR 1127, *per* Waite J at 1129.

pursue such a practice.[102] The express deed of trust should be reviewed periodically with the benefit of legal advice, and replaced by a new deed, if necessary, to reflect the parties' changed circumstances and expectations. The law's ideal is, however, unrealistic. It is hard to imagine cohabitees, and perhaps least of all newly-weds, choosing to regularize their property ownership by means of an express trust unless their solicitor advises them to do so in the course of a house purchase. The point at which a relationship is strong enough to contemplate sharing property communally is the very point at which the parties to the relationship are least likely to feel the need to regularize their property ownership by means of a formal piece of paper.

The Law Commission has rejected calls for 'informal' cohabitants to be given the same rights as married couples and civil partners in the event of separation.[103] This is not surprising. It is hard enough to define 'cohabitant', let alone to draft laws to govern fair property distribution when cohabitants go their separate ways. The Law Commission has, however, sought to disperse some of the dark clouds hanging over informal cohabitation. It acknowledges that the current law that governs property disputes between cohabitees on separation '*is unclear and complicated*' and that it '*can produce unfair outcomes*'. It has therefore proposed a scheme to make the law better reflect the '*economic impact of the parties' contributions to the relationship*':

> Unlike in cases of divorce, cohabitants would not be expected to meet each other's future needs by means of maintenance payments and there would be no principle that the parties should share their assets equally.

It is intended that the scheme would apply to couples who have had a child together or who have lived together for a minimum period of, say, two to five years; and couples will have the right to opt out of the scheme by written agreement. In any proceedings the primary consideration will always be the welfare of any dependent children of the couple, and of course it will not be possible to opt out of that.[104]

The current absence of any presumption of communal ownership, combined with the failure of the vast majority of cohabitees to place their home-sharing on a formal legal basis, means that the legal status of a significant proportion of home ownership does not reflect the parties' own understanding of the basis on which they share their home. In one recent case, Waite LJ identified the problem of the gap between law and reality in the context of home-sharing, stating that it would be wrong

> to create a range of home-buyers who were beyond the pale of equity's assistance...simply because they had been honest enough to admit that they never gave ownership a thought or reached any agreement about it.[105]

---

[102] In *Carlton v. Goodman* [2002] EWCA Civ 545, CA, Ward LJ despaired: '*Perhaps conveyancers do not read the law reports. I will try one more time: always try to agree on and then record how the beneficial interest is to be held. It is not very difficult to do.*'

[103] *Cohabitation: The Financial Consequences of Relationship Breakdown*, The Law Commission (Law Com No. 307) Cm. 7182, July 2007. Following Law Commission Consultation Paper No. 179, 4 May 2006.

[104] Text in quotation marks is taken directly from the Law Commission's press release, July 2007.

[105] *Midland Bank plc v. Cooke* [1995] 4 All ER 562, CA, *per* Waite LJ at 575D.

Throughout the remainder of this chapter, we will see that the courts have not lacked creativity in their efforts to extend legal regulation to the unique social problem of home-sharing, as well as to other informal dealings with land occurring outside the context of home-sharing.

Difficulties in determining the property rights of cohabitees and other persons deal-ing informally in land stem from the absence of an express trust or contract, or the absence of the formalities necessary to give effect to an express trust or contract, so the judicial solution has been to discover, within the parties' dealings, binding arrange-ments which do not depend upon formality. A number of such arrangements have been and gone in the recent history of the English courts, including such innovations as the 'deserted wife's equity' and the remedial constructive trust (or 'constructive trusts of the new model'[106] as Lord Denning called them), but the most significant to survive are the resulting trust, the constructive trust, and proprietary estoppel. The reason for the success of the resulting trust and the constructive trust is straightforward: s. 53(2) of the Law of Property Act 1925 expressly exempts 'resulting, constructive and implied trusts' from statutory formality requirements. Applying the usual rule of statutory construction, *expressio unius exclusio alterius* ('express reference to a particular case excludes implied reference to another'), the absence of any express reference to propri-etary estoppel in s. 53(2) of the Law of Property Act 1925 could, and perhaps should, have prevented the use of proprietary estoppel as a device for giving effect to informal dealings with land[107]—but the conceptual and remedial flexibility of the proprietary estoppel has ensured not only its survival, but also its great success. In fact, in *Yaxley v. Gotts*,[108] the Court of Appeal held that the statutory 'constructive trust' exception to the requirement of contractual formality should be taken to embrace any cases of proprietary estoppel which might equally well have been categorized as cases of con-structive trust.[109] We will see that proprietary estoppel has had its wings clipped in 'commercial' contexts,[110] but that it still thrives in more 'familial' contexts.[111]

In *Yaxley v. Gotts*, Robert Walker LJ opined that at a '*high level of generality, there is much common ground between the doctrines of proprietary estoppel and the constructive trust*', in that they are both '*concerned with equity's intervention to provide relief against unconscionable conduct*'.[112] This typifies the highly pragmatic approach that many judges have taken to the problem of informal home-sharing. In *Lloyds Bank v. Rosset*,[113] one of the leading decisions of the House of Lords in this area, the terms 'constructive trusts' and 'proprietary estoppel' were used interchangeably. In *Gissing v. Gissing*, another

---

[106] *Eves v. Eves* [1975] 1 WLR 1338.

[107] See *United Bank of Kuwait plc v. Sahib* [1995] 2 WLR 94, in which Chadwick J made a similar (obiter) observation at 129.   [108] [2000] Ch 162.

[109] Ibid. at 193B–F, *per* Beldam LJ. See also Law Commission, *Transfer of Land: Formalities for Contracts of Sale, etc.* (1987) Report No. 164 at paras 5.4–5.5.

[110] *Yeoman's Row Management Ltd v. Cobbe* [2008] UKHL 55, [2008] 1 WLR 1752.

[111] *Thorner v. Major* [2009] UKHL 18. [2009] 1 WLR 776.

[112] See, also, the comments of Patten J in *Brian Turner v. Kim Jacob* [2006] EWHC 1317 (Ch).

[113] [1991] 1 AC 107.

leading House of Lords case, Lord Diplock even held that, for the purpose of determining co-ownership of a matrimonial home (in the days before the Matrimonial Causes Act 1973), it is 'unnecessary' to distinguish between resulting, constructive, and implied trusts.[114] Taken together, these cases might suggest that there is no significant difference between constructive trusts, resulting trusts, and proprietary estoppel in the context of informal dealings with land. We will see that the concepts certainly have a great deal in common, in so far as they are all employed pragmatically to give effect to the perceived underlying justice of the case, based on the parties' intentions and mutual expectations, but we will also see that there are very definite conceptual distinctions between them.

A final introductory point to bear in mind as we examine the cases is that claims to informally created ownership interests in land do not always arise in the context of relationship breakdown between cohabitees. Very often, a non-owning cohabitee will wish to establish a beneficial interest in land, because a third party (typically a mortgagee) has commenced proceedings (typically possession proceedings) against the cohabitee who is the legal owner of the property.

Establishing an interest

In the absence of an express trust, the first thing to ask is whether the land is in joint names or in a sole name. If the land is in joint names, the second thing to ask is whether the land is a 'family home'. If it is, there is a strong presumption that ownership in equity is also joint, leading to an equal division of sale proceeds in the event of sale. This presumption has been established by the decision of the House of Lords in the important case of *Stack v. Dowden*.[115] Most of the cases come down to disputes about the parties' respective financial interest in the shared home, but it should not be forgotten that the property is a home first and financial asset second, thus in *Holman v. Howes*[116] the Court of Appeal ordered that a woman should be permitted to remain in occupation of the house she had acquired jointly with her ex-husband, because she had been assured from the outset that he would not evict her.

The family home for which legal title is in joint names

The transfer of land into joint names automatically produces a joint tenancy of legal title[117] and, as a result of the decision of the House of Lords in *Stack v. Dowden*, the transfer of a family home into joint names raises a very strong presumption that equitable ownership, like legal ownership, is joint.[118] This is in accordance with the maxim

---

[114] [1971] AC 886 at 905.

[115] [2007] UKHL 17, [2007] 2 AC 432. Noted A. J. Cloherty and D. M. Fox (2007) 66(3) CLJ 517–20; P. Kenny (2007) Conv 364; R. Bailey-Harris (2007) 37 Fam Law 593; R. Probert (2007) 37 Fam Law 924; W. Swadling (2007) 123 LQR 511.   [116] [2007] EWCA Civ 877.

[117] Law of Property Act 1925, s. 34.

[118] The most significant feature of a joint tenancy is the 'the right of survivorship', which provides that when a joint tenant dies, the surviving joint tenant remains owner of the whole.

'equity follows the law'.[119] According to Baroness Hale, who delivered the leading speech of the four-to-one majority: '*cases in which the joint legal owners are to be taken to have intended that their beneficial interests should be different from their legal interests will be very unusual*'.[120] Before *Stack*, in contrast, it had been very easy to displace the presumption that equity follows the law where land was acquired in joint names:[121] if parties had contributed unequally to the purchase of land acquired in joint names, the presumption of joint ownership was rebutted in favour of the presumption of resulting trust (i.e. the presumption that the parties own distinct equitable shares in proportion to their individual financial contributions to acquisition).[122]

Mr Stack and Ms Dowden began cohabiting in the early 1980s, in a house that was in Ms Dowden's sole name. Mr Stack may have contributed to the deposit on that house, but the deposit was paid out of Ms Dowden's account and she provided the balance by means of a mortgage loan, which she repaid. They had four children and, in 1993, moved into a new home. Title to that house was registered in their joint names. There was a new mortgage on that house under which both Stack and Dowden were liable, and under which they both made repayments. Ms Dowden paid all of the domestic bills. They separated in 2002 and Mr Stack brought proceedings to establish a beneficial share in the house. He was awarded a half-share at first instance, but the Court of Appeal reduced that to one-third (35 per cent, in fact) and that was upheld by the House of Lords. It is interesting to observe that the value of the family home was divided between them in almost exactly the same proportions in which, at the end of their relationship, Mr Stack and Ms Dowden had been bringing income into the 'family finances': Ms Dowden, '*the most highly qualified woman electrical engineer in the London area*', earned a £42,000 salary, representing 63 per cent of the whole their income; Mr Stack earned £24,000, representing 37 per cent. Baroness Hale of Richmond delivered the leading speech for the majority, with the concurrence of Lords Hoffmann, Walker, and Hope. Lord Neuberger agreed in the result, but on a more traditional resulting trust basis.

The case presented the House of Lords with its first opportunity to consider a property dispute arising from the breakdown of the relationship between a non-married couple. It also provided the first opportunity for the House of Lords to scrutinize a purchase in the joint names of cohabiting parties, as part of which they had failed to declare the size of their respective beneficial interests. It is important to note that their Lordships did not consider the situation, still very common in practice, where legal

---

[119] *Per* Lord Walker at [33].

[120] At para. [69]. The strong presumption in favour of joint beneficial ownership, where land is held in joint names, was applied in *Fowler v. Barron* [2008] EWCA Civ 377; [2008] 2 FLR 831. This strong presumption may be restricted to 'romantic' cohabitation. Even if it applies to other forms of family co-ownership—such as that between mother and daughter—it will not apply where the land is acquired in both names merely as a commercial investment (*Laskar v. Laskar* [2008] EWCA Civ 347, [2008] 1 WLR 2695—distinguished in *Agarwala v. Agarwal* [2013] EWCA Civ 1763).

[121] *Mckenzie v. Mckenzie* [2003] EWHC 601; *Goodman v. Gallant* [1986] 2 WLR 236, 246.

[122] *Springette v. Defoe* [1992] 2 FCR 561; *Pettitt v. Pettitt* [1970] AC 777, HL, *per* Lord Upjohn at 814; *Dyer v. Dyer* (1788) 2 Cox Eq Cas 92.

title is in the sole name of one of the cohabitants. It follows that nothing said in *Stack v. Dowden* is binding in that situation, although elements of their Lordships' reasoning will be highly persuasive even in the context of sole ownership. Where property is purchased or held in the name of a sole legal owner that person will prima facie be the sole beneficial owner as well.

Despite insisting that there should be a very strong presumption that equity follows the law and that it should be 'very unusual' to rebut that presumption, their Lordships held that, on the facts of *Stack v. Dowden*, the strong presumption in favour of joint equitable ownership had, indeed, been rebutted, with the result that a larger share went to the party who had made the biggest financial contribution. Apart from the fact that Mr Stack paid less and could have paid more, it is hard to identify any factor that would justify the discrepancy in the shares awarded to the parties, which begs the question: did their different financial contributions really make this case 'very unusual'?

Leaving those concerns aside, the case confirms that the best way to establish a trust of any land is to use an express trust setting out all of the rights and entitlements of the parties having an interest in the land. As Baroness Hale said: '*No-one now doubts that such an express declaration of trust is conclusive unless varied by subsequent agreement or affected by proprietary estoppel.*'[123] Ideally, an express trust will deal with such matters as whether the equitable interest in the land is owned jointly or in shares. If the express trust declares that the co-owners own distinct equitable shares in the land, the trust should also express the size of the parties' distinct shares. The problem is that not everyone takes the sensible precaution of drawing up an express trust. In this respect, the parties in *Stack v. Dowden* are typical: all that they did was to sign a conveyance, which provided that the survivor could 'give a valid receipt for capital money arising on a disposition of the land'. It was held that this mere form of words did not constitute an express declaration of trust.

Before *Stack v. Dowden*, a party claiming an interest under an informal trust of the family home was allowed two bites at the cherry: she could argue that she had an interest under a resulting trust, or, in the alternative, an interest under a constructive trust. Following *Stack*, it would appear that the resulting trust alternative is now no longer available to the claimant. That alternative died when the House of Lords held that, if land is held in joint names, it is presumed that beneficial ownership is also joint and that the presumption of joint ownership is not rebutted by the mere fact of unequal contributions to purchase price.

To reduce the influence of resulting trusts in land acquisition is, at first sight, a welcome innovation, because any case of disputed ownership of the family home that can be dealt with by resulting trust can be dealt with by constructive trust. However, even if constructive trust can do the job of resulting trust, it cannot do it anywhere near as efficiently. The presumption of a resulting trust is based on the single factor of financial contributions to the initial purchase price, whereas *Stack v. Dowden* (as we will shortly see) requires

---

[123] At para. [49], approving *Goodman v. Gallant* [1986] 2 WLR 236.

the court to consider a wide range of factors. Another criticism of the decision in *Stack v. Dowden* is that it is so radical it must be read restrictively to 'family' or 'romantic domestic' contexts or it will threaten to subvert general property law principles. The problem with this requirement is that it proceeds on the assumption that there is a fundamental and clear distinction between the family home and other sorts of property, including other sorts of land. In an age when the family home is often used as a place of work and frequently serves as mortgage security for business loans, it is not clear that the family home is altogether distinct from commercial property. The difficulty of trying to restrict *Stack* to a context that is hard to define perhaps explains why the Court of Appeal has since suggested that there is prima facie no substantial difference between domestic and business contexts when deciding fair shares under a constructive trust.[124] When a family home is remortgaged, it may be done to raise cash for purposes that are wholly unrelated to enhancing the house as a shared home, in which event, the home is being used as a commercial resource. Yet according to *Stack v. Dowden* and despite concerns raised by Lord Neuberger, the presumption of joint tenancy will apply just as much to remortgage situations as to home acquisition. This is despite the fact that transfer into joint names on remortgage may be in no way intended to express the parties' understanding as to their relative entitlement, but is generally an artificial step inserted merely to placate the lender.

A more general difficulty with the decision in *Stack v. Dowden* is that, in one fell swoop, it has made the application of the well-settled property doctrine of resulting trust turn upon such relatively ill-defined concepts as 'family' and 'shared home'—and to what end? The majority of their Lordships ousted the orthodox weak presumption of resulting trust in favour of a new extremely strong presumption of equality, only to decide, on the particular facts of *Stack v. Dowden*, that the extremely strong presumption of equality had been rebutted. They decided that the parties should have interests in the property proportionate to their financial contributions to acquisition—precisely the same outcome as would have been reached on a resulting trust approach.

To understand *Stack v. Dowden*, it has to be read in the wider historical context of property law. It can be seen as the latest significant step in a general move away from mechanistic doctrine based on rigid *probanda* (particular requirements which have to be met) towards more flexible remedial approaches based on consideration of a broad range of factors. A majority of their Lordships agreed that the following list of factors will be amongst those that a court might consider when seeking to determine the parties' intentions regarding ownership of the shared home:[125]

1. the parties' financial contributions to the acquisition of the property;
2. any advice or discussions at the time of the transfer that cast light upon their intentions then;

---

[124] *Gallarotti v. Sebastianelli* [2012] EWCA Civ 865; [2012] Fam Law 1206—a case of two 'friends' living together. Note that a case is to be characterized as commercial or domestic according to the nature of the parties' dealings, not the nature of the type of property involved (*Whittaker v. Kinnear* [2011] EWHC 1479 (QB)—a proprietary estoppel case).

[125] Mostly taken from the speech of Baroness Hale of Richmond at paras [69]–[70].

3. the reasons why the home was acquired in their joint names;

4. the reasons why (if it is the case) the survivor was authorized to give a receipt for the capital monies;

5. the purpose for which the home was acquired;

6. the nature of the parties' relationship;

7. whether they had children for whom they both had responsibility to provide a home;

8. how the purchase was financed, both initially and subsequently;

9. how the parties arranged their finances, whether separately or together, or a bit of both;

10. how they discharged the outgoings on the property and their other household expenses;

11. the parties' individual characters and personalities;

12. the fact that one party has financed (or constructed himself) an extension or substantial improvement to the property, so that what they have now is significantly different from what they had initially;[126]

13. any other factors that indicate that the parties' intentions have changed over time.

Baroness Hale emphasized that this list is not exhaustive and she made the general observation that:

> [i]n the cohabitation context, mercenary considerations may be more to the fore than they would be in marriage, but it should not be assumed that they always take pride of place over natural love and affection.

In a similar vein, Lord Neuberger cautioned against inferring a constructive trust of the shared home based only on the way the cohabitants manage their finances and share their other property.[127] Baroness Hale also confirmed that the court must not seek 'the result which the court itself considers fair', but rather the result which the parties 'must, in the light of their conduct, be taken to have intended'.[128] This was followed in *James v. Thomas*,[129] which was in turn followed in *Morris v. Morris*,[130] where a husband successfully appealed against the judge's finding that his wife had acquired a share in the family farm he had inherited from his mother, and on which he had encouraged his wife to pursue her horse riding business. The Court of Appeal held that courts should be slow to interpret the actions of spouses and cohabitees in relation to a property as necessarily granting some form of beneficial interest, and here neither party had expressly

---

[126] This factor is, of course, very significant, given that few people can now afford to move to bigger houses and therefore prefer to extend their existing house.

[127] At paras [113], [132]. In *James v. Thomas* [2007] EWCA Civ 1212 it was held that courts should be especially slow to impose a trust on land which had been acquired before the relationship between the cohabitants began.   [128] At para. [61]

[129] [2007] EWCA Civ 1212, CA.   [130] [2008] EWCA Civ 257; [2008] Fam Law 521.

discussed the matter of her entitlement to some interest, and the wife had never raised the matter of her own volition. Her financial contributions were mitigated by the contributions she, in turn, received in order to set up the business.

Resulting trust

Resulting trusts were considered at length in Chapter 5. After the cases of *Stack v. Dowden* and *Jones v. Kernott*, the status of the resulting trusts of land is rather uncertain. According to strict legal method, the decisions of such powerful courts should be read restrictively. Such an approach would mean that the presumption of resulting trust still applies to land where legal title is held in one name, and to land held in joint names unless it is a family home. According to orthodoxy, the presumption arises where B makes a voluntary payment to A or pays (wholly or in part) for the purchase of property that is vested either in A alone or in the joint names of B and A. There are two significant drawbacks to the use of a resulting trust to establish a beneficial interest in co-owned land. The first is that the resulting trust arising where B acquires property in the name of A arises at the moment of purchase and not later,[131] hence it is sometimes referred to as a 'purchase money resulting trust'. The second is that, although a resulting trust is adequate to establish *some* interest in A's land, the size of B's interest will be limited to the size of B's contribution to the value of A's land, albeit expressed as a proportion of the total value of the land. So if B contributes one-third of the cost of acquiring A's land, B will be entitled to one-third of the capital proceeds when the land is eventually sold. In the meantime, B will be entitled to occupy the land[132] and, if the land is leased out, B will be entitled to one-third of the rent.

Section 60(3) of the Law of Property Act 1925

We have seen that, when property is voluntarily transferred and there is no evidence of the transferor's reasons for making the transfer, a resulting trust will automatically be 'presumed'. In the case of land, however, the Law of Property Act 1925 expressly provides that:

> In a voluntary conveyance a resulting trust for the grantor shall not be implied merely by reason that the property is not expressed to be conveyed for the use or benefit of the grantee.[133]

In *Lohia v. Lohia*,[134] Judge Nicholas Strauss QC concluded that the subsection has removed the presumption of a resulting trust on the voluntary conveyance of land, but that it does not preclude the possibility that a resulting trust may be inferred in the case of a voluntary conveyance, provided that the resulting trust is not based 'merely' upon the absence of express words confirming that the grantee is to take beneficially.[135]

---

[131] *Curley v. Parkes* [2004] EWCA Civ 1515, CA.

[132] Trusts of Land and Appointment of Trustees Act 1996, s. 12.

[133] Law of Property Act 1925, s. 60(3).

[134] [2001] WTLR 101 at 113. See also *Ali v. Khan* [2002] EWCA Civ 974, CA.

[135] His Honour referred to a discussion in R. Chambers, *Resulting Trusts* (Oxford: Clarendon Press, 1997) at 18–19. See, further, J. Mee, 'Resulting trusts and voluntary conveyances of land' (2012) 4 Conv 307–26.

Constructive trust

This section should be read in the light of the earlier lengthy discussion of *Stack v. Dowden*. For the reasons discussed there, it is still unclear to what extent and in what ways *Stack* will change the existing law on cohabitation constructive trusts outside the context of a family home held in the joint names of the cohabitees. The leading case in the law before *Stack* was the decision of the House of Lords in *Lloyds Bank v. Rosset*.[136] Mr Rosset had received a loan to buy a derelict house on the understanding that the house would be in his name alone. Mrs Rosset did a limited amount of work towards the renovation of the house: in particular, she helped with the interior decorations. However, the vast bulk of the work was carried out by contractors paid for by the husband. Following matrimonial problems, the husband left home, leaving his wife and children in the premises. The loan that the husband had taken out was not, in the event, repaid. Consequently, the bank brought proceedings for possession. The husband raised no defence to that action, but the wife did resist. She claimed to have a beneficial interest in the house under a trust. The House of Lords held that she did not.

His Lordship held that Mrs Rosset would succeed if she could show that it was the parties' common intention that she should have a beneficial interest in the land, for in such circumstances it would be unconscionable for Mr Rosset to deny her the intended interest. His Lordship identified two alternative routes to establishing the common intention necessary to raise the trust: first, that there had been some express understanding between Mr and Mrs Rosset that they would share the property beneficially in equity; second, that she had made substantial direct financial contributions to the land.

Route one: express understanding plus detrimental reliance

According to Lord Bridge, the first route to establishing a beneficial interest under a constructive trust is to establish that, prior to the acquisition of the home ('or exceptionally at some later date'), the legal owner and the claimant reached an express agreement, arrangement, or understanding to share the beneficial ownership of the home. Provided that the arrangement was expressed in discussion between the parties, it does not matter that the terms were imprecise and that the parties' recollection of the express agreement is 'imperfect'. In addition to proving that there was an express agreement or arrangement, the claimant must also '*show that he or she acted to his or her detriment or significantly altered his or her position in reliance on the agreement*'.[137]

In Chapter 3, we noted that courts are reluctant to discover express trusts arising from 'loose conversations', so it seems somewhat surprising that Lord Bridge was prepared to recognize a constructive trust on the basis of an imperfectly remembered agreement comprising imprecise terms. The criteria laid down by Lord Bridge for the recognition of trusts of this sort are not particularly stringent and the danger is that they will encourage the fanciful recollection of discussions that never, in fact, took place. However, the potential for injustice to a bank, such as Lloyds, may not be statistically

---

[136] [1991] 1 AC 107.   [137] *Lloyds Bank v. Rosset* [1991] 1 AC 107 at 132.

significant. Even where there has been an agreement between the cohabitees, it will only bind the bank where the agreement was concluded before the bank took the mortgage, and, before taking the mortgage, the bank (like any purchaser) should have carried out a prudent search for evidence of any such pre-existing agreement by making an inquiry into the rights of all occupiers of the land.

Express

The relevant understanding between the parties must be expressed; it is not enough that the parties happened to be '*thinking on the same lines in his or her uncommunicated thoughts*'.[138] Nevertheless, this has not deterred the courts from *interpreting* express statements according to the uncommunicated thoughts of the persons making them, sometimes in ways that seem entirely inconsistent with the actual words employed. In *Grant v. Edwards*[139] and *Eves v. Eves*,[140] the claimants established beneficial interest in the defendants' land even though the expressed understanding between the parties in each case was that the defendant had no intention of placing the claimant's name on the legal title. In *Grant v. Edwards*, the defendant explained that he did not want to place the claimant's name on the title because it might prejudice matrimonial proceedings pending between the defendant and his wife. In *Eves v. Eves*, the defendant explained that he would not be placing the claimant's name on the legal title because (which was not, in fact, true) she was too young. In both cases, the courts held that the express 'explanations' were, in reality, 'excuses' and that they therefore constituted express evidence of an unspoken understanding between the parties that the claimant was entitled to a beneficial interest in the land. As Nourse LJ put it in *Grant v. Edwards*: '*these facts raise a clear inference that there was an understanding... otherwise no excuse for not putting her name onto the title would have been needed*'.[141] Simon Gardner has criticized this type of reasoning:

> If I give an excuse for rejecting an invitation to what I expect to be a dull party, it does not mean that I thereby agree to come: on the contrary, it means that I do not agree to come, but for one reason or another I find it hard to say outright.[142]

The case of *Rowe v. Prance*[143] illustrates how different the law's response to trusts of *personal* property can be, compared to trusts of land. On facts otherwise reminiscent of *Grant v. Edwards*, the cohabitees bought a boat to live on. The man paid for it, but frequently stated that the boat belonged to them both. His explanation ('excuse') for not registering the woman as joint owner was that she did not possess 'a relevant certificate'. The court held that he had constituted himself an *express* trustee of the boat for himself and the woman in equal shares. The clear implication is that cases such as *Grant v. Edwards* and *Eves v. Eves* would also be treated as express trusts were it not for

---

[138] *Springette v. Defoe* [1992] 2 FLR 388, CA, *per* Dillon LJ at 393G.   [139] [1986] Ch 636, CA.
[140] [1975] 1 WLR 1338, CA.
[141] [1986] Ch 636, *per* Nourse LJ at 649. Compare *Williamson v. Sheikh* [2008] EWCA Civ 990, Court of Appeal, where a constructive trust was found despite the parties' deliberate choice not to make it express; the man was held to the terms of the formal trust on the ground that the only reason he had not executed it had been an expression of informal trust between the parties.
[142] 'Rethinking family property' (1993) 109 LQR 263 at 265.   [143] [1999] 2 FLR 787.

the fact that they would then be unenforceable due to lack of the formalities required where the subject matter of the trust is land. In *Rowe v. Prance*,[144] Nicholas Warren QC declined to judge the merits of a constructive trust claim pleaded in the alternative to the express trust.[145]

Understanding

The relevant transaction between the trustee and the beneficiary is an '*agreement, arrangement or understanding reached between them that the property is to be shared beneficially*'.[146] Accordingly, constructive trusts of land have frequently been referred to as 'common intention' constructive trusts,[147] although the requirement of an inferred 'common intention' has been criticized.[148] It is certainly clear from cases such as *Grant v. Edwards* and *Eves v. Eves* that it is not necessary for there to have been an actual *subjective* agreement; agreement can be objectively assessed. It is also clear from the cases that it is not necessary that the agreement should contain a consensus as to the size of the parties' respective shares under the trust.[149] It must, though, be an agreement to share beneficial ownership of the land. In *Buggs v. Buggs*,[150] a husband and wife used a common fund of money to purchase a house for the husband's mother. When the mother died, the wife (then divorced) sought to claim a share in the house. She failed. The judge held that the wife had intended to enjoy some future use of the house as a daughter-in-law, but had not intended to acquire a beneficial share.[151]

The date of the agreement will usually be prior to or concurrent with the financial outlay of the claimant, but Fox LJ in *Burns v. Burns*[152] held that, even if

> initially, there was no intention that the claimant should have any interest in the property, circumstances may subsequently arise from which the intention to confer an equitable interest upon the claimant may arise.[153]

Lord Bridge in *Rosset* also accepted that the agreement between the parties need not be established prior to acquisition, but may (exceptionally) occur '*at some later date*'.[154] Certainly, when it comes to *quantifying* the claimant's share, the timing of the agreement relative to acquisition is basically unimportant.[155]

---

[144] Ibid.   [145] Ibid. at 795F–G.   [146] *Lloyds Bank v. Rosset* [1991] 1 AC 107 at 132.

[147] *Pettitt v. Pettitt* [1970] AC 777, *per* Lord Diplock at 822–3; *Gissing v. Gissing* [1971] AC 886, HL at 905–6.

[148] See J. Montgomery, 'A question of intention?' [1987] Conv 16; N. Glover and P. Todd, 'The myth of common intention' (1996) 16 Legal Studies 325.

[149] *Drake v. Whipp* [1996] 1 FLR 826, *per* Peter Gibson LJ at 830D–831H.

[150] [2003] EWHC 1538; [2004] WTLR 799.

[151] The decision has been criticized for drawing a false distinction between acquiring land as a joint venture and acquiring land as an owner (M. P. Thompson, 'The obscurity of common intention' (2003) Conv 411).

[152] [1984] Ch 317.   [153] Ibid. at 327.   [154] [1991] 1 AC 107 at 132.

[155] *Gissing v. Gissing* [1971] AC 886, *per* Lord Diplock at 909D; *Mortgage Corporation v. Shaire* [2001] Ch 743, *per* Neuberger J at 750, approving *Stokes v. Anderson* [1991] 1 FLR 391.

Detrimental reliance

In *Grant v. Edwards*,[156] Browne-Wilkinson VC stated, following Fox LJ in *Midland v. Dobson*,[157] that:

> mere common intention is not by itself enough: the claimant has also to prove that she has acted to her detriment in the reasonable belief by so acting she was acquiring a beneficial interest.[158]

There are two main obstacles to proof of detrimental reliance. The first is to demonstrate that the claimant has suffered a detriment. On one (deliberately overstated) view, the claimant who gives up a career to care for a home and children has been liberated from the need to work, has enjoyed the delight of daily contact with his or her children, and has lived rent free for several years in a house that is legally owned by someone else. Browne-Wilkinson VC was alert to these obstacles in *Grant v. Edwards*, when he held that:

> setting up house together, having a baby and making payments to general housekeeping expenses ... may all be referable to the mutual love and affection of the parties and not specifically referable to the claimant's belief that she has an interest in the house.[159]

However, their Lordships decided that Mrs Grant had acted to her detriment and granted her a half-share in the house. Nourse LJ described detrimental reliance as '*conduct on which the woman could not reasonably be expected to embark unless she was to have an interest in the home*'.[160] Mrs Grant's detrimental reliance comprised her conduct in making substantial indirect contributions to mortgage instalments by way of contribution to household expenses, which liberated the defendant to spend his money on direct repayment of the mortgage. The second obstacle the claimant will face, assuming a detriment has been established, is to prove that the detriment was suffered as a causal consequence of the express arrangement between the parties. As Browne-Wilkinson VC put it: '*there has to be some "link" between the common intention and the acts relied on as a detriment*'.[161] We might add a third potential obstacle, which is judicial reluctance to recognize conduct as 'detrimental' to a private party where there is arguably a public interest in supporting the conduct. We might put 'bringing up children' in this category. The Court of Appeal in *Smith v. Bottomley* declined to decide whether accepting an offer of marriage might amount to a detriment.[162] Perhaps it was reluctant to undermine the public interest in promoting stable long-term relationships.

Route two: direct financial contribution

In any case in which there is no evidence of detrimental reliance upon an express agreement, arrangement, or understanding to share, the parties' 'common intention' to share

---

[156] [1986] Ch 638 at 656.
[157] [1986] 1 FLR 171 and Lord Diplock in *Gissing v. Gissing* [1971] AC 886 at 905D.
[158] [1986] 1 FLR 171 at 174.   [159] [1986] Ch 638 at 657.   [160] Ibid. at 648.
[161] [1986] Ch 683 at 656, referring to *Eves v. Eves* [1975] 1 WLR 1338.
[162] *Smith v. Bottomley* [2013] EWCA Civ 953, Court of Appeal (Civil Division).

must be inferred instead from their conduct. Direct contributions to the purchase price by the claimant '*whether initially or by payment of mortgage instalments*' will suffice, but Lord Bridge thought it '*extremely doubtful whether anything less will do*'.[163] Thus it has been held that where land, having already been acquired, is subsequently mortgaged to raise money for some other purpose, repayment of instalments on that mortgage will not be qualifying 'direct' contributions.[164] In any event, initial direct contributions to purchase price (by way of deposit, say) are preferable to contributions by way of mortgage instalments, because the payment of mortgage instalments can be ambiguous in the absence of an agreement expressly relating to that type of payment. Payment of mortgage instalments could, for instance, be construed to be merely a payment made instead of rent.[165]

Direct contribution

In the years immediately preceding the Matrimonial Causes Act 1973, courts were willing to recognize a common intention based on indirect contributions to the acquisition of the matrimonial home. In *Falconer v. Falconer*,[166] Lord Denning MR observed that contributions

> may be indirect as where both go out to work and one pays the housekeeping and the other the mortgage instalments...so long as there is a substantial financial contribution towards the family expenses it raises the inference of a trust.[167]

In *Gissing v. Gissing*,[168] Lord Diplock observed that:

> It may be no more than a matter of convenience which spouse pays particular household accounts, particularly when both are earning, and if the wife goes out to work and devotes part of her earnings or uses her private income to meet joint expenses of the household which would otherwise be met by the husband, so as to enable him to pay the mortgage instalments out of his moneys, this would be consistent with and might be corroborative of an original common intention that her payments of other household expenses were intended by both spouses to be treated as including a contribution by the wife to the purchase price of the matrimonial home.[169]

The enactment of the Matrimonial Causes Act 1973, which conferred wide powers on the courts to adjust the property rights of married couples on divorce, reduced the need to recognize beneficial interests arising from indirect contributions in cases of marital breakdown. In that light, one can see why, in *Lloyds Bank v. Rosset*, Lord Bridge restricted the circumstances in which a non-owning spouse would be entitled to take priority over a secured lender on the basis of mere indirect financial contributions to the matrimonial home. Why should a lender, without whose direct financial assistance neither husband nor wife would have a home, concede priority to a spouse who has made only indirect

---

[163] *Lloyds Bank v. Rosset* [1991] 1 AC 107 at 133.   [164] *McKenzie v. McKenzie* [2003] EWHC 601 (Ch).
[165] See *Barrett v. Barrett* [2008] EWHC 1061 (Ch) and *Carlton v. Goodman* [2002] EWCA Civ 545; 2 FLR 259.   [166] [1970] 1 WLR 1333.
[167] Ibid. at 1336.   [168] [1971] AC 886.   [169] Ibid. at 907–8.

contributions to the home? Nevertheless, the problem with Lord Bridge's refusal to recognize indirect financial contributions as a basis for a constructive trust—appropriate though it may be to married couples since the 1973 Act—is that it also applies to unmarried cohabitees who, as yet, have no equivalent to the 1973 Act on which to fall back in the event of their relationship breaking down. The Civil Partnership Act 2004 offers a partial solution,[170] but it only confers marriage-like property rights on registered relationships between two people '*of the same sex*'.[171] The increased incidence of non-married cohabitees since *Rosset* would, it is submitted, justify a return to the *Gissing v. Gissing* approach of allowing beneficial interests to be based on indirect financial contributions, especially where financial contributions to the family finances by one party 'enable' the other party to pay the mortgage instalments. Indeed, there is recent authority for such an approach, albeit that the authority was at first instance and involved a married couple.[172]

Financial contribution

Judicial opinion may vary on the question of whether the contributions prerequisite to a constructive trust interest may be indirect, but judicial opinion is agreed that, whether direct or indirect, the contributions must be financial. Against this consensus, there is no shortage of commentators who argue that substantial, indirect, non-financial contributions—such as long-term childcare and the carrying out of domestic chores, such as cooking, and maintenance of the house and garden—ought to burden the conscience of the legal owner every bit as much as the contribution of cash. There is certainly merit in this argument when one considers that childcare, cooking, cleaning, and gardening are all tasks that a homeowner might have to pay a professional to perform if there were no cohabitee willing to perform them for free. However, as the law presently stands, there is a major obstacle in the way of property rights based on indirect non-financial contributions. It stems from the current belief that the legal owner's conscience is only burdened if he knew that the contributions he received were made with the intention of acquiring a beneficial interest in the land. The problem with non-financial contributions in this respect is that there will nearly always be an alternative explanation for the contribution.[173] In the case of childcare, for example, the courts have tended to identify

---

[170] Section 65 provides that a substantial contribution by a civil partner to the improvement of real or personal property in which either, or both, of the civil partners has, or have, a beneficial interest will give that partner a share enlarged to such an extent as may have been then agreed, or in default of such agreement, as may seem, in all of the circumstances just to the court. Section 66 provides that, in any question between the civil partners as to title to, or possession of, property, the High Court or county court '*may make such order with respect to the property as it thinks fit (including an order for the sale of the property)*'. The Act came into force on 5 December 2005.

[171] Section 1(1).

[172] *Le Foe v. Le Foe* [2001] 2 FLR 970 per Nicholas Mostyn QC at 982, at [50]. The Law Commission approved this case in *Sharing Homes: A Discussion Paper* (2002).

[173] See *Burns v. Burns* [1984] 2 WLR 582: '*It is true that she contemplated living with the defendant in the house and, no doubt, that she would do housekeeping and look after the children. But those facts do not carry with them any implication of a common intention that the plaintiff should have any interest in the house*' (per Fox LJ at 327).

the carer's motive to be *'love and affection'*.[174] However, motivations may be mixed: a cohabitee might care for a child out of love, affection, a sense of responsibility, but also for such ulterior purposes as maintaining a romantic relationship with the child's parent, or living in the home of the child's parent, or qualifying for local authority housing. Surely somewhere down the list of reasons why a long-term cohabitee would gratuitously care for a child of the relationship, or mow the lawn, or paint a wall, is an expectation that he or she would acquire an interest in the land sufficient to provide a home for him or her and the child, and to allow him or her to enjoy the lawn and wall. Why, it might be asked, should such an intention to acquire a beneficial interest in the land be required to appear at the very top of the list of motives in order to qualify as a basis for a constructive trust? The relevant question, surely, is whether the intention is sufficiently clear to burden the conscience of the legal owner. However, the courts have not yet demonstrated a willingness to infer 'mixed' or 'sub' intentions.

Simon Gardner has argued that *'the position of the law regarding the discovery of a common understanding—and so of the constructive trust itself—is very far from neutral'*.[175] He argues that there are two major concerns to counter the social imbalance against women in respect to ownership of family assets. The first is based on the idea of the family as a communal entity:

> The argument is that it is adventitious that the man undertakes the income-generating work which enables him to acquire assets, while she undertakes domestic functions; both roles are equally essential to the success of the family as a whole.[176]

The second is based on an unjust enrichment, which should be addressed: in that *if the woman is earning* money herself,

> her earnings are . . . more likely to be spent on fungibles (food, clothes, etc.), which are wasting assets at best, while the man's go, in particular, to buying the house, with its capital appreciation.[177]

Gardner argues that the law's orthodox 'referability rules' redress the second kind of imbalance, but not the first. This, he submits, means that help is withheld where it is most needed.[178] J. W. Harris has argued, on the other hand, that recognition of non-financial contributions relies upon the artificial assumption that people carry in their pockets *'so much cash and a fixed quantity of labour-power'*.[179]

Improvements to land subsequent to acquisition

It is unclear whether or not substantial direct improvements to land subsequent to acquisition, such as paying for an extension, are a sufficient basis on which to establish a constructive trust within Lord Bridge's scheme. It may be that improvements should be dealt with by proprietary estoppel where the legal owner acquiesces in the non-owner's expenditure. When, in 1969, the question arose for consideration in *Pettitt v. Pettitt*,[180]

---

[174] *Grant v. Edwards* [1986] Ch 638 at 657.
[175] *An Introduction to the Law of Trusts* (Oxford: Clarendon Press, 1990) at 238.   [176] Ibid. at 519G–H.
[177] Ibid.   [178] See, further, S. Gardner, 'Rethinking family property' (1993) 109 LQR 263.
[179] 'Doctrine, justice, and home-sharing' (1999) 19(3) OJLS 421.   [180] [1970] AC 777.

there was no clear outcome. Of their Lordships who expressed an opinion on the point, Lord Reid was satisfied that improvements do qualify, but Lord Hodson was equally convinced that they do not. The following year, s. 37 of the Matrimonial Proceedings and Property Act 1970 resolved the question in relation to married couples (and couples engaged to be married),[181] but the question remains unresolved as regards unmarried cohabitees—subject to any influence that the 1970 Act might exert in such cases.

Section 37 of the Matrimonial Proceedings and Property Act 1970 provides that where a spouse makes a substantial contribution in money or money's worth to the improvement of property in which either or both have a beneficial interest, the spouse will get a share or enlarged share in the property unless there is any express *or implied* agreement to the contrary. The share will be that which has been agreed or, in the absence of agreement, whatever would be fair. The fact that an interest under s. 37 is subject to contrary agreement caused the claim in *Thomas v. Fuller-Brown* [182] to fail. The improvements in that case had been very substantial, but the court held that they had been made in return for rent-free accommodation, rather than for any interest in the house itself.

There are obiter dicta in *Stack* which suggest that the two *Rosset* routes to a constructive trust interest (express agreement plus detrimental reliance *or* substantial direct financial contribution to purchase) may be too restrictively framed.[183] It was suggested, for example, that making improvements that add significant value to the property should be sufficient to generate an interest. Lord Walker opined that '*the law has moved on* [*since* Rosset], *and your Lordships should move it a little more in the same direction*'.[184] This has since been approved by Baroness Hale in the Privy Council in *Abbott v. Abbott*.[185] Simon Gardner argues that, following *Stack v. Dowden* and *Abbott v. Abbott*, intention can apparently be imputed where no intention actually exists, so that it is illogical to require one of the parties to have acted (as *Rosset* requires) upon intention.[186] It is submitted that Gardner should attach more weight to the fact that *Rosset* was a case in which land was in a sole name and *Stack* was a case in which land was in joint names. As regards sole legal owner cases, no court will be bound to prefer their Lordships' analysis in *Stack* to their Lordships' analysis in *Rosset*. I would go further and suggest that *Stack* does not have the authority to justify a departure from the *Rosset* orthodoxy in sole legal owner cases. The key innovation in *Stack* was to revitalize the maxim 'equity follows law'. It follows that if anything should be implied from *Stack* for sole owner cases, it should be that 'equity follows the law'. This would raise a very strong presumption that a sole legal owner is the sole beneficial owner, which (surprising as it may seem) would make it harder to claim a beneficial interest against a sole legal owner under *Stack* than under *Rosset*.

---

[181] Law Reform (Miscellaneous Provisions) Act 1970, s. 2(1).   [182] [1988] 1 FLR 237.
[183] [2007] UKHL 17, [2007] 2 AC 432, *per* Lord Hope at [12], Lord Walker at [36] and Baroness Hale at [70].
[184] Para. [27].   [185] [2007] UKPC 53.   [186] 'Family Property Today' (2008) 124 LQR 422.

Quantifying the interest under the trust

Establishing that the claimant has *some* interest under a trust of land is only stage one; stage two is to establish *the size* of that interest. The size of the cohabitees' respective shares is determined according to the terms of the express trust, if they ever created one.[187] In the absence of any express trust, the question of quantification depends upon the facts of the case. The difference between resulting and constructive trusts of land is crucial when it comes to quantifying the size of a claimant's beneficial interest. Under a resulting trust, the contributor merely recovers the value of her contribution as a proportion of the total value of the land: so if B contributed one-tenth of the purchase price of the land, she will today be entitled to only one-tenth of the land's current sale value, regardless of the fact that she has cohabited with the legal owner for the past 30 years. If, on the other hand, the claimant had established a common intention that she should have some interest under a constructive trust, the court has a wide discretion, when it comes to quantifying her interest, to fix the size of her interest at whatever level is necessary to discharge the burden on the conscience of the constructive trustee.

If the claimant has established *some* interest under a constructive trust by either of the *Rosset* routes, but there is no evidence that the parties expressly agreed the size of their respective shares, it falls to the court to identify the shares that they probably intended, on the basis of '*a survey of the whole course of dealing between the parties relevant to their ownership and occupation of the property*'.[188] This survey can include such matters as labour, housework, childcare, and so on.[189] We have already considered quantification in cases where a family home is transferred into cohabitants' joint names;[190] here, we consider other types of case. It should be borne in mind, however, that the factors listed by their Lordships in *Stack v. Dowden* as bearing on quantification[191] are bound to exert an influence beyond the particular situation of a family home in joint names. It appears that the courts have given up any attempt to produce a rigid doctrine to determine quantification, preferring instead to rely upon a broad discretion based on a wide range of factors. Let us consider two cases in which a claimant was awarded a one-third interest in the land under a constructive trust when they would have recovered much less if they had sought judgment under a resulting trust. In the first, *Cooke v. Head*,[192] the couple worked together to build a bungalow on a plot of land which they had bought for that purpose. The woman's financial contribution to the joint venture was one-twelfth the size of the man's and, under a resulting trust, the size of her beneficial share would, accordingly, have been one-twelfth. However, she was awarded an enlarged share under

---

[187] *Goodman v. Gallant* [1986] 2 WLR 236.

[188] In *Midland Bank plc v. Cooke* [1995] 4 All ER 562, *per* Waite LJ at 563.

[189] This represents a departure from the inflexible approach laid down by the Court of Appeal in *Burns v. Burns* [1984] Ch 317, in which May LJ held (at 344) that the court was only entitled to take into account direct financial contributions.

[190] See the section entitled 'The family home for which legal title is in joint names'.

[191] See *Stack v Dowden* [2007] 2 AC 432.   [192] [1972] 1 WLR 518, CA.

a constructive trust, because, when the house was being renovated, she did (in Lord Denning's, let us say 'quaint', terminology)

> quite an unusual amount of work for a woman. She used a sledge hammer to demolish some old buildings. She filled the wheelbarrow with rubble and hard core and wheeled it up the bank.[193]

In the second case, *Drake v. Whipp*,[194] a man and woman purchased a barn to convert into a joint residence, but it was conveyed into the man's name alone. He contributed 60 per cent of the purchase price and she contributed 40 per cent, but he contributed the vast majority of the extensive costs of the subsequent conversion work. She pleaded resulting trust, which would have given her approximately one-fifth of the value of the converted barn, but the Court of Appeal held that she should be entitled to a one-third share under a constructive trust. Peter Gibson LJ held that the court should take a '*broad*' approach, '*looking at the parties' entire course of conduct together*'.[195] Incidentally, in the cases of *Eves v. Eves* and *Grant v. Edwards* considered earlier, the claimants would have been able to establish no interest whatsoever under a resulting trust, because they had made no substantial direct financial contribution. A constructive trust solution in those cases produced awards of one-quarter and one-half, respectively.

The 'one-third cases', *Cooke v. Head* and *Drake v. Whipp*, concerned relatively short-term childless relationships of four and eight years, respectively. In the former case the parties never actually lived together in the bungalow, while in the latter case the period of cohabitation was a mere four years. *Eves v. Eves* concerned an equally short-term relationship, but one that produced two children, whereas *Grant v. Edwards*, which also involved children, involved a relationship of some 11 years.

According to a recent decision of the UK Supreme Court, after land has been acquired in cohabitees' joint names (i.e. a *Stack* type of case), the parties' dealings *inter se* are only relevant to the extent that such dealings elucidate their intentions regarding sharing beneficial ownership of the land.[196] The cohabitants in *Jones v. Kernott*[197] expressly agreed, when their relationship broke down and Mr Kernott left the family home in 1993, that they were at that time beneficial joint owners in equity. Thereafter Ms Jones remained in occupation and met all future expenses related to maintenance of the premises and paying off the mortgage. Some years later, Mr Kernott purported to sever and recover his half-share of the land, but the county court judge awarded Ms Jones 90 per cent of the value of the land on the basis that this was 'fair and just'. That decision was upheld in the High Court. The Court of Appeal allowed Mr Kernott's appeal by a majority of two to one, where their Lordships emphasized that (following *Stack v. Dowden*) the judges in the lower courts ought to have respected the parties' agreement to share equally in the event of sale and, in the absence of compelling evidence that the parties' intentions had changed, that the initial agreement should stand.[198] However, when the

---

[193] Ibid. *per* Lord Denning MR at 5196G–H.   [194] [1996] 1 FLR 826, CA.   [195] Ibid. at 831.
[196] Ibid.   [197] [2011] UKSC 53; [2011] 3 WLR 1121.
[198] [2010] EWCA Civ 578; [2010] 3 All ER 423.

matter came before the UK Supreme Court, their Lordships held that the parties' intentions *had* changed during the period of Mr Kernott's absence from the shared home and, allowing the appeal, upheld the decision of the county court judge. Their Lordships favoured fair maintenance of the current occupants (the woman and the children of her cohabitation with Kernott) over a strict allocation on the basis of initial financial contribution to purchase, or to put it in the legal terms they adopted, their Lordships held that purchase-money resulting trusts do not determine the outcome of cohabitation cases and that the court should look instead to fulfil the parties' actual intentions by means of a constructive trust. In short, they confirmed what had been said by the House of Lords in *Stack v. Dowden*. This approach might work justice in some cases, but it is equally liable to work injustice, for the parties' 'intentions' can only ever be whatever the court finds them to be 'on the balance of probabilities'. The outcome of any given 'cohabitation case' is as unpredictable as ever as a result of *Jones v. Kernott*, and it is fair to say that judicial discretion in this area is now so wide that courts are not far off the broad approach to allocation that is required by statute when married cohabitants divorce, but which Parliament has so far not seen fit to grant to (or impose upon) unmarried cohabitants. Lord Walker and Lady Hale summarized their judgment[199] by saying that 'where a family home is bought in the joint names of a cohabiting couple who are both responsible for any mortgage, but without any express declaration of their beneficial interests', the starting point is that 'equity follows the law and they are joint tenants both in law and in equity'.[200] This 'presumption can be displaced by showing (a) that the parties had a different common intention at the time when they acquired the home, or (b) that they later formed the common intention that their respective shares would change'. In the same place, their Lordships state, following Lord Diplock in *Gissing v. Gissing*,[201] that common intention is to be deduced objectively from the parties' words and conduct. Their Lordships note that examples of relevant evidence are given in *Stack v. Dowden*, at para. 69.[202] In their Lordships' judgment '"the whole course of dealing... in relation to the property" [a phrase borrowed from Chadwick LJ in *Oxley v. Hiscock* [2005] Fam 211, para. 69] should be given a broad meaning, enabling a similar range of factors to be taken into account as may be relevant to ascertaining the parties' actual intentions', adding that every case turns on its own facts.

The 'new model constructive trust'

In the early years after *Gissing v. Gissing*,[203] encouraged by Lord Diplock's statement that a constructive trust will arise '*whenever the trustee has so conducted himself that it would be inequitable to deny the* cestui que trust *a beneficial interest in the land acquired*',[204]

---

[199] Ibid. para. [51].

[200] In light of this, their Lordships' earlier attempt (at para. [19]) to disparage or downplay the maxim by labelling it a mere 'mantra' looks rather unconvincing. Their fear, presumably, is that in cases of sole legal ownership the maxim, if too strictly applied, might raise a strong presumption that the legal owner is absolute owner.

[201] [1971] AC 886, 906.

[202] [2007] 2 AC 432.   [203] [1971] AC 886.   [204] Ibid. at 905.

Lord Denning MR sought to bring a new, flexible version of the constructive trust to the assistance of married and unmarried cohabitees. *Cooke v. Head*[205] and *Hussey v. Palmer*[206] are good examples of his efforts. A distinctive feature of Lord Denning's so-called 'new model constructive trust' is that it does not depend upon proof of any common intention between the parties that the claimant should acquire a beneficial interest in the land. The only requirement is that the claimant be able to establish a claim to a beneficial interest, which it would be inequitable for the defendant to deny: it is '*a liberal process, founded on large principles of equity*'.[207] So, in *Eves v. Eves*, the case in which the married man told his young girlfriend (quite insincerely, as it turned out) that he would have placed the house in their joint names if she had been older, Lord Denning MR held that the man '*should be judged by what he told her—by what he led her to believe—and not by his own intent which he kept to himself*'.[208] Another distinctive feature of Lord Denning's 'new model constructive trust' is that it does not appear to depend upon a financial contribution to the land. Any substantial contribution will suffice. The claimant in *Cooke v. Head*[209] had made a small financial contribution to the house, but Lord Denning MR did not consider this to be essential to finding a trust. The crucial feature was that the house had been acquired by their 'joint efforts', financial contribution being merely one possible example of a 'joint effort'.

In *Eves v. Eves*,[210] the woman '*did not make any financial contribution but she contributed in many other ways. She did much work in the house and garden. She looked after him and cared for the children.*'[211] Lord Denning considered *Eves v. Eves* to be a case requiring the assistance of his 'constructive trust of a new model',[212] but the majority of their Lordships in that case (Browne LJ and Brightman J) found a constructive trust on the basis of an understanding reached between the parties—what we would today recognize as a *Rosset* constructive trust by 'route one'. Brightman J even went so far as to intimate that, were it not for lack of appropriate formalities, the trust in *Eves v. Eves* would have been an ordinary express trust.[213] (Curiously, Lord Denning MR also suggested that the defendant's conduct was equivalent in some way to a declaration of trust).[214]

In 1983, the year after Lord Denning's retirement, the Court of Appeal in *Burns v. Burns*[215] brought down the curtain on his 'new model constructive trust'. Their Lordships affirmed the requirement laid down in *Gissing v. Gissing* of financial contributions referable to a common intention that the contributor should acquire an interest in the property. The decision of the Court of Appeal in *Burns v. Burns* was strongly endorsed by the House of Lords in *Winkworth v. Edward Baron Development*.[216] *Burns v. Burns* demonstrates how harsh the results can be when unmarried cohabitees are left

---

[205] [1972] 1 WLR 518, CA.   [206] [1972] 1 WLR 1286, CA.   [207] Ibid. at 1290.

[208] [1975] 1 WLR 1338 at 1342E.   [209] [1972] 1 WLR 518.   [210] [1975] 1 WLR 1338.

[211] Ibid. at 1341G.   [212] Ibid. at 1341G.

[213] An informal express trust is not enough by itself to create a beneficial interest in her favour; there would at best be a mere 'voluntary declaration of trust', which would be 'unenforceable for want of writing' (*Gissing v. Gissing* [1971] AC 886, *per* Lord Diplock at 905).   [214] [1975] 1 WLR 1338 at 1342F.

[215] [1984] Ch 317.   [216] [1987] 1 All ER 114.

to their strict proprietary entitlements. Mrs Burns had lived with Mr Burns as his wife (although they were not in fact married) for nearly two decades. They had two children together and she gave up work to look after them. Later on, she returned to work, and her earnings were spent on household expenses and purchases. The family home in which they were living when their relationship broke down had been acquired in Mr Burns's sole name during the course of their relationship. The Court of Appeal held that Mrs Burns had no beneficial interest in it, because there had been no common intention to that effect and she had made no substantial direct financial contribution to the property.

Commonwealth jurisdictions

There is not the space here to do more than indicate, in broad outline, the approach taken to constructive trusts of land in other commonwealth jurisdictions. In fact, this short section is really included not so much to provide information, but rather to provide inspiration to look at this subject (and other subjects) through the eyes of others: we cannot comprehend, unless we compare. As Kipling wrote: what do '*they know of England who only England know*'?[217]

Canada

In Canada, the constructive trust of land is considered to be a remedial device for the reversal of unjust enrichment.[218] In this respect, it is closer to the approach taken in the USA than to the approach taken in England and Wales. The leading Canadian case is *Pettkus v. Becker*.[219] The facts were that Miss Becker had worked for 14 years on a honey farm owned by her cohabitee, Mr Pettkus. The Supreme Court of Canada, led by Dixon J, granted her a half-share in Mr Pettkus's property under a constructive trust in order to remedy his unjust enrichment at her expense. According to the judge, this 'unjust enrichment' arises where there is '*an enrichment, a corresponding deprivation and absence of any juristic reason for the enrichment*'.[220] Gardner has observed, however, that the first and third elements are problematic: the first, because the defendant can simply deny that he has been enriched by the plaintiff's services unless the enrichment was financial and obvious; the third, because it is never easy to show that an enrichment has been unjustly received when it was consensually conferred.

Australia

In Australia, constructive trusts have been granted in order to remedy the 'unconscionability' of the legal owner. At first sight, this seems to resemble the English basis

---

[217] 'The English flag' (1891).
[218] S. Gardner, 'Rethinking family property' (1993) 109 LQR 263 at 269–74.
[219] (1980) 117 DLR (3d) 257.   [220] Ibid. at 274.

for constructive trusts, but the English idea of unconscionability is more narrow and defined. In English law, the only relevant unconscionability is unconscionable denial of the claimant's subsisting proprietary interest, or unconscionable denial of a common understanding between claimant and defendant that the claimant should be entitled to a beneficial interest in the property. In Australia, 'unconscionability' is simply that which one party *'ought not in conscience, as between* [the parties] *be allowed to do*',[221] and the Australian constructive trust is:

> a remedial institution which equity imposes regardless of actual or presumed intention ... to preclude the retention or assertion of beneficial ownership of property to the extent that such retention or assertion would be contrary to equitable principle[222] ... [or] ... to the extent that it would be unconscionable.[223]

It has been observed that, in the leading Australian case, *Baumgartner v. Baumgartner*,[224] the High Court seemed to reject any suggestion that unconscionability should be based on *'idiosyncratic notions of what is fair and just'*, but then proceeded to invoke those very notions.[225]

Proprietary estoppel

A proprietary estoppel is a cause of action that arises in equity to prevent ('stop') the legal owner of certain property (A) from denying that another person (B) has, or might have, a proprietary interest in that property:

> 'it is the first principle upon which all courts of equity proceed',[226] that it will prevent a person from insisting on his strict legal rights—whether arising under a contract, or on his title deeds, or by statute—when it would be inequitable for him to do so having regard to the dealings which have taken place between the parties.[227]

The 'dealings' essential to establishing an estoppel are now taken to be:

1. a representation made, or assurance given, by the owner of land (A) to another person B;

2. to the effect that B will acquire some interest in A's land;

3. upon which assurance B has reasonably relied by act or omission;[228]

4. in such a way that it would be detrimental to B (and unconscionable of A) if A were subsequently to resile from his representation or assurance and assert his ownership of the land unencumbered by any rights claimed by B.

---

[221] *Commonwealth v. Verwayen* (1990) 170 CLR 394, *per* Deane J at 441.

[222] *Muschinski v. Dodds* (1985) 160 CLR 583, *per* Deane J at 451.   [223] Ibid. at 455.

[224] (1987) 164 CLR 137, in which Deane J appeared again, but this time with Wilson J and Mason CJ in the High Court of Australia.   [225] S. Gardner, 'Rethinking family property' (1993) 109 LQR 263 at 275.

[226] *Hughes v. Metropolitan Railway Co* (1877) LR 2 App Cas 439, *per* Lord Cairns LC at 448.

[227] Lord Denning MR in *Crabb v. Arun District Council* [1976] Ch 179 at 187.

[228] A detriment can be reasonably incurred even if the defendant did not expressly agree to it (*Parris v. Williams* [2008] EWCA Civ 1147).

These elements of estoppel are not to be regarded as entirely distinct from one another. They are frequently compounded or amalgamated on particular sets of facts; thus the nature of the assurance will often be bound up in the extent to which the reliance was reasonable and the nature of the reliance will often be inseparable from the detriment. This point was forcefully made by Robert Walker LJ in *Gillett v. Holt*,[229] where his Lordship emphasized that 'detriment' is '*not a narrow or technical concept*':

> The detriment need not consist of the expenditure of money or other quantifiable financial detriment, so long as it is something substantial. The requirement must be approached as part of a broad enquiry as to whether repudiation of an assurance is or is not unconscionable in all the circumstances.[230]

This flexible approach displaces the previous approach according to which proprietary estoppel had depended upon satisfaction of certain fixed *probanda* (matters to be proved), including proof that the claimant had acted on the basis of a mistake as to her legal entitlement in the land.[231] Of course, it goes without saying that the basic ingredients of representation and detrimental reliance must still be proved, and that the court will scrutinize the facts very carefully. Thus, if a representation is made on certain conditions, it is not enough to prove the representation merely; it is also required to prove that the conditions have been met.[232] Likewise, it is not enough to show mere reliance on the representation; it is also necessary to show that reliance was reasonable in the circumstances.[233] And it is not enough to show detriment, unless the detriment flowed from reasonable reliance on the representation.[234] *Powell v. Benney*[235] illustrates these points. The owner of a number of properties promised Mr and Mrs Powell that he would leave the properties to them in his will. They proceeded to improve the properties *on their own initiative*. When the representor died he left no will and his property passed to Benney on intestacy. The Court of Appeal called this a 'non-bargain' estoppel and upheld the first instance award of £20,000 as reasonable to meet the Powells' expectations.

The facts of *Gillett v. Holt* read like a Dickens novel.[236] Mr Gillett was 12 years old when Mr Holt (then a 38-year-old gentleman farmer) took him under his wing. At Mr

---

[229] [2001] Ch 210.   [230] Ibid. at 232.

[231] See *Wilmot v. Barber* (1880) LR 15 Ch D 96; *Matharu v. Matharu* (1994) 68 P & CR 93, *per* Roch LJ at 102. Even prior to *Gillett v. Holt*, there was some support for a more flexible approach; see, for example, *Taylors Fashions Ltd v. Liverpool Victoria Trustees Co Ltd* [1982] 1 QB 133, *per* Oliver J at 154.

[232] *Hunt v. Soady* [2007] EWCA Civ 366, CA (Civ Div).

[233] In *Hunt v. Soady* (ibid.) an estoppel claim failed on proof that the person who made the representation had later revoked it by letter before there had been detrimental reliance by the representee.

[234] Ibid.   [235] [2007] EWCA Civ 1283.

[236] [2001] Ch 210. Compare the similar facts of *Murphy v. Burrows* [2004] EWHC 1900 (Ch), which the judge in that case described as 'Dickensian', and compare *Century (UK) Ltd SA v. Clibbery* [2004] EWHC 1870 (Ch). If *Gillett v. Holt* belongs in a novel by Charles Dickens, the facts of *Century (UK) Ltd SA v. Clibbery*, involving a Panamanian company, a racehorse trainer, and numerous mistresses, would be at home in a novel by Jilly Cooper.

Holt's suggestion, Mr Gillett left school at the age of 16 and began a long career working on Mr Holt's farm. Mr Gillett's wife and children became, in due course, a surrogate family to Mr Holt (who had no immediate family of his own)—a fact confirmed by Mr Holt's frequent assurances (often in public) that Mr Gillett would one day inherit the farm. However, the relationship between the men eventually cooled and, ultimately, broke down entirely. Mr Holt wrote Mr Gillett out of his will and Mr Gillett commenced action seeking to establish an interest in the farm under proprietary estoppel, on the basis of Mr Holt's assurances and Mr Gillett's detrimental reliance upon them. The judge at first instance held that Mr Holt's representation could not be considered irrevocable and that, in any event, Mr Gillett had suffered no detriment in reliance upon them. The Court of Appeal rejected any need to show that the assurance was irrevocable and held that, despite the obvious material benefits of Mr Holt's patronage, it would be detrimental to deny him an interest in the farm, because he had forgone the opportunity to educate himself, and to make alternative provision for his retirement and old age. A most interesting feature is the detriment that Mr Gillett was held to have suffered when Mr Holt paid the private school fees of Mr Gillett's eldest son. How is that detrimental one might ask? The answer is that Mr Gillett had another son whom he then felt obliged to educate privately at his own expense.

Gillett v. Holt was followed by the Court of Appeal in *Lloyd v. Dugdale*,[237] where their Lordships confirmed that, if the person to whom an assurance is made forsakes an opportunity, he can be said to have suffered a detriment. So if X declines to take up an advantageous lease of Blueacre because he has been assured a lease of Redacre, the person giving the assurance may be estopped (assuming he is the owner of Redacre) from denying X's right to a lease of Redacre.

The requirement to demonstrate an assurance given by A to B that B will acquire some interest in A's land, upon which assurance B has reasonably relied by act or omission, is generally more easily demonstrable on the facts of a case than is the requirement to show that detriment to B makes it unconscionable for A to resile from the assurance. Robert Walker LJ has observed that, in cases in which the claimant's expectations are not clearly set out in a quasi-contractual way, '*the court has to exercise a wide judgmental discretion*'.[238] His Lordship set out a non-exhaustive list of factors bearing on the exercise of that discretion: misconduct of the claimant; particularly oppressive conduct on the part of the defendant; the need for a clean break; alterations in A's assets and circumstances; the length of the period during which A's assurance was given and B's detriment was suffered; the likely effect of taxation; (to a limited degree) the other claims (legal

---

[237] [2001] EWCA Civ 1754.

[238] *Jaggard v. Sawyer* [2002] EWCA Civ 159; [2003] 1 FCR 501, CA at [52]–[53]. See S. Gardner, 'The remedial discretion in proprietary estoppel—again' (2006) 122 LQR 492. Gardner argues that the wide judicial discretion involved in estoppel represents '*an unacceptable degree of rule by men (the individual judges), not laws*', but he welcomes the initial efforts of Robert Walker LJ to limit that discretion by reference to certain guiding considerations.

and moral) on the benefactor or his or her estate; crucially 'proportionality' between remedy and detriment.[239]

In *Yeoman's Row Management Ltd v. Cobbe*[240] the House of Lords took the opportunity to rein in the scope of proprietary estoppel in commercial contexts, by holding that estoppel should not be allowed to disturb normal commercial dealings. *Yeoman* is a so-called 'bargain case', albeit one in which the bargain was still under negotiation as regards certain terms. In *Yeoman's*, a property developer entered into an oral agreement with the owner of a block of flats under which the developer undertook to obtain planning permission to demolish the block and replace it with new town houses. A formula was agreed on price and division of profits from the development. The developer spent 18 months acquiring planning permission to demolish the block and build the town houses. It was after planning permission had been obtained that the owner of the block purported to withdraw from the agreement. In the Court of Appeal, a proprietary estoppel was recognized in favour of the developer, which was remedied by awarding the developer a share in the increased value of the property attributable to the planning permission, but this was overturned by the House of Lords. It was held that there was no proprietary estoppel on these facts, so the developer was awarded a mere *quantum meruit* (sum deserved) sufficient to ensure that the land owner had not been unjustly enriched by the time and labour expended by the developer in pursuing the planning permission in accordance with the informal agreement. It was held that the developer had assumed the risk that the owner of the block would withdraw. The fact that withdrawal was unconscionable in the abstract did not suffice; it had to be shown that the owner had behaved in a manner traditionally considered to be unconscionable in this context. The evidence was the other way—namely, that the traditional practice was to allow parties to withdraw from an informal contract in such a case. The claimant's argument that both parties considered themselves to be bound 'in honour' to perform the contract was rejected.

In the same way that the radical decision in *Stack v. Dowden* ought to be read so as to restrict it to its facts (i.e. domestic or 'romantic' joint legal ownership cases), so the *Yeoman* case ought to be construed restrictively to apply only to commercial cases (and perhaps only to joint venture cases). It is clear that proprietary estoppel will continue to thrive in non-commercial cases, as the decision in *Thorner v. Major*[241] makes clear. In this case, the legal owner had left his farm to the claimant by will, but subsequently destroyed the will and died intestate. The claimant had worked for the deceased for nearly 30 years in the reasonable expectation (based on various hints, but no express representation)

---

[239] Robert Walker LJ approved the judgment of Hobhouse LJ in *Sledmore v. Dalby* (1996) 72 P & CR 196, who had identified the need for proportionality: '*The essence of the doctrine of proprietary estoppel is to do what is necessary to avoid an unconscionable result, and a disproportionate remedy cannot be the right way of going about that*' (at 209). In *Sledmore v. Dalby*, the Court of Appeal held that, although there may have been grounds for an estoppel in the past, it was no longer inequitable to allow the expectation created by A to be defeated. See, also, *Clark v. Clark* [2006] EWHC 275 (Ch).   [240] [2008] UKHL 55; [2008] 1 WLR 1752.

[241] [2009] UKHL 18; [2009] 1 WLR 776. For application of this case see, for example, *Suggitt v. Suggitt* [2011] EWHC 903 (Ch).

that he would inherit the farm. Proprietary estoppel was found in favour of the claimant and he was awarded the farm. It should be noted that in so-called 'bargain' cases, where an agreement gives rise to a proprietary estoppel, the terms of the agreement must be sufficiently certain, but need be no more certain than normal contractual terms.[242] It is a nice question whether the promisor's estate is reduced for inheritance tax purposes from the moment the promise is made[243] or, in the case of a promisor who has not fulfilled his promise, only from the date of the promisor's death.[244]

If the reader suffers under any lingering doubt as to the importance of our subject, it will be noted the authors McFarlane and Robertson write about *Cobbe* under the title 'The Death of Proprietary Estoppel' and about *Thorner* under the title 'Apocalypse averted'![245] Their Lordships might have narrowly missed apocalypse, but arguably they also missed the opportunity presented by *Cobbe* and *Thorner* to explore the potential of 'unconscionability' to provide a framework for law in this area.[246]

Proprietary estoppel having arisen, B's actual remedy against A is uncertain because it is 'inchoate', which means it is incomplete and is therefore dependent upon a court judgment. However, in the interests of certainty and because the estoppel might lead to a proprietary right in or over A's property, the estoppel is deemed to bind third parties who acquire A's property with notice of it. Furthermore, if the property is land with registered title and the register indicates that A is the absolute owner of the land, a purchaser cannot rely upon the register, because B's estoppel is said to override it (assuming B is in actual occupation of the land).[247]

If a proprietary estoppel, having arisen, comes before a court, the court will then decide how the proprietary estoppel should be satisfied or 'fed'. The Court of Appeal, following *Jennings v. Rice*,[248] has confirmed that the remedy satisfying a proprietary estoppel should attempt to achieve an outcome that is fair and proportionate between the parties, rather than seeking merely 'the minimum equity to do justice', which was the traditional formula.[249]

The possible remedies range from mere 'damages'[250] (an estoppel remedied by an award of cash would have been an alternative to the decision to award a *quantum meruit*

---

[242] *Herbert v. Doyle* [2010] EWCA Civ 1095, CA.

[243] C. Whitehouse, 'Further thoughts on the inheritance tax implications of proprietary estoppel' (2010) 2 PCB 91–4.

[244] P. Reed QC, 'Proprietary estoppel: the law after *Cobbe* and *Thorner* and its impact on inheritance tax' (2010) 1 PCB 49–57.

[245] B. McFarlane and A. Robertson, 'The Death of Proprietary Estoppel' [2008] LMCLQ 449; 'Apocalypse averted: proprietary estoppel in the House of Lords' (2009) 125 LQR 535.

[246] M. J. Dixon, 'Proprietary estoppel: a return to principle?' (2009) 3 Conv 260.

[247] Land Registration Act 1925, s. 70(1)(g); confirmed in the Land Registration Act 2002, s. 116. See, generally, M. Dixon, 'Protecting third party interests under the Land Registration Act 2002: to worry or not to worry–that is the question' in M. Dixon and G. Ll. H. Griffiths (eds), *Contemporary Perspectives on Property, Equity and Trust Law* (Oxford: Oxford University Press, 2007).   [248] [2003] 1 P & CR 8.

[249] *Joyce v. Epsom* [2012] EWCA Civ 1398. See also *Suggitt v. Suggitt* [2012] EWCA Civ 1140.

[250] Strictly speaking, 'equitable compensation'. Cash was awarded to satisfy the estoppel in *Lloyd v. Sutcliffe* [2008] EWHC 1329 (Ch).

instead of estoppel in the *Yeoman's* case) through to conveyance of the fee simple,[251] and everything in between, such as the giving of period of notice to remedy the expectation of a tenancy,[252] compensation secured on the land by a charge,[253] a life interest in the land,[254] and, most common of all, an interest under a constructive trust. If a constructive trust is the remedy deemed to be appropriate to satisfy the proprietary estoppel, the claimant will end up with a trust that will be identical in *operation*[255] (if not in theory) to a constructive trust construed directly from the facts—that is, a constructive trust of the *Rosset* type. It is hardly surprising, therefore, that the use of the terms 'proprietary estoppel' and 'constructive trust' have frequently been used interchangeably by the courts.[256]

It has been argued that there is no relevant distinction between proprietary estoppel and constructive trusts awarded as the result of the court's discretion.[257] This, it is submitted, is perfectly true, provided that it is acknowledged that there is this small, but significant, theoretical distinction between the two concepts: namely, that the proprietary estoppel *pre-dates* (indeed, requires) the court's discretionary choice of appropriate outcome as between the parties, whereas the constructive trust is an outcome declared *after* the court has exercised its discretion. However, even though the constructive trust is, in this respect, a remedy, it is not a 'remedial constructive trust' as that term was used earlier; it is an institutional constructive trust, because it is awarded in satisfaction of an estoppel raised according to an institutional notion of unconscionable denial of the claimant's prior entitlement (based on factors such as assurance and detrimental reliance) to a proprietary interest in the defendant's land. It is because it is institutional that a purchaser from the legal owner ought to be able to discover, by asking appropriate questions of a claimant in occupation, whether or not representations have been made to the claimant and acts of reliance carried out by her, which are likely to have given rise to a proprietary estoppel in her favour. Indeed, it is because the facts giving rise to a proprietary estoppel are reasonably discoverable by inquiry that a proprietary estoppel arising in favour of a person in actual occupation of registered land will bind a purchaser from the registered owner, even though it has not been protected by entry on the register.[258]

---

[251] *Pascoe v. Turner* [1979] 1 WLR 431. [252] *Parker v. Parker* [2003] EWHC 1846 (Ch).

[253] *Campbell v. Griffin* [2001] EWCA Civ 2001, 27 June 2001. [254] *Inwards v. Baker* [1965] 2 QB 29.

[255] For the purposes, *inter alia*, of the Trusts of Land and Appointment of Trustees Act 1996.

[256] *Hammond v. Mitchell* [1991] 1 WLR 1127, *per* Waite J at 1137B; *Van Laethem v. Brooker* [2005] EWHC 1478 (Ch), Ch D. Contrast Lord Walker in *Stack v. Dowden* [2007] 2 AC 432, who (at para. [37]) re-emphasized the difference between them.

[257] D. Hayton, 'Equitable rights of cohabitees' [1990] Conv 370 and 'Constructive trusts of homes: a bold approach' (1993) 109 LQR 485, but see P. Ferguson, 'Constructive trusts: a note of caution' (1993) 109 LQR 114. The issue is still live (*Yaxley v. Gotts* [2000] Ch 162, CA, at 180B–F; *Jiggins v. Brisley* [2003] All ER (D) 319 (Apr); *Hyett v. Stanley* [2004] 1 FLR 394). *Aspden v. Elvy* [2012] EWHC 1387 (Ch); [2012] 2 FLR 807 is a typical case of a judge leaping straight to the constructive trust remedy and considering it irrelevant to discuss the initial stage at which proprietary estoppel was the cause of action giving rise to the remedy of constructive trust.

[258] Land Registration Act 2002, s. 116; Sch. 3, para. 2(c).

The most obvious role for proprietary estoppel is to remedy those cases, not covered by purchase money resulting trust, in which the claimant expends money or labour improving the defendant's property in the expectation, induced by the defendant, that she will thereby acquire a beneficial interest in the land. *Inwards v. Baker* [259] is a classic case of this sort. Baker junior was keen to build himself a bungalow, but he could not afford the price of a vacant site. His father had some spare land. Baker senior said to his son: 'Why don't you build the bungalow on my land and make it a bit bigger?' Baker junior did exactly that and made the bungalow his permanent home. All was well while both senior and junior were alive, but when senior died, his will (made long before the bungalow was built) did not leave the land to Baker junior, but to Inwards. Inwards brought proceedings to possess the bungalow, but he failed in a Court of Appeal led by Lord Denning MR. Danckwerts LJ, concurring with the conclusion of the Master of the Rolls, stated that this was '*one of the cases of an equity created by estoppel, or equitable estoppel*'.[260] Lord Denning MR held that '*the court must look at the circumstances in each case to decide in what way the equity can be satisfied*'.[261] In this case, their Lordships did not expressly identify the nature of the son's equitable right, but it seems fairly clear from the judgment of the Master of the Rolls that the son had acquired an equitable life interest.[262]

Some years ago, Sir Christopher Slade, who was a member of the Court of Appeal in *Springette v. Defoe*,[263] urged a threefold distinction between:

(1) implied and resulting trusts arising by virtue of contributions to the cost of acquisition of land; (2) constructive trusts arising by virtue of the doctrine of proprietary estoppel; [and] (3) other cases of constructive trusts.[264]

It is only a pity that Sir Christopher's lecture was delivered after the landmark decision in *Burns v. Burns*,[265] because it is, it is respectfully submitted, a logical and comprehensive tripartition of the law relating to the recognition of informal trusts of land, and one that deserved to have a greater influence than it appears to have had.

Further reading

In addition to the following print sources, the Online Resource Centre accompanying this book contains web links to further reading as well as guide answers to assessment questions relevant to this chapter.

BROWNE-WILKINSON, SIR NICOLAS, 'Constructive trusts and unjust enrichment' (1996) 10(4) Tru LI 98–101.

COOKE, E., *The Modern Law of Estoppel* (Oxford: Oxford University Press, 2000).

---

[259] [1965] 2 QB 29.   [260] Ibid. at 38F.   [261] Ibid. at 37.
[262] Ibid. But see *Dodsworth v. Dodsworth* (1973) 228 EG 1115, CA.   [263] [1992] 2 FLR 388.
[264] *The Informal Creation of Interests in Land*, The Child & Co. Oxford Lecture, 2 March 1984.
[265] [1984] 2 WLR 582.

Dixon, M. J., 'Proprietary estoppel: a return to principle?' [2009] Conv 260.

Elias, G. C. A., *Explaining Constructive Trusts* (Oxford: Oxford University Press, 1990).

Etherton, Sir Terence, 'Constructive Trusts and Proprietary Estoppel: The Search for Clarity and Principle' [2009] Conv 104.

Getzler, J., 'Quantum meruit, estoppel, and the primacy of contract' (2009) 125 LQR 196.

Hopkins, N., 'The *Pallant v. Morgan* "equity"?' [2002] Conv 35.

Hopkins, N., 'How should we respond to unconscionability? Unpacking the relationship between conscience and the constructive trust', in *Contemporary Perspectives on Property, Equity and Trust Law* (M. Dixon and G. L. H. Griffiths, eds) (Oxford: Oxford University Press, 2007) 3–18.

McFarlane, B., 'Constructive trusts arising on a receipt of property *sub conditione*' (2004) 120 LQR 667.

Millett, sir peter, 'Restitution and constructive trusts' (1998) 114 LQR 399.

Mitchell, C. (ed.), *Constructive and Resulting Trusts* (Oxford: Hart Publishing, 2010).

Neuberger of Abbotsbury, Lord, 'The stuffing of Minervás Owl? Taxonomy and taxidermy in equity' (2009) 68(3) CZJ 537.

Oakley, A. J., *Constructive Trusts*, 3rd edn (London: Sweet & Maxwell, 1997).

Rickett, C. and Grantham, R., 'Toward a more constructive classification of trusts' [1999] LMCLQ III.

Sherwin, E., 'Constructive trusts in bankruptcy' (1989) U Ill L Rev 297.

Waters, D. W. M., *Constructive Trusts* (London: The Athlone Press, 1964).

PART III

The Regulation of Trusts

9

Flexibility of benefit

The beneficiaries of an expressly created private trust may bring the trust to an end if they are in unanimous agreement and are all competent adults, and are, between them absolutely entitled to the trust property. This is the so-called 'rule in *Saunders v. Vautier*'.[1] Having terminated the trust, each beneficiary will be entitled to take her share of the fund as an absolute owner. When beneficial ownership returns to absolute ownership, it is then at its most flexible, because an absolute owner has virtually unrestricted rights to use and dispose of her property as she wishes.[2] In the meantime, before the trust is brought to an end, the nature and extent of a beneficiary's beneficial ownership is limited by the terms of the trust. The trust may provide that the beneficiary's interest will vest in possession at the moment the trust is created; alternatively, her interest may be deferred until some future date (for example, 'the year 2010' or 'the date of her father's death'), or it may be expressly contingent upon the happening of some future event that may or may not occur (for example, 'when she qualifies as a barrister' or 'when she reaches the age of 25'). The central question to be addressed in this chapter is to what extent beneficiaries may be able to take benefits under a trust despite limitations on their beneficial ownership, and to what extent limitations on their beneficial ownership may be varied or entirely removed. In short, we are concerned with the issue of 'flexibility of benefit'.[3]

We will identify, for example, what may be done if a trust confers a benefit on X at the age of 25 and it is thought that X would benefit during her infancy from the payment of trust income towards school fees, or that she would benefit at the age of 21 from a lump sum of capital to pay for the legal practice course. We will see that, subject to contrary provision in the trust instrument, the Trustee Act 1925 grants trustees a discretionary power—called 'the power of maintenance'—to apply income for the benefit of infant beneficiaries and a similar discretionary power—called 'the power of advancement'—to apply capital for the benefit of a beneficiary (infant or adult) out of her anticipated entitlement to the trust fund. In fact, if the trust instrument so provides, it is even possible for trustees to exercise the 'power of advancement' so as to allow a beneficiary to

---

[1] (1841) 4 Beav 115.   [2] See Chapter 1.
[3] A variation on Moffat's description. See G. Moffat, *Trusts Law Text and Materials*, 5th edn (Cambridge: Cambridge University Press, 2009) ch. 7.

take her entire presumptive share under the trust even though her interest has not yet, and might never, vest in possession. The availability, operation, and extent of the powers of maintenance and advancement are the first major topic in this chapter.

Occasionally, more fundamental flexibility may be called for. Events might occur for which the settlor had made no express provision, such as the divorce of a beneficiary or a change in the tax laws. Another possibility is that one beneficiary may wish to reduce the size of her share in favour of another beneficiary. Faced with a need for fundamental flexibility of this kind, the beneficiaries could agree to bring the trust to an end under the rule in *Saunders v. Vautier*, thereby taking their shares absolutely or resettling them on new trusts, but this will not be possible if, for example, an adult beneficiary wishes to reduce the size of her share in favour of an infant beneficiary. It was in response to problems of this sort that Parliament enacted the Variation of Trusts Act 1958. The Act confers a right on any interested party to seek the court's approval for proposals to vary or revoke expressly created trusts. A variation under the Act operates, like the rule in *Saunders v. Vautier*, on the basis of the unanimous consent of the beneficiaries. So if the court approves a proposal to vary beneficial interests under a trust, or to bring the trust to an end, it gives its consent on behalf of any beneficiary who, as a matter of fact or law, is incapable of giving her own consent to the proposal. All other beneficiaries must give their own consent before the proposal can be approved. The second major topic in this chapter is the variation of beneficial interest under private trusts. The Variation of Trusts Act 1958 forms the major part of that topic, but other modes of varying beneficial interests under private trusts are also considered.

In this chapter, we are mainly concerned with flexibility that is available as a matter of general law, but it should always be borne in mind that the trust instrument can, subject to limitations of public policy,[4] override the general law. Thus it is common practice for a modern trust deed to grant the trustees an overriding power of appointment by which they may terminate the interest of the principal beneficiary and appoint the benefit in favour of members of a defined class of alternative beneficiaries.

The chapter concludes with a brief reference to the variation of trust administration, which is included in order to contrast administrative flexibility with flexibility of benefit.

Maintenance

Consider the traditional settlement trust 'to A for life, to B in remainder'. The settlor has expressed an intention as regards the extent of the beneficial entitlements under the trust: the two beneficiaries are to have vested interests. A will have an interest vested 'in possession' now and B's entitlement will be vested 'in interest' until A's death, when it will vest in possession. Do the settlor's intentions end there? Suppose that A is currently

---

[4] See further Chapter 6.

in urgent need of financial assistance, but, being an infant, is not yet absolutely entitled to the income from the trust. It is natural to presume that the settlor's general intention to confer a benefit on A extends to providing for A in these circumstances, so the Trustee Act 1925 implies a power to maintain an infant beneficiary out of trust income, provided that the gift to that beneficiary includes income arising between the creation of the trust and the date the beneficiary's interest vests in possession.[5] This 'power of maintenance' is fiduciary, which means that the trustees must consider whether or not to exercise it, bearing in mind the purposes of the trust and the interests of all of the beneficiaries, and, if the trustees decide to exercise the power, they must exercise it for the benefit of the beneficiaries and for their benefit alone.[6] The statutory power of maintenance can be extended, modified, or excluded by the express terms of the trust instrument.[7]

The statutory power

Section 31 of the Trustee Act 1925 provides that trustees may '*at their sole discretion*' apply the whole or any part of the income from trust assets for '*the maintenance, education or benefit*' of an infant beneficiary. An 'infant' is any person under the age of 18.[8]

Limitations on the exercise of the statutory power

Even though the statutory power provides that the exercise of the power of maintenance is at the trustees' 'sole discretion', s. 31(1) lays down a number of limitations on its exercise.

1. The power cannot be exercised in conflict with the rights of persons with prior interests. So if the trust is for A for life and for B in remainder, A is absolutely entitled to all of the income from the fund and no income can be applied to maintain B unless A consents.

2. When income is applied to maintain an infant, it should not be paid directly to the infant: it should be paid to the infant's parent or guardian, or directly to address the particular financial need. If, for example, the payment of income is intended to meet the infant's school fees, the trustees should make the payment to the child's guardian or to the school direct. Trustees cannot safely pay income to an infant beneficiary, even if her interest in income has vested in possession, because an infant beneficiary cannot (unless she is married)[9] give a valid receipt for income,[10] with the result that she could demand the money *again* upon attaining majority.

3. The maintenance payment must be reasonable in all of the circumstances. In determining what is reasonable, the trustees must have regard to the '*age of the infant and his requirements and generally to the circumstances of the case, and in particular to what other income, if any, is applicable for the same purposes*'.[11]

---

[5] Trustee Act 1925, s. 31.   [6] Subject to permissible incidental benefits to non-beneficiaries.
[7] Trustee Act 1925, s. 69(2).   [8] Family Law Reform Act 1969, s. 1.
[9] Law of Property Act 1925, s. 21.   [10] Trustee Act 1925, s. 31(1), (2).   [11] Ibid. s. 31(1).

4. If the trustees have notice that more than one fund is available to meet the infant's particular financial need, the trustees should not meet that need entirely out of income from the trust fund. Contribution from the trust income should be made pro rata to contributions from other sources. Thus if the other available funds are together twice as large as the trust fund, the trustees should pay out only half as much as those other funds towards the beneficiary's maintenance. If it is not practicable to make a proportional contribution, or if the court otherwise directs, the trustees may meet the particular financial need entirely out of trust income. This might be necessary if, for example, the other available funds have already been allocated to other purposes or have otherwise been exhausted.[12]

Gifts carrying intermediate income

As stated earlier, the statutory power of maintenance can only be exercised in favour of a beneficiary under a trust if the gift to that beneficiary includes income arising between the creation of the trust and the date the beneficiary's interest vests in possession. In legal language, it is said that the gift must '*carry the intermediate income of the property*'.[13] To determine whether or not a gift carries the intermediate income is a very technical question, the answer to which is hidden in a mixture of statutory provisions and judicial decisions. Before an attempt is made to summarize these technical rules in as straightforward a way as possible, it is necessary to reacquaint ourselves with the meaning of certain terms.

Future and contingent gifts

A 'future' or 'deferred' gift is a gift that is expressed to vest in possession at some future date. An example would be a gift to X in 2015, or a gift to Y when her Uncle Jack dies. Typically, a future gift is one that will not vest in possession until some time after the trust comes into effect. However, testamentary trusts do not come into effect until the death of the testator, so there is every possibility that, by then, the future date to which the beneficiary's interest was deferred will already have passed, as would be the case if Uncle Jack were to predecease the testator in the example given earlier. The crucial point, however, is that a future gift is one that will certainly vest in possession. Short of divine intervention, the year 2015 will be reached and Uncle Jack will certainly die. This is the feature that distinguishes future gifts from contingent gifts. A contingent gift is a gift subject to a condition that may or may not be fulfilled. An example would be a gift to Z when Z qualifies as a solicitor. To confuse matters somewhat, it is possible to have a future contingent gift. An example would be a gift to Q in 2015 *if* Q has qualified as a solicitor by that date.

Devise, bequest, and legacy

'Devise', 'bequest', and 'legacy' are all types of testamentary gift. Such gifts come into effect on the death of the testator or testatrix and must comply with the formalities of

---

[12] Ibid.   [13] Ibid. s. 31(3).

the Wills Act 1837. A devise is simply a testamentary gift of 'real' property, which, for testamentary purposes, means all interests in land apart from leases (for historical reasons, leases are said to fall within the testator's personal estate and not his real estate). A bequest is simply a testamentary gift of personal property or 'personalty', which is property other than real property, and a legacy is a testamentary gift of cash. 'Legacy' is sometimes used more casually to refer to a testamentary gift of property of any type, so the term 'pecuniary legacy' is sometimes used to remove any doubt that the legacy is of cash. Finally, we must be aware of the distinction between 'specific' testamentary gifts and 'residuary' testamentary gifts. If T makes a gift to S of the freehold title to 'Linacre Farm' and leaves the rest of his real estate to R, S is said to be the beneficiary of a specific devise and R is said to be the beneficiary of a residuary devise. If T leaves his Rolls-Royce Corniche Convertible to S, and the rest of his personalty to R, S is said to be the beneficiary of a specific bequest and R is said to be the beneficiary of a residuary bequest.

Express and implied exclusion by the trust instrument

The express terms of the trust instrument or deed of gift are conclusive on the issue of whether or not a gift carries the intermediate income, so if the trust instrument says that a gift to beneficiary A does not carry the intermediate income, it does not carry it.[14] Conversely, if the trust instrument says that a gift to beneficiary A does carry the intermediate income, then so it does. Let us assume, however, that the trust instrument is silent on the point. In such a case, it is important to distinguish between gifts of income and gifts of capital. If a trust is established for A for life and B in remainder, the gift to A is a gift of all income arising from the trust property so long as she lives and the gift to B is a gift of the capital remaining when A has died. There is no point debating whether or not the gift to B carries the income between the creation of the gift and A's death, because the gift to B does not carry income in any circumstances at all. This does not mean that it is impossible to maintain B, but that, to do so, the court will have to exercise its special inherent jurisdiction to maintain an infant out of capital. The court is unlikely to do so apart from where the legacy is small and the infant has no other means of being maintained.[15] Where the fund is small, so that the cost of an application to court would be disproportionate to the size of the fund, a trustee will probably be justified in maintaining a beneficiary out of capital without the express authority of the court order.[16] However, by applying capital by way of maintenance, it may be regarded as taxable income, so it generally makes more sense to pay capital by way of advancement. Another possibility is to sell the property to which the infant is entitled and use the capital proceeds for her benefit.[17]

---

[14] Law of Property Act 1925, s. 69(2).   [15] *Re Mary England* (1830) 1 Russ & M 499.
[16] *Lee v. Brown* (1798) 4 Ves 362.   [17] Trustee Act 1925, s. 53; *Re Meux* [1958] Ch 154.

Testamentary gifts: the general position

An important distinction is between a gift conferred by an *inter vivos* trust and a gift conferred by a testamentary trust: the former will generally carry the intermediate income, whereas the latter is subject to more complex rules. If a testamentary gift is absolute, it vests in possession immediately; there is no intermediate period between the creation of the trust and the beneficiary's interest vesting in possession, so the question of entitlement to intermediate income simply does not arise. The position is more complex, however, when a testamentary gift is deferred to the future, or expressed to be contingent upon the happening of an event which may or may not occur. Here, the general position can be summarized by saying that future testamentary gifts *do not* carry the intermediate income unless the gift is a specific devise[18] or specific bequest,[19] whereas contingent testamentary gifts *do* carry the intermediate income[20] unless the gift is a pure pecuniary legacy.[21] A contingent pecuniary legacy will only carry the intermediate income in special circumstances:[22]

1. where the legacy was conferred by the parent of the legatee or a person standing *in loco parentis*;[23]

2. if the testator has elsewhere demonstrated an intention to maintain the beneficiary;[24]

3. the legacy is held on trusts distinct from the trusts to which the testator's other property is subject.[25]

If a residuary bequest is both future and contingent, it will not carry the intermediate income[26] and, logically, the same will follow in the case of a future-contingent residuary devise.

Residuary gifts are a special case, because trust income that is not otherwise disposed of automatically falls into residue. A beneficiary of a *contingent* residuary bequest can be maintained from intermediate income acquired indirectly in this way[27] and the same is presumably true of the beneficiary of a *contingent* residuary devise, but the beneficiary of a *future* residuary devise cannot,[28] and the same is true of the beneficiary of a *future* residuary bequest.[29]

Accumulation of income during infancy

Trustees do not have a *duty* to maintain an infant beneficiary when the gift to the beneficiary carries the intermediate income: they merely have a *power* to do so. Accordingly, it may be that the intermediate income arising in any given year will not be applied

---

[18] Law of Property Act 1925, s. 175. This section applies to wills coming into effect after 1925.
[19] Ibid. [20] Ibid. [21] *Re Raine* [1929] 1 Ch 716.
[22] See, generally, B. S. Ker, 'Trustees' powers of maintenance' (1953) 17 Conv 273.
[23] Trustee Act 1925, s. 31(3). Unless the person *in loco parentis* has provided another fund for the purpose of maintaining the infant, or the legacy was contingent upon the legatee attaining an age greater than 18 (*Re Abrahams* [1911] 1 Ch 108).   [24] *Re Churchill* [1909] 2 Ch 431.
[25] *Re Medlock* (1886) 54 LT 828.   [26] *Re Geering* [1964] 3 All ER 1043, *per* Cross J.
[27] *Re Adams* [1893] 1 Ch 329, *per* North J.   [28] *Re McGeorge* [1963] Ch 544, *per* Cross J.
[29] *Re Oliver* [1947] 2 All ER 162, *per* Jenkins J.

by way of maintenance. If this is the case, the unapplied income must be accumulated *'in the way of compound interest'*,[30] which means that last year's unapplied income is treated as if it were capital and added to the main capital of the trust, so the beneficiary can be maintained this year out of income arising on last year's accumulated income in addition to the usual income arising on the main trust capital. Thus, even though the accumulated income is treated for most purposes as if it were capital,[31] it can still be used to maintain the infant beneficiary in future years as if it were income arising in those years, provided that the infant is still entitled to be maintained out of income arising in those future years. If a beneficiary dies during infancy, the accumulations on that beneficiary's share are added to the capital of the trust as a whole, and not only to that beneficiary's share of the capital, so the deceased beneficiary's accumulations will not devolve as part of his estate. This is so even though the infant had a vested interest in the income during its life.[32]

Allocation of income after infancy

When the infant beneficiary attains majority (reaches the age of 18), or marries under that age, the trustees must add accumulated income to the main trust capital from which that beneficiary's accumulated income arose. There are, however, two exceptions to this rule.[33] When either of those exceptions applies, the trustees will not add the accumulations to the main capital, but will hold them on trust for the beneficiary absolutely, so that the accumulations may be paid to the beneficiary and the beneficiary's receipt will discharge the trustee. The first covers cases where the beneficiary already had a vested interest in the income *before* she attained majority (or earlier marriage). The second exception is when the beneficiary's contingent interest in the income vests absolutely *at the date* that she attains majority (or earlier marriage); this exception will apply when the gift is in the form 'to X when she reaches 18' or 'to Y when she marries'.

If neither exception applies—as would be the case if the gift was, for example, £1,000 'to Y when she reaches the age of 21'—the income accumulated on the £1,000 during Y's infancy will be added to the main capital (the £1,000) when she reaches the age of 18. Thereafter, she can no longer be maintained and she cannot take the accumulated income, but she is absolutely entitled to all income arising thereafter on the combined fund of capital and accumulations until she becomes absolutely entitled at the age of 21.[34] This concession ensures that income is not accumulated long enough to infringe the rule against excessive accumulation.[35]

Class gifts

If there is a gift to a class, contingent upon its members attaining the age of 21 or some other age, the class will be closed on a provisional basis, for the purpose of maintenance, when the first member attains that age. The provisional class will include all members

---

[30] Trustee Act 1925, s. 31(2).   [31] See Chapter 6 ('The rule against excessive accumulation of income').
[32] *Re Delamere's ST* [1984] 1 WLR 813.   [33] Trustee Act 1925, s. 31(2).   [34] Ibid. s. 31(1)(ii).
[35] See Chapter 6.

living at the date on which the class is closed. The trustees may then maintain that beneficiary out of the income attributable to her notional share. If a new beneficiary is born
later, the class is enlarged to include the new beneficiary, reclosed again on a provisional
basis, and a fresh allocation of notional shares is made. This reallocation occurs every
time a member of the class attains the contingent age or a new member is born.

Inherent jurisdiction to maintain

Even when a trust requires all income on a gift to be accumulated, which would normally be clear evidence that the settlor intended to exclude the statutory power of maintenance, the court has an inherent jurisdiction to maintain an infant if there are no
other funds available for its maintenance.[36] The assumption is that the settlor, having
demonstrated an intention eventually to confer a benefit on the infant, would not have
intended it to go without basic necessities in the meantime.

Advancement

Advancement is the power to pay trust capital for the advantage of an adult or infant
beneficiary. Usually, the capital is applied by means of a formal deed of advancement,
but such a deed is not strictly necessarily. The exercise of the power usually confers benefits on the beneficiary 'in advance' of the beneficiary's interest vesting in possession,
but, in this context, 'advancement' actually means 'to confer an advantage'. There are
suggestions, particularly in some of the earlier cases, that 'advancement' necessitates a
contribution to the 'early period' of the beneficiary's life—part of the process of 'getting
them started'—but it is now established that the power can be exercised at any stage to
further '*the establishment in life of the beneficiary*'.[37] Examples include payment of capital to support an apprenticeship, to purchase a commission in the army,[38] to purchase
an interest in a business,[39] to provide a dowry on the marriage of a girl,[40] to pay off the
beneficiary's inheritance tax,[41] and to establish the beneficiary's spouse in business.[42]

The fiduciary aspect

The power to make an advancement is a fiduciary power. Therefore the trustees must
weigh the interests of other beneficiaries against the advantage to the beneficiary who
is the object of the advancement.[43] They must also ensure that the capital monies paid

---

[36] *Re Walker* [1901] 1 Ch 879.   [37] *Pilkington v. IRC* [1964] AC 612, *per* Viscount Radcliffe at 634.
[38] *Cope v. Wilmot* (1772) Amb 704.   [39] *Re Mead* (1919) LT 724, CA.
[40] *Lloyd v. Cocker* (1860) 27 Beav 645.   [41] *Klug v. Klug* [1918] 2 Ch 67.
[42] *Re Kershaw's Trusts* (1868) LR 6 Eq 322.
[43] *Re Pauling's ST* [1964] Ch 303. In this case, the power should have benefited children but instead it placed
money in the hands of their parents who wasted it on their own living expenses.

to the object beneficiary are used by her for the purpose intended by the trustees. In *Re Pauling's Settlement Trusts*, the trustee bank had been advised by counsel that it could pay capital monies directly to the adult beneficiary by way of advancement and what the beneficiary did with them thereafter was his own concern. The Court of Appeal came to a different view. Wilmer LJ held that trustees are not permitted to prescribe a particular purpose, and then raise and pay the money over to the advancee leaving him or her entirely free, legally and morally, to apply it for that purpose or to spend it in any way he or she chooses, without any responsibility on the trustees even to inquire as to its application.[44]

If monies paid by way of advancement are not used for the prescribed purpose and the trustees receive notice of that fact, they are under a duty to make no further advances without first being satisfied that the monies will be properly applied.

The statutory power

Section 32 of the Trustee Act 1925 provides that trustees may apply 'capital money' for the advancement or benefit of a beneficiary, regardless of whether the beneficiary is an infant or an adult. The reference to 'benefit' in the statutory power widens the ambit of the power beyond mere 'advancement' in its traditional sense, so the power of advancement is now truly a power of applying capital so as to confer an 'advantage' of any kind. This means, for example, that the statutory power can be applied to paying off a beneficiary's debts,[45] whereas a mere power of 'advancement' cannot.[46] We will see shortly that the word 'benefit' has a very wide meaning indeed. The statutory power has no application to Settled Land Act settlements; in relation to other trusts, the statutory power is subject to express contrary provision in the trust instrument.[47]

Capital money

The reference to 'capital money' in s. 32 is misleading. There is no requirement to sell trust assets so as to realize capital money for the purpose of advancement; it is possible to apply capital assets directly for the advancement of the beneficiary. This occurred in *Re Collard's Will Trusts*.[48] The capital asset in that case was a farm to which the beneficiary was entitled under a will. Buckley J observed that the trustees had the power to advance £20,000 in capital monies to the beneficiary and then to sell the farm to the beneficiary at that price, so he concluded that the farm could be given to the beneficiary directly. R. E. Megarry described this as the '*healthy realism*' of equity.[49] It is worth digressing to note, briefly, that this 'healthy realism' is exhibited in other contexts. There is even a maxim which states that 'equity will not act in vain'. This maxim must be carefully applied according to the particular context of each case, but it can apply, for example, as a basis for refusing an injunction where it is incapable of practical enforcement.[50]

---

[44] [1964] Ch 303 at 334.   [45] *Lowther v. Bentick* (1874) LR 19 Eq 166.
[46] *Talbot v. Marshfield* (1868) LR 3 Ch App 661.   [47] Trustee Act 1925, s. 69(2).
[48] [1961] 1 All ER 821.   [49] (1961) 77 LQR 161 at 163 (a note on *Re Collard's WT*, ibid.).
[50] *Derby & Co Ltd v. Weldon* [1990] Ch 65.

The meaning of benefit

The example of the farm in *Re Collard's Will Trusts* demonstrates that advancement need not involve the conferral of financial benefits. The beneficiary in that case received far more than money—he received a livelihood and a place to live. Even though the immediate benefits of advancement take the form of money or valuable assets, the trustees must be satisfied that the payment of the money or valuable assets will achieve some ulterior benefit for the beneficiaries.[51] There is no defined limit to the range of benefits that will justify the exercise of the power of advancement. 'Benefit' is '*the widest possible word one could have*'.[52] Contribution to the costs of a wedding confers the social benefit of marriage, contribution to professional training confers the social benefit of a professional qualification, and so on. *Re Clore's Settlement Trusts*[53] illustrates the potential breadth of the concept. The beneficiary's father had established a charitable foundation to which the beneficiary felt morally obliged to contribute. It was more tax-efficient for a donation to be made by the trustees out of the trust capital than to be made by the beneficiary out of his private funds, so the trustees made the contribution by exercising their power of advancement in favour of the beneficiary. At one level, the benefit to the beneficiary was nothing more remarkable than the benefit of a tax saving, but, at another level, the benefit was assistance in fulfilling a moral obligation.

Re Clore's Settlement Trusts was applied in *X v. A*.[54] In that case, trustees of a marriage settlement had exercised their power of advancement to give the life tenant (the wife of the settlor) £350,000 in 1996 and £500,000 in 2000, which sums she had given to charity in accordance with her Christian beliefs. The trustees now applied for directions as to whether it was open to them to give her a very substantial part of the remaining trust capital for the purpose of enabling her to devote it to charitable causes. The judge did not criticize the earlier payments, but refused to authorize further advancement on the ground that the sums proposed to be released were too large a proportion of the whole. The implication that trustees can apply funds to discharge a moral burden on the beneficiary's conscience, but only to a limited extent, betrays the law's inherent bias towards maintaining material wealth at the expense of moral considerations.[55]

It might even be beneficial for the trustees to exercise the power of advancement temporarily to *prevent* a beneficiary from receiving wealth that would otherwise be due to her. Suppose a beneficiary's interest under a trust was contingent upon her attaining the age of 25, but evidence suggested that the beneficiary was immature, reckless, or a spendthrift. It might be to the benefit of the beneficiary for the trustees to exercise the power of advancement by resettling her capital on new trusts under which her interest will not vest until she reached the age of 30 (see the section headed 'Advancement by resettlement'). Incidentally, the notion of beneficial postponement has also been applied to justify the variation of a trust under the Variation of Trusts Act 1958.[56]

---

[51] *Moxon's Will Trusts* [1958] 1 WLR 165.   [52] Ibid. *per* Danckwerts J at 168.
[53] [1966] 1 WLR 955.   [54] [2006] 1 WLR 741.
[55] Compare the law's attitude towards ethical investment in Chapter 12.
[56] *Re T's Settlement Trusts* [1964] Ch 158.

Incidental beneficiaries

We have already observed that it is a valid exercise of the statutory power of advancement to pay off a beneficiary's debts and, in another case, to set the beneficiary's spouse up in business. In these cases, it is clear that the beneficiary's creditors and spouse are incidental beneficiaries of the exercise of the trustees' power. This, however, does not make the exercise of the power invalid. As Viscount Radcliffe stated in *Pilkington v. IRC:*[57] '*It is no objection to the exercise of the power that other persons benefit incidentally from the exercise of the power.*'[58] In that case, Miss Pilkington was the principal object of the power of advancement. The trustees had proposed to exercise their power of advancement by resettling capital monies on new trusts for her benefit. The proposal was approved despite the fact that the children of the principal beneficiary, who would have received nothing under the original trusts, would take as 'incidental beneficiaries' of the new trusts if she were to die under the age of 30 and they were to survive her.

Although incidental beneficiaries are usually permitted, it will be a breach of their fiduciary duty for trustees to exercise the power of advancement knowing that one or more *of the trustees* will take some incidental benefit in the trust capital paid in exercise of the power.[59]

Provisos to the statutory power of advancement

Section 32 of the Trustee Act 1925, as well as providing the statutory power of advancement, lays down the following limitations on its exercise.

Advancement limited to one half of the beneficiary's presumptive share

A settlor might include a clause in his trust authorizing the trustees to apply the entirety of a beneficiary's interest by way of advancement, but money paid for the advancement or benefit of a beneficiary under the statutory power '*shall not exceed altogether in amount one-half of the presumptive or vested share or interest of that person in the trust property.*'[60] Consider a typical gift on trust 'of £10,000 to A at the age of 25': if A is presently only 15 years old, it is clear that his interest has not yet vested in possession. His interest has, however, 'vested in interest', which means that he has a 'presumptive' interest in the subject matter of the gift. Accordingly, the trustees have the power to distribute half of the trust capital (£5,000) to A even though he has not yet met the contingency. What is more, even if A fails to satisfy the contingency, he will be under no obligation to repay the £5,000.

Trustees should be wary of exercising their power to the full extent, because, once they have distributed the entire one-half of a beneficiary's presumptive share, the power is exhausted as regards that beneficiary[61] (subject to the possibility of varying the beneficial interests under the trust by application to the court under the Variation

---

[57] [1964] AC 612, HL.   [58] Ibid. at 636.   [59] *Molyneux v. Fletcher* [1898] 1 QBD 648.
[60] Trustee Act 1925, s. 32(1)(a).   [61] *Re Marquess of Abergavenny* [1981] 1 WLR 843.

of Trusts Act 1958, considered later).[62] Suppose that a gift of £100,000 had been made on trust for A and B in equal shares upon their qualification as medical doctors. If, today, the trustees pay the full one-half of A's presumptive share (£25,000) by way of advancement, A can be given no further payments of capital until she actually qualifies as a medical doctor. This is so even if the remaining £75,000 worth of trust property subsequently increases in value to £300,000. Despite the increased value of the fund, the trustees have no authority to exercise their statutory power of advancement in favour of A, the power having already been exercised to the full. The trustees will, however, be able to exercise the statutory power of advancement for the first time in favour of B up to the value of £81,250, being half of B's presumptive share. B's total presumptive share is worked out by adding the current fund of £300,000 to the £25,000 paid out to A and dividing the total fund value of £325,000 between A and B in equal shares, making B's total presumptive interest in the £300,000 the princely sum of £162,500. A's presumptive interest in the £300,000 is the remaining £137,500. (This represents her total presumptive entitlement of £162,500 less the £25,000 she has already received.)

The preceding example appears to treat A and B equally, but it may be that B suffered a disadvantage when the power of advancement was exercised in favour of A. When we examine trustee investment in Chapter 12 we will see that, as a basic rule, the larger the fund, the better the investment opportunities and the lower the risk. When A received one-quarter of the total fund by way of advancement, it would have seriously weakened the investment potential of the remaining three-quarters. There would be nothing unfair in this if A's interest in the final value of the fund were limited to one more quarter (that is one-third of the remaining three-quarters of the fund), but at present the rule is distinctly more generous to A. In our example, A was entitled to £137,500 of the final fund value of £300,000, but if she had been restricted to one-third of the £300,000 (on the basis that the £300,000 represents three-quarters of the original fund), A would have been entitled to a mere £100,000. The Law Commission has expressed concern with the present state of affairs and has recommended that, when the beneficiaries become absolutely entitled to the capital, any beneficiary (such as A) who received capital early by way of advancement should account, not merely for the nominal cash value of the capital at the date of the advancement (£25,000 in our example), but for its value *as a proportion of the fund at the date of the advancement*.[63]

---

[62] This occurred in *CD (a minor) v. O* [2004] EWHC 1036 (Ch), Ch D, in which the one-half limit was exceeded in favour of a child (indeed, it was held that the child's *entire* presumptive share could be used) in order to pay her school fees. This decision seems a somewhat radical departure from the statutory rule restricting advancement to one-half of a beneficiary's presumptive share, but the judge was rightly fortified by the fact that the beneficiary in this case was solely entitled to the fund and would (but for her age) have been entitled to bring the trust to an end.

[63] Law Reform Committee 23rd Report, *The Powers and Duties of Trustees* (1982) Cmnd. 8733, paras 4.43–4.47.

The 'hotchpot' rule

Section 32(1)(b) of the Trustee Act 1925 provides that, if a beneficiary becomes absolutely and indefeasibly entitled to a share of trust property, the money she has already received by way of advancement must be brought into account as part of her share. The process is called 'hotchpot', and we saw an illustration of its operation in the previous section in the example of the gift on trust to A and B on their qualification as medical doctors. We noted that, when A qualified as a medical doctor, she was not entitled to a full half-share of the final value of the fund; on the contrary, A had to account in 'hotchpot' for the £25,000 she had received by way of advancement at an earlier date.

The statutory power cannot be exercised prejudicially to prior entitlements

Section 32(1)(c) of the Trustee Act 1925 provides that trustees are not permitted to make a payment by way of advancement if to do so would prejudice any person with a prior interest in the fund, unless the person with the prior interest gives consent in writing to the advancement. The written consent of a person with a prior interest will still be required, despite a clause in the trust instrument dispensing with the requirement[64] (a rare instance of the settlor being unable to oust the provisions of the general law by the express terms of the trust instrument). So if a trust provides for A for life and for B in remainder, the trustees will not be permitted to apply any capital money for the advancement or benefit of B unless A has first given her consent in writing. This is because A has a vested interest in income arising on the capital of the trust and the payment of capital to B will reduce A's income. However, if A is merely a potential object of a discretionary trust, her consent will not be required.[65]

Advancement by resettlement

The power of advancement may be exercised by resettling the trust capital on new trusts, but Upjohn J stated, in *Re Wills WT*, that:

> Trustees cannot under the guise of making an advancement create new trusts merely because they think they can devise better trusts than those which the Settlor has chosen to declare. They must honestly have in mind some particular circumstances making it right to apply funds for the benefit of an object or objects of the power.[66]

In addition to the requirement that the resettlement is beneficial to the beneficiary, the resettlement must not infringe the rule against inalienability of capital and must not involve the unauthorized delegation of a basic discretion. As to the last requirement, Upjohn J stated that '*a settlement created in exercise of the power of advancement cannot in general delegate any powers or discretion, at any rate in relation to beneficial interests*',[67] but his Lordship made it clear that such delegation may be expressly authorized by the trust instrument. When considering the advancement by resettlement in *Pilkington*

---

[64] *Henley v. Wardell, The Times*, 29 January 1988. The report carries the witty caption, 'Will power doesn't override consent'.   [65] *Re Beckett's Settlement* [1940] Ch 279.

[66] *Re Wills' WT* [1959] Ch 1, *per* Upjohn J at 14.   [67] Ibid. at 12, 13.

v. IRC,[68] Viscount Radcliffe confirmed that '*the law is not that a trustee may not delegate; it is that trustees may not delegate unless they have authority to do so*'.[69] The resettlement in *Pilkington v. IRC* was successfully carried out for the avoidance of death duties (the precursor to inheritance tax), but, nowadays, a resettlement of trust capital on distinct trusts may give rise to a chargeable gain.[70] Today, there may also be adverse inheritance tax implications to such an arrangement.[71]

Exclusion of the statutory powers

The powers conferred on trustees by the Trustee Act 1925, including the powers of maintenance and advancement, are in addition to the powers conferred by the trust instrument, if any, but, according to s. 69(2) of the Act, they apply only so far as a contrary intention is not expressed in the instrument.[72] In *IRC v. Bernstein*,[73] the settlor had directed that the income on his trusts should be accumulated during his lifetime, and this was held to be evidence of an intention to exclude the statutory powers of maintenance and advancement. In *Re Ransome*,[74] a similar direction to accumulate income was held to be evidence of an intention to exclude the trustees' usual duty to pay income on accumulations under the Trustee Act 1925, s. 31(1)(ii).[75] The beneficiary in that case got the worst of both worlds, because the direction to accumulate was held to be good evidence of an intention that the beneficiary should not be able to take income by way of maintenance, but the direction to accumulate was otherwise void for perpetuity, so the beneficiary was also disabled from taking income by way of accumulation. Accordingly, the settlor's fundamental intention to benefit the beneficiary was thwarted by the unintended, and unforeseen, combined effect of s. 69(2) of the Trustee Act 1925 and the rule against excessive accumulation.[76]

The Variation of Trusts Act 1958

If a dispute arises as to the proper construction to be given to the words of a trust instrument, it goes without saying that the courts are its most expert arbiters. However, a practice grew up whereby parties interested in varying the terms of a trust for the benefit of the beneficiaries would produce a sham dispute and, having agreed a 'compromise' in terms favourable to the beneficiaries, would seek a court order approving the parties' agreed interpretation of the trust. This practice continued until it was brought to an end by the House of Lords in the case of *Chapman v. Chapman*.[77] The House of Lords insisted that courts should no longer approve the compromise of sham disputes, but the consequence was to deprive the courts of a flexible and useful jurisdiction to

---

[68] [1964] AC 612.　　[69] Ibid. at 639.
[70] Inland Revenue *Statement of Practice* SP7/84; *Swires v. Renton* [1991] STC 490.
[71] See N. Hassall, 'Powers of advancement: how far can *Pilkington* be stretched' (2007) 4 PCB 282.
[72] Trustee Act 1925, s. 69(2).　　[73] [1961] 1 Ch 399.　　[74] [1960] Ch 444.　　[75] See earlier.
[76] See J. G. Riddall's imaginative article, '*Re Ransome* revisited or "first the good news"' (1979) 43 Conv 423.
[77] [1954] AC 429.

vary trusts. It was in response to *Chapman v. Chapman* that the Law Reform Committee proposed that Parliament should grant the courts an '*unlimited jurisdiction to sanction*' variation of trusts[78] and it was in response to that proposal that the Variation of Trusts Act 1958 was swiftly passed into law.

The essence of the 1958 Act is that it confers a jurisdiction on the Chancery Division of the High Court to approve an arrangement varying or revoking all, or any part, of any expressly created private trust. This jurisdiction cannot be excluded by the express terms of the trust.[79] The Act lists four categories of beneficiary on whose behalf the court can give substituted consent, but all other beneficiaries have the right freely to decide on their own behalf whether or not to approve a proposed variation.

The most common reason for seeking a variation of beneficial interests under trusts is to reduce the beneficiaries' tax liabilities, with the result that the 1958 Act has become something of a tax-avoidance facility. It is perfectly acceptable for an individual to arrange his property and affairs so as to reduce his tax burden, but it is surely doubtful that the courts should take so active a role in reducing the public revenue. The contrast with the law of charitable trusts, where public benefit is a precondition to the judicial grant of fiscal immunity, could hardly be more stark. Nevertheless, the courts have turned a blind eye to the moral problem of judicially assisted tax avoidance, being content to make it their 'moral' imperative to advance the best interests of the beneficiaries. The Revenue is more concerned with public fiscal responsibilities than private financial rights, and is reported to have discontinued its practice of giving advance opinions on proposed arrangements to vary trusts under the 1958 Act.[80] Of course, not every variation is made to achieve tax advantages. Thus in one recent unreported case the 1958 Act was used to vary a settlement made following a divorce. The original trust had settled cash on the ex-husband for the purpose of buying a house in which to see his children. The house was never bought, so the court approved the ex-wife's application to vary the trust so as to partition the cash between the ex-husband and their children and any children (presumably step-children) yet to be born.[81] Sometimes there is undoubtedly a public interest in varying a trust. An example would be any trust containing a condition tending to racial prejudice. We shall consider some cases in this category later.

The theoretical basis of variations under the Act

In theory, a variation under the 1958 Act is based on the consent of the beneficiaries; it is a statutory extension of the rule in *Saunders v. Vautier*. In *Re Holmden's Settlement Trusts*,[82] Lord Reid stated that:

> The beneficiaries are not bound by variations because the court has made the variation. Each beneficiary is bound because he has consented to the variation. If he was not of full

---

[78] Law Reform Committee 6th Report, *Court's Power to Sanction Variation of Trusts* (1957) Cmnd. 310, para. 13.

[79] '[E]*ven the most determined settlor or testator cannot exclude the jurisdiction of the court under the 1958 Act*' (*per* Mummery LJ in *Goulding v. James* [1997] 2 All ER 239 at 251d–e).

[80] *Wyndham v. Egremont* [2009] EWHC 2076 (Ch).   [81] *Re King*, Ch D, 15 December 2010.

[82] [1968] AC 685, HL.

age when the arrangement was made he is bound because the court was authorised by the Act [1958] to approve of it on his behalf and did so by making an order. If he was of full age and did not in fact consent he is not affected by the order of the court and he is not bound.[83]

However, the power of the beneficiaries must not be overstated. The court is never obliged to vary a trust under the Act, even if the beneficiaries are all adults and all consent to the variation. The Act merely authorizes the court to approve the arrangement. Section 1 states that the court may '*if it thinks fit*' approve:

> any arrangement... varying or revoking all or any of the trusts, or enlarging the powers of the trustees of managing or administering any of the property subject to the trusts.

The machinery of the Act

Who should apply?

Section 1 of the Act provides that the court has authority to approve an arrangement '*by whomsoever proposed*', but, in keeping with the principle of consent on which the jurisdiction is based, it is accepted that adult beneficiaries should normally be the ones to apply to vary or revoke their trust. Trustees should not make the application themselves unless they believe, first, that the variation would be for the benefit of the beneficiaries and, second, that there is no adult beneficiary willing to make the application for a variation.[84] In fact, far from being applicants, trustees should be joined as defendants to the application, because it is they who have the fiduciary duty to protect the interests of all of the beneficiaries under the trust and they who should raise objections if the proposed variation appears to benefit some, but not all, of the beneficiaries. If the beneficiaries are not unanimous in making the application, the non-applicant beneficiaries should be joined as additional defendants. In keeping with the notion that the settlor's intentions are a 'serious' consideration, the settlor should be joined as a defendant if variation of an *inter vivos* trust is proposed and the settlor is still alive.[85] The form of the application to vary a trust under the Act is an originating summons exhibiting a draft scheme of arrangement.

How does the variation occur?

According to Megarry J in *Re Holt's Settlement*,[86] any beneficiary who gives her own consent to a variation disposes of her original equitable interest the moment the application to vary is approved by the court, but his Lordship reluctantly yielded to counsel's submission that this disposition should be an exception to the usual requirement[87] that dispositions of equitable interests must be made in writing. This means that consent can be given informally, with the result that there will be no document liable to *ad valorem* stamp duty.[88] A reversal of this concession would go some way to countering the tax

---

[83] Ibid. at 701. Followed in *Goulding v. James* [1997] 2 All ER 239.
[84] *Re Druce's ST* [1962] 1 WLR 363.   [85] RSC Ord. 93, r. 6(2).   [86] [1969] 1 Ch 100.
[87] Law of Property Act 1925, s. 53(1) and (1)(c). See Chapter 6.   [88] Stamp Act 1891, s. 54.

benefits that usually accompany a variation of trust. There is, however, little prospect of such a reversal, because, as Megarry J observed, the practice of informal consents has been accepted by HM Revenue and Customs, and by the courts for many years '*in some thousands of cases*'.[89]

Consents given by the court

The Act lists four categories of beneficiary on whose behalf the court may give substituted consent, but all other beneficiaries have the right freely to decide on their own behalf whether or not to approve a proposed variation. The four categories of beneficiary on whose behalf the court may grant consent are set out in paras (a), (b), (c), and (d) of s. 1(1) of the Act. The para. (b) category is the most difficult and will therefore be considered last.

Persons under a disability: s. 1(1)(a)

This class includes minors (infants) and any other beneficiaries, including those of unsound mind and those suffering from a relevant physical disability, who are incapable of giving their own consent to the proposed arrangement to vary the trusts. If it seems surprising that the consent of an adolescent should be treated in like manner to the consent of a person of unsound mind, it should be borne in mind that, in practice, the court will take into account the expressed wishes of persons approaching majority even though their lack of consent cannot be a conclusive consideration. The power of the court to substitute its own consent for that of minors is a recognition that infants (even those aged 17) may still be under parental influence, with the very real possibility that their parents might try to influence the exercise of their child's consent for their own ends.

A long-established Chancery practice of requiring counsel's opinion when proceedings are compromised in which an infant is interested has been extended to all cases '*where any infants or unborn beneficiaries will be affected by an arrangement*' under the 1958 Act:[90]

> such a written opinion is helpful, and in complicated cases it is usually essential to the understanding of the *guardian ad litem* and the trustees, and to the consideration by the court of the merits and the fiscal consequences of the arrangement.[91]

The unborn: s. 1(1)(c)

The court may consent to an arrangement on behalf of any person unborn. This class is not restricted to persons in the womb. It would include 'the children of X', even if X were an avowed celibate. Even if X were a female octogenarian, the court would take the precaution of consenting on behalf of her unborn issue.

---

[89] [1969] 1 Ch 100 at 115.   [90] *Vice Chancellor's Practice Direction of 27 July 1976* [1976] 1 WLR 884.
[91] Ibid.

Discretionary beneficiaries under protective trusts: s. 1(1)(d)

A protective trust is a trust under which the principal beneficiary has a determinable life interest that, if it determines due to the bankruptcy or such like of the principal beneficiary, is replaced by a discretionary trust for a secondary class of potential beneficiaries.[92] According to s. 1(1)(d), the court may provide the consent of any beneficiary of the discretionary trust so arising.

Persons with mere expectations: s. 1(1)(b)

According to s. 1(1)(b), the court may, if it thinks fit, approve a variation on behalf of:

> Any person (whether ascertained or not) who may become entitled, directly or indirectly, to an interest under the trusts as being at a future date or on the happening of a future event a person of any specified description or a member of any specified class of persons

but with the following proviso:

> this paragraph shall not include any person who would be of that description or a member of that class, as the case may be, if the said date had fallen or the said event had happened at the date of the application to the court.

The key to understanding s. 1(1)(b) is to identify those persons on whose behalf the court can give consent and to contrast them with the persons described in the proviso. The court has no authority to consent on behalf of the persons described in the proviso.

Persons on whose behalf the court can give consent under s. 1(1)(b) have no certain entitlement to the trust property, but merely an expectation of attaining an interest under the trust. Their interests in the trust have not vested in interest, let alone vested in possession. It is for this reason that they are not required to give their own consent and that the court is authorized to consent on their behalf. The essential words of s. 1(1)(b) identify the person with a mere expectation as someone who '*may become entitled... at a future date or on the happening of a future event*' if he then falls within a '*specified description*' or a '*specified class of persons*'. The most straightforward example of a person falling within s. 1(1)(b) is a person, E, who may be entitled to an interest under a trust when X dies, as being, at that time, X's next of kin. E satisfies all of the key ingredients of s. 1(1)(b). He 'may become entitled' (but may not) 'on the happening of a future event' (the death of X), as being at that date within a 'specified description or specified class' (X's next of kin). The reason why we say that E has a mere expectation is because, even if X is unmarried today and E is X's only child, there is still the possibility that E may not be X's next of kin by the time that X dies. If E predeceases X, or if X marries and is survived by his spouse, E will not be X's next of kin. In short, one can never say for certain until a person dies who will be their next of kin. An old maxim puts it this way: *nemo est heres viventis* ('the living have no heirs').

Consider the facts of *Re Moncrieff's Settlement Trust.*[93] The primary beneficiary, Mrs Parkin, applied to court for an order approving an arrangement to vary the trusts under

---

[92] See Chapter 6.   [93] [1962] 1 WLR 1344.

which she was entitled. Mrs Parkin had an adopted son, Alan. In the event of Alan prede-
ceasing Mrs Parkin, her next of kin would be the four infant grandchildren of her mater-
nal aunt. The judge was able to consent on behalf of Alan, because Alan was still an infant
and therefore fell within s. 1(1)(a) of the Act. However, s. 1(1)(a) only applies to persons
'having' an interest under the trust, so the four infant grandchildren, having mere expectations of an interest under the trust, did not fall within s. 1(1)(a). The crucial question
was whether they fell within s. 1(1)(b) as being persons who *may become entitled...on
the happening of a future event*, as falling within a specified description or class. The question was answered in the affirmative. At the date of the court hearing, it could be said
that the cousins 'may' fall in the specified class of 'next of kin' on the future event of Mrs
Parkin's death. However, the court then took into account the important proviso to s. 1(1)
(b), which states that s. 1(1)(b) does not include any person who *would be* a member of
the specified class if the said future event had happened *at the date of the application to
the court*. So the court asked itself whether the four infant grandchildren *would have been*
'next of kin' if Mrs Parkin had died on the date of the application to the court. The court
answered this question in the negative. If Mrs Parkin had died at the date of the application to the court, Alan, not the four infant grandchildren, would have been her next of
kin. Hence the court was able to consent on behalf of the four infant grandchildren to the
arrangement proposed by Mrs Parkin. Buckley J observed that the four infant grandchildren '*may never fall within the class of beneficiaries because they may predecease the settlor
or the first respondent* [Alan] *may survive the settlor*'.[94] His Lordship took the view that the
interests of the four infant grandchildren could be adequately looked after by the trustees.

The facts of *Re Suffert's Settlement*[95] were broadly similar to those of *Re Moncrieff's
Settlement Trust*. Under the terms of the original settlement, Miss Suffert had a life
interest under a protective trust with a power to appoint her successor. If she were to die
without issue, having failed to exercise her power of appointment, the fund would pass
in trust to her statutory next of kin. Miss Suffert applied to court for an order approving
a variation of the protective trusts. She was a 61-year-old spinster, who had no children
and her only ascertainable relations were three adult first cousins. One of the cousins
had joined Miss Suffert in making the application to the court, but that still left two
adult cousins who had not given their consent to the proposed variation. The question
arose whether the court could consent on their behalf. The court held that it could not
consent on behalf of the cousins, because they fell within the proviso to s. 1(1)(b). If
the future event (Miss Suffert's death) had happened '*at the date of the application to
the court*'—that is, the date of the court hearing—the three cousins *would be* entitled
immediately as next of kin to an interest under the trust.

A vested interest, albeit remote and contingent, is more than a mere expectation
In *Knocker v. Youle*,[96] Mrs Youle, the settlor's daughter and primary beneficiary, had a
life interest in income under the trust. The remainder of the fund would pass to persons

---

[94] [1962] 1 WLR 1344 at 1346.   [95] [1961] Ch 1.   [96] [1986] 1 WLR 934.

appointed by the primary beneficiary in her will. If she made no appointment, the remainder interest would pass to the following persons or classes of person in the following strict order: the settlor's son, Mr Knocker; if he were dead, to the settlor's sisters; if they were dead, to the sisters' issue at the age of 21. The settlor's daughter and son applied to court for an order approving a variation of the trusts. The settlor's sisters had all died. The question arose whether the sisters' issue had to give their consent to the arrangement, or whether the court was able to consent on their behalf under s. 1(1)(b). The court concluded that the sisters' issue were not persons who 'may' be entitled upon the happening of a future event, etc., but were persons who 'would' be entitled upon the happening of a future event—that is, Mrs Youle's omission to appoint beneficiaries by her will). As Warner J stated:

> Each of them is...entitled now to an interest under the trusts, albeit a contingent one (in the case of those under 21, a doubly contingent one) and albeit also that it is an interest that is defeasible on the exercise of the general testamentary powers of appointment vested in Mrs Youle and Mr Knocker.[97]

Warner's J's reading of the word 'may' works very well in the case of any of the sisters' issue aged over 21, but is less convincing in relation to any under the age of 21. The interest of any of the sisters' issue under the age of 21 depends upon *two* contingencies being met: Mrs Youle's omission to appoint beneficiaries by her will *and* their attaining the age of 21. Those beneficiaries cannot say that that they 'would' be entitled upon the happening of *a* (singular) future event; the most that can be said is that they 'may' be entitled upon the happening of *a* future event. However that may be, Warner J was making the point that, in contrast with the 'next of kin' referred to in *Re Suffert's* and *Re Moncrieff's*, persons with remote and doubly contingent interests have more than a mere specious hope of attaining a vested interest, and should therefore have the opportunity to give or refuse consent. In any event, Warner J went on to state that, even if the applicants had been able to argue a way around the importance that he had attached to the word 'may', the variation would still have depended upon the sisters' issue giving their own consent, because, like the cousins in *Re Suffert's Settlement*, the sisters fell within the proviso to s. 1(1)(b).

The benefit requirement

The main statutory prerequisite to the grant of the court's approval to a proposal to vary or revoke trusts is that the proposal must be beneficial to beneficiaries falling within s. 1(1)(a), (b), and (c). In exercising its discretion, '*the function of the court is to protect those who cannot protect themselves*'.[98] Even if the proposal is beneficial to beneficiaries within the three relevant categories, it does not follow that the court is obliged to approve the variation. The court still has discretion to withhold its approval. Persons falling within s. 1(1)(d) are expressly excluded from the benefit requirement, so their

---

[97] Ibid. at 937B–C.   [98] *Re Weston's Settlements* [1969] 1 Ch 223, *per* Lord Denning MR at 245.

consent may be given even if the arrangement will not be, or may not be, for their benefit.[99]

The Act does not define what may constitute a 'benefit', or how benefit and detriment are to be weighed, but the cases indicate that benefit has a wide meaning:

> The court's concern involves, *inter alia*, a practical and business-like consideration of the arrangement, including the total amounts of the advantages which the various parties obtain, and their bargaining strength.[100]

Financial benefits

In the great majority of cases, the benefit provided by the Act is a tax-planning advantage and so, ultimately, a financial one. The jurisdiction can therefore appear to serve the more financially privileged members of society 'at the expense' of the ordinary taxpayer. Of course, should the very wealthy benefit from a variation under the Act, they would no doubt argue that they are extraordinary taxpayers attempting merely to retain their private wealth and that ordinary taxpayers would be well advised to do the same wherever possible. Less controversial, one assumes, would be a variation designed to avoid, for example, the payment of tax on a damages award held in trust to maintain a person who had been seriously injured in a road-traffic accident.[101]

Social and moral benefits

In *Re Holt's Settlement*,[102] Megarry J held that benefit is '*not confined to financial benefit, but may extend to social or moral benefit*'.[103] The reader might recall the case of *Re Weston's Settlements*,[104] in which the Court of Appeal led by Lord Denning refused to approve of an arrangement that would have provided a tax-planning advantage, and thus a financial benefit, to the beneficiaries. The transaction proposed the export of a trust to Jersey and entailed a temporary change of the residence of infant beneficiaries from England to Jersey. Lord Denning observed that:

> the court should not consider merely the financial benefit to the infants or unborn children, but also their educational and social benefit. There are many things in life more worth while than money.[105]

Benefit by deferral

In *Re Towler's Settlement Trusts*,[106] it was accepted that it might be beneficial to defer the vesting of a gift until the beneficiary was more mature and responsible, thereby protecting her from creditors, exploitation, and her own folly.[107] In *Re Holt's Settlement*,[108]

---

[99] *Re Turner's WT* [1960] 1 Ch 122.

[100] *Re Van Gruisen's Will Trusts* [1964] 1 All ER 843, *per* Ungoed-Thomas J at 844.

[101] In practice, such a variation would usually be unnecessary, because damages for personal injury automatically enjoy exemption from income tax (Income and Corporation Taxes Act 1988, s. 329) and capital gains tax (Taxation and Chargeable Gains Act 1992, s. 51(2)). See, generally, J. Lomas, 'The use of trusts in personal injury cases' (2002) JPIL 307–9.   [102] [1969] 1 Ch 100.

[103] Ibid. at 121D.

[104] [1969] 1 Ch 223.   [105] Ibid. at 245.   [106] [1964] Ch 158, *sub nom. Re T's Settlement Trusts*.

[107] The variation in this case was refused on other grounds.

[108] [1969] 1 Ch 100. Postponement in the interest of saving tax and life insurance justified the variation in *Re RGST* [2007] EWHC 2666 (Ch).

it was seen to be a benefit to the beneficiaries to defer the vesting of the gift until they were reasonably advanced in a career and settled in life. This involved a deferral of the contingent age from 21 to 30. Megarry J stated that he did not require evidence of special immaturity or irresponsibility. Of course it cannot be presumed beneficial to defer the coming into possession of a valuable interest under a trust. In *Wright v. Gater*[109] an application to postpone from age 18 to age 30 was rejected on the ground that no benefit had been shown, and because the variation would come close to being a resettlement.

The benefit of familial harmony

In some cases, applicants for a variation have sought to set the benefit of familial harmony against the reduced financial benefits that would flow from the new arrangement. They have not always been successful. In *Re Tinker's Settlement*,[110] a fund was held on trust for the settlor's son and daughter in equal shares. The daughter's share was contingent upon her attaining the age of 30, failing which, it would pass to her issue, or to her brother if she were to die without issue. The brother's share was given upon a similar contingency, but with no gift over to his issue should he fail to attain the age of 30; instead, his share would pass to his sister. This crucial difference between the two gifts was quite reasonably presumed to have resulted from an inadvertent omission in the drafting of the settlement. By applying to court for an order approving an arrangement varying the trusts, it was hoped to rectify the error so as to allow the brother's children to take if he were to die before the age of 30. The application failed and approval was refused. The court had to be satisfied that the new arrangement would be for the benefit of unborn beneficiaries within s. 1(1)(c) of the Variation of Trusts Act 1958. The daughter's unborn children could not possibly benefit financially from the arrangement, as they had a financial advantage over the brother's unborn children according to the terms of the original settlement. Russell J was not persuaded that the advantage of familial harmony outweighed the financial loss that the daughter's unborn children would incur if the proposal were approved. His Lordship did not regard family harmony '*as a benefit in itself*'.[111]

In *Re Remnant's Settlement Trust*,[112] the testator left a fund upon trust, ultimately, to the issue of his two daughters. However, he provided that any child who, on the death of its mother, was 'practising Roman Catholicism' (which included being married to a Roman Catholic) should forfeit any interest. The forfeited share was directed to be passed to the issue of the other sister. One of the daughters had become a Roman Catholic and it was likely that her children would forfeit their interests under the terms of the will. Both daughters disliked the forfeiture clause and they applied, within less than two years of their father's death, for a variation of the trusts to excise the forfeiture clauses. The new arrangement also proposed to accelerate the interests of the sisters' children in £10,000 of the fund, which would be set aside for that purpose.

Pennycuik J took into account the fact that the forfeiture clause might '*operate as a deterrent to each of the . . . children in the selection of a husband when the time comes*' and

---

[109] [2011] EWHC 2881.   [110] [1960] 1 WLR 1011.   [111] Ibid. at 1014.   [112] [1970] 1 Ch 560.

'*might well cause very serious dissension between the families of the two sisters*'.[113] These considerations, together with the fact that each of the sisters' issue had an accelerated financial entitlement, persuaded the judge to approve the arrangement. As he said:

> I have not found this an easy point, but I think that I am entitled to take a broad view of what is meant by 'benefit', and so taking it, I think this arrangement can fairly be said to be for their benefit.[114]

In *Re Tinker's Settlement*, it was proposed to give a beneficial interest to a beneficiary who would have had nothing under the original settlement, whereas in *Re Remnant's ST*, the proposal did not give any beneficiary anything that they did not already have, but simply removed a forfeiture provision that could have stripped them of their entitlement and accelerated certain other benefits. The judge in *Re Remnant's ST* acknowledged that the new arrangement '*defeats this testator's intention*', but stated that this had to be set against the fact that '*forfeiture provisions are undesirable in themselves*'.[115]

In *Ridgwell v. Ridgwell*[116] the court held that children having benefits under a trust set up by their father might benefit if the trust were varied to postpone their interests whilst granting the settlor's spouse a life interest on the settlor's death. In terms of financial benefits, it is hard to see how the children benefitted from this tax-avoidance arrangement except very indirectly. It might have been more convincing to acknowledge that this is an area in which financial benefits might be relevant where they are conferred on a close family unit (rather than upon each individual member of the family), or to acknowledge that financial benefits should sometimes give way to the broader benefit of familial harmony.

Risks of detriment

What if the proposed variation would, in the normal course of events, be for the benefit of all of the beneficiaries, but carries a risk that certain potential beneficiaries might suffer a detriment rather than a benefit? How much weight should be attached to that possibility? The question is of particular relevance when the court comes to consider whether the arrangement would be for the benefit of unborn beneficiaries under s. 1(1)(c).

In *Re Cohen's Will Trusts*,[117] Danckwerts J held that, in exercising its discretion to consent to a variation under the Act, the court must take the sort of risk, on behalf of persons for whom it was providing consent, that an adult beneficiary might be prepared to take on her own behalf. In a different case, of similar name,[118] approval for an arrangement was refused, because the prospects for one unborn person under the arrangement would have been hopeless whatever events might happen to pass. In *Re Holt's Settlement*, there was a risk that one of the unborn beneficiaries would receive no interest under the trust if their mother were to die during, or shortly after, childbirth.

---

[113] Ibid. at 566D–E.   [114] Ibid. at 566 F.   [115] [1970] 1 Ch 560 at 561C.
[116] [2007] EWHC 2666 (Ch).   [117] [1959] 1 WLR 865.
[118] *Re Cohen's Settlement Trusts* [1965] 1 WLR 1229.

However, this risk had to be balanced against the possibility that the mother might survive for a reasonable, or indeed substantial, period after the birth, whereupon the infant would undoubtedly receive a benefit under the new arrangement. In *Re Holt's Settlement*, Megarry J concluded that the risk was one that an adult would be prepared to take in order to secure the benefit. Accordingly, he gave approval for the new arrangement.

If the proposed arrangement involves a risk of detriment (including the risk that anticipated benefits might not materialize), the court may require the trustees to take out insurance against that risk, even at the expense of that beneficiary's income,[119] unless the insurance premiums would involve an excessive drain on trust income.

The hypothesis that an adult would have taken the sort of risk that the court took on behalf of the unborn beneficiary in *Re Holt's Settlement* involves the court in mental gymnastics. The court in *Re CL*[120] carried out a similar exercise when it provided the consent of a mentally unsound beneficiary,[121] on the basis that the beneficiary would have given their own consent had they been in a position to do so. This was despite the fact that the new arrangement removed the beneficiary's interest under the trust and conferred benefits on other persons instead. Cotterell has observed in relation to this case that '*it is hard to avoid the conclusion that benefit and the measure of it is simply what the court says it is*'.[122]

The settlor's intentions

Judges demonstrate a basic fidelity to the settlor's intentions—'[a] *court will not re-write a trust*'[123]—but when deciding whether or not to approve applications under the Act, the court must weigh in the balance the equitable property rights of the persons beneficially entitled under the trust against the wishes of the person who set up the trust in the first place. It follows that, even though consideration of the settlor's intentions may, in some cases, be '*relevant and weighty*'[124] or '*serious*',[125] it is '*by no means conclusive*'.[126] It has even been said that '[f]*idelity to the settlor's intention ends where equitable property begins*'.[127] This view is confirmed by cases such as *Re Remnant's ST* and *Re CL*, which we considered in the previous section, and by the Court of Appeal in *Goulding v. James*.[128]

In *Goulding v. James*, the testatrix provided by her will that her residuary estate should be divided equally between her daughter, June, and her daughter's husband, Kenneth, but the testatrix later revoked that will and replaced it with a new will which provided for the creation of a trust under which June would have a life interest in possession of

---

[119] *Re Robinson's Settlement Trusts* [1976] 1 WLR 806.   [120] [1969] 1 Ch 587.

[121] Under s. 1(1)(a).

[122] R. Cotterell, 'The requirement of "benefit" under the Variation of Trusts Act' (1971) 34 MLR 96 at 98.

[123] *Re Downshire Settled Estates* [1953] Ch 218 at 248, *per* Lord Evershed MR.

[124] Mummery LJ in *Goulding v. James* [1997] 2 All ER 239 cited *Re Steed's Will Trusts* [1960] 1 Ch 407 as such a case.   [125] *Re Remnant's Settlement Trusts* [1970] 1 Ch 560.

[126] Ibid. at 567.   [127] J. W. Harris, *Variation of Trusts* (London: Sweet & Maxwell, 1975) at 2.

[128] [1997] 2 All ER 239.

the residue, with June's son, Marcus, taking the residue after June's death, but not before he attained the age of 40. If Marcus were to predecease the daughter, or die before attaining the age of 40, the trust provided that his children living at the date of his death would take absolutely by substitution. When the testatrix died, June and Marcus applied to the court for a variation of the will trusts. They proposed that the will trust should be varied to provide that the testatrix's residuary estate be held 45 per cent for June absolutely, 45 per cent for Marcus absolutely, and 10 per cent on trust for Marcus's children. The applicants wished the variation to operate retrospectively—in other words, they sought a declaration from the court that the residuary estate should be deemed to have devolved according to the new terms since the date of the testatrix's death.

The judge at first instance dismissed the application, on the ground that the testatrix clearly intended to postpone her grandson's interest in capital until he reached the age of 40 and, as the revocation of her first will showed, clearly did not intend that her daughter should get any interest in capital at all. Nevertheless, the applicants appealed successfully to the Court of Appeal. Their Lordships held that the judge had erred by allowing extrinsic evidence of the testatrix's subjective wishes to outweigh considerations of objective and substantial benefit to unborn great-grandchildren falling with s. 1(1)(c) of the Act. The Court of Appeal held that, in deciding whether or not to grant approval under that section, the court's only concern should be to ensure that the arrangement was 'beneficial' to those on whose behalf the court had been asked to consent. The purpose of s. 1 of the Act was merely to enable a *Saunders v. Vautier* type of arrangement to take place where it would otherwise be precluded because there were beneficiaries who could not give their own consent.

Resettlement or variation?

Related to the problem of fidelity to the settlor's intentions is the problem of where to draw the line between a genuine variation of trust and the creation of a wholly new trust. In *Re T's Settlement*,[129] a mother wished to prevent her immature and irresponsible daughter becoming entitled to trust capital at the age of 21, so she applied for an order approving an arrangement under which her daughter's share would be transferred to a new trust under which the fund would be held on a protective trust for the daughter's life, with remainder to her issue. Wilberforce J refused to approve the proposal on the ground, *inter alia*, that the mother was not proposing a variation but rather an entirely new settlement. In *Re Ball's Settlement*,[130] Megarry J proposed the following test for distinguishing variation from resettlement:

> if an arrangement, while leaving the substratum, effectuates the purpose of the original trust by other means, it may still be possible to regard the arrangement as merely varying the original trusts, even though the means employed are wholly different and even though the form is completely changed.[131]

---

[129] [1964] Ch 158.   [130] [1968] 1 WLR 899.   [131] Ibid. at 905C.

This so-called 'substratum test' sounds simple enough, but it is by no means straightforward to apply in practice. Where is the line to be drawn between a mere change in the form of a trust and an alteration to the substratum of the trust? In *Re Ball's Settlement* itself, the settlor's life interest was removed, but this was held to be a mere formal change, because the varied trusts were '*still in essence trusts of half of the fund for each of the two named sons and their families*'.[132] Perhaps the substratum of the trust and the original purpose of the trust are one and the same thing. Perhaps they are simply shorthand for the settlor's basic intention to confer beneficial entitlement. If the issue were purely academic, it would make sense to abandon any attempt to draw a distinction between variation and resettlement, but where there is a resettlement there are potential (capital gains) tax consequences, so to recognize when a variation involves a resettlement is a practical necessity. In *Roome v. Edwards*,[133] Lord Wilberforce suggested that a new settlement (one that does not leave the old substratum intact) might be indicated by such factors as 'separate and defined property; separate trusts; and separate trustees' and, perhaps, 'a separate disposition bringing the separate settlement into existence'.[134] An advancement by way of resettlement is more likely to be permitted where it varies the trusts applicable to *part* only of the beneficial interests in the trust property.[135]

Other modes of varying private trusts

Variation of 'strict settlements'

Since the coming into force of the Trusts of Lands and Appointment of Trustees Act, on 1 January 1997, it has not been possible to create a new 'strict settlement' under the Settled Land Act 1925, but existing settlements remain subject to the Act.[136] The Act provides that the court may sanction any transaction that is beneficial to the settled land or the beneficiaries of the settlement.[137] A 'transaction' includes '*any compromise or other dealing, or arrangement*',[138] including the conveyance of the settled land to trustees to hold on protective trusts.[139]

Matrimonial jurisdiction

The Matrimonial Causes Act 1973[140] grants to the courts a wide power to vary beneficial interests under trusts in order to achieve a fair distribution of property upon the pronouncement of a decree of divorce or nullity of marriage. In this context, tax avoidance will not be a factor in determining the exercise of the court's discretion.[141]

---

[132] Ibid. at 905F.   [133] [1982] AC 279.
[134] Ibid at 292–3. Followed in *Wyndham v. Egremont* [2009] EWHC 2076 (Ch).
[135] *Southgate v. Sutton* [2011] EWCA Civ 637, CA, following *Pilkington v. IRC* [1964] AC 612.
[136] Trusts of Land and Appointment of Trustees Act 1996, s. 2(1).   [137] Section 64.
[138] Section 64(2).   [139] *Hambro v. Duke of Marlborough* [1994] Ch 158.
[140] Section 24 as substituted by the Family Law Act 1996, s. 15, Sch. 2, para. 6.
[141] *Thomson v. Thomson and Whitmee* [1956] P 384.

Mental Capacity Act jurisdiction

The Mental Capacity Act 2005 grants the court the jurisdiction to create a trust of property of a person lacking mental capacity.[142] Supplementary provisions in Sch. 2 of the Act provide that these trusts can be varied later if there is a significant change of circumstances: for example, if the patient ceases to be of unsound mind.

Revocation

It is possible for a settlor to revoke a trust if the trust instrument so authorizes. If the settlor exercises this power, the trust will be brought to an end even though it had been entirely valid. In the absence of such a power of revocation, the settlor can only bring the trust to an end if he can satisfy the court that the trust was created as a result of fraud, undue influence, or mistake.[143] It may be that the settlor of an *inter vivos* trust is under a fiduciary duty to the beneficiary with regard to the exercise of any vestigial power or status, such as his power to revoke the trust.[144]

Rectification of wills

If a court is satisfied that, as a result of a clerical error or a failure to understand the testator's instructions, a will is so expressed that it fails to carry out his intentions, it may order that the will be rectified.[145] The meaning of 'clerical error' was considered in *Re Segelman (deceased)*.[146] The error in that case was a solicitor's failure to remove a drafting inconsistency between a will and a schedule to it. The test applied by the court was whether or not the solicitor had applied his mind to the significance and effect of the words used. Chadwick J held that the solicitor in the instant case had not, so he had committed an error through mere inadvertence, with the result that the will should be rectified. A will can also be rectified on grounds of fraud.[147]

Administrative variations

So far, we have been considering the variation of beneficial interests under trusts. In the following sections, we will examine the modes of varying the administration of trusts.

Trustee Act 1925, s. 57

The Variation of Trusts Act 1958 permits changes to the administration of a trust if they are incidental to the remoulding of beneficial interests under the trust. However, where

---

[142] Sections 16, 18(1)(h).   [143] *Wright v. Carter* [1903] 1 Ch 27.
[144] W. F. Fratcher, *Scott on Trusts*, 3rd edn (Boston: Little Brown & Co, 1967) vol. III, para. 331 ff.
[145] Administration of Justice Act 1982, s. 20(1).   [146] [1996] 2 WLR 173.
[147] *Collins v. Elstone* [1893] P 1.

all that is required is an administrative variation, an order should be sought under the Trustee Act 1925, s. 57. Section 57 permits variations in the way that the trust is managed;[148] it does not authorize the remoulding of the beneficial interests under the trust, but does permit administrative changes that cause merely 'incidental' variation of beneficial interests.[149] It operates by inserting an 'overriding power' in the trust instrument so as to permit the trustees to act in accordance with the variation ordered by the court.[150] In the words of the section, it allows the court to authorize the trustees to carry out any transaction '*in the management or administration*' of the trust property where such transaction is '*expedient*'. It was suggested, in *Re Downshire SE*,[151] that the section would permit '*specific dealings*' with the trust property, which the court might not otherwise be authorized to permit under its inherent jurisdiction. So, for example, variation of investment powers should normally be sought under this section.[152] Another example arises in the context of trusts of land. The court has a broad power to make any order that it thinks fit in relation to the exercise by trustees of land of any of their 'functions'.[153] However, this jurisdiction probably does not extend to authorizing the sale of trust property where the settlor has removed the trustees' power of sale by including an express clause to that effect in the trust instrument.[154] In such cases, an order for sale must be sought under the general jurisdiction conferred by s. 57 of the Trustee Act 1925.[155]

Trustee Act 1925, s. 53

Under this section, the trust may be varied for the maintenance, education, or benefit of an infant beneficiary. The variation is effected by making a conveyance on sale of the beneficiary's interest. The capital proceeds of the sale, and income made thereon, are then 'applied' for the maintenance of the infant. This power is most useful where the beneficiary has an interest only in capital under the trust and in other situations in which the trustees will not have the usual power to maintain the beneficiary.[156]

Variation under the court's inherent jurisdiction

The court has always had an inherent jurisdiction to vary the manner in which a trust is administered in cases of 'salvage' and 'emergency', although the courts now prefer

---

[148] The section applies to 'the management or administration of any property vested in trustees'.

[149] *Southgate v. Sutton* [2011] EWCA Civ 637, Court of Appeal. In this case, an order was granted under s. 57 to create a sub-trust for the benefit of US-resident beneficiaries with a view to avoiding the 28% rate of capital gains tax charged against UK trustees. *Southgate* was followed in *Re English & American Insurance Co Ltd* (Chancery Division, Unreported) 9 October 2013.   [150] *Re Mair* [1935] Ch 562.

[151] [1952] 2 All ER 603.   [152] *Anker-Petersen v. Anker-Petersen* (1991) 16 LS Gaz 32.

[153] Trusts of Land and Appointment of Trustees Act 1996, ss. 14–15.

[154] In accordance with the power conferred on settlors by the Trusts of Land and Appointment of Trustees Act 1996, s. 8(1).

[155] G. Watt, 'Escaping section 8(1) provisions in "new style" trusts of land' (1997) 61 Conv 263. *Alexander v. Alexander* [2011] EWHC 2721 is a case in which the court used s. 57 to reinstate the trustees' power of sale which the settlor had removed.

[156] On the power of maintenance see the start of this chapter.

that such variations be sought under s. 57 wherever appropriate. 'Salvage' cases almost exclusively involve infants. In such cases, the administration of the trust may be varied in the interests of the infant beneficiary, but only in situations of absolute necessity. An example might be where one part of the property is mortgaged to raise monies to prevent another part of the property from becoming valueless—as where Greenacre is mortgaged to prevent Green Mansion from falling down. Trusts may be varied in situations of 'emergency' without there being any need to show that the variation is absolutely necessary. 'Emergency' refers to situations which the settlor had not foreseen. A variation under this heading can therefore be made entirely in keeping with the settlor's presumed intention for the trust.

In *Re New*,[157] the trustees wished to approve a proposal to reorganize a limited company in which the trust owned shares, but neither they, nor the beneficiaries, had power to give such approval (the beneficiaries were not all *sui juris* and so the rule in *Saunders v. Vautier* could not assist). Romer LJ stated that the court will not be justified in sanctioning every act desired by the trustees and beneficiaries '*merely because it may appear beneficial to the estate*',[158] but there were suggestions in the judgment that the court might vary the administration of the trust under its inherent jurisdiction in cases where the variation would be desirable, even if it was not, in fact, essential.

Further reading

In addition to the following print sources, the Online Resource Centre accompanying this book contains web links to further reading as well as guide answers to assessment questions relevant to this chapter.

HARRIS, J. W., *Variation of Trusts* (London: Sweet & Maxwell, 1975).

KER, B. S., 'Trustees' powers of maintenance' (1953) 17 Conv 273.

RIDDALL, J. G., 'Does it or doesn't it? Contingent interests and the Variation of Trusts Act 1958' [1987] Conv 144.

STIBBARD, P., 'Jersey court upholds variation of trust to avoid capital gains tax liability of the settlor' (2001) 1 PCB 35.

---

[157] [1901] 2 Ch 534.   [158] Ibid. at 545.

10

The fiduciary duty

The fiduciary duty comprises a number of overlapping obligations concerned to promote loyalty or faithfulness. It is the defining duty of trusteeship. The principal obligations that make up the fiduciary duty are the trustee's duty not to put himself in a position of potential conflict with the interests of the trust and his duty not to make an unauthorized profit from the trust property, or from his position of trust.[1] In certain circumstances, the fiduciary duty will also apply to a person who is not a trustee properly so called. In such a case, the person subject to the duty is said to be a fiduciary. The word 'fiduciary' simply means 'trust-like' or 'appertaining to trust', and, although its roots are Latin,[2] it has flowered in England and in Commonwealth jurisdictions derived from the English model. According to one French observer, the word '*plays in the spirit of English jurists*'.[3] If that is true, then in the common law of Canada it has become something of a national sport, for it is said that in Canada there are only three categories of people: 'those who are fiduciaries, those who are about to become fiduciaries, and judges'.[4] Canadian courts have even held that a parent is in a fiduciary relationship to their child.[5] The fiduciary duty was developed in Chancery, and it is equitable in the sense that it is, broadly speaking, concerned to restrain unconscionable abuse of legal power and position, but it is not equitable in the usual sense of being concerned to achieve justice between the parties in a particular case. It is not concerned to achieve fairness between the trustee and the beneficiaries of his trust, or between a fiduciary and his principal. On the contrary, it is a rule of public policy that is strictly applied against trustees in order to set an example and to encourage good behaviour in all who hold positions of trust.[6] One senior judge has efficiently

---

[1] These opening lines are intended to echo Professor Paul Finn's seminal analysis of the subject (see P. Finn, *Fiduciary Obligations* (Sydney: Law Book Co, 1977) and 'Fiduciary law' in *Commercial Aspects of Trusts and Fiduciary Obligations* (E. McKendrick, ed.) (Oxford: Oxford University Press, 1992)) as approved in the important judgment of Millett LJ in *Bristol and West BS v. Mothew* [1998] Ch 1 at 18.

[2] From the Latin *fides* (faith) and *fiducia* (trust).

[3] J.-P. Béraudo, *Les Trusts Anglo-Saxons et Le Droit Français* (Paris: LGDA, 1992) at 9, para. 21: '*le mot fiduciaire joue dans l'esprit des juristes anglo-saxons comme une sorte de signal*'. This might be translated: 'The word "fiduciary" rouses the spirit of Anglo-Saxon jurists like a sort of alarm.'

[4] Attributed to Chief Justice Mason of the High Court of Australia (quoted in M. McInnes, 'A new direction for the Canadian law of fiduciary relations?' (2010) 126 LQR 185).   [5] *M (K) v. M (H)* [1992] 3 SCR 6.

[6] Matthew Conaglen argues in his article 'The nature and function of fiduciary loyalty' (2005) 121 LQR 452, that the fiduciary duty is purely accessory or 'subsidiary' to non-fiduciary duties, the function of

characterized the rules governing the fiduciary duty to avoid conflicts of interest as being 'simple, strict and salutary'.[7]

This is the first of a series of chapters, which will take us to the end of the book, in which we will be examining the major obligations of trusteeship and considering the implications, for trustees, beneficiaries, and third parties, of breach of those obligations. One of the main tasks of Chapter 11 is to consider the trustee's duty of care and to distinguish it from the trustee's fiduciary duty; it should therefore be borne in mind, as we progress through the present chapter, that not every duty of a person in a fiduciary office is necessarily a fiduciary duty.[8]

The strict rule of exemplary fiduciary propriety

Fiduciary obligations are rigorously enforced on grounds of public policy.[9] When it is established that a trustee has placed himself in a position of *potential* conflict, it is generally no defence for him to prove that *actual* conflict is unlikely to arise and, when a trustee makes an unauthorized profit, it is generally no defence to demonstrate that the trust has suffered no harm. Insistence upon exemplary fiduciary propriety encourages other persons in positions of trust to fulfil the requirements of their office.

As Professor Jones once put it: '*there are cases where the innocent fiduciary must suffer, like Admiral Byng. Policy may demand a public sacrifice of the fiduciary's profit*.'[10] John Byng was an English Admiral sent, in 1756, to relieve Minorca from the French. He failed and was unfairly court-martialled for dereliction of duty. Having been found guilty, he was executed on the quarterdeck of his own ship, leading the French satirist and philosopher Voltaire to suggest that, in England, it is deemed good to kill an Admiral from time to time '*pour encourager les autres*'.[11] The fiduciary duty has the same prophylactic, or preventative, aim of encouraging good behaviour in persons other than the parties in the instant case. This has been

---

fiduciary duties being merely '*to protect the proper performance of non-fiduciary duties*' (480) by prohibiting '*the fiduciary from acting in a situation where he has a personal interest which is inconsistent with his non-fiduciary duty*' (462). It is a sophisticated analysis, but it may be unlikely to influence or predict the outcome of cases. We will see throughout this chapter that the enforcement of fiduciary duties is, as Conaglen himself admits, '*ultimately one of public policy*' (478). The same author has more recently extended his argument (that fiduciary duties are merely subsidiary to non-fiduciary duties) to the fiduciary duty to avoid conflicts between duties to different principals ('Fiduciary regulation of conflicts between duties' (2009) 125 LQR 111–41).

[7] *Towers v. Premier Waste Ltd* [2011] EWCA Civ 923; [2012] 1 BCLC 67, CA, *per* Mummery LJ at para. [2]. His Lordship was speaking in the context of company directors' fiduciary duties.

[8] *New Zealand Netherlands Society v. Kuys* [1973] 1 WLR 1126, PC, *per* Lord Wilberforce at 1130.

[9] *Regal (Hastings) Ltd v. Gulliver (Note)* [1967] 2 AC 134 at 157B, HL; Law Commission Consultation Paper No. 151, *The Limitation of Actions*, para. 13.100 and Law Reform Committee, *Twenty-First Report (Final Report on Limitation of Actions)* (1977) Cmnd. 6923 at para. 3.82.

[10] G. Jones, 'Unjust enrichment and the fiduciary's duty of loyalty' (1968) 84 LQR 477 at 487.

[11] 'To encourage the others': F.-M. A. Voltaire, *Candide* (1759) ch. 23.

called the policy of 'prophylaxis',[12] but we will refer to it as the policy of exemplary fiduciary propriety.

In *Parker v. McKenna*,[13] James LJ went so far as to say that the strict enforcement of exemplary fiduciary propriety is required for '*the safety of mankind*'.[14] In one case, the court insisted that '*in order to set an example to the world*', a trustee in bankruptcy should repay money that he had been paid under a mistake of law.[15] This all sounds very dramatic, but it must be borne in mind that not only private persons, but public bodies also, assume trust-like obligations. The strict enforcement of fiduciary duties is therefore exemplary ('sets a positive example') to all who hold positions of trust—whether the trust is a political trust 'in the higher sense'[16] or a fiduciary office that is justiciable in the courts in the usual way at the behest of a private beneficiary or principal.

Of course, it should not be thought that all fiduciaries owe the same fiduciary duties. The fiduciary duties owed by an express trustee will not be precisely the same as those owed by a fiduciary agent.[17] Some form of the basic rules against conflicts and unauthorized profits will apply to all fiduciaries, but the nature and extent of the fiduciary duties owed in any particular case is qualified by reference to the particular relationship, including any underlying contractual relationship, between the parties.[18] Neither should it be thought that a contract which binds the parties to work together for a common purpose (such as a joint venture) necessarily imposes fiduciary duties between the parties.[19] As we saw in Chapter 2, a fiduciary duty '*cannot be prayed in aid to enlarge the scope of contractual duties*'.[20]

The duty of good faith

Good faith has been described as '*an apocryphally indefinite term*'.[21] At its most basic, it merely describes the absence of dishonesty. It is used in this sense to describe the bona fide or 'good faith' purchaser.[22] The *duty* of good faith is more substantial, but equally

---

[12] P. Birks, *An Introduction to the Law of Restitution* (Oxford: Clarendon Press, revd edn 1989) at 339, 332–3, referring to King LC in *Keech v. Sandford* (1726) Sel Cas Ch 61 at 62. 'Prophylaxis' is derived from the Greek for 'to guard against'.   [13] (1874) LR 10 Ch App 96.

[14] Ibid. at 125.

[15] *Re Condon* (1874) LR 9 Ch App 609 at 614. Approved in *R. v. Tower Hamlets LBC, Ex p Chetnik Developments Ltd* [1988] AC 858, *per* Lord Bridge of Harwich at 874, HL.

[16] See *Kinloch v. Secretary of State for India* (1882) LR 7 App Cas 619 and *Tito v. Waddell (No. 2)* [1977] Ch 106 at 221.

[17] *Henderson v. Merrett Syndicates Ltd* [1995] 2 AC 145, HL, at 206B, *per* Lord Browne-Wilkinson.

[18] Ibid.

[19] In *Button v. Phelps* [2006] EWHC 53; 2006 WL 584571 (Ch D) the defendant's liability for promoting a rival bid when contractually bound to promote another bid was held to be limited to contractual damages, rather than liability for an account of profits for breach of fiduciary duty.

[20] *Clark Boyce v. Mouat* [1994] 1 AC 428, *per* Lord Jauncey of Tullichettle at 437g–h.

[21] D. W. M. Waters, 'The protector: new wine in old bottles?' in *Trends in Contemporary Trust Law* (A. J. Oakley, ed.) (Oxford: Clarendon Press, 1996) 63 at 101.

[22] *Pilcher v. Rawlins* (1872) LR 7 Ch App 259; *Taylor v. London and County Banking Co* [1901] 2 Ch 231, CA, at 256.

hard to define. Some consider the duty of good faith to be the positive aspect of the fiduciary duty. They contrast it with negative aspects of the fiduciary duty, such as the duty *not* to put oneself in a position of potential conflict and the duty *not* to make an unauthorized gain. However, this distinction is not convincing. Even the so-called 'negative' fiduciary rules have their positive counterparts. Hence a fiduciary has a positive duty, unless he is authorized to the contrary, to extricate himself from any position of actual conflict and to disgorge any gain made from his position of trust.

Whether or not it is a fiduciary duty properly so-called, the duty of good faith is certainly a duty that is owed by fiduciaries in relation to the exercise of their powers and discretions.[23] So, if a fiduciary has been authorized to act for two principals with potentially conflicting interests,

> [h]e must act in good faith in the interests of each and must not act with the intention of furthering the interests of one principal to the prejudice of those of the other.[24]

A trustee of a traditional settlement trust is in a broadly similar position. He is obliged to exercise his powers and discretion in good faith for the purposes of the trust, which means that he is not permitted to prefer the interests of one class of beneficiary to the exclusion of the interests of any other competing class of beneficiary. He cannot be exclusively loyal to either class of beneficiary. This duty is considered further in Chapter 11 in the context of investment.

Fiduciary relationships and fiduciary duties

A question of some theoretical and practical importance is whether fiduciary duties can only ever be owed by persons who occupy a recognized form of fiduciary office—such as agent, banker, company director,[25] partner[26]—or whether fiduciary duties may be free-standing—that is, owed by persons who are not parties to any established form of 'fiduciary relationship'. The answer to the question was settled by the Court of Appeal in *Bristol and West BS v. Mothew*.[27] The fact that a person is not a party to a recognized category of fiduciary relationship does not mean that he does not owe a fiduciary duty—if a person owes a fiduciary duty, he is a fiduciary: '*he is not subject to fiduciary obligations*

---

[23] 'A fiduciary must act in good faith': *per* Millett LJ in *Mothew* at 18.

[24] Finn (1977, n. 1) at 48.

[25] '*A corporate body can only act by agents, and it is of course the duty of those agents so to act as best to promote the interests of the corporation whose affairs they are conducting. Such agents have duties to discharge of a fiduciary nature towards their principal*': *Aberdeen Railway Co v. Blaikie Bros* (1854) 1 Macq 461, HL (SC), *per* Lord Cranworth LC at 471–2, applied in *Guinness plc v. Saunders* [1990] 2 WLR 324, HL.

[26] Each partner is both principal and fiduciary to every other partner in relation to matters within the ambit of partnership business. See *Aas v. Benham* [1891] 2 Ch 244 at 256. Considered in *Boardman v. Phipps* [1967] 2 AC 46, *per* Viscount Dilhorne at 70.

[27] [1998] 1 Ch 1. See, also, *Lac Minerals Ltd v. International Corona Resources Ltd* [1990] FSR 441, Supreme Court of Canada, *per* Wilson J (at 444) and La Forest J (at 455).

because he is a fiduciary; it is because he is subject to them that he is a fiduciary.[28] Sir George Jessel made a similar observation more than a hundred years earlier:

> What is a fiduciary relationship? It is one in respect of which, if a wrong arise, the same remedy exists against the wrongdoer on behalf of the principal as would exist against a trustee on behalf of the cestui que trust.[29]

So a fiduciary duty may arise independently of any established category of 'fiduciary relationship', but in what circumstances will the duty arise? Again, an answer was provided in *Mothew*:[30]

> A fiduciary is someone who has undertaken to act for or on behalf of another in a particular matter in circumstances which give rise to a relationship of trust and confidence.[31]

However, a fiduciary duty will not arise in every case in which one party reposes trust in another.[32] There must also be an obligation on the fiduciary to prefer the interests of his principal to the exclusion of his own interests, at least to the extent of the fiduciary's undertaking and the extent of the trust reposed by his principal. In short, a fiduciary relationship is defined as much by the absence of self-interest as by the presence of trust, or, as a leading Canadian judge put it: '*The fiduciary relationship has trust, not self-interest, at its core*.'[33] This explains why, when a banker or other agent is permitted to make use of his client's money for his own business purposes, profit, or otherwise for his own benefit, the banker or agent is '*not in any fiduciary relation whatever*' with the client.[34]

The trust '*has always been the paradigm for all fiduciary relationships*'.[35] In the trust relationship, the fiduciary duties are '*peculiarly intense*'[36] and all fiduciary relationships are, to a greater or lesser extent, trust-like. Having said that, it was accepted as long ago as 1866, in the case of *Tate v. Williamson*,[37] that the courts do not place limits on the varieties of fiduciary relationship.[38] Tate was an indebted student who had turned to his uncle for help. His uncle's son (Williamson), having undertaken to act as his father's deputy, arranged to purchase a share of freehold land from Tate for the price of £7,000. Williamson knew that the land was actually worth £20,000, but he did not reveal the true valuation to Tate. Tate died of drink at the tender age of 24 and his next of kin filed a bill to impeach the sale to Williamson. The bill was successful and the sale was set aside on grounds of breach of fiduciary duty.[39]

---

[28] Ibid. *per* Millett LJ at 18, approving the analysis of Finn, *Fiduciary Obligations* (1977, n. 1) at 2. See also P. Finn, 'Fiduciary law and the modern commercial world' in *Commercial Aspects of Trusts and Fiduciary Obligations* (E. McKendrick, ed.) 1992 (n. 1) at 7.   [29] *Re Hallett's Estate* (1880) LR 13 Ch D 696 at 712.

[30] [1998] 1 Ch 1.   [31] [1998] 1 Ch 1 at 18.

[32] According to Lord Mustill in *Re Goldcorp Exchange* [1995] 1 AC 74 at 98: '*high expectations do not necessarily lead to equitable remedies*'. See also R. P. Austin 'Moulding the content of fiduciary duties' in *Trends in Contemporary Trust Law* (A. J. Oakley, ed.) (Oxford: Clarendon Press, 1996) at 161.

[33] *Norberg v. Wynrib* (1992) 92 DLR (4th) 449 (SCC) *per* McLachlin J at § 68.

[34] *Burdick v. Garrick* (1869–70) LR 5 Ch App 233, 240.

[35] R. P. Austin, 'Moulding the content of fiduciary duties' in *Trends in Contemporary Trust Law* (A. J. Oakley, ed.) (Oxford: Clarendon Press, 1996) at 169.

[36] W. Fratcher, *Scott on Trusts*, 4th edn (Boston: Little Brown & Co, 1987) at 43.

[37] (1866) LR 2 Ch App 55.   [38] Ibid. at 60–1.   [39] Compare *O'Sullivan v. MAM Ltd* [1985] QB 428.

It is probably accurate to say that the recognition of a fiduciary duty now depends less upon the nature of the parties' relationship to each other than upon the assumption by one of an obligation to the other. There is, in short, a discernible trend from status to consensus as a basis for the imposition of a fiduciary duty. In this vein, Sealy has observed that the emphasis has gradually shifted from the defendant to the claimant and from '*the notion of selflessness*' to '*features such as the "vulnerability" of the beneficiary*'. He suggests that this trend might eventually cause the fiduciary principle to lose '*vital links with its roots*'.[40] Austin argues that, as the basis of the fiduciary duty changes, there may be implications for its content: '*If we move comprehensively from fiduciary relationship to fiduciary duties, a momentum will have been generated to reduce fiduciary law into the general law of obligations*'.[41]

Despite this, Austin is confident that '*the movement from relationship to obligation need not cause the fiduciary standard to be diluted from a proscriptive, prophylactic rule to a prescriptive but less demanding one*'.[42] This is surely correct. The fact that the source of the fiduciary duty may be the voluntary assumption of a personal responsibility rather than the status of the parties should not, of itself, detract from the strict enforcement of the fiduciary duty on grounds of public policy.

The fiduciary duty to avoid conflicts of interest

The fiduciary duty to avoid conflicts of interest is basically fourfold: first, not to place oneself in a position of potential conflict of interest; second, not to carry out a transaction in conflict of interest; third, to remove oneself from a position in which one is inhibited from acting due to potential conflict of interest; fourth, to remove oneself from a position in which one is bound to transact in conflict of interests. Breaches of the first two 'prohibitive' aspects of the duty might be referred to as 'positional' and 'transactional' breaches, respectively. Breach of the third and fourth 'mandatory' aspects are breaches of what Millett LJ has referred to, respectively, as the '*no inhibition principle*' and the '*Actual Conflict Rule*'.[43] The usual response to a conflict of interest is to resign from the trust, but this will not always be in the best interests of the trust. The court has been known to authorize a trustee to stay in post if it is satisfied that the trustee can discharge his duties to the trust without ever having to choose between the trust and his private interests.[44]

Before we go any further, we should, of course, address a preliminary question: 'What *is* a conflict of interest?' The short answer is that there are two types of conflict of interest: the first is conflict between the interests of the principal and the personal interests of the fiduciary; the second is conflict between the interests of the principal and the

---

[40] L. S. Sealy, 'Fiduciary obligations, forty years on' (1995) 9 JCL 37 at 40.
[41] R. P. Austin, 'Moulding the content of fiduciary duties' in *Trends in Contemporary Trust Law* (A. J. Oakley, ed.) (Oxford: Clarendon Press, 1996) 153 at 174.   [42] Ibid. at 175.
[43] *Bristol and West Building Society v. Mothew* [1998] 1 Ch 1, *per* Millett LJ at 19.
[44] *Public Trustee v. Cooper* [2001] WTLR 901.

fiduciary's duty to advance the interests of another principal or third party. A conflict of the second type is a breach of the 'double employment' rule or, to put it another way, a breach of the obligation of 'undivided loyalty'.[45] The informed consent of both of the fiduciary's principals is a defence to breach of the double employment rule.[46] The main focus of the following sections is to see how these rules operate in the context of a trustee's fiduciary duty to his trust, but it should be borne in mind that the rules apply equally to, and many of the authorities involve, fiduciaries who are not trustees per se.

Positional breach of fiduciary duty

A trustee is subject to a duty never to *put himself* in a position of *potential conflict* with the interests of his trust. According to Nourse LJ in the Court of Appeal in *Sargeant v. National Westminster Bank plc*,[47] the rule is prophylactic: it '*holds that prevention is better than cure*'.[48] The rule is breached only if the trustee *puts himself* in the position of potential conflict, so if the settlor puts him in the position of potential conflict, there will be no breach.[49] In *Sargeant*, a testator had appointed his children to be trustees of the freehold title to certain farms of which they were already tenants. They therefore became, at the same time, both landlords and tenants, with an obvious potential for conflict of interest. However, there was no positional breach of trust, because the testator had put them in that situation.[50] In *Mothew*, a mortgage lender claimed, *inter alia*, that its solicitor had put himself in a position of potential conflict with its interests, because the solicitor was also acting for the borrowers (the purchasers) in connection with a conveyance of land. The claim failed because the mortgagee '*knew that the defendant was acting for the purchasers when it instructed him*'.[51] If, however, the testator in *Sargeant* or the mortgagee in *Mothew* had not known of the potential breach of trust, their intended trustee or fiduciary would have been obliged to decline the appointment.[52]

The rule against 'positional breach' of trust is strictly applied; it is irrelevant that there will probably be no actual conflict or any actual harm to the trust. The inquiry according to which one determines whether there is a conflict of interest is to ask 'what might be done':[53]

> it is a rule of universal application, that no one, having [fiduciary] duties to discharge, shall be allowed to enter into engagements in which he has, or can have, a personal interest

---

[45] Ibid. at 18–19.

[46] *Clark Boyce v. Mouat* [1994] 1 AC 428, PC, *per* Lord Jauncey of Tullichettle at 435G; *Kelly v. Cooper* [1993] AC 205, PC.   [47] (1990) 61 P & CR 518.

[48] Ibid. at 519.   [49] *Kelly v. Cooper* [1993] AC 205.

[50] The principle that a trustee conflict will not be actionable if it was created by the appointment of the trustee also applies in Scotland; see *The Earl of Cawdor's case* [2006] CSOH 141; 2006 SLT 1070.

[51] Millett LJ in *Bristol and West Building Society v. Mothew* [1998] 1 Ch 1 at 19A. See also Finn, 'Fiduciary obligations' (1977) (n. 1) 254.

[52] See *Wight v. Olswang* [2001] Lloyds' Rep PN 269, in which a solicitor was held to have placed himself in an untenable position for a trustee.

[53] *Wright v. Morgan* [1926] AC 788, *per* Viscount Dunedin at 798.

conflicting, *or which possibly may conflict*, with the interests of those whom he is bound to protect.[54]

In fact, the rule is not strictly speaking 'universal'. It is more accurately described as a 'general' rule, because cases are frequently decided as exceptions to it:

> The general rule of equity is that no one who has duties of a fiduciary nature to perform is allowed to enter into engagements in which he has or can have a personal interest conflicting with the interests of those whom he is bound to protect.[55]

One case decided as an exception to the general rule is *Re Drexel Burnham Lambert UK Pension Plan*.[56] In this case, a scheme to distribute surplus assets in a pension fund was approved, even though it had been proposed by trustees who were beneficiaries under the scheme. Lindsay J recognized that there were many exceptions to the general rule and that the trustees in this case had doubtless been selected as persons able to exercise their discretion properly, despite the potential conflict of interest.

'Transactional breach' of fiduciary duty

A trustee must not carry out any transaction in breach of his fiduciary duty. In particular, he must not grant or sell any trust property to himself (this is the rule against self-dealing), and, if he purchases an equitable interest in trust property from a beneficiary, the onus is on the trustee to prove that the purchase was fair and that he took no advantage of his position (this is the fair dealing rule). Related to these rules, there is another, more general, rule that a trustee is not permitted to make an unauthorized profit by reason of his position of trust or his use of trust property. It is crucial to realize that, even if a trustee has been placed in a position of *potential* conflict, he is obliged to avoid any transaction which is actually in conflict of interest. So, although the tenants of the farms in *Sargeant* had committed no 'positional' breach of trust by accepting trusts of the freeholds, they would have been guilty of a transactional breach of trust if they had proceeded to take advantage of their position by charging themselves a reduced rent. Generally speaking, it would also have been a breach of trust (a straightforward case of self-dealing) if they had attempted to sell the freeholds to themselves. However, in that case, the tenants' right to purchase the freeholds pre-dated their acceptance of the trust. Accordingly, the court declared that the tenants would be permitted to purchase freehold title off themselves in their capacity as trustees.[57] Nevertheless, the onus, '*on grounds of public policy*',[58] is on the trustee to show that no advantage has been taken of their position.

---

[54] *Aberdeen Railway Co v. Blaikie Bros* (1854) 1 Macq 461, HL (SC), *per* Lord Cranworth LC at 471–2 (emphasis added).

[55] *Regal (Hastings) Ltd v. Gulliver* [1967] 2 AC 134, HL(E), HL, *per* Viscount Sankey at 137G.

[56] [1995] 1 WLR 32.

[57] Transactions pursuant to rights arising before trusteeship, and transactions occurring after retirement from trusteeship, are considered later.

[58] *Goldsworthy v. Brickell* [1987] 2 WLR 133, CA, *per* Nourse LJ at 150B.

The self-dealing and fair dealing rules contrasted

The self-dealing and fair dealing rules are distinct, but connected. They are both concerned to prevent a trustee from carrying out a transaction in conflict with the interests of the trust, but, whereas the self-dealing rule is 'prohibitory', the fair dealing rule is merely 'regulatory'.[59] In *Tito v. Waddell (No. 2)*,[60] Megarry VC summarized them in the following terms:

> The self-dealing rule is (to put it very shortly) that if a trustee sells the trust property to himself, the sale is voidable by any beneficiary *ex debito justitiae*,[61] however fair the transaction. The fair-dealing rule is (again putting it very shortly) that if a trustee purchases the beneficial interest of any of his beneficiaries, the transaction is not voidable *ex debito justitiae*, but can be set aside by the beneficiary unless the trustee can show that he has taken no advantage of his position and has made full disclosure to the beneficiary, and that the transaction is fair and honest.[62]

Vinelott J, who had appeared as counsel in *Tito v. Waddell*, was the judge in the later case of *Re Thompson's Settlement*.[63] In *Re Thompson's*, his Lordship observed that fair dealing can involve a genuine contract between two independent parties, whereas self-dealing cannot,[64] because in a case of self-dealing, at least one person will appear as a party on both sides of the transaction. If *all* of the parties are exactly the same on both sides, it will not merely be voidable at the instance of a beneficiary; it will be void *ab initio*, because there can be no contract between identical parties.[65] Despite that rule, a conveyance by trustees of a legal estate in land will be effective even if the trustees on both sides of the conveyance are identical.[66] The explanation for this exception may be that agreement is a fundamental requirement of a contract, but not of a conveyance.

The self-dealing rule

Where trustees sell trust property to one or more of their number, the trust will notionally continue to bind both the trust property and the proceeds of its sale until the beneficiary is required to elect between the property or its proceeds. If the beneficiary elects to adopt the sale, the trust will bind the proceeds of sale in the hands of the vendor-trustees. If the beneficiary elects to rescind the sale, it must be set aside no matter how fair, or even generous, may have been the price paid. Where the sale is set aside, the original trusts will remain binding on the trust property in the hands of the trustee-purchaser so far as possible as if it had never been sold. Self-dealing by a trustee is contrary to the public interest in exemplary fiduciary propriety and cannot be allowed to stand once a beneficiary's complaint has brought it into

---

[59] Hon. Mr Justice B. H. McPherson CBE, 'Self-dealing trustees' in *Trends in Contemporary Trust Law* (A. J. Oakley, ed.) (Oxford: Clarendon Press, 1996) 135 at 150.   [60] [1977] Ch 106.

[61] 'Out of a debt to justice'.   [62] [1977] Ch 106 at 241A–B.   [63] [1986] Ch 99.

[64] Ibid. at 115H–116A.

[65] *Mainwaring v. Newman* (1800) 2 Bos & Pul 120, 126 ER 1190; *Ellis v. Kerr* [1910] 2 Ch 529 at 534–6; *Boyce v. Edbrooke* [1903] 1 Ch 836; Hon. Mr Justice B. H. McPherson CBE, 'Self-dealing trustees' in *Trends in Contemporary Trust Law* (A. J. Oakley, ed.) (Oxford: Clarendon Press, 1996) 135.

[66] Law of Property Act 1925, s. 72(3), (4).

the public domain. However, beneficiaries will be unable to assert their right to have the transaction set aside if they gave fully informed consent to the self-dealing or have acquiesced in it, or if they have delayed too long in seeking to have it set aside.

Long delay is a bar because, whereas the policy of exemplary fiduciary propriety presumes *against* the righteousness of a fiduciary transaction and requires a self-dealing to be set aside *ex debito justitiae*, the public interest is in favour of quiescence of title.[67] As Bowen LJ stated in *Re Postlethwaite*: '[T]*he general presumption which the law makes is in favour of the good faith and validity of transactions, and not against them*.'[68] These two conflicting policies must eventually cancel each other out so as to allow a trustee to retain property which it is alleged was obtained in breach of fiduciary duty.[69] In *Re Postlethwaite*, that point was reached after 34 years. After very long delay, private interests do not readily enter into the picture.[70]

As with many other features of trust law, the rule against self-dealing has been the subject of special consideration in the pensions context: so, for example, there is no hard and fast rule requiring negotiations between pension fund trustees and the employer company to be set aside simply because one or more of the trustees happens to be a director of the company.[71]

The fair dealing rule

This is a rule designed to regulate contracts made between beneficiaries and their trustees. Such contracts may be genuine contracts between independent parties and are therefore not subject to the same fundamental criticisms that are raised when a trustee deals with himself. Nevertheless, a contract between beneficiaries and their trustees, or between a principal and his fiduciary, must '*be watched with infinite and the most guarded jealousy*'.[72] Accordingly, any trustee entering into a transaction with a beneficiary should protect himself by ensuring that the beneficiary does not enter the transaction without first taking competent and independent advice.[73]

The burden of proof that the transaction was a righteous one rests upon the trustee, who is bound to produce clear affirmative proof that the parties were at arms' length, that the *cestui que* trusts had the fullest information on all material facts, and that, having this information, they agreed to and adopted what was done.[74]

If the trustee fails to make full disclosure to the beneficiaries, even inadvertently, the beneficiaries may elect to rescind the transaction.[75]

---

[67] '[I]*t is the public policy that possession should remain undisturbed*': *Chalmondeley v. Clinton* (1821) 4 Bligh 1, *per* Lord Redesdale at 74–5.   [68] (1889) 60 LT Rep 514 at 520.

[69] See G. Watt, 'Laches election and estoppel' in *Breach of Trust* (P. Birks and A. Pretto, eds) (Oxford: Hart Publishing, 2002) at 354.

[70] J. Brunyate, *Limitation of Actions in Equity* (Cambridge: Cambridge University Press, 1932) at 243–4.

[71] *Edge v. Pensions Ombudsman* [2000] Ch 602 at 632.

[72] *Ex p. Lacey* (1802) 8 Ves Jun 625 at 626; 31 ER 1228.

[73] *Rhodes v. Bate* (1865–6) LR 1 Ch App 252 at 257; *BCCI v. Aboody* [1990] 1 QB 923, CA at 964.

[74] *Williams v. Scott* [1900] AC 499, *per* Sir Ford North at 508.

[75] Millett LJ speaking obiter in *Mothew* [1998] 1 Ch 1 at 18D.

Transactions authorized before acceptance of trusteeship

We noted earlier that the tenants in the *Sargeant* case had a right to purchase the freeholds of which they were tenants and that this right was not lost when they were subsequently appointed trustees of those freeholds. The reason, as Wynn-Parry J observed of similar facts in *Re Mulholland WT*,[76] is that:

> the existence of the fiduciary relationship creates an inability in the trustee to contract in regard to the trust property [but] does not touch the position arising where the contract in question has been brought into existence before the fiduciary relationship.[77]

Transactions carried out after retirement from trusteeship

Continuing trustees are permitted to sell trust property to a retired trustee as long as '*there is nothing to show that at the time of retirement there was any idea of a sale*'.[78] The onus, as always where a transactional breach is alleged, is on the trustees to prove that the transaction was a righteous one. One way in which to prove the transaction was 'righteous' is to demonstrate that it was carried out with the sanction of the court.[79] To prove that a transaction was righteous is no easy task for a retired trustee. In one case, the purchase of trust property by a trustee 12 years after his retirement was allowed to stand,[80] but, in another case, a trustee who retired in order to purchase land was required to give it up even though he had paid a price determined by independent valuers.[81] In the latter case, Viscount Dunedin held that whether the trustee had actually paid a fair or unfair price was irrelevant: '*the criterion . . . is not what was done, but what might be done*'.[82]

Courts have sometimes seen fit to relax the strict rule. In *Holder v. Holder*,[83] a testator was survived by his widow, eight daughters, and two sons. Included in his estate were a number of farms. Having performed some minor administrative functions as one of the executors of his father's estate, the younger son purported to renounce the executorship in order to purchase certain of the farms at a fair price at public auction. The elder son, who attended the auction with his solicitor, made no objection at that stage, but later, repeating a theme of great antiquity,[84] he disputed the younger son's right to the farms. He alleged that the younger son, having acted briefly as an executor of the estate, had barred himself from purchasing trust property. The Court of Appeal allowed the purchase to stand, even though the younger son, having failed effectively to renounce his executorship, remained an executor at the time of the sale. Harman LJ acknowledged that '*there must never be a conflict of duty and interest*', but held that '*in fact there was none here*', on '*the very special circumstances of this case*'. Although this case is generally

---

[76] [1949] 1 All ER 460.   [77] Ibid. at 463.   [78] *Re Boles* [1902] 1 Ch 244, *per* Buckley J.
[79] See, for example, *Holder v. Holder* [1968] Ch 353, *per* Danckwerts LJ at 398D.   [80] Ibid.
[81] *Wright v. Morgan* [1926] AC 788, PC.   [82] Ibid. at 798.   [83] [1968] Ch 353.
[84] The Book of Genesis relates how Esau was usurped by Jacob. Jacob was victorious then, and the younger brother was victorious in *Holder v. Holder*. (His name, Victor James Holder, was therefore appropriate on three counts—'James' is a westernized version of the Hebrew 'Jacob').

cited as an exception to, or relaxation of, the strict rule against potential conflicts of interest, it might be better understood as a case in which the trustee was allowed to retain the fruits of the transaction because, as a matter of fact, there was insufficient *causal connection* between his gain and his position of trust. Harman LJ acknowledged that the younger son had acquired his knowledge of his farms, not by reason of his brief status as executor, but in his capacity as a tenant of one of the farms before his father's death. We return to the issue of causation later.

The 'no inhibition' principle

A fiduciary must not carry out any transaction in breach of his fiduciary duty, but it is also true that a fiduciary must not, in breach of his fiduciary duty, decline to carry out a transaction or to exercise a power or discretion. A '*fiduciary must not be inhibited by the existence of his other employment from serving the interests of his principal as faithfully and effectively as if he were the only employer*'.[85] If, because of a conflict of interest, a fiduciary abstains from exercising a power, he '*must be held to all the same consequences as though that power had been exercised*'.[86]

The 'actual conflict' rule

We have considered the rule which prohibits fiduciaries from carrying out a transaction in conflict of interest and the rule which prohibits inhibition (by reason of conflict of interest) in the exercise of fiduciary powers, but what happens if a fiduciary is placed in a position in which it is inevitable, if he is to discharge his duties properly, that he will sooner or later breach one of these rules? Suppose, for example, that an estate agent with existing instructions to assist in the purchase of certain land is appointed executor of an estate containing the same land. This fiduciary has been placed in a position of actual conflict where he '*cannot fulfil his obligations to one principal without failing in his obligations to the other*'.[87] Consequently, '*he may have no alternative but to cease to act for at least one and preferably both*'.[88] Note, however, that an estate agent is permitted to act for two or more principals competing to acquire the same property, just as he is able to act for two vendors trying to sell similar neighbouring properties,[89] '*otherwise he could not carry on his business*'.[90]

Conflicting interests and confidential information

Solicitors,[91] estate agents, accountants, and similar commercial agents are often fiduciaries, and they often associate in commercial partnerships or firms. It is clear that any

---

[85] Millett LJ in *Mothew* at 19F.

[86] *Gilbert's Case* (1869–70) LR 5 Ch App 559 at 566. For discussion of a recent example, see *Wight v. Olswang* [2001] Lloyds' Rep PN 269.   [87] *Mothew* (n. 1) at 19G.

[88] Ibid. at 19G–H, *per* Millett LJ, referring to *Moody v. Cox* [1917] 2 Ch 71 and *Commonwealth Bank of Australia v. Smith* (1991) 102 ALR 453.   [89] *Kelly v. Cooper* [1993] AC 205, PC.

[90] R. Goode, *Commercial Law*, 2nd edn (London: Penguin, 1995) at 177.

[91] See F. M. B. Reynolds, 'Solicitors and Conflicts of Duties' [1991] 107 LQR 536.

individual fiduciary who finds himself acting for two clients with conflicting interests must cease to act for one, or *'preferably both'*,[92] but what if a fiduciary is already acting for a principal when another fiduciary in the same firm wishes to accept instructions from another principal in circumstances where there is a potential for conflict between the interests of the two principals? The answer to that question is clear. Unless the fiduciaries have the fully informed consent of both principals, their firm should decline to accept the new, potentially conflicting, instructions.

Less clear-cut is the situation in which an agent *used to act* for a client (Alpha), and another agent in the same firm wishes to accept instructions from a new client—or new instructions from an existing client—in circumstances where there is a potential for conflict between the interests of Alpha and the client (Omega) who is offering new instructions. Because Alpha is no longer instructing the firm and his agent no longer has power to transact in his name, it is arguable that there is no longer any risk (unless the firm fraudulently represents itself still to be Alpha's agent) of positional or transactional breach of fiduciary duty. This certainly appears to be Lord Millett's assessment of such a situation. His Lordship takes the view that the termination of Alpha's instructions terminates the fiduciary relationship and thereby terminates the fiduciary duties owed to Alpha.[93] That view is hard to reconcile with his Lordship's view, expressed elsewhere, that a fiduciary relationship arises out of a fiduciary duty, rather than vice versa.[94] However that may be, his Lordship recognizes that, even if there is no risk of breach of fiduciary duty per se after the termination of Alpha's instructions, there is a risk that confidential information relating to Alpha may be disclosed (albeit inadvertently) to Omega. If that risk is real (it need not be a substantial risk, but it must be more than merely *'fanciful'*),[95] the firm must decline to act for Omega unless Alpha and Omega are fully aware of the potential conflict of interest, and still consent to the firm accepting Omega's instructions.

So, are there any circumstances in which a firm may accept instructions from Omega (whose interests are potentially adverse to those of Alpha) without increasing to any 'real' extent the risk that confidential information relating to Alpha will be disclosed to Omega? The answer is 'yes'. In *Rakusen v. Ellis Munday & Clarke*,[96] both partners of a small firm of solicitors carried on separate practices, each with his own clients and without any knowledge of the other's clients. The claimant (Alpha) consulted one of the partners in relation to a contentious matter and, after he had terminated his instructions, the other partner, who had never met Alpha and was not aware that Alpha had consulted his partner, was instructed by Omega (the party on the other side in the same contentious matter). An injunction restraining the firm from acting for Omega was granted at first instance, but discharged by the Court of Appeal on the ground that there was no risk of disclosure of confidential information.

---

[92] See the previous section on the actual conflict rule.
[93] In *Jefri Bolkiah v. KPMG* [1999] 2 AC 222 at 234.   [94] *Mothew*, n. 1.
[95] Lord Millett in *Jefri Bolkiah v. KPMG* [1999] 2 AC 222. See also Lightman J in *Re a firm of solicitors* [1995] 3 All ER 482 at 488–9; [1997] Ch 1 at 9; Drummond J in *Carindale Country Club Estate Pty Ltd v. Astill* (1993) 115 ALR 112.   [96] [1912] 1 Ch 831.

The question in each case is whether the separation between the members of the firm is such that Omega's instructions can be accepted without any real increase in the risk of disclosure of confidential information relating to Alpha. This was precisely the question that fell to be considered by the House of Lords in *Jefri Bolkiah v. KPMG (a firm)*.[97] The firm in this case was a global firm of chartered accountants, which had carried out an annual audit for the Brunei Investment Agency (Omega) since 1983. Prince Jefri (Alpha) is the youngest brother of the Sultan of Brunei. Over a period of 18 months between 1996 and 1998 the firm was retained by one of Alpha's companies on his behalf and at his request to undertake a substantial investigation in connection with major litigation in which he was personally involved. In the course of the investigation, the firm was entrusted with, or acquired, extensive confidential information concerning Alpha's assets and financial affairs. On 14 May 1998, Alpha terminated his instructions to the firm and, two months later, Omega approached the same department of the firm with a view to instructing it to carry out certain financial investigations, including investigations into transactions carried out by Alpha. The firm took the view that there was no conflict of interest, because it had ceased to act for Alpha and there was no longer a client relationship with him, but it nevertheless took the precaution of putting special arrangements in place designed to prevent the disclosure of confidential information between the relevant departments. The creation of this information barrier or 'Chinese wall' involved a number of steps, including interviews of all staff to ensure that nobody engaged in work for Omega had confidential information relating to Alpha. A separate office, with a separate computer server, was established to carry out work on behalf of Omega and information relating to Alpha was deleted from the firm's computers. Nevertheless, the House of Lords held that such measures had been inadequate to protect Alpha's interests, because they had been created ad hoc in order to obtain Omega's instructions. The Chinese wall would only have been effective if it had been in place before Omega had offered to instruct the firm in matters potentially adverse to the interests of Alpha. As in the *Rakusen* case, an effective Chinese wall is an '*established organisational arrangement*';[98] it is not created ad hoc in response to events.[99]

The 'consent' defence

At no stage in the facts of *Jefri v. KPMG* did the firm seek Prince Jefri's consent before accepting instructions from the Brunei Investment Agency that were potentially adverse to the Prince's interests. The majority of the Court of Appeal suggested that there had been some element of inferred consent, because Prince Jefri knew that the firm already had a long-standing relationship with Brunei Investment Agency, which the firm would not wish to prejudice. On appeal, Lord Millett accepted that consent could sometimes be inferred, especially in the case of auditors,[100] because '*large accountancy*

[97] [1999] 2 AC 222.   [98] Lord Millett's term. Ibid. at 238B.

[99] See, generally, the Core Conduct of Business Rules (Financial Services Authority) and Law Commission Consultation Paper No. 124, *Fiduciary Duties and Regulatory Rules* (1992).

[100] And in relation to estate agents: see *Kelly v. Cooper* [1993] AC 205, PC.

firms commonly carry out the audit of clients who are in competition with one another'
and the *'identity of their audit clients is publicly acknowledged',*[101] but his Lordship held
that the consent defence is only relevant where a fiduciary is presently acting (or, presumably, where a fiduciary intends to act) for clients with conflicting interests. It has no
relevance where the fiduciary no longer acts for the principal whose interests are at risk.
His Lordship's reasoning appears to be that, in such a case, there is no risk of conflict
per se and so the consent of the former client, to the acceptance of 'potentially adverse'
instructions, is irrelevant.

The burden of proof

According to Lord Millett in *Jefri v. KPMG*, the burden of proof is on the former principal (Alpha)[102] to establish two things before he will be able to restrain his former fiduciary from acting in a matter for another client (Omega): first, that the former fiduciary is
in possession of information that is confidential to Alpha; second, that the information
is or may be relevant to the new matter in which the interests of Omega may be adverse
to his own. However, this burden of proof on Alpha is *'not a heavy one'.*[103] The first
requirement *'may readily be inferred'* and the second requirement *'will often be obvious'.*[104] His Lordship also suggested that Alpha must prove that he did not consent to the
disclosure of the information and that such lack of consent may be inferred. However,
this aspect of his Lordship's analysis is, with respect, questionable. Alpha's consent is
no doubt a defence which the former fudiciary could raise to Alpha's complaint—but
it is hard to see why Alpha should be required to prove his own lack of consent as an
element of his cause of action. The burden should surely be on the former fiduciary to
prove that Alpha provided express, or inferred, consent.

Once Alpha has proved the two elements—first, possession of confidential information, which, second, may be relevant to a new client (Omega) whose interests are potentially adverse to Alpha—the burden of proof shifts to the defendant to show that there
is no real risk that the confidential information will come into Omega's possession. On
the facts of *Jefri v. KPMG*, Lord Millett was not satisfied that the firm had discharged
this 'heavy burden'. So, leaving aside the controversial question of which party must
plead and prove the issue of consent, we may summarize the law by saying that there is
a 'light' burden of proof upon the former principal to establish the factual elements of
an adverse disclosure of confidential information, and that there is a 'heavy' burden of
proof on the former fiduciary to show that, despite those factual prerequisites, there is
no real risk of such disclosure.

The policy behind 'Chinese walls'

We have seen that, as a matter of policy, fiduciary duties are strictly enforced to set an
example to others. The same policy would explain why a perfectly effective Chinese

---

[101] *Jefri Bolkiah v. KPMG* [1999] 2 AC 222 at 235A.   [102] Alpha and Omega are the author's terms.
[103] *Jefri* [1999] 2 AC 222 at 235E.   [104] Ibid.

wall will be torn down if it is created ad hoc. However, according to Lord Millett in *Jefri v. KPMG*, Chinese walls are not designed to advance the policy of exemplary fiduciary propriety; they are simply a practical measure designed to prevent a real risk of disclosure of confidential information. Nevertheless, when the information is not merely confidential, but also privileged—as is frequently the case in relation to information acquired by a solicitor from his client—the prevention of disclosure becomes a matter of '*perception as well as substance*'.[105] This is not because of the policy of exemplary fiduciary propriety, but because of the policy on which legal professional privilege is based: '*It is of overriding importance for the proper administration of justice that a client should be able to have complete confidence that what he tells his lawyer will remain secret.*'[106]

The fiduciary duty to account for unauthorized profits

A trustee or other fiduciary is under a personal obligation to account for any unauthorized profit or gain accruing to him by reason of his office or position of trust, unless all of the persons to whom he is obliged to account freely give their fully informed consent to his retention of it. The rules of the Supreme Court[107] provide a procedure by which the fiduciary duty to account may be summarily enforced. It is a procedure that is '*often resorted to*'.[108] In any case in which there is an allegation of fiduciary relationship or duty, but no allegation of any impropriety, the court tends not to make any order in respect of costs of the summary application, reserving them instead until the final account has been taken. This is because:

> if the accounting party is innocent and produces a true and good account, it would be quite wrong that the cost of carrying out that duty should be thrown upon the innocent accounting party.[109]

The duty to account does not preclude the trustee's right to be reimbursed '*expenses properly incurred by him when acting on behalf of the trust*',[110] because expenses cannot properly be described as 'gains'. However, the trustee's right to be indemnified, which is secured as a 'lien' or 'equitable charge' over the trust fund, only covers out-of-pocket *financial* expenses (albeit future and contingent expenses as well as those already incurred).[111] Until recently, trustees had no right to be indemnified in respect of expenditure of *time and trouble*, except where remuneration had been specifically authorized.[112]

---

[105] Ibid. at 236G.   [106] Ibid   [107] Order 43.

[108] Harman J, *AG v. Cocke* [1988] Ch 414 at 420F.

[109] Ibid. at 420–1, approving *Re Richardson* [1920] 1 Ch 423, CA.

[110] Trustee Act 2000, s. 31(1), replacing the provision to like effect in Trustee Act 1925, s. 30(2).

[111] *X v. A* [2000] 1 All ER 490.

[112] Russell J in *Williams v. Barton* [1927] 2 Ch 9 at 11: '[o]*n the same principle* [that a trustee may not profit from their trust] *a trustee has no right to charge for his time and trouble*'; Paul Baker QC in *Foster v. Spencer* [1996] 2 All ER 672 at 678.

Today, as a result of the Trustee Act 2000,[113] certain types of trustee (trust corporations and professional trustees) are presumed to be entitled to reasonable remuneration.[114] Remuneration is considered later in this chapter.

Unauthorized profits: an inflexible rule?

According to Lord Herschell in *Bray v. Ford*, the rule that requires a fiduciary to account for unauthorized profits is '*an inflexible one*',[115] but, in the same case, his Lordship acknowledged that the rule might be departed from '*without any breach of morality, without any wrong being inflicted, and without any consciousness of wrongdoing*'.[116] In a more recent case, a judge suggested that the rule is '*riddled with exceptions*'.[117] Amongst the exceptional circumstances in which a fiduciary has been permitted to retain all, or part, of his gain are cases where the gain was merely trifling,[118] cases where the fiduciary had acted honestly and for the benefit of the trust such that he should be entitled to a *quantum meruit* ('sum deserved'),[119] and cases where the principal or beneficiaries would otherwise have been unjustly enriched at the fiduciary's expense.[120] These exceptions, and the last one in particular, seem at first sight to cut at the very root of the rule and to make a mockery of Lord Herschell's suggestion that the rule is an inflexible one. However, contrary to first impressions, it is possible to reconcile the inflexible nature of the rule with the significant, extensive exceptions to its operation. One simply has to appreciate that the rule and the exceptions have different concerns.

The rule is inflexible, because it seeks to maintain exemplary fiduciary propriety for symbolic and prophylactic reasons. It was to maintain the symbol or example of fiduciary propriety that Sir Eric Sachs once held that, when a fiduciary duty is established, it is '*contrary to public policy that the benefit of the transaction be retained by the person under the duty unless he positively shows that the duty of fiduciary care has been fulfilled*'.[121] And it was for prophylactic reasons that Lord Herschell upheld the inflexible nature of the rule in *Bray v. Ford* itself:

> It does not appear to me that this rule is, as has been said, founded upon principles of morality. I regard it rather as based on the consideration that, human nature being what it is, there is a danger... of the person holding a fiduciary position being swayed by interest rather than by duty, and thus prejudicing those whom he was bound to protect.[122]

The exceptions to the rule are designed to allow the fiduciary to retain unauthorized gains whenever justice between the fiduciary and his principal requires it. In short, the

---

[113] Part V, which came into force on 1 February 2001.

[114] The presumption may be rebutted by express contrary provision in the trust instrument or statute.

[115] [1896] AC 44 at 51.   [116] Ibid.

[117] Lindsay J in *Regal (Hastings) v. Gulliver* [1967] 2 AC 134 at 137. In *Murad v. Al-Saraj* [2005] EWCA Civ 959, CA, Arden LJ stated, obiter, that it '*may be... the court should revisit the operation of the flexible rule*' (at. [8.2]).

[118] *Rhodes v. Bate* (1865–6) LR 1 Ch App 252: '*the conferment of a trifling benefit will not be undone without evidence of* mala fides' (at 258).   [119] *Boardman v. Phipps* [1967] 2 AC 46.

[120] *Foster v. Spencer* [1996] 2 All ER 672.   [121] *Lloyds Bank Ltd v. Bundy* [1975] QB 326 at 346B.

[122] *Bray v. Ford* [1896] AC 44. Lord Herschell's exposition was described by Lord Upjohn in *Boardman v. Phipps* [1967] 2 AC 46 at 123 as being the best statement of the rule.

inflexible rule that a fiduciary must account for unauthorized gains is strictly enforced in the interests of the public at large, whereas the many exceptions to the rule are admitted when justice between the parties to the particular case so requires. So, contrary to first impressions, it appears that the rule itself is not 'equitable' in the functional sense,[123] but that the exceptions are.

The strictness of the rule

It is no defence to breach of the rule for the fiduciary to prove that he acted honestly or innocently. Nor is it a defence to prove that the principal suffered no harm, nor indeed to show that the principal *gained* as a result of the fiduciary's action.

No defence of honesty and bona fides

In *Regal Hastings v. Gulliver*, Lord Russell of Killowen observed that '[t]*he profiteer, however honest and well-intentioned, cannot escape the risk of being called upon to account*'.[124] This observation was applied by the House of Lords in *Boardman v. Phipps*,[125] where the fiduciary was held liable to account even though, as Lord Hodson observed, there had been no question of fraud and no suggestion that the fiduciary had acted other than in '*an open and honourable manner*'.[126] Lord Cohen even went so far as to state that the fiduciary had '*acted with complete honesty throughout*'.[127] Boardman was a solicitor acting on behalf of a trust, who, in that capacity and acting as proxy to the trustees, had attended the annual general meeting of a company in which the trust had a substantial shareholding. Unhappy with the state of the company, he and one of the beneficiaries (his co-defendant) decided to launch a takeover bid for those shares in the company that were not already owned by the trust. Boardman wrote to the beneficiaries outlining his plans to take a personal interest in the company, thereby giving them an opportunity to raise any objections they might have to his so doing. No objections having been made, the defendants proceeded with the takeover. In the event, the takeover was very successful and the value of the shares in the company greatly increased in value, to the great profit of the trust and the defendants. Despite this, one of the trust beneficiaries (Phipps) brought an action against Boardman for an account of the unauthorized profits he had made in his fiduciary capacity. The trial judge, Wilberforce J, found, as a fact, that Phipps had not been fully informed by Boardman as to the precise nature of his plans and ordered him to make the account. That order was ultimately upheld by a bare majority of the House of Lords (Lord Upjohn and Viscount Dilhorne dissenting), and their Lordships also upheld the judgment of Wilberforce J that Boardman should be paid a *quantum meruit* out of the trust fund '*on a liberal scale*', by way of remuneration for his hard work in service of the trust.

The fact that honesty and good faith are no answer to the fiduciary duty to account demonstrates that the strict rule against unauthorized gains is not concerned with wrongdoing. It is not even concerned with wrongful omission—namely, the fiduciary's

---

[123] See Chapter 1.   [124] [1967] 2 AC 134 at 144G–145A.   [125] [1967] 2 AC 46.
[126] [1967] 2 AC 46 at 105G.   [127] Ibid. at 104E.

failure to disgorge unauthorized gains. The duty to account does not depend upon the fiduciary's behaviour or culpability at all, even though there will inevitably be cases in which the fiduciary has made his unauthorized gain through some conscious and wrongful act or omission. Rather, the duty is concerned to address a wrongful state of affairs—namely, the retention by a fiduciary of unauthorized gains acquired by reason, and by reason only,[128] of his position of trust. From the fact that the duty to account is not a response to wrongdoing, it necessarily follows that the duty to account cannot properly be described as a forfeiture or a penalty, even though respected authors have described it in such terms in the past.[129] This conclusion should not surprise us. The Court of Chancery, which established the fiduciary duty, never did uphold a forfeiture[130] or exercise a penal jurisdiction.[131]

No requirement of harm to the principal

The fiduciary duty to account for unauthorized gains applies even where the fiduciary's gain was made without harm or expense to his principal, a point made forcefully by James LJ in *Parker v. McKenna*:

> this Court…is not entitled, in my judgment, to receive evidence, or suggestion, or argument as to whether the principal did or did not suffer any injury in fact by reason of the dealing of the agent; for the safety of mankind requires that no agent shall be able to put his principal to the danger of such an inquiry as that.[132]

The point was taken up by Lord Wright in *Regal (Hastings) Ltd v. Gulliver*:[133]

> both in law and equity, it has been held that, if a person in a fiduciary relationship makes a secret profit out of the relationship, the court will not inquire whether the other person is damnified or has lost a profit which otherwise he would have got. The fact is in itself a fundamental breach of the fiduciary relationship.[134]

Regal Ltd had been financially unable to take up a business opportunity due to limited finances and so the company's directors took up the opportunity on their own behalf. They were held liable to account to the company for the gains they had made. The outcome would have been the same even if the business opportunity had never been offered to the company, but had instead been offered directly to the directors personally.[135] Only if the offer had been made to the defendants independently of their status as directors would they have been permitted to take it up on their own account.

---

[128] This causation-based qualification is the subject of debate. See later.

[129] A. J. Oakley refers to this, *Constructive Trusts*, 3rd edn (London: Sweet & Maxwell, 1997) at 236 as '*the penal attitude displayed by the authorities*'; G. Jones, 'Unjust enrichment and the fiduciary's duty of loyalty' (1968) 84 LQR 472.

[130] G. Watt, 'Property rights and wrongs: the frontiers of forfeiture' in *Modern Studies in Property Law: Property 2000* (E. Cooke, ed.) (Oxford: Hart Publishing, 2001) vol. I at 115.

[131] *Vyse v. Foster* (1872) LR 8 Ch App 309.   [132] (1874) LR 10 Ch App at 124, 125.

[133] [1967] 2 AC 134.   [134] At 154F.

[135] *Industrial Development Consultants Ltd v. Cooley* [1972] 1 WLR 443.

In *Keech v. Sandford*,[136] a trustee sought to take advantage of an opportunity to renew a lease when the landlord made it clear that he would not offer the renewal to the beneficiary of the trust who was the current tenant. The trustee's gain was, in no sense, made at the expense of the trust, but the trustee was still barred from taking the renewal. Lord King LC held that:

> This may seem harsh that the trustee is the only person of all mankind who might not have the lease; but it is very proper that the rule should be strictly pursued, and not in the least relaxed.[137]

It may be that, by excluding entirely any inquiry into harm to the principal, the inflexible rule goes too far. The prophylactic aims of the policy of exemplary fiduciary propriety would be served sufficiently well by restricting the duty to account to cases in which there is at least *a real risk of harm*. However, the merit of excluding all inquiry into harm is the merit of simplicity. If harm is irrelevant, the principal is only required to show that his fiduciary made a gain without authority and by means of his position of trust. The rule is therefore easily understood and the onus will undeniably be upon the fiduciary to anticipate its effects by gaining his principal's authority or consent before obtaining or retaining any such gain.

John H. Langbein argues that the technique of avoiding all possible conflicts sometimes obstructs the aim of serving the beneficiaries' best interest and he calls for the law to '*allow inquiry into the merits of a trustee's defense that the conduct in question served the best interest of the beneficiary*'.[138] He identifies four historical trends, which he says justify a relaxation of the strict rule: first, the courts are more efficient in fact-finding than they were when the strict rule was established, so there is no need for '*crude over-deterrence*'; second, the shift from reliance upon the unskilled gentleman amateur trustee to the skilled paid professional trustee; third, improvements in trust accounting and information retention brought about by the IT revolution; fourth,

> Professional trustees do not serve for honor, they serve for hire; accordingly, they serve not in the sole interest of the beneficiary but also to make money for themselves and their shareholders.

Significant though these trends are, only the first and third indicate clearly that the original reasons for the rule might no longer apply. If anything, the historical moves towards paid professionalism (Langbein's second and fourth trends) suggest that the strict rule may be more necessary than ever. One thing is clear: in this jurisdiction, any relaxation of the strict equitable principle must be left to the House of Lords.[139]

No defence of harm to the fiduciary

Boardman v. Phipps illustrates that a fiduciary will be required to account for unauthorized gains even if they are, to a large extent, attributable to the fiduciary's hard

---

[136] (1726) Sel Cas Ch 61.

[137] *Keech v. Sandford* (1726) Sel Cas Ch 61 at 62. In *Re Biss, decd* [1903] 2 Ch 40, CA.

[138] 'Questioning the trust law duty of loyalty: sole interest or best interest?' (2005) 114 Yale LJ 929; 987–90.

[139] *Murad v. Al-Saraj* [2005] EWCA Civ 959, *per* Arden LJ at [82]; *Wrexham Association Football Club Ltd v. Crucialmove Ltd* [2006] EWCA Civ 237; [2007] BCC 139, CA, *per* Sir Peter Gibson at [51].

work. Regardless of the hardship to the fiduciary, he has a duty to account if the gains could not have been made without his position of trust. Professor Peter Birks has criticized cases such as *Boardman*, because they tend to produce '*windfalls to rather sharp plaintiffs at the expense of honest and industrious defendants*'.[140] That may be true, but the fiduciary duty to account is not susceptible to a straightforward restitutionary critique, as Birks himself acknowledges.[141] If it were, every account would be limited to the reversal of the fiduciary's unjust enrichment, and, a fortiori, no account could be so extensive as to unjustly enrich the principal at the fiduciary's expense. Justice between the particular fiduciary and the particular principal is not the only matter with which the duty to account is concerned. The gist of the fiduciary duty to account for unauthorized gains is the maintenance of exemplary fiduciary propriety, not the reversal of unjust enrichment of the particular parties. As one Australian judge put it: '*the law relating to sustaining the integrity of fiduciary relationships enunciates the* [sic] *higher principle than that of* restitutio in integrum'.[142]

Exceptions to the rule

There is no doubt that strict enforcement of the fiduciary duty to account can produce an unfair imbalance between fiduciaries and principals in individual cases. Therefore, although public policy requires that the rule be maintained in its strict form in the generality of cases, in particular cases, the courts are willing to employ a number of techniques to ensure that the rule does not produce harsh results. Even if courts were not motivated by a basic concern for *inter partes* justice to create exceptions to the strict rule, they might be motivated by pragmatic and policy reasons to maintain some reasonable relation between the obligations of fiduciaries and the rights of their principals—because the policy of exemplary fiduciary propriety must be weighed against the public interest in attracting persons to accept fiduciary obligations in the first place.

The quantum meruit exception

A trustee or fiduciary may be awarded a *quantum meruit* (a 'sum deserved') in respect of past service he has rendered to the trust or to his principal. The office of trustee or fiduciary is, essentially, unremunerated, so a *quantum meruit* will only be awarded by way of reduction of any unauthorized gain for which the trustee or fiduciary is obliged to account to his trust or principal. It should not be regarded as an award of remuneration per se. It will only be awarded in exceptional circumstances and it will not be awarded if it might induce the fiduciary to act in conflict of interest,[143] because that would undermine the policy on which the general duty to account is based.

---

[140] 'Civil wrongs: a new world', Butterworth Lecture, 1990 (London: Butterworths, 1991) 55 at 97.
[141] P. Birks, *An Introduction to the Law of Restitution* (Oxford: Clarendon Press, revd edn 1989).
[142] *Maguire v. Makaronis* 1995 VIC LEXIS 1425, 17 August 1995, Supreme Court of Victoria, Appeal Division, *per* Nathan J at 48; but see the dissenting judgment of Brooking J at 32.
[143] *Guinness plc v. Saunders* [1990] 2 AC 663 at 694.

We have already noted that, where the fiduciary is innocent of any wrongdoing, as was the case in *Boardman v. Phipps*, the *quantum meruit* may be awarded on a 'liberal scale'. The measure of the award to the fiduciary reflects the fiduciary's deserts. In the next section, we will consider whether the size of the fiduciary's account should be reduced to prevent enrichment of the principal.

Is there an 'unjust enrichment' exception?

Professor Gareth Jones argued many years ago that as a general rule the fiduciary duty to account should be restricted to cases in which the fiduciary had been unjustly enriched at his principal's expense and that making a public example of innocent fiduciaries, who had caused no harm, should be the exception rather than the rule.[144] That position has not been adopted by the English courts, but the point can be turned on its head, to ask whether a fiduciary should be required to account if the account might *unjustly enrich his principal*. In other words, is there an unjust enrichment exception to the general duty to account? The Australian High Court has answered that question in the affirmative: '*the liability of the fiduciary should not be transformed into a vehicle for the unjust enrichment of the plaintiff*'.[145] In *Crown Dilmun v. Sutton*,[146] Peter Smith J did not rule out the possibility that the fiduciary's liability to account may be reduced where it would otherwise unjustly enrich his principal, but noted that in this area, '*the law favours conferring benefits on the wronged even though that is at the expense of the wrongdoer*'[147] and stressed that, if the fiduciary has acted dishonestly, there can be no question of reducing his liability to account.

In *Foster v. Spencer*,[148] Paul Baker QC J made an award of remuneration to trustees of a cricket club in respect of past service to the trust. Refusal of the award, he said, would '*result in the beneficiaries being unjustly enriched at the expense of the trustees*'.[149] The judge held the enrichment to be unjust, because the trustees had assumed office at a time when the club could not afford to offer remuneration and, in the years following their appointment, the trustees' service to the club was far more extensive than they could have anticipated at the date of their appointment. It is arguable that such special facts justify the decision in *Foster v. Spencer*, but in the generality of cases, trustees assume office knowing that, unless authorized to the contrary, they are obliged to provide their services for free. So, in the vast majority of cases, there can be no suggestion that services provided by trustees have *unjustly* enriched the beneficiaries and the existence of an unjust enrichment exception should be considered doubtful at best.

The 'practical justice' exception

We have seen that the fiduciary duty to account, although a product of Chancery, is equitable in name only: it is not concerned with fairness, but with the maintenance of

---

[144] 'Unjust enrichment and the fiduciary's duty of loyalty' (1968) 84 LQR 472 at 502.
[145] *Warman International Ltd v. Dwyer* (1995) 128 ALR 201 at 211–12.
[146] [2004] 1 BCLC 468; [2004] EWHC 52 (Ch).   [147] Ibid. at [212].   [148] [1996] 2 All ER 672.
[149] At 681B–C.

exemplary fiduciary propriety. It follows that the duty is usually enforced as a matter of course and that the court has no real discretion to refuse to order an account where a fiduciary has made unauthorized gains from his position of trust. Its only discretion in the usual course of events is to order the fiduciary to account in full, but to make a *quantum meruit* award in favour of the defendant where appropriate, and to set off the *quantum meruit* against the account. Suppose, however, that a court were asked to rescind a transaction, carried out by a fiduciary with his principal's consent, on the ground that the principal's consent had been obtained by undue influence. An example would be a financially unfavourable contract entered into by a young and inexperienced 'pop star' under the undue influence of their manager. In such a case, the manager's fiduciary duty to account for his illegitimate fiduciary gains is not an automatic duty, but one that is indirectly dependent upon judicial discretion to order rescission on the ground of undue influence. The court's discretion to decline to award rescission in such a case has sometimes been seized upon as a basis for introducing considerations of fairness and justice between the parties into the quantification of the account. Thus, in a case concerning a young pop star, 'Gilbert O'Sullivan', who successfully claimed that he had signed an unfavourable contract due to his manager's undue influence, Dunn LJ held that:

> in taking the account the defendants are entitled to an allowance . . . for reasonable remuneration, including a profit element, for all work done in promoting and exploiting O'Sullivan and his compositions.[150]

Crucially, his Lordship held that:

> although equity looks at the advantage gained by the wrongdoer rather than the loss to the victim, the cases show that in assessing the advantage gained the court will look at the whole situation in the round.[151]

In reaching this conclusion, his Lordship applied the maxim 'he who seeks equity must do equity'.[152]

Defences to the enforcement of the rule

Lord Hodson summarized the fiduciary duty to account in the following terms:

> no person standing in a fiduciary position, when a demand is made upon him by the person to whom he stands in the fiduciary relationship to account for profits acquired by him by reason of his fiduciary position . . . is entitled to defeat the claim upon any ground save that he made profits with the knowledge and assent of the other person.[153]

---

[150] *O'Sullivan v. MAM Ltd* [1985] QB 428 at 459. The manager's efforts must have been very considerable indeed. O'Sullivan met the agent in 1969, having had no real success on his own and yet, by 1972, he was the biggest selling solo artist in the world.   [151] Ibid. at 458.

[152] For further application of this maxim, see *Re Berkeley Applegate Ltd* [1989] Ch 32, *per* Edward Nugee QC, and *Spence v. Crawford* [1939] All ER 271 at 288–9.

[153] In *Boardman v. Phipps* [1967] 2 AC 46 at 105.

This summary suggests that two major defences are available to the fiduciary when called upon to account: the first is the causation defence—for the account only applies where the unauthorized gains were acquired *by reason of* his fiduciary position; the second is the consent defence.

The causation defence

A fiduciary is only required to account for unauthorized gains made *by reason of* his fiduciary position. He is not required to account for gains acquired by other means, for '*it is one thing to strip a fiduciary of profit without much enquiry; it is another to hold him accountable for all loss without enquiring into relative causes*'.[154] Hence Lord Cohen's observation in *Boardman v. Phipps*:[155] '*had the company been a public company and had the appellants bought the shares on the market, they would not, I think, have been accountable*'.[156] Viscount Sankey had reached a similar conclusion in *Regal (Hastings) Ltd v. Gulliver*:[157]

> having obtained . . . shares by reason and only by reason of the fact that they were directors of Regal and in the course of the execution of that office, [they] are accountable for the profits which they have made out of them.[158]

The words 'by reason only' must not be taken too literally. We observed earlier that a fiduciary will typically still have to account even if his unauthorized gains are, to a large extent, attributable to his own hard work. Lord Porter's summary in the same case is actually more accurate:

> The legal proposition may, I think, be broadly stated by saying that one occupying a position of trust must not make a profit which he can acquire only by use of his fiduciary position, or, if he does, he must account for the profit so made.[159]

The preceding dicta are, at first sight, hard to reconcile with the judgment of Morritt LJ in the Court of Appeal in *United Pan-Europe Communications NV v. Deutsche Bank AG*,[160] where his Lordship said:

> If there is a fiduciary duty of loyalty and if the conduct complained of falls within the scope of that fiduciary duty . . . then I see no justification for any further requirement that the profit shall have been obtained by the fiduciary 'by virtue of his position'.[161]

The implication of this statement is that a solicitor, such as Mr Boardman, should sometimes be disqualified from purchasing shares even if they are quoted on the public stock exchange and that directors, such as those in *Regal*, should sometimes be accountable for profits made on shares, even if they might have been acquired independently of their fiduciary position. In *United Pan-Europe* itself, the defendant had received documents from the claimant in confidence and, on the basis of information contained within

---

[154] J. D. Heydon, 'Causal relationships between a fiduciary's default and the principal's loss' (1994) 110 LQR 328 at 332.   [155] [1967] 2 AC 46, HL.
[156] Ibid. at 100–1.   [157] [1967] 2 AC 143.
[158] Ibid. at 149.   [159] Ibid. at 158E–F. See also Lord Macmillan at 153D–E; Lord Wright at 154B.
[160] [2000] 2 BCLC 461.   [161] Ibid. 484A–B.

the documents, had proceeded to purchase shares in competition with the claimant. However, Morritt LJ does not remove considerations of causation entirely. His Lordship still requires that the conduct complained of must '*fall within the scope of* ' the fiduciary duty. There must, in other words, be a basic factual connection between the particular gains and the defendant's lack of authority to retain such gains. His Lordship's point is that the duty to account should arise directly when profits are made in breach of fiduciary duty without any additional requirement to prove that such profits arise from a fiduciary position as such. Read in this way, his Lordship's dictum can be seen as an inevitable next step in the movement (established by Millett LJ, as he then was, in the *Mothew* case) to describing remedies against fiduciaries in terms of the fiduciary's duty, as opposed to the fiduciary's 'status', or 'relationship', or 'position'. Because a fiduciary duty can arise independently of any traditional category of fiduciary position (solicitor, agent, director, etc.), it follows that there is no need to prove that an unauthorized profit was made by virtue of a fiduciary position in order to establish a fiduciary duty to account for it. In fact, the explanation for Morritt LJ's dictum may be even more straightforward than this: it may be nothing more than a restatement of the principle that the burden of proof in fiduciary transactions rests heavily upon the fiduciary. If either of these analyses is correct, his Lordship's dictum is significant in at least two respects: first, it supports the argument that the claimant should be under no obligation to prove causation as an element of his cause of action; second, it leaves open the possibility that the defendant will be able to raise the absence of basic factual causation as a *defence*.

The consent defence

The basic rule is that, apart from statute, a fiduciary may only make or retain a relevant personal gain if authorized to do so by his principal or by the court. Likewise, a trustee may be authorized by the trust instrument, or by the trust beneficiaries, or by the court. However, in the absence of advance authority to make a gain, it is nevertheless a good defence to an action for an account for the fiduciary or trustee to prove that his principal (or every beneficiary) has given their fully informed consent to the retention of the gain.[162] Furthermore, a principal is not permitted to gamble at his fiduciary's expense, so if he is aware that his fiduciary has made an unauthorized gain—for example, the purchase of profitable shares with his own money as a result of information acquired in his fiduciary capacity—the principal must call for an account without undue delay or he may be taken to have acquiesced in the fiduciary's retention of the unauthorized gain.

Is there a duty to account for gains made from trust 'information'?

A fiduciary will be liable to account for any gain made by virtue of his position of trust or his use of trust property. We have so far assumed that Mr Boardman was accountable

---

[162] Lord Cohen confirmed that the consent must be '*informed consent*' (*Boardman v. Phipps* [1967] 2 AC 46 at 101).

because of his position of trust, but he wasn't actually a trustee, so the question arises: in what sense was he acting in a fiduciary capacity for the trust? The answer seems to be that he had voluntarily assumed a fiduciary position, but their Lordships' judgments on this point were not clear. Two of their five Lordships (Lords Guest and Hodson) upheld, as an alternative basis for the account, the view taken by Wilberforce J at first instance that Boardman was liable to account not merely because he had held a fiduciary position, but because his gains were derived from the use of trust property.[163] The relevant trust property was the 'knowledge' that Boardman had acquired in the course of acting as a solicitor to the trust and, in particular, that which he had acquired when acting as proxy to the trustees at the annual general meeting of the trust-owned company. Lord Upjohn and Viscount Dilhorne dissented from this analysis of the case. Lord Upjohn held that information relating to a trust '*is not property in any normal sense but equity will restrain its transmission to another if in breach of some confidential relationship*'.[164] The 'casting vote' on this possible ratio of the decision fell to Lord Cohen and his Lordship declined to exercise it, stating simply that '[i]*nformation is, of course, not property in the strict sense of that word*'.[165] Echoing this, Sir Peter Millett, writing extrajudicially, has suggested that '*the categorisation of information as property owes more to metaphor than to legal accuracy*'.[166]

Trustee remuneration

It is hard to say whether trustee remuneration properly belongs in this chapter or the next, so it may serve as a bridge between the two. The justification for placing the topic in this chapter is the basic presumption that a trustee is not entitled to remuneration unless directly or indirectly authorized by the trust instrument. This rule of 'gratuitous service' is an extension of the rule that a fiduciary is not entitled to unauthorized gains acquired by virtue of his fiduciary position. However, the argument for placing this topic in the next chapter is that the law relating to trustee remuneration has been amended by Part V of the Trustee Act 2000,[167] which applies regardless of when the trust was created. Since the Act came into force, on 1 February 2001, the basic presumption of gratuitous service no longer applies to a trust corporation that is not a charitable trust,[168] nor to a trustee '*acting in a professional capacity*',[169] provided that

---

[163] [1964] 1 WLR 993 at 1012. See, further, Russell LJ's vigorous defence of this view in the Court of Appeal ([1965] Ch 992 at 1031).   [164] *Boardman v. Phipps* [1967] 2 AC 46 at 128A.

[165] Ibid. at 102G.

[166] 'Remedies: the error in *Lister v. Stubbs*' in P. Birks, ed., *The Frontiers of Liability* (Oxford: Oxford University Press, 1994) 51 at 53; echoing in turn F. Gurry, *Breach of Confidence* (Oxford: Clarendon Press, 1984) at 46–8.

[167] Sections 28–33.   [168] Section 29(1).

[169] A trustee acts in a professional capacity if '*he acts in the course of a profession or business which consists of or includes the provision of services in connection with (a) the management or administration of trusts generally or a particular kind of trust, or (b) any particular aspect of the management or administration of trusts generally or a particular kind of trust, and the services he provides to or on behalf of the trust fall within that description*' (s. 28(5)).

he is not a sole trustee and provided that his remuneration has been agreed in writing by every other trustee.[170] Such trustees are now entitled to reasonable remuneration out of the trust fund *if the trust instrument is silent* on the issue of remuneration.[171] 'Reasonable remuneration' means such remuneration as is reasonable in the circumstances for the provision of trust services. Expressly included are reasonable banking charges levied by trustees who are authorized institutions (typically, banks) under the Banking Act 1987.[172] Also included is remuneration for services that a lay trustee could have provided.[173]

Cases decided before the 2000 Act demonstrate that, when the presumption of the general law was against trustee remuneration, the courts were not slow to find that a trust instrument had indirectly authorized remuneration. Thus in *Re Llewellin's Will Trust*,[174] Jenkins J allowed a clause in a trust instrument its ordinary construction even though this meant that the trustees would be able to appoint themselves to be directors of a company the shares of which they held on trust. As directors, they were empowered to award themselves remuneration at a level that they themselves could fix.[175] Now that the presumption in the case of trust corporations and professional trustees is in favour of remuneration, it will be interesting to see if the courts will be as quick to treat the indirect provision of remuneration by the trust instrument as a sufficient basis for *excluding* such trustees' statutory right to reasonable remuneration.

Where the trust instrument expressly authorizes the remuneration of a trust corporation or professional trustee, such a trustee is deemed to be entitled under the trust instrument to receive payment in respect of services even if they are services which are capable of being provided by a lay trustee.[176] However, this provision only applies to a professional trustee of a charitable trust if he is not a sole trustee and if he has the agreement of a majority of the other trustees.[177]

Apart from the case of trust corporations and trustees acting in a professional capacity, as outlined earlier, the general rule is still that trustees must act gratuitously. The Act also confirms the established rule that a trustee's right to be remunerated from the trust is not a beneficial interest in the trust fund,[178] but merely a personal entitlement, albeit one secured by an equitable charge over the trust fund.

The court's inherent jurisdiction to award prospective remuneration

Courts have an inherent jurisdiction to grant or to increase prospective (future) remuneration to trustees (whether corporate, professional, or lay) if it is in the interests of

---

[170] Section 29(2).   [171] Section 29(5) and subject to any legislation to the contrary.
[172] Section 29(3).   [173] Section 29(4).   [174] [1949] 1 Ch 225.
[175] See, also, *Guinness plc v. Saunders* [1990] 2 WLR 324, HL.   [176] Section 28(1), (2).
[177] Section 28(3)(b). In the case of charitable trusts, s. 30 of the Act provides that the Secretary of State may make special provision for the remuneration of professional trustees and trust corporations.
[178] Section 28(4).

the beneficiaries on the facts of a particular case.[179] This inherent jurisdiction may be exercised even when the trust instrument authorizes remuneration:

> One can...see some force [in the] view that, as a matter of policy the court should *not* exercise its jurisdiction to bail out professional trustees who have made a bad bargain. But given that a trustee may retire and that there is no means of compelling him to continue in office, the fact must be faced that there will often be a stark choice between increasing the remuneration of a skilled trustee familiar with the trust property and being forced to look for new trustees who may well not undertake the office without the inducement of higher fees.[180]

Lord Herschell had made the same observation in *Bray v. Ford*:

> it might sometimes be to the advantage of the beneficiaries that their trustee should act for them professionally rather than a stranger, even though the trustee were paid for his services.[181]

However, a trustee cannot, by merely threatening to resign, coerce the court into awarding remuneration. In *Foster v. Spencer*,[182] which concerned trustees of a cricket club, the judge was satisfied that the trust business was not unduly complex and that other trustees could be found who would be willing to discharge it without remuneration.

Further reading

In addition to the following print sources, the Online Resource Centre accompanying this book contains web links to further reading as well as guide answers to assessment questions relevant to this chapter.

BIRKS, P. B. H., 'The content of fiduciary obligation' (2002) 16(1) TLI at 34–52.

CONAGLEN, M., 'The nature and function of fiduciary loyalty' (2005) 121 LQR 452.

CONAGLEN, M., 'Fiduciary regulation of conflicts between duties' (2009) 125 LQR 111.

CONAGLEN, M., *Fiduciary Loyalty: Protecting the Due Performance of Non-Fiduciary Duties* (Oxford: Hart Publishing, 2010).

EDELMAN, J., 'The Fiduciary Self-Dealing Rule' in J. Glister and P. Ridge (eds.) *Fault Lines in Equity* (Oxford: Hart Publishing, 2012).

FINN, P., *Fiduciary Obligations* (Sydney: Law Book Co, 1977).

FINN, P., 'Fiduciary law' in *Commercial Aspects of Trusts and Fiduciary Obligations* (E. McKendrick, ed.) (Oxford: Oxford University Press, 1992).

HICKS, A. D., 'The remedial principle of *Keech v Sandford* reconsidered' (2010) CLJ 287.

HILLIARD, J., 'The flexibility of fiduciary doctrine in trust law: how far does it stretch in practice?' (2009) 23(3) Tru. LI 119–29.

JONES, G., 'Unjust Enrichment and the Fiduciary's Duty of Loyalty' (1968) 84 LQR 477.

---

[179] *Re Duke of Norfolk's ST* [1981] 3 All ER 220, CA, *per* Fox LJ.
[180] K. Hodkinson (1982) 46 Conv 231 at 233.
[181] [1896] AC 44 at 52.
[182] [1996] 2 All ER 672.

LANGBEIN, J. H., 'Questioning the trust law
duty of loyalty: sole interest or best interest?' (2005) 114 Yale LJ 929.

NOLAN, R.C., 'Controlling Fiduciary Power'
(2009) 68(2) CLJ 293–323.

SALZEDO, S. and HOLLANDER, C., *Conflicts of
Interest and Chinese Walls* (London: Sweet
& Maxwell, 2000).

SEALY, L. S., 'Fiduciary obligations, forty years
on' (1995) 9 JCL 37 at 40.

SIMPSON, E., 'Conflicts' in *Breach of Trust*
(P. Birks and A. Pretto, eds) (Oxford: Hart
Publishing, 2002), ch. 3, at 75–94.

11

Fulfilling and filling the office of trustee

Trustees are the legal owners of trust property and as such they have all the legal powers of an absolute owner, including the power to sell, lease, mortgage, and otherwise manage and invest trust assets.[1] Trusteeship is not, however, merely a way of holding property belonging to another; it also entails the responsibility of managing trust property in accordance with the terms of the trust instrument and the general law. '*Trust is patrimony, plus office*',[2] or, to put the same point another way, '*it is the office that makes the difference between entrusting and trust*'.[3] In short, trustees do not have the freedom of an absolute owner. They must exercise their trust powers for the exclusive benefit of the trust beneficiaries[4] or otherwise for the purposes of the trust, and they must exercise their powers unanimously with the other trustees.[5] Trustees may even be liable, in certain circumstances, for omitting to exercise their powers.[6]

Unless the provisions of his particular trust instrument provide to the contrary, a trustee is subject to a number of duties laid down by the general law. One of these, the fiduciary duty, was considered at length in the preceding chapter; the others, including the duty of care and the duty to exercise a sound discretion, are introduced in this chapter and demonstrated in the next chapter, in the context of trustee investment. When we examined the fiduciary duty, we observed that it is strictly enforced in the public interest. We also observed, however, that, despite the public interest in exemplary fiduciary propriety the courts have admitted many exceptions to the strict fiduciary duty to

---

[1] In the case of trusts of land (trusts comprising or including land), there is statutory authority to this effect (Trusts of Land and Appointment of Trustees Act 1996, s. 6).

[2] G. L. Gretton, 'Trusts without equity' (2000) 49 ICLQ 599 at 618.

[3] A. Honoré, 'Obstacles to the reception of trust law? The examples of South Africa and Scotland' in A. M. Rabello, *Aequitas and Equity: Equity in Civil Law and Mixed Jurisdictions* (Jerusalem: Hebrew University of Jerusalem, Sacher Institute, 1997) at 793.

[4] J. W. Harris, *Property and Justice* (Oxford: Clarendon Press, 1996) at 74.

[5] *Luke v. South Kensington Hotel Co* (1879) LR 11 Ch D 121, *per* Jessel MR at 125. Trustees may validly exercise trust powers without unanimity when authorized by the court (*Cowan v. Scargill* [1985] Ch 270 at 297), by the trust instrument (*Re Butlin's Settlement Trusts* [1976] Ch 251), or by statute. However, the powers of charity trustees may be validly exercised by a bare majority (*Re Whiteley* [1910] 1 Ch 600) or, in some cases, a two-thirds majority (Charities Act 1993, s. 74(3)).

[6] See 'The duty to exercise a sound discretion', later.

account. We even discovered that part of the reason for the court's willingness to relax the strict enforcement of the fiduciary duty, especially in the context of trustee remuneration, is a pragmatic concern to ensure that people are not dissuaded from accepting trusteeship in the first place. There is even a case for saying that the *'strong public interest in having persons and institutions ready and willing to be trustees'*[7] ought to be set against the public interest in exemplary fiduciary propriety. The office of trustee must be filled if it is to be fulfilled. This point will be borne in mind throughout the first two-thirds of this chapter, as we consider the various ways in which the law maintains a fine balance between the strict enforcement of trust duties and the need to attract persons to accept trust office. In the final third of the chapter, we will consider the ways in which the law ensures that the office of trustee does not remain vacant for long.

The significance of the trust instrument

The trust instrument plays a significant role in defining the nature and extent of a trustee's duties, and, as we will see in Chapter 13, the nature and extent of a trustee's liability for breach of his duties.[8] As Lord Browne-Wilkinson has said, the *'basic right of a beneficiary is to have the trust duly administered in accordance with the provisions of the trust instrument, if any, and the general law'.*[9] The general law of trusts is really little more than the background against which settlors set out the rules that are to govern their particular trust and trustees. Indeed, much of the general law has itself been laid down in response to the general practice of settlors and trust practitioners; when practitioners who draft trusts routinely disapply some aspect of the general law, this is often taken to be a sign that the general law is in need of reform.[10] The question therefore arises whether there is a point beyond which the trust instrument is not permitted to go in modifying or excluding the general law of trustee obligations. This question may be the single most important question in trusts law, because it is basically a question about the essence or 'core'[11] of the trust.

It is not a new question. In 1861, it arose in the case of *Wilkins v. Hogg*,[12] in which the testator expressly provided that:

> any trustee who shall pay over to his co-trustee or shall do or concur in any act enabling his co-trustee to receive any moneys... shall not be obliged to see to the application thereof; nor

---

[7] R. Niles and B. Schwartz, 'Breach of trust: recent developments' (1944–45) NYULR 165 at 183.

[8] See the section on exemption clauses in particular.

[9] *Target Holdings Ltd v. Redferns (a firm)* [1996] 1 AC 421, *per* Lord Browne-Wilkinson at 434A.

[10] Sir W. Goodhart QC, 'Trust law for the twenty-first century' in *Trends in Contemporary Trust Law* (A. J. Oakley, ed.) (Oxford: Clarendon Press, 1996) 257 at 263.

[11] In *Armitage v. Nurse* [1998] Ch 241, CA, Millett LJ sought to identify those aspects of the trust that cannot be removed by the terms of the trust instrument, which his Lordship referred to, at 253, as the '*irreducible core*' of the trust. See also David Hayton, 'The irreducible core content of trusteeship' in *Trends in Contemporary Trust Law* (A. J. Oakley, ed.) (Oxford: Clarendon Press, 1996) at 47.

[12] (1861) 31 LJ Ch 41.

shall such trustee be subsequently rendered responsible by an express notice or intimation of the actual misapplication of the same moneys.[13]

It was held that the express terms of the trust absolved two co-trustees of responsibility for trust money that had been lost after they permitted it to pass to a third co-trustee. Lord Westbury LC accepted that the terms of the trust could not absolve a trustee from liability for knowingly participating in a fraudulent breach of trust by his co-trustee, but, in the absence of evidence of fraud, the settlor could, as Millett LJ put it in a later case, '*limit the scope of the trustee's liability in any way*'.[14]

Hayim v. Citibank[15] provides another stark demonstration of the way in which the express terms of a trust may limit the extent of a trustee's duties. *Hayim* concerned two wills that had been executed by the same testator, one in respect of his property in the USA and one in respect of his property in Hong Kong. The executors of the two wills were different persons. The dispute concerned a particular residential property in Hong Kong. Although the Hong Kong executors held legal title to the residence, they had no power to sell it without the consent of the US executors. An express clause in the trust instrument relieved the US executors of any responsibility in respect of the Hong Kong property, as long as the testator's elderly brother and sister remained alive, unless the US executors received the proceeds of sale of the Hong Kong residence in the meantime. The beneficiaries of the US will were entitled to the proceeds of sale of the Hong Kong residence and so they requested that the residence be sold. When the US executors refused consent to a sale (so as to allow the existing occupiers, the testator's elderly brother and sister, to remain in occupation), the beneficiaries of the US will brought the present action against the US executors and against the Hong Kong executors. In other words, the claimants issued proceedings against all of the trustees of both trusts. Despite this, the claimants failed. It was held that the Hong Kong executors owed no trust duties to the beneficiaries of the US will and that the US executors had no trust duties, because the Hong Kong residence had not yet been sold—so, for a short period of time no trustee was liable to account to the US beneficiaries with respect to the Hong Kong residence. Lord Templeman observed that:

> It is of course unusual for a testator to relieve the trustee of his will of any responsibility or duty in respect of the trust property, but a testator may do as he pleases.[16]

It is no doubt true that there 'can be no trust where the trustee is not accountable to someone',[17] but *Hayim* illustrates that 'in special circumstances minimal accountability may subsist for a period'.[18]

---

[13] Ibid.

[14] *Armitage v. Nurse* [1998] Ch 241 at 254, approving *Wilkins v. Hogg* and *Pass v. Dundas* (1880) 43 LT 665.

[15] [1987] AC 730, PC.   [16] Ibid. at 744F.

[17] P. Matthews, 'The new trust: obligations without rights?' in *Trends in Contemporary Trust Law* (A. J. Oakley, ed.) (Oxford: Clarendon Press, 1996) 1 at 26.

[18] David Hayton, 'The irreducible core content of trusteeship' in *Trends in Contemporary Trust Law* (A. J. Oakley, ed.) (Oxford: Clarendon Press, 1996) at 54–5.

The duty of care

Trustees do not owe a common law duty of care to their beneficiaries, but they owe a duty of care in equity. The duty of care is one of the *'two great principles of trust fiduciary law'*,[19] the other being the fiduciary duty that we considered in the previous chapter. It is important to appreciate that the fiduciary duty and the duty of care are distinct duties. One can breach the fiduciary duty without breaching the duty of care—as would occur if a trustee, without authority, were to make an objectively prudent investment of trust monies in his own business. Conversely, one can be careless without being disloyal. As Millett LJ observed in *Bristol and West v. Mothew*:[20]

> Breach of fiduciary obligation . . . connotes disloyalty or infidelity. Mere incompetence is not enough. A servant who loyally does his incompetent best for his master is not unfaithful and is not guilty of a breach of fiduciary duty.[21]

Mothew concerned a solicitor acting for a purchaser and the purchaser's mortgagee in relation to the purchase of land. In the course of the conveyancing and in response to the usual inquiries, the solicitor assured the mortgagee that the purchaser had not borrowed, and would not be borrowing, any monies other than those secured by the mortgagee's charge. The solicitor had acted honestly in giving that assurance, but he had mistakenly omitted to mention an arrangement under which the purchaser's overdraft at his bank was to be secured by a charge on the purchased land. The Court of Appeal held that there had been a breach of the solicitor's duty of care, but no breach of trust or fiduciary duty.

Defining the trustee's duty of care

The extent to which a trustee's duty of care applies to the exercise of his powers is determined by the terms of the trust instrument, but in so far as the trust instrument does not exclude or modify it,[22] his duty of care will be that set out in s. 1 of the Trustee Act 2000. Section 1 provides that a trustee must exercise *'such care and skill as is reasonable in the circumstances'* and, according to s. 2, the trustee's duty of care will apply to those matters set out in the first schedule to the Act—including investment,[23] acquisition of land, the appointment of agents, nominees, and custodians,[24] and the insurance of trust property.[25]

The duty to invest with prudence, which is a significant aspect of the trustees' duty of care, is considered in detail in Chapter 12. Here we are concerned with identifying some general features of the duty of care. The first point to make is that it is a positive

---

[19] J. H. Langbein, 'The secret life of the trust: the trust as an instrument of commerce' (1997) 107 Yale LJ 165 at 182.						[20] [1998] 1 Ch 1.

[21] Ibid. at 18, *per* Millett LJ.	[22] Sch. 1, para. 7.	[23] Sch. 1, para. 1.

[24] See 'The duty of personal service'.	[25] Sch. 1, para. 5.

duty, which means that it may be breached by acts omitted as well as by acts committed. A careful trustee does not sit back and allow events to run their own course; he must act—and he must act carefully. The question is: just how careful must he be? The answer is that a trustee '*is not bound to avoid all risks and act as an insurer of the trust fund*';[26] he is not liable '*for mere errors of judgment provided he acts with reasonable care, prudence, and circumspection*'.[27] In fact, a trustee is, prima facie, '*only*' required '*to conduct the business of the trust in the same manner that an ordinary prudent man of business would conduct his own*'.[28] This may not sound unduly onerous, but it is, of course, an objective standard. So a trustee who fails to meet the 'ordinary prudent man of business' standard will breach his trust even if he is accustomed to devoting a lesser degree of care to the conduct of his own business and personal affairs, and even though he had acted carefully according to his own relatively low standards.

In one exceptional case, the court, taking pity on an unpaid, non-professional trustee whose agent had absconded with the trust money, relieved the trustee of liability on the ground that his neglect had not been deliberate.[29] The reasoning in that case has been criticized,[30] even though it is widely accepted that the result was a fair one.[31] Indeed, at least one commentator has argued that all amateur unremunerated trustees should be assessed by a subjective standard.[32] Nevertheless, the Trustee Act 2000 confirms the objective standard of care and it is a higher standard than it might at first appear, especially as regards the investment of the trust fund. Even if prudent persons of business might take certain risks on their own account when acting in their own affairs, a trustee may be liable for breach of trust if he takes equivalent risks on behalf of the trust. The trustee's objective duty of prudence is said to be analogous to a moral duty:

> The duty of the trustee is to take such care as an ordinary prudent man of business would take if he were minded to make an investment for the benefit of other people for whom he felt morally obliged to provide.[33]

It could be argued that embellishing the trustee's duty of care with reference to morality adds nothing but a symbolic dimension to the trustee's duty of care, even in the investment context. Ultimately, the extent of one's belief that a trustee will, and ought to, conduct trust business more carefully if reminded of his 'moral' obligation to the

---

[26] *Re Godfrey* (1883) LR 23 Ch D 483 at 493, *per* Bacon VC.

[27] *Re Chapman* [1896] 2 Ch 763 at 778, *per* Lopes LJ.

[28] *Re Speight* (1883) LR 22 Ch D 727, *per* Jessel MR at 739, *per* Bowen LJ at 762; applied *sub nom. Speight v. Gaunt* (1883) LR 9 App Cas 1, *per* Lord Blackburn at 19. See, generally, R. P. Austin, 'Moulding the content of fiduciary duties' in *Trends in Contemporary Trust Laws* (A. J. Oakley, ed.) (Oxford: Clarendon Press, 1996) 153 at 169–70.　　　　　　　　　　　　　　　　　　　　　　　　　　[29] *Re Vickery* [1931] 1 Ch 572.

[30] G. H. Jones, 'Delegation by trustees: a reappraisal' (1959) 22 MLR 381.

[31] Ibid. at 338. The authors of *Parker and Mellows' The Modern Law of Trusts* (A. J. Oakley, ed.) 6th edn (London: Sweet & Maxwell, 1994) also express the view that the result in the case was arguably 'desirable', despite the fact that it was 'technically incorrect', at 405.

[32] D. R. Paling, 'The trustee's duty of skill and care' (1973) 37 Conv 48.

[33] *Re Whiteley* (1886) LR 33 Ch D 347 CA, *per* Lindley LJ at 355 (later approved in the House of Lords). See also *King v. Talbot* 40 NY 76 (1869).

beneficiaries may correspond to the extent to which one believes that a driver will, and ought to, take more care when informed that the car in front has a 'baby on board'.

The objective standard of care under the Trustee Act 2000, s. 1(1), can also be raised to take account of the subjective characteristics of the particular trustee. Thus 'a bank which advertises itself largely in the public press as taking charge of administration is under a special duty'.[34] Yet, despite the high standards to which professional trustees are held, many of them are able, by means of exculpatory clauses in their trust instruments, to exclude liability for failure to meet those high standards.[35]

The judge in *Jobson v. Palmer*[36] did not consider remuneration in itself to be a factor that should lead to a higher standard of care, but a paid trustee is less likely than an unpaid trustee to be relieved of liability under the Trustee Act 1925, s. 61.[37]

Comparison with the common law tort of negligence

According to the explanatory notes that accompany the Trustee Act 2000, the phrase 'duty of care' means '*a duty to take care to avoid causing injury or loss*', but it operates to the exclusion of '*any common law duty of care which might otherwise have applied*'.[38] This is no doubt a restatement of the orthodox position according to which the beneficiaries' rights against their trustee are recognized in equity and not at law, but it begs the question of whether the duty of care to which trustees are subject in equity is, in essence, the same as the duty of care recognized by the common law tort of negligence. In theory, the law distinguishes between the fiduciary's duty of care and the tortious duty of care; they are not coterminous.[39] However, '*the standard of care of fiduciaries is increasingly being treated as merely an application of the common law of negligence*',[40] as the following statement demonstrates:

> The liability of a fiduciary for the negligent transaction of his duties is not a separate head of liability but the paradigm of the general duty to act with care imposed by law on those who take it upon themselves to act for or advise others.[41]

It is notable that, in the investment context, the trustees' duty of care was traditionally described as a duty to act 'prudently', which suggests a duty to be careful by exercising caution, whereas the new statutory duty of care expresses the trustees' duty in the more neutral language of 'reasonableness'. According to the 'Explanatory notes' accompanying the 2000 Act, the new statutory duty of care makes 'explicit' the traditional duty, which measures trustee investment behaviour against that expected of the ordinary

---

[34] *Re Waterman's WT* [1952] 2 All ER 1054, *per* Harman J at 1055.

[35] See 'Exemption clauses' in Chapter 13.   [36] [1893] 1 Ch 71.

[37] *Bartlett v. Barclays Bank (No. 1)* [1980] Ch 515 at 526A. See Chapter 13.

[38] Explanatory notes to Trustee Act 2000 (London: HMSO, 2000).

[39] *Henderson and Os v. Merrett Syndicates Ltd* [1995] 2 AC 145, HL; see also *Hedley Byrne & Co Ltd v. Heller & Partners Ltd* [1964] AC 465.

[40] R. P. Austin, 'Moulding the content of fiduciary duties' in *Trends in Contemporary Trust Law* (A. J. Oakley, ed.) (Oxford: Clarendon Press, 1996) 153 at 169.

[41] Lord Browne-Wilkinson in *Henderson v. Merrett Syndicates Ltd* [1995] 2 AC 145, HL at 205F.

prudent man of business, but the Act makes no explicit reference to 'prudence' at all. It is as if the parliamentary draftsman wanted to have his cake and eat it. By removing any express reference to prudence, the draftsman has removed the language of caution from trustee investment behaviour, to which it is deemed to be inappropriate in modern investment conditions,[42] but by informing us in the notes that 'reasonable' really means 'prudent' in the context of trustee investment, he has changed the form of words while purporting to leave the substance intact. It is an attempt at statutory 'spin'. The trouble is, of course, that the explanatory notes prepared by the Lord Chancellor's department have not, as their own introduction admits, '*been endorsed by Parliament*'. Only the actual wording of the Act has been endorsed by Parliament and a straightforward reading of s. 1 tells us that the language of 'reasonableness', which hitherto belonged to the duty of care at common law,[43] has been brought into the mainstream of trusts law. We can only assume that, when the section refers to such care and skill as is reasonable '*in the circumstances*', we are to take it as read that investment 'circumstances' call for such skill and care as hitherto went by the name of prudence.

The duty to exercise a sound discretion

The basic rule is that '*[t]he purported exercise of a discretionary power on the part of trustees will be void if what is done is not within the scope of the power*'.[44] The exercise of a discretion will also be void if it breaches an aspect of the general law, such as the rule against perpetuities.[45] An exercise of trustee discretion is also liable to be set aside if there is some formal or procedural irregularity (for example, if the trustee failed to obtain the necessary prior consent of a third party) and it is certain to be set aside if there was a distribution to the wrong beneficiaries or if there was a fraud on the trustee's power (an example would be trustees distributing benefits to the beneficiaries on the understanding that the beneficiaries will pass the benefits back to the trustees).[46]

Furthermore, trustees are obliged to exercise a *positive* discretion. They are not permitted to stand by and allow the trust to manage itself, and apparent decisions will be set aside if it appears that the trustees gave no actual thought to them (as occurred in one case where the trustees simply signed whatever documents their legal advisers put in front of them).[47] Of course trustees are obliged to exercise their discretions and reach their decisions unanimously, unless the trust instrument or statute provides to the contrary. No trustee is permitted to 'sleep' while the others discharge the trust. In addition,

---

[42] See Chapter 12.

[43] Apart from in the context of relieving trustees of liability for breach under the Trustee Act 1925, s. 61. See Chapter 13 and, generally, A. M. Kenny, 'The reasonable trustee' (1982) 126 SJ 631.

[44] *Pitt v. Holt; Futter v. Futter* [2011] EWCA Civ 197, *per* Lloyd LJ at para. [96].   [45] Ibid.

[46] In *Cloutte v. Storey* [1911] 1 Ch 18, the trustees were the parents of the beneficiaries.

[47] *Turner v. Turner* [1984] Ch 100.

they should reach their decisions honestly, in good faith, fairly, and without caprice. They should also take advantage of expert opinion and advice where appropriate.

A trustee who omits to exercise a trust discretion,[48] or places himself in a position in which he is not able freely to exercise it, may be held liable for the consequences, including any loss caused to the fund through his failure to act.[49] However, where the trust instrument gives the trustee the choice whether or not to exercise a discretionary power, the trustee owes no duty of care in respect of his decision '*whether to exercise that discretionary power in the first place*'.[50]

Trustees proposing to exercise their discretion in a particular way may apply to court for approval of their proposal. The court will tend to approve the proposal if it is within the scope of the trustees' authority and if it is reasonable for the trustees to believe that the proposal is in the best interests of the beneficiaries. Subject to these requirements, the court will presume that the discretion is exercised validly unless there is evidence to the contrary, always bearing in mind that '*one consequence of authorising the trustees to exercise a power is to deprive the beneficiaries of any opportunity of alleging that it constitutes a breach of trust*'.[51]

When the duty is qualified by express words

It is not uncommon for a trust instrument to authorize the trustees to exercise a discretion 'as they think fit'. The trust instrument may even grant a discretion that is in terms 'uncontrollable' or 'absolute'. Such qualifying words cannot oust the jurisdiction of the court, but, in exercising their jurisdiction to construe trust instruments, courts tend to give effect to the ordinary meaning of such words:

> The court cannot exercise a personal discretion connected with a trustee's personality or experience ... but, if there are well-established objective canons of construction, on which the trustee cannot be so well informed as the court, the court will not permit usurpation by the trustee, even under the terms of the trust, of jurisdiction to construe a trust document.[52]

'As the trustees think fit'

The fiduciary in *Bishop v. Bonham*[53] had been authorized to exercise an administrative discretion 'as he thought fit'. Slade LJ held that:

> the natural construction of words authorising a person to carry out such a transaction in such manner and upon such terms and for such consideration 'as you may think fit' is as authorising that person to carry out the transaction in such manner (and so on) as he thinks

---

[48] In *Turner v. Turner* [1984] Ch 100, the trustees did not realize that they had a discretion at all.

[49] See *Wight v. Olswang* [2001] Lloyd's Rep PN 269. Before accepting trusteeship, an intended trustee must reveal facts that may inhibit him (*Galmerrow Securities Ltd v. National Westminster Bank plc* (2000) 14 Tru LI 158 at 173).   [50] The explanatory notes to the 2000 Act, note 39.

[51] *Richard v. Mackay*, unreported, 4 March 1987, *per* Millett J at para. [8] of the official transcript.

[52] A. Kiralfy, 'A Limitation on the discretionary powers of trustees' (1953) 17 Conv (NS) 285 at 285.

[53] [1988] 1 WLR 742.

fit, *within the limits of the duty of reasonable care imposed by the general law*—no more, no less.[54]

Courts are generally more reluctant to intervene in the case of a dispositive discretion. Indeed, the only reported cases found by this author in which the exercise of a dispositive discretion had been set aside on the ground that the trustee had simply made a 'bad choice' are both old cases in which the trustee was a woman.[55] It may be that they can be dismissed as having been decided on a paternalistic, rather than a principled, basis.

Absolute and uncontrollable discretion

Gisborne v. Gisborne[56] concerned a will trust that granted the trustees an absolute discretion and 'uncontrollable authority' over the fund. Lord Cairns LC stated that:

> larger words than these, it appears to me, it would be impossible to introduce into a will. The trustees are not merely to have a discretion, but they are to have 'uncontrollable', that is, 'uncontrolled', authority. Their discretion and authority, always supposing that there is no *mala fides* with regard to its exercise, is to be without check or control from any superior tribunal.[57]

The terms of the settlement in *Re Locker's Settlement Trusts*[58] granted the trustees an 'absolute and uncontrolled' discretion in relation to the distribution of income. Goulding J, following *Gisborne v. Gisborne*, acknowledged that this prevented interference by the court in a bona fide exercise of that discretion, but held that it did not prevent the court's intervention in a case in which the trustees had totally failed to act. The settlor in this case requested that the trustees accumulate the trust income for several years, which, in breach of trust, they did. They then took out a summons for directions as to how the income ought to be distributed. The court decided that it would be in the best interests of the beneficiaries for the court to direct the distribution. However, the court did state that, if the trustees had been willing and fit to exercise their discretion, albeit late, the court would normally encourage them to do so. As Goulding J acknowledged: '*A tardy distribution at the discretion of the trustees is ... nearer to ... what the settlor intended, than tardy distribution by the trustees at the discretion of someone else.*'[59]

The rise and fall of the rule in *Hastings-Bass*

The so-called 'rule' in *Hastings-Bass*[60] is pragmatic. It provides that a trustees' decision, even if it was based on unsound reasoning, should not be reviewed by the courts or sent back to the trustees for reconsideration if, were the trustees to reconsider the

---

[54] Slade LJ, ibid. at 753E.

[55] *Re Roper's Trust* (1879) LR 9 Ch D 272 is one. Another is a case referred to in R. Francis, *Maxims of Equity* (1727) (at 17), in which the testator's widow was required to hold her husband's personal estate on trust for his children '*as she shall think fit*'. When she remarried, she divided the estate '*very unequally*' between the children and the court set her distribution aside (*Craker v. Parrott* (1677) 2 Chan (as 228) 355, 414).

[56] (1877) LR 2 App Cas 300, HL.   [57] Ibid. at 305.   [58] [1977] 1 WLR 1323.

[59] [1977] 1 WLR 1323 at 1325.

[60] *Re Hastings-Bass* [1975] Ch 25. In *Re Hastings-Bass* itself, the Court of Appeal refused to interfere with the trustees' decision to exercise their power of advancement by means of a sub-settlement which they had

issue on a sound basis, they might simply confirm their original decision. (Note that the rule allows the court to set aside a trustee's discretionary judgment in a particular case, but does not allow the court to replace the trustees' decision with a decision of its own.)[61] Sir Robert Walker, as he then was, suggested extra-judicially that the rule promotes practical certainty and gives trustees confidence to make decisions without fear of constant challenge.[62] His Lordship acknowledged that practical certainty may come at the cost of perfectly informed decision making and that there is a balance to be struck between the two. Whether the rule actually achieved an appropriate balance in practice was open to debate and Sir Robert Walker subsequently argued extra-judicially that the debate was in need of resolution by a superior court.[63] That resolution has since come in the decision of the Supreme Court in the twin appeals in *Futter v. HMRC Commissioners*; *Pitt v. HMRC Commissioners* (hereafter 'Futter' unless otherwise stated),[64] and specifically in the speech of Lord Walker of Gestingthorpe (the same Sir Robert Walker, as was) with whom Lord Neuberger, Lady Hale, Lord Mance, Lord Clarke, Lord Sumption, and Lord Carnwath agreed. So far as the *Hastings-Bass* rule was concerned, Lord Walker was largely in agreement with Lloyd LJ in the Court of Appeal and accordingly, on the *Hastings-Bass* aspect, his Lordship dismissed the appeals in *Futter* and *Pitt*. However, his Lordship set aside the error in *Pitt* under the court's inherent equitable jurisdiction to rectify mistakes.[65] The facts of *Futter* concern incorrect advice given by solicitors as to the capital gains tax implications of gains realized by non-resident trustees.[66] The facts of *Pitt* concerned the failure of Frenkel Topping, a firm of financial advisers professing to specialize in personal injury trusts, to take account of the inheritance tax implications of a settlement designed to hold funds for a man who, as a result of an accident, had been rendered incapable of caring for himself.

Lord Walker held that the court should not interfere with a trustee's decision except where the outcome is unauthorized by the power conferred upon the trustee.[67] In so deciding, his Lordship approved the judgment of Lightman J in *Abacus Trust Co (Isle of Man) v. Barr*,[68] where Lightman J had made the following observation:

---

not appreciated would be void for perpetuity. Lord Walker retained the description 'the rule in *Hastings-Bass*' in his speech in the Supreme Court in *Futter v. HMRC Commissioners*; *Pitt v. HMRC Commissioners* [2013] UKSC 26, but his Lordship also acknowledged (at para. [1]) that the description is a misnomer and that, if anything, the rule should be named after *Mettoy Pension Trustees Ltd v. Evans* (a case his Lordship was critical of). In *Mettoy*, Warner J had suggested that the rule requires the courts to ask three questions: 1) What were the trustees under a duty to consider? 2) Did they fail to consider it? 3) If so, what would they have done if they had considered it?   [61] *Smithson v. Hamilton* [2008] 1 WLR 1453.

[62] 'Trust principles in the pension context' in *Trends in Contemporary Trust Law* (A. J. Oakley, ed.) (Oxford: Clarendon Press, 1996) at 129.

[63] Sir R. Walker, 'The Limits of the Principle in *Re Hasting-Bass*' (2002) 4 PCB 226–40, based on a lecture given at King's College, London on 26 February 2002.   [64] [2013] UKSC 26; [2013] 2 WLR 1200.

[65] See Chapter 16.

[66] In particular, they failed to give correct advice concerning the Taxation of Chargeable Gains Act 1992, s.87.

[67] *Futter* [2013] UKSC 26; [2013] 2 WLR 1200 at para. [26].

[68] [2003] Ch 409. *Futter* [2013] UKSC 26; [2013] 2 WLR 1200 at paras [39]–[41].

...If the trustee has in accordance with his duty identified the relevant considerations and used all proper care and diligence in obtaining the relevant information and advice relating to those considerations, the trustee can be in no breach of duty and its decision cannot be impugned merely because in fact that information turns out to be partial or incorrect.

Lord Walker also approved Lloyd LJ in *Sieff v. Fox*,[69] who had drawn a 'very important distinction' between a trustee's error in going beyond the scope of a power (so-called 'excessive execution') and a trustee's error in failing to give proper consideration to relevant matters in making a decision within the scope of the relevant power (so-called 'inadequate deliberation').[70] His Lordship added that 'a fraudulent appointment (that is, one shown to have been made for a positively improper purpose) may need a separate pigeonhole somewhere between the categories of excessive execution and inadequate deliberation'.[71] His Lordship also clarified that a standard trustee exculpatory clause[72] will not apply to oust the application of the *Hastings-Bass* rule, 'if it were otherwise applicable'.[73]

The 'rule' was designed to protect trustees' decision-making from external challenge, but over time it came to be used by trustees as a way of setting aside their own decisions. In fact, the proper course for redress (where the trustees had made a genuine mistake) would be the traditional equitable remedy of rectification of mistakes.[74] On the question whether a trustee's decision is void or voidable if it falls foul of the rule in *Hastings-Bass*, Lord Walker expressed his agreement with the following part of Lloyd LJ's judgment in *Sieff v. Fox*:

> if an exercise by trustees of a discretionary power is within the terms of the power, but the trustees have in some way breached their duties in respect of that exercise, then (unless it is a case of a fraud on the power) the trustees' act is not void but it may be voidable at the instance of a beneficiary who is adversely affected.[75]

No duty to give reasons for decisions

Trustees have no duty to disclose the reasons for the decisions they reach. In *Re Beloved Wilke's Charity*,[76] the Lord Chancellor suggested that trustees would be '*most prudent and judicious*' simply to state '*that they have met and considered and come to a conclusion*'.[77] One obvious reason for this immunity is to protect trustees' decisions from constant challenge so that they may be free to manage the trust as they think fit. Other reasons include: the duty of confidentiality that the trustees owe to each beneficiary not to disclose personal information about that beneficiary to the other beneficiaries; the public interest in family harmony; and the public interest, referred to earlier, in

---

[69] *Sieff v. Fox* [2005] EWHC 1312 (Ch). Lloyd LJ sat in this case as a judge of the Chancery Division.
[70] *Futter* para. [60].   [71] *Futter* para. [62].   [72] See Chapter 13.
[73] *Futter* para. [89].   [74] See Chapter 16.   [75] *Sieff v. Fox* [2005] EWHC 1312 (Ch) at para. [99].
[76] (1851) 3 Mac & G 440 at 448.   [77] Ibid. at 448.

ensuring that people are not dissuaded from acting as trustees. According to Salmon LJ in *Re Londonderry*:[78]

> Nothing would be more likely to embitter family feelings and the relationship between the trustees and members of the family, were trustees obliged to state their reasons for the exercise of the powers entrusted to them. It might indeed be difficult to persuade any persons to act as trustees were a duty to disclose their reasons, with all the embarrassment, arguments and quarrels that might ensue, added to their present not inconsiderable burdens.[79]

However, if the trustees fail to give reasons for their decision, the court may be more likely to conclude that their decision should be struck down on the ground that no reasonable trustee could have reached it—that is, on the ground, in a word, of 'irrationality'. If the beneficiaries allege that the absence of reasons is due to the fact that the trustees had failed to exercise any discretion at all, the 'no reasonable trustee' test does not apply, but the trustees will be required to demonstrate that they had considered the matter. So held Mummery LJ in *Wight v. Olswang*,[80] where trustees had decided to sell the shares, but in the event failed to sell them:

> The beneficiaries are at least entitled to an explanation as to why the decision to sell half the shares was not implemented and, in the absence of a satisfactory explanation, to invite the court to infer that there was a dereliction of duty amounting to a breach of trust.[81]

An interesting question is how the trustees' duty to account can be reconciled with the absence of any duty to give reasons for trust decisions. The question is especially acute where the trustees' decision-making process is recorded in the trust documentation, because the trustees' duty to account extends beyond the fiduciary duty to account for unauthorized gains, to include a duty to produce full and accurate trust accounts, and trust documentation upon request.[82] The beneficiaries have a proprietary interest in trust documentation, just as they have a proprietary interest in all trust assets and so, prima facie, they are entitled to possession of trust documents on demand. However, beneficiaries' possession of trust assets is always subject to the terms of the trust and the obligations to which the trustees are subject; proprietary access to trust documentation cannot be permitted to undermine the trustees' proper discharge of their office:

> The beneficiaries' rights to inspect trust documents are now seen as better based not on equitable proprietary rights but on the beneficiaries' rights to make the trustees account for their trusteeship.[83]

In *Re Londonderry's Settlement*,[84] the Court of Appeal held that trustees are not required to disclose trust documentation that contains reasons for their decisions. Harman LJ decided that, 'if necessary', the principle of non-disclosure should override

---

[78] [1965] Ch 918.   [79] Ibid. at 937.   [80] [2001] Lloyd's Rep PN 269.   [81] Ibid at [18].

[82] *Tiger v. Barclays Bank Ltd* [1951] 2 KB 556, CA.

[83] D. Hayton, 'The irreducible core content of trusteeship' in *Trends in Contemporary Trust Law* (A. J. Oakley, ed.) (Oxford: Clarendon Press, 1996) 47 at 52, citing *Hartigan Nominees Pty Ltd v. Rydge* (1992) 29 NSWLR 405 at 432.   [84] [1964] 3 All ER 855.

the beneficiaries' entitlement to inspect trust documents. Salmon LJ even suggested that, if any part of a document contains information that the beneficiaries are not entitled to know, such a document should not be regarded as being a trust document. *Re Londonderry's* was followed in *Wilson v. Law Debenture Trust Corp plc*.[85] The facts of *Wilson* were essentially the same as those of the *Stannard* case set out in the previous section. After an employer transferred its business and its employees transferred their pensions, a member of the pension scheme issued a summons requiring his former pension trustees to disclose the basis on which they had calculated the sum to be transferred to the new pension. Rattee J dismissed the summons, holding that, in the absence of disclosure of evidence that the trustee had acted improperly, the court would not require disclosure of the basis of the trustee's discretion. In *Schmidt v. Rosewood Trust Ltd*,[86] the Privy Council held that trust beneficiaries are not entitled to disclosure of trust documents, but that disclosure may be ordered on a case-by-case basis as part of the courts' inherent jurisdiction to ensure the proper administration of trusts. In *Breakspear v. Ackland*,[87] a settlor set up a discretionary trust for the benefit of himself and his children and by a contemporaneous non-binding 'wish letter' requested that the trustees should take stated matters into account when exercising their dispositive powers. The claimants, three of the beneficiaries, asked for disclosure of the wish letter in order to evaluate their future expectations under the trust. Ordering disclosure, the Privy Council held that trustees and the court should not approach a request for disclosure of a wish letter as an issue turning on the beneficiaries' entitlement to see trust documents, but as an issue calling for the exercise of discretion on the facts of each case. It should be noted that a professional trustee may, in certain circumstances, raise professional privilege as a defence to a summons to disclose trust documents. In order to displace this professional privilege, the beneficiaries must make out a prima facie case of fraud.[88]

The duty to act fairly

Sometimes, a trustee will find himself faced with a choice between two beneficiaries, or classes of beneficiary, whose interests are in competition with each other: he cannot be completely loyal to one class of beneficiaries without prejudicing the other class. Accordingly, his duty in such a case is not one of absolute loyalty to either class, but of acting fairly in the interests of each.

The duty to act fairly comes to the fore when a trustee chooses how to invest the trust fund, so it is considered in depth in Chapter 12. In summary, beneficiaries with a present interest in possession will typically prefer investments that yield high income,

---

[85] [1995] 2 All ER 337.   [86] [2003] 2 WLR 1442, PC.
[87] [2008] EWHC 220; [2009] Ch 32, Ch D.
[88] *O'Rourke v. Darbishire* [1920] AC 581, HL.

whereas beneficiaries interested in remainder will typically prefer investments that maintain, or increase, the value of the capital. The interests of the two classes of beneficiary are therefore in competition with each other and so the trustee must make investments that are fair to both. However, fairness does not always mean equality.[89] If the life beneficiaries are closely related to the settlor and the remainder beneficiaries are distant relations, it may be that an equal balance between the interests of the life and remainder beneficiaries will be unfair.

Fair investment and the impact of The Trusts (Capital and Income) Act 2013 is discussed further in Chapter 12. Here it is worth noting that trustees' expenses, like trust investments, must be apportioned appropriately, but in relation to expenses the general rule is that expenses incurred for the benefit of both the income and capital beneficiaries should be charged against capital. Unless the trust instrument or the court otherwise directs, it is only expenses incurred exclusively for the benefit of the income beneficiaries that may be charged against income.[90]

Of course, the resolution of competing interests by reference to the underlying intentions of the settlor is only possible in trusts, such as traditional settlement trusts, in which the trust has an 'independent' settlor. In simple bare trusts of the commercial variety and in simple fiduciary relationships, the creator of the duty and the object of the duty are usually the same person. Accordingly, if the fiduciary is acting for two principals whose interests conflict, or may conflict, there is no scope to resolve the conflict by reference to a notion of 'fairness' derived by reference to the inferred intentions of a fair-minded settlor. It follows that the fiduciary must '*serve each as faithfully and loyally as if he were his only principal*'.[91] He must act '*in good faith in the interests of each and must not act with the intention of furthering the interests of one principal to the prejudice of those of the other*'.[92]

The duty to act fairly applies in the pensions context. *Edge v. Pensions Ombudsman*[93] concerned a case in which a pension fund was in surplus. The trustees decided to alter the rules of the fund so as to reduce the level of employees' contributions. The plan was to keep existing employees and attract new employees, and thereby to ensure the future viability of the pension fund. However, retired employees (pensioners) complained to the Ombudsman that the trustees had breached their trust by preferring the interests of current employees over those of current pensioners. The Ombudsman found for the pensioners, but his decision was overturned. The Court of Appeal held that it would make no sense to apply the duty of impartiality where the rules of the fund allowed the trustees a discretionary power to choose between beneficiaries for in such a case the trustees are permitted to prefer one class over another provided that in doing so they do not take into account '*irrelevant, irrational or improper factors*'.[94]

---

[89] *Per* Hoffmann J in *Nestle v. National Westminster Bank plc* (1996) 10 TLI 112 at 115.

[90] *Commissioners for HM Revenue & Customs v. Trustees of the Peter Clay Discretionary Trust* [2008] EWCA Civ 1441.   [91] Millett LJ in *Mothew* [1998] 1 Ch 1 at 19E.

[92] Ibid. at 19D and P. Finn, *Fiduciary Obligations* (Sydney: Law Book Co, 1977) at 48.

[93] [1998] Ch 512, CA.   [94] Ibid. at 533.

The duty of personal service

A corollary of the trustees' duty to make decisions on behalf of the trust is a presumption that trustees may not delegate their decision making to others. The presumption is encapsulated in the maxim *delegatus non potest delegare* ('a person to whom responsibility has been delegated has no power to delegate'). In other words, trustees are presumed to be subject to a duty of personal service. Lindley LJ expressed the duty in the following terms in *Speight v. Gaunt*:[95]

> A trustee has no business to cast upon brokers or solicitors or anybody else the duty of performing those trusts and exercising that judgment and discretion which he is bound to perform and exercise himself.[96]

Of course, that statement begs the question: *which* trusts, judgments, and discretions are trustees bound to exercise themselves? In *Speight v. Gaunt*, their Lordships accepted that it was reasonable for a trustee to employ a stockbroker to make investments as directed by the trustee, so we know that the delegation of mere ministerial acts is permitted, to the extent that such delegation is prudent. This position was confirmed by the Trustee Act 1925, which authorized trustees to employ agents to '*transact any business or do any act required to be transacted or done in the execution of the trust*' and relieved trustees of liability for the defaults of such agent employed in good faith.[97] However, the delegation of ministerial acts is not the same thing as the delegation of fiduciary discretions. So far as the delegation of discretion is concerned, the rule is that '*trustees cannot delegate unless they have authority to do so*'[98] and, in the absence of authority in the trust instrument, or the authority of the court,[99] a trustee is only permitted to delegate to the extent authorized by statute.

Statute lays down powers of collective delegation and powers of individual delegation. The former must be exercised by the trustees acting unanimously as a group; the latter may be exercised by a single trustee acting unilaterally.

Statutory powers relating to collective delegation

We have seen that the Trustee Act 1925 permitted delegation of ministerial acts, but, apart from the case of property situated abroad,[100] it granted no authority to delegate more fundamental choices relating to fund management, such as whether to increase the proportion of the fund held in bonds and whether to lease trust property instead

---

[95] (1883) LR 22 Ch D 727.
[96] Ibid. at 756, CA. This echoes *Turner v. Corney* (1841) Beav 515, *per* Lord Langdale MR at 517.
[97] Section 23(1). Repealed by the Trustee Act 2000, which now provides a far larger authority to delegate.
[98] *Pilkington v. IRC* [1964] AC 612, HL, *per* Viscount Radcliffe at 639.
[99] For example, by an order made under the Trustee Act 1925, s. 57.
[100] Trustee Act 1925, s. 23(2) (repealed).

of selling it.[101] In its Consultation Paper on trustees' powers and duties,[102] the Law Commission identified the rule against delegation of fiduciary discretions to be one of two major constraints upon the effective management of trusts (the other being the inability of trustees to vest legal title to trust property in nominees).

The report that followed the Consultation Paper identified four recent developments in the investment of shares and securities that suggested a need for wider powers of trustee delegation:[103] first, the practice of employing nominees; second, the widespread employment of discretionary fund managers; third, the introduction of the CREST system;[104] fourth, the introduction of five-day rolling settlement in relation to the purchase of shares and securities on the London Stock Exchange. The report even suggested that the then existing restrictive rules on delegation '*may force trustees to commit breaches of trust in order to achieve the most effective administration*';[105] it therefore recommended that trustees should be permitted to delegate their fiduciary discretions, with the exceptions of discretion relating to '*the distribution of the income or capital of the trust for the benefit of its objects*'[106] and discretion relating to the appointment or replacement of trustees.[107]

Delegable functions

The Law Commission recommendations were enacted as the Trustee Act 2000, which came into force on 1 February 2001. Part IV of the Act reforms the law relating to collective delegation in order to facilitate the liberalized investment scheme that is the main aim of the Act. It divides trustee functions into those that are delegable and those that are non-delegable, and provides that trustees may authorize any person to exercise any, or all, of their delegable functions as their agent, subject to the rest of Part IV[108] and subject to other legislation, or the trust instrument, providing to the contrary.[109] 'Non-delegable' functions are listed as follows:[110] the distribution of trust assets;[111] the choice whether to meet the financial commitments of the trust out of income or capital; the appointment of trustees, agents, nominees, and custodians.[112] All other trustee functions are now delegable.[113]

In the case of charitable trusts, on the other hand, all trustee functions are non-delegable, with the exception of the following, which are delegable: investment (which includes the management of land acquired as an investment); the practical

---

[101] *Robson v. Flight* (1865) 4 De GJ & S 608 at 614.

[102] Law Commission for England and Wales, Consultation Paper No. 146, *Trustees' Powers and Duties* (1997). [103] Report No. 260, *Trustees' Powers and Duties* (1999) para. 2.8.

[104] Computerized or Electronic Share Transfer system.

[105] Report No. 260, *Trustees' Powers and Duties* (1999) para. 4.6. [106] Ibid. para. 4.9(2).

[107] Ibid. para. 4.9(1). [108] Trustee Act 2000, s. 11(1). [109] Section 26(b).

[110] In s. 11(2)(a)–(d). [111] For example, under a discretionary trust, see Chapter 3.

[112] Trustee Act 2000, s. 24 provides that '[a] *failure by the trustees to act within the limits of the powers conferred by this Part (a) in authorising a person to exercise a function of theirs as an agent, or (b) in appointing a person to act as a nominee or custodian, does not invalidate the authorisation or appointment*'.

[113] Section 11(1).

implementation of decisions made by trustees;[114] fund-raising.[115] 'Fund raising' does not include the production of profits from a trade, even though the trade is an integral part of the trust's charitable purpose. A trade is 'integral' in this sense if the profits are applied solely to the purposes of the trust and the trade is exercised in the course of carrying out a primary purpose of the trust, or if the work in connection with the trade is mainly carried out by beneficiaries of the trust.[116] (A charity—such as Oxfam— that raises some of its funds through high-street trade would fall within this category.) Other functions may be delegated only if the Secretary of State makes an order granting the necessary authority.[117]

Choice of agent

The fiduciary duty and the duty of care apply to the appointment and supervision of agents, just as they apply to the exercise of every other trust power. So, unless authorized to do so, a trustee must not appoint his own firm to act as an agent to the trust and, if he does, he will be subject to a fiduciary duty to account for any commission or other such gains.[118] The trustees must also choose an agent suited to the task[119] and keep a watchful eye on his activities,[120] or they may be liable for breach of their duty of care.

Persons who may be appointed as agents to the trust include current nominees or custodians of the trust,[121] and even one or more of the trustees themselves,[122] but beneficiaries (including those who are also trustees) may not be appointed,[123] unless the trust instrument provides to the contrary. The appointment of two (or more) persons as agents is only permitted when they are to exercise their functions jointly.[124]

In the context of the investment of pension funds, it has recently been proposed that the employment of agents should be opened up to competitive tender and that pension trustees '*should be prepared to pay sufficient fees for each service to attract a broad range of kinds of potential provider*', bearing in mind that '*the level of fees should properly relate to the contribution they can make to the fund's investment performance*'.[125]

Terms of appointment

Trustees may authorize an agent, nominee, or custodian (hereafter the term 'agent' can be taken to include nominees and custodians if the context permits) to act on such terms as they may determine, even with regard to remuneration,[126] and if he is engaged on terms entitling him to be remunerated,[127] the trustees may pay him such remuneration as is reasonable in the circumstances.[128] The trustees may also reimburse all of the agent's expenses properly incurred by him in exercising functions as an agent.[129]

---

[114] Section 11(3).   [115] Section 11(3)(c).   [116] Section 11(4).   [117] Section 11(3)(d).
[118] *Williams v. Barton* [1927] 2 Ch 9, Ch D.   [119] *Fry v. Tapson* (1884) LR 28 Ch D 268.
[120] *Speight v. Gaunt* (1883) LR 22 Ch D 727, CA.
[121] Trustee Act 2000, s. 12(4). The terms 'nominee' and 'custodian' are explained later.
[122] Section 12(1).   [123] Section 12(3).   [124] Section 12(2).
[125] *Myners Review: Institutional Investment in the UK*, 6 March 2001, para. 80 and 'Recommendations'.
[126] Trustee Act 2000, s. 14.   [127] Section 32(2)(a).   [128] Section 32(2)(b).   [129] Section 32.

There are, however, certain terms that, according to s. 14 of the Trustee Act 2000, trustees are not permitted to include unless '*it is reasonably necessary for them to do so*'.[130] The prohibited terms are those that would permit agents to appoint substitutes,[131] to restrict the agent's (or substitute's) liability,[132] or to permit the agent to act in circumstances that are capable of giving rise to a conflict of interest.[133] The fear must be that trustees will not struggle to satisfy the requirement of 'reasonable necessity', raising the spectre of well-paid sub-agents with limited liability acting in positions of conflict. It is clear that the statutory *powers* of delegation are subject to express contrary provision in the trust instrument,[134] but it is debatable whether the s. 14 *limitations* on the powers of delegation are so subject.

The Act does not allow agents a completely free hand in relation to 'asset management functions'—a description that covers the investment, acquisition, and management of trust property, including the creation or disposition of interests in such property.[135] The Act provides that trustees are not permitted to authorize an agent to exercise asset management functions except by an agreement evidenced in writing, in which the agent undertakes to comply with a 'policy statement' provided by the trustees. The trustees are obliged to provide the statement as a guide to the exercise of asset management functions in the best interests of the trust.[136] The trustee may revise the policy statement from time to time[137] and the agent must agree to be bound by any such revisions.[138] The policy statement (and any revisions of it) must be in writing or evidenced in writing.[139] A clue to the appropriate content of the policy statement is provided by s. 35 of the Pensions Act 1995, which provides that the trustees of a pension scheme must ensure that there is prepared, maintained, and, from time to time, revised a written statement covering their policy regarding a number of investment matters. Those matters include the kinds of investments to be held, the balance between different kinds of investments, the expected return on investments, the realization of investments, and the levels of risk.

What is not entirely clear from the wording of the Act is whether the requirement to produce written policy statements applies to trustees who, under a power granted by their trust instrument, had already delegated asset management functions to agents prior to the Act coming into force. Until the point is resolved, such trustees should err on the side of caution and assume that the requirement applies to them directly, because, even if it does not, courts will almost certainly come to regard policy statements as an essential feature of prudent investment. This is especially the case when the trust has appointed a discretionary fund manager, for such a person acts on his own discretion without making continual reference to the client. The appointment of a discretionary fund manager is a practical necessity when the trust fund is very large,[140] and

---

[130] Section 14(2).   [131] Section 14(3)(a).   [132] Section 14(3)(b).   [133] Section 14(3)(c).
[134] Section 26(b).   [135] Section 15(5).   [136] Section 15(1).   [137] Section 22.
[138] Section 15(2)(b)(ii).   [139] Section 15(4).
[140] *Steel v. Wellcome Custodian Trustees Ltd* [1988] 1 WLR 167 at 174.

the appointment of professional fund managers in relation to the investment of pension funds is now a legal requirement.[141]

Supervision of agents and review of appointments

Trustees will be liable for the default of any agent[142] if they failed to meet the required standard of care[143] when choosing the agent and arranging the appointment.[144] They will also be liable if they fail to discharge their duty of care as regards the supervision and control of their agents, because the Act requires trustees to review the arrangements under which their agents act and how those arrangements are being put into effect.[145] This includes a duty to assess whether the current policy statement on asset management is being complied with.[146] If circumstances make it appropriate to do so, trustees must consider whether to exercise any power they might have to give directions to their agents, or even to revoke their agents' authority.[147] The trustees must exercise their powers of intervention whenever appropriate.[148] However, apart from these circumstances outlined, trustees will not be liable for the defaults of their agents; nor will trustees be liable for the defaults of substitutes appointed by their agents, unless the trustee was careless when supervising the agents or careless when agreeing to allow the appointment of substitutes in the first place.[149]

Given that trustees must supervise their agents, it makes sense that they should be aware of the restrictions to which their agents are subject in the exercise of delegated functions. The trust instrument may impose certain restrictions, such as requiring that an agent report to the trustees at given intervals. However, even if there are no restrictions apparent from the trust instrument, agents will be subject to statutory restrictions specific to the particular functions they are to carry out.[150] So, for example, if a person is authorized to *invest* on behalf of the trust, that person is subject to the usual statutory requirements relating to *investment*, such as the requirement to invest in accordance with the statutory '*standard investment criteria*'.[151] It follows that, if a trustee appoints a discretionary fund manager, any term purporting to free the manager from 'fiduciary or equitable duties' will be ineffective.[152]

---

[141] Financial Services Act 1986, s. 191. *Allan v. Rea Bros Trustees Ltd* [2002] EWCA Civ 85, CA.

[142] Which term, for present purposes, includes a nominee or custodian.

[143] Trustee Act 2000, Sch. 1, para. 3.

[144] Section 23(1)(a). See the facts of *Fry v. Tapson* (1884) LR 28 Ch D 268.

[145] Section 22(1)(a).   [146] Section 22(2)(c).   [147] Section 22(1)(b).

[148] Section 22(1)(c). The sole trustee in *Re Lucking's WT* [1968] 1 WLR 866 would today be liable under this subsection. He had appointed a director to the board of a company in which the trust had a majority shareholding and signed blank cheques payable to the director to cover his expenses. It became apparent that the director was making withdrawals for his own ends, but the trustee took no remedial action. The director was declared bankrupt, owing £15,890 to the company. The trustee, himself a beneficiary, was held liable to compensate the other beneficiaries for the devaluation in the shares owned by the trust.

[149] Trustee Act 2000, s. 23(2).   [150] Section 13.   [151] See Chapter 12.

[152] Terms of this sort are apparently quite common in such agreements (Law Commission Consultation Paper No. 146 *Trustees' Powers and Duties* (1997) para. 2.18 ff).

Nominees and custodians

A nominee is a person in whose name trust assets are vested without any intention that that person should become a trustee—one estimate suggests that over half (by value) of the shares in the UK are held in this way.[153] When a nominee holds legal title to trust assets, his title is, quite literally, nominal: he holds it purely for administrative purposes. Accordingly, the main benefit of using a nominee is speedy and smooth administration, especially in relation to share dealings; a nominee is spared the need to obtain the trustees' signatures and authority prior to dealing.

A custodian is a person who 'undertakes the safe custody of the assets or of any documents or records concerning the assets'.[154] According to HM Treasury, 'custody is now an integral part of modern investment business and is often seen as best practice'.[155] Some trusts, including charitable trusts in which the assets are vested in the official custodian for charities, had custodian trustees before the coming into force of the Trustee Act 2000, and many trust instruments expressly grant a power to appoint nominees and custodians. The Act now extends that power to trustees generally.[156] In fact, if the trust holds 'bearer securities' (securities payable to the bearer), it is now a requirement that a custodian be appointed.[157]

The appointment of a nominee must be in writing, or evidenced in writing, and may relate to such assets as the trustees determine. The trustees are authorized to take such steps as are necessary to vest the relevant assets in the nominee.[158] The appointment of a custodian must also be in writing or evidenced in writing.[159] Section 19 states that the only persons permitted to act as nominees or custodians to trusts are corporations controlled[160] by the trustees, corporations recognized under the Administration of Justice Act 1985,[161] and persons whose business includes acting as a nominee or custodian. Subject to these limitations, trustees may appoint one of their number to act as a nominee or custodian, or two (or more) of their number to act jointly in that capacity, and they may appoint the same person (or persons) to be nominee, custodian, and agent.[162] Very often, the nominee chosen by the trustees will be the trustee's broker or a company controlled by the broker.

When a trustee vests legal title to trust property in a nominee, it appears, at first sight, that the trustee no longer has any interest in the trust property: he never had any

---

[153] Central Statistical Office, *Share Ownership: The Share Register Survey Report* 1993, para. 3.1. On nominees generally, see M. Heneker, 'Shares in nominee names' (1995) 139 SJ 531; A. Butterworth, 'Regulating custody' (1996) 9 CM Monitor 78.

[154] Trustee Act 2000, s. 17(2).

[155] *Custody: A Consultation Document*, June 1996, para. 12(c). This paper sought views on what subsequently became the Financial Services Act 1986 (Extension of Scope of Act) Order 1996 (SI 1996, No. 2958). See, generally, J. Benjamin, *The Law of Global Custody* (1996) ch. 11 at 148, 151, 160.

[156] Sections 16–20.

[157] Unless the trust instrument or other legislation provides to the contrary in relation to a particular trust (s. 18).

[158] Section 16.   [159] Section 17.

[160] To be determined in accordance with the Income and Corporation Taxes Act 1988, s. 840.

[161] Trustee Act 2000, s. 9.   [162] Section 20.

equitable entitlement and he has transferred his legal entitlement. However, subject to contrary expression in the trust instrument, the trustee must retain those functions that statute identifies to be non-delegable. So, by virtue of the statute, the trustee retains his status as trustee despite the transfer of formal legal ownership to the nominee. Furthermore, the trustee has a right, normally a contractual right, to recover the trust property from the nominee and that right is a chose in action that is itself a trust asset. So the trustee holds his right against the nominee on trust for the beneficiaries.[163] In the event of the nominee becoming insolvent, the trustee's chose in action against the nominee will be a mere personal claim against the nominee, which has no priority over other personal claims against the nominee. However, the trustee's residual trust (comprising his non-delegated and statutorily non-delegable trust functions) does confer priority on the trustee ahead of persons with mere personal claims against the nominee.

Delegation risk

There are several risks associated with the use of nominees and custodians. They include: theft; misappropriation through forgery and fraud; wilful or accidental destruction of trust property; loss in transit; unauthorized delivery to a third party; misapplication of trust investments to satisfy obligations due to the nominee's or custodian's other clients; unauthorized use of trust investments for the nominee's or custodian's own purposes; failure to maintain proper records; mixing trust investments with those of the nominee or custodian, so as to place them at risk in the event of the insolvency of the nominee or custodian.[164]

To these drawbacks can be added the loss of shareholder rights, with the reduced opportunity for corporate governance that such loss entails:[165]

> The investor's name does not appear on the register, the broker rather than the investor is entitled to receive the company's annual report and accounts and the shareholder perks, and it is the broker that is entitled to attend and vote at company meetings.[166]

A balance must always be struck between managing the risks inherent in the investment of a trust fund, what we might call 'investment risks',[167] and the risks inherent in appointing expert agents to manage investments, what we might call 'agency risks'. The Trustee Act 2000 anticipated that balance between investment risks and agency risks would be achieved by increasing agency risks through the relaxation of the rule against trustee delegation, but by the time the Act came into force many professional fund managers had decided to move their funds into lower risk investments due to the poor

---

[163] Law Commission Consultation Paper No. 146 *Trustees' Powers and Duties* (1997) note 67.

[164] Law Commission Report No. 260 *Trustees' Powers and Duties* (1999) para. 2.14.

[165] Ibid. para. 2.16. In November 1996, the Department of Trade and Industry and HM Treasury issued a joint consultative document, *Private Shareholders: Corporate Governance Rights*. For the significance of corporate governance to ethical investment, see Chapter 12.

[166] B. Ludlow, 'CREST goes active' (1996) 9 CM 13 at 14.

[167] Different types of investment risk are examined in Chapter 12.

performance of the stock market. That trend has continued until the time of writing, so it appears in retrospect that the Act may have increased agency risks unnecessarily.

Statutory powers relating to individual delegation

Unilateral delegation by a single trustee is useful in the event of a trustee becoming ill or being absent abroad. Section 25 of the Trustee Act 1925 provides that an individual trustee may delegate the execution or exercise of all, or any, of the trusts, powers, and discretions vested in him as trustee or in him as one of a body of trustees. Because this power permits a trustee to delegate even the most basic of his trust discretions, s. 25 also lays down strict limitations on its exercise. In summary, they are:

1. Delegation must be by power of attorney, which that means the trustee making the delegation must execute a formal deed.

2. The period of the delegation may not exceed 12 months.

3. The individual trustee making the delegation should give notice to the other trustees of that fact.[168]

4. An individual trustee who delegates in this way remains liable for the acts and defaults of his attorney as if they were the trustee's own acts and defaults.[169]

Insurance

As a general rule, trustees do not have a duty to insure trust property against events, such as theft, fire, and flood, by purchasing insurance cover in the usual way. They do, however, have a power to take out such insurance and to pay premiums out of the trust funds,[170] and their statutory duty of care extends to any exercise of this statutory power, so they may be personally liable if the chosen insurance is inadequate or inappropriate.[171]

Trustees are well advised to take out private insurance, but the Financial Services Compensation Scheme provides insurance of last resort to customers of authorized investment firms when the firms become insolvent, or otherwise go out of business. Beneficiaries of trusts will qualify as 'customers' provided that they would have qualified as private customers if they had invested directly.[172] The Financial Services Act 1986 recognizes two types of 'private customer': the 'small business investor' is one—trustees fall within this class;[173] the other is 'an individual... who is not acting in the course of carrying on investment business'[174]—beneficiaries fall into this class. However,

---

[168] Trustee Act 1925, s. 25(1), as amended by the Trustee Delegation Act 1999, s. 5.

[169] Ibid. s. 5(7).   [170] Trustee Act 2000, s. 34, replacing the Trustee Act 1925, s. 19.

[171] Trustee Act 2000, s. 2 and Sch. 1, para. 5.

[172] Part II of the Financial Services (Compensation of Investors) Rules 1994. The maximum level of compensation under the scheme is currently £48,000.

[173] Unless the trust has assets that currently exceed £10m or have done so during the previous two years.

[174] Financial Services Authority, *Financial Services Core Glossary*, 3rd edn (1991).

compensation is only available to the extent that loss can be proven, and even then it is usually only available in cases of insolvency.[175]

Filling the office of trustee

If the reader wonders why a whole section of this chapter is devoted to the topic of trustee appointments, the answer is simple: if a mistake is made in this practical aspect of trusts law, the consequences can be disastrous. The recent case of *Jasmine Trustees v. Wells & Hinds*[176] illustrates the point. The case, which was a professional negligence action brought against various solicitors' firms, arose from a 1982 deed of appointment and retirement of trustees that appointed a Mr Thornton and a trust company to act as new trustees. The new trustees were based in the Isle of Man and that was the problem. In 1982, trustees could retire, provided that the trustees they left behind were at least two humans or one trust corporation.[177] Unfortunately, in this case, the retiring trustees left behind one human and one trust company, which (because it was incorporated outside the EU) could not be regarded as a trust corporation. The retirement of the trustees had been invalid and the retired trustees continued to be liable for trust matters.[178] The knock-on effect of the new trustees being unaware of the fact that the trust was now invalid in the UK was to render subsequent trustees appointments void. The trustees might have hoped that this would get them off the hook, but even though they were not true trustees, they continued to be liable to the trust as 'trustees *de son tort*'[179] and liable to pay tax on the trust (which is why the *Jasmine* case was brought). They could also, conceivably, have been required to account for two decades of wrongfully received remuneration, plus compound interest, and without any hope of relief from liability. The lesson is never to accept appointment to the office of trustee without first checking that all trustees have been correctly appointed in the past. If an error is found at any stage, all relevant parties, if living, might be persuaded to correct the error by mutual deed.[180] Failing that, the court should be called upon to rectify the situation to whatever extent it can.

Given the onerous duties of trusteeship and the potentially serious consequences of breaching those duties, one would be forgiven for thinking that neither 'love nor money' could tempt someone to be a trustee. As Lord Hardwicke LC observed long ago, the office of trustee '*is attended with no small degree of trouble*', so that '*it is an act of great kindness in anyone to accept it*'.[181] In fact, if nobody can be found to accept trusteeship out of love, there will invariably be somebody willing to accept it for money.[182] There

---

[175] Rule 2.01.   [176] [2007] EWHC 38 (Ch).   [177] Section 37(1)(c), Trustee Act 1925.

[178] Section 37(1)(c) has since been amended, so this particular case would not have arisen had the deed of appointment and retirement been made today.   [179] See Chapter 15.

[180] J. Morris and C. O'Sullivan '*Jasmine* trustees: tangles in the trusteeship chain—Part 1' (2007) 5 PCB 347.

[181] *Knight v. Earl of Plymouth* (1747) 1 Dick 120, *per* Lord Hardwicke LC at 126–7.

[182] '[H]*uman goodwill and the profit motive between them can be relied upon to produce a supply of people prima facie willing to be trustees*': S. Gardner, *Introduction to the Law of Trusts* (Oxford: Clarendon Press, 1990) at 165.

may be few people nowadays who are willing and able to devote their time gratuitously to the complex business of trusteeship[183] (although one study has suggested that '*private individuals who agree to act as trustees usually regard it as an honour and not as a chore*'),[184] but there is no shortage of trust corporations and professional trustees willing to undertake trusteeship for the right price.

When the original trustees have been appointed and the trust has been fully constituted, the trust will not fail even if all of the trustees are subsequently removed from office or die (or, in the case of trust corporations, are dissolved). Trustees hold their legal title as joint tenants, which means that they each own the whole of the legal title; legal title is never shared. The distinguishing feature of a joint tenancy is that, when a joint tenant dies, the surviving joint tenant, or joint tenants, continue to own the whole land by 'right of survivorship'. It is said that a trust will never fail for want of a trustee and that, as a last resort, '*the court itself can execute the trust*'.[185]

Capacity to act as a trustee

Capacity means '*legal competency or qualification*'.[186] A human person will lack capacity to act as a trustee if he is an infant[187] or '*lacks mental capacity*' so to act.[188] In the case of an express trust, an infant cannot be appointed to the office of trustee[189] and can be removed if so appointed.[190] In the case of a non-express trust, such as a resulting or constructive trust, an infant may become a trustee of personal property, but not of land.[191] Any attempt to convey legal title in land to a minor will operate as a declaration of trust under which the transferor becomes the trustee and the infant transferee becomes the beneficiary,[192] although if land is conveyed jointly to an infant and an adult, the adult will take the legal title on trust for himself and the infant.[193]

A corporate person will lack capacity to act as a trustee unless it is authorized to act as such by the legal documentation by which it is constituted. The objects clause in a company's memorandum of association is the place that one would typically expect to find such authority. It should be noted that the description 'trust corporation', should be reserved for particular types of corporate trustees. When judges refer to 'trust corporations' they are usually referring to corporate trustees that carry out trust business for profit and advertise their services. There is nothing to prevent the appointment of such trust corporations and human trustees to the same trust.[194] When statutes refer to 'trust corporations', they are usually referring to corporate trustees, such as the Public Trustee,[195]

---

[183] G. W. Keeton, 'Modern developments in the law of trusts' (1971) NI LQ at 13.

[184] C. Bell, 'Some reflections on choosing trustees' (1988) January TL&P 86.

[185] Lord Eldon LC in *Morice v. Bishop of Durham* (1805) 10 Ves 539.   [186] *Oxford English Dictionary*.

[187] A person who has not attained 18 years of age (known as the age of majority): Family Law Reform Act 1969.

[188] Mental Capacity Act 2005, Sch. 6, para. 3(3) (which came into force on 1 October 2007).

[189] Law of Property Act 1925, s. 20.   [190] See s. 36(1) later in the chapter.

[191] Law of Property Act 1925, s. 1(6).

[192] Trusts of Land and Appointment of Trustees Act 1996, Sch. 1, para. 1.   [193] Paragraph 2.

[194] See later.   [195] Section 4(3).

trustees appointed under the Public Trustee Act 1906,[196] trustees appointed as custodian trustees under the Public Trustee Rules 1912,[197] and trustees in bankruptcy—in other words, to corporate trustees with a public dimension to their trust.

The number of trustees

Subject to special statutory exceptions, the maximum number of trustees of any 'trust of land'[198] created after 1925 is four.[199] The special statutory exceptions include trusts established for charitable, ecclesiastical, or public purposes.[200] In such cases, there is no specified maximum number of trustees. Neither is there a specified maximum number of trustees for a trust of pure personalty, although it is ill advised ever to appoint more than four trustees to a private trust. This is not merely because the trustees may wish to acquire land at some point, but because the greater the number of trustees, the harder it will be to achieve the required unanimity in the exercise of trust powers.

A trust will not fail for want of a trustee

More pertinent than the maximum permitted number of trustees is the minimum per-mitted number of trustees. In accordance with the maxim 'a trust does not fail for want of a trustee', a trust can, in theory, *exist* without any identified trustee, but it cannot be *fulfilled* without at least one trustee. Indeed, it is advisable to have at least two trustees or a trust corporation wherever the trust assets include, or might in the future include, land. This is because of the statutory rule that a purchaser of land who pays purchase monies to all the trustees of the land need not be concerned with any beneficial interests under trusts of that land, provided that he pays the trust monies to at least two trustees or a trust corporation.[201]

The right of survivorship

Where there are two or more trustees, they will hold the legal title to the trust property as joint tenants, so that, if one dies (or, in the case of a corporation, is dissolved), legal title will remain vested in the surviving trustees by 'right of survivorship'. The 'right of survivorship' has at least two significant advantages: first, there is no need to vest the trust property in the surviving trustees every time a trustee dies; second, there is no question of the deceased trustee disposing of legal title by his will, because trusteeship cannot be inherited.

Disclaimer of the trust

A person nominated to be a trustee of an express trust should disclaim the trust at the earliest opportunity if he does not wish to accept office. The disclaimer will ideally be

---

[196] Rule 30. One example is corporate trustee of a pension fund (r. 30(11)).

[197] Bodies Corporate (Joint Tenancy) Act 1899; Trustee Act 1925, s. 42.

[198] That is, a trust comprising or including land—Trusts of Land Act and Appointment of Trustees 1996, s. 1.

[199] Trustee Act 1925, s. 34(2).   [200] Ibid. s. 34(3).

[201] Law of Property Act 1925, ss. 2 and 27, etc. The purchaser is said to 'overreach' beneficial interests in the land.

made in the form of a deed. If the trustee acts in performance of the trust, it will then be too late to disclaim. Even if the intended trustee is inactive, there is a risk that he will be said to have accepted trusteeship by acquiescence if he stands by while trust business is conducted in his name.[202]

No partial disclaimer

A trustee is not permitted to '*accept the office as to some part of the estate and not accept it as to the rest*'. This is how Lindley LJ expressed the rule in a case in which a trustee of real and personal property, some existing in England and some abroad, purported to disclaim the trust except as to the property abroad.[203] The main reason for the rule against partial disclaimer is to provide certainty to persons who purchase trust property from the trustees.

Failure of the trust due to disclaimer

There are two types of situation in which a trust will fail if the intended 'trustee' disclaims the trusteeship. If this happens, the trust is said to have been void *ab initio*, which means that it is treated as never having come into being. This does not infringe the maxim 'a trust does not fail for want of a trustee', because that maxim only applies to trusts which have been successfully created.

The first situation arises when it is prerequisite to the existence of the trust that a particular named trustee accepts office. As Buckley J held in *Re Lysaght*:[204]

> If it is of the essence of a trust that the trustees selected by the settlor and no one else shall act as the trustees of it and those trustees cannot or will not undertake the office, the trust must fail.[205]

In that case, money had been endowed on the Royal College of Surgeons to fund a studentship in medicine for the sons of male medical practitioners, provided that the students were 'not of the Jewish or Roman Catholic faith'. The Royal College objected to the religious limitations and declined the trusts subject to the removal of the 'invidious' proviso. No body other than the Royal College had authority to train doctors, so the judge held that the trust had failed and would have to be applied to charitable purposes as near as possible in kind to those intended by the donor.[206] In the event, the 'next-best' charitable purpose was to fund a studentship at the Royal College, but with the invidious religious limitations removed.

The second situation arises when an *inter vivos* trust is disclaimed before it is fully constituted. Apart from cases in which a settlor declares himself to be a trustee, an *inter vivos* trust is not fully constituted until the trust property has been transferred to the trustees. From this, it ought to follow that an *inter vivos* trust will be void *ab initio* if the trustees disclaim the trust before the trust property is transferred to them.[207] However,

---

[202] *Montford v. Cadogan* (1810) 17 Ves Jr 485.
[203] *Re Lord and Fullerton's Contract* [1896] 1 Ch 228, CA at 232.   [204] [1966] 1 Ch 191, Ch D.
[205] [1966] 1 Ch 191, *per* Buckley J at 207A.   [206] According to a doctrine called cy-près (see Chapter 7).
[207] P. Matthews, 'The constitution of disclaimed trusts *inter vivos*' (1981) 45 Conv 141.

we know that judges sometimes take a pragmatic approach to the constitution of trusts in order to give effect to the settlor's basic intentions.[208] So in *Mallott v. Wilson*,[209] where the trustee disclaimed the trust 'as soon as he heard of it' and the trust property was never transferred to him, the judge decided that the trust had been valid until it was disclaimed. It could therefore take effect with a new trustee.

Replacement and additional trustees

The Trustee Act 1925 provides that, whenever a trustee dies, remains out of the UK for more than 12 months, desires to be discharged, refuses to act, is unfit to act, or is incapable of acting, replacement trustees may be appointed by writing.[210] Replacement trustees may also be appointed if a trustee is removed under a power contained in the trust instrument.[211] The instrument by which a replacement trustee is appointed should state the name of the former trustee and the reason why he was replaced. Such statements are conclusive evidence in favour of a person who purchases land from the trust.[212]

Subject to the usual restrictions on the maximum number of trustees, a trustee may be replaced by one new trustee or by more than one new trustee.[213] However, the statute does not permit the appointment of a person to act as the sole trustee of a trust, unless it is a trust corporation or otherwise able to give valid receipts for all capital money arising under the trust.

Who may appoint trustees?

The trust instrument might nominate a person or persons for the express purpose of appointing new trustees.[214] This is frequently the case in large institutional trusts, such as pension funds and charitable trusts. However, the extent of the nominee's authority is determined by the express wording of the instrument.[215] So, if the clause nominates X as the person able to appoint trustees 'in the event of the death of any of the current trustees', X has no power to appoint new trustees on the occurrence of the other events listed in s. 36 (bankruptcy, retirement, and so on). An infant may be nominated to exercise the power of appointing new trustees even though an infant cannot act as a trustee, but an appointment made by an infant is liable to be set aside if the appointment is prejudicial to the infant, or could affect her interest under the trust, or is otherwise imprudent.[216]

If there is no such person nominated for the purpose of appointing trustees, then the beneficiaries—if they are of full age and capacity, and are together absolutely entitled to the trust property—have the power to appoint new trustees. The beneficiaries may, in writing, direct the existing trustees (or, if there are none, the personal representatives

---

[208] See Chapter 4.   [209] [1903] 2 Ch 494.

[210] Trustee Act 1925, s. 36(1), although if a trustee is incapable within the meaning of the Mental Capacity Act 2005, and is also entitled to a beneficial interest in possession, no replacement trustee may be appointed without the leave of the authority having jurisdiction under the Mental Capacity Act 2005 (Trustee Act 1925, s. 36(9)).

[211] Trustee Act 1925, s. 36(2).   [212] Ibid. s. 38(1).   [213] Ibid. s. 36(1).   [214] Ibid. s. 36(1)(a).

[215] *Re Wheeler* [1896] 1 Ch 315.   [216] *Re Parsons* [1940] 1 Ch 973.

of the last surviving trustee) to appoint by writing such person or persons as they specify.[217] Where a trustee lacks capacity (within the meaning of the Mental Capacity Act 2005), the beneficiaries may give a similar written direction to that trustee's receiver or attorney.[218]

If there is no person nominated for the purpose of appointing trustees, or if that person is unable or unwilling to act and if the beneficiaries do not direct an appointment,[219] then the power to appoint replacement trustees lies with the surviving or continuing trustees. If all of the trustees have died, the power to appoint replacement trustees lies with the personal representatives of whichever trustee died last.[220] This introduces the possibility that, when a trustee nominated in a will dies before the testator, the power to appoint trustees might pass to the personal representatives of the nominated trustee, even though the nominated trustee never actually assumed office.[221]

If a trustee lacks capacity (within the meaning of the Mental Capacity Act 2005) to exercise his functions as trustee, *and* there is no person who is entitled, willing, and able to appoint a trustee in place of him under s. 36(1) of the Trustee Act 1925, *and* the beneficiaries under the trust are of full age and capacity, *and* (taken together) are absolutely entitled to the property subject to the trust, the beneficiaries may give a written direction to appoint a specified person in place of the incapable trustee. Such a direction may be given to a deputy appointed for the trustee by the Court of Protection, an attorney acting for him under the authority of an enduring power of attorney or lasting power of attorney registered under the Mental Capacity Act 2005, or a person authorized for the purpose by the Court of Protection.[222]

The appointment of additional trustees

So far, we have been considering the appointment of trustees as replacements for former trustees, but sometimes it will be expedient to appoint additional trustees without replacing any of the existing trustees. Such 'additional trustees' may be appointed by writing where, in the case of any trust, there are currently not more than three trustees.[223] The total number of trustees after additions cannot exceed four.

Replacement and additional trustees have the same powers, authorities, and discretions, and may, in all respects, act as if they had been originally appointed trustees by the trust instrument.[224]

Fiduciary nature of the power

The power to appoint new trustees is a fiduciary power, which means that it must be exercised exclusively for the benefit of the beneficiaries. Prima facie, this does not

---

[217] Trusts of Land etc. Act 1996, s. 19.   [218] Ibid. s. 20, as amended.
[219] Under s. 19 or 20 of the 1996 Act.   [220] Section 36(1)(b).   [221] Section 36(8).
[222] Section 20 of the Trusts of Land and Appointment of Trustees Act 1996 (as amended by the Mental Capacity Act 2005).
[223] Section 36(6), as amended by the Trusts of Land and Appointment of Trustees Act 1996, s. 25(1), Sch. 3, para. 3(11).   [224] Section 36(7).

prevent the holder of the power appointing himself to be a replacement trustee, because trusteeship confers no benefit on the trustee,[225] but self-appointment ought properly to be reserved to exceptional cases. Be that as it may, the holder of the power must never appoint himself to be an *additional* trustee in any case in which the settlor originally appointed fewer than the maximum number of trustees. The reason is simple: the nominated appointer cannot appoint himself to be a trustee when the settlor clearly intended that the nominated appointer should not be a trustee.[226]

Appointment of new trustees by the court

Whenever it is expedient to appoint a new trustee or new trustees, and it is found to be inexpedient, difficult, or impracticable to do so without the assistance of the court, s. 41 of the Trustee Act 1925 authorizes the court to appoint a new trustee with, or without, replacing the existing trustees;[227] indeed, it may be that there is no existing trustee. A trustee appointed by the court may act in every respect just as if they were one of the original trustees.[228]

Situations in which it might be inexpedient for a trustee to be appointed without the assistance of the court include the liquidation or dissolution of a trust corporation, the bankruptcy, incapacity or bodily infirmity[229] of a human trustee, and the inability of the persons nominated to appoint new trustees to agree upon an appointment.[230] This list is not exhaustive. In *Re May's Will Trusts*,[231] a trustee was trapped in territory occupied by the Germans during World War II, but the existing trustees had no authority to replace her under s. 36, because she was not deemed to be 'incapable' in the s. 36 sense. It was therefore inexpedient to appoint a replacement trustee without the court's assistance.

A factor that the court will consider when appointing a trustee under s. 41 is the intentions of the settlor. If the settlor clearly (whether expressly or implicitly) disapproved of a certain person acting as his trustee, the court will not appoint him.[232] Nor will the court appoint a person whose appointment might be expected to impede the efficient and fair administration of the trust. Hence the court is careful not to appoint a trustee who is supported by some of the beneficiaries, but opposed by others.[233] Likewise, the court inclines against the appointment of a beneficiary or a beneficiary's spouse to the office of trustee.[234] However, if the current trustee or trustees unreasonably refuse to cooperate with a new trustee whose appointment is proposed by the court, the court might proceed with the appointment and remove the current trustees in order to ensure that the trust is properly administered.[235] The courts are disinclined to appoint a person, no matter how honest, to be the sole trustee of a valuable fund.[236]

---

[225] With the exception, of course, of trustee remuneration, if that is available.
[226] *Re Power's Settlement Trusts* [1951] 1 Ch 1074.
[227] Subject to the usual maximum number of trustees.   [228] Trustee Act 1925, s. 43.
[229] *Re Lemann's Trust* (1883) LR 22 Ch D 633.
[230] As occurred in *Re Tempest* (1866) LR 1 Ch App 485.   [231] [1941] Ch 109.
[232] *Re Tempest* (1866) LR 1 Ch App 485 at 487.   [233] Ibid. at 487–8.
[234] *Re Kemp's Settled Estate* (1883) LR 24 Ch D 485, CA.   [235] *Re Tempest* (1866) LR 1 Ch App 485 at 490.
[236] *Re Parsons* [1940] 1 Ch 973, *per* Bennett J.

Choosing trustees

A modern survey of solicitors engaged in trust business revealed that a non-professional trustee should ideally demonstrate a number of positive attributes, including a genuine interest in the objects of the trust, financial acumen, business experience, sound judgement, common sense, and the strength of character to deal with difficult beneficiaries.[237] A professional trustee ought, of course, to demonstrate these attributes as a matter of course.

It would be ill advised to choose a person to act as a trustee if he is an undischarged bankrupt, has current convictions for offences involving dishonesty, is disqualified from acting as a company director, or is otherwise unfit for the office of trustee. The court will never appoint such a person to any trust and it is a criminal offence to appoint such a person to be a trustee of a charitable trust. Nor should persons be chosen who, on account of mental disorder, ill health, or some other relevant disability, are incapable of acting. Whether it is appropriate to appoint persons resident abroad is debatable.[238]

The duties of a newly appointed trustee

In the sport of cricket, the person who has just come in to bat is generally more vulnerable than the person who has already scored a few runs. The same may be true of trustees: a new trustee is vulnerable and may be more likely than established trustees to commit an inadvertent breach of trust. Accordingly, the first duty of a new trustee is to become acquainted with the trust instrument, the trust accounts, and other trust documentation. The documentation should confirm that the new trustee has been validly appointed. It will also identify the beneficiaries, and the nature and extent of their interests under the trust. If the beneficiaries have sold or otherwise dealt with their interests, memoranda on the trust instrument will inform the new trustee of that fact. (The assignee of a beneficial interest under a trust will give notice of the assignment to the trustees or risk losing his priority over other persons who might claim to be assignees of the same interest.)[239] The trust documentation will also reveal the nature of the trust property.

If a new trustee is appointed by deed, much of the trust property will automatically vest in him and the continuing trustees under s. 40 of the Trustee Act 1925. Any property that does not vest under s. 40 must be 'got in'. *Re Brogden*[240] illustrates the potentially devastating personal liability that may befall a new trustee who fails to bring the trust property under his control. The trustee of a marriage settlement, the inappropriately named Mr Budgett, delayed too long in his attempt to get in certain monies due from his co-trustees. Although his neglect was attributed to his being '[f]*earful of the disruption of family relations*',[241] Fry LJ stated that a trustee's discretion in the discharge

---

[237] C. Bell, 'Some reflections on choosing trustees' (1988) January TL&P 86.
[238] See Chapter 2 ('Non-resident trusts').
[239] *United Bank of Kuwait plc v. Sahib* [1995] 2 WLR 94, *per* Chadwick J. See the rule in *Dearle v. Hall*, Chapter 4.   [240] (1888) LR 38 Ch D 546.
[241] Ibid. at 575.

of his office *'is never an absolute one; it is always limited by the duty—the dominant duty, the guiding duty—of recovering, securing and duly applying the trust fund'.*[242] In the event, the trust suffered a loss of £17,250, which today would be roughly equivalent to £1.2m.[243] Mr Budgett was held personally liable to compensate the trust.

A new trustee is under no duty to search for evidence of wrongdoing by the former and continuing trustees. A trustee is not a private detective, but a trustee is obliged to act on any facts that raise suspicion of wrongdoing. Suspicion of wrongdoing may require the trustee to issue legal proceedings against his co-trustees or former trustees, but there will be no such requirement if the new trustee reasonably considers that taking legal action would be fruitless. The Charity Commission issues special guidance for newly appointed charity trustees.[244]

Retirement from the trust

Although it is undoubtedly true that no trustee *'accepts the responsibility for the term of his natural life, or for more than a reasonable period',*[245] he cannot retire on a whim. A trustee remains subject to the trust, and to liabilities (such as tax liability)[246] associated with trusteeship, until formal retirement.

A trustee may retire whenever the trust instrument entitles him to do so, or, as a last resort, whenever the court approves an application for retirement. He can even be forced to 'retire' by the beneficiaries of the trust if, being competent adults and between them absolutely entitled to the fund, they issue a written direction to that effect.[247] Otherwise, a trustee may only retire by one of the modes set out in the Trustee Act 1925. The first mode is retirement under s. 36, which requires that at least one new trustee be appointed in the place of the retiring trustee. If two or more trustees retire, the appointment of a sole replacement trustee is incapable of discharging them from the trust.[248]

---

[242] Ibid. at 571.

[243] C. H. Feinstein, *National Income, Expenditure and Output of the United Kingdom 1855 to 1965* (Cambridge: Cambridge University Press, 1972) tables 3 and 5. Cited in R. Twigger, *Inflation: The Value of the Pound 1750–1998* (House of Commons Library Research Paper 99/20, 23 February 1999) at 6.

[244] Charity Commission publication RS10, *Start as you mean to go on: Trustee Recruitment and Induction* (July 2005); available at www.charity-commission.gov.uk/publications/.

[245] *Re Chetwynd's Settlement* [1902] 1 Ch 692 at 694, *per* Farwell J.

[246] *Adam & Co International Trustees Ltd v. Theodore Goddard (a firm), The Times,* 17 March 2000, 97(13) LSG 44.　　　　　　　　　　　　　　[247] Trusts of Land and Appointment of Trustees Act 1996, s. 19(2)(a).

[248] Section 37(1)(c) of the Trustee Act 1925 provides that *'it shall not be obligatory to appoint more than one new trustee where only one trustee was originally appointed but a retiring trustee shall not be discharged from his trust unless he leaves behind a trust corporation or at least two persons to act as trustees to perform the trust'.* The word 'persons' was substituted for 'individuals' by the Trusts of Land and Appointment of Trustees Act 1996, s. 25(1), so whereas previously a retiring trustee would need to leave two humans behind, he can now leave a human and a company or other 'person'. See *Jasmine Trustees v. Wells & Hinds* [2007] EWHC 38 (Ch). Trustee Act 1925, s. 37(1) contains other supplemental provisions as to appointment of trustees, including: (a) the possibility of increasing the number of trustees on any appointment; (b) the possibility of appointing a separate set of trustees, not exceeding four, for any part of the trust property held on trusts distinct from those relating to any other part or parts of the trust property.

The second mode is retirement under s. 39.[249] According to this mode, the trustee who retires is not replaced.

A number of conditions must be satisfied before a trustee retiring under s. 39 is fully discharged from his trust: first, the trustee must, by deed, express his intention to retire; second, the trustee must obtain the consent of the other trustees and any person who is empowered to appoint new trustees; third, such consent must be given by deed, and must approve of the retirement and of the vesting of the trust property in the remaining trustees alone; fourth, the retirement will only be valid if two trustees or a trust corporation remain after the retirement.[250] The section also provides that '[a]*ny assurance or thing requisite for vesting the trust property in the continuing trustees alone shall be executed or done*'.[251] The vesting of trust property is considered in the next section.

If retirement is effective, the trustee will be discharged from any continuing obligations under the trust. He will only be liable for breaches of trust that occurred when he was a trustee, although he will be liable for a breach occurring after his retirement if he retired in order to facilitate it,[252] or if he retired with a negligent regard for the future well-being of the trust fund, or ought to have concluded that his successor was likely to misapply it.[253] Furthermore, it is not sufficient for liability to prove that the former trustee facilitated, or even intended, a breach of trust if, in the event, it was never committed.[254]

Vesting of trust property on appointment or retirement

When a new trustee is appointed by deed or when an existing trustee retires by deed, any land, chattel, or chose in action that is subject to the trust will, unless the deed provides to the contrary, automatically vest in the new and/or continuing trustees as joint tenants without any need for a conveyance or assignment.[255] The following interests, however, do not automatically vest in the new and/or continuing trustees:

1. land conveyed by way of mortgage for securing trust money (except land conveyed on trust for securing debentures or debenture stock);[256]

2. subject to certain highly technical exceptions, land held under a legal or equitable lease or underlease the terms of which prohibit assignment or disposition without the landlord's consent (unless consent has already been obtained);[257]

3. perhaps most significantly, company shares and any other property that is only transferable in books kept by a company or other body, or in a manner directed by or under an Act of Parliament;[258]

---

[249] As amended by the Trusts of Land and Appointment of Trustees Act 1996, s. 25(1), Sch. 3, para. 3(13).
[250] Section 39(1).   [251] Section 39(2).
[252] *Re Boles and British Land Company's Contract* [1902] 1 Ch 244, Ch D; *Wright v. Morgan* [1926] AC 788, PC.   [253] *Head v. Gould* [1898] 2 Ch 250, Ch D, *per* Kekewich J.
[254] Ibid. at 274.   [255] Trustee Act 1925, s. 40.   [256] Section 40(3)(a).
[257] Section 40(3)(b).   [258] Section 40(3)(c).

4. title to registered land does not vest until the register has been amended to reflect the new legal proprietorship.[259]

Removal of trustees

Trustees may be removed from office against their will. They may be removed under a power contained in the trust instrument, in which event, they may be replaced under s. 36 of the Trustee Act 1925 as if they had died. Alternatively, they may be removed if all of the beneficiaries of the trust are competent adults who, in writing, so direct, although the relevant statutory provision euphemistically refers to such removal as obligatory 'retirement'.[260] Finally, the court has the power to remove trustees under its inherent jurisdiction.

Where the facts that constitute the grounds for removal are not disputed, the court may remove trustees under s. 41 of the Trustee Act 1925 when appointing one or more replacement trustees under that section.[261] In any other case, the court may remove a trustee under its inherent jurisdiction. According to Lord Blackburn, speaking in the Privy Council in *Letterstedt v. Broers*,[262] when exercising the 'delicate' jurisdiction of removing trustees, the court's '*main guide must be the welfare of the beneficiaries*'.[263] It follows that trustees will be removed if the court believes that the trust property is endangered by their continuing in office.[264] Accordingly, a trustee whose acts or omissions show '*a want of honesty, or a want of proper capacity to execute the duties, or a want of reasonable fidelity*'[265] will be removed, and personal hostility between a trustee and the beneficiaries may be a factor influencing the removal of a trustee.[266] However, a trustee will not be removed simply because he has interests in conflict with the trust, provided the trust can function properly without him ever having to choose between the trust and his private interests,[267] and an occasional error by a trustee is not of itself a ground for removal.[268] In one case a trustee who had wrongfully assumed that she was beneficially entitled to the trust property was permitted to continue in office once the court had pointed out her error.[269] If the trust fund is small and the trustee contests

---

[259] Land Registration Act 1925, s. 47.

[260] Trusts of Land and Appointment of Trustees Act 1996, s. 19.

[261] *Re Henderson* [1940] Ch 764. In this case, a trustee was replaced because she initially stated her wish to retire from the trust, but, at a later date, insisted that she would not retire unless certain conditions were met.

[262] (1884) LR 9 App Cas 371.   [263] Ibid. at 386.

[264] Ibid. at 386; see also *Titterton v. Oates* [2001] WTLR 319 Supreme Court (Australian Capital Territory).

[265] *Story's Equity Jurisprudence* at [1289].

[266] *Letterstedt v. Broers* (1884) LR 9 App Cas 371; followed in *The Thomas and Agnes Carvel Foundation v. Carvel* [2007] EWHC 1314 (Ch), in which 'intense hostility' led to the removal of a personal representative from office. Hostility between siblings is a common cause of such cases. See, for example *Jones v. Firkin-Flood* [2008] EWHC 2417 (Ch) and *Re E A Scott (1991 Children's Settlement N1); Scott v. Scott* [2012] EWHC 2397 (Ch).

[267] *Public Trustee v. Cooper* [2001] WTLR 901.

[268] *Isaac v. Isaac* [2005] EWHC 435 (Ch), at [73].   [269] *Rafferty v. Philp* [2011] EWHC 709 (Ch).

the grounds for removal, the administrative expense of removing the trustee might persuade the court to allow him to continue in office.[270]

The office of judicial trustee

'*As it is a maxim, that the execution of a trust shall be under the control of the court . . . the court itself can execute the trust.*'[271] However, to have a court carry out the administrative functions of a trustee is very expensive and inconvenient, so the Judicial Trustees Act 1896 was passed to allow a judicial trustee to be appointed where administration of the trust by the ordinary trustees has failed. The remuneration of a judicial trustee must be justified, reasonable, and proportionate, and is generally limited to 15 per cent of the capital value of the trust property.[272] A judicial trustee has all the powers of ordinary trustees, but, as an officer of the court, he or she also has ready access to the court's directions regarding administration of the trust. As Jenkins J stated in *Re Ridsel*:[273] '*a judicial trustee . . . acts in close concert with the court and under conditions enabling the court to supervise his transactions*'.[274] Any fit and appropriate person may be appointed to be a judicial trustee. One such fit and appropriate person is the Public Trustee.

The office of the Public Trustee

The Public Trustee is a 'corporation sole' established by the Public Trustee Act 1906.[275] The incumbent for the time being is an individual, but he or she is regarded as 'a corporation sole' by virtue of the perpetual, successive nature of his or her office.[276] The role of the Public Trustee is to administer trusts—typically, private, non-business trusts—no matter how small, for which no other trustee can be found. Although the court will take into account the wishes of the settlor when choosing new trustees, the settlor cannot exclude appointment of the Public Trustee in an appropriate case.[277] It is in the office of the Public Trustee that the maxim 'a trust will never fail for want of a trustee' finds its ultimate expression.

Fulfilling and filling the office of trustee

At the outset of this chapter, we observed that a balance must be struck between ensuring that the office of trustee is properly fulfilled and ensuring that the obligations of trusteeship are not so onerous that people are dissuaded from acting as trustees: '*The Court has laid down a rule with regard to the transactions . . . of trustees, so as not to strike a terror into mankind acting for the benefit of others.*'[278]

---

[270] See *Re Wrightson* [1908] 1 Ch 798.
[271] As Lord Eldon LC acknowledged long ago in *Morice v. Bishop of Durham* (1805) 10 Ves 522 at 539.
[272] Judicial Trustee Rules 1983, r. 11(1)(a); Practice Direction [2003] All ER (D) 93 (Jul).
[273] [1947] Ch 597.   [274] Ibid. at 605.   [275] Section 1.
[276] The present incumbent is Nick Crew.   [277] *Re Duxbury's Settlement Trusts* [1995] 1 WLR 425.
[278] Lord Hardwicke in *Ex p. Belchier* (1754) Amb 218, *per* Lord Hardwicke at 219: '*if Mrs Parsons is chargeable in this case, no man in his senses would act as assignee under commission of a bankrupt*'.

We have seen that the rule 'laid down' is expressed in many different ways. It prevents review of a trustee's discretion apart from when the decision reached is one that no reasonable trustee could have reached. It allows trustees to delegate fiduciary discretions and ministerial acts, and, crucially, it does not require perfection from trustees:

> It never could be reasonable to make a trustee adopt further and better precautions than an ordinary prudent man of business would adopt, or to conduct the business in any other way. If it were otherwise, no one would be a trustee at all.[279]

Further reading

In addition to the following print sources, the Online Resource Centre accompanying this book contains web links to further reading as well as guide answers to assessment questions relevant to this chapter.

BELL, C., 'Some reflections on choosing trustees' (1988) TL&P, January.

HAYTON, D., 'Liability of trustees to third parties: the Scottish Law Commission's proposals' (2008) Edin LR 446.

HILLIARD, J., 'Limiting *Re Hastings-Bass*' (2004) Conv 208.

KIRALFY, A., 'A limitation on the discretionary powers of trustees' (1953) 17 Conv (NS) 285.

KIRKLAND, K., 'Recruiting, selecting and inducing charity trustees' (2002) 4 PCB 253.

MATTHEWS, P., 'The constitution of disclaimed trusts *inter vivos*' (1981) Conv 141.

MORRIS, J. and O'SULLIVAN, C., 'Jasmine Trustees: tangles in the trusteeship chain: Parts 1 and 2' (2007) 5 Private Client Business 347; 6 Private Client Business 442.

NOLAN, R. and CLOHERTY, A., 'Taxing Times For *Re Hastings-Bass*' (2010) 126 LQR 513.

---

[279] *Speight v. Gaunt* (1883) 22 Ch D 727, *per* Sir George Jessel MR at 739–42.

12

Trustee investment

There are a number of reasons for devoting a whole chapter to trustee investment: first, and most obvious, it is an almost universal obligation of trusteeship; second, reform of trustee investment was the principal motivation behind the Trustee Act 2000; third, it provides a context in which to examine the interplay of a number of significant trustee duties, including the duty of care, the duty to act fairly, the duty to exercise a sound discretion, and even the fiduciary duty; fourth, it represents a significant interface between trustees' obligations and beneficiaries' proprietary rights; last, and by no means least, the social significance of trustee investment, and the investment of pension funds in particular, cannot be overstated.

A matter of choice

Trustees must invest in a manner that is prudent in the light of current investment practice and fair as between beneficiaries with competing interests in the fund. If they breach their trust in either of these respects, they may be personally liable to compensate for any loss caused. This sounds straightforward enough; the authorities suggest, however, that disappointed beneficiaries find it hard to establish that their trustees have invested improperly, let alone that improper investment has actually caused the trust fund to suffer a quantifiable loss. It is difficult to prove a breach of trust, because prudent trustees choose to invest similar funds in widely divergent ways and because it is reasonable for trustees to have quite different views as to which investments are likely to achieve a fair balance between beneficiaries with competing interests in the fund. It is difficult to prove and to quantify the loss suffered by the fund, because of fundamental definitional problems as to what constitutes loss: is it to be assessed in nominal terms or real terms, and how does one quantify real loss? Most difficult of all, however, is the task of proving causation. Even if the trustees were to concede that they had invested imprudently and that the trust fund had suffered a loss, the significant obstacle would remain of proving that the trustees' imprudence had caused the loss. In short, as the law currently stands, there will, in many cases, be no effective remedy for improper trustee investment. Given the vast amount of social wealth that is held in trust, this should be a cause for concern, but we will see that the modern trend in trustee investment is towards liberalization, towards freedom of choice and the free participation of trust funds in investment markets. In such a climate, a weak regulatory scheme will be tolerated and may even be desired.

A matter of time

Investment returns are compensation for postponed consumption. If I spend my money today on consumables, such as food, or a 'wasting' (depreciating) asset, such as a mass-produced television or a car, it is only a matter of time before I have little, or nothing, to show for it. Conversely, if I purchase shares or land with my money, there is a possibility that I will receive income (in the form of dividends and rent) and long-term capital growth. Land rarely disappoints as an investment over the longer term, because, as Mark Twain once said, '[t]*hey aren't making it any more*.'[1] However, I should be wary of short-term investments: not only because markets for equities (shares) and real estate (land) are notoriously volatile in the short term, but because the purchase of investments incurs transaction costs, such as agents' fees and stamp duty, which will rarely be offset by returns made in the very short term. Sound investment takes time. A short-term venture '*in which the object is the chance of reaping a rapid advantage by a sudden rise in the market price*' is not investment, but speculation.[2]

If time is essential to sound investment, the good news is that many trusts have time in abundance. Indeed, the private trust has been described as a '*gift projected on the plane of time and, meanwhile, in need of management*'.[3] The leading cases on trustee investment have tended to involve trusts established for the medium to long term. These include charitable trusts, pension trusts, and traditional settlement trusts of the form 'to A for life and to B in remainder'. But what happens when time runs out? Taking the example of our traditional settlement trust, what is the effect on the trustee's investment duties if, when A dies, B is *sui juris* and (as the sole beneficiary under a 'bare trust') is able to bring the trust immediately to an end? In such circumstances, uncertainty as to the duration of the trust renders the trustee unable to implement a prudent investment policy. In short, because time is essential to sound investment and time is not a feature of a bare trust, a 'bare' trust can, in no meaningful sense, be 'invested'.[4] Indeed, it is usually said that the trustee of a 'bare trust' has no authority to exercise a positive discretion, but is only required to act according to the beneficiary's instruction.[5]

The goals of trustee investment

The goals of trustee investment depend upon the goals of the particular trust. According to one distinguished commentator, '*the lodestar which should guide* [trustees] *is the promotion of the purposes of their trust, that is, the best interests of the beneficiaries*',[6] but

---

[1] Quoted in *The Business*, June 2002.   [2] *Compact Oxford English Dictionary*, 2nd edn (1993) at 874.
[3] 44 MLR 610 at 610. See also F. H. Lawson and B. Rudden, *The Law of Property*, 2nd edn (Oxford: Clarendon Press, 1982) at 55.   [4] A fitting conclusion, given that 'invest' derives from the Latin 'to clothe'.
[5] *Christie v. Ovington* (1875) LR 1 Ch D 279, *per* Hall VC at 281, but contrast Jessell MR, who was of the view that trusteeship necessarily connotes positive duties and discretion (*Morgan v. Swansea Urban Sanitary Authority* (1878) LR 9 Ch D 582 at 584).
[6] Lord Nicholls of Birkenhead, 'Trustees and their broader community: where duty, morality and ethics converge' (1995) 9(3) TLI 71 at 76.

the purposes of the trust vary from trust to trust. In the case of a charitable trust, the goals of trustee investment should be aligned with the charitable purposes,[7] but in most trusts, the aim is to provide financial benefits to the beneficiaries. Where that is the case, '*the best interests of the beneficiaries are normally their best financial interests*'.[8] This means that, in most trusts, the immediate goal of investment, no matter how worthy the ulterior goal, is the selfish, materialistic goal of wealth maximization. With the exception of freehold land, which can now be acquired for occupation by the beneficiary,[9] it is still true that trustee investments must produce wealth and that '*property which is acquired merely for use and enjoyment is not an investment*'.[10]

So, the goals of trustee investment are usually financial, but the question is: which financial goals? It has been said that a balanced portfolio will have three basic characteristics: namely, liquidity, stability, and growth.[11] The liquid component of a portfolio will be readily available as cash and can be used to deal with emergencies, such as repairs to a trust-owned house. The smaller the fund, the greater the proportion that is likely to be kept in a 'liquid' state. Far more complex, however, is the task of identifying the proportions of the fund that should be devoted to stability and growth, respectively.

In *Nestle v. National Westminster Bank plc*,[12] Leggatt LJ asserted that '*the importance of preservation of a trust fund will always outweigh success in its advancement*',[13] which, at first sight, suggests a bias in favour of stability and against growth. However, the statement begs two significant questions: first, is the real value of the fund to be preserved, or merely its nominal value?[14] Second, what qualifies as 'success' in the advancement of a trust fund? On the facts of *Nestle*, the nominal value of the fund increased fivefold over a 60-year period, but, in the same period, its real value decreased fourfold.[15] Is that success? Leggatt LJ's question is unhelpful, because it suggests that the trustees' duty is to achieve particular outcomes. This ought not to be the case, as Hoffmann J stated at first instance in the same case:

> Preservation of real values can be no more than an aspiration which some trustees may have the good fortune to achieve...a rule that real capital values must be maintained would be unfair to both income beneficiaries and trustees.[16]

The trustees' investment duty is not to achieve a particular outcome, but rather to invest the fund in a particular way, namely prudently and fairly.[17] However, before we consider trustees' duties in detail, we must first examine the scope of their powers.

---

[7] *Harries v. Church Commissioners* [1992] 1 WLR 1241.
[8] *Cowan v. Scargill* [1985] Ch 270, *per* Megarry VC at 287.   [9] Trustee Act 2000, s. 8.
[10] *Re Peczenik's Settlement* [1964] 1 WLR 720 Ch D, *per* Buckley J at 723.
[11] J. Stephens, 'Designing an investment portfolio for trustees' (1994) 1 T&T 12.
[12] [1993] 1 WLR 1260, CA.   [13] Ibid. at 1284G.
[14] The same question was left unanswered in *Re Whiteley* (1886) LR 33 Ch D 347, in which Cotton LJ held (at 350) that trustees are '*bound to preserve the money for those entitled to the corpus in remainder, and they are bound to invest it in such a way as will produce a reasonable income for those enjoying the income for the present*' (confirmed on appeal in *Re Whiteley* (1887) LR 12 App Cas 727).
[15] See later.   [16] *Nestle v. National Westminster Bank plc* [1988] (1996) 10(4) TLI 112 at 115.
[17] It is respectfully submitted that Lightman J was wrong to suggest in *Don King Productions Inc v. Warren* [1998] 2 All ER 608 at 634a that '*the first duty of a trustee is to preserve the trust property*'. The first duty of the trustee is to pursue a prudent course *with a view* to preservation of the trust property. There is no duty actually to preserve it.

Trustees' investment powers

The first guide to a trustee's investment powers is the trust instrument governing his particular trust.[18] The terms of the trust instrument in relation to investment powers are always to be given their natural construction.[19] Subject to what the trust instrument might say to the contrary, one would expect a trustee, as legal owner of the trust property, to have the same powers as any other legal owner of property. In fact, it was only as recent as the Trustee Act 2000 that the law was reformed to allow trustees to make 'any kind of investment', as if they were 'absolutely entitled to the assets' of the trust. Pension trustees were the first to benefit from these wide investment powers.[20] Now, subject to certain exceptions,[21] the Trustee Act 2000 extends them to all trustees,[22] including trustees who, prior to the Trustee Act 2000, were authorized to invest without limitation in accordance with the Trustee Investments Act 1961.[23] (Any limitations set out in trust instruments prior to the 2000 Act will, however, still apply unless made before 3 August 1961.)[24] The Trustee Act 2000 even authorizes trustees to hold investments jointly or in common with persons who are not trustees.[25] As things turned out, the timing of the Trustee Act 2000 could not have been worse. It changed the law to allow trustees unrestricted power to invest in stock markets just as stock markets reached all-time highs. (At the end of 2011, stock markets had still failed to attain the levels they had achieved at the very end of 1999.)

The Trustee Investments Act 1961, which was repealed by the Trustee Act 2000, had restricted trustees to certain types of so-called 'safe' investments, such as gilt-edged securities,[26] bank accounts, and shares in quoted public limited companies with a good track record and a strong financial base.[27] More creative investment had been permitted only if authorized by the trust instrument or by the court.[28] The 'authorised list' approach laid down by the 1961 Act denied conscientious trustees the freedom to invest positively in accordance with the best available techniques (and, in particular, in accordance with modern portfolio theory),[29] and it also encouraged the indolent to restrict themselves to investments on the 'authorised list' even when they had express

---

[18] Trustee Act 2000, s. 6(1)(b). If the trust instrument was made before 3 August 1961, see later.

[19] *Re Harari's Settlement Trusts* [1949] 1 All ER 430.   [20] Pensions Act 1995, s. 34.

[21] Such as occupational pension trusts (Trustee Act 2000, s. 36(3)), authorized unit trusts, and certain schemes under the Charities Act 1993.

[22] Trustee Act 2000, Part II, s. 3(1). The new, wider default power is referred to in the Act as the *'general power of investment'*.

[23] Section 7(6).   [24] Section 7(5).

[25] Explanatory notes to the Trustee Act 2000 (note 20).   [26] Defined later.

[27] Part IV of the first Schedule to the 1961 Act. Furthermore, according to the Trustee Investments Act 1961, s. 2, trustees were permitted to devote a maximum of 50 per cent of the fund to such investments (although the greater profitability of shares, along with other factors, tended over time to increase the proportion actually held). Not until 1996 was the 50:50 rule modified for private companies to allow three-quarters of the fund to be devoted to investment in shares in quoted companies (SI 1996, No. 845). Under the Trustee Act 2000, there is no requirement that any part be held in so-called 'safe' investments.

[28] *Re Kolb's WT* [1962] 1 Ch 531; *Mason v. Farbrother* [1983] 2 All ER 1078; *Trustees of the British Museum v. AG* [1984] 1 All ER 337.   [29] See later.

authority to invest beyond it.[30] There were even adverse consequences for third parties who had commercial dealings with trusts, because if a trustee purchased investments beyond his authority to do so, the unpaid vendor of such investments would be unable to seek reimbursement from the trust fund in the event of the trustee's personal insolvency.[31]

Types of investment

Although the 'general power of investment' provided by s. 3(1) of the Trustee Act 2000 authorizes trustees to 'make any kind of investment', the meaning of 'investment' is nowhere defined in the Act. There is a good reason for this omission: some transactions, if considered in isolation, do not appear to be investments at all. Suppose, for example, that a trustee holds shares worth £100 each and sells X an option to purchase the shares if their value reaches £110 per share.[32] Is the sale of the option an investment? It looks more like a *'relatively short-term bet'*[33] that the value of the shares will not rise much above £110 each. However, to judge the option in isolation is entirely to miss the point. The option only makes sense as an investment when it is considered alongside another investment—namely, the shares themselves—whereupon it is immediately clear that the purpose of the option was to insure against any future fall in the value of the shares. Had the shares dropped below £100, the loss to the trust fund would have been reduced by the gain made on the sale of the option.

A 1986 survey of trustees and other fiduciary fund managers in the USA[34] revealed that 42 per cent of all respondents were using options and 35 per cent were using futures.[35] The fact that stock index futures had only been approved for trading by the US Securities and Exchange Commission at the end of 1982 suggests that options and futures were very popular.[36] The author of the survey recognized that such investments are, on the traditional view, *'suspect to varying degrees'*,[37] but argued that, in modern

---

[30] As occurred in *Nestle v. National Westminster Bank plc* [1988] (1996) 10(4) TLI 112.

[31] See *Re Johnson* (1880) LR 15 Ch D 548 at 552 and *Re Frith* [1902] 1 Ch 342 at 345–6. Two papers critical of this fact appeared in April 1997: *Rights of Creditors Against Trustees and Trust Funds: A Consultation Paper* (the Trust Law Committee), and *Financial Dealings with Trustees* (the Financial Law Panel).

[32] E. Ford, 'Trustee investment and modern portfolio theory' (1996) 10(4) TLI 102–4 at 102.

[33] B. Longstreth, *Modern Investment Management and the Prudent Man Rule* (New York, Oxford: Oxford University Press, 1986) at 133.　　　　　　　　　　　　　　　　　　　　　　　　[34] Ibid.

[35] Under a futures contract, a price is agreed for the sale of an asset, but the payment of the price and the delivery of the asset are postponed until a future date. Whereas an option is exercisable by only one of the parties, a future can be enforced by either of the parties.

[36] It is notable that, in the UK, options are one of the assets listed as an 'investment' in Part I of Sch. 1 to the Financial Services Act 1986. Others include: company stocks and shares; debentures; government and public securities; warrants, certificates, or other instruments entitling the holder to, or representing, shares or securities; units in a 'unit trust' company or other collective investment scheme, and futures contracts made for investment (not commercial) purposes. At the time of writing, the Law Commission has just published an advice on *Property Interests in Inrermediated Securities*, which proposes new protection for trustee (and private) investors in collective schemes such as unit trusts.

[37] B. Longstreth, *Modern Investment Management and the Prudent Man Rule* (New York, Oxford: Oxford University Press, 1986) at 4.

investment conditions, no type of investment should be ruled out. He suggested that it should be left to the trustees of individual trusts to determine whether a particular investment is suitable to their trust. This argument was accepted and became law in the USA as the prudent investor rule.[38] HM Treasury[39] and the Law Commission[40] proposed that the English law of trusts should undergo a similar reform, and the Trustee Act 2000 was the result. The hallmarks of a 'suitable' investment are set out in the 2000 Act and are considered later, but first we must examine certain types of investment that raise special considerations for trustees.

Government bonds and Treasury bills

Government bonds (known as 'gilt-edged securities' or 'gilts') are sold by the government for the purpose of long-term borrowing. Treasury bills are similar, but are sold for borrowing over the short term: for example, three months. They both yield income in the form of a lump-sum dividend called a 'coupon' and, on the redemption date, they yield capital equivalent to their nominal face value (known as the 'par' value).[41]

Investments of this type are said to be virtually risk-free. (It is more accurate to say that they are as financially secure as the government that grants them.) They yield a guaranteed fixed rate of income and the nominal value of the capital is secure. However, because the level of guaranteed income is usually very low and there is no prospect of a capital gain (unless the bonds are acquired below 'par'),[42] the real value of the bonds, which is determined according to their purchasing power, will decrease as the price of standard commodities rise. This general rise in prices, known as 'inflation', is now an endemic feature of the economic landscape.[43] In fact, between 1750 and 1998, prices rose 118-fold, including a 61-fold increase since the outbreak of World War I.[44] The corresponding effect on the nominal value of sterling is dramatic: *'one (decimal) penny in 1750 would have had greater purchasing power than a pound in 1998'.*[45]

---

[38] The American Law Institute, *Restatement of the Law of Trusts* (3rd edn): *The Prudent Investor Rule*, adopted 18 May 1990 (St. Paul: American Law Publishers, 1992). B. Longstreth (author of *Modern Investment Management and the Prudent Man Rule*) was one of the advisers to the American Law Institute in relation to the prudent investor rule.

[39] *Investment Powers of Trustees: A Consultation Document*, May 1996.

[40] Law Commission Report No. 260: *Trustees' Powers and Duties* (1999). The Scottish counterpart was Report No. 172.

[41] Gilts can now be traded electronically. The Central Gilts Office runs a system of dematerialized gilts. See Gilt-edged Securities (CGO Service) Regulations 1985 (SI 1985, No. 1144) and J. Benjamin, *The Law of Global Custody* (London: Butterworths, 1996) ch. 11 at 148, 151, 160.

[42] That is, below nominal face value.

[43] Although the annual average increase in underlying inflation for 2000 was, at 2.1%, the lowest since 1976 (T. Edmonds, *Economic Indicators*, Research Paper 01/13, 1 February 2001 (Economic Policy and Statistics Section, House of Commons Library) at 10).

[44] R. Twigger, *Inflation: The Value of the Pound 1750–1998*, Research paper 99/20, 23 February 1999 (Economic Policy and Statistics Section, House of Commons Library).

[45] Ibid. at 3. See also O. Newman and A. Foster, *The Value of the Pound*, Office of National Statistics (1995).

These statistics suggest that it would be imprudent to leave a significant proportion of a trust fund in gilts and other so-called 'risk-free' investments over the longer term. This is particularly true of large funds, for which prudent investment would typically lead to a much larger holding of shares relative to gilts. Records show that £1m invested in 1963 and performing in line with the FTSE[46] All Share Index would, in 1994, have been worth £1.5m in real terms—that is, having taken inflation into account. Over the same period, £1m performing in line with the FT 15-Year Gilt Index would have been worth a mere £62,000 in real terms.[47] Having said that, the hallmark of a prudent trustee is that he exercises a sound discretion; a trustee should not assume that what was prudent last year will be prudent this year. If economic indicators suggest, as they do at the time of writing, that there will be low inflation and poor share performance over the next few years, a larger proportion of gilts might well be justified.

Shares

Investment in a company can take a number of forms. A trustee may, for example, make a loan to a company at an agreed rate of interest, in return for which the company will issue a promise to repay, in the form of a 'debenture'. Ideally, the debenture will be secured against the company's assets, but it might take the form of an unsecured 'bond'. However, the most common form of investment in a company is in shares.[48] The typical ordinary share is attractive to trusts, because it yields an income (called a 'dividend') and the possibility of capital growth. If the company is successful and market conditions are favourable, the capital value of ordinary shares in that company will rise. Another significant feature of ordinary shares is that they confer voting rights. Most significant resolutions will be passed if they attract the votes attaching to 75 per cent of the shares; some only require the support of 51 per cent of the shares. This means that a trust that holds anything above 26 per cent of the total shareholding can exert a considerable influence over the company's policy. However, with this power comes responsibility.

In *Bartlett v. Barclays Bank (No. 1)*,[49] the trust held a 99.8 per cent shareholding in a company. Despite this, the trust corporation had been content to receive no more information than an ordinary shareholder would have obtained at the annual general meeting. Brightman J held that this was not the behaviour of a prudent trustee. A prudent trustee

---

[46] Financial Times Stock Exchange.

[47] HM Treasury Consultation Document, *Investment Powers of Trustees*, May 1996 at 6, n. 5 (quoting Phillips & Drew Fund Management Ltd).

[48] The CREST system for electronic transfer on the London and Dublin Stock Exchanges came into operation on 15 July 1996. See C. Marquand, 'CREST and the shareholder' (1996) 140 SJ 668; 'CREST goes active' (1996) 9 CM 15. Trustees may wish to continue to hold shares in certified (i.e. documentary) form, but they are permitted by the Uncertificated Securities Regulations 1995 (SI 1995, No. 3272) to hold their shares in uncertified (i.e. electronic) form by becoming sponsored members of CREST—unless the particular trust instrument provides otherwise. (See Law Commission Report No. 260 *Trustees' Powers and Duties* (1999) at para. 2.30.) Brokerage fees are generally cheaper for uncertified share dealing than for certified dealing. CREST is a loose acronym for Computerized or Electronic Share Transfer.   [49] [1980] Ch 515.

would have ensured that the investment was adequately supervised. It would probably have appointed a director or nominee to the board in order to represent the interests of the trust, and to supply the trustees with copies of the agenda and minutes of the board meetings.

Land and loans secured on land

If the trust property currently includes land, the trust is a 'trust of land' and the trustees have, in relation to the land subject to the trust, all of the powers of an absolute owner for the purpose of exercising their functions as trustees.[50] This includes the power to acquire land.[51] In exercising their powers, the trustees must have regard to the rights of the beneficiaries[52] and the duty of care under s. 1 of the Trustee Act 2000 applies to them.[53] Beneficiaries who are beneficially entitled to an interest in possession in land subject to a trust of land are entitled to occupy the land at any time.[54]

The 'general power of investment' contained in Part II of the Trustee Act 2000[55] does not permit the trustees to make investments in land, although it does permit them to be parties to a mortgage.[56] However, Part III of the Act provides that trustees may acquire freehold or leasehold land in the UK as an investment, for occupation by a beneficiary, or for any other reason.[57] For the purpose of exercising his functions as a trustee, a trustee who acquires land under this section has all of the powers of an absolute owner in relation to the land. Previously, trustees were only permitted to invest in freehold land if the trust contained freehold land from the outset,[58] or if the trust instrument expressly authorized investment in land; now, trustees have the power to invest in legal freehold and leasehold estates in land[59] (apart from in cases of settled land and university land),[60] although the trust instrument or other legislation may exclude or restrict that power.[61]

Like 'investment', 'land' is nowhere defined in the 2000 Act. An explanatory note to the Act[62] suggests that the definition of land in Sch. 1 to the Interpretation Act 1978 should apply. That Schedule defines land as including buildings and other structures, land covered with water, and any estate, interest, easement, servitude, or right in, or over, land. However, according to the actual text of the 2000 Act, express power to invest in land is restricted to investment in mortgages,[63] and the legal estates of freehold and leasehold. This produces an odd (and presumably unintended) contrast with trustees of trusts that already include land. Such trusts are 'trusts of land' within the Trusts of Land and Appointment of Trustees Act 1996 and the trustees of such trusts are permitted to invest in any interest in land as if they were absolute owners of the fund.[64]

---

[50] Trusts of Land and Appointment of Trustees Act 1996, s. 6(1) and (2).
[51] Section 6(3) (acquisition is effected under the power conferred by the Trustee Act 2000, s. 8, see later).
[52] Trusts of Land and Appointments of Trustees Act 1996, s. 6(5).   [53] Ibid. s. 6(9).
[54] Provided that the purposes of the trust include making the land available for occupation by beneficiaries, or the land is held by the trustees so as to be so available (ibid. s. 12).   [55] Trustee Act 2000, s. 3.
[56] Section 3(3).   [57] Section 8(1).   [58] Trusts of Land and Appointments of Trustees Act 1996.
[59] Trustee Act 2000, s. 8.   [60] Section 10(1).   [61] Section 9.   [62] Note 22.
[63] There is no requirement that the mortgage be legal.   [64] Section 6(1).

One reason for the law's traditional reluctance to authorize trustee investment in land may have been the problem of valuation.[65] The accurate valuation of land is a task requiring professional expertise and knowledge of the local property market.[66] Mark Twain's advice—'buy land, they aren't making it anymore'—just isn't detailed enough.

Even if the trust is not purchasing land, but merely lending money secured on land, it is crucial that an accurate valuation is obtained. If a trustee lends money without taking expert advice, or lends contrary to expert advice, such failure is prima facie imprudent[67] and the trustee is liable to the full extent of any loss incurred by the trust fund as a result of the breach.

A loan secured on land made before the Trustee Act 2000 came into force is still subject to special rules laid down in the Trustee Act 1925. Those rules provide that, if the trustee took expert advice as to the value of the land intended to be security for the loan and loaned no more than two-thirds of the expert valuation, he will not be liable if the land is subsequently shown to be inadequate security.[68] So, if land is valued at £150,000, the trustee will incur no liability if he lends no more than £100,000, even if the land turns out to be worth, for example £50,000. The rules also provide that even if the trustee loans more than two-thirds of the expert's valuation, his liability will be limited to the extent of the excess.[69] So, if land is valued at £150,000 and the trustee lends £110,000, the trustee will only be liable to pay £10,000 compensation if the land turns out to be worth £50,000.

Borrowing to invest

If mortgage interest rates are low, it might make sound financial sense to borrow money on the security of trust-owned land and to reinvest the borrowed funds elsewhere. Such borrowing is, in fact, authorized by most modern trust deeds. In 1996, HM Treasury declined to recommend that such a power should be extended to trustees generally,[70] but Part II of the Trustee Act 2000 now permits trustees to invest in loans secured on land,[71] regardless of whether the trustees are borrowers or lenders.[72] Accordingly, unless the trust instrument provides to the contrary, there is nothing to prevent trustees from borrowing for investment purposes.

Personal loans

Secured loans must be contrasted with loans made by trustees on no security other than the borrower's personal promise to repay. Such 'personal loans' are inherently risky, and not merely because the borrower might break his promise. The borrower might be quite

---

[65] See G. Lightman QC, 'Sales at valuation by fiduciaries' [1985] Conv 44.

[66] In *Fry v. Tapson* (1884) LR 28 Ch D 268 Kay J said: '*I am most reluctant to visit trustees acting* bona fide *with the consequences of a want of due caution, but... they most incautiously employed the mortgagor's agent... although he was a London surveyor, and it was most important to obtain the opinion of some experienced local surveyor'* (at 282).   [67] *Palmer v. Emerson* [1911] 1 Ch 758.

[68] Trustee Act 1925, s. 8.   [69] Ibid. s. 9.

[70] HM Treasury Consultation Document, *Investment Powers of Trustees*, May 1996 at 12, n. 25.

[71] Section 3(3).   [72] Section 3(4).

willing to repay the loan, but may be unable to do so due to insolvency or impecuniosity. For this reason, it has been said that *'loans on no security beyond the liability of the borrower to repay... are not investments'*.[73] In fact, prior to the Trustee Act 2000, it was clear that trustees were only permitted to invest by means of personal loans if the trust instrument expressly authorized such investments.[74] Since the Act came into force, it is a moot point whether personal loans are authorized under the general power of investment.[75] If one takes the view that personal loans 'are not investments', they will not be authorized by the Trustee Act 2000. However, the better view may be to acknowledge that a personal loan is a type of investment, but one that should be presumed imprudent.

Trustees' investment duties

The law recognizes trustees as having the same investment powers as absolute owners, but whereas an absolute owner may use his property as he pleases—choosing, if he wishes, to gamble and speculate—trustees' legal powers are constrained by their duty to invest prudently and fairly.[76] Absolute owners invest on their own account; trustees are accountable to beneficiaries. This does not mean that trustees are required to make up from their own funds every loss that befalls the trust fund. They are not insurers of the fund:[77]

> All that can be required of a trustee to invest, is, that he shall conduct himself faithfully and exercise a sound discretion. He is to observe how men of prudence, discretion and intelligence manage their own affairs, not in regard to speculation, but in regard to the permanent disposition of their funds, considering the probable income, as well as the probable safety of the capital to be invested.[78]

This passage from a leading US case sets out the essential trustee duties in relation to investment:

1. The trustee must be faithful: he must not invest in companies he owns or otherwise place himself in a position of conflict.

---

[73] *Khoo Tek Keon v. Chen Joo Tuan Neoh* [1934] AC 529, *per* Lord Russell of Killowen at 536. In *Re Peczenik's Settlement* [1964] 1 WLR 720, Buckley J also cast doubt upon investments *'merely upon personal security'* (at 723). In that case, a clause that authorized the trustees to invest *'in any shares stocks property or property holding company as the trustees in their discretion shall consider to be in the best interests of* [the beneficiary]' was held not to authorize personal loans.

[74] The trust instrument in *Re Laing's Settlement* [1899] 1 Ch 593 authorized investment *'upon such personal credit without security as the trustees... think fit'.*

[75] Trustee Act 2000, s. 3.

[76] See *Nestle v. National Westminster Bank plc* [1988] (1996) 10(4) TLI 112, *per* Hoffmann J at 115.

[77] The engagement into which institutional trustees enter *'is not one of insurance. They do not guarantee results',* *per* Hoffmann J in the High Court in *Nestle*, ibid. This statement, taken from the original transcript of the conclusion to his Lordship's judgment does not appear in the report of the case (ibid.). A similar statement was made by Bacon VC in *Re Godfrey* (1883) LR 23 Ch D 483 at 493.

[78] *Harvard College v. Amory*, 26 Mass (9 Pick) 446 (1830), *per* Putman J at 461.

2. He must exercise a positive discretion: he must make choices in relation to all aspects of investment management, such as when to sell and acquire investments, which investments to sell and acquire, whether or not to delegate investment functions, when to delegate and to whom.

3. The discretion he exercises must be a sound one. This is judged objectively, the question being whether the trustee exercised his discretion prudently and fairly.

4. Speculation is *ipso facto* imprudent and is not permitted. It is sometimes said that one must 'speculate to accumulate' but 'select to protect' is a more appropriate motto for the trustee.

5. The trustee should have regard to both income and capital returns. This latter requirement is especially relevant to traditional trusts under which there is a life tenant and remainderman. Generally speaking, the life tenant is interested in income and the remainderman is interested in capital.

The duty to exercise a sound discretion

Prudence and fairness, the principal characteristics of a sound discretion, are considered in detail later. There are, however, several other aspects to the duty to exercise a sound discretion. One is that trustees must not allow the exercise of their discretion to be influenced by matters unrelated to the purposes of the trust.[79] They must manage the fund in the way that is most beneficial to the beneficiaries, even if such a course conflicts with their personal morality[80] (a fiduciary cannot '*make moral gestures*',[81] or political opinions,[82] or any other extraneous consideration).[83] Related aspects of the duty are that a trustee must not exercise his discretion dishonestly, or capriciously, or, subject to the trust instrument providing to the contrary, for his own benefit. However, the most basic aspect of the duty to exercise a sound discretion is sometimes overlooked. It is simply this: that trustees are not permitted to abdicate responsibility for decision making,[84] nor are they permitted unduly to restrict the choices available to them, nor are they permitted to place themselves in a position in which they are powerless to exercise a free discretion. In short, trustees must exercise *some* discretion if they are to exercise a *sound* discretion.[85]

---

[79] *Balls v. Strutt* (1841) 1 Hare 146, *per* Sir James Wigram VC at 149.

[80] '*Trustees may...have to act dishonourably (though not illegally) if the interests of their beneficiaries require it*' (*Cowan v. Scargill* [1985] 1 Ch 270, *per* Megarry VC at 287–8, citing *Buttle v. Saunders* [1950] 2 All ER 193, *per* Wynn-Parry J at 195).

[81] *Re Wyvern Developments Ltd* [1974] 1 WLR 1097, *per* Templeman J at 1106.

[82] *Cowan v. Scargill* [1985] 1 Ch 270, *per* Megarry VC at 288A.

[83] *R. v. Lewisham LBC, Ex p Shell UK Ltd* [1988] 1 All ER 938, *per* Neill LJ: '*The wish to change the Shell policy towards South Africa was inextricably mixed up with any wish to improve race relations in the borough and this extraneous and impermissible purpose has the effect of vitiating the decision as a whole.*'

[84] See *Orr-Ewing v. Orr-Ewing* (1884) 11 R 600 at 627; *Gisborne v. Gisborne* (1877) LR 2 App Cas 300.

[85] *Wight v. Olswang* [2001] Lloyd's Rep PN 269.

The duty to invest with prudence

Prudence is a word that describes a process.[86] One may describe an investment as having been prudently (or imprudently) selected, managed, and retained, but it makes no sense to describe a particular investment asset (such as 'shares in X Co') as being per se prudent or imprudent.[87] As one commentator has put it: '[P]*rudence is demonstrated by the process through which risk is managed, rather than by the definition of specific risks that are imprudent.*'[88] To a layperson, the word 'risk' has negative connotations, but to an economist it is a neutral concept. There is a risk that a trust fund will perform well and a risk that it will perform badly. A prudent trustee recognizes that, whatever he does, the fund is exposed to some form of risk—hence the advice offered to trustees in an old US case: '*Do what you will, the capital is at hazard.*'[89] Even if it is relatively easy to maintain the nominal value of the fund by placing it in a bank account,[90] there is always the risk that inflation, or devaluation of currency for some other reason,[91] will cause the value of the fund to fall in real terms while it is resting in the account.

It may be no coincidence that the trustee's duty of prudence was established in the Victorian era. Those were the days of the gold standard, when the value of a pound sterling was directly linked to, and therefore remained as stable as, the value of gold.[92] The idea of prudence meant something then. A prudent trustee knew that capital could be made safe, and an income guaranteed, merely by purchasing gilts or placing trust money on deposit with a respected bank. Why expose the fund to unnecessary risk by purchasing company shares? Times change, however, and '*investments which were imprudent in the days of the gold standard may be sound and sensible in times of high inflation*'.[93] It is therefore to the credit of the Victorian courts that, by requiring a trustee to '*conduct the business of the trust in the same manner that an ordinary prudent man of business would conduct his own*',[94] they laid down a standard of trustee prudence that is adaptable to changing economic circumstances and investment practice. In Victorian times, prudence could reasonably be equated with caution, but it is clear from the leading Victorian case on trustee investment that the overriding

---

[86] The *Oxford English Dictionary* defines prudence as the '*ability to discern the most suitable, politic, or profitable course of action, especially as regards conduct, practical wisdom, discretion*'.

[87] See B. Longstreth, *Modern Investment Management and the Prudent Man Rule* (New York, Oxford: Oxford University Press, 1986), esp ch. 4, 'A modern paradigm of prudence', at 111.

[88] Ibid. Nor is it '*inherently negligent for a trustee to retain stock in a period of declining market values*' (*Jones v. AMP Perpetual Trustee Company NZ Ltd* [1994] 1 NZLR 690 at 706–7).

[89] *Harvard College v. Amory* (1830) 26 Mass (9 Pick) 446, *per* Putman J at 461.

[90] Or in a hole in the ground: see the New Testament 'parable of the talents', in which the faithful servants applied their master's money profitably, whereas the unfaithful servant 'dug a hole and hid his master's money' and boasted that it was safe (Matt. 25: 14–30, *New Testament*, New International Version).

[91] Leaving the European Exchange Rate Mechanism in 1992 produced a dramatic devaluation in the pound.

[92] The gold standard was finally abandoned in 1927.

[93] *Per* Hoffmann J in *Nestle v. National Westminster Bank plc* [1988] (1996) 10(4) TLI 112.

[94] *Re Speight* (1883) LR 22 Ch D 727.

duty is not to be cautious,[95] but to invest in a way that is calculated to provide for the beneficiaries:

> The duty of a trustee is not to take such care only as a prudent man would take if he had only himself to consider; the duty rather is to take such care as an ordinary prudent man would take if he were minded to make an investment for the benefit of other people for whom he felt morally bound to provide.[96]

The merit of this formulation is that it holds trustees to certain standards of conduct.[97] The alternative approach,[98] which would require trustees to achieve particular outcomes, may have been appropriate to Victorian England, but it is not appropriate in today's uncertain investment climate.

A paradigm of prudence that judges trustees according to the current practice of ordinary persons of business is bad news and good news for trusts. The bad news is that trustees may be encouraged to adopt popular practice, even if it is detrimental. It has been suggested, for example, that modern investment practice has become increasingly concerned with the short term, because professional fund managers are in competition and keen to produce early rewards to attract investors.[99] The good news, on the other hand, is that the trustees are encouraged continually to review best practice. The paradigm might, for instance, encourage 'ethical' or 'socially responsible' investment if society's increasing concern for such issues suggests that ethical investment may be financially viable in the medium to long term. It might also encourage a return to investment in bonds and gold,[100] in the light of the serious underperformance of the stock market in recent years. However, the main advantage of a flexible paradigm of prudence is that it allows trustees to invest according to modern portfolio theory. Investment according to that theory is *'the modern paradigm of prudence'.*[101]

---

[95] HM Treasury consultation document, *Investment Powers of Trustees*, May 1996, para. 30: '*The duty to act prudently may be breached if the trustees are insufficiently cautious, but also if they are too cautious.*' See also *Melville v. Noble's Trustees* (1896) 24 R 243.

[96] *Re Whiteley* (1886) LR 33 Ch D 347 at 355, *per* Lindley LJ. Approved in *Nestle v. National Westminster Bank* [1993] 1 WLR 1260, *per* Dillon LJ at 1267H. See, also, on the moral provision aspect: *King v. Talbot*, 40 NY 76 (1869).

[97] See also *Harvard College v. Amory* 26 Mass (9 Pick) 446 (1830) at 461: the trustee should '*conduct himself faithfully and exercise a sound discretion*'.

[98] Endorsed by another of their Lordships in the same case: '*Trustees are bound to preserve the money for those entitled to the corpus in remainder, and they are bound to invest it in such a way as will produce a reasonable income for those enjoying the income for the present*', *per* Cotton LJ (*Re Whiteley* (1886) LR 33 Ch D 347 at 350).

[99] S. Gardner, *An Introduction to The Law of Trusts* (Oxford: Clarendon Press, 1990) at 125–6.

[100] During the period 1999–2009, when stock markets generally fell, gold has more-or-less tripled in value. Economic studies indicate that gold is effective as a hedge against stock market risk in the long term. R. Aggarwal, 'Gold Markets' in *The New Palgrave Dictionary of Money and Finance* (P. Newman, M. Milgate, and J. Eatwell, eds) (Basingstoke: Macmillan, 1992) vol. 2, 257; D. Ghosh, E.J. Levin, P. MacMillan, and R.E. Wright, 'Gold as an inflation hedge?' (2004) 22 Studies in Economics and Finance 1.

[101] This is the title to ch. 4 of Longstreth, *Modern Investment Management and the Prudent Man Rule* (New York, Oxford: Oxford University Press, 1986). See also also J. H. Langbein and R. Posner, 'Market funds and trust: investment law' (1976) 1 American Bar Foundation Res J, 3; Friedman, 'The dynastic trust' (1964) 73 Yale LJ 547, 553; M. A. Shattuck, 'The development of the prudent man rule for fiduciary investment in the United States in the twentieth century' (1951) 12 Ohio St LJ 491, 492; S. Lofthouse, *Equity Investment Management*, 1st edn, at 9; J. H. Langbein, 'The Uniform Prudent Investor Act and the future of trust investing' (1996) 81 Iowa LR 641; J. R. Hicks, *Value and Capital* (1938) at 177.

Modern portfolio theory

In 1988, just two years after the deregulation of investment business in the UK[102] and the publication of Longstreth's seminal work, *Modern Investment Management and the Prudent Man Rule*,[103] Hoffmann J held that:

> Modern trustees acting within their investment powers are entitled to be judged by the standards of current portfolio theory, which emphasises the risk level of the entire portfolio rather than the risk attaching to each investment taken in isolation.[104]

That judgment was reported in 1996 and was referred to, with approval, by HM Treasury in its consultation document published that year.[105] Since then, the Trustee Act 2000 has laid down '*standard investment criteria*',[106] which, according to the explanatory notes accompanying the Act, are intended to facilitate trustee investment in accordance with modern portfolio theory.[107]

The major insight offered by modern portfolio theory is that risks specific to investment in any particular company may be virtually eliminated by holding a diverse portfolio of shares in other companies. Portfolios containing investments other than shares also benefit from diversification, but the theory is most applicable to shares, and especially to shares in public companies. The values of shares in public companies are quoted on the stock exchange, so the market in such shares is efficient relative to other markets, in the sense that the quoted value of the shares ought to be an accurate reflection of all published information relating to those shares.

Types of investment risk

To understand portfolio theory, it is necessary to distinguish two types of investment risk. The first is 'specific risk', which is risk associated with a particular company, say Z plc. The second is 'market risk' or 'systemic risk', which is risk associated with the entire market in shares. Systemic risk is the risk that the whole market or 'system' will fail. It is sometimes said that the stock market lurches like a roller coaster, and certainly the descriptions for various degrees of systemic failure reflect that: there are 'dips', 'slumps', 'dives', and, if things are really bad, a 'crash'.

Diversification within an equities market (such as the FTSE 100 or the FTSE All Share) does nothing to reduce the systemic risk of failure across the market as a whole. Such risk is therefore said to be non-diversifiable. However, diversification of shareholdings across companies *within* the market does reduce the risks associated with the failure of any particular company. This is the major insight of modern portfolio theory.

---

[102] The so-called 'Big Bang' brought about by the Financial Services Act 1986. See Gardner, *An Introduction to The Law of Trusts* (Oxford: Clarendon Press, 1990) at 122.

[103] Longstreth, *Modern Investment Management and the Prudent Man Rule* (New York, Oxford: Oxford University Press, 1986). See, especially, ch. 4: A modern paradigm of prudence.

[104] *Nestle v. National Westminster Bank plc* [1988] (1996) 10(4) TLI 112 at 115.

[105] HM Treasury Consultation Document, *Investment Powers of Trustees*, May 1996 at paras 40(iii) and 35(ii).

[106] See later.   [107] Note 25.

Non-diversifiable risks

'Non-diversifiable' or 'systemic' risks include changes in the tax regime, interest rate, and the rate of inflation. Political changes, such as the election of a left-wing government, may also have an immediate detrimental effect on the value of the stock market as a whole.[108]

A particularly potent form of non-diversifiable risk is the fraud or incompetence of human agents; 'agency risk' of this sort has even been described as the primary risk that investors face.[109] Trustees are authorized to insure the fund against loss howsoever caused[110] and statutory insurance is available via the Financial Services Compensation Scheme,[111] but the problem is that investment losses are hard to prove. If an agent absconds with trust funds, loss will be obvious, but if the investments yield a return, it will be much harder to establish that the level of return has been reduced due to incompetence or fraud.[112]

Reducing risk through diversification

If the portfolio is so diverse that it mirrors the composition of the market, specific risks will be entirely eliminated as regards that market, because the portfolio will rise and fall in line with the movement of the market quite regardless of what happens to individual companies quoted on it. Such a market- or index-tracking portfolio can be created by holding shares in every company within the market, the size of each shareholding being proportionate to the capitalized value of the company in which it is held.[113] Of course, it is not possible to track markets in other assets, such as land, in this way.

Few trusts have the means to hold directly the required number of shares to match the market, and if they did the transaction costs and governance duties would probably be prohibitive.[114] Trustees can, instead, invest in tracker funds managed by external fund managers, but that is merely to replace risks specific to particular company shares with risks specific to particular fund managers, including such matters as their honesty, competence, and the level of their charges.

It is at this point that we return to the problem of trustee decision making. A trustee is breaching his trust if he rigidly adheres to an index-tracking portfolio in the belief that modern portfolio theory has absolved him of the need to make investment decisions.

---

[108] K. Redhead, *Introduction to Financial Investment* (Harlow: Prentice Hall/Woodhead-Faulkner, 1995) at 7.
[109] J. A. Franks and C. Mayer, *Risk, Regulation, and Investor Protection* (Oxford: Clarendon Press, 1989) ch. 6 at 151, part C, para. 2.15.   [110] See Chapter 11.
[111] See ibid.   [112] See later.
[113] '*The most ardent practitioners of modern portfolio theory, when they invest in the share market, construct a portfolio which exactly replicates it*': W. A. Lee, 'Modern portfolio theory and the investment of pension funds', ch. 10 in *Equity and Commercial Relationships* (P. Finn, ed.) (North Ryde, NSW: The Law Book Co, 1987) 284 at 298. See also Butler (1995) 16 NZULR 349.
[114] One alternative is the use of common investment funds (CIFs). These allow trusts (typically charitable trusts) to pool their funds for investment purposes. However, one disadvantage of CIFs (as with unit trusts) is that investors may not entirely appreciate the nature of their shareholdings (see D. Morris, 'Charity investment in the UK' (1995) 3 Web JCL1.). Charities may also use common deposit funds (CDFs) to pool cash on deposit in order to obtain higher returns of interest.

A trustee is entitled to be judged by the standards of modern portfolio theory, but he is neither required, nor permitted, slavishly to adhere to that theory. His duty to exercise a positive discretion may require him to remove a company from his portfolio if any prudent person would regard it as a poor investment.

The good news for trustees of funds that are too small to track the entire market is that even a relatively small amount of diversification will offset the greater part of the risk: even investment in two companies is better than investment in one.[115] And, if a trustee is careful which two companies he chooses, the risks associated with one company can be offset quite significantly by investment in the other. So, for example, the risk of investment in an umbrella manufacturer will, in theory, be better offset or 'hedged' by investment in a manufacturer of sunglasses than by investment in waterproof jackets. Further good news for trusts which are too small to hold an index-tracking portfolio of investments is that diversification across different domestic markets (for example, shares, land, and bonds) and different international markets (for example, the UK, the USA, and Hong Kong) produces greater insulation against overall risk than diversification within any single market.[116] Of course, the downside to an international portfolio is increased management and transaction costs, and increased numbers of managers means an increased risk of fraud and error.

Risk management

Historically the trustee investor avoided risk, but today the trustee investor manages risk. As Lord Nicholls of Birkenhead has said:

> traditional warnings against the need for trustees to avoid speculative or hazardous invest-
> ments are not to be read as inhibiting trustees from maintaining portfolios of investments
> which contain a prudent and sensible mixture of low risk and higher risk securities. They are
> not to be so read, because they were not directed at a portfolio which is a balanced exercise
> in risk management.[117]

This does not mean that trustees are permitted to invest in individual investments that are speculative or hazardous: '*The distinction is between a prudent degree of risk on the one hand, and hazard on the other.*' [118] Nor does it mean that trustees are no longer accountable for risk associated with the investments they choose; it means only that trustees will be judged by the risk associated with the portfolio as a whole and not merely by the risk associated with individual investments.

The question therefore arises: what level of total portfolio risk is appropriate to trusts? An economic model known as the 'capital asset pricing model' demonstrates

---

[115] Witness the disaster that befell the trust fund in *Wight v. Olswang* [2001] Lloyd's Rep PN 269.

[116] In 'Time for change: charity investment and modern portfolio theory' (1995) 3(2) CL&PR, Harvey P. Dale and Michael Gwinell suggest that the choice of asset type is estimated to account for 80–90% of portfolio performance, but only 10–20% reflects choice between investments of that type.

[117] Lord Nicholls of Birkenhead, 'Trustees and their broader community: where duty, morality and ethics converge' (1995) 9(3) TLI 71.

[118] *Bartlett v. Barclays Bank Trust Co (No. 1)* [1980] Ch 515, *per* Brightman J at 531G.

that, having taken into account the level of returns that is expected from the 'risk-free' portion of a portfolio (that part comprising gilt-edged securities, three-month Treasury bills, etc.), additional expected returns will rise in direct proportion to increased risk. This linear correlation is known as the security market line. At the heart of this model is common sense. The model is based on expectations and expectations are based on information. If we assume a world in which accurate information about investments is freely and instantly available (only the market in publicly quoted shares comes close to this), it will follow that the value of an investment as currently quoted will be an accurate reflection of its true underlying value. In this 'efficient market', the hypothetical 'rational' investor will run greater risks only if there is a corresponding expectation of greater returns.[119] In short, returns can be expected to rise as risk rises, so the question 'What risks is it appropriate for trustees to take?' becomes 'What returns is it appropriate for trustees to seek?'

It is at this point that the process of trustee investment must be concerned with outcomes. The trustee's first hope—in a traditional settlement trust, at least—is to preserve the real value of the capital and to produce an income. This means that the trustee should seek a portfolio with a low overall risk quotient. In other words, the prudent trustee will be cautious or 'risk-averse' as regards the total portfolio, but he will ensure that assets within the portfolio are exposed to risk, albeit in a managed way.

Of course, the law does not *require* trustees to invest according to modern portfolio theory; it merely *facilitates* it. There are alternatives for the prudent trustee. One of these is to have a smaller, but more carefully selected, portfolio:

> many people believe that by restricting the stocks a manager can invest in must inhibit performance. A simple answer to this is that focussing attention on a smaller universe of stocks can lead to improved quality and quantity of research.[120]

In other words, the most prudent course may be to follow the advice given (so it is said) by the famous industrialist, Andrew Carnegie: '*Put your eggs in one basket. And watch the basket. That's the way to make money.*'[121]

Obstacles to modern portfolio theory in English law

Prior to the Trustee Act 2000, the English law of trusts presented a number of obstacles to the implementation of modern portfolio theory. The 2000 Act removes them all, either directly or indirectly.

The primary obstacle was the fact that trustees were limited to certain types of investment. Trustees were not even permitted to invest in private company shares, unless authorized by the trust instrument or the court. What is more, when, in the 1980s and 1990s, many prudent investors were purchasing shares in denationalized

---

[119] The capital asset pricing model is based on this 'efficient market hypothesis'.

[120] John Thornton (of Friends Provident): a paper delivered to the NAPF Euro-Pensions Conference 1996. (The author is grateful to the Institute of Actuaries for providing a copy.)

[121] Of course, the advice given was originally aimed at entrepreneurs, rather than trustees.

utilities, trustees were unable to do so, because the new public limited companies (such as British Gas plc and British Telecom plc) had no track record and therefore failed to meet the stringent criteria laid down by the Trustee Investment Act 1961 for investment in quoted companies.[122] Now, as we have seen, the Trustee Act 2000 permits any type of investment.

A second obstacle, related to the first, was the assumption that the trustees' duty of prudence required trustees to avoid risky investments. We have seen that the trust fund is always subject to risk, if only the risk of inflation. To make gains sufficient to offset the effect of inflation, trustees must expose the fund to a degree of risk. If the exposure to risk is planned (by means of an appropriately balanced portfolio), it will be prudent. According to the modern paradigm of prudence, exposure to risk will be considered imprudent or speculative only if it is unplanned, or planned badly.

A third obstacle was the so-called 'anti-netting rule', or the rule against 'set-off'. This rule insists that trustees may not set off gains made by one breach of trust against losses arising from another breach of trust.[123] However, the rule against 'set-off' only presents an obstacle to portfolio investment if the purchase of individual assets in the portfolio is viewed in isolation, because then there will be no possibility of reducing a loss made by investing in asset A by the gain made by investing in asset B. In fact, even before the Trustee Act 2000, there was judicial support for assessing linked transactions together, so as to limit the trustee's liability to the net loss arising from the linked transactions.[124]

A fourth obstacle was the old rule that trust investments had to yield an income.[125] In essence, it was a rule designed to preserve capital, for if a beneficiary's needs could not be met out of income, the capital would have to be sold.[126] The rule unduly limited the range of possible trust investments and therefore reduced the trustees' ability to create a balanced portfolio. Now, as the explanatory notes that accompany the Trustee Act 2000 make clear, the general power of investment[127] permits trustees to invest in assets that are expected to yield capital growth instead of (or in addition to) income.[128] However, the notes also confirm that one factor relevant to determining the suitability of a particular investment is '*the need to produce an appropriate balance between income and capital growth*'.[129] What is appropriate will depend upon the '*needs of the trust*'. Certain formal rules used to apply to trusts, but they have been abolished by the Trusts (Capital and Income) Act 2013 for new trusts coming into force after its commencement (on

---

[122] Trustee Investment Act 1961, Sch. 1 Pt. IV (repealed).   [123] *Dimes v. Scott* (1828) 4 Russ 195.

[124] *Bartlett v. Barclays Trust (No. 1)* [1980] Ch 515, *per* Brightman J.

[125] See E. M. David, 'Principal and income: obsolete concepts' (1972) 43 PA Bar Assoc Q at 247.

[126] By keeping the capital (the means of income production) in private hands, the trust, especially the traditional settlement trust, demonstrates its capitalist credentials (see Karl Marx, *Das Kapital*, for a wider conception of capital as the 'means of production').   [127] Trustee Act 2000, s. 3.

[128] Judges had begun to relax the rule even prior to the Act: '*prima facie the purposes of the trust will be best served by the trustees seeking to obtain therefrom the maximum return, whether by way of income or capital growth, which is consistent with commercial prudence*', *per* Sir Donald Nicholls VC in *Harries v. Church Commissioners* [1992] 1 WLR 1241 at 1246. See also Megarry VC in *Cowan v. Scargill* [1985] Ch 270 at 287. The decisions of the Charity Commissioners Vol. 3, No. 4, Dec. 1995 confirmed that capital growth is a form of investment return acceptable to a charity.   [129] Note 23.

31 January 2013).[130] In the case of charities, the 2013 Act empowers trustees to free the endowment fund, or a portion of it, from restrictions with respect to expenditure of capital in order that they might operate total return investment (i.e. investment which ignores the distinction between income and capital).

The statutory 'standard investment criteria'

According to the Trustee Act 2000, trustees must have regard to the '*standard investment criteria*'[131] when investing on behalf of the trust. It defines the 'standard investment criteria' as 'suitability' and 'diversity'. The type of investment—for example, land—must be suitable to the trust, as must the particular investment of that type—for example, The Old Vicarage, Warwick[132]—and diversification must be pitched at a level appropriate to the '*circumstances of the trust*'.[133] Furthermore, the trust investments must be reviewed '*from time to time*' and the trustees must consider, in the light of the standard investment criteria, whether to vary them.[134]

The explanatory notes that accompany the 2000 Act confirm that courts should judge the *suitability* of particular investments in the light of the overall portfolio of investments. It appears that the size and risk of the investment, the need to produce an appropriate balance between income and capital growth, and 'ethical considerations' will all be relevant in judging whether the portfolio is a 'suitable' one.[135]

Obtaining and considering proper advice

Before exercising any power of investment or implementing any decision to vary investments as a result of a review, trustees must '*obtain and consider proper advice about whether, having regard to the standard investment criteria*', they should proceed.[136] This statutory duty is really nothing more than a specific instance of the duty to invest with prudence. Obviously 'obtain and consider' does not mean 'follow': trustees are obliged to exercise an independent discretion. Having said that, trustees depart from expert advice at their peril. Portfolio management is not for amateurs.[137] Indeed, the move to portfolio-based investment has made it necessary to take advice even in relation to investments, such as bank accounts and gilts, which, prior to the 2000 Act, could be made without advice.

---

[130] See the section on the 'duty to invest fairly',

[131] Trustee Act 2000, s. 4(1). This section is essentially a re-enactment of the Trustee Investments Act 1961, s. 6(1). [132] Section 4(3)(a).

[133] Section 4(3)(b). The same words, which appeared in s. 6(1) of the 1961 Act, were held to include circumstances such as the size of the trust fund. As Megarry VC stated in *Cowan v. Scargill* [1985] Ch 270, '*the degree of diversification that is practicable and desirable for a large fund may plainly be impracticable or undesirable (or both) in the case of a small fund*' at 289E–F. Another relevant circumstance is the presence of beneficiaries with competing interests in the fund (see 'The duty of fairness', later).

[134] Section 4(2). The duty to conduct periodic reviews was recognized before the 2000 Act: *Nestle v. National Westminster Bank plc (No. 2)* [1993] 1 WLR 1260, *per* Leggatt LJ at 1282G.

[135] These factors are listed in note 23 of the explanatory notes accompanying the Act.

[136] Trustee Act 2000, s. 5(1) and (2).

[137] J. H. Langbein, 'Reversing the non-delegation rule of trust-investment law' (1994) 59 MLR 105, 110.

'Proper advice' is 'the advice of a person who is reasonably believed by the trustee to be qualified by his ability in and practical experience of financial and other matters relating to the proposed investment'.[138] There is no requirement that the advice be given or confirmed in writing, but 'to do so will no doubt be regarded as best practice in many circumstances, and may be necessary for trustees to show compliance with the general duty of care in section 1'.[139] If one of the trustees is qualified to give advice, the trustees are together entitled to rely on the advice of the 'expert' trustee.[140]

There is, however, an important exception to the duty to obtain and consider proper advice: 'a trustee need not obtain such advice if he reasonably concludes that in all the circumstances it is unnecessary or inappropriate to do so'.[141] One relevant 'circumstance' is the size of the investment: if the proposed investment is small, the cost of obtaining advice might be disproportionate to the benefit.[142]

The duty to invest fairly

Beneficiaries with life interests and beneficiaries with interests in remainder will agree that their trust should be administered prudently by trustees who have powers adequate for the task. So, when the trustees in *Anker-Petersen v. Anker-Petersen*[143] applied to court to have their investment powers extended, the judge held that he was not required to give consent on behalf of every category of beneficiary separately, but could consider the beneficiaries' interests collectively in income and in capital. With regard to certain matters, however, the interests of different classes of beneficiary are essentially in direct competition with each other. Thus, whereas the life tenant's interest is in high-income assets with limited scope for capital appreciation (or even scope for depreciation), the remainder-man's interest is firmly in capital retention at the expense of income. The law recognizes this conflict and takes the view that, in exercising their investment discretion, trustees should invest fairly in the interests of every beneficiary and every class of beneficiary:

> it is of the essence of the duty of every trustee to hold an even hand between the parties interested under the trust. Every trustee is in duty bound to look to the interests of all, and not of any particular member or class.[144]

The duty is sometimes expressed as a duty to maintain a fair balance between the beneficiaries. In fact, the word 'balance' can be misleading in so far as it suggests equality.[145]

---

[138] Trustee Act 2000, s. 5(4).   [139] Explanatory notes accompanying the 2000 Act (note 28).

[140] Section 12(1).   [141] Section 5(4).

[142] Explanatory notes accompanying the Act (note 26).   [143] (1991) 16 LS Gaz 32, Ch D.

[144] *Re Tempest* (1866) LR 1 Ch App 485, CA, *per* Sir G. J. Turner LJ at 487.

[145] Hoffmann J disagreed with the view of Sir Robert Megarry VC in *Cowan v. Scargill* [1985] 1 Ch 270 at 286–8, that the trustees' duty is to hold '*the scales impartially between different classes of beneficiaries*'. He disagreed partly because it suggests equality, but partly because '*the image of the scales suggests a weighing of known quantities whereas investment decisions are concerned with predictions of the future ... but there is always a greater or lesser risk that the outcome will deviate from those expectations. A judgment on the fairness of the choices made by the trustees must have regard to these imponderables*' (*Nestle v. National Westminster Bank plc* [1988] (1996) 10(4) TLI 112 at 115).

Fairness between competing beneficiaries need not import equality, because an equal approach would automatically place the life tenant (who may be, and often is, the sett-lor's surviving spouse) on the same footing as the remainderman (who may be a cousin or other remote relative). In such a case, '[equality] *is surely the last thing the settlor ever intended*'.[146] These are the words Lord Wilberforce used in connection with discretion-ary trusts and it is not by accident that they are used here. The discretion that a trustee must exercise when determining a fair balance of investments is equivalent in breadth to the dispositive discretion that trustees exercise when distributing the trust fund under a discretionary trust. In both situations, the trustees are required, in essence, to second-guess what the settlor would have wanted to provide for the particular benefi-ciaries. As Hoffmann J said in *Nestle*:

> The trustees have in my judgment a wide discretion. They are for example entitled to take into account the income needs of the tenant for life or the fact that the tenant for life was a person known to the settlor and a primary object of the trust whereas the remainderman is a remoter relative or a stranger ... It would be an inhuman law which required trustees to adhere to some mechanical rule for preserving the real value of the capital when the tenant for life was the testator's widow who had fallen upon hard times and the remainderman was young and well off.[147]

Specific duties in relation to original investments

Implicit in the general investment power[148] is a power to retain or sell the original invest-ments. There are, however, situations in which this power is replaced by a *duty* to retain or sell the investments in their original form. Family heirlooms, for example, must be retained[149] unless the court orders their sale in an emergency.[150] The duty to sell origi-nal investments is more complicated. It may be that the original fund consists solely of gold bullion that is producing no income at all. Or maybe it consists solely of shares in a gold-mining company that are expected to produce great income in the short term but will be worthless within a few years because the mine is nearly exhausted. How are the respective interests of the life tenant and remainderman to be satisfied? Is it encum-bent upon the trustee to redress the balance between capital and income? Or, to put it another way, is there a duty to convert the fund?

The basic principle is that, in the absence of any express direction appearing in the trust instrument, the trustee will be obliged to convert only to the extent necessary to give effect to the settlor's intentions. The law that has developed from this principle states that there is no duty to convert specific gifts such as 'freehold title to Greenacre', '£20,000', and 'the Red Ferrari registration F1 DE'. The fact that the specific gift may be

---

[146]   *McPhail v. Doulton* [1971] AC 424, HL, *per* Lord Wilberforce at 451.

[147]   *Nestle v. National Westminster Bank plc* [1988] (1996) 10(4) TLI 112. See D. Hayton, 32 Vand J Transnat'l 555 at 561: '*This duty to act fairly confers a wide discretion upon trustees enabling them to act partially but honestly.*'   [148]   Trustee Act 2000, s. 3.

[149]   See *Re Hope* [1899] 2 Ch 679.   [150]   See Chapter 9.

incapable of providing income for the life tenant and capital for the remainderman is none of the trustee's concern, because the settlor is presumed to have intended to make the particular gift despite its inherent limitations. It follows that the duty to convert is limited to residuary gifts and therefore, by definition, to testamentary gifts. The duty is also limited to personalty, because real estate is, in principle, always capable of providing capital security for the remainderman and present enjoyment for the life tenant. Limiting the duty to personalty also relieves the trustee of any duty to sell the family home or ancestral seat.

In summary, then, the duty to convert—which is known as the rule in *Howe v. Earl Dartmouth*[151]—extends only to residuary bequests. However, in practice, it rarely extends even that far. The duty to convert, together with the rigid and complex rules as to apportionment of income and capital that accompany it, are ill-suited to modern investment practice and they are usually excluded by the express terms of trust instruments. Indeed, as a result of the Trusts (Capital and Income) Act 2013 this apportionment rule and others like it are no longer law as regards trusts coming into effect after 31 January 2013.[152] Arguably the Trustee Act 2000 s. 4(2), which requires trustees periodically to review the suitability to the trust of the current investments, is sufficient on its own to achieve the fundamental aims of conversion and apportionment.

Liability for improper investment by trustees

At the very start of this chapter, the reader was alerted to the difficulties that beneficiaries face when trying to establish that their trustees are liable for improper investment. We noted that there are challenges at every stage, from proving that there has been a breach of trust (which we now know requires proof of imprudence or unfairness),[153] to proving that the trust has suffered a loss (and the size of the loss), to proving that the loss was caused by the breach. The beneficiaries' task is not made any easier by the decision in the leading modern case on liability for imprudent trustee investment, *Nestle v. National Westminster Bank plc*.[154]

'*How do you make a small fortune? Give a bank a large one to manage in trust*.'[155] The joke could have been based on *Nestle v. National Westminster Bank plc*. William

---

[151] (1802) 7 Ves 137.

[152] Other traditional rules on apportionament of capital and income include the rule that income beneficiaries are entitled only to that part of the trust income that accrued during their period of entitlement (Apportionment Act 1870, s. 2); the rule that protects income beneficiaries against the trustees' decision to retain investments in capital form (the rule in *Re Earl of Chesterfield's Trusts* (1883) 24 Ch D 643), and the rule that apportions between capital and income residuary beneficiaries any liabilities falling to be paid out of the residuary estate (the rule in *Allhusen v. Whittell* (1867) LR 4 Eq 295).

[153] Proof that the statutory 'standard investment criteria' of 'suitability' and 'diversity' were not adhered to is prima facie evidence of a breach of trust, and can be pleaded in addition to a plea based on the common law duties of prudence and fairness.   [154] [1993] 1 WLR 1260, CA.

[155] J. Dukeminier and J. E. Krier, 'The rise of the perpetual trust' (2003) 50 UCLA L 1303, 1335.

David Nestle died in 1922, leaving a fund worth approximately £54,000 on trust for various descendants. The claimant, the testator's only granddaughter, became solely and absolutely entitled to the fund in 1986, by which date the nominal capital value of the fund had increased to nearly £270,000. However, had the real value of the fund been maintained, it would have been worth around £1m in 1986. What is more, the claimant alleged that she would have received almost double that (around £1.8m) had the original portfolio balance between equities and gilts been maintained until 1986. The trustee, the National Provincial Bank (later the National Westminster Bank), had misinterpreted the powers of investment granted to it by the terms of the trust and, choosing to err on the side of caution, had reduced the proportion of the portfolio devoted to equities. The claimant alleged that the bank had done so imprudently and, furthermore, that, through the purchase or retention of fixed interest securities in preference to ordinary shares, the bank had unfairly favoured the life beneficiaries over her.

The Court of Appeal considered it 'inexcusable that the bank took no steps at any time to obtain legal advice as to the scope of its power to invest in ordinary shares'.[156] Their Lordships also held that the bank should have undertaken regular reviews of the investments under its control. Leggatt LJ reached the damning conclusion that '[n]o testator, in the light of this example, would choose this bank for the effective management of his investment'.[157] Yet despite these sentiments, the claimant failed. This led commentators to ask whether there is any effective legal remedy for improper trustee investment:[158]

> Some people might see it as remarkable that the bank incurred no liability notwithstanding the fact that they plainly misconstrued the scope of their investment powers especially since the trustee was a paid professional who supposedly owes higher duties of care.[159]

The outcome in *Nestle* may not be remarkable when one considers how broad is the trustee's discretion to determine a *fair* balance within the portfolio between the interests of life and remainder beneficiaries, but it is most remarkable when one considers the high objective standards of *prudence* against which trustees are supposed to be assessed. The main reason why the trustee in *Nestle* escaped liability for the losses that probably resulted from its undoubted imprudence, was that the three basic elements of liability (breach, loss, and causation) were not kept sufficiently distinct—especially in so far as questions of outcome (loss) were allowed to impinge upon questions of process (breach of duty). The following passage from the judgment of Staughton LJ exemplifies the confusion:

> The misunderstanding of the investment clause and the failure to conduct periodic reviews do not by themselves, whether separately or together, afford the plaintiff a remedy. They were symptoms of incompetence or idleness...they were not, without more, breaches of

---

[156] Ibid. *per* Dillon LJ at 1265 E–F.   [157] Ibid. at 1284 G–H.
[158] G. McCormack, 'Liability of trustees for negligent investment decisions' (1997) 13(2) *Professional Negligence* at 45; G. Watt and M. Stauch, 'Is there liability for imprudent trustee investment?' (1998) 62 Conv 352.
[159] G. McCormack, ibid. at 50.

trust. The plaintiff must show that, through one or other or both of those causes, the trustees made decisions which they should not have made or failed to make decisions which they should have made… The judge took the view that 'the bank had acted conscientiously, fairly and carefully throughout the administration of [the] trust'. I cannot join in that accolade. But it is not shown that there was loss arising from a breach of trust for which the trustees ought to compensate the trust fund.[160]

His Lordship was quite correct to suggest that the trustee's defaults '*do not by themselves, whether separately or together, afford the plaintiff a remedy*', but his Lordship was, it is submitted, wrong to suggest that '*they were not, without more, breaches of trust*'. The behaviour of a professional trust corporation is judged by a high standard and there can be no doubt that the trustee in *Nestle* had breached its trust. The only scope for argument relates to the quite distinct questions that follow: did the trust fund suffer an identifiable and quantifiable loss, and did the trustee's breach of trust cause that loss? It undermines the deterrent and symbolic aims of high standards of fiduciary behaviour to dismiss a breach of trust as immaterial merely because the uncertainties inherent in the investment process have made it practically impossible to prove that the breach went on to cause a quantifiable loss.[161]

Staughton LJ suggests that, in order to prove a breach of trust, it is insufficient to demonstrate merely that the trustee was incompetent and idle. It is also necessary to show that the trustee made bad decisions as a result. There is nothing wrong with that approach in so far as it suggests that a finding of breach of trust should be based on the totality of the investment process and the manner in which the trustee exercises his discretion. However, it can be read as suggesting that there is no breach of trust—no matter how improper the trustee's decision-making process—as long as the trustee's ultimate decisions are unimpeachable. On that reading, a trustee who selects his portfolio by randomly pricking a pin in the shares pages of the *Financial Times* might be beyond reproach. The process is completely imprudent and involves a total abdication of discretion, but who is to say that a trustee investing prudently would necessarily have chosen a different portfolio? The judgment of Leggatt LJ seems to confirm that this latter, albeit pessimistic, interpretation of Staughton LJ's words is the one that their Lordships approve:

> it does not follow from the fact that a wider power of investment was available to the bank than it realised either that it would have been exercised or that, if it had been, the exercise of it would have produced a result more beneficial to the bank than actually was produced. Loss cannot be presumed, if none would necessarily have resulted.[162]

The problem with this approach is that it puts a heavy burden on the claimant to prove not only that the trustee acted imprudently or unfairly—by, say, taking inappropriate matters into account or failing to take appropriate matters into account (as in *Nestle*)— but also that the ultimate outcome of these errors was 'necessarily' worse than that

---

[160] [1993] 1 WLR 1260, CA.   [161] See the quotation from the judgment of Leggatt LJ, next.
[162] [1993] 1 WLR 1260, CA, *per* Leggatt LJ at 1283B.

which would have occurred in the absence of default. If we have learned anything about the process of investment in this chapter, we have surely learned that one can never say of any investment process that it will 'necessarily' produce such and such an outcome; still less can it be said that a trustee's investment would 'necessarily' have yielded such and such an outcome in the absence of default—for that calculation would require one to overcome the unpredictability of the investment market and to overcome the unpredictability of trustee decision making. We have seen that decisions relating to trustee investment involve very broad discretions, in relation to both 'prudence' and 'fairness'. The sheer breadth of such discretions makes it impossible to establish what a trustee would 'necessarily' have done but for his default.

There are many possible explanations for the approach taken by their Lordships in *Nestle*. One is that their Lordships deliberately wished to promote a liberal regulatory regime for trustee investment, one in which trustees would feel safe to participate in the most up-to-date investment techniques. However, against this explanation stands their Lordships' apparent assumption that inactivity is the best guarantee of the fund's success:

> Inevitably, a trustee in the bank's position wears a complacent air, because the virtue of safety will in practice put a premium on inactivity. Until the 1950s active management of the portfolio might have been seen as speculative, and even in these days such dealing would have to be notably successful before the expense would be justified.[163]

This reasoning cannot be appropriate in the light of endemic inflation and the insights of modern portfolio theory.

The approach in *Nestle* should be contrasted with that adopted by the court in *Re Mulligan (deceased)*,[164] a New Zealand case. There, the testator had died in 1949, leaving his widow a substantial legacy and a life interest in a farm. The widow was one of the trustees of the estate. The farm was sold in 1965 and the estate invested in fixed-interest securities until the widow died in 1990. The other trustee had, between 1965 and 1990, tried to persuade the widow to invest in shares to counter inflation, but she had adamantly refused to do so. That trustee (a trust corporation) was held to be in breach of trust, because it had appreciated the corrosive effect of inflation on the estate capital (which was held to be reliable evidence of the standard of prudence in the industry at the time), but had nevertheless deferred to the widow's wishes. The merit of this approach, over that adopted in *Nestle*, is that breach of trust was determined by reference to the trustee's conduct and not by reference to the outcomes that conduct happened to produce. Although, ironically, if presented with the facts[165] in *Re Mulligan*, it is possible that their Lordships in *Nestle* would also have found for the plaintiff. As Dillon LJ stated:

> If what had happened in the present case had been that the bank, through failure to inform itself as to the true scope of its investment powers, had invested the whole of the annuity

---

[163] Ibid. *per* Leggatt LJ at 1284H.   [164] [1998] 1 NZLR 481.
[165] The court in *Re Mulligan* distinguished *Nestle* on its facts.

fund in fixed interest securities, and no part in equities…then, as on the evidence loss would clearly have been proved to have been suffered, the appropriate course would have been to require the bank to make good to the trust fair compensation—and not just the minimum that might have got by without challenge.[166]

Finally, it must be stressed that it is not enough to prove that a trustee's investment choices 'caused' the trust to suffer a loss. Trustees are only liable for losses that they have caused *by breaching their trust*. If a trustee chooses to invest in X Co and X Co fails, it is clear that, factually speaking, the trustee's choice was one cause of any loss suffered by the trust fund: 'but for' the trustee's choice to invest in X Co, the fund would not have suffered a loss when X Co failed. It does not follow, however, that trustees should be liable as a matter of law to compensate for every loss they cause as a matter of fact. If, on the other hand, a trustee imprudently makes an investment (such as the retention of dilapidated land) which by pure chance happens to do well (due, say, to a general increase in land values),[167] the trustee will escape liability on the *Nestle* principle that imprudent investment does not lead to liability in the absence of proof of loss.

In *Bartlett v. Barclays Bank Trust Co (No. 1)*,[168] Brightman J warned that courts must not 'be astute to fix liability upon a trustee who has committed no more than an error of judgment, from which no business man, however prudent, can expect to be immune'.[169] The settlor, and, by implication, the beneficiaries, 'must take the consequences of having intrusted their monies to persons of sanguine temperament who have made a purchase which turns out to be a bad one'.[170] In short, 'lack of clairvoyance is not negligence'.[171] The merit of these dicta is that they focus on the blameworthiness, or otherwise, of the trustee's conduct as a basis for any liability. In contrast, their Lordships in *Nestle* placed undue emphasis upon outcomes. So when Leggatt LJ accepted counsel's submission that 'loss' will be incurred by a trust fund 'when it makes a gain less than would have been made by a prudent businessman',[172] his Lordship made no reference to the fact that even prudent businessmen are not exempt from bad luck.

Related to the problem of causation is the problem of quantification. Liability will be difficult to establish if it is not possible to say *how much* loss a breach has caused.

Quantification is relatively straightforward where the trustee was directed to invest in particular investments and failed to do so,[173] but, as with everything in the law of

---

[166] *Nestle v. National Westminster Bank* [1993] 1 WLR 1260 at 1268H.

[167] See *Jeffrey v. Gretton and Russell* [2011] WTLR 809 (Ch D), which the judge described as *'fortunate for the trustees, but…fortuitous. This is not a case of a judicious breach of trust; it is a case of a thoughtless breach of trust that happens to have turned out well'* (para. [84]). [168] [1980] Ch 515.

[169] Ibid. at 531H. Trustees *'do make mistakes from time to time'* (Lord Nicholls of Birkenhead, 'Trustees and their broader community: where duty, morality and ethics converge' (1995) 9(3) TLI 71 at 73).

[170] *Overend, Gurney & Co v. Gurney* (1868–69) LR 4 Ch App 701 at 720.

[171] *Hamilton v. Nielsen*, 678 F.2d 709 (1982), *per* Circuit Judge Posner at 713.

[172] *Nestle v. National Westminster Bank* [1993] 1 WLR 1260 at 1283C.

[173] *Re Massingberd's Settlement Trusts* (1890) 63 LT 296. See *Shepherd v. Mouls* (1845) 4 Hare 500.

trustee investment, it is far from straightforward where the trustee has a broad discretion. It has even been said that:

> The discretion given to the trustees to select an investment among several securities makes it impossible to ascertain the amount of the loss (if any) which has arisen to the trust fund from the omission to invest.[174]

Nowadays, with the advent of shares indexing, this ceases to be a valid objection: the loss, if any, caused to the fund through an imprudently chosen portfolio can at least be estimated by comparing the performance of that portfolio to the performance of a 'control' portfolio over the same period. The control portfolio should be a balanced portfolio resembling as nearly as possible the disputed portfolio, but varied to estimate what might have been included or omitted had the trustees not breached their trust. Once it is established that the trustee breached its trust and that the breach probably caused loss to the fund, the constitution of the control portfolio will ideally be agreed between the parties, but, in default of agreement, it could be proposed by an independent financial expert acting as *amicus curiae*.

Ethical investment

Earlier, we noted that trustees must set aside their own political or moral views in order to advance the beneficiaries' best interests, but what if the beneficiaries themselves have strongly held religious, political, or moral convictions? Are the trustees permitted—even required—to take such beliefs into account when investing the fund? The courts have answered this question in the negative. Where the trust exists for the purpose of financial provision (as most private trusts do), the trustees are obliged to pursue the beneficiaries' best *financial* interests. The only exceptions to this are where the trust instrument authorizes ethical investments,[175] or the beneficiaries are unanimously opposed to particular investments. As Sir Robert Megarry VC stated in *Cowan v. Scargill*:[176]

> if the only actual or potential beneficiaries of a trust are all adults with very strict views on moral and social matters, condemning all forms of alcohol, tobacco and popular entertainment, as well as armaments, I can well understand that it might not be for the 'benefit' of such beneficiaries to know that they are obtaining rather larger financial returns under the trust by reason of investments in those activities than they would have received if the trustees had invested the trust funds in other investments...the burden would rest, and rest heavy, on him who asserts that it is for the benefit of the beneficiaries as a whole to receive less by reason of the exclusion of some of the possibly more profitable forms of investment.[177]

---

[174]　Ibid. at 504.

[175]　As Sir Donald Nicholls VC acknowledged in *Harries v. The Church Commissioners for England* [1992] 1 WLR 1241, '*trustees would be entitled, or even required, to take into account non-financial criteria... where the trust deed so provides*'.

[176]　[1985] Ch 270. If the trust was a pension fund trust and, as such, was a trust for the provision of financial benefits.　　　　　　　　　　　　　　　　　　　　　　　　　　　[177]　At 288E–G.

Of course, the purpose of certain trusts—most notably charities—is not merely to make financial provision, but to achieve ulterior social goals. Such trusts are permitted to advance those goals by the manner of their investment, as well as by the way in which they distribute the trust income.[178] It would be perverse if a charity for the protection of the environment through the promotion of bicycling[179] were required to invest some part of the fund in the motor industry.

It is difficult for trustees to establish that ethical investments ought, on financial grounds, to be preferred. In *Cowan v. Scargill*,[180] one half of the management committee of the National Coal Board's pension trust sued the other half, which comprised Mr Arthur Scargill and four other officials of the National Union of Mineworkers (NUM). The complaint was that the NUM trustees had refused to invest the pension fund in certain overseas industries. The NUM trustees objected to the fact that the overseas industries were competitors of the British mining industry. They defended their refusal to invest as being in the beneficiaries' best interests. The beneficiaries were, of course, retired British mineworkers. Sir Robert Megarry VC held that:

> the broad economic arguments of the defendants provide no justification for the restrictions that they wish to impose. Any possible benefits from imposing the restrictions under the scheme...are far too speculative and remote.[181]

In theory, trustees are not even permitted to prefer the 'more ethical' of two investments with near-identical financial potential, although, in practice, no action could be taken on such a breach, because it would be impossible to prove that it had caused a loss to the fund.[182] However, Lord Nicholls of Birkenhead, writing extra-judicially, has expressed his opinion that the range of investments available to trustees is sufficiently extensive to allow trustees '*to give effect to moral considerations, either by positively preferring certain investments or negatively avoiding others, without thereby prejudicing beneficiaries' financial interests*'.[183]

We should not expect the courts to abandon overnight their long-held assumption that beneficiaries' best interests are their best financial interests. Indeed, Lord

---

[178] The Charity Commission's website confirms that '*charities may pursue their charitable purposes...through the provision of loans, loan guarantees or the subscription or purchase of shares or through the letting of land and buildings*', collectively known as 'social investments' (publication *Charities and Social Investment*). Richard Nobles, in 'Charities and Ethical Investment' (1992) 56 Conv 115, forcefully makes the point that charity trustees are permitted to *give away* trust property to meet the charitable purposes of the trust, and so logically they should be permitted a wider discretion to *invest* with a view to meeting the charitable purposes. It is not, however, always clear what those purposes are: in *Harries* (earlier) Sir Donald Nicholls held that the trustees of a Church of England organization were not obliged by their Christian ethics to sell trust-owned land at an undervalue in order to assist low-income families when '*the local planning authority has taken a different view*'.

[179] *Sustrans* is one such charity.   [180] [1985] 1 Ch 270.   [181] Ibid. at 296.

[182] Megarry VC in *Cowan v. Scargill* [1985] 1 Ch 270. '*The assertion that trustees could not be criticised for failing to make a particular investment for social or political reasons is one that I would not accept in its full width. If the investment in fact made is equally beneficial to the beneficiaries, then criticism would be difficult to sustain in practice, whatever the position in theory*' at 297F.

[183] Lord Nicholls of Birkenhead, 'Trustees and their broader community: where duty, morality and ethics converge' (1995) 9(3) TLI 71.

Nicholls himself has described ethical investment as '*an example par excellence of an instance where, if social conditions today are thought by some to dictate a need for a change in the law, the change ought to be made by the legislature*'.[184] Nevertheless, we know that the paradigm of prudence shifts in line with trends in good investment practice and it may be that, one day, the hypothetical 'prudent investor' will also be an ethical investor.[185] Evidence is growing to suggest that ethical portfolios may be a financially strong alternative to comparable, but less ethical, portfolios,[186] especially over the long term.[187]

The Trustee Act 2000 represented an opportunity for legislative change, but the statute makes no express reference to ethical investment. The Act does, however, require trustees to consider the 'suitability' of investments when exercising their investment powers and the explanatory notes accompanying the Act confirm that suitability '*will…include any relevant ethical considerations as to the kind of investments which it is appropriate for the trust to make*'.[188] It remains to be seen what weight the courts will attach to that note. They will probably conclude that 'relevant ethical considerations' should be identified in the same limited way after the Act as before, but, at the very least, trustees should now be required to show that they have considered the possible relevance of ethical considerations—even if they conclude that there is none. Such an approach is already required in the case of pension trusts.[189] One survey shows that 21 of the 25 largest pension funds intend to implement a policy of socially responsible investing. These include the three largest funds: British Telecom plc, the Universities Superannuation Scheme…and British Coal![190]

---

[184] Lord Nicholls of Birkenhead, 'Trustees and their broader community: where duty, morality and ethics converge' (1995) 9(3) TLI 71 at 75. Social conditions do indeed appear to be changing: a survey carried out by the Ethical Investment Research Service (EIRIS) in February 1999 found that 73% of the UK adult population would like to have pension funds run on ethical lines. Perhaps more surprisingly, almost a third of those questioned would have been prepared to accept some reduction in their pension benefits as a result (*The Independent*, 10 March 1999).

[185] See J. H. Langbein and R. Posner, 'Social investing and the law of trusts' [1980] 79 Michigan LR 72. The 1997 Social Investment Forum (SIF) Report on Responsible Investing Trends in the USA found that 10% of all managed funds were managed in some consciously socially responsible way.

[186] The CAPS survey of UK equity pooled funds at 30 June 1996 showed that the largest ethical fund manager (Friends Provident Stewardship) had outperformed the Median UK Equity Fund year on year for the previous ten years. In the same ten-year period, the Median outperformed the market (the FT All Share Index) only once.

[187] '*A good environmental record may be a sign of long-term potential*' (*The Ethical Investor*, EIRIS November/ December 1999).   [188] Note 23.

[189] From 3 July 2000 pension scheme trustees must disclose '*the extent to which social, environmental, or ethical considerations are taken into account in the selection, retention and realisation of investments*': the Occupational Pension Schemes (Investment, and Assignment, Forfeiture, Bankruptcy etc.) Amendment Regulations 1999 (SI 1999, No. 1849). The Regulations do not require trustees to adopt an ethical policy, but they must state that they have no ethical policy if there is none, although no reasons need be given to explain the absence of an ethical policy.

[190] E. Borremans makes reference to the survey, carried out by Environmental Resource Management, in 'New policies, new demands', *Pensions Management*, August 2000.

Ethical investment policies

There are, of course, a number of reasons why the courts will be reluctant to admit ethical considerations as a straight alternative to financial considerations. For one thing, there are the inevitable dilemmas that ethical questions throw up: is it wrong, for example, for a cycling charity to invest in a supermarket that sells petrol? Does it matter that only a small portion of the company's trade conflicts with the trust's purposes or the beneficiaries' views? What if the company invested in is itself ethically sound, but has subsidiaries or associates that are not? What if a company makes its money in ethically dubious ways, but makes a positive social contribution in other ways, as might a chocolate company that exploits producers in developing countries, but sponsors the provision of computers to schools in the UK? The latter example highlights a key distinction between ethical investment policies—the distinction between *excluding* investments which are unethical and *including* those which are ethical. Often, when reference is made to ethical 'investment' by trustees, what is really being referred to is ethical 'disinvestment'. Ethical disinvestment, because it is exclusionary, represents a threat to portfolio diversity. Indeed, some approaches would restrict trustees to a list of investments that are authorized on ethical grounds in much the same way that the Trustee Investments Act 1961 used to restrict trustees to a list of investments authorized on grounds of low risk. The sad fact is that over half of the FTSE 100—the top 100 quoted companies in the UK—could be excluded on commonly used ethical measures.[191] This problem was recognized in *Harries v. Church Commissioners*,[192] where the Church Commissioners' existing investment policy already excluded investment in 13 per cent (by value) of listed UK companies, and the Bishop of Oxford proposed further ethical exclusions that would have brought the total level of exclusion to 37 per cent of the total market.

However, is the threat to portfolio diversity overstated? Certainly, an exclusionary approach to ethical investment will render it almost impossible to participate in a full market-tracking strategy, unless the market chosen is a specialist ethical investments market,[193] but, short of that, it is surprising how few investments are required to create a reasonably diverse portfolio. As Sir Donald Nicholls VC observed:

> It is not easy to think of an instance where in practice the exclusion ... of one or more companies or sectors from the whole range of investments open to trustees would be likely to leave them without an adequately wide range of investments from which to choose a properly diversified portfolio.[194]

The greater danger posed by an exclusionary approach to ethical investment may be that it tends to exclude larger companies, because the scale of their enterprise makes some unethical activity virtually inevitable, and therefore drives trusts to invest in smaller

---

[191] A FTSE 4 Good Index Series has been implemented, which purports to 'measure the performance of companies that meet globally recognised corporate responsibility standards'.

[192] *Harries v. Church Commissioners for England* [1992] 1 WLR 1241, Ch D.   [193] See earlier.

[194] *Harries v. Church Commissioners for England* [1992] 1 WLR 1241 at 1246H.

companies for which the risk of company failure may be higher than for larger concerns. There is, nevertheless, a significant financial advantage associated with a negative (that is a 'disinvestment') strategy. It stems from the fact that campaigners are usually far more vociferous in publishing and denouncing unethical activity than in promoting positive ethical activity. Campaigns *against* nuclear armament, animal cruelty, apartheid, and child labour tend to make headlines in ways that campaigns *promoting* wind farms and free range eggs do not. A consequence of this is that potential donors to trusts will be put off if the trust holds 'tainted' investments.[195] A trust that merely fails to hold ethically positive investments will be less likely to lose donors. Of course, one alternative to disinvestment in a dubious company is to take advantage of the opportunities for corporate governance that accompany a shareholding in the company.[196] One such opportunity might be to prevent company directors from awarding themselves so-called 'fat cat' salaries.[197]

Possibilities for reform of the law on ethical investment

Unanimity between beneficiaries on ethical issues will sometimes be hard to establish, even amongst persons who share the same fundamental beliefs. As Sir Donald Nicholls VC observed in *Harries v. Church Commissioners*: '*different minds within the Church of England, applying the highest moral standards, will reach different conclusions*' as to the merits of a particular investment.[198] Accordingly, in that case, the Commissioners were vindicated in their decision not to prefer one ethical view over another '*beyond the point at which they would incur a risk of significant financial detriment*'.[199] An argument in favour of unanimity is administrative simplicity. Another is that simple wealth maximization does not impinge upon beneficiaries' freedom to spend their wealth as they please, whereas an ethical investment policy might impinge upon beneficiaries' wealth for the sake of ethical views to which they do not subscribe. The converse of the latter argument is that people are increasingly concerned that their wealth should be acquired in ways of which they approve, and not merely spent in ways of which they approve. As for the administrative simplicity of unanimity-based ethical investment: this need not to be sacrificed completely if, instead of insisting on unanimity, it were possible to identify those issues about which a majority, say three-quarters (by value), of the beneficiaries feel strongly. It could also be made a statutory requirement of trustee investment that the trustees consult the beneficiaries and consider their views.[200]

---

[195] Ibid. at 1247A.

[196] *The Merlin Ecology Research Bulletin*, Winter 1989, at 3 (Merlin Jupiter Unit Trust Management).

[197] Lord Nicholls of Birkenhead, 'Trustees and their broader community: where duty, morality and ethics converge' (1995) 9(3) TLI 71 at 76–7.

[198] *Harries v. Church Commissioners* [1992] 1 WLR 1241 at 1251H. See an open letter to the Bishop of Coventry that appeared in *The Independent* on 9 February 1995 outlining contrasting views within the Church of England on the issue of animal welfare. See, also, 'Differing over a religious matter: Church Commissioners' investment in armaments', an article in *The Standard*, 28 June 1985.

[199] *Harries v. Church Commissioners* [1992] 1 WLR 1241 at 1251.

[200] There is a precedent for this in relation to trusts of land (Trusts of Land and Appointment of Trustees Act 1996, s. 11).

Conclusion

The law relating to the investment powers of trustees has come a long way since *Anker-Petersen v. Anker-Petersen* was reported.[201] In that case, the trustees sought a variation of their investment powers to allow them to invest in assets of any kind as if they were beneficial owners, to delegate to investment managers, to hold investments through nominees, and to borrow money for any purpose. In retrospect, those requests read like a reform agenda, because every one of the powers requested then is available today as a matter of course to the vast majority of trustees as a result of the Trustee Act 2000. The exercise of their enlarged powers is, of course, subject to the usual trustee duties and, in particular, to the duty to exercise a positive discretion in good faith. The investment discretion must be exercised prudently and fairly, and, above all, in a manner that is appropriate to the particular trust. At least that is the position in theory. In practice, however, the vagaries of the investment environment make it very difficult for disappointed beneficiaries to prove that their trustees have breached their investment duties and caused the fund to suffer a quantifiable loss.

If there is a silver lining to that dark cloud, it is that trust funds will participate more freely in the economy, the fewer the practical constraints on trustees. Trustees may even have the practical freedom to invest in socially responsible ways that would not be possible if the strict letter of the law were obeyed. In fact, it is so difficult to prove liability for improper investment that trustees might sometimes 'get away with' actually preferring ethical to financial ends.[202]

Further reading

In addition to the following print sources, the Online Resource Centre accompanying this book contains web links to further reading as well as guide answers to assessment questions relevant to this chapter.

AMERICAN LAW INSTITUTE, *Restatement of the Law of Trusts (3rd edn): The Prudent Investor Rule* (St. Paul, Minn: American Law Publishers, 1992).

BRITISH COLUMBIA LAW INSTITUTE, *Total Return Investing by Trustees*, Rep. No. 16 (August 2001).

DALE, H. P., and GWINELL, M., 'Time for change: charity investment and modern portfolio theory' (1995) 3(2) CL&PR 89.

DAVID, E. M., 'Principal and income: obsolete concepts' (1972) 43 PA Bar Assoc Q 247.

---

[201] (1991) 16 LS Gaz 32, Ch D, Transcript, 6 December 1990.

[202] D. Hayton, *Underhill & Hayton's Law Relating to Trusts and Trustees*, 14th edn (London: Butterworths, 1987) at 530: *'trustees can quietly invest ethically… because the uncertainty in the stock market acts as a shield to liability'.* See also P. Docking and I. Pittaway, 'Social investment by English pension funds: can it be done?' (1990) Feb. TL&P, at 25.

DOCKING, P. and PITTAWAY, I., 'Social investment by English pension funds: can it be done?' (1990) TL&P 25.

FORD, E., 'Trustee investment and modern portfolio theory' (1996) 10(4) TLI 102.

HM TREASURY, *Investment Powers of Trustees: A Consultation Document* (May 1996).

LAW COMMISSION OF ENGLAND AND WALES, *Trustees' Powers and Duties* Rep. No. 260 (1999).

LONGSTRETH, B., *Modern Investment Management and the Prudent Man Rule* (New York, Oxford: Oxford University Press, 1986).

LORD NICHOLLS OF BIRKENHEAD, 'Trustees and their broader community: where duty, morality and ethics converge' (1995) 9(3) TLI 71.

MCCORMACK, G., 'Liability of trustees for negligent investment decisions' (1997) 13(2) Professional Negligence 45.

MCCORMACK, G., 'Sexy but not sleazy: trustee investments and ethical considerations' (1998) 19(2) The Company Lawyer 39.

MCCORMACK, G., 'OEICS and trusts: the changing face of English investment law' (2000) 21(1) The Company Lawyer 2.

NOBLES, R., 'Charities and ethical investment' (1992) 56 Conv 115.

RICHARDSON, B.J., *Socially Responsible Investment Law: Regulating the Unseen Polluters* (New York, Oxford: Oxford University Press, 2008).

13

Breach of trust: the personal liability of trustees

In the three chapters immediately preceding this we identified the main duties of trusteeship. In this chapter we will examine the nature and potential extent of trustees' liability for breach of those duties.

Trustees' powers are incidents of their legal ownership of the trust property, but their duties are incidents of their personal office. It follows from this that the beneficiaries' principal remedies in an action for breach of trust will be against the trustees personally. This is not to say that individual trustees owe a direct personal obligation to individual beneficiaries: generally speaking, trust obligations are owed by the trustees collectively to the beneficiaries collectively. A beneficiary, unless he is the sole beneficiary of a bare trust, does not claim that the trustees owe him an individual duty of loyalty or care, he merely claims '*to have the trust duly administered in accordance with the provisions of the trust instrument, if any, and the general law*'.[1]

Typically, then, the trust fund or 'estate' mediates the relationship between the trustees and the beneficiaries. This is most clearly seen in the trustees' duty to invest the trust fund fairly in the interests of all classes of beneficiary, as we noted in the previous chapter. However, many trusts do not involve a fund in need of investment. Trusts created in commercial contexts are very often 'bare trusts', in which the trustees' only duty is to hold the trust property to the beneficiary's order and to apply it in accordance with the beneficiary's instructions. A typical example of such a trust is the trust under which a solicitor holds clients' monies. The direct, bi-party nature of such trusts is analogous to the sort of relationships that give rise to contractual and tortious obligations; indeed, it is normal for such trusts actually to arise in accordance with the terms of a contract between the parties. It is interesting to note, therefore, how common law concepts, such as causation, remoteness of damage, and contributory negligence, are increasingly being introduced to limit trustees' liability for breaches of bare trusts in commercial contexts.[2]

---

[1] In *Target Holdings Ltd v. Redferns (a firm)* [1996] AC 421, *per* Lord Browne-Wilkinson at 434A.
[2] See, generally, P. Birks, 'The content of fiduciary obligation' (2002) 16(1) TLI at 34–52.

Holding these perspectives in mind, the aim of this chapter is to consider the nature and extent of the remedies that are available against trustees when they breach their trust. We will also consider defences that may be available to trustees in breach and, in the absence of defences, whether trustees may be relieved of liability.

Locus standi

This Latin phrase, which means 'a place to stand', is used to describe a claimant's right to be heard in a court of law—sometimes referred to simply as a claimant's 'standing'. The beneficiary of any trust, even if it is a discretionary trust, has *locus standi* to bring an action against her trustees for breach of trust. This is so whether her interest is contingent or vested. However, a person with nothing more than a speculative hope (a mere '*spes*') of becoming entitled to an interest in an estate has no *locus standi* in relation to that estate; one example is anyone who hopes to be entitled as 'next of kin' to the estate of someone who has not yet died.

Where there is more than one beneficiary interested in the action, the court may, in the interests of efficient justice, make a representation order allowing one or more claimants to represent the interests of the others with whom they have an identity of interest.[3] Such orders were granted to protect the interests of the 800 or so mail-order customers in *Re Kayford Ltd (in liquidation)*,[4] the thousands of investors in *Barlow Clowes International Ltd (in liquidation) v. Vaughan*,[5] the persons in *Foskett v. McKeown*[6] who had paid deposits on the purchase of land in the Algarve, and, more prosaically, the nieces and nephews in *Re Hay's Settlement Trusts*.[7] When an order is made allowing certain members of an occupational pension trust to represent the interests of all the members, the representative action is said to be analogous to a derivative action brought by a minority shareholder on behalf of a company.[8] The court also has power to make a representation order on behalf of an unborn beneficiary.[9] If no representation order is made on behalf of an unborn beneficiary, the judgment of the court may not be binding on the child when it is subsequently born.[10]

It is not only the beneficiaries who have *locus standi* to bring action against trustees who have breached their trust; trustees have *locus standi* to bring claims against their co-trustees.[11]

---

[3] Civil Procedure Rules 1998 (SI 1998, No. 3132) (CPR), rr. 19.6–19.7 (incorporated by the Civil Procedure (Amendment) Rules 2000 (SI 2000, No. 22 and replacing Ord. 15, r. 13(1) and (2) of the old Rules of the Supreme Court).   [4] [1975] 1 WLR 279.

[5] [1992] 4 All ER 22, CA, see Chapter 14.

[6] See the decision of the Court of Appeal at [1998] 2 WLR 298. For the decision in the House of Lords, see Chapter 14.   [7] [1982] 1 WLR 202.

[8] *McDonald v. Horn* [1994] 1 All ER 961, CA.

[9] CPR, r. 19.7(2)(a), r. 19.7(1)(b). For an Australian example, see *Yunghanns v. Candoora No. 19 Pty Ltd* [2000] 2 ITELR 589, in which a father was appointed to represent the interests of his unborn child.

[10] *Blathwayt v. Baron Cawley* [1976] AC 397, HL, at 403C.

[11] RSC, Ord. 15, r. 14. See also CPR, r. 50.

Breach without liability

The title of this chapter indicates that a trustee will be personally liable for breach of trust, but breach of trust does not always lead to liability. Breach will only lead to liability if the breach produced an unauthorized gain for the trustee or caused a loss to the trust. This was starkly illustrated by the *Nestle* case in the previous chapter, where we noted that a trustee was not liable to compensate, because it had not been proved that its breach had caused a loss. As Leggatt LJ stated: '*Loss cannot be presumed, if none would necessarily have resulted.*'[12] It is clear, then, that a trustee can escape liability for imprudently making an investment which by pure chance happens to do well,[13] but even when a trustee *deliberately* breaches his trust, by making an investment that he knows he has no authority to make, he will escape liability unless loss is proved:

> Say, as often occurs, a trustee commits a judicious breach of trust by investing in an unauthorised investment which proves to be very profitable to the trust. A carping beneficiary could insist that the unauthorised investment be sold and the proceeds invested in authorised investments: but the trustee would be under no liability to pay compensation either to the trust fund or to the beneficiary because the breach has caused no loss to the trust fund.[14]

It has even been suggested, somewhat tongue in cheek, that 'the main duty' of a trustee is to commit 'judicious' breaches of trust.[15]

Even where there is no difficulty in establishing that a breach of trust has produced a loss to the trust or an unauthorized gain for the trustee, the trustee might still escape liability if he can successfully raise a defence to the beneficiary's claim. The defendant may plead statutory limitation or 'laches', both of which are concerned with preventing claims from being brought too long after the occurrence of the alleged breach. Appropriately worded exculpatory clauses in trust instruments may also be relied upon to defend allegations of breach. Most defences operate merely to excuse a breach of trust, but defences which might be said actually to justify the breach include the advance authority of a court and the advance unanimous consent of the beneficiaries. The various defences are considered later in the chapter. We will also consider the possibility of a trustee being relieved of some or all of his liability in cases where he does not have a defence as such.

Liability for breach of trust

There are basically two distinct measures of trustee liability for breach of trust. One measure is determined by the loss caused to the trust and is typically remedied by

---

[12] In *Nestle v. National Westminster Bank plc* [1993] 1 WLR 1260, *per* Leggatt LJ at 1283B.
[13] *Jeffrey v. Gretton* [2011] WTLR 809 (Ch).
[14] *Target Holdings* (n. 1), *per* Lord Brown-Wilkinson at 433G. See also *Re Brogden* (1888) 38 Ch D 546, CA at 557.
[15] Attributed to Selwyn LJ by Sir Nathaniel Lindley MR in *Perrins v. Bellamy* [1899] 1 Ch 797, CA at 798.

monetary compensation,[16] the trustee's obligation being to restore the trust to the position it was in before the breach;[17] the other measure is determined by the trustee's unauthorized gains and is typically remedied by requiring the trustee to account for the gains.[18] Liability on either measure is personal, which means that the trustee is liable to satisfy the beneficiary's claim out of his personal funds, and the success of the beneficiary's claim is not dependent (as a proprietary claim would be) upon proof that the trustee is still in possession of trust property (including any unauthorized gains). Of course, if the trustee *is* still in possession of the trust property or its traceable proceeds or substitutes, the beneficiaries will also have their usual proprietary rights in the trust property in addition to their rights against the trustee personally, in respect of the breach of trust.

The fact that a trustee's liability to compensate losses and account for gains is personal means that in an extreme case liability may bring about the financial ruination of the trustee, even if the trustee's breach was honest.[19] This is exacerbated by the fact that trustees are jointly and severally liable for their joint breaches of trust: each one of the trustees is potentially liable for the entire sum claimed.[20] A trustee is not, however, *vicariously* liable for the defaults of his co-trustees if he was not a party to the breach. A trustee is only liable for his own defaults, whether committed alone or jointly with the other trustees.

It is not unusual for a single breach of trust to give rise to potential liability both to compensate losses and to account for gains. If, for example, a trustee has wrongfully appropriated trust property to his own use, the trust will have suffered a loss and the trustee will have made a gain. Or, to take another example, a trustee might wrongfully have sold a specific item of trust property and made a secret commission on the sale, in which event the beneficiaries may seek its return or compensation for its lost value, as well as requiring the trustee to account for the secret commission. However, in such cases, the remedies of compensation and account will be alternative bases of recovery, which means that the beneficiaries must elect between them before judgment is entered in their favour.[21] So a trustee who misappropriates an item of trust property will not be liable to account both for his gain of that item and for the trust's loss of that item. In such a case gain and loss are said to be alternative and 'inconsistent' bases of recovery.[22]

Before we continue, it will be useful to clarify the meaning of the term 'account' in the context of trustee liability. The term has two quite distinct meanings: first, there is liability to account for unauthorized gains, mentioned earlier,[23] second, there is account

---

[16] See, generally, J. D. Heydon QC, 'The negligent fiduciary' (1995) 111 LQR 1; C. E. F. Rickett, 'Where are we going with equitable compensation?' in *Trends in Contemporary Trust Law* (A. J. Oakley, ed.) (Oxford: Clarendon Press, 1996) at 177.

[17] *Nocton v. Lord Ashburton* [1914] AC 932, HL, *per* Lord Haldane LC at 952.   [18] See Chapter 10.

[19] Witness the unfortunate plight of Mr Budgett in *Re Brogden* (1888) 38 Ch D 546, which is discussed in Chapter 11.   [20] Subject to 'contribution', see later.

[21] See 'Election', later.

[22] The argument that a defendant's unauthorized gain is a gain that the claimant might have made, and is therefore a loss, does not withstand close scrutiny, but see S. Stoljar, 'Restitutionary relief for breach of contract' (1989) 2 JCL 1.   [23] This is considered at length in Chapters 8 and 10.

as a method of compensation. Beneficiaries can bring an action for 'an account' at any time. This, as its name suggest, requires the trustees to account for trust assets that ought to be in their hands. If the account falls short, the trustees can then be ordered to account to the trust for the shortfall by reinstating specific assets, or reinstating the fund, or, in an appropriate case, compensating individual beneficiaries directly. Each of these circumstances is considered in the following sections.

Specific 'restitution'

If trustees distribute or sell a particular trust asset, say 1,000 ordinary shares in Trade Ltd, which they were obliged to retain, their basic obligation is to restore the trust fund to the position it was in before the breach. This may be achieved by specific 'restitution',[24] which is the process of restoring to the trust the asset that has been misapplied. However, if it is not possible to purchase another 1,000 ordinary shares in Trade Ltd, the trustees will be liable to compensate the trust for the value of 1,000 ordinary shares in Trade Ltd,[25] calculated at the date of the court's judgment in the matter.[26] Thus the remedy of specific 'restitution' is a personal remedy against the trustee which does not rely for its success upon the property actually being in the defendant's hands.[27]

The same rule applies where the trustees are directed to invest in specific investments—for example, 1,000 ordinary shares in Commerce Co—but invest (or leave) the trust money elsewhere instead; they may be charged '*with the amount of the stock which they might have purchased with the money*'.[28] This remedy will be most attractive to the beneficiaries where the value of the desired stock has risen since the date on which the trustee ought to have purchased it, for the trustee may now be required, at the option of the beneficiaries, to purchase the same stock using only the same amount of trust money as would have been required to make the purchase in the first place.[29] In other words, the trustee will be required to make up the difference between the original and the present purchase price out of his own pocket. If the particular stock is no longer for sale, or if the beneficiaries no longer want it, the trustee must pay the difference between the original purchase price and the present value of the stock out of his own pocket by way of compensation in cash.

Despite its traditional name, the remedy of specific 'restitution' should not be confused with the more usual meaning of 'restitution', which, as we saw in Chapter 2, is the label attached to the remedial processes by which ill-gotten wealth or proprietary benefits are stripped from a recipient. Specific 'restitution' is really specific 'compensation'.

---

[24] For consideration of the distinction between 'restitution' to a trust fund and restitution as a remedy for the reversal of unjust enrichment, see the end of this section.

[25] *Caffrey v. Darby* (1801) 6 Ves Jr 488; *Target Holdings v. Redferns* [1996] AC 421, HL, at 434.

[26] *Re Bell's Indenture* [1980] 1 WLR 1217.

[27] A. J. Oakley calls this 'restitutionary obligation' an obligation of a 'personal character'. ('The liberalising nature of remedies for breach of trust' in *Trends in Contemporary Trust Law* (A. J. Oakley, ed.) (Oxford: Clarendon Press, 1996) 217 at 220.)

[28] *Shepherd v. Mouls* (1845) 4 Hare 500, 504. How much the trustee might have purchased will be difficult to establish by evidence.   [29] *Re Massingberd's Settlement* (1890) 63 LT 296, CA.

Compensation for loss: general

We noted earlier that a breach of trust will not found liability unless it is demonstrated to have caused a loss. We will now see that the converse is also true: that a loss suffered by a trust will not found liability unless it is shown to have been caused by a breach of trust.[30] Accidents happen; trustees are not insurers of the fund. It is said that '*equity relieves against accidents*',[31] so a trustee is under no obligation to account personally for trust property destroyed by flood or fire through no fault of his own. However, although a trustee is not liable for losses that were not the result of any breach of trust, a trustee who has breached his trust may be liable for the consequences if his breach exposes the trust to accidental damage. This is discussed further later.

It is important to recall that a trustee's honesty is no defence to a claim based on a breach of his duty of care. So when a trust suffers a loss, as might be caused by a dishonest agent employed by the trust, the court is sometimes presented with an invidious choice: whether the loss should be borne by the honest trustee or the innocent beneficiaries.[32] The outcome depends upon whether the trustee has breached his trust, however honestly. If the trustee is in breach, perhaps because he failed adequately to supervise an agent who was thereby able to steal trust property, the trustee will bear the loss. If the trustee is not in breach, the loss will fall upon the trust fund.

Compensation for breach of trust compared to common law damages

According to Brightman LJ in *Bartlett v. Barclays Bank Trust Co Ltd (Nos 1 and 2)*,[33] compensation for breach of trust is '*not readily distinguishable from* [common law] *damages except with the aid of a powerful legal microscope*'.[34] This is true, in as much as both are monetary awards made by way of remedy for loss. However, it is equally true, as Brightman LJ observed in the same case, that '*the obligation of a trustee who is held liable for breach of trust is fundamentally different from the obligation of a contractual or tortious wrongdoer*'. Whereas a contractual or tortious wrongdoer must compensate the losses suffered by the particular claimant, the trustee's obligation 'is to restore to the trust estate the assets of which he has deprived it',[35] irrespective of the level of harm that particular beneficiaries, or classes of beneficiary, may have actually suffered as a result of the breach.

Traditional settlement trusts: the duty to reconstitute the fund

It is worth reciting the following extract from the speech of Lord Browne-Wilkinson in the House of Lords in *Target Holdings v. Redferns*.[36] His Lordship expressly had in

---

[30] Only if some relevant right has been infringed so as to give rise to a loss is it necessary to consider the extent of the trustee's liability to compensate for such loss (*Target Holdings* at n. 1).

[31] R. Francis, *Maxims of Equity* (1727) Maxim VII, p. 27, case 4.

[32] *Re Rosenthal, decd* [1972] 1 WLR 1273, *per* Plowman J at 1276 G–H: '*The question is where is the loss to fall?*'   [33] [1980] Ch 515.

[34] Ibid. at 545B.   [35] At 545C.   [36] *Target Holdings Ltd v. Redferns (a firm)* [1996] 1 AC 421, HL.

mind a case of a breach of trust '*involving the wrongful paying away of trust assets*',[37] but the principle has also been applied to cases of loss arising from negligent investment:[38]

> in relation to a traditional trust where the fund is held in trust for a number of beneficiaries having different, usually successive, equitable interests, (eg A for life with remainder to B), the right of each beneficiary is to have the whole fund vested in the trustees so as to be available to satisfy his equitable interest when, and if, it falls into possession...Courts of Equity did not award damages but, acting *in personam*, ordered the defaulting trustee to restore the trust estate.[39]

The strict duty to restore the trust fund to a state in which it will be able to satisfy the claims of the various beneficiaries is usually referred to as the trustee's duty to make 'restitution' to the trust estate, but that is apt to mislead,[40] so it is submitted that 'reconstitution' is a better description. In *Bartlett v. Barclays Bank Trust Co Ltd (Nos 1 and 2)*,[41] a case of loss caused by poor investment, Brightman LJ acknowledged that in the context of reconstituting the trust fund '*so-called restitution...is in reality compensation for loss suffered*'.[42] Distinguished counsel in that case summarized perfectly the precise nature of the trustee's liability. It is, first and foremost, a duty to account,[43] second, a duty to reconstitute, and third, a duty to compensate:

> Equity does not award damages: it requires the trustee to account, and if necessary to reconstitute the trust fund, or if that is not literally possible, to restore to the trust estate the monetary value of what should have been there had there been no breach of trust.[44]

The significance of the 'estate reconstitution' measure of compensation is that it requires the defendant to restore the trust to the state it was in prior to his breach, even if the consequence may be to overcompensate individual beneficiaries at the defendant's expense. So if the trustee's breach reduces the level of trust income and thereby has the incidental effect of reducing the tax burden on individual beneficiaries, the trustee's liability is not reduced to take the beneficiaries' tax savings into account.[45] Just as there is no inquiry designed to limit the level of compensation to losses actually suffered by individual beneficiaries, neither is there any detailed inquiry into the causal relevance of the defendant's action. The trustee will have a valid defence if 'but for' the breach of trust precisely the same loss would

---

[37] Ibid. at 434.

[38] See *Bartlett v. Barclays Bank Trust Co Ltd (Nos 1 and 2)* [1980] Ch 515, later in the chapter.

[39] His Lordship cites *Nocton v. Lord Ashburton* [1914] AC 932, *per* Viscount Haldane LC at 952, 958.

[40] C. Rickett has highlighted the conflict of usage. See *Trends in Contemporary Trust Law* (A. J. Oakley, ed.) (Oxford: Clarendon Press, 1996) at 183: '*This use of the term restitution must be distinguished clearly from the meanings assigned the term by those who theorize about the law of restitutionary recovery*'. He observes that making restitution to a trust fund '*is more closely related to compensatory damages at common law than it is to gain-based or property-based restitution*'.   [41] [1980] Ch 515.

[42] Ibid. at 545A; R. P. Austin refers in 'Moulding the content of fiduciary duties' in *Trends in Contemporary Trust Law* (A. J. Oakley, ed.) (Oxford: Clarendon Press, 1996) 153 at 170 to '*the restitutionary nature of equitable compensation for breach of trust*'; see *Caffrey v. Darby* (1801) 6 Ves 488.

[43] The procedure and remedy of account is considered later.

[44] E. G. Nugee QC and J. Sher (now QC) for the claimants.

[45] See *O'Sullivan and Another v. Management Agency and Music Ltd* [1985] QB 428, Court of Appeal.

certainly have occurred, but the onus will be upon the trustee to prove that fact. So if a trustee breaches his trust by, for example, storing trust-owned antiques on display in his own home, he will suffer the full consequences of any accident, such as his house being burned to the ground,[46] that befalls the antiques by reason of their being in his house.

Is estate reconstitution an equitable hybrid of contractual and tortious damages?

To the extent that estate reconstitution enables the proper (usually 'future') distribution of the estate in accordance with the terms of the trust, it replicates the 'obligation-fulfilling' function that we normally associate with contractual damages—namely, to put the claimant in the position *she would have been in* had the defendant fulfilled his legal obligation—but in so far as it compensates individual beneficiaries for losses they have already incurred, it replicates the compensatory function usually associated with tortious damages, which is to put the claimant, so far as possible, in the position *she was in* before the defendant breached his legal duty. In any trust where a fund is managed for present and future beneficiaries (such as a traditional settlement trust or a pension trust), the nature of the loss suffered by present beneficiaries is different from the nature of the loss suffered by future beneficiaries, so, in very broad terms, estate reconstitution by trustees may be regarded as a functional hybrid of common law damages for contractual breach and common law damages for tortious injury.

Bare trusts: direct equitable compensation

According to Lord Browne-Wilkinson in *Target Holdings v. Redferns*,[47] the duty to compensate by restoring the trust fund (what we have called the duty of 'estate reconstitution') which applies to subsisting settlement trusts will normally have no application to a settlement that has come to an end leaving a remainder beneficiary solely entitled to the fund.[48] Provided that the remainder beneficiary is a competent adult, the trustee is no longer under a duty to reconstitute the trust fund in the event of a breach of trust causing loss; instead, he is under a duty to compensate the beneficiary directly for the loss. His Lordship illustrated the point by reference to the case of *Bartlett v. Barclays Bank Trust Co Ltd (Nos 1 and 2)*[49] where, by the date of judgment, some of the interests settled by the trust deed had become absolutely vested in possession, with the result that compensation was payable directly to the beneficiaries, rather than indirectly via the fund. This duty to compensate directly also applies to any other sort of bare trust, such as those that frequently arise in commercial contexts. The trust in *Target Holdings*[50] was itself of this kind.

---

[46] *Caffrey v. Darby* (1801) 6 Ves Jr 488 at 496 establishes that a trustee in breach will be liable for the consequences of '*fire, lightning or any other accidents*'.

[47] [1996] 1 AC 421, HL. See, generally, D. Capper, 'compensation for breach of trusts' (1997) 61 Conv 14.

[48] Followed in *Hulbert v. Avens* [2003] EWHC 76 (Ch).   [49] [1980] Ch 515.

[50] *Target Holdings Ltd v. Redferns (a firm)* [1996] AC 421.

The claimant in *Target* was a finance company that had entered into an arrangement to advance a loan secured by way of mortgage on a commercial property. The defendant was a firm of solicitors instructed by the claimant to act on its behalf in connection with the transaction. The defendant firm had also been instructed by the borrower, who had informed the claimant that the commercial property (the intended security for the loan) had been valued by a firm of surveyors at £2m. The borrower failed to reveal that it had, in fact, paid only £775,000 for the commercial property. Relying on the false valuation, the claimants gave the solicitors £1.5m to be held on bare trust until completion of the mortgage in its favour, at which point, the defendant firm was authorized to pay the loan monies to the borrower. In the event, the defendant firm advanced the monies to the borrower before completion of the mortgage and untruthfully informed the claimant that the mortgage had already been completed. The mortgage was not, in fact, completed until almost one month later. When the claimant decided subsequently to enforce its security and sell the commercial property, it found that the property was worth (at that time) only £500,000. The claimant therefore brought an action against the solicitors alleging, *inter alia*, breach of trust and claiming an account for the entire advance of £1.5m. The Court of Appeal held that, in the circumstances, the defendant was liable to replace all of the monies paid away in breach of trust, subject only to the claimant giving credit for any monies recoverable on the sale of the commercial property. The solicitors appealed.

The House of Lords held that the rule applicable to traditional settlement trusts, which requires trustees fully to reconstitute the trust fund to its original state, has no application to bare trusts arising in commercial contexts. On the contrary, the quantum of compensation should be assessed at the date of judgment as the figure necessary to put the beneficiary in the position he would have been in if there had been no breach. On the facts the claimant had not shown that it was entitled to any compensation since it had obtained precisely that which it would have acquired 'but for' the breach of trust, namely, a valid security for the sum advanced.

The decision in *Target* establishes that a common-sense approach to causation should be applied to bare trusts in a commercial context. If, at the date of the court hearing, the facts demonstrate, with *'the full benefit of hindsight'*,[51] that the claimant's loss would have been incurred even if there had been no breach, the trustee will not be liable. Correspondingly, if the facts demonstrate that part of the loss would have occurred but for the trustee's breach, the trustee will be liable to compensate *only* to the extent of the part he caused even though transfer of the entire sum had been in breach of trust.[52] The previous rule, which had required a trustee in breach to compensate for all losses incurred through the tainted transaction, even if they would have occurred regardless of his breach,[53] was overruled.

---

[51] [1996] 1 AC 421, HL at 438H.

[52] *AIB Group (UK) Plc v. Mark Redler & Co Solicitors* [2013] EWCA Civ 45; [2013] PNLR 19.

[53] See, for example, *Jaffray v. Marshall* [1993] 1 WLR 1285.

Target was followed in *Swindle v. Harrison.*[54] In that case, a firm of solicitors knew that one of its clients would probably fail to raise certain finance she needed in order to purchase a hotel, so it loaned her the money itself. However, it failed to reveal that it knew the hotel to have a poor commercial history. In due course, the hotel turned out to be a financial failure, the client defaulted on repayment of the loan, and the solicitors issued proceedings to recover the outstanding sum. The client then counterclaimed for compensation for her losses on the ground that she would not have proceeded with the purchase of the hotel if the solicitors had discharged their duty to make full disclosure of all the information they had in relation to the hotel. Following *Target*, Evans LJ dismissed the counterclaim on the ground that the client had failed to prove that her loss had been caused, on any common-sense view, by the solicitors' breach of fiduciary duty:

> Since she would have accepted the loan and completed the purchase, even if full disclosure had been made to her, she would have lost the value of the equity in her home in any event.[55]

His Lordship confirmed that the aim of compensation in a bare trust of this type is to put the claimant in the position she would have been in at the date of the court hearing had the breach of trust not been committed.[56]

There are dicta in *Target* and *Swindle* to suggest that cases such as these are considered to be analogous to cases in which the common law tort of negligence is alleged, which is why an analogous common-sense test should be applied to determine whether the defendant's wrongdoing had caused harm. However, if a fiduciary defendant had acted dishonestly, as would almost certainly have been the case if the solicitors in *Swindle* had *known* that the hotel was going to be a financial failure but had nevertheless advised and induced their client to proceed with the purchase, the more appropriate analogy would be to the common law tort of deceit.[57] In such a case, the fiduciary defendant will be liable for any losses to which his dishonest acts or omissions were a contributory cause, even if the losses might have been incurred despite his default.[58]

The relevance of the claimant's behaviour

We have seen that, in the case of a bare trust, the date for determining causation is the date of judgment and that the extent of the losses caused by the defendant is determined by taking a common-sense retrospective view of all of the facts, but does this mean that the claimant's own behaviour should be relevant when determining the extent of the losses caused by the defendant's breach? On any common-sense view the claimant's behaviour ought to be relevant, but the orthodox approach to trustee liability was, as we have seen, to focus exclusively upon the behaviour of the defendant trustee. This is in contrast with the common law approach, which has always taken the claimant's loss as

---

[54] [1997] 4 All ER 705, CA.   [55] Ibid. at 718.   [56] Ibid. at 714.

[57] As to which, see Lord Steyn in *Smith New Court Securities Ltd v. Scrimegeour Vickers (Asset Management) Ltd* [1997] AC 254.

[58] *Nationwide BS v. Various Solicitors* [1999] PNLR 606; *The Times*, 5 February 1998.

the basic measure of the defendant's liability,[59] so it used to be said that equitable compensation '*is not limited to common law principles governing remoteness of damage*.'[60]

Recent decisions demonstrate, however, that there is growing judicial acceptance of common law concepts (or language) in the determination of the extent to which a trustee is liable for losses of which his breach was a contributory cause. In *Nationwide BS v. Various Solicitors*,[61] for example, Blackburne J held that the conduct of the person to whom a fiduciary duty was owed could be relevant and that there may come a point, following the breach of fiduciary duty, at which the loss would be 'too remote' to be said to flow from the breach. His Lordship seems to have had a more loose idea of 'remoteness' in mind than the technical idea of 'remoteness of damage' that applies in the common law of negligence.[62] His Lordship added that he could see no reason why the inquiry should be concerned only with the behaviour of the defendant: '*I do not see why equity should close its eyes to what the beneficiary would have done if there had been no misrepresentation or the appropriate disclosure had been made*.'[63]

The litigation in *Nationwide BS v. Various Solicitors* concerned a number of mortgages made by the claimant in which the defendant firms had acted on behalf of the claimant and, as is quite usual, on behalf of the borrower at the same time. All of the mortgages had unusual features, such as an agreement by the borrower immediately to sell the land onwards after acquiring the mortgage monies, or a misrepresentation by the borrower as to the true value of the land. The claimant had made losses on all of the mortgages and claimed that it would not have made these losses if the solicitors had discharged their duty to disclose the unusual features of the various mortgages. In some cases, in which the defendant firms were held liable in the common law tort of negligence, their liability was reduced because of the contributory negligence of the claimants (elements of contributory negligence included the claimants' failure to exercise industry-recommended levels of prudence in lending, including failure to emphasize the adequacy of underlying security and the borrower's financial well-being). However, Blackburne J refused to accept that liability for breach of trust or fiduciary duty might be similarly reduced to take account of the beneficiaries' contributory fault. In a subsequent case, Patten J agreed that the plea of contributory negligence '*has no application to liability for breach of trust or for breach of fiduciary duty*.'[64] This accords with the position in Australia, where the focus in this context is still exclusively upon the wrongdoer,[65] but it contrasts with the approach in New Zealand[66] and Canada,[67] where liability for breach of trust or fiduciary duty may be reduced to take account of the beneficiaries' contributory fault.[68]

---

[59] Apart from such exceptional cases as exemplary and punitive damages.
[60] *Re Dawson* [1966] 2 NSWR 211.   [61] [1999] PNLR 606.
[62] *Overseas Tankship (UK) Ltd v. Morts Dock and Engineering Co Ltd, 'The Wagon Mound'* [1961] AC 388, PC.
[63] *Nationwide BS v. Various Solicitors* [1999] PNLR 606, at heading 9.
[64] *De Beer v. Kanaar & Co. (a firm)* [2002] EWHC 688, per Patten J at [92].
[65] *Pilmer v. Duke Group Ltd (in liq)* (2001) 207 CLR 165, 201 (High Court of Australia).
[66] *Day v. Mead* [1987] 2 NZLR 443, CA, *per* Sir Robin Cooke, P at 451.
[67] *Canson Enterprises Ltd v. Boughton & Co* (1991) 85 DLR 4th 129 (Supreme Court of Canada).
[68] See, generally, R Mulheron, 'Contributory negligence in equity: Should fiduciaries accept all the blame?' (2003) 19(3) Professional Negligence 422.

Matthew Conaglen contends that '[i]t *would be anathema to the nature and function of fiduciary liability for* [contributory fault] *pleas to be accepted*' to reduce a fiduciary's liability,[69] but this extreme position is somewhat at odds with Conaglen's own theory that fiduciary duties are merely subsidiary to non-fiduciary duties (see Chapter 10). If fiduciary duties were utterly free-standing duties established in the public interest to prevent abuse of trust, to reduce a fiduciary's liability on account of the principal's fault ought then to be prohibited or wholly exceptional, but if the most important duties owed by a fiduciary to their principal are non-fiduciary duties, as Conaglen argues, it is then not difficult to imagine cases in which the fiduciary's personal liability ought in fairness to be reduced to take account of the principal's contribution to their own loss. To reduce a trustee's liability on account of a trust beneficiary's fault will not be appropriate to all trusts, but a compromise may be to admit the plea in simple cases of bare trust, since such trusts involve a tort-like direct duty of care owed by one party (the trustee) to another (the sole adult beneficiary).[70]

Liability to account

Account is a procedure and a remedy. As a procedure, it involves the production of the trust's financial accounts and requires the trustee to give an account of his dealings with the trust property. As a remedy, it requires the trustee to account personally to the trust for any trust property or money which, according to the procedure or otherwise, is, or ought to be, in the trustee's possession or under his control.

Summary order for an account

When proceedings against a trustee involve the taking of an account, any party can apply to the Chancery Division of the High Court for an order directing the requisite accounts and inquiries to be undertaken on a summary basis—that is, without a full hearing of the merits of the case.[71] Provided that the trustees have acknowledged service, or the court otherwise sees fit, the court can enter summary judgment against any trustee for the amount certified on the account whenever the court adjudges that there is no reason for the case to proceed to a full trial. Summary judgment is unlikely in any case where the trustee has a real prospect of making out a successful defence.

The remedy of account

A trustee account can be calculated in one of two ways: calculation on the normal 'common' basis, or calculation 'on the basis of wilful default'.

The common basis of account

This basis of account requires a trustee to account personally for trust property that is, or ought still to be, in his possession. The fact that the duty to account is 'personal' means

---

[69] 'Remedial ramifications of conflicts between a fiduciary's duties' (2010) 126 LQR 72–101.
[70] G. Watt, 'Contributory fault and breach of trust' (2005) 5(2) OUCLJ 205.   [71] CPR, Pt 24.

that it extends to trust property that has passed through the trustee's hands, whether or not it remains in his hands at the date of the account. The fact that an account on the common basis extends to trust property that 'ought' still to be in the trustee's possession means that it can be used to establish a trustee's liability to compensate the trust for any losses caused. The common basis of account does not itself allege wrongdoing, but where a shortfall is established, the beneficiaries can then claim an account on the basis of willful default.[72] Indeed, it has been suggested that the recent popularity of equitable compensation in relation to actions against fiduciaries *'tends to obscure the fact that the account remains the main method of compelling trustees to pay compensation for breach of trust'.*[73]

Accounting on the basis of wilful default

Account on the basis of wilful default must be specifically pleaded or further inquiry requested.[74] The burden is on the claimant to prove the alleged default, but, if proved, the corresponding benefit to the claimant is that the defendant will be subjected to a more intensive inquiry. The defendant will be liable to account not only for property and monetary gains that he has, or has had, in his possession or under his control, but also for that which he could, and should with reasonable diligence, have had in his possession or under his control.[75] Suppose, for example, that a trust owns a house that the trustee has neglected to rent out, so that it stands empty. The beneficiaries have the option of seeking compensation for lost rents or requiring the trustee to account for lost rents on the basis of wilful default.

Although an account on the basis of wilful default must, in theory, be specifically pleaded and proved,[76] it appears that the courts sometimes order similar accounts of their own volition. Thus, in *Re Howlett*,[77] a trustee, who for several years had been using trust-owned land without paying rent, was held to be in possession of, and liable to account for, 'notional' trust property in the form of unpaid rent; in *Re Brogden*,[78] the trustee was personally liable to account for funds which he ought to have 'got in' for the trust, but did not. In neither case was an account on the basis of wilful default specifically pleaded.

Interest

Courts have discretion to award interest on any sum awarded to a successful claimant. When judgment is awarded against a trustee in an action for breach of trust, the type of interest will be simple interest unless it is alleged that the defendant has committed a fraud or made an unauthorized gain, in which case the court may award compound interest.[79] (At present, the courts have no power to award compound interest on

---

[72] *Partington v. Reynolds* (1858) 4 Drew 253, 255–6. R. Chambers, 'Liability' in P. Birks and A. Pretto (eds), *Breach of Trust* (Oxford: Hart Publishing, 2002) 1 at 18.   [73] Ibid. at 21.

[74] Practice Direction, Pt 16, 11.2(7).   [75] *Armitage v. Nurse* [1998] Ch 241, *per* Millett LJ at 252C, CA.

[76] See earlier.   [77] [1949] 2 All ER 490.   [78] (1888) LR 38 Ch D 546, CA.

[79] *President of India v. La Pintada Compania Navigacion SA* [1985] AC 104, 116; *Westdeutsche Landesbank Girozentrale v. Islington LBC* [1996] AC 669.

common law debts or damages.)[80] Simple interest is awarded at a fixed rate for every year that the judgment debt remains outstanding, the rate of interest lying in the discretion of the court.[81] Compound interest is interest on interest: in practice, this means that simple interest will be awarded on the judgment in the first year, with the first year's interest being added to the judgment debt; in the second year, the same fixed rate of interest will be charged on the combined sum of judgment debt plus the interest from the first year; and so on in future years.

Compound interest is not awarded as a punishment.[82] The object of the award is to ensure that the trustee does not retain any unauthorized profit at the expense of the trust:[83] this is why it is routine for the court to consider an award of compound interest on the judgment debt when a trustee or fiduciary is required to account for unauthorized gains.[84] In fact, it has even been suggested obiter that compound interest should be limited to cases in which the trustee or fiduciary has used unauthorized gains in the course of his own trade or business,[85] but that is probably a restriction too far. However that may be, it is certainly the case that, whenever a defendant trustee improperly uses trust assets for the purposes of his own trade or business, the claimant must elect either to take the portion of trade profits made with trust assets or compound interest on the account for trust assets so used.[86] To recover both would be to give the claimant a double satisfaction.[87] Having said that, '*the court will think hard before enforcing an election against the plaintiff where the trustee has deliberately loaned trust money (in breach) to himself and to others*'.[88]

If the claimant fails to establish that the defendant was a trustee or fiduciary, an award of compound interest will not be possible. The appropriate award will be simple interest, which is the only award possible when interest is awarded on a judgment debt at common law.[89] Thus in *Westdeutsche Landesbank Girozentrale v. Islington LBC*,[90] where it was held that the recipient of monies paid under a void contract did not hold those monies on a resulting trust, the House of Lords held[91] that, in the absence of fraud or a

---

[80] The Law Commission proposed reform of this rule for judgments over £15,000 (*Pre-Judgment Interest on Debts and Damages*, Report No. 287, 24 February 2004, para. 5.69), but the government's response (16 September 2008) was not enthusiastic.

[81] In *Wallersteiner v. Moir (No. 2)* [1975] 1 QB 373, the interest was fixed at 1% above the minimum bank lending rate. In *Bartlett v. Barclays Bank (No. 1)* [1980] Ch 515, it was fixed at the rate from time to time allowed on the court's short-term investment account. In *West v. West* [2003] All ER (D) 17 (Jun), the rate of judgment interest was fixed at 1% over the High Court's special account rate for the time being (usually between 6% and 8%).

[82] *Wallersteiner v. Moir (No. 2)* [1975] 1 QB 373.   [83] See Chapter 10.

[84] *Wallersteiner v. Moir (No. 2)* [1975] 1 QB 373.

[85] *O'Sullivan and Another v. Management Agency and Music Ltd* [1985] QB 428, CA, *per* Dunn LJ at 461: '*it is only in cases of breaches of fiduciary duty that compound interest can be awarded, since at common law the position is governed by s. 3(1) of the Law Reform (Miscellaneous Provisions) Act 1934, which provides that interest cannot be charged on interest. But in equity compound interest can be charged where the profits made in breach of a fiduciary duty have been used in trade.*'

[86] *Vyse v. Foster* (1872–3) LR 8 Ch App 309, *per* Sir W. M. James LJ at 329, 334.   [87] See 'Election'.

[88] *Vyse v. Foster* (1872–3) LR 8 Ch App 309 at 334.

[89] Law Reform (Miscellaneous Provisions) Act 1934, s. 3(1).   [90] [1996] 2 WLR 802.

[91] Lord Goff of Chieveley and Lord Woolf dissenting.

fiduciary relationship, the proper award was of simple interest only. This rule has since been relaxed. In *Sempra Metals Ltd (formerly Metallgesellschaft Ltd) v. IRC*[92] it was held by a bare majority of the House of Lords that the court has power to make an award of compound interest in a claim for restitution where such an award is necessary to achieve full justice for the claimant. As a result of a decision of the Court of Justice of the European Communities which had held certain UK tax provisions to be in contravention of Art. 52 (now Art. 43) of the EC Treaty, numerous taxpayers sought restitution of tax paid. It was held that the detriment suffered by a taxpayer by the premature payment of tax was loss of use of the money for the period of prematurity and such loss included interest paid on borrowing substitute money during that period. Alternatively, if the taxpayer's reparation claim was framed in restitution, the Revenue had been unjustly enriched by the tax and by interest earned on it. Accordingly, an award of compound interest 'was necessary to achieve full restitution and, hence, a just result'.[93]

It was held in another case that there is no jurisdiction to award compound interest against a fiduciary on damages for deceit unless the deceit relates to the use of a fund held by the fiduciary, since the purpose of the award of compound interest is to ensure that the defendant does not profit from his breach.[94] When the same case went to appeal, it was indicated that the essentially contractual nature of the council's rights (in *Westdeutsche*) might have barred the award of compound interest even if the claimant had been able to establish fiduciary liability alongside liability in contract.[95]

Costs

The general rule of trusts law is that a trustee is entitled to be indemnified out of the trust fund whenever he embarks upon litigation in connection with trust business, but where the trustee is held liable for breach of trust, the general rule of costs in hostile litigation applies—namely, that the unsuccessful party must pay the costs of the successful party.[96] However, the court has discretion to reduce the award of costs against the trustee if, for example, he has remedied, or attempted to remedy, his breach before judgment[97] or can point to gains that he has made for the trust.[98] Trustees who are solicitors may be ordered to indemnify trustees who are not,[99] and an entirely innocent trustee who is joined as a defendant to an action against the trustee who committed the breach may be indemnified out of the trust fund in respect of any costs that he was unable to recover from the trustee in breach.[100]

Tax

When the value of a trust fund is reduced because of a trustee's breach of trust, it will very often follow that the tax liability of the beneficiaries will also be reduced. So if, for

---

[92] [2007] UKHL 34; [2008] 1 AC 561. [93] [2008] 1 AC 561, 605.
[94] *Black v. Davies* [2004] EWHC 1464, QBD. [95] *Black v. Davies* [2005] EWCA Civ 531, CA (Civ Div).
[96] *McDonald v. Horn* [1995] 1 All ER 961 at 972j. CPR, r. 44.3.
[97] *Peacock v. Colling* (1885) 54 LJ Ch 743 at 746, CA. [98] *Knott v. Cottee* (1852) 16 Beav 77.
[99] *Lockhart v. Reilly* (1856) 25 LJ Ch 697. [100] *Cook v. Addison* (1869) LR 7 Eq 466 at 471.

example, a life tenant receives less income due to the trustee's breach, she will pay less income tax. This raises the question of whether a trustee will be permitted to reduce his liability to compensate by the amount of tax that his breach has 'saved' the beneficiaries. The courts have tended to answer that question in the negative.[101] In *Bartlett v. Barclays Trust (No. 2)*,[102] Brightman LJ stated that:

> the tax liability of individual beneficiaries... do not enter into the picture because they arise not at the point of restitution to the trust estate but at the point of distribution of capital or income out of the trust estate. These are different stages.[103]

The rule prohibiting deduction of tax seems fair enough in any case in which a trustee has deliberately misappropriated trust assets for his own benefit or for the benefit of a third party, as was the case in *Re Bell's Indenture*,[104] to which Vinelott J applied it,[105] but it does seem somewhat harsh in any case in which the breach of trust was merely negligent, as it was in *Bartlett* itself.

Of course, not every fiduciary is a trustee of the traditional sort, with duties to manage and invest a trust estate. Consider, for example, a mere fiduciary who is called to account for unauthorized gains. *O'Sullivan v. MAM Ltd*[106] was such a case. There, the fiduciary (a manager who had profited from an unfair contract obtained by his undue influence over a naive young pop star) was given credit for tax that it had already paid on its improper profits and which (having been paid more than six years ago) it would be unable to reclaim from the Inland Revenue. However, it was not permitted to deduct tax that it still had time to recover from the Inland Revenue.[107]

Election

An election is the choice that any claimant must make when presented with two 'mutually exclusive' courses of action. Two types of election are of special relevance to cases of breach of trust, both of them having a 'procedural' rather than a 'substantive' quality. The first is the choice whether or not to pursue a remedy at all. Thus beneficiaries must decide whether to avoid a voidable transaction (such as self-dealing by their trustee),[108] whether to claim unauthorized profits made by their trustee from his position of trust,[109] and whether to complain when their trustee has used trust funds to make an unauthorized purchase of an asset.[110] The second type of election is the choice between alternative inconsistent remedies, the classic instance being the choice between the remedy of account and the remedy of compensation where the trustee has misappropriated trust

---

[101] Nicholls LJ in *John v. James* [1986] STC 352, 361h.   [102] [1980] Ch 515.

[103] [1980] Ch 515 at 545C.   [104] [1980] 1 WLR 1217.   [105] Ibid. at 1235H–1236A, 1237B–C.

[106] [1985] QB 428.   [107] Ibid. at 460 G–H.

[108] The beneficiary might elect instead to adopt, confirm, or ratify the transaction, or might by his conduct or acquiescence be said to have elected to waive his remedy.

[109] For example, on facts such as those in *Keech v. Sandford* (1726) Sel Cas Ch 61.

[110] 'The fact that he does not... complain of the acquisition of the asset but seeks to take advantage of it does not mean that he adopts or ratifies it—he will almost certainly plead that it was a breach of trust—it means only that he does not seek a remedy in respect of it' (per Millett LJ in *Boscawen v. Bajwa* [1996] 1 WLR 328 at 342B).

property to his own use.[111] These procedural forms of election, and the second species in particular, are sometimes called election 'at common law',[112] but that label is not especially helpful. They are best considered as forms of procedural election that can apply in common law or equitable contexts. The label 'election at common law' is no doubt a reaction to the existence of the special 'equitable doctrine of election', which requires a party to choose between accepting an instrument or judgment in its entirety, or rejecting it in its entirety.[113]

The first type of election, between pursuing a remedy and foregoing a remedy, must be made within a reasonable time. It is a close relation to laches.[114] If we take the example of the claimant's decision whether or not to avoid a self-dealing by her trustee, such as the unauthorized purchase by the trustee of trust-owned shares, it is clear that the claimant who delays her election is able, in effect, to gamble on a certainty at the defendant's expense. If the shares do well, the claimant will seek to have the self-dealing set aside; if the shares do badly, the claimant will allow the self-dealing to stand. Clearly, the claimant cannot be permitted to delay her election until such time as the shares start to look attractive.

The second type of election, election between alternative inconsistent remedies, is quite different. It applies when litigation has already commenced. In such a case, the claimant has taken the risk that she will lose the proceedings and be ordered to pay the costs.[115] She cannot be said to be gambling solely at the defendant's expense and it follows that there is no requirement that an election of this type must be made within a reasonable time; the only requirement is that it must be made before judgment is entered.

Part of the reason why the claimant is required to elect between inconsistent alternatives is simple fairness between the parties,[116] for an election will prevent the 'double satisfaction' of the claimant. Suppose that a trustee were to steal the ubiquitous antique vase from his trust. It would clearly be unfair to require him to return the vase in an action for specific 'restitution' (or to return its value in an action for an account) and *in addition* to require him to compensate the trust for the loss of the vase. The claimant must choose between an award based on the trustee's gain and an award based on the trust's loss. However, the doctrine of election is not concerned solely with fairness between the parties to the litigation; it is also concerned with the wider public interest in the conduct of judicial proceedings.[117] The doctrine of election prevents two logically

---

[111] See *Tang Man Sit (decd) (personal representative) v. Capacious Investments Ltd* [1996] 1 AC 514.

[112] *Nexus Communications Group Ltd v. Lambert* [2005] EWHC 345.   [113] See Chapter 16.

[114] J. Brunyate, *Limitation of Actions in Equity* (Cambridge: Cambridge University Press, 1932) observes (at 189). See also *Allcard v. Skinner* (1887) LR 36 Ch D at 145 and *Edwards v. Carter* [1893] AC 360.

[115] See the previous section.

[116] In *Johnson v. Agnew* [1980] AC 367, HL, Lord Wilberforce stated (at 398) that '[e]*lection, though the subject of much learning and refinement, is in the end a doctrine based on simple considerations of common sense and equity'.* In *Tang Man Sit v. Capacious Investments Ltd* [1996] 1 AC 514, Lord Nicholls approved this dictum (at 522B–C).

[117] See *Tang Man Sit* (ibid.) at 521H–522B. G. Watt, 'Laches, estoppel and election', in *Breach of Trust* (P. Birks and A. Pretto, eds) (Oxford: Hart Publishing, 2002) at 354.

inconsistent awards appearing in the same judgment and therefore prevents the judicial process from being brought into disrepute.

If judgment is mistakenly entered before an election is made, the claimant will still be required to make an election in order to prevent a double satisfaction. This is what occurred in the leading case, *Tang Man Sit (decd) (personal representative) v. Capacious Investments Ltd*.[118] Tang was the owner of land and a party to a joint venture for the building of houses on it. As part of the joint venture, he agreed to assign some of the houses to the claimant after completion of the building works. No assignment was made. Instead, Tang let out the houses as homes for the elderly without the claimant's knowledge or approval. The presence of the tenants in the flats produced rents, but it reduced the letting value of the flats; their presence therefore produced a gain and caused a loss. Accordingly, the claimant sought, on the one hand, to recover the unauthorized rents, and, on the other hand, to be compensated for lost use and occupation (and diminution in the value) of the property, due to wrongful use and occupation. The judge entered judgment in the claimant's favour, in respect of both the restitutionary award and compensation, before the claimant had had the opportunity to consider fully its preferred remedy. The claimant was still required to make an election between the two remedies, not only to prevent a 'double satisfaction', but also to prevent an internally inconsistent judgment from remaining on the public record. Clearly, an award could not be permitted to stand which, at one and the same time, assumed the flats were *vacant* for the purpose of assessing the claimant's loss and *occupied* for the purpose of assessing the defendant's gain.

Defences

We have seen that, when a trustee is called upon to account for unauthorized gains, it is no defence for him to show that the trust has suffered no loss,[119] and that, when a trustee is called upon to compensate a loss caused to the trust, it is no defence for the trustee to show that he has made no gain.[120] There are, however, a number of defences that trustees may raise to actions for breach of trust.

Limitation of actions

The Limitation Act 1980 lays down time limits within which certain legal actions must be commenced or the cause of action lost. The Act is the latest in a long line of statutes of limitation which give effect to the public interest in an end to civil litigation (*interest reipublicae ut sit finis litium*) and the related public interest in certainty of proprietary title, which requires that, after a sufficient time, the possessor of property should be presumed entitled to it, so as to be 'quieted' in possession.[121]

---

[118] Ibid.   [119] This was considered in Chapter 10.
[120] *Lord Mountford v. Lord Cadogan* (1810) 17 Ves Jr 485 at 489.
[121] *Chalmondeley v. Clinton* (1821) 4 Bligh 1, *per* Lord Redesdale at 124.

On 9 July 2001, the Law Commission for England and Wales published a report recommending reform of the law relating to the limitation of actions.[122] The report was accompanied by a Limitation Bill. The Law Commission's proposed reforms are considered later, but, at the time of writing, the Bill has still not passed into law.

The limitation period for breach of trust

Ever since the Limitation Act 1623, the general limitation period for a breach of trust has been six years. As the 1980 Act now recites: *'an action by a beneficiary to recover trust property or in respect of any breach of trust shall not be brought after the expiration of* six years *from the date on which the right of action accrued'*.[123] Certain cases are not subject to this six-year period. Cases excepted by the statute itself include cases of *'fraud or fraudulent breach of trust to which the trustee was a party or privy'*,[124] cases where the claimant is under a disability, and cases where the defendant concealed the cause of action. Cases where the trust property, the proceeds of trust property, or notional trust property[125] are still in the possession of the trustee or have been converted to the trustee's use are also excepted.[126] A further exception, recognized by the courts, is breach of the self-dealing and fair dealing rules.[127]

Where an action is brought by the Attorney General against the trustees of a charity, the Limitation Act has no application, because the 'beneficiary' of a charitable trust is 'the public at large'[128] and it cannot sensibly be said that a cause of action has 'accrued' to the public at large as that term is employed in the Limitation Act.

Accrual of the right of action

The right of action may accrue to different beneficiaries at different times. Under a traditional settlement trust 'for A for life and B in remainder', B's interest will not vest in possession until A's death. Accordingly, if the trustees commit a breach of trust during A's lifetime, A will have six years within which to bring an action for breach of trust, but time does not begin to run against B until B's interest falls into possession at the date of A's death.[129]

---

[122] Law Commission Report No. 270, *Item 2 of the Seventh Programme of Law Reform: Limitation of Actions* (2001).

[123] Limitation Act 1980, s. 21(3). The Law Commission has proposed a number of fundamental changes to the law relating to limitation of actions. These are considered later.

[124] Ibid. ss. 21(1)(a) and 32(1)(a). In *Armitage v. Nurse* [1997] 2 All ER 705, the Court of Appeal held that proof of actual dishonesty is required to establish 'fraud' under s. 21(1)(a) (but see Goff and Jones, *The Law of Restitution*, 5th edn (London: Sweet & Maxwell, 1998) at 858. In *Gwembe Valley Development Company Ltd v. Koshy* [2003] EWCA Civ 1478 a trustee who had dishonestly concealed the fact that he had a personal interest in a trust transaction was held to have acted fraudulently for the purposes of s. 21(1)(a) Limitation Act 1980. (Note that certain other aspects of the decision in *Gwembe* have since been disapproved by the Court of Appeal, in *Green v. Gaul* [2007] 1 WLR 591.)

[125] The facts of *Re Howlett* [1949] 2 All ER 490, illustrate how notional trust property can be said to remain in the possession of the trustee.

[126] Limitation Act 1980, s. 21(1)(b). See *Nelson v. Rye* [1996] 1 WLR 1378.

[127] See *Tito v. Waddell (No. 2)* [1977] Ch 106, *per* Megarry VC at 248–9.

[128] *AG v. Cocke* [1988] Ch 414, *per* Harman J at 419E.　　[129] *Re Allsop* [1914] 1 Ch 1, CA.

The disability exception

Infants and persons of unsound mind are treated as being under a disability for the purposes of the Act.[130] If the claimant was under a disability at the date on which the right accrued to him, he may bring his action within six years from the date on which he ceased to be under the disability.[131] This rule applies even if he ceases to be under the disability by reason of death, because in that case, his personal representatives may bring the action on behalf of his estate.

The concealment exception

If a trustee deliberately conceals any fact relevant to a right of action against him, the period of limitation will not begin to run until the claimant becomes aware of the concealment.[132] To be 'deliberate', concealment must be intentional, but need not be dishonest.[133] Concealment is only relevant where it is the intentional act of the defendant; concealment by another party is not sufficient to disapply the limitation period. This is demonstrated by *Thorne v. Heard*.[134] Heard was the first mortgagee of certain land and Thorne was second mortgagee of the same land. The land had been sold and the solicitor employed by Heard paid off the first mortgage from the proceeds of sale. The solicitor should then have accounted to Thorne for part of the balance. Instead, he kept that part of the proceeds to himself and continued secretly to pay off the second mortgage by the usual instalments. Thorne had a right of action against Heard, because Heard's agent (the solicitor) had failed to hand over the proceeds of sale. However, Thorne's right of action was held to be time-barred, because it had been concealed, not by Heard, but by Heard's solicitor. Heard could not be imputed with the consequences of his agent having acted fraudulently and beyond his authority.

The 'trustee still in possession of trust property' exception

According to s. 21(1)(b) of the Limitation Act 1980, no period of limitation under the Act shall apply to actions '*to recover from the trustee trust property or the proceeds of trust property in the possession of the trustee, or previously received by the trustee and converted to his use*'. However, the statute does place a limit on trustees' liability for actions brought under this section: a claim brought after the limitation period has expired against a trustee who is *also* a beneficiary under the trust is limited to property in *excess* of that trustee's proper share under the trust.[135]

The rationale behind s. 21(1)(b) may be that a trustee in possession of trust property is under an ongoing obligation to account for that property to the beneficiaries of the trust. When Romer J applied the old Statute of Limitations[136] against a husband who held his wife's property as a trustee, his Lordship observed that he '*was her trustee at*

---

[130] Limitation Act 1980, s. 38(2).   [131] Ibid. s. 28.   [132] Limitation Act 1980, s. 32(1).

[133] *Liverpool Roman Catholic Archdiocese Trustees Inc v. Goldberg, The Times*, 18 July 2000, Ch D.

[134] [1895] AC 495.   [135] Section 21(2).

[136] 1623 (21 Jac. 1, c. 16). The Real Property Limitation Acts of 1833 (3 & 4 Wm 4, c. 27) and 1874 (37 & 38 Vict., c. 57) have also gone under the name 'statute of limitations'. For a comprehensive analysis of the statutory history, see W. Swadling, 'Limitation' in *Breach of Trust* (P. Birks and A. Pretto, eds) (Oxford: Hart Publishing Ltd, 2002) at 319.

first, and never ceased to be her trustee.[137] In a sense, therefore, a fresh duty to account arises each day and the corresponding cause of action accrues to the beneficiary on a daily basis. A limitation period can have no sensible application to this sort of situation, hence its express exclusion by s. 21(1)(b).

In *Re Howlett*,[138] the beneficiary of a trust waited for more than six years before bringing an action for an account against the trustee's estate. The complaint was that the trustee had been using trust-owned land without paying rent and was therefore liable for several years' unpaid back rent. The beneficiary had waited for so long, because the trustee in question was his own father and he had been reluctant to litigate the matter while his father was alive. It was held that the claimant was not subject to the usual limitation period, because the trustee's estate was still in possession of 'notional' trust property in the form of unpaid rent.

In *Nelson v. Rye*,[139] the defendant was an agent who, in the words of Millett LJ in the later case of *Paragon Finance plc v. D. B. Thakerar & Co (a firm)*,[140] was

> entitled to pay receipts into his own account, mix them with his own money, use them for his own cash flow, deduct his own commission, and account for the balance to the plaintiff at the end of the year.[141]

Millett LJ observed (in *Paragon*) that an agent of this sort is not a constructive trustee, even if he is in a fiduciary relationship with the person to whom he must account, since a trustee is, by definition, required to keep trust money separate from his own.[142] Accordingly, such an agent does not have trust property within his possession and is able to rely upon the usual six-year limitation period applicable to the personal duty to account. His Lordship also observed that certain types of constructive trustee never actually commit a 'breach of trust' properly so-called and are therefore not subject to the onerous 'trustee still in possession of trust property' exception,[143] since that exception applies to the six-year limitation period for breach of trust.[144] Far from being liable for breach of trust, 'constructive trustees' of this sort become 'constructive trustees' because they have breached some other duty, such as the fiduciary duty not to misappropriate their employer's property.[145] A very clear example of a defendant who is said to be a constructive trustee, but never holds trust property and never commits a breach of trust, is the person who dishonestly assists in a breach of trust and is held liable to account *as if* he were a constructive trustee.[146] He is not, in fact, a trustee and is not subject to the limitation period for breach of trust.[147] The Supreme Court has confirmed that persons liable for dishonestly assisting in the misapplication of trust funds by the trustee, or for knowingly receiving trust funds in breach of trust, are not true trustees.[148]

---

[137] *Wassell v. Leggatt* [1896] 1 Ch 554 at 558.   [138] [1949] 2 All ER 490.
[139] [1996] 1 WLR 1378.   [140] [1999] 1 All ER 400, CA.   [141] Ibid. at 416b.
[142] Ibid. at 416c.   [143] Limitation Act 1980, s. 21.   [144] Ibid. s. 21(1b).
[145] See Chapter 8.   [146] See Chapter 15.
[147] *Cattley v. Pollard* [2006] EWHC 3130 (Ch), [2007] 2 All ER 1086.
[148] *Williams v. Central Bank of Nigeria* [2014] UKSC 10, Supreme Court.

It is not always straightforward to identify who is, and who is not, a constructive trustee.[149] In *Martin v. Myers*,[150] the issue was whether a surviving cohabitee who remained in the home that she had shared with her deceased partner had become a constructive trustee for their children (who were entitled on her partner's intestacy) so as to be barred under s. 21(1)(b) from relying on the Limitation Act 1980 to claim title to the house by long possession. It was held that the surviving cohabitee never became a constructive trustee for her children, because her conscience was never affected by knowledge of any entitlement that her children might have in the house.

Time bars 'by analogy' to the Limitation Act 1980

Where equity exercises a concurrent jurisdiction (giving the same or corresponding relief) as the common law, the exercise of such equitable jurisdiction will be time-barred by analogy to the time-bar under the Act in relation to the comparable common law jurisdiction.[151] Thus, in *Coulthard v. Disco Mix Club Ltd*,[152] an equitable claim based on breaches of fiduciary duty by way of deliberate and dishonest under-accounting, arising from facts analogous to those which would give rise to an action in fraud at common law fraud, was held to be subject to the limitation period for common law fraud.

Of course, equity, by its nature, will not apply the statute if, on the particular facts of the case, it would be unjust to bar the claim.[153]

In *P & O Nedlloyd B V v. Arab Metals Co*,[154] the Court of Appeal concluded that, in claims for the equitable remedy of specific performance, it is never appropriate to apply a limitation period by analogy to the common law, because specific performance has no common law counterpart.[155] In reaching this conclusion, Moore-Bick LJ observed that the facts giving rise to specific performance are not always the same as those giving rise to contractual damages for breach of contract,[156] noting, in particular, that a contract is specifically enforceable from the moment it is made, with the result that the cause of action would accrue then and the six-year period might run its course before there is even any suggestion of breach. This reasoning is plausible where the contract is one for which (as in the case of a contract to acquire land) specific performance is generally available, but even with such a contract, it is not necessary to suppose that the cause of action for specific performance commences the moment the contract is made, since in theory, the award depends upon the court's discretion.[157] Given the broad public

---

[149] See, generally, Chapter 8.   [150] [2004] EWHC 1947 (Ch).

[151] Limitation Act 1980, s. 36(1); *Knox v. Gye* (1872) LR 5 App Cas 656, 674.   [152] [1999] 2 All ER 457.

[153] *Companhia de Seguros Imperio v. Heath (REBX) Ltd* [2001] 1 WLR 112, CA, approving Spry, *The Principles of Equitable Remedies*, 5th edn (London: Sweet & Maxwell, 1997) (now in its 6th edition, 2001).

[154] [2006] EWCA Civ 1717.

[155] On the application of statutory time-bars to specific performance, see J. Beatson, 'Limitation Periods and Specific performance' in *Contemporary Issues in Commercial Law, Essays in Honour of Professor A. G. Guest* (Lomnicka and Morse, eds) (London: Sweet & Maxwell, 1997) at 9–23.

[156] Cases such as *Hasham v. Zenab* [1960] AC 316 illustrate the point.

[157] For specific performance, see Chapter 16. There is authority for the view that '*the vendor is a constructive trustee for the purchaser of the estate from the moment the contract is entered into*' (*Lysaght v. Edwards* (1876) LR 2 Ch D 499 at 506–10), and this assumes that specific performance is available the moment the contract is made, but the fact remains that the assumption is only generally, and not universally, accurate.

interest against late claims, the decision in the *P & O* case might be said to rest upon a rather technical analysis of 'cause of action' as it applies to s. 36(1), but the Court of Appeal was no doubt comforted by the availability of the doctrine of laches as an alternative basis for barring a tardy equitable claim.[158]

Reform

Under the new Limitation Act proposed by the Law Commission,[159] actions for breaches of trust which are not at present subject to the six-year limitation period will become subject to the new standard statutory limitation periods. The new statutory limitation periods conclude three years from the date the defendant knew of the claim or 10 years from the date on which the cause of action first arose, whichever is the shorter.[160] In private trusts, the standard statutory periods for breach of trust will only be relaxed if the claimant is a child,[161] is under a disability,[162] or has an interest that has not vested in possession.[163]

Laches

The doctrine of laches[164] bars an action by reason of the 'staleness' of a claim in situations in which the statutory limitation period does not apply either expressly or by analogy. The doctrine '*renders it necessary to consider the time which has elapsed and the balance of justice or injustice in affording or refusing relief*'.[165] The doctrine also applies where the Act expressly disapplies the usual statutory limitation period, as it does, for example, where the trustee is still in possession of trust property.[166] A beneficiary's claim to recover property from the trustee of an express trust will not be barred by laches unless there has been a breach of trust giving rise to a cause of action, but a claim to assert proprietary rights under a constructive trust might be barred by laches, regardless of the merits of the claim.[167]

The modern formulation of the doctrine holds that what is required is 'a broad approach, directed to ascertaining whether it would in all the circumstances be unconscionable for a party to be permitted to assert his beneficial right'.[168] According to this formulation, the public interest has nothing to do with the doctrine. It is true, of course,

---

[158] For laches, see later.

[159] In the form of a Limitation Bill appended to Law Commission Report No. 270, *Item 2 of the Seventh Programme of Law Reform: Limitation of Actions* (2001). [160] Limitation Bill, ibid. at cl. 1.

[161] Ibid. at cl. 28. [162] Ibid. at cl. 29. [163] Ibid. at sub-cl. 22(1).

[164] The word laches (pronounced 'lay-cheese') has its root in the Latin *laxus*, meaning 'loose'. Even in everyday speech, we might describe as 'lax' a person who acts in a tardy manner.

[165] *Re Sharpe* [1892] 1 Ch 154, *per* Lindley LJ at 168.

[166] Under Limitation Act 1980 s. 21(1)(b), see *Green v. Gaul* [2007] 1 WLR 591, CA (dismissing an appeal from the decision of Lawrence Collins J in *Re Loftus (decd)* [2005] EWHC 406 (Ch)).

[167] *Burdick v. Garrick* (1870) LR 5 Ch App 233 at 243; *Mills v. Drewitt* (1855) 20 Beav 632, *per* Sir John Romilly MR at 638; *Re Ashwell's Will* (1859) Johns 112, *per* Sir W. Page Wood at 117; *Wedderburn v. Wedderburn* (1838) 4 My & Cr 41, *per* Cottenham LC at 53.

[168] *Frawley v. Neill* [2000] CP Rep 20, CA, *per* Aldous LJ (at the conclusion of his judgment); followed in *Patel v. Shah* [2005] EWCA Civ 157, CA, and *Green v. Gaul* [2007] 1 WLR 591, CA.

that, after long delay, '[i]t is immaterial to the public at large whether the estate belongs to A or B', as Lord Redesdale put it, but he immediately went on to say that 'it is material, that the person in possession, should be quieted in that possession'.[169] This interest in 'quiescence of title' is a public interest as much as it is a private one and, if one goes a little further back in the authorities, it is clear that laches was deeply concerned with the public interest in bringing civil dispute to an end:

> A Court of Equity, which is never active in relief against conscience, or public convenience, has always refused its aid to stale demands, where the party has slept upon his right, and acquiesced for a great length of time... 'Expedit reipublicae ut sit finis litium', is a maxim that has prevailed in this court in all time.[170]

The irony is that these earlier formulations of the doctrine, which take into account the public interest as well as the private interests of the parties, are, at first blush, better suited to the modern system of civil litigation, with its emphasis on efficiency, than is the modern formulation of the doctrine of laches,[171] although the very fact that civil procedure as a whole has been systemically attuned to the public interest in efficiency might explain why the courts have recently been prepared to reformulate the doctrine of laches in terms of fairness between the particular litigants without reference to the public interest.

A beneficiary's claim to recover property from the trustee of an express trust will not be barred by laches unless there has been a breach of trust giving rise to a cause of action, but a claim to assert proprietary rights under a constructive trust might be barred by laches, regardless of the merits of the claim.[172]

Reform of laches

At present, the doctrine of laches only applies to breaches that are not subject to a statutory limitation period, of which the most significant are those committed fraudulently, those involving an infringement of the rules on 'self-' or 'fair' dealing, and cases in which the trustee is still holding trust property. However, under the new Limitation Act,[173] these three situations will be subject to the standard statutory limitation periods of three and 10 years, respectively, so the new Limitation Act will reduce significantly the circumstances in which the doctrine of laches, as currently understood, will apply to breaches of trust. This is despite the assertion in the draft Limitation Bill that nothing in the proposed new Limitation Act will affect 'any equitable jurisdiction to refuse relief on the ground of delay, acquiescence or otherwise'.[174]

---

[169] *Chalmondeley v. Clinton* (1821) 4 Bligh 1, *per* Lord Redesdale at 124.

[170] *Smith v. Clay* (1767) 3 Bro CC 639n, *per* Lord Camden. See also *Hercy v. Dinwoody* (1793) 2 Ves Jun 87 at 93 and *Pickering v. Stamford* (1794) 2 Ves Jun 581 at 582–3, both *per* Sir R. P. Arden, MR.

[171] G. Watt, 'Laches, estoppel and election' in *Breach of Trust* (P. Birks and A. Pretto, eds (Oxford: Hart Publishing, 2002) 353.

[172] *Burdick v. Garrick* (1870) LR 5 Ch App 233 at 243; *Mills v. Drewitt* (1855) 20 Beav 632, *per* Sir John Romilly MR at 638; *Re Ashwell's Will* (1859) Johns 112, *per* Sir W. Page Wood at 117; *Wedderburn v. Wedderburn* (1838) 4 My & Cr 41, *per* Cottenham LC at 53.

[173] Proposed by the Law Commission in Law Commission Report No. 270, *Item 2 of the Seventh Programme of Law Reform: Limitation of Actions* (2001).   [174] Paragraph 34(2) of the report.

Release, acquiescence, concurrence, and instigation

A beneficiary may, by his own acts and omissions, lose his right to take action against a defaulting trustee.

The most straightforward method of precluding a right of action is to execute a formal release or confirmation: the former releases the trustee from liability; the latter confirms the righteousness of the trustee's acts or omissions. A trustee should ensure, before potential claimants execute such forms, that the potential claimants are in possession of all relevant facts, have independent legal advice, and are free from undue influence. When a trustee makes the final distribution of the fund so that he no longer has any trust fund in his possession, he is well advised to seek a release from the beneficiaries and, preferably, in the form of a deed. A trustee is not entitled to demand a release except where the beneficiaries have requested the trustee to breach the express terms of his trust.[175]

More problematic than formal release or confirmation is the possibility of informal 'acquiescence' in a breach of trust, which can take effect by words, or conduct, or omissions. Acquiescence cannot be pleaded against a claimant unless he is *sui juris* and has full knowledge of the facts upon which his right of action is based,[176] but a claimant who fails to complain of a breach of trust when in possession of all of the relevant and necessary facts may be held to have acquiesced in the breach even though he was not aware that, as a matter of law, those facts constituted a breach of trust.[177]

Acquiescence is frequently confused with laches, but the two doctrines are quite different. Acquiescence is purely concerned with justice between the parties, whereas laches is also concerned with the public interest in an end to litigation and the public interest in certainty of ownership of property. The defence of laches may be based on long periods of mere delay, but, for acquiescence, there must be delay combined with knowledge of the facts on which the breach of trust is based, such that it would be inequitable as between the parties for the claimant to bring an action for breach after such a long time.

If informal acquiescence may be a defence to an action for breach of trust, then a fortiori it will be a valid defence if the defendant can show that the claimant has consented to, or even instigated, a breach:

> The court has to consider all the circumstances in which the concurrence of the *cestui que trust* was given with a view to seeing whether it is fair and equitable that, having given his concurrence, he should afterwards turn around and sue the trustees.[178]

However, the defendant trustee cannot rely upon the claimant's release or concurrence as a defence to an action brought by another claimant, so a trustee who proposes deliberately to commit a technical breach of trust (a so-called 'judicious' breach of trust)[179]

---

[175] *King v. Mullins* (1852) 1 Drew 308.   [176] *Holder v. Holder* [1968] Ch 353.
[177] Wilberforce J in *Re Pauling's ST* [1962] 1 WLR 86.   [178] Ibid. at 108.
[179] See the beginning of this chapter.

for the benefit of the beneficiaries must be careful to get the consent of all present and future beneficiaries of the trust, preferably in writing and ideally under seal. Of course, the concurrence of unborn beneficiaries will be unobtainable and the concurrence of infant beneficiaries will not be effective to preclude the minor from bringing a claim on attaining majority, unless the minor beneficiary had fraudulently induced the trustee to rely on her consent by, for example, representing that she was an adult.[180] Any beneficiary who concurs in a breach of trust may be required to indemnify the trustees out of his or her share against liability arising from an action brought by non-concurring beneficiaries.[181]

Exemption clauses

An exemption clause is a clause in a trust instrument that excludes or limits a trustee's liability for breaches of trust. The leading case is the decision of the Court of Appeal in *Armitage v. Nurse*,[182] in which a clause of a traditional settlement trust provided that the trustee would not be 'liable for any loss or damage which may happen from any cause whatsoever unless such damage shall be caused by his own actual fraud'. Such clauses are construed fairly without preference for either party,[183] but any ambiguity in the wording of an exemption clause is construed strictly *contra proferentem* (*'against the one who seeks to benefit from it'*).[184] There was no ambiguity in the wording of the clause in *Armitage v. Nurse*, so the court simply had to determine whether it was proper, as a matter of law, principle, and policy, that such a wide exemption clause should be permitted to operate according to its natural construction. The Court of Appeal held that it should.

At first instance, Jacob J held that the trust had been *'undertaken by trustees who knew they would not be liable unless they were fraudulent'*, so that it would be *'wrong to impose . . . any liability for honest acts'*, even if those acts were deliberate or reckless. This suggests that his Lordship viewed the trust deed as a form of contract between the settlor and the trustees. The Court of Appeal upheld the judgment of Jacob J and appeared to lend some support to his contractual analysis of the arrangement made between the settlor and trustees. Their Lordships declined to strike out the clause as being repugnant to the public interest, on the ground that a clause excluding liability for ordinary negligence or want of care had never been deemed contrary to public policy in the law of contract.[185] However, if such similar policies apply to trust deeds as apply to contracts, it may be wondered why the Court of Appeal in *Re Duke of Norfolk's Settlement Trusts*[186] held that the Unfair Contract Terms Act 1977 does not apply to exemption clauses in

---

[180] *Overton v. Banister* (1844) 3 Hare 303.   [181] See 'Impounding a beneficiary's interest', later.
[182] *Armitage v. Nurse* [1998] Ch 241.   [183] *Bogg v. Raper, The Times*, 22 April 1998, CA.
[184] *Wight v. Olswang, The Times*, 18 May 1999.
[185] In the USA exculpation (exemption) clauses are set aside as being contrary to public policy in some such cases (see D. Waters, 'The protector: new wine in old bottles' in *Trends in Contemporary Trust Law* (A. J. Oakley, ed.) (Oxford: Clarendon Press, 1996) 63 at 100).   [186] [1982] Ch 61.

trusts[187] and cautioned against taking the contractual analysis of the deal between settlor and trustee too far.[188]

Dishonesty, recklessness, gross negligence, and negligence

'Gross negligence may be evidence of *mala fides* but is not the same thing:'

Goodman v. Harvey (1836) 4 A & E 870, 876, *per* Lord Denman CJ.[189]

The Court of Appeal in *Armitage v. Nurse* held that a clause purporting to exclude all liability apart from liability for actual fraud is effective to exclude liability for deliberate breaches of trust which the trustee honestly believed to be in the best interests of the beneficiaries.[190] The definition of actual fraud is an act or omission, involving some element of dishonesty or deceit, which is intended to harm the beneficiaries' interests. In a later case, the Court of Appeal held that a trustee might be found to have been dishonest in this context if no reasonable solicitor-trustee would have considered the trustee's actions to be in the best interests of the beneficiaries, even if the trustee genuinely believed that they were.[191] The decision of the Court of Appeal in *Bonham v. David Fishwick*[192] suggests that trustees who follow legal advice will be able to rely on a clause exempting them from liability for wilful default. The honesty of a trustee's conduct is judged according to what an objective trustee, looking on, would make of it—it is not judged subjectively according to the trustee's own beliefs.[193]

Their Lordships in *Armitage v. Nurse* held that an exemption clause is unable to remove liability for fraudulent and dishonest breaches of trust, but that an appropriately worded clause is able to remove liability for mere negligence and gross negligence.[194] The question to which no definite answer was given is whether liability for recklessness can be removed by an appropriately worded exemption clause. The judgment of Millett LJ in *Armitage v. Nurse* is inconclusive on this issue, although his Lordship does indicate that there is a distinction between gross negligence, which is inactive, and recklessness, which is active. Reading between the lines of the judgment, it would

---

[187] A distinguished commentator once argued that it should (Sir William Goodhart QC (1980) 44 Conv 333), but withdrew his argument at a later date: Sir William Goodhart QC 'Trust law for the twenty-first century' in *Trends in Contemporary Trust Law* (A. J. Oakley, ed.) (Oxford: Clarendon Press, 1996) 257 at 270). He defended the principle, however, that '*paid trustees should not be permitted to be exempt from collective or personal liability for negligence, except in special circumstances*'.

[188] For a comparison between contract and trust, see Chapter 2.

[189] Approved as common law doctrine in *Spread Trustee Company Ltd v. Hutcheson* [2011] UKPC 13, Privy Council, at para. [46], where it was contrasted with the doctrine in civil law jurisdictions.

[190] [1998] Ch 241 at 251B–D, 252G.   [191] *Walker v. Stones, The Independent*, 27 July 2000.

[192] [2008] EWCA Civ 373.   [193] *Barnes v. Tomlinson* [2006] EWHC 3115; [2007] WTLR 377.

[194] Contrast the approach of Scots law, under which gross negligence is considered to be inconsistent with bona fides and therefore inconsistent with trust: *Knox v. MacKinnon* (1883) LR 13 App Cas 753, 765. In *Rae v. Meek* (1889) LR 14 App Cas 558 HL (SC) an exculpatory clause '*was held to be ineffectual to protect a trustee against the consequences of* culpa lata, *or gross negligence on his part, or of any conduct which is inconsistent with bona fides*' (*per* Lord Herschell at 573).

appear that recklessness—what is sometimes referred to as the attitude of someone who *'couldn't care less'*[195]—is inconsistent with the bona fide or 'honest' state of mind that is essential to trusteeship. It follows that an exemption clause will probably be ineffective, no matter how it is worded, to exclude or reduce liability for reckless breaches of trust.

The irreducible core of trust obligations

An exemption clause does not define the nature and extent of a trustee's obligations; it is merely concerned to define the nature and extent of liability for the breach of those obligations. One consequence of this is that a trustee cannot rely upon an exemption clause to justify a proposed course of action. Such a course would be regarded as a reckless breach of trust.[196] Another consequence is that conclusions as to the scope of exemption clauses should not, and logically cannot, form the basis for conclusions about the essential nature of trusteeship. It is this writer's respectful submission that Millett LJ was therefore mistaken to conclude, as he did in *Armitage v. Nurse*, that the *'irreducible core of obligations'* owed by trustees to the trust beneficiaries does not include *'the duties of skill and care, prudence and diligence'*. His Lordship put it this way:

> The duty of the trustees to perform the trusts honestly and in good faith for the benefit of the beneficiaries is the minimum necessary to give substance to the trusts, but in my opinion it is sufficient.[197]

Such a radical observation on the nature of the trust was unnecessary to dispose of the issues in *Armitage v. Nurse* and is, as such, obiter dicta. In any event, it is this writer's belief that the statement is wrong in principle. It is submitted that the duty of care is a fundamental feature of trusts, such as traditional settlement trusts of the *Armitage v. Nurse* variety, under which the trustees manage a fund for beneficiaries who have competing interests in it. In such trusts, the trustees' duty prudently to maintain a fairly invested fund in accordance with the terms of the trust becomes a surrogate for, or summary of, the fiduciary duty and duty of care that, in a bare trust, would be owed to individual beneficiaries or individual classes of beneficiary. If a clause in the trust instrument of such a trust were competent to exclude trustees' liability for negligence, even gross negligence, it would surely come close to being a trust with no meaningful trust obligations. Of course, the beneficiaries would still have rights enforceable against rogue trustees in relation to fraudulent breaches, dishonest breaches, bias, perverse exercise of discretion, and so on, but they would be left with little recourse against the typical trustee in relation to that most practically significant of duties—caring for the fund.

To put the point another way, it can be argued that the problem with Millett LJ's analysis in *Armitage v. Nurse* is that it concentrates on the trustee's obligations to the beneficiaries to the near exclusion of the trustee's obligations in relation to the trust

---

[195] D. Hayton, 'The irreducible core content of trusteeship' in *Trends in Contemporary Trust Law* (A. J. Oakley, ed.) (Oxford: Clarendon Press, 1996) 47 at 59.

[196] Millett LJ in *Armitage v. Nurse* [1998] Ch 241: *'a trustee who relied on the presence of a trustee exemption clause to justify what he proposed to do would thereby lose its protection: he would be acting recklessly in the proper sense of the term'* (at 254A). [197] Ibid. at 253–4.

property.[198] It is true that an absolute owner of property is free to destroy it or to agree to its destruction by another party, but it is quite another thing to suppose that an absolute owner should be permitted to settle his property on trust for the benefit of someone else with trustees who have no duty to care for the property. A reason for the undue emphasis on obligation at the expense of property rights may be that a great many of the trusts that nowadays fall to be considered by the courts are bare trusts in which the trustees' obligations to the beneficiaries are not mediated through the trust fund, but it should not be forgotten that *Armitage v. Nurse* was a traditional settlement trust, not a bare trust. Even if it had been, it could be argued that there must be an irreducible core of trustee obligations correlating to the beneficiary's irreducible core of proprietary rights in the trust assets.[199] As Lord Kerr opined in *Spread Trustee Company Ltd v. Hutcheson*:[200]

> If...placing of reliance on a responsible person to manage property so as to promote the interests of the beneficiaries of a trust is central to the concept of trusteeship, denying trustees the opportunity to avoid liability for their gross negligence seems to be entirely in keeping with that essential aim.[201]

If contract has the power to strip the trust of that core content, as, rightly or wrongly, the Court of Appeal in *Armitage v. Nurse* concluded it has, then the power of contract must be restrained in the interest of maintaining public confidence in the trust institution. This is an especially important consideration if the trustee is a professional, or is otherwise paid to discharge his trust. However, the restraint of contract is, as Millett LJ observed, a task for Parliament.[202]

Relief

If trustees are unable to raise a defence to a breach of trust, or if the defence can only be raised against some of the beneficiaries, trustees may nevertheless be relieved of all, or some, of their liability.

---

[198] In a similar vein, J. Penner has argued that there must be an irreducible core of trustee obligations correlating to the beneficiary's irreducible core of proprietary rights in the trust assets ('Exemptions' in *Breach of Trust* (P. Birks and A. Pretto, eds) (Oxford: Hart Publishing, 2002) at 259).

[199] For a sophisticated version of this argument, see J. Penner, 'Exemptions', ibid. at 259 ff.

[200] [2011] UKPC 13, Privy Council.   [201] Ibid. at para. [180].

[202] [1998] Ch 241 at 256B–D, 264B. On 19 July 2006, the Law Commission for England and Wales published a report on *Trustee Exemption Clauses* (Law Commission Report No. 301) containing its recommendations for reform. It is recommended that '[a]*ny paid trustee who causes a settlor to include a clause in a trust instrument which has the effect of excluding or limiting liability for negligence must before the creation of the trust take such steps as are reasonable to ensure that the settlor is aware of the meaning and effect of the clause*'. The Law Commission expects that this will ensure that exemption clauses will in future, '*represent a proper and fully informed expression of the terms on which settlors are willing to dispose of their property on trust*' (para. 1.19). The report follows a consultation paper on the same subject (*Trustee Exemption Clauses* (2003) Law Commission Consultation Paper No. 171).

Set-off

The general rule is that, if a trustee makes a gain in one breach of trust, he cannot set off that gain against a loss arising out of another breach of trust,[203] but, if transactions are connected as part of a larger transaction—as is the case when individual investments form part of a portfolio of investments—a loss in one transaction may be set off against a gain in another transaction.[204]

Contribution

Trustees are liable only for their own defaults; they are not vicariously liable for breaches committed by their co-trustees[205] (or their agents).[206] Trustees are, however, jointly and severally liable for breaches to which they have together been parties, and, if one trustee commits a breach of trust, the other trustees will be jointly and severally liable if, with adequate supervision of their co-trustees, they could have prevented the breach.[207] There is, however, a significant palliative to the pain of joint and several liability—namely, that a trustee may recover a contribution under the Civil Liability (Contribution) Act 1978 from any other person (typically another trustee) who is liable in respect of the same damage. The Act applies if the breach occurred after 1978 and if all relevant trustees were appointed after 1978.[208] Under the Act, the court may apportion liability between trustees who are *'jointly and severally liable'* for the same breach of trust, according to whatever is *'just and equitable'*. Apportionment is effected by requiring one trustee to make a financial contribution to another trustee in reduction of the latter's liability to the trust. The Act confirms that a person is liable to contribute whether his liability is based in *'tort, breach of contract, breach of trust or otherwise'*.[209] A person who is liable for knowing receipt of property misapplied in breach of trust is also liable to contribute under the Act.[210]

Indemnity

A trustee who is liable to the beneficiaries for a breach of trust may claim an indemnity from a co-trustee, if that co-trustee committed the breach fraudulently, or if the co-trustee exclusively benefited from the breach,[211] or if the co-trustee is a solicitor-trustee

---

[203] *Dimes v. Scott* (1828) 4 Russ 195.

[204] *Bartlett v. Barclays Bank Trust Co (Nos 1 and 2)* [1980] Ch 515. In truth, the discussion in *Bartlett v. Barclays Bank Trust Co Ltd* on the issue of set-off was not relevant to the facts of that case. The facts did not concern a distinct gain and loss, but merely a loss in the form of a drop in value of trust-owned shares.

[205] See, generally, G. E. Dal Pont, 'Wilful default revisited: liability for a co-trustee's defaults' (2001) at Conv 376–86.　　　　　　　　　　　　　　[206] Trustees' liability for the acts of their agents is considered in Chapter 11.

[207] *Bahin v. Hughes* (1886) LR 31 Ch D 390.

[208] Section 7(2); *Lampitt v. Poole Borough Council* [1991] 2 QB 545.　　　[209] Section 6(1).

[210] *Charter plc v. City Index Ltd (Gawler, Part 20 defendants)* [2008] EWCA Civ 1382; [2008] 2 WLR 950 (noted G. Virgo, 'Contribution Revisited' (2008) 67 CLJ 254). For 'knowing receipt', see Chapter 15.

[211] *Chillingworth v. Chambers* [1896] 1 Ch 685, CA.

whose controlling influence over the other trustees caused the breach.[212] (Note, however, that it will not be *presumed* that a solicitor has a controlling influence.)[213]

Where the benefits of a breach of trust fall exclusively on a particular trustee and that trustee is a beneficiary under the trust, he will be liable to indemnify his co-trustees up to the extent of his beneficial interest under the trust. This has been described as the co-trustee's 'lien'.[214] This rule does not apply, however, where the defendant is beneficially interested under trusts distinct from those under which the claimant is entitled. So, in *Re Towndrow*,[215] the rule had no application due to the fact that the defendant trustee was entitled to a specific legacy under a will, whereas his breach had caused a loss to the residue of the testator's estate, and the legacy and residue were held upon distinct trusts.

Impounding a beneficiary's interest

The court has the power to impound a beneficiary's interest under the trust in certain circumstances. That impounded interest can then be used, in whole or in part, to relieve a trustee of his liability to the other trustees. The court can impound under its inherent jurisdiction if the beneficiary instigated or requested the breach with the intention of obtaining a personal benefit, or if the beneficiary consented to the breach and *actually benefited* from it. The court can impound under the Trustee Act 1925 if the beneficiary instigated or requested the breach, or consented in writing to the breach.[216]

Section 61 of the Trustee Act 1925

Under s. 61 of the Trustee Act 1925, the courts may relieve a trustee of some, or all, of his liability for breach of trust if he acted honestly and reasonably, and ought fairly to be excused. If these three requirements are met, the award of relief is in the discretion of the court. The section was first introduced in 1896,[217] in response to a perceived shortfall in the number of persons willing to act as trustees,[218] and consolidated in the 1925 Act. The section is little used because it is hard for a trustee to demonstrate that conduct amounting to a breach was 'reasonable', but it has, for example, assisted trustees of land used by a tennis club who omitted to charge rent because they (erroneously) believed that the land was held on charitable trusts for the benefit of the club members.[219] It has been suggested that the section '*offers a viable but as yet unexplored base for a change*

---

[212] *Re Partington* (1887) 57 LT 654.

[213] *Head v. Gould* (1898) 2 Ch 250.   [214] *Chillingworth v. Chambers* [1896] 1 Ch 685.

[215] [1911] 1 Ch 662.   [216] Trustee Act 1925, s. 62.

[217] Judicial Trustees Act 1896, s. 3.

[218] J. Lowry and R. Edmunds, 'Excuses' in *Breach of Trust* (P. Birks and A. Pretto, eds) (Oxford: Hart Publishing, 2002) 269 at 272–6. The concern was such that extracts from the proceedings of the Select Committee on Trusts Administration chaired by Sir R. T. Reid, Attorney General, made the newspapers (see, for example, *The Times*, 9 March 1895); D. R. Paling, 'The Trustee's duty of skill and care' [1973] 37 Conv 48.

[219] *Re St Andrew's (Cheam) Lawn Tennis Club Trust (sub nom Philippe v. Cameron)* [2012] EWHC 1040 (Ch); [2012] 3 All ER 746.

of position defence where a defendant has become a constructive trustee due to his receipt of trust property belonging to another.[220] Chambers accepts that it may be that innocent recipients of another's trust property should always be excused from liability '*until they become (or ought to have become) aware of the obligation to restore the trust property*', but he suggests it would be unacceptable if innocent recipients were required to seek statutory 'forgiveness' under s. 61.[221] Section 61 also offers a possible (although not the only, or best) basis for reducing trustee liability to take account of a beneficiary's contributory fault.[222] However, the courts are reluctant to infer such a possibility into the section when Parliament was free (but declined) to extend the section by express words.[223]

Reasonably

Objective reasonableness is not a defence to breach of trust in the way that it is a defence to certain heads of common law tortious liability, such as negligence and nuisance. Acting 'reasonably' is merely one of the factors that a trustee must establish before a court will consider the grant of statutory relief from liability for breach of trust under s. 61. The trustee's basic liability for breach of trust is based on a finding that the trustee acted imprudently in the light of the usual paradigm of trustee behaviour, so it might be thought almost impossible for the trustee to demonstrate that he nevertheless acted reasonably according to some other objective standard. Professional trustees will find it especially hard to escape liability, for a single error can undermine the regime to protect beneficiaries from risk.[224]

In practice, the section appears to be most useful in the case of a non-professional trustee who makes a reasonable error of judgement that is technically in breach of trust. An example is the case of *Re Evans*.[225] The defendant was the daughter of a man who had died intestate. His estate had passed to her on the usual statutory trusts to distribute it between herself and her brother in equal shares. However, she had not heard from her brother for 30 years, so, having taken out missing beneficiary insurance,[226] she distributed the entire estate in favour of herself on the assumption that her brother was dead. When her brother reappeared four years later, he sued his sister on the ground that the insurance cover had been inadequate. She was held to have breached her trust, but, applying s. 61, the judge limited her liability to whatever sums might be forthcoming from the sale of a trust-owned house that had not yet been sold. Judges have expressly stated that s. 61 is more likely to be applied to relieve unpaid amateur trustees than trustees who are remunerated[227] or professional.[228] However, the courts will relieve a professional trustee under s.61 where the trustee inadvertently hands trust money to a

---

[220] G. Elias, *Explaining Constructive Trusts* (Oxford: Clarendon Press, 1990) at 20.

[221] R. Chambers, *Resulting Trusts* (Oxford: Clarendon Press, 1997) at 212.

[222] G. Watt, 'Contributory fault and breach of trust' (2005) 5(2) OUCLJ 205–24. For the situation in tort see the Law Reform (Contributory Negligence) Act 1945.

[223] *Lloyds TSB Bank Plc v. Markandan & Uddin (a firm)* [2010] EWHC 2840 (Ch).

[224] *Santander UK v. RA Legal Solicitors* [2014] EWCA Civ 183, Court of Appeal.

[225] [1999] 2 All ER 777.   [226] See Chapter 3.

[227] *Bartlett v. Barclays Bank (No. 1)* [1980] Ch 515.

[228] *Re Rosenthal, decd* [1972] 1 WLR 1273, Ch D.

fraudster, assuming that the trustee's behaviour wasn't otherwise a cause of the beneficiaries' loss.[229] It has been said that the law 'leans towards confining the responsibility of professional people to a duty to take reasonable care, and . . . does not readily impose on them responsibility for loss resulting from the fraud of others'.[230]

Ought fairly to be excused

The question of whether a trustee ought fairly to be excused arose for consideration in *Marsden v. Regan*.[231] The claimant was a personal creditor of a deceased debtor. He brought this action against an executrix who had paid off all of the deceased's business creditors out of the deceased's estate, but had not paid the claimant. The claimant had been the landlord of the premises from which the deceased had conducted his business, so, when the defendant sought relief under s. 61, the claimant argued that it would not be fair to relieve the defendant of her liability to account to him. The judge at first instance held that the defendant had acted honestly and reasonably, and ought fairly to be excused. In the Court of Appeal, Denning LJ doubted that the defendant ought fairly to be excused, but he felt that it would not be proper to interfere in the fully informed exercise of the judge's discretion at first instance. In the same case, Evershed MR made it clear that it will not be sufficient, by itself, for a trustee seeking relief from liability to say, '*I acted throughout on solicitor's advice*'.[232]

Further reading

In addition to the following print sources, the Online Resource Centre accompanying this book contains web links to further reading as well as guide answers to assessment questions relevant to this chapter.

BIRKS, P. B. H. and PRETTO, A. (eds), *Breach of Trust* (Oxford: Hart Publishing, 2002).

BRUNYATE, J., *The Limitation of Actions in Equity* (London: Stevens & Sons, 1932).

CAPPER, D., 'Compensation for breach of trusts' (1997) 61 Conv 14.

CONAGLEN, M. D. J., 'Equitable compensation for breach of fiduciary dealing rules' (2003) 119 LQR 246.

DAL PONT, G., 'Wilful default revisited: liability for a co-trustee's defaults' [2001] Conv 376.

ELLIOTT, S., and EDELMAN, J., '*Target Holdings* considered in Australia' (2003) 119 LQR 545.

GLISTER, J., 'Equitable Compensation' in *Fault Lines in Equity* (J. Glister and P. Ridge, eds) (Oxford: Hart Publishing, 2012).

HAYTON, D., 'The irreducible core content of trusteeship' (1996) 5(1) J Int P 3.

LAW COMMISSION OF ENGLAND AND WALES, *Limitation of Actions* Report No. 270 (2001).

---

[229] *Santander UK Plc v. RA Legal Solicitors* [2013] EWHC 1380 (QB); [2013] PNLR 24.

[230] Ibid. at para. [72], citing *Platform Funding Ltd v. Bank of Scotland Plc* [2008] EWCA Civ 930, para. 48.

[231] [1954] 1 WLR 423.   [232] Ibid. at 434–5.

MATHER, J., 'Fiduciaries and the law of limitation' [2008] JBL 344.

MCCORMACK, G., 'The liability of trustees for gross negligence' [1998] Conv 100.

MCGEE, A., *Limitation Periods*, 6th revsd edn (London: Sweet & Maxwell, 2010).

OAKLEY, A. J., 'The liberalising nature of remedies for breach of trust' in *Trends in Contemporary Trusts Law* (A.J. Oakley, ed.) (Oxford: Clarendon Press, 1996) at 217.

PALING, D. R., 'The trustee's duty of skill and care' (1973) 37 Conv 48.

PART IV

Trusts and Third Parties

14

Tracing and recovering trust property

In this chapter and the next, we are concerned with situations in which trust property has passed into the hands of a third party 'stranger'—a 'stranger' being someone other than a trustee or beneficiary of the trust. Our principal aim in the present chapter is to identify the circumstances in which a claimant, typically a beneficiary of the trust, is able to trace trust property into the hands of a stranger and recover it by means of a proprietary remedy. In the course of this chapter and the next, we will also examine personal remedies against strangers, based on their receipt of trust property.

Personal and proprietary remedies against strangers are particularly valuable where actions against the original trustee (actions of the sort considered in the previous three chapters) are inadequate to satisfy the claimant. In practice, a claimant will pursue every arguable proprietary and personal claim at the same time, against the trustees and the strangers, because she is unlikely to know at the commencement of her action which remedy is likely to be most beneficial by the time judgment is finally entered. If, at the date of the final judgment, the defendant no longer holds the trust property or its traceable proceeds, the claimant will elect to take judgment on her personal claims against that defendant. If, on the other hand, the defendant is still holding trust property or its traceable proceeds, the claimant may elect to assert her proprietary rights against the property in the defendant's hands. A proprietary claim will be particularly valuable if, at the date of judgment, the defendant is insolvent and therefore unable to meet all of his personal liabilities in full. The claimant may even be awarded judgment on a combination of personal and proprietary remedies, as long as the remedies are logically consistent with each other and do not confer an unjust windfall on the claimant in the nature of a 'double recovery' or 'double satisfaction'.

It is not only in relation to the final remedy that the claimant must make choices. The tracing process, which supplies the evidence that a stranger has received trust property, may require the claimant to 'elect' between evidential alternatives. From the moment the trust property leaves the trustee's hands the claimant will attempt to follow or trace it into the hands of every subsequent holder. However, having been transferred, the trust property cannot, at one and the same time, be in the hands of the transferor and the transferee. Suppose that the trustee has given the trust property (a valuable vase) to stranger 'A', who then proceeds to exchange it, with 'stranger B', for a painting. If we assume that neither stranger can establish the defence of bona fide purchase without notice of the claimant's interest, the claimant has a choice. She is not permitted to follow the vase into the hands of 'stranger B' and, at the same time, to trace the proceeds of the vase into the painting held by 'stranger A'; she has to choose which of the two 'assets' (the vase or the painting) represents her trust property and, accordingly, which of the two defendants she will take judgment against. That choice must, like the 'election' between alternative remedies, be made before judgment. Naturally, the claimant will elect to trace the value of her property into whichever asset is worth more at the date of judgment. The choice will be an easy one if, say, the vase had been broken prior to judgment.

Of course, the claimant's choices in relation to the tracing process and her ultimate remedy are not entirely private choices. They are constrained at every turn by considerations of public policy, reflected in the legal presumptions, or 'rules', that govern tracing and the recovery of property. Thus 'the policy of the insolvency acts', which requires the fair and final distribution of an insolvent's estate among his creditors, yields to the policy that a beneficiary should be permitted to recover her property from the hands of an insolvent trustee in priority to the claims of the trustee's personal creditors; the policy of protecting a beneficiary's proprietary interest in her assets yields, in turn, to the overriding policy that innocent persons who purchase legal title to those assets for valuable consideration and without notice of the beneficiary's interest must take free of the beneficiary's interest.

The subject matter of this chapter is divided into two halves to reflect the elements of 'tracing' and 'recovery' appearing in the title. However, 'recovery' is really shorthand for 'remedies for recovering trust property', so the chapter is actually concerned with tracing and 'remedies'. The decision to consider remedies in the first half of the chapter and tracing in the second reflects the author's belief that this is the most logical approach. Tracing is merely a process of collecting evidence to support a claim to recover trust property, whereas the remedy is the motive for carrying out the process in the first place.

Remedies

The claimant's remedies for recovery of her trust property, or its value, may be awarded in equity or at law, and may be proprietary or personal.[1] Another significant distinction, although it is questionable that it should be so, is between remedies for the recovery of money and remedies for the recovery of other forms of property. This distinction is significant, because most of the cases with which we are concerned involve the misapplication of money and, although a claimant might be said to have a proprietary 'claim' to money at common law—in as much as he claims that the money in the defendant's hands *belongs to him at law or represents profits made by the use of money which belonged*

---

[1] *El Ajou v. Dollar Land Holdings* [1993] 3 All ER 717.

to him at law'[2]—there is no common law proprietary remedy for the recovery of money from the hands of a stranger. Only equity grants such a remedy. At another level of refinement, it may be helpful to think of beneficiaries' proprietary rights against third parties as being in a separate category from their rights against their trustees (indeed, that is why they are treated in different parts of this book). It has been suggested that the distinction lies in the fact that beneficiaries' rights against third parties do not yield a right to positive performance of duties, but merely yield a right to exclude third parties from the benefits of the trust assets.[3]

Having considered equitable and common law remedies, this section concludes with a brief examination of restitution, which, its proponents argue, transcends the distinction between law and equity.

Equitable proprietary remedies

Proprietary rights are vigorously protected in law: the criminal law, the law of tort, and human rights law[4] all play a part in vindicating ownership. Except in very exceptional circumstances,[5] ownership will only come to an end according to rules established institutionally by the law of property.

In Chapter 5, we observed that, when a purported transfer by the beneficial owner of an asset fails to transfer the entirety of the transferor's beneficial interest according to property law, equity will require the transferee to hold the undisposed of benefits on resulting trust for the transferor. In this chapter, we will see that, when a person, such as a trustee, who has power to dispose of property to which someone else is beneficially entitled misapplies that property, the first instinct of the law is again to vindicate or 'uphold' the proprietary rights of the beneficial owner. Lord Millett has confirmed that '*this branch of the law is concerned with vindicating rights of property*'.[6]

The only valid defences to an equitable proprietary claim to recover property from the hands of a stranger are the traditional defences to ownership claims. The defendant must prove either that the claimant's property is not in his hands, or that the property in his hands now belongs to him because he purchased it in good faith for value and without notice of the claimant's interest:

> The tracing claim in equity gives rise to a proprietary remedy which depends on the continued existence of the trust property in the hands of the defendant. Unless he is a bona fide purchaser for value without notice, he must restore the trust property to its rightful owner if he still has it.[7]

---

[2] In *Jones & Sons (a firm) v. Jones* [1997] Ch 159, CA at 168.
[3] R. C. Nolan, 'Equitable property' (2006) 122 LQR 232.
[4] European Convention on Human Rights (Rome: 1950) Protocol 1.
[5] Such as compulsory purchase, criminal confiscation, forfeiture on special grounds of public policy, and cases of *bona vacantia*.
[6] *Foskett v. McKeown* [2001] 1 AC 102 at 132. (Noted J. Stevens, 'Vindicating the proprietary nature of tracing' [2001] Conv 94.)
[7] Millett J in *Agip (Africa) Ltd v. Jackson* [1990] 1 Ch 265 at 290G (affirmed [1991] Ch 547, CA).

It is no defence for the defendant to establish that he has substituted the claimant's property for other property. If the defendant still holds the substitute property, the claimant can assert his proprietary rights in the substitute. This is a straightforward case of 'clean substitution'. Neither is it a defence for the defendant to establish that he had contributed to the acquisition of the substitute asset and that '*the claimant's property has contributed in part only*'[8] towards it. This is a straightforward case of 'mixed substitution'. The claimant's proprietary entitlement to that part of the mixed substitute representing his original property must be vindicated. If the value of the mixed substitute has decreased, the value of the claimant's share will have decreased; if the value of the mixed asset has increased, the value of the claimant's share will increase: '*The primary rule in regard to a mixed fund, therefore, is that gains and losses are borne by the contributors rateably*.'[9]

Although this is the primary rule, the claimant has an alternative remedy where the defendant, knowing of the claimant's interest, wrongfully mixed the claimant's property with his own in the acquisition of the new, substitute asset. This alternative remedy is also available against persons deriving title from the wrongdoer 'otherwise than for value'. In such cases, the beneficiary may elect, instead of taking a proportionate proprietary share, to take an equitable charge (a 'lien') over the mixed substitute as security for a personal claim against the defendant for the full value of the claimant's property at the date it came into the defendant's hands. This secured personal claim for the 'receipt' value will be most useful where, due to a fall in the value of the mixed substitute, the claimant is unlikely to be satisfied by the award of a proportionate proprietary share in the mixed asset. It is arguable that where the value of the claimant's proportionate proprietary share of the mixed asset is greater than the value of his property at the date it was received by the defendant, the defendant may be able to insist that the claimant take a proportionate proprietary share instead of a lien, but it is hard to imagine a case in which he would want to.

In the following sections, we examine equity's two main proprietary remedies—the proportionate proprietary share and the lien—in greater detail.

Proportionate share of a mixed substitute

Where the claimant has successfully traced his property or its substitute into the defendant's hands, the claimant is entitled to recover it. If the claimant's property is still in its original form, the claimant will simply require specific restitution—the defendant will be required to return the property to the claimant. The same remedy will be awarded if the claimant's property has been directly substituted for another asset, by what is known as a 'clean substitution'. According to Lord Millett, there is no difficulty with '*the transmission of a claimant's property rights from one asset to its traceable proceeds*',[10] but that is not altogether true. There is invariably one significant difficulty lurking behind every case of substitution—the so-called problem of 'geometric multiplication'[11]—which

---

[8] Lord Millett in *Foskett v. McKeown* [2001] 1 AC 102.   [9] Ibid. at 132.   [10] Ibid. at 127.
[11] L. Smith, *The Law of Tracing* (Oxford: Clarendon Press, 1997) at 322.

arises when, for example, a trust-owned car is wrongfully exchanged for a vase, which, in turn, is wrongfully exchanged for a block of shares, which, in turn, is wrongfully exchanged for premium bonds. It is impossible for every one of the assets to belong to the trust, but the claimant nevertheless has a potential claim to each. However, in practice, the problem only becomes relevant if more than one of the assets is still in the hands of a person or persons having no defence to the beneficiary's claim to recover the assets. Even then, the problem is overcome for practical purposes by requiring the beneficiary to elect which asset to take and by the rule against double recovery, which prevents the defendant recovering the value of his property twice over. However, the problem remains a real one in theory, for why should beneficial entitlement to multiple assets held by multiple defendants, each of whom is equally liable to make restitution, be determined by the choice of a claimant who cannot possibly be the owner of all the assets?

To these complications we can add a whole new layer of complexity in any case where the substitute asset was not acquired wholly with the claimant's asset, but, in part, by the defendant contributing some of his own money or property towards the acquisition of the substitute. Such cases are referred to as 'mixed substitutions'.

In the leading case, *Foskett v. McKeown*,[12] it was not immediately apparent whether the claimant had contributed to the acquisition of the asset in which the claimant claimed to have a proprietary interest, or whether the claimant had merely contributed to the improvement of the defendant's property. The facts of the case were unusual. A number of persons paid deposits to Mr Murphy for the sole purpose of purchasing land in Portugal and it was agreed that Mr Murphy would hold the deposits on trust until transfer of the land to the purchasers. In the event, the land was never developed and Mr Murphy, in breach of trust, paid their money into his own account and used the mixed monies to pay two premiums towards a life assurance policy, having previously paid two premiums with his own money. Later, having by deed divested the beneficial interest in the policy in favour of his three children, Mr Murphy committed suicide. The claimant, one of the prospective purchasers, brought an action against Mr Murphy's children. The action was brought on behalf of all of the purchasers with the aim of recovering the proceeds of the policy, which came to around £1m.

The trial judge decided that the claimants were entitled to 53.46 per cent of the proceeds of the policy, which he calculated on the assumption that the proceeds of the insurance policy were the direct product of the four insurance premiums, two paid by Mr Murphy and two paid using trust money. The children appealed and the Court of Appeal held, by a majority, that, since Mr Murphy had not had any beneficial interest in the insurance policy at the time the misappropriated money was used to pay the premiums, no resulting or constructive trust could be imposed upon the proceeds of the policy in favour of the claimants. Accordingly, the claimants were only entitled to recover the money used to pay for the premiums plus interest.[13] In reaching this decision, the

---

[12] [2001] 1 AC 102, HL.   [13] *Foskett v. McKeown* [1998] Ch 265, CA.

Court of Appeal stated that the authorities were against the conclusion that the payment of the premiums meant that the payer became part-owner of the policy and part-owner of the proceeds of the policy at 'pay-out'. Hobhouse LJ took the view that the payment of premiums on a policy held in someone else's name was analogous to expenditure on the improvement of another person's land. If the expenditure of £500 on the improvement of someone else's land happens to increase its value by £5,000 it does not follow that the contributor of the £500 should, in addition to the return of his £500, plus interest, be awarded a proportionate share of the £4,500 'profit' made by the landowner.

The decision of the Court of Appeal was appealed to the House of Lords, where Lord Browne-Wilkinson identified the central issue to be whether the payment of insurance premiums should be regarded as:

> analogous to the expenditure of cash on the physical property of another or as analogous to the mixture of moneys in a bank account. If the former analogy is to be preferred, the maximum amount recoverable by the purchasers will be the amount of the...premiums [paid using trust money] plus interest: if the latter analogy is preferred the children and the other purchasers will share the policy moneys pro rata.[14]

His Lordship held that the proper analogy is to the mixture of monies in a bank account:

> Where a trustee in breach of trust mixes money in his own bank account with trust moneys, the moneys in the account belong to the trustee personally and to the beneficiaries under the trust rateably according to the amounts respectively provided. On a proper analysis, there are 'no moneys in the account' in the sense of physical cash. Immediately before the improper mixture, the trustee had a chose in action being his right against the bank to demand a payment of the credit balance on his account. Immediately after the mixture, the trustee had the same chose in action (i.e. the right of action against the bank) but its value reflected in part the amount of the beneficiaries' moneys wrongly paid in. There is no doubt that in such a case of moneys mixed in a bank account the credit balance on the account belongs to the trustee and the beneficiaries rateably according to their respective contributions.[15]

Lord Millett agreed that '[t]*here is no analogy with the case where trust money is used to maintain or improve property of a third party*' and held that '[t]*he nearest analogy is with an instalment purchase*'.[16]

Is there a trust of the claimant's proportionate share?

When a claimant establishes that he is beneficially entitled to a proprietary share in property held by the defendant, the question arises whether the defendant holds the claimant's share *on trust* for the claimant. We know from the detailed discussion in Chapter 1 that separating the legal title from the equitable title to an asset necessarily creates a trust. However, to conclude that the defendant holds the mixed substitute on trust is not without difficulties, particularly, as we noted in Chapter 1,[17] when the claimant's property was already subject to a trust before it came into the defendant's hands, for in such a case the defendant will only be liable as a trustee if he had the requisite

---

[14] [2001] 1 AC 102 at 110.   [15] [2001] 1 AC 102 at 110.   [16] Ibid. at 137.
[17] At 'Separation of legal and equitable title'.

notice or knowledge of the pre-existing trust.[18] The person claiming a proportionate share had not entrusted his property to the defendant as a settlor entrusts property to the trustee of an expressly intended trust. On the contrary, the trust is likely to have been completely unintended and, from the point of view of an innocent defendant, the trust may have been entirely unforeseen. The defendant may have received the claimant's money, mistakenly believing it to be a valid gift, and then proceeded innocently to mix the claimant's money with his own in order to purchase a new asset—a mixed substitute asset. It would be wholly inappropriate for the defendant to be personally liable for breach of trust if, reasonably believing the mixed asset to be entirely his own to do with as he wished, he failed to care for it or even chose to destroy it. Analytically, there are at least two alternative solutions for ensuring that an innocent defendant avoids personal liability for breach of trust in such a case.

The first solution is to say that he does not become a trustee until he has knowledge of the claimant's proprietary right. This approach has the merit of being consistent with Lord Browne-Wilkinson's view that a person cannot be a trustee of property that he receives until his conscience is affected by knowledge of another's beneficial interest in the property. However, the drawback in endorsing his Lordship's approach is that it proceeds on the highly unorthodox assumption that legal ownership may be split from equitable ownership without necessarily creating a trust. However, leaving aside that assumption, there is no reason why it should not be presumed that a defendant holds mixed assets on trust, but will not be personally liable for breaches of trust innocently committed prior to his having knowledge of the claimant's interest. So if the defendant happens, say, to have destroyed the asset, he should be permitted to rely upon a change of position defence if his behaviour had been innocent. If he has not destroyed it, he should be liable to account to the claimant for his share from the moment the defendant is aware that he is a trustee. The obligations vacuum, prior to the defendant's knowledge of the claimant's claim, is filled in part by the fact that the alleged trustee is a beneficial owner of the mixed asset. Fiduciary duty is defined in contrast to self-interest, but joint contributors to an asset have a mutual self-interest positively to preserve and increase the value of the mixed asset. Therefore, what one contributor (the trustee) does on his own behalf in relation to the mixed asset can be presumed to be done on behalf of his co-contributor (the beneficiary). Accordingly, the trust to which a defendant is subject, when he unwittingly holds an asset in which a claimant has a proprietary share, is not a trust under which the defendant owes fiduciary duties in any meaningful sense, for his fiduciary duty is automatically aligned with his self-interest.

A possible objection to this first solution is that the innocent defendant may be required to account to the claimant for the claimant's share in circumstances that will produce personal hardship to the defendant. He might, for example, have bought a new house with a mixture of the claimant's money and his own money. Must the defendant be required to sell the house to make restitution to the claimant? An initial solution to

---

[18] See Chapter 8.

this drawback is that it may be open to the defendant to avoid a sale by 'buying out' the claimant's share, but such a course may be beyond the defendant's means. The solution in such a case should, it is submitted, lie in the discretion of the court, just as it does when co-owners of land cannot agree upon a sale of the land.[19] An order for sale of the mixed asset, possibly suspended for a period, is likely to be the right solution in most cases.

The second alternative solution to the problem is analytically not as satisfactory as the first, although it shares with the first solution the practical merit of placing discretion in relation to the sale of the mixed asset in the hands of the court. The second solution holds that a claimant is never permitted to claim a proportionate proprietary share of a mixed substitute. Instead, the claimant is limited to a lien (equitable charge) over the mixed asset, which then acts as proprietary security for a personal claim against the defendant for recovery of the value of the claimant's trust property. This solution was advanced in a statement made obiter by Jessel MR in *Re Hallett's Estate*,[20] but it has since been decisively rejected by Lord Millett in *Foskett*. The arguments for and against Jessel MR's approach, and the nature of the lien, are considered in the next section.

Lien

A 'lien', or equitable charge, is a form of proprietary security interest. The fact that it is a *security* interest means that it does not give the claimant a proportionate share of property in the defendant's hands; it merely confers on the claimant the right to be satisfied out of the proceeds of sale of that property, and to be satisfied ahead of the defendant and ahead of any of the defendant's unsecured creditors. The fact that it is *proprietary* means that the lien will continue to bind the defendant's property even in the event of the defendant's insolvency. It therefore takes effect in priority to all personal claims, whether secured or unsecured, against the insolvent defendant.

The facts of *Re Hallett's Estate*[21] were that Mr Hallett had held certain bonds as bailee[22] for Mrs Cotterill, and had received the income arising from the bonds and accounted to her for the exact amount every half-year. He therefore stood in a fiduciary position towards Mrs Cotterill, but, in breach of his fiduciary duty, he had improperly sold the bonds and put the proceeds in his personal bank account, where they remained mixed with his own money at his death. Sir George Jessel MR considered the remedies available to a trust beneficiary, such as Mrs Cotterill, whose trust monies had been used in the purchase of substitute assets:

> Now, what is the position of the beneficial owner as regards such purchases? I will, first of all, take his position when the purchase is clearly made with what I will call, for shortness, the trust money, although it is not confined, as I will show presently, to express trusts. In that case, according to the now well-established doctrine of Equity, the beneficial owner

---

[19] Trusts of Land and Appointment of Trustees Act 1996, ss. 14–15.   [20] (1880) LR 13 Ch D 696, CA.
[21] Ibid.   [22] See 'Bailment', Chapter 2.

has a right to elect either to take the property purchased, or to hold it as a security for the amount of the trust money laid out in the purchase; or, as we generally express it, he is entitled at his election either to take the property, or to have a charge on the property for the amount of the trust money. But in the second case, where a trustee has mixed the money with his own, there is this distinction, that the cestui que trust, or beneficial owner, can no longer elect to take the property, because it is no longer bought with the trust-money simply and purely, but with a mixed fund. He is, however, still entitled to a charge on the property purchased, for the amount of the trust-money laid out in the purchase; and that charge is quite independent of the fact of the amount laid out by the trustee.[23]

This conclusion, that a claimant cannot assert a proprietary share in a mixed substitute, but is restricted to a charge over the mixed substitute by way of security for the recovery of a sum equivalent to the trust monies used to acquire it, can produce quite artificial results. Jessel MR virtually admitted as much when citing the example of a trustee who mixes 1,000 trust-owned sovereigns in a bag containing one of the trustee's own sovereigns. Describing the remedy available to the beneficiaries of the trust, his Lordship said: '*I do not like to call it a charge of 1,000 sovereigns on the 1,001 sovereigns, but that is the effect of it.*'[24]

The House of Lords has since concluded that Jessel MR's view—that a claimant cannot recover a proportionate proprietary share in a mixed substitute—is without any principled justification.[25]

No lien over a mixed substitute in the hands of an innocent defendant

Where the mixing is carried out by an innocent party, the claimant cannot elect to take a lien—he is limited to a proprietary share. Although election normally gives the claimant the option to wait and see which remedy will be most beneficial to him, the law will not permit a claimant to 'gamble' at the expense of an innocent defendant.

Where the claimant's original property was in the form of security

Where the claimant's original property was in the form of security (such as a debenture or mortgage), as opposed to a beneficial ownership interest (such as absolute ownership or a share under a trust), the claimant will be restricted to a lien, itself a security interest, against the defendant. Only if the claimant had a beneficial proprietary interest in the original property will the claimant be able to elect to take a proprietary share of the property in the defendant's hands.[26]

---

[23] (1880) LR 13 Ch D 696, CA, at 710–11.   [24] Ibid. at 711.

[25] *Foskett v. McKeown* [2001] 1 AC 102 at 131, *per* Lord Millett, a conclusion previously reached in Australia in *Scott v. Scott* (1963) 109 CLR 649 at 661–2; see also *Re Tilley's Will Trusts* [1967] Ch 1179, in which Ungoed-Thomas J accepted obiter (at 1186) that, if a trustee deliberately uses a mixture of trust money and his own money to buy property in his own name, '*the beneficiaries are entitled to the property purchased* and any profits *which it produces to the extent to which it has been paid for out of trust moneys*' (original emphasis).

[26] See L. Smith, *The Law of Tracing* (Oxford: Clarendon Press, 1997) at 348–9.

Election between a proprietary share and a lien

Election has at least one feature in common with ratification, in that '*it cannot be relied upon so as to render an innocent recipient a wrongdoer*',[27] but it is important that the claimant's election is not mistaken for ratification or approval of the defendant's actions:

> The fact that he does not . . . complain of the acquisition of the asset but seeks to take advantage of it does not mean that he adopts or ratifies it—he will almost certainly plead that it was a breach of trust—it means only that he does not seek a remedy in respect of it.[28]

Advantages and disadvantages of a lien compared to a proportionate share

The major advantage of a lien is that the whole of an asset acquired with a mixture of trust money and the defendant's own money is subject to a charge that can only be removed when the defendant repays, in full, the trust money he wrongfully misapplied. A lien over the defendant's asset will tend to be more advantageous than a proprietary share in the asset in any case in which the asset has decreased in value since the defendant received the trust money used to acquire it. Suppose that £10,000 of trust money is wrongfully mixed with £10,000 of the defendant's own monies and a car is purchased for £20,000 for the defendant's own use. The current second-hand value of the car is £14,000. A personal claim for the original £10,000 will be more than adequately secured by a lien over the £14,000 asset, whereas a proportionate half share in the acquisition value of the asset will now be worth only £7,000. Conversely, the major disadvantage of a lien compared to a proportionate share in the mixed asset is that a lien is security for a claim fixed at the value of the claimant's misapplied money; the claimant is not entitled to share in any increase in the value of the defendant's asset. In practice, this means that a claimant will almost invariably elect to take a proportionate share in any case in which the mixed asset has increased in value since the defendant acquired it and will elect to take a lien in any case in which the mixed asset has decreased in value since the defendant acquired it. There is no objection to the claimant choosing the best of both worlds when making his election, because:

> the trustee cannot be allowed to make a profit from the use of the trust money, and if the property which he wrongfully purchased were held subject only to a lien for the amount invested, any appreciation in value would go to the trustee.[29]

Advantages of equitable proprietary remedies

Proprietary remedies, which are awarded because the claimant has a right in the trust asset, have several advantages over personal remedies, which are awarded when the claimant has a mere right against the defendant personally. We have already referred to some of these advantages. They can be summarized as follows.

---

[27] *Lipkin Gorman v. Karpnale Ltd* [1991] 2 AC 548, *per* Lord Goff of Chieveley at 573.

[28] *Per* Millett LJ in *Boscawen v. Bajwa* [1996] 1 WLR 328 at 342B.

[29] S. Williston, 'The right to follow trust property when confused with other property' (1880) 2 Harv LR 28 at 29.

Insolvency is no bar to recovery

A proprietary claim is a claim to recover property from the defendant that never belonged to the defendant personally. It follows that a proprietary claim is not defeated or diminished by the defendant's personal insolvency.

Increases in value are recoverable

When a claimant successfully recovers his property (whether in the form of an entire asset or as a proportionate proprietary share of a mixed asset) from the defendant's hands, the claimant will recover his property regardless of any increase or decrease in its value. This is so even if the defendant had contributed his own time and labour to an increase in the value of the claimant's property, although, in such a case, the defendant may have a legitimate counterclaim to prevent the claimant from being unjustly enriched at the defendant's expense.[30]

Injunctions are available to protect property rights

The success of a proprietary claim depends upon the continued existence of the property in the defendant's hands, so it follows that a claimant requires some legal means to prevent the defendant from disposing of 'target' assets prior to the court hearing. The most effective legal device is a freezing injunction, which, as its name suggests, has the effect of freezing the defendant's assets so as to prevent their disposal.[31] One reason why an injunction is so effective is because breach of its terms is contempt of court punishable by a fine, or even by imprisonment for a term of up to two years.[32] Another reason for the effectiveness of the injunction is that it operates *in personam*—that is, it binds a defendant to proceedings in a domestic court personally, even if his assets are held in a foreign jurisdiction. However, a freezing injunction will not be granted in support of an action under way in a foreign court against a foreign-resident defendant,[33] and it will only be granted against a foreign-resident defendant if the injunction against the foreign-resident is incidental to, and dependent upon, a substantive claim against a defendant within the domestic jurisdiction.[34] In *Cardille v. LED Builders Pty Ltd*,[35] a freezing injunction was granted on this basis against a husband resident abroad whose wife, the defendant to a substantive claim within the English jurisdiction, held certain assets in the English jurisdiction on trust for her husband.

Statutory limitation periods do not apply

Whereas personal actions may be time-barred under the Limitation Act 1980, or by analogy to it, the Act will usually have no application to a claim to recover property from a trustee. However, the doctrine of laches may still apply to bar such a claim.[36]

---

[30] L. Smith, *The Law of Tracing* (Oxford: Clarendon Press, 1997) at 350, citing *Brooks v. Conston*, 364 Pa. 256, 72 A2d 75 (1950).

[31] The 'freezing injunction' was formerly known as the 'Mareva' injunction (CA, in *Mareva Compania Naviera SA v. International Bulkcarriers SA (1975)* [1980] 1 All ER 213).

[32] Contempt of Court Act 1981, s. 14. On injunctions, generally, see Chapter 16.

[33] *Mercedes-Benz AG v. Leiduck* [1996] 1 AC 210.   [34] *Cardille v. LED Builders Pty Ltd* (1999) ALR 294.

[35] Ibid.   [36] See Chapter 13.

Limitations on equitable proprietary remedies

The observant reader will note that the limitations on equitable proprietary rights, as set out in the order which follows, spell out a useful acronym.

Fiduciary required

Proprietary rights generally depend on equity and therefore, as things presently stand, they depend upon equitable tracing, which, in turn, depends upon proof of a prior fiduciary relationship.[37] This requirement has been widely criticized, as we shall see when we come to consider equitable tracing later in this chapter.

Innocent volunteer recipients

When the claimant's property has passed into the hands of an innocent volunteer (a recipient who did not give valuable legal consideration—'payment'—for the property), he is entitled to recover it in the usual way. However, where the claimant's property has become mixed with the defendant's property and has been used to acquire a mixed asset or is sitting in a mixed bank account, the innocent volunteer, whose conscience is clear in the eyes of equity, is under no obligation to prefer the claimant's proprietary claims to his own. Accordingly, the presumption is that defendant and claimant are entitled to the mixed asset in shares proportionate to their respective contributions to its acquisition.

The facts of *Re Diplock*[38] demonstrate how these issues can arise in practice. The executors of an estate had mistakenly paid money to certain charities. The claimants were the persons who had a legitimate entitlement to those monies under the will. Equity had a dilemma: the claimants and the defendants were both innocent, and there was nothing to choose between them in terms of conscience, apart from the fact that, by the date of the court hearing, the charities had discovered that they had benefited from a mistake at the claimants' expense. The court held that the claimants were permitted to trace their property into the defendants' hands, but that the innocent volunteers (the charities) were not obliged to prefer the claimants' rights. Lord Greene MR held that:

> if the volunteer innocently mixes the money with money of his own, or receives it mixed with his own money from a fiduciary agent, he must admit the claim of the true owner, but is not precluded from setting up his own claim in respect of the moneys which he has contributed to the mixed fund, the result being that they share *pari passu*, neither being entitled to priority.[39]

Destruction or dissipation of the claimant's property

Any proprietary claim against a defendant depends for its success on the defendant having the claimant's property (or its 'substitute' or 'value') in his hands at the date of judgment. It follows that the physical destruction of property destroys the claimant's proprietary claim. The point was made in *Re Diplock*:[40]

---

[37] See later in this chapter, where this is discussed in the context of the equitable tracing process.
[38] [1948] Ch 465, CA.   [39] Ibid. at 539.   [40] [1948] Ch 465, CA.

The equitable remedies pre-suppose the continued existence of the money either as a sepa-rate fund or as part of a mixed fund or as latent in property acquired by means of such a fund. If, on the facts of any individual case, such continued existence is not established, equity is as helpless as the common law itself. If the fund, mixed or unmixed, is spent upon a dinner, equity, which dealt only in specific relief and not in damages, could do nothing.[41]

Of course, even when property is destroyed or consumed, it very often leaves a by-product, such as ashes, and, in theory, the claimant ought to be able to assert a claim to the physical product of the destruction process where it can be shown to be the sub-stitute for the claimant's original asset. The fact is, of course, that few claimants would wish to expend time and money in pursuing a claim to ashes.[42]

In other cases, the claimant's asset might have been subjected to a chemical or physi-cal process leading to the production of an asset to which the claimant may desire to be entitled, but which is so different from his original asset that his original asset is deemed to have been destroyed.[43] In such cases, equitable tracing is still possible, but tracing at common law (which depends upon the traced assets remaining in an identifiable form) is not.

In still other cases, it may be practically impossible to determine whether or not the claimant's property remains in the defendant's hands. In *Space Investments Ltd v. Canadian Imperial Bank of Commerce Trust Co. (Bahamas) Ltd*,[44] for example, the defendant trustee bank had deposited trust monies with itself, as it had been author-ized to do. The Privy Council held that beneficiaries cannot claim trust monies lawfully deposited by a trustee bank with itself as banker in priority to other depositors and unsecured creditors of the trustee bank. As Lord Templeman explained:

> A bank in fact uses all deposit moneys for the general purposes of the bank. Whether a bank trustee lawfully receives deposits or wrongly treats trust money as on deposit from trusts, all the moneys are in fact dealt with and expended by the bank for the general purposes of the bank. In these circumstances it is impossible for the beneficiaries interested in trust money misappropriated from their trust to trace their money to any particular asset belonging to the trustee bank.[45]

However, his Lordship went on to state, obiter, that beneficiaries might be awarded a charge over all of the assets of the bank in any case in which a trustee bank had *unlaw-fully* deposited trust monies with itself:

> But equity allows the beneficiaries, or a new trustee appointed in place of an insolvent bank trustee to protect the interests of the beneficiaries, to trace the trust money to all the assets of the bank and to recover the trust money by the exercise of an equitable charge over all the assets of the bank.[46]

---

[41] Ibid. at 521.

[42] One exception is a regrettable case in which divorced parents attempted to assert rights (probably 'pos-sessory' rather than 'property' rights) in the ashes of their cremated child (*Fessi v. Whitmore* [1991] 1 FLR 767).

[43] See the discussion of *accessio* and *specificatio* later in this chapter.   [44] [1986] 1 WLR 1072.

[45] [1986] 1 WLR 1072 at 1074.   [46] Ibid. at 1074C–D.

These observations have been supported by some commentators,[47] but Professor Goode[48] suggests that they are inconsistent with the dicta of the Court of Appeal in *Re Diplock* with which we commenced this section. It is the present author's submission that everything turns upon Lord Templeman's distinction between an authorized deposit of trust monies and an unauthorized deposit of trust monies. Where a trustee has authority to deposit trust monies within its general holdings, the trustee is under no immediate binding obligation, as a trustee, to separate the trust monies from the monies of other depositors. That situation must be contrasted with the situation where the trustee deposits trust property with itself in breach of trust. Here, the trustee is under an immediate binding obligation to separate the trust monies again.[49] It may be that the identity of the trust monies within the general funds is uncertain, but the trustee has the power (and the duty) to separate the trust monies from the mass of deposited funds and thereby to ascertain which money belongs to the trust. The trustee cannot be heard to say that he is unable to identify the trust property, when it is within his power to say that he can, because 'equity imputes an intention to fulfil an obligation'.[50] It follows that, in the event of the trustee's insolvency, the trustee's successor is also conscience-bound to separate the claimant's trust property out of the insolvent trustee's estate *before* distributing it amongst the trustee's general creditors (the other depositors in the *Space Investments* case). Lord Templeman proposed that the claimant in a case such as *Space Investments* would have a mere charge over the trustee bank's general funds if the trustee had lacked authority to deposit trust monies with itself, but the advantage of a 'conscientious obligation to separate' analysis is that it would recognize that the beneficiaries have a beneficial proprietary interest in the monies deposited at the bank. A charge, because it is a mere security interest, could more fairly be accused of undermining the policy of the Insolvency Acts in relation to the distribution of the estate of an insolvent corporation than would a beneficial proprietary interest under a trust. The latter stands 'outside' the Insolvency Acts' scheme.

'Equity's darling'

An equitable proprietary remedy is available against a recipient to whom a trustee has made a gift of trust property in breach of trust and against a recipient who buys trust property with knowledge of the breach, but it will not be awarded against a bona fide purchaser for value of a legal estate without notice of the claimant's interest. Such a defendant is sometimes referred to as 'equity's darling', because he is said to have an unanswerable defence to any person claiming to have had an equitable interest in, or equitable claim against, the property before it came into the defendant's hands.[51]

---

[47] P. Birks, in *An Introduction to the Law of Restitution* (1989) at 370 (ff. 472–3), and R. Goff and G. H. Jones, *The Law of Restitution*, 4th edn (London: Sweet & Maxwell, 1993) esp. at pp. 73–5.

[48] R. M. Goode, 'Ownership and obligation in Commercial Transactions' (1987) 103 LQR 433, 445–7.

[49] *Re Hallett's Estate* (1980) LR 13 ChD 696, CA.   [50] Chapter 16.

[51] *Pilcher v. Rawlins* (1872) LR 7 Ch Ap. 259, CA.

Where a defendant wrongfully uses trust monies to pay off a private debt, the payee (the former creditor) is equity's darling if he had no notice that the repayment monies had been misappropriated from a trust. Analytically, the payee is said to have purchased legal title to the repayment monies in return for the value of his loan. The claimant will therefore have no proprietary claim against the defendant, because the trust monies are no longer in his hands, and no proprietary claim against the payee, because he is equity's darling. However, the outcome is quite different where a defendant pays away trust monies in order to redeem a secured loan. In such a case, the claimant will be able to claim that the value of her trust property has been transferred to the defendant's assets against which the defendant's loan had been secured: the defendant cannot be permitted to redeem his property at the claimant's expense. So if the defendant had borrowed £10,000 secured by a mortgage on his home and he used £10,000 of the claimant's monies to pay off the loan, the claimant would be entitled to a proprietary remedy in the form of a charge for £10,000 secured over the defendant's home. Another way of explaining the same facts is to say that the claimant has stepped into the shoes of the lender and has been 'subrogated' to the lender's security over the land. This has been described as 'reviving subrogation',[52] because it has the effect of reviving the claimant's proprietary interest.

Personal remedies in equity

In Chapter 15, we will consider remedies that may be awarded in equity against defendants personally on account of their knowing receipt of trust property or dishonest assistance in breaches of trust. For the purposes of the present chapter, we will restrict ourselves to consideration of the personal remedy that arises in equity whenever the executors of a deceased person's estate distribute the estate incorrectly under some mistake of fact or law, with the result that some beneficiaries of the estate, or even non-beneficiaries, are overpaid at the expense of the intended beneficiaries. The facts of *Re Diplock*[53] typify the circumstances in which the remedy arises. It will be recalled that, in that case, the executors had mistakenly distributed the deceased's estate to certain charities. Although the charities had been entirely innocent beneficiaries of the mistake, it was held that they were personally liable to account to the true intended beneficiaries. This personal action in equity is available to an unpaid or underpaid creditor, legatee, or next of kin, but is not available to the beneficiaries under an *inter vivos* trust. The equitable action arises because the conscience of the defendant is affected by the fact that he has received some share of the estate to which he was not entitled.

It should be noted, however, that the personal claim in equity is enforceable against the overpaid defendant only to the extent that the monies are irrecoverable from the executor whose error was responsible for the mistaken payment in the first place. It should also be noted that the personal action in equity to recover an overpayment is analogous to the common law action for money had and received, which is considered next.

---

[52] C. Mitchell, *The Law of Subrogation* (Oxford: Clarendon Press, 1994) at ch. 5.   [53] [1948] 1 Ch 465.

Common law remedies

It is important to be aware from the outset that common law remedies differ according to whether the claimant's property is a sum of money or a chattel.[54] There are limited proprietary remedies for the recovery of a chattel at common law, but the common law recognizes no proprietary remedy for the recovery of money.

A claimant who makes a valid transfer of his chattel to another is precluded by the rule against 'derogation from grant' from reasserting his title at a later date, but if the claimant's chattel is misapplied by some other party, the claimant can trace his legal title into the recipient's hands because, in accordance with the maxim *nemo dat non quod habet*, a recipient cannot acquire good title from a person who was incapable of granting good title. Money is a significant exception to the maxim *nemo dat non quod habet*.[55]

Money

A claimant might be said to have a proprietary *claim* to money at common law—inasmuch as he claims that the money in the defendant's hands '*belongs to him at law or represents profits made by the use of money which belonged to him at law*'[56]—but there is no common law proprietary *remedy* for the recovery of money. To recover misapplied money, a claimant must resort to a personal action for money had and received.

The action for 'money had and received' to the defendant's use

According to Millett J (as he then was) in *Agip v. Africa*:[57]

> The cause of action for money had and received is complete when the plaintiff's money is received by the defendant. It does not depend on the continued retention of the money by the defendant. Save in strictly limited circumstances it is no defence that he has parted with it. A fortiori it can be no defence for him to show that he has so mixed it with his own money that he cannot tell whether he still has it or not.[58]

Just as receipt of the claimant's money is the basis for liability, the amount received establishes the measure of liability.[59] So the action for money had and received is genuinely restitutionary in that it reverses the process by which the defendant was enriched at the claimant's expense. Lionel Smith has advanced an unorthodox analysis which, if accepted, would greatly simplify our conceptual understanding of the action for money had and received. Smith notes that, because the action for money had and received is a common law action, courts usually seek to explain it without relying on the (equitable) law of trusts. This, he says, is a '*misunderstanding*', for '*all of the cases in which the action for money had and received is deployed in relation to the surviving proceeds of an unauthorised disposition can be understood as allowing a common law claim in respect of*

---

[54]   Chattel is used in distinction to money, although money (in the form of coins and notes) is a type of chattel.
[55]   There are other exceptions that lie outside the scope of this book. See R. Goode, *Commercial Law*, 2nd edn (London: Butterworths, 1995) 451–82.
[56]   In *Jones & Sons (a firm) v. Jones* [1996] 3 WLR 703, CA at 710F.   [57]   [1990] 1 Ch 265.
[58]   Ibid. at 285C.   [59]   Ibid.

a determined sum of money held in trust for the claimant, being the traceable proceeds of an unauthorised disposition of trust property or of the claimant's legal property'. Hence, 'the only kinds of rights held in the proceeds of an unauthorised disposition are equitable rights arising under a trust'. In short, 'the law in these cases follows equity ... by allowing claimants to use common law claims to vindicate equitable interests under a trust'.[60]

The remaining personal remedies in this section are compensatory, rather than restitutionary; they are not established or quantified on the basis of the defendant's enrichment, but on the basis of the claimant's loss.

Chattels

The following remedies are considered in greater depth in books on the common law (or laws) of torts.[61]

Compensation

The usual remedy against a defendant who has directly interfered with the claimant's *possession* of a chattel is compensatory damages for 'wrongful interference',[62] which term covers 'conversion of goods',[63] trespass to goods, and negligence resulting in damage to goods or to an interest in goods.[64]

An award of compensatory damages is the usual remedy against a defendant who has *dealt with* the claimant's chattel in a manner inconsistent with the claimant's rights in or over it and therefore has committed 'conversion'. The claimant's right may be absolute ownership, bare legal title, equitable ownership under a trust, an equitable charge (lien), mere possession, or even the mere right to immediate possession. As between mere possessors, the first to possess is able to bring an action in conversion against the subsequent possessor. In one case, a boy found a jewel and took it to a jeweller for valuation. When the jeweller attempted to keep the jewel for himself, the boy successfully sued the jeweller in conversion.[65] Any deliberate dealing with the claimant's property, in a manner inconsistent with the defendant's title, will be an actionable conversion even if the defendant believed the chattel to be his own, or otherwise had an innocent state of mind.

The appropriate claimant in an action for trespass to goods will be the person with an immediate right to possession of the chattel. Where the chattel is trust property, the trustees are deemed to have an immediate right to possession of it, and so it is they who are entitled to bring the action in trespass.

One difference between the action for trespass and conversion is that trespass is only ever concerned with interference with the claimant's possession, whereas conversion is concerned to protect a much greater range of the claimant's property rights, possession included. However, the key difference is that conversion is concerned with dealings

---

[60] L. Smith, 'Simplifying Claims to Traceable Proceeds' (2009) 125 LQR 338 at 346–7.

[61] See B. S. Markesinis and S. F. Deakin, *Tort Law* (Oxford: Oxford University Press, 1999), and P. Cane, *Tort Law and Economic Interests*, 2nd edn (Oxford: Clarendon Press, 1996).

[62] Torts (Interference with Goods) Act 1977.   [63] Also called trover (traditional) and replevin (US).

[64] Torts (Interference with Goods) Act 1977, s. 1.   [65] *Armory v. Delamirie* (1721) 1 Stra 505.

with the claimant's chattel, whereas trespass is concerned merely with interference with the claimant's property. So, subject to very limited exceptions,[66] mere receipt of the claimant's chattel will give rise to liability in trespass, but not conversion. Simply returning a chattel to the person who gave it to the defendant will not render an innocent defendant liable in conversion, for such an act does not amount to 'a dealing' with the claimant's chattel.[67]

The award of damages for trespass or conversion is quantified according to the relevant diminution in the market value of the chattel *plus* any additional special loss that the claimant can demonstrate.[68] So loss of one of a matching pair of antique vases will be compensated at the market value of the lost vase *plus* the amount by which the value of the matching pair exceeded the value of the two vases valued separately. Where the chattel is a cheque or some other negotiable instrument, the value of the chattel is its monetary value, not the value of the paper.

Delivery up of chattels

This statutory remedy is awarded in response to the tort of conversion or trespass to goods.[69] It is analogous to the equitable remedy of specific 'restitution', in that it tends to be applied only to unique goods, because, in such cases, the usual remedy of compensation in damages will be inadequate.

Restitution

Restitution has been considered at several points throughout this book. It is descriptive of all remedies that reverse the unjust enrichment of a defendant when that enrichment was made at the claimant's expense. The idea that unjust enrichment should be a basis for a restitutionary remedy independent of proof that any orthodox legal or equitable right has been infringed is not a new one to English law. As long ago as 1914, in the case of *Sinclair v. Brougham*,[70] Lord Dunedin appeared to advocate an autonomous remedy based on the reversal of unjust enrichment. Several years later, the Court of Appeal[71] acknowledged that this approach would offer a way around the orthodox rule that equitable proprietary rights must be restricted to cases in which the claimant's property had, at some stage, been held in a fiduciary capacity, but '*apart from the possible case of Lord Dunedin's speech*' their Lordships could not find '*any principle so wide in its operation... enunciated in English law*'.[72]

However, the House of Lords, in the case of *Lipkin Gorman v. Karpnale*,[73] has now accepted the existence of an independent restitutionary remedy for unjust enrichment.

---

[66] According to the Torts (Interference with Goods) Act 1977, s. 11(2), '[r]*eceipt of goods by way of pledge is conversion if the delivery of the goods is conversion*'. So pawn brokers (who receive goods by way of pledge) must be astute to check that the person delivering the pledged goods is entitled to do so.

[67] *Hollins v. Fowler* (1875) LR 7 HL 757.

[68] See, generally, A. M. Tettenborn, 'Damages in conversion: exception or anomaly' [1993] Cam LJ 128.

[69] Torts (Interference with Goods) Act 1977, s. 3(3)(a).   [70] [1914] AC 398.

[71] *Re Diplock* [1948] Ch 465.   [72] Ibid. at 420–1.   [73] [1991] 2 AC 548.

The facts of the case were that a partner in a firm of solicitors had used monies from his firm's client account in order to gamble at the 'Playboy Club' casino in London. The casino was the defendant to the action. Lord Templeman identified the relevant issue in restitutionary terms: '*The question is whether the club which was enriched by £154,695 at the date when the solicitors sought restitution was unjustly enriched*.'[74]

The casino argued that it should not be required to make restitution to the claimant, because it had provided consideration for the monies it had received—namely, the provision of gambling services. The House of Lords accepted that the giving of legal consideration could be a valid defence to a claim based in unjust enrichment, but held that the defence was not available to the casino, because a contract for gambling services is not a legally enforceable contract, so consideration given under such a contract was not 'legal' consideration of the type capable of supplying the necessary defence.[75] The casino was held to have been unjustly enriched. However, the casino argued further, that even if it were liable to make restitution, it should only be liable to make restitution *net* of winnings that it had paid out to the rogue solicitor. It would be unjust, it argued, to require it to repay all the money that it had received without taking account of the money that it had paid out in good faith. This time the House of Lords accepted the casino's argument.

Defences to a restitutionary claim

A defendant's liability to account to a claimant for unjust enrichment is strict, in so far as liability does not depend upon proof that the defendant was at fault. The only requirement is to prove that the defendant was in fact enriched at the claimant's expense, and unjustly. It follows that liability to make restitution on the basis of unjust enrichment can only be justified if accompanied by generous defences. The most significant defence is the 'innocent change of position defence', which reduces the defendant's liability to account to the extent that he has innocently altered his financial and other affairs due to receipt of the claimant's property. Another important defence is one that we considered earlier: the bona fide purchaser defence. Although this defence is referred to as the defence of 'equity's darling', the bona fide purchaser defence is in truth based on a fundamental policy of protecting purchasers that transcends the distinction between law, equity, and restitution.

Innocent change of position
Innocent

Unjust enrichment gives rise to an entitlement to restitution unless it would be inequitable in all the circumstances to require the recipient of the benefit to make restitution in full or in part.[76] It is clear that mere negligence on the part of the recipient is not sufficient to deprive him of the defence of change of position.[77] The defence will only be denied to a party who fails to satisfy the requirement of 'innocence'.

---

[74] Ibid. at 560E. [75] Gaming Act 1845, s. 18.

[76] *Lipkin Gorman v. Karpnale Ltd* [1991] 2 AC 548, followed in *Niru Battery Manufacturing Co v. Milestone Trading Ltd* [2002] All ER (D) 206, *per* Moore-Bick J.

[77] *Dextra Bank & Trust Co Ltd v. Bank of Jamaica* [2002] 1 All ER (Comm) 193, PC.

Change of position

According to the speech of Lord Goff in *Lipkin Gorman*:[78]

> where an innocent defendant's position is so changed that he will suffer an injustice if called
> upon to repay or to repay in full, the injustice of requiring him so to repay outweighs the
> injustice of denying the plaintiff restitution.[79]

Suppose that a chronically arthritic person had always wished to own a swimming pool to provide pain-free exercise, but had been unable to afford one until he received £20,000 from a wealthy friend. He genuinely believed the £20,000 to be a gift, but his 'friend' had, in fact, misappropriated the monies from a company of which he was a director. If the recipient proceeded to use the entire £20,000 on the installation of a swimming pool in his garden, it would surely be unjust to require him to account to the company for the £20,000 he had received, especially as this would probably necessitate the sale of his house or taking out a loan secured on the house. This is the sort of scenario in which the defence of innocent change of position would succeed.

Lord Templeman suggested other examples in *Lipkin Gorman*, including that of a donee who spends the gift on a trip around the world '*which he would not have undertaken without the gift*', and '*the purchase of a motor car which he would not have purchased but for the gift*'. In the latter case, the donee '*has only been unjustly enriched to the extent of the second hand value of the motor car at the date when the victim of the theft seeks restitution*'.[80] It could be argued that our swimming pool owner should also be required to sell the swimming pool and account for its second-hand value, but the swimming pool, assuming that it is a fairly substantial installation, will probably be considered to have been irreversibly incorporated into the defendant's land.[81]

Applying the innocent change of position defence to the facts of *Lipkin Gorman* itself proved to be far from straightforward. The casino had no doubt acted innocently, but, at first sight, it is hard to see that the casino had changed its position due to the receipt of the monies gambled by the solicitor. The facts of *Lipkin Gorman* could hardly be further from the swimming pool example set out earlier. The actions of the casino with regard to the bets placed by the rogue solicitor were precisely the same as its actions with regard to the bets placed by every other gambler. (No doubt that very fact was evidence of the casino's innocence.) In what sense, then, did the casino 'change' its position? Lord Goff admitted that the result may not have been 'entirely logical', but any reservation was seemingly overborne by his Lordship's desire to introduce the change of position defence into English law: '*The principle is widely recognised throughout the common law world . . . The time for its recognition in this country is, in my opinion, long overdue.*'[82] And, of course, by his Lordship's assessment of the justice of the case:

> it would be inequitable to require the casino to repay in full without bringing into account
> winnings paid by it to the gambler on any one or more of the bets so placed with it.[83]

---

[78] [1991] 2 AC 548.　　[79] Ibid. at 579E–F.　　[80] [1991] 2 AC 548 at 560C.

[81] Under the rule relating to fixtures, see later.　　[82] [1991] 2 AC 548 at 580.　　[83] Ibid. at 582–3.

The property law–restitution debate

There is a danger, inherent in the redescription of traditional equitable and common law remedies in terms of the reversal of unjust enrichment, that the orthodox remedies will be inappropriately distorted. Lord Browne-Wilkinson was alert to this danger in *Westdeutsche Landesbank Girozentrale v. Islington LBC*,[84] when he expressed his opinion that '*the search for a perceived need to strengthen the remedies of a plaintiff claiming in restitution involves . . . a distortion of trust principles*'.[85] Lord Millett has also confirmed, in *Foskett*,[86] that tracing and recovering trust property '*is concerned with vindicating rights of property and not with reversing unjust enrichment*'.[87]

Lord Millett's speech is implicitly critical of the 'unjust' element in 'unjust enrichment':[88]

> The transmission of a claimant's property rights from one asset to its traceable proceeds is part of our law of property, not of the law of unjust enrichment. There is no 'unjust factor' to justify restitution (unless 'want of title' be one, which makes the point). The claimant succeeds if at all by virtue of his own title, not to reverse unjust enrichment. Property rights are determined by fixed rules and settled principles. They are not discretionary. They do not depend upon ideas of what is 'fair, just and reasonable.' Such concepts, which in reality mask decisions of legal policy, have no place in the law of property.[89]

If the law concerned with the reversal of unjust enrichment is to develop along lines consistent with long-established principles and doctrines of common law and equity, it is essential that the 'unjust' element of the unjust enrichment is an element that would be considered unjust according to established principles. As Lord Goff stated in *Lipkin Gorman*:

> A claim to recover money at common law is made as a matter of right; and even though the underlying principle of recovery is the principle of unjust enrichment, nevertheless, where recovery is denied, it is denied on the basis of legal principle.[90]

In cases decided shortly after *Lipkin Gorman*, one can identify the same desire to maintain a connection between the unjust element of the enrichment, and established legal and equitable principles. One such case is *South Tyneside MBC v. Svenska International plc*.[91] The claimant local authority had entered into an interest swap agreement with the defendant bank. (Under such an agreement, one party pays a fixed rate of interest on a sum of money, while the other party pays a variable rate of interest on the same sum.) Shortly after the claimant local authority had entered into the interest swap agreement, it was established (in another case)[92] that such an arrangement was ultra vires the powers of local authorities. Accordingly, the bank refused to fulfil the agreement, even though it owed the authority nearly £700,000 under the agreement.[93] The local authority brought

---

[84] [1996] AC 669.   [85] Ibid. at 709.   [86] [2001] 1 AC 102.   [87] Ibid. at 132.
[88] Compare the observations made on restitution in Chapter 2.   [89] [2001] 1 AC 102 at 127.
[90] [1991] 2 AC 548 at 578.   [91] [1995] 1 All ER 545.
[92] *Hazell v. Hammersmith and Fulham London Borough Council* [1992] 2 AC 1, HL, restoring the decision of the Divisional Court ([1990] 2 QB 697).
[93] Similar facts gave rise to the important case of *Westdeutsche Landesbank Girozentrale v. Islington LBC* [1996] AC 669, HL, except the bank claimed the overpayment in *Westdeutsche*.

the present action in restitution to recover money had and received, on the basis of the defendant's unjust enrichment. The defendant sought to show that it had changed its position in good faith due to the receipt of the monies. Clarke J held that the bank had been unjustly enriched and could not rely upon the defence of change of position.

Crucially, his Lordship held that the bank had been unjustly enriched because it had received money that in equity belonged to the council and which both law and equity said should be repaid to the payer. Academic proponents of the law of restitution have frequently been less accommodating of orthodox principles of law and equity, arguing instead for a free-standing law of restitution in which the unjust element of the enrichment is established by reference to autonomous factors which have no necessary connection with orthodox principles of law and equity.[94]

There is no doubt that restitution sometimes provides solutions to problems when the law of property does not. Suppose, for example, that B's trust money is misapplied by her trustee and comes into the possession of a third party, A, who innocently uses the money to pay rent which A would otherwise have had to pay using his own money.

The law of property, as we noted earlier, considers B's money to have been 'spent' or 'dissipated' and therefore to be irrecoverable. The law of restitution, on the other hand, considers A to have been unjustly enriched at B's expense and so requires A, who cannot rely upon the change of position defence, to repay the money to B.[95] Nevertheless, it is submitted that restitution exceeds its usefulness, and even becomes detrimental, when it seeks to provide a solution to a perceived injustice in a particular case even when an adequate solution can be found by applying orthodox property law principles.

Professor Birks' argument is that a free-standing law of restitution based on the reversal of unjust enrichment is sometimes more appropriate than orthodox property law and the law of obligations to deal with problems arising from the misapplication of trust money, because property law and obligations law construct general responses to sets of facts, whereas unjust enrichment is a basic fact: '*Property and obligations are co-ordinate categories of response to events, while unjust enrichment is an event*.'[96] That argument is, with respect, unconvincing: 'enrichment' might be an event, but 'unjust enrichment' is a secondary construction. In fact, it is arguable that the misappropriation of B's property by A is a more fundamental 'event', given political commitment to proprietary entitlement, than the unjust enrichment of A on the same facts. Arguably, A can only be said to have been unjustly enriched *because* he has B's property.[97]

Tracing

As one reads through the cases and academic commentaries on this area of law, one occasionally sees references to the 'tracing remedy'. It is a description that is nowadays

---

[94] See, for example, A. Burrows, *The Law of Restitution*, 2nd edn (London: Butterworths, 2002) at 41–5, where he lists as examples such factors as 'mistake', 'exploitation', and 'duress'.

[95] P. Birks in *Breach of Trust* (P. Birks and A. Pretto, eds) (Oxford: Hart Publishing, 2002) at 236.

[96] Ibid at 220.   [97] See, further, Chapter 2 where 'restitution' is discussed.

considered to be unhelpful, because it tends to confuse the process of tracing property into the hands of various recipients with the remedies that might ultimately be available against them. Tracing is nothing more than the process which supplies the evidence that a defendant has received trust property. It is detective work carried out according to a set of legal (including equitable) rules and principles. The rules establish a number of presumptions that determine whether the claimant's property, or its substitute (its value represented in a new form), has ever passed through the defendant's hands. Because tracing is an evidential matter, most of the tracing presumptions are rebuttable by clear evidence in the form of written accounts, memoranda, and similar documentary statements. Of course, in the typical case of misapplication of trust property, such documentary evidence (if there is any at all) is unlikely to produce a comprehensive and true picture of what has happened.

Tracing and following contrasted

'Just... follow the money'

All the President's Men (Warner Bros., 1976)[98]

At its most simple, tracing merely involves following a particular trust asset, such as an antique vase, as it passes from the trustee to 'stranger A' to 'stranger B' to 'stranger C', and so on. In fact, this simple process is usually referred to as 'following' in order to distinguish it from the more sophisticated process of 'tracing' the value of an asset into substitute assets for which the original asset has been exchanged.[99]

If a trustee sells a trust-owned antique vase to an innocent purchaser, the beneficiaries will, as a simple matter of factual evidence, be able to 'follow' the vase into the purchaser's hands, but they will be unable to recover it. It will therefore be more profitable to them to 'trace' the value of the vase into the sale proceeds in the trustee's hands. They can even trace the value of their vase *into* the trustee's bank account, despite the fact that his account may also contain the trustee's own money. Furthermore, they are (in equity, but not at common law) able to trace *through* the bank account into assets purchased with monies from the account, even if those assets have been acquired with a mixture of trust monies and the trustee's own money. The claimant can trace the money '*not because it is the claimant's, but because it is derived from a fund which is treated as if it were subject to a charge in the claimant's favour*'.[100]

---

[98] The quote is from William Goldman's script of the film that starred Robert Redford and Dustin Hoffman as the *Washington Post* reporters Carl Bernstein and Bob Woodward. The script was based on Bernstein and Woodward's eponymous novel about the famous 'Watergate' affair, which they had helped to disclose and which led to the resignation of President Nixon. '*Follow the money*' was the advice of William Mark Felt Sr, the deputy director of the FBI, who secretly leaked information to the reporters. He was referred to in the novel and the film by the pseudonym 'Deep Throat'.

[99] Lord Millett in *Foskett*: '*Following is the process of following the same asset as it moves from hand to hand. Tracing is the process of identifying a new asset as the substitute for the old*' ([2001] 1 AC 102 at 127).

[100] *London Allied Holdings Ltd v. Lee* [2007] EWHC 2061 (Ch), *per* Etherton J at [257], citing *El Ajou v. Dollar Land Holdings* [1993] 3 All ER 717, *per* Millet J at 735j–736a. *London Allied Holdings Ltd v. Lee* involved a fake sale of London's Ritz Hotel—the definitive 'putting on the Ritz'.

One way of understanding the tracing process is to regard it as the process by which a claimant establishes a transactional or factual connection between his original assets and its 'exchange products', or 'substitutes'. As Lord Millett observed in *Foskett v. McKeown*:[101]

> We speak of tracing money into and out of the account, but there is no money in the account. There is merely a single debt of an amount equal to the final balance standing to the credit of the account holder. No money passes from paying bank to receiving bank or through the clearing system (where the money flows may be in the opposite direction). There is simply a series of debits and credits which are causally and transactionally linked.[102] We also speak of tracing one asset into another, but this too is inaccurate. The original asset still exists in the hands of the new owner, or it may have become untraceable. The claimant claims the new asset because it was acquired in whole or in part with the original asset. What he traces, therefore, is not the physical asset itself but the value inherent in it.[103]

Foskett v. McKeown is, in Lord Millett's words, '*a textbook example of tracing through mixed substitutions*'.[104] His Lordship analysed the facts in that case[105] as a simple sequence of substitutions.

> The claimants were '*beneficially entitled under an express trust to a sum standing in the name of Mr. Murphy in a bank account*'.[106]

> When these monies were placed in Mr Murphy's personal bank account the balance of that account, could be treated as a substitute asset, because a credit balance in a bank account is a debt owed by the bank to its customer and a debt is an asset.[107]

> When monies were drawn to acquire life insurance, the debt owed by the bank was substituted by another asset—namely, '*the debt prospectively and contingently due from an insurance company to its policyholders*'.[108]

> The debt owed by the insurance company was (as a result of Mr Murphy's death) substituted by insurance proceeds paid into the bank account of Mr Murphy's trustees—that is, the debt owed by the insurance company was substituted by a debt owed to the trustees (the defendants in this case) by their bank.

Hence the claimants were able to trace the value of their trust property from the original account into each of the substitute assets and, ultimately, into the trustees' bank

---

[101] [2001] 1 AC 102.

[102] There is, in a sense, a 'money transfer without money movement'. This is the description used by Interpol to describe the '*hawala*' system of banking, which for hundreds of years, has been a favoured method of international cash transfer between Muslims (P. M. Jost and H. S. Sandhu, *The* Hawala *Alternative Remittance System and its Role in Money Laundering* (Interpol: Lyon, 2000) at 5). The fact that the *hawala* banking and the '*Western*' system both involve '*money transfer without money movement*' suggests that the systems are not as diametrically opposed as the Interpol document assumes. The *hawala* system works on the basis of personal trust between sending and receiving brokers, who do not actually send and receive the sum transferred, but keep accounts and settle balances. This trust-based banking is a good thing in itself. The problem is that no permanent records are kept and this produces potential for illegal money laundering. On money laundering, generally, see the Money Laundering Regulations 2007 (SI 2007, No. 2157) as amended (SI 2007, No. 3299).

[103] [2001] 1 AC 102 at 128.   [104] Ibid. at 126.   [105] *Foskett v. McKeown* [2001] 1 AC 102.

[106] Ibid. at 126.   [107] Technically speaking, a chose in action (chose means 'thing').

[108] [2001] 1 AC 102 at 126.

account, against which they were then able successfully to assert their proprietary rights.[109]

Following fails when property is destroyed

The process of following a particular trust asset will fail if the asset is physically destroyed or if, having been subjected to some physical or chemical process, the asset is deemed to have lost its identity. So, for example, it is impossible to follow a moveable item of trust property, such as a statue or a tapestry, if it has been fixed to land. (A chattel is said to become a 'fixture' when it is annexed to the land with a sufficient degree of physical permanence and with the intention that it should enhance the land as part of the land.)[110] The rule relating to fixtures on land is derived from the maxim *quicquid plantatur solo, solo cedit* ('that which is fixed to the soil accedes to the soil'). It is a particular application of the ancient doctrine of accession, which provides that, when an inferior asset has, for practical purposes, been irreversibly co-joined with a superior asset, the identity of the inferior asset is destroyed and the identity of the superior asset survives. The doctrine of *accessio* was created in Roman law, where it applied to such basic problems as the application of A's thread, by embroidery, to B's garment (in which case, the owner of the garment was considered to be the owner of the whole). According to Professor Roy Goode, whichever of the constituents '*predominates as a distinct entity*' is that which survives.[111] Professor Lionel Smith[112] illustrates this point with some modern examples: an engine accedes to a truck,[113] a meter accedes to a taxi,[114] and spare parts accede to a vehicle.[115]

Distinct from the doctrine of accession is the doctrine of specification, derived from the Roman law doctrine of *specificatio*.[116] Whereas, in a case of accession, the character of the superior asset survives joinder with the inferior asset (diamonds incorporated in a diamond tiara are still diamonds) and it is usually possible to reduce the co-joined asset into its constituent parts, a case of specification joinder produces an entirely new species of asset in which the character of its constituent parts is lost and cannot be separated. *Borden (UK) Ltd v. Scottish Timber Products*[117] is a classic case of specification, for there the claimant's resin had been incorporated with other ingredients to create a product (chipboard) which bore no resemblance to any of the ingredients that had gone

---

[109] The requirement to show that the claimant's property is in the defendant's hands, and that it can be traced from the claimant to the defendant by an unbroken chain of connections, applies just as rigorously in the context of claims against criminal assets 'frozen' under the Proceeds of Crime Act 2002 (see *The Serious Fraud Office v. Lexi Holdings PLC (In Administration)* [2008] EWCA Crim 1443; [2009] QB 376).

[110] *Berkeley v. Poulett* (1976) EG 911, *per* Scarman LJ. In *Elitestone Ltd v. Morris* [1997] 1 WLR 687, a wooden bungalow was held to be a fixture. It was resting on concrete pillars embedded in the ground and could only be removed by demolition.

[111] In *Hire-Purchase Law and Practice*, 2nd edn (London: Butterworths, 1970). Referred to in L. Smith, *The Law of Tracing* (Oxford: Clarendon Press, 1997) at 105.   [112] Ibid.

[113] *Lincoln Bank & Trust Co v. Netter*, 253 SW2d 260 (Ky. 1952).

[114] *Schofield & Co v. Amer* (1931), 26 MCR 164 (NZ Mag. Ct).

[115] *Andrew v. The New Jersey Steamboat Co*, 11 Hun's SCR 490 (NY 1877).

[116] R. B. Slater, '*Accessio, Specificatio* and *Confusio*: three skeletons in the closet' (1959) 37 Can BR 597.

[117] [1981] Ch 25.

to make it. It has been suggested that the doctrine of specification has no application to English law.[118] It is submitted, however, that specification does defeat the process of following a particular asset, even if it does not defeat the process of tracing its value.

Tracing at common law and in equity

At the time of writing, the law still makes a distinction between tracing at common law and tracing in equity. A claimant wishing to subject a defendant to a common law claim must establish that his property can be traced *at common law* into the defendant's hands. Conversely, a claimant wishing to subject a defendant to a proprietary or personal claim *in equity* must establish that the trust property can be traced *in equity* into the defendant's hands. Our study of tracing will be set out under orthodox headings of tracing at common law and equity, because it remains a useful way of organizing existing law—but it should be borne in mind that the House of Lords might well remove the distinction between common and equitable tracing at the first opportunity. The distinction has already been expressly disapproved of by Lords Millett and Steyn in the House of Lords in *Foskett v. McKeown*, but that case did not present an appropriate occasion to remove the distinction entirely, because, as Lord Millett acknowledged, the claimants in *Foskett* were successful even according to the traditional equitable tracing rules. Lords Millett and Steyn referred with approval to Professor Birks's essay on 'The necessity of a unitary law of tracing',[119] which Lord Steyn described as a 'crystalline' analysis of the issues.[120] Birks's argument, as summarized by Lord Steyn, is that '*tracing is a process of identifying assets: it belongs to the realm of evidence. It tells us nothing about legal or equitable rights to the assets traced.*'[121]

However, even if the House of Lords were unanimously resolved to abolish the distinction between legal and equitable tracing at the earliest opportunity, it will be no straightforward matter to do away with it entirely. The legal and equitable nature of the ultimate remedies inevitably has a reflex effect upon the nature of the evidence relied upon to support them. Every evidential question begs the incidental question: evidence of 'what'? So if the tracing process is, at its most basic, the evidential question, 'Where has the value of my property gone?', it is hard to avoid such incidental questions as: 'What is "property"?'; 'What is "my" property?'; 'What do we mean by "value"?'; even, as seen most starkly in the context of resulting trusts, 'What do we mean by "gone"?' The answer provided by the common law to each of these questions differs, to a greater or lesser extent, from the answer provided by equity. Even Lord Millett, an advocate of unitary tracing, once acknowledged that the existence of different tracing rules at law and in equity is '*unfortunate though probably inevitable*', because sometimes differences may be '*required by the different nature of legal and equitable doctrines and remedies*'.[122]

---

[118] P. Matthews, '"*Specificatio*" in the common law' (1981) 10 Anglo-American LR 121.

[119] In *Making Commercial Law: Essays in Honour of Roy Goode* (R. Cranston, ed.) (Oxford: Clarendon Press, 1997) 239 at 258.   [120] Lord Steyn in *Foskett* [2001] 1 AC 102 at 113.

[121] Ibid.

[122] *Trustee of the Property of F. C. Jones and sons (a firm) v. Jones* [1996] 3 WLR 703, CA, at 702, *per* Millett LJ.

It may be particularly hard to sever the theoretical connection between the process and the remedy where a claimant wishes to employ common law rules of tracing as a precursor to an equitable claim, because the common law rules are inevitably more formal than their equitable counterparts. There is however '*less merit in the present rule which precludes the invocation of the equitable tracing rules to support a common law claim*',[123] because it is entirely consistent with equity's traditional role of supplementing common law remedies for equitable tracing to be available to ensure that a substantially meritorious common law claim does not fail due to non-compliance with the common law rules of tracing.[124]

Tracing at common law

The most straightforward way to understand the nature of common law tracing is to appreciate its limitations. Subject to its limitations, tracing at common law is a simple process of following an original asset into new hands or tracing the value of an original asset into substitute assets.

The limits to tracing at common law

There are limits to tracing at common law.[125] In *Lipkin Gorman v. Karpnale Ltd*,[126] a firm of solicitors[127] opted to use the common law rules to trace clients' monies into the hands of a casino, the casino having acquired the monies from a rogue partner in the claimant firm who had gambled there. Lord Goff held that common law tracing had been successful. Originally, the firm had a 'chose of action' against its bank to recover the monies held in its client account. This chose in action could be traced at common law into its 'substitute' or 'exchange product', namely the monies withdrawn by the rogue solicitor. As Lord Goff put it:

> 'Tracing' or 'following' property into its product involves a decision by the owner of the original property to assert his title to the product in place of his original property.[128]

Trust beneficiaries cannot trace at common law Trust beneficiaries are able to rely on equity's generous tracing rules and it is therefore unlikely in practice that they would prefer to trace at common law. This is perhaps just as well because, according to orthodoxy, the common law rules of tracing are not available to trace equitable property, such property being recognizable in equity, but not at common law. There are,

---

[123] Ibid. at 712B.

[124] See Atkin LJ's obiter dicta in *Banque Belge pour L'Etranger v. Hambrouck* [1921] 1 KB 321 at 335–6. Note that in *Federal Republic of Brazil v. Durant International Corp* [2013] JCA 071, Jersey's Court of Appeal confirmed the approach taken by The Royal Court of Jersey, which had held that tracing is an evidential process in which the challenge is the pragmatic one of demonstrating that current assets may be considered the substitutes of original assets. The process, in contrast to the tracing process in England, is not concerned to distinguish tracing in law from tracing in equity.

[125] See P. Matthews, 'The legal and moral limits of common law tracing' in P. B. H. Birks, *Laundering and Tracing* (Oxford: Clarendon Press, 1995) at 23–71.

[126] [1991] 2 AC 548.   [127] For the facts, see earlier.   [128] [1991] 2 AC 548 at 573F–G.

however, circumstances in which beneficiaries can take advantage of common law rights indirectly.[129]

Common law tracing through 'clean' and 'mixed' substitutions

The common law is said to allow a claimant to *trace* the value of his original property through 'clean substitutions',[130] but not through 'mixed substitutions'.[131] To put it another way, property may be traced at common law only so long as it remains in an identifiable form, so that the claimant could, at every stage of the process, point to his property and say 'that is mine'. It is important to note that, although the property must remain in an *identifiable* form, it does not matter that its legal or factual form has changed, say from coins to notes, or from cash to cheque, or from cash paid into a bank account to the chose in action (debt) enforceable against the bank to recover the balance of the account. In the 1815 case of *Taylor v. Plumer*,[132] Lord Ellenborough stated that:

> the product of or substitute for the original thing still follows the nature of the thing itself, as long as it can be ascertained to be such, and the right only ceases when the means of ascertainment fail, which is the case when the subject is turned into money, and mixed and confounded in a general mass of the same description.[133]

Although this suggests that common law tracing into a mixed account is impossible, we will see later that the rule is not that clear-cut. What is clear, however, is that equity has no such limitations. In the 1879 case *Re Hallett's Estate*,[134] the Court of Appeal upheld the decision of Fry J to allow a trust beneficiary to trace its money into an account where it had been mixed with the trustee's own money. In *Banque Belge pour L'Etranger v. Hambrouck*,[135] Lord Atkin LJ observed that '*if in 1815 the common law halted outside the bankers' door, by 1879 equity had had the courage to lift the latch, walk in and examine the books*'.[136]

Banque Belge is a textbook example of tracing through clean substitutions. A cashier stole money from his employer, paid it into a new bank account, and later made certain withdrawals. He paid some of the money to his mistress by way of gift, who, in turn, paid the money into her own deposit account. She later spent the majority of the money, so that only £315 remained in her account at the date of the court hearing. It was held that the bank was entitled to trace its money, at common law. The £315 could be identified as the product of, or substitute for, the original money, because the misapplied monies were identifiable at every stage. A crucial factor in the decision was that the only money in the accounts of the cashier and the mistress was money misappropriated from the claimant.

The case of *Jones & Sons (a firm) v. Jones*[137] provides another good example of tracing at common law through clean substitutions. In 1984, a firm of potato growers got into financial difficulties, and the partners committed an act of bankruptcy and were adjudicated bankrupt. After the act of bankruptcy, but before the adjudication, the defendant

---

[129] See Chapter 2.   [130] See 'Equitable proprietary remedies' at the beginning of this chapter.
[131] Ibid.   [132] (1815) 3 M & S 562.   [133] Ibid. at 575.   [134] (1879) LR 13 Ch D 696.
[135] [1921] 1 KB 321.   [136] Ibid. at 335–6.   [137] [1996] 3 WLR 703, CA.

(the wife of one of the partners) opened an account with commodity brokers in order to deal in potato futures and paid in the proceeds of cheques totalling £11,700 drawn by her husband on a joint bank account held in his name and that of one of the other partners. The defendant received £50,760 from her dealings, which was then paid into a deposit account with R plc. The Official Receiver informed R plc of its claim to the money in the account, whereupon the defendant immediately demanded its release to her. R plc interpleaded and the money was paid into court. The proceedings were transferred to the Chancery Division, with the trustee in bankruptcy as claimant. The judge ordered the money to be paid out to the trustee in bankruptcy. The Court of Appeal dismissed the defendant's appeal on the ground that, from the date of the act of bankruptcy, the money in the bankrupts' joint bank account had belonged to the trustee in bankruptcy, so the defendant's husband had no title, whether at law or in equity, to the £11,700 he had paid to the defendant and therefore he could confer no title on her.

According to Millett LJ, as he then was, the deposit of the money under the terms of the contract between the defendant and the commodity brokers was substituted for a chose of action against the brokers, which, although vested in the defendant's name, in reality belonged to the trustee in bankruptcy. The chose in action conferred on the trustee in bankruptcy the right to claim the balance, whether greater or less than the amounted deposited. Accordingly, the trustee was entitled both to the £11,700 and to the profits made by the defendant's use of that sum.

Tracing through clean substitutions is straightforward enough, but '*tracing runs into problems when it encounters mixing*'.[138] A claimant is permitted to trace at common law *into* a mixed substitute if the defendant carried out the mixing, but the claimant is not permitted to trace at common law *through* that mixed substitute and into the hands of another defendant. Suppose that a trustee paid trust money into his own private bank account, so that, immediately upon receiving the trust money for his own use, it was mixed with his own money and rendered indistinguishable from it. If the common law literally '*stopped at the door of the bank*',[139] a fraudster could (by the simple expedient of paying misappropriated monies into his own current account) escape personal liability at common law for the tort of money had and received. In *Agip (Africa) Ltd v. Jackson*, Millett J put it this way:

> Mixing by the defendant himself must … be distinguished from mixing by a prior recipient. The former is irrelevant, but the latter will destroy the claim, for it will prevent proof that the money received by the defendant was the money paid by the plaintiff.[140]

In *Agip (Africa) Ltd v. Jackson*, a senior officer of A Ltd innocently signed a payment order for around US$500,000, which a fraudulent employee of the company then altered in favour of Baker Oil Ltd, a company created and controlled by the defendants (the defendants were accountants who had been instructed throughout by their fraudulent clients). The employee took the order to A Ltd's Tunisian bank and the Tunisian bank executed it,

---

[138] P. Birks, 'Mixing and tracing: property and restitution' (1992) 45 CLP 69–98.
[139] [1921] 1 KB 321 at 335–6.   [140] Millett in *Agip (Africa) Ltd v. Jackson* [1990] 1 Ch 265 at 285G–H.

by debiting the claimant's account and telexing instructions to Lloyds in London to pay the US$500,000 into the account of Baker Oil, which was an account holder with Lloyds. At the same time, the Tunisian bank telexed instructions to its correspondent bank in New York to reimburse Lloyds through the New York clearing system. Lloyds made the payment, believing that it would be reimbursed by the Tunisian bank's partner bank in New York, but, in so doing, it took a delivery risk, because the New York bank had not yet opened for business. By the time that Lloyds had discovered the fraud, the payment had already left Baker Oil's account and passed to various accounts held in the name of the defendants. The defendants refused Lloyds' request to have the monies returned and, in accordance with the instructions of its clients (the fraudsters), the defendants paid all of the money away apart from US $43,000 that remained in the defendants' accounts at the date of the action. The defendants claimed that they had acted innocently throughout.

The claimant's action to recover the US$500,000 from the defendants was success-ful at first instance, where the judge was Millett J.[141] That judgment was upheld on appeal.[142] Common law tracing failed, but tracing in equity was successful. The defend-ants were, in addition, personally liable as accessories to the fraud. We will consider the defendants' accessory liability in the next chapter and we will consider equitable tracing later in this. Here, we are interested in the reasons why common law tracing failed.

At least three reasons were given by their Lordships, either at first instance or on appeal. The most significant reason for failure of common law tracing was that Lloyds had paid its own monies into the Baker Oil account and the money by which it was reimbursed could not be identified except through the New York clearing system, where it was mixed with other money. Tracing at common law therefore failed, because it depended upon tracing through a mixed substitution. A second, related, reason for the failure of common law tracing was that the value of the claimant's money could not be followed directly from the Tunisian bank to Lloyds, because Lloyds had credited the Baker Oil account *before* the Tunisian monies had actually arrived from New York— Lloyds had taken a delivery risk. If one sees tracing as following actual property or its 'value', this reasoning must be right, but if tracing is more accurately regarded as fol-lowing property through substitutes that are transactionally linked, it is hard to see how Lloyds' delivery risk can be an adequate ground for the failure of common law tracing. Lloyds' advance payment into the Baker Oil account was clearly 'transactionally linked' to the later receipt from the New York bank. Even less convincing is the third reason given in *Agip* for the failure of common law tracing—namely, that, because of the use of telegraphic transfer (telex), '*nothing passed between Tunisia and London but a stream of electrons*',[143] with the result that the claimant's property could not be identified at every stage, as is required for successful tracing at common law. It is hard to see why the com-mon law should suffer a Luddite inability to deal with the technological realities of the commercial world.

---

[141] *Agip (Africa) Ltd v. Jackson* [1990] 1 Ch 265.   [142] *Agip (Africa) Ltd v. Jackson* [1991] Ch 547.
[143] Millett J [1990] 1 Ch 265 at 286C.

Tracing in equity

Equity follows the law, so it is possible to trace in equity through clean substitutions. However, whereas, at common law, it is possible to trace into mixed funds in the defendant's hands if the defendant carried out the mixing, only in equity is it possible to trace *through* mixed substitutions into the hands of third-party recipients from the defendant.[144] This is the great advantage of equitable tracing over common law tracing. According to Lord Greene MR in *Re Diplock*:

> Equity adopted a more metaphysical approach. It found no difficulty in regarding a composite fund as an amalgam constituted by the mixture of two or more funds each of which could be regarded as having, for certain purposes, a continued separate existence. Putting it in another way, equity regarded the amalgam as capable, in proper circumstances, of being resolved into its component parts.[145]

Another major advantage of equitable tracing over common law tracing, which will remain so long as the type of remedy depends upon the tracing process used to support it, is that equitable tracing is the only way to provide the evidence necessary to support an equitable proprietary claim.

Nevertheless, for all its obvious advantages, tracing in equity is subject to one significant limitation: equitable tracing depends upon proof that the claimant's property has, at some point in the tracing process, been held by someone subject to a fiduciary duty.

The fiduciary requirement

A claimant is not permitted to take advantage of equity's tracing rules unless he can show that the property he is tracing had '*been the subject of fiduciary obligations before it got into the wrong hands*'.[146] Millett J referred to this as the '*only restriction on the ability of equity to follow assets*',[147] which is true inasmuch as it is the only restriction which has no counterpart in common law tracing. His Lordship suggested that the requirement '*depends on authority rather than principle*',[148] and here his Lordship expressly had in mind the authority of the Court of Appeal in *Re Diplock*.[149]

However, the *Diplock* case does reveal an attempt to provide a principled justification for the fiduciary requirement. Lord Greene MR took the view that a fiduciary obligation was required *in order to establish a proprietary basis* for the claimant's ultimate proprietary claim:

> equity may operate on the conscience not merely of those who acquire a legal title in breach of some trust, express or constructive, or of some other fiduciary obligation, but of volunteers provided that as a result of what has gone before some equitable proprietary interest has been created and attaches to the property in the hands of the volunteer.[150]

---

[144] '[W]*hat the Roman lawyers, if they had had an economy which required tracing through bank accounts, would have called* confusio', *per* Lord Hoffmann in *Foskett* [2001] 1 AC 102 at 115.

[145] *Re Diplock* [1948] 1 Ch 465, Ch D at 520.

[146] *Agip (Africa) Ltd v. Jackson* [1990] Ch 265, *per* Millett J at 290B.

[147] Ibid. at 290A.   [148] Ibid.   [149] [1948] Ch 465.   [150] Ibid. at 530.

His Lordship purported to follow the reasoning of Lord Parker and Lord Haldane who, in *Sinclair v. Brougham*,[151] had held that a right of property recognized by equity '*depends upon there having existed at some stage a fiduciary relationship of some kind (though not necessarily a positive duty of trusteeship) sufficient to give rise to the equitable right of property*'.[152]

The requirement that a claimant should establish a proprietary base or 'history' before he can be awarded a proprietary remedy is logical enough;[153] less logical is the way in which the courts in *Diplock* and *Sinclair v. Brougham* intimate (it is never made explicit)[154] that an equitable proprietary right cannot be established without a prior fiduciary relationship. It seems strange that an absolute owner should be less able to take advantage of equity's tracing rules, leading as they do to proprietary remedies, than an owner whose property has, at some point, been held in trust or otherwise held subject to fiduciary obligations. Why, for instance, should an absolute owner whose property has been stolen be unable to trace in equity into the hands of the thief merely on account of a fiduciary relationship being absent?[155] In *Re Hallett's Settlement Trusts*,[156] Jessel MR observed that there is no '*distinction between an express trustee, or an agent, or a bailee, or a collector of rents, or anybody else in a fiduciary position*'[157] as regards the right to trace in equity, on the ground that '*the beneficial ownership is the same, wherever the legal ownership may be*'.[158] Why, then, should equitable tracing be denied simply because legal ownership happened, at first, to be in an absolute owner and was never held by a fiduciary? The answer, surely, is that it should not be denied. Further support for this view can be found later in the judgment of Sir George Jessel MR, where he stated that it should make no difference '*in a Court of Equity*'[159] whether a man vests legal title to goods in someone else as his trustee or simply deposits the goods with him as bailee or agent '*so that the legal ownership remains in the beneficial owner... he being entire beneficial owner in both cases*'.[160]

In cases in which the claimant is the beneficiary of an express trust, whether traditional or commercial, he will *ipso facto* be able to show that his property had been held subject to fiduciary obligations before it came into the defendant's hands. Yet, even in cases that do not involve express trusts, claimants will very often be able to establish that the property had, at some stage, been held by someone who owed the claimant duties of a fiduciary nature. Consider the facts of *Agip* itself, where the fraudster was an employee of the claimant who, having been entrusted with possession of the signed payment order, must have been subject to a fiduciary duty not to use the payment order for his own purposes.

---

[151] [1914] AC 398.   [152] Lord Greene's summary of *Sinclair* at *Re Diplock* [1948] Ch 465 at 540.

[153] Birks suggests that a 'proprietary base' is needed ('Mixing and tracing: property and restitution' (1992) 45 CLP 69–98 and *An Introduction to the Law of Restitution*, revd edn (Oxford: Clarendon Press, 1989) at 378).

[154] A. J. Oakley, *Trends in Contemporary Trust Law* (Oxford: Clarendon Press, 1996) at 252, argues that it is 'questionable' whether *Diplock* and *Sinclair* really are authority for the proposition that one has to have '*an initial fiduciary relationship*' (see *Chase Manhattan Bank v. Israel-British Bank (London) Ltd* [1981] 1 Ch 105) as a foundation for equitable tracing.

[155] C. Band, 'The development of the tracing rules in commercial cases' [1997] LMCLQ 65.

[156] (1880) LR 13 Ch D 696.   [157] Ibid. at 709.   [158] Ibid. at 710.   [159] Ibid.   [160] Ibid.

The judge in *Chase Manhattan Bank v. Israel-British Bank (London) Ltd*[161] would doubtless have abandoned the fiduciary requirement entirely had the requirement not been settled by numerous decisions of superior courts. Instead, he chose to relax the requirement in the interests of the justice of that case, by discovering a fiduciary relationship in circumstances that surely did not warrant such a finding. The facts concerned a mistaken overpayment of US$2m made by the claimant bank to the defendant bank. The money overpaid had not previously been subject to any trust or fiduciary obligation, but Goulding J held that the conscience of the defendant bank became subject to a fiduciary duty to respect the claimant's proprietary right *upon receipt* of the plaintiff's monies. Accordingly, *Chase Manhattan* is authority for the proposition that equitable tracing is permissible even when the fiduciary obligation does not arise until the moment at which the claimant's property passes into the defendant's hands.[162] However, since *Chase Manhattan* was decided, Lord Mustill has urged greater restraint in the discovery of fiduciary relationships.[163]

Equitable tracing through mixed substitutions

The process of tracing in equity varies according to whether the substitution was carried out by a wrongdoer or by an innocent party. Professor Smith has observed that the rules of tracing '*subordinate the interests of wrongdoers, and attempt to deal equitably with everyone else*';[164] thus innocent claimants to a mixed fund will be satisfied ahead of the claims of the person who wrongfully carried out the mixing.

Substitution carried out by a defendant who is an innocent volunteer

In *Re Diplock*,[165] Lord Greene MR held that a claimant is entitled to trace into mixed funds and assets acquired with mixed funds, even where an innocent volunteer had effected the mixing. He disagreed with the view, adopted by the judge at first instance, that tracing should only be permitted where the mixing takes place in breach of trust, actual or constructive, or in breach of some other fiduciary relationship. However, as we saw when we considered remedies, his Lordship stated that a volunteer recipient of property belonging in equity to another:

> is under no greater duty of conscience to recognise the interest of the equitable owner than that which lies upon a person having an equitable interest in one of two trust funds of 'money' which have become mixed towards the equitable owner of the other. Such a person is not in conscience bound to give precedence to the equitable owner of the other of the two funds[166] ... Equity will not restrain a defendant from asserting a claim save to the extent that it would be unconscionable for him to do so.[167]

---

[161] [1981] 1 Ch 105.

[162] Ibid. *per* Goulding J at 119B–C; *Neste Oy v. Lloyds Bank plc* [1983] 2 Lloyd's Rep 658 at 666.

[163] *Re Goldcorp Exchange Ltd* [1995] 1 AC 74 at 98.

[164] L. Smith, *The Law of Tracing* (Oxford: Oxford University Press, 1997) 278. See also Lord Millett in *Foskett* [2001] 1 AC 102 at 132.   [165] [1948] Ch 465, CA.

[166] Ibid. at 524.   [167] Ibid. at 532.

Lord Millett has since confirmed that:

> [w]here the beneficiary's claim is in competition with the claims of other innocent contributors, there is no basis upon which any of the claims can be subordinated to any of the others.[168]

Substitution carried out by a defendant who is a trustee or other wrongdoer

In *Boscawen v. Bajwa*,[169] the registered proprietor of certain land charged it to a building society and contracted to sell the land to a purchaser who had obtained a mortgage offer from a bank. The bank transferred cash to the purchaser's solicitors for the sole purpose of completing the purchase. The purchaser's solicitors transferred the money to the vendor's solicitors, who then paid it on to the building society in repayment of the vendor's mortgage debt. The building society duly discharged the vendor's mortgage and forwarded the title deeds to the property to the vendor's solicitors. However, the vendor subsequently became insolvent and the sale was never completed. The claimant (who was an ordinary judgment creditor of the vendor) obtained a charging order absolute against the property. The question was whether the claimant's charge had priority over the bank's equitable claim.

The Court of Appeal held that, because the bank's money could be traced into the payment to the building society and had been used towards the discharge of the latter's charge, the bank was entitled to a charge on the property by way of subrogation to the rights of the building society, to the extent that the money had been used to redeem the charge and in priority to any interest of the claimant. Millett LJ rejected the claimant's argument (based upon *Re Diplock*) that the vendor and the bank had both contributed to the discharge of the building society's charge, and should therefore be entitled to the property in proportion to their contributions, thus allowing the plaintiff to assert its charge against the vendor's part. His Lordship considered the present case to be very different to *Re Diplock*. In *Re Diplock*, volunteers had innocently mixed trust monies with their own monies; in the present case, the vendor and his solicitors were not innocent volunteers, although it was true that their actions fell short of dishonesty (because the vendor had relied upon the solicitors and the solicitors had honestly believed that completion was imminent). The vendor must have known that any monies received by his solicitors would only be available to the vendor *on completion* of the sale of the property and after discharge of the vendor's mortgage. He cannot have believed in good faith that he could, at one and the same time, retain possession of the property and use and enjoyment of the proceeds of sale. The vendor's behaviour had not been wholly innocent, so it followed that the more favourable tracing rules that are available to an innocent volunteer could not be relied upon by the vendor or by his successor, the claimant.

In such a case, we know that a claimant is entitled to elect between a proportionate share in the mixed fund and a lien over it. We can now add that this election is available whether the trustee mixed the trust money with his own in a single fund before

---

[168] *Foskett v. McKeown* [2001] 1 AC 102 at 132.   [169] *Boscawen v. Bajwa* [1996] 1 WLR 328.

using it to acquire the mixed substitute or made separate (simultaneous or sequential) payments out of differently owned funds at the moment of acquisition of the mixed substitute.[170] We should also note that, according to the doctrine in *Lupton v. White*,[171]

> if a trustee or agent mixes and confuses the property which he holds in a fiduciary character with his own property, so as that they cannot be separated with perfect accuracy, he is liable for the whole.[172]

In *Re Hallett's*,[173] a trustee died leaving sufficient money in his bank account to satisfy the beneficiaries, but the trustee's general creditors argued that the money in the bank account had been the trustee's own money, not trust money, and claimed that they should therefore be entitled to be satisfied out of the balance ahead of the beneficiaries. It was held that the balance in the account must be treated as belonging to the beneficiaries, because the trustee should be presumed to have withdrawn his own money first rather than to have withdrawn the trust money in breach of trust. A trustee cannot assert that he has done an act improperly which it is open on the facts to find that he has done properly.[174] This rule against 'improper assertion' appears to share the rationale of the maxim 'equity imputes an intention to fulfil an obligation'. However, Professor Smith has argued[175] that there is no need to resort to the subtle equitable 'fiction' of a righteous wrongdoer, when the competition between the claimant and the wrongdoer's creditors can be resolved by following the simple rule that the interests of the wrongdoer (and his personal creditors) should be subordinated to the interests of an innocent claimant.[176]

By extension of *Re Hallett's*, a beneficiary will only be entitled to trace into the '*lowest intermediate balance*' of a mixed bank account.[177] In other words, the beneficiaries will not be entitled to recover the entire value of their claim from the final balance of a mixed account, if, at some time between their monies being paid in and the date of the final balance, the balance of the account dropped below the value of the amount they are claiming. The simple logic to this restriction is that the claimant's property cannot possibly have remained in the account throughout the entire intermediate period if, at some point, withdrawals from the account had reduced the balance to below the sum claimed.

Where there is an insufficient intermediate balance, but a sufficient final balance, the claimant will only be entitled to complete satisfaction of his claim if he can demonstrate that the payments which returned the balance to sufficiency were specifically credited to him. So if a trustee placed £10,000 of trust monies in his private account and then

---

[170] *Foskett v. McKeown* [2001] 1 AC 102 at 131, *per* Lord Millett.

[171] (1808) 15 Ves 432, *per* Lord Eldon.

[172] As expounded by Sir John Stuart VC in *Cook v. Addison* (1869) LR 7 Eq 466 at 470. See the arguments of counsel in *Re Tilley's Will Trusts* [1967] Ch 1179 at 1183.　　　　　　　　　　[173] (1880) LR 13 Ch D 696.

[174] Jessel MR in *Re Hallett's* (1880) LR 13 Ch D 696 at 727.

[175] L. Smith, *The Law of Tracing* (Oxford: Clarendon Press, 1997).

[176] Simon Gardner has also suggested that the presumption that the trustee has withdrawn his or her own monies first is made on the basis that the trustee has been culpable in mixing the fund in the first place and therefore should be the one who suffers the loss: *An Introduction to the Law of Trusts* (Oxford: Clarendon Press, 1990) at 201–2.　　　　　　　　　　[177] *Roscoe v. Winder* [1915] 1 Ch 62, Ch D.

withdrew the entire balance of that account, but later paid a different £10,000 into the account, the beneficiaries will only be entitled to the £10,000 if the payment in had been accompanied by some memorandum or other evidence that the deposit was intended to be to the credit of the beneficiaries. This appears to be an overly formal rule when applied to facts, such as these, which seem to indicate that the trustee *must* have intended to fulfil his obligation to the trust. However, the 'lowest intermediate balance' rule has frequently been reaffirmed. It was even applied in one of the cases arising out of the Robert Maxwell scandal,[178] in which a pension account ended up in credit, but the liquidators were unable to trace into those monies on behalf of defrauded pensioners because there had previously been a nil balance in the account (in fact, the account had been overdrawn).[179]

However, the 'lowest intermediate balance' rule does not mean that trust monies will always be deemed to have been the last monies withdrawn from a mixed account. The principle underlying the decision in *Re Hallett's* was, as we have seen, that the rights of an innocent claimant should be preferred to those of the wrongdoer. This will occasionally lead to a finding that the trustee withdrew trust money first and left his own money in the bank account. Such a finding will be most appropriate where money was withdrawn to acquire a valuable asset that still exists, while the money remaining in the account after the withdrawal has since been expended on assets that have been destroyed, dissipated, or lost. Consider *Re Oatway*:[180] the trustee bought shares with monies from a mixed account, comprising his own monies and those of the trust. At the time of the purchase of the shares, enough money remained in the account to meet the claims of the trust beneficiaries, but, later, the balance in the account was dissipated. Holding that the claimant beneficiaries were able to trace their part of the mixed fund into the shares, Joyce J stated that:

> Whatever alteration of form any property may undergo, the true owner is entitled to seize it in its new shape if he can prove the identity of the original material.[181]

The 'lowest intermediate balance' rule suggests that it would be highly unorthodox to allow tracing into an asset which the defendant acquired before the claimant's money had been misappropriated.[182] And yet, where a debt is incurred to acquire an asset (such as a loan to acquire a car), and the debt is incurred with the intention of repaying it with misapplied trust money and the debt is actually repaid in whole or in part with misapplied trust money, it is arguable that the beneficiaries of the trust are permitted (by 'backward tracing')[183] to trace their money into the asset, to the extent that it has been redeemed (from the debt) by their money.[184]

---

[178] *Bishopsgate v. Homan* [1994] 3 WLR 1270.

[179] *Barlow Clowes International Ltd (in liquidation) and Ors v. Vaughan and Ors* [1992] 4 All ER 22, CA, *per* Woolf LJ.

[180] [1903] 2 Ch 356.

[181] Ibid. at 359. See also *Re Tilley's Will Trusts* [1967] Ch 1179, *per* Ungoed-Thomas J at 1183–4.

[182] *Bishopsgate Investment Management Ltd (in liquidation) v. Homan* [1995] Ch 211, *per* Leggatt LJ at 221. See, generally, M. Conaglen, 'Difficulties with tracing backwards' (2011) 127 LQR 432.

[183] L. Smith, 'Tracing into the payment of a debt' (1995) 54 CLJ 290.

[184] *Bishopsgate Investment Management Ltd (in liquidation) v. Homan* [1995] Ch 211, CA, *per* Dillon LJ at 216. Backward tracing was also approved by a majority of the Court of Appeal in *Foskett v. McKeown* [1998] Ch 265, although that decision was subsequently overturned by the House of Lords on other grounds.

The rule in Clayton's Case

If a trustee places £10,000 belonging to trust A into a current account that already holds £10,000 belonging to trust B, which trust is entitled to the £10,000 balance of the account if the trustee withdraws the other £10,000 and spends it on a luxury cruise? Here is equity's traditional dilemma: which of two innocent parties is to bear the loss? The usual rule for the convenient determination of priority between two innocent equitable claimants is to prefer whichever claim arose first. This is in accordance with the maxim 'where equities are equal, the first in time prevails'.[185] However, a different rule of convenience applies to determine entitlement to the balance of a simple current bank account. The rule, which does not apply in any other context,[186] is called the rule in *Clayton's Case*.[187] It provides that the first payment into the account is presumed to have been withdrawn first, that the second payment is presumed to have been withdrawn second, and so on. Ironically, then, this rule of convenience achieves the opposite result to the maxim. The balance of a bank account will belong to the persons who made the most recent payments into it, so the last in time becomes the first in right.

Applying the rule in *Clayton's Case* to the dispute between trust A and trust B, A will be entitled to the entire balance in the account. This result does not seem at all fair. A rule that was designed to achieve a convenient solution to the complex accounting problems arising where there are numerous and frequent payments into and out of simple bank accounts produces a palpably inequitable result in the context of the dispute between the beneficiaries of trust A and the beneficiaries of trust B. Sir George Jessel MR described the rule in *Clayton's Case* as

> a very convenient rule, and I have nothing to say against it unless there is evidence either of agreement to the contrary or of circumstances from which a contrary intention must be presumed.[188]

In the dispute between trusts A and B, it must surely be presumed that the beneficiaries of the two trusts would have intended some other outcome than the 'all or nothing' solution produced by the rule in *Clayton's Case*. A fairer result would have been for A and B to share the balance in the account in proportion to (*pari passu*) their contributions. Having made equal contributions, they ought to share the balance equally.

This approach was adopted in *Sinclair v. Brougham*.[189] In that case, a building society had been wound up and the question of priority arose between outside creditors, shareholders, and depositors. The assets remaining to be distributed could not satisfy all the claims in full, so the assets were divided *pari passu* between the claimants, according to the amounts credited to them in the books of the society at the commencement of the winding up.[190] It

---

[185] Which we will consider further in Chapter 16.

[186] *Per* Lord Halsbury LC in *Cory Bros & Co Ltd v. Turkish Steamship Mecca (owners), The Mecca* [1897] AC 286 at 290–1. See, also, *Re Diplock* [1948] 1 Ch 465, Ch D.

[187] (1816) 1 Mer 572, *per* Sir William Grant MR at 608–9.

[188] *Re Hallett's Estate* [1880] LR 13 Ch D 696 at 728.   [189] [1914] AC 398.

[190] *Sinclair v. Brougham* was considered by the House of Lords in *Westdeutsche Landesbank Girozentrale v. Islington LBC* [1996] AC 669. Their Lordships declined to follow *Sinclair v. Brougham*, but in relation to a different point.

was confirmed in *El Ajou v. Dollar Land Holdings plc*[191] that the rule in *Clayton's Case* must yield to the contrary intentions of the parties involved. Neither will it apply if it would produce unjust results, provided a practical, alternative method of distribution presents itself. In *Barlow Clowes International Ltd (in liquidation) v. Vaughan*,[192] an investment company went into liquidation, leaving insufficient funds to satisfy the claims of all of its investors. The judge at first instance held that investors should be able to trace into the funds on a 'first in, first out' basis, following the rule in *Clayton's Case*. This was reversed on appeal, where it was held that '[b]*ecause of their shared misfortune, the investors will be presumed to have intended the rule not to apply*';[193] instead, the investors were entitled to claim shares in the final fund in proportion to the size of their original investment. The *Barlow Clowes* approach to the rule in *Clayton's Case* was confirmed in *Commerzbank AG v. IMB Morgan plc*,[194] where it was also held that the rule would not be applied, irrespective of the parties' intentions, if it would produce an unjust result. In fact the so-called 'rule' in *Clayton's Case* is nowadays so often disapplied in the interests of justice that one judge has renamed it the 'exception' in *Clayton's Case*.[195]

Further reading

In addition to the following print sources, the Online Resource Centre accompanying this book contains web links to further reading as well as guide answers to assessment questions relevant to this chapter.

BANT, E., *The Change of Position Defence* (Oxford: Hart Publishing, 2009).

BIRKS, P. B. H., 'Misdirected funds: restitution from the recipient' [1989] LMCLQ 296.

BIRKS, P. B. H., 'Misdirected funds again' (1989) 105 LQR 528.

BIRKS, P. B. H., 'Mixing and tracing: property and restitution' (1992) 45 CLP 69.

BIRKS, P. B. H., 'Persistent problems in misdirected money: a quintet' [1993] LMCLQ 218.

BIRKS, P. B. H., 'Establishing a proprietary base' [1995] Restitution LR 83.

BIRKS, P. B. H., (ed.), *Laundering and Tracing* (Oxford: Clarendon Press, 1995).

BIRKS, P. B. H., 'The necessity of a unitary law of tracing' in *Making Commercial Law: Essays in Honour of Roy Goode* (Oxford: Clarendon Press, 1997) at 239.

FOX, D., *Property Rights in Money* (Oxford: Oxford University Press, 2008).

GROSSEY, S., *The Money Laundering Training Manual* (London: Informa, 2002).

GULLIFER, L., 'Recovery of misappropriated assets: orthodoxy re-established?' [1995] LMCLQ 446.

KHURSHID, S. and MATTHEWS, P., 'Tracing confusion' (1979) 95 LQR 78.

MATTHEWS, P., '"*Specificatio*" in the common law' (1981) 10 Anglo-American LR 121.

---

[191] [1993] 3 All ER 717.
[192] *Sub nom. Vaughan v. Barlow Clowes International Ltd* [1992] 4 All ER 22, CA.
[193] Woolf LJ at 42G–H.
[194] [2005] 1 Lloyd's Rep 298.
[195] *Russell-Cooke Trust Co v. Prentis* [2003] 2 All ER 478, *per* Lindsay J at [55].

MATTHEWS, P., 'The legal and moral limits of common law tracing' in *Laundering and Tracing* (P. Birks, ed.) (Oxford: Clarendon Press, 1995) at 23.

MILLETT, SIR PETER, 'Tracing the proceeds of fraud' (1991) 107 LQR 71.

OAKLEY, A. J., 'The prerequisites of an equitable tracing claim' (1975) 28 CLP 64.

PAWLOWSKI, M., 'Constructive trusts, tracing and the requirement of a fiduciary obligation' (2005) 11 *Trusts and Trustees* 10.

PEARCE, R. A., 'A tracing paper' (1976) 40 Conv 277.

SMITH, L., 'Tracing in *Taylor v. Plumer*: equity in the Court of King's Bench' [1995] LMCLQ 240.

SMITH, L., 'Tracing into the payment of a debt' [1995] CLJ 290.

SMITH, L., *The Law of Tracing* (Oxford: Oxford University Press, 1997).

SMITH, L., 'Simplifying Claims to Traceable Proceeds' (2009) 125 LQR 338.

STEVENS, J., 'Vindicating the proprietary nature of tracing' (2001) Conv 94.

THOMAS, S. B., 'Electronic funds transfer and fiduciary fraud' [2005] JBL 48.

WILLISTON, S., 'The right to follow trust property when confused with other property' (1880) 2 Harv LR 29.

15

The equitable personal liability of strangers to the trust

The reader will recall from the previous chapter that, even where a trust beneficiary has successfully traced misappropriated trust property, the equitable tracing process will only lead to a proprietary remedy against a stranger who still has the trust property in his possession or under his control. If a stranger received trust property, but has not retained it, the beneficiary's proprietary claim will fail. In such a case, the beneficiary (or the trustee)[1] may, however, be able to bring a claim against the stranger personally if the receipt was wrongful. The receipt will be wrongful if the stranger received the trust property for his own benefit knowing that he was doing so against the interests of the true beneficial owner. The receipt will also be wrongful if, having at first received the property legitimately, he later misappropriated it to his own benefit knowing that he was doing so against the interests of the true beneficial owner. The receipt will also be wrongful if a stranger received the trust property as an accessory to a breach of trust even though he never held the trust property for his own benefit. Finally, a stranger may be personally liable as an accessory to a breach of trust even though he never received the trust property at all. Liability 'as an accessory' means liability for dishonest assistance in, or procurement of, a breach of trust. In the previous chapter, we considered how a stranger might be personally liable at common law for having and receiving another person's money or for interfering with another person's property; in this chapter, we are interested in the circumstances in which a stranger may be personally liable in equity for analogous wrongs.

Strangers: who are they?

For present purposes, a stranger to a trust is anyone who is not a trustee or beneficiary of the trust, and a stranger to a fiduciary relationship is anyone who is not the principal

---

[1] It has been said that '*public policy positively requires*' a trustee to take action to recover trust property whenever the trustee has misapplied it in breach of trust (*Montrose Investment Ltd v. Orion Nominees Ltd* [2004] EWCA Civ 1032, CA, *per* Waller LJ at [24]).

or fiduciary in that relationship. On one view, a properly appointed agent to a trust or fiduciary relationship is not a stranger to it, but we will include agents within our definition of stranger. However, the fact that agents may be given legitimate control of trust assets means that they are a somewhat special case, as we will see when we consider liability for inconsistent dealing with trust property.

Strangers who make the most attractive defendants are very often solicitors, accountants, banks, and building societies, because they have 'deep pockets' and tend to be well insured, and because it is hard for expert commercial agents of this sort to convince a court that they were ignorant of the wrongful nature of their activities.

Although we are mainly concerned with the liability of strangers, it is implicit from the judgment of the Court of Appeal in *Re Montagu's Settlement Trusts*,[2] a case in which the court was willing to consider an action brought by one beneficiary against the estate of another beneficiary, that personal liability of the sort considered in this chapter might in an appropriate case be extended to beneficiaries. Normally this is not necessary, of course, because of the possibility of impounding the beneficiaries' interest,[3] but, in *Re Montagu's*, the defendant beneficiary, being a deceased life tenant, no longer had any interest under the trust that could be impounded.

Policy and practice

In the light of the fact that commercial agents make attractive targets for claimant beneficiaries, a number of policy considerations and practical measures have been introduced to give strangers some degree of protection.

Policy

Judges bear in mind a number of important policy considerations when formulating the laws to govern the liability of strangers. First, they presume against any rule that will cause an honest, competent, commercial party to be forever looking over his shoulder and watching his back when the efficiency of commerce demands that he should keep his eyes on the task in hand. Second, and related to the first, courts are mindful of the need to ensure a constant flow of persons willing to act as agents to trusts and, because such persons automatically assume contractual and tortious obligations to the trustees, the courts are concerned that they should only become personally liable to the beneficiaries in very limited circumstances.[4] In his seminal judgment in *Barnes v. Addy*,[5] Lord Selborne LC stated that strangers are not to be made liable '*merely because they act as the agents of trustees in transactions within their legal powers, transactions perhaps, of which a Court of Equity may disapprove*',[6] but he held that they may be liable

---

[2] [1987] Ch 264.   [3] See Chapter 13.
[4] Lord Selborne in *Barnes v. Addy* (1874) LR 9 Ch App 244.   [5] (1874) LR 9 Ch App 244.
[6] Ibid. at 251.

for wrongful receipt of trust property or wrongful assistance in a breach of trust. Third, mindful of the potentially disastrous implications for careers and livelihoods, judges are especially concerned to exercise caution before finding that a person, especially a professional person, has acted dishonestly. Fourth, a basic principle of economic efficiency and justice, that loss should be borne first by those who assume the risk of such loss and are best able to avoid it,[7] inclines the courts to hold that losses flowing from a trustee's breach of trust should be borne first by the beneficiaries, rather than by an innocent third party who happened to have dealings with a rogue trustee.[8] The argument that a fair allocation of risk raises a presumption that the beneficiaries should bear the loss is strongest where beneficiaries have the power to remove their trustees[9] (especially where they are able to do so without bringing the trust to an end).[10]

Practice

Any commercial agent in a real dilemma as to the propriety of a proposed course of action can apply to the court for a 'binding declaration' that the proposed course of action is proper,[11] or for directions as to the best way to proceed. If the declaration is granted and the agent acts according to its terms, the agent will be immune to any subsequent action brought by a beneficiary, even if the court's guidance is later overturned on appeal or disapproved by a higher court:

> it seems almost inconceivable that a bank which takes the initiative in seeking the court's guidance should subsequently be held to have acted dishonestly so as to incur accessory liability.[12]

The problem with this approach is that it represents a severe deviation from the policy that a commercial person should not be required to take time-consuming defensive measures. It also seems far from certain that the courts will be willing to exercise their jurisdiction to sanction transactions in advance when there is a risk that to do so might prejudice interested parties. So the judge in *United Mizrahi Bank Ltd v. Doherty*,[13] although accepting that it could not be right for solicitors to be looking over their shoulders when acting for a defendant in a suit for breach of trust, stopped short of allowing the solicitors to take their fees out of money that was the subject matter of the claim. The judge explained that, if the solicitors took their fees prior to the conclusion of the matter, they would assume the risk, albeit a small one, that they might be held personally liable, in the event of their client losing the case, for wrongful receipt of trust money.

---

[7] See, generally, G. Watt, 'Personal liability for receipt of trust property: allocating the risks' in *Modern Studies in Property Law* (E. Cooke, ed.) (Oxford: Hart Publishing, 2005) vol. III, 91.

[8] *Hunter v. Walters* (1871–2) LR 7 Ch App 75 at 85.

[9] *Saunders v. Vautier* (1841) 10 LJ Ch 354; *Re Brockbank* [1948] Ch 206.

[10] Trusts of Land and Appointment of Trustees Act 1996, s. 19.   [11] CPR, r. 40.20.

[12] *Governor and Company of the Bank of Scotland v. A Ltd* [2001] 1 WLR 751, *per* Lord Woolf CJ at 768D.

[13] [1998] 2 All ER 230.

Even if a stranger omits to take such precautions and finds himself in court, he can take advantage of another rule of practice: the privilege against self-incrimination. This rule permits a defendant to a civil action to refuse to give evidence that might be used against him in subsequent criminal proceedings. Obviously, a defendant who is accused of dishonest assistance in or procurement of a breach of trust runs the very real risk of a criminal action being brought against him.[14] The privilege against self-incrimination has been described as an *'archaic and unjustifiable survival from the past'*,[15] but, as a result of the enactment of the Human Rights Act 1998, it may be likely to remain.[16]

The nature of liability

A person who knowingly receives a beneficiary's or principal's property transferred in breach of trust or fiduciary duty will be personally liable to account to the beneficiary or principal for the amount received plus any personal profits made by the recipient while in possession of the property. Of course, if he is still in possession of the property and the profits, the beneficiary will simply trace them into the defendant's hands and recover them by asserting his proprietary entitlement to them. However, to recover assets or monies *'which the defendants have paid away the plaintiffs must subject them to a personal liability to account as constructive trustees'*.[17]

Personal liability in equity

When trustees appoint an agent, he generally assumes personal obligations to the trustees under the common law of agency, contract, and tort. In the ordinary course of events, he will not assume direct obligations to the beneficiaries under the trust[18] and the beneficiaries are, generally speaking, unable to bring a common law action against the agent.[19] The agent will only be personally liable in equity to the beneficiaries directly if his conduct is out of the ordinary as being a wrongful receipt of trust property or wrongful assistance in a breach of trust.

A personal action against a stranger is most useful where a proprietary claim to recover trust assets or their value in substitute assets will be inadequate. This will be the case if the defendant has no relevant 'target' assets in his possession, so that a proprietary claim cannot be brought at all, and if the defendant does have such assets in his possession, but they have decreased in value or extent while in his hands. A practical way of looking at the latter situation is to say that personal liability for knowing receipt

---

[14] C. Harpum, 'Accessory liability for procuring or assisting a breach of trust' (1995) 111 LQR 545.

[15] *AT & T Istel Ltd v. Tully* [1993] AC 45, HL, *per* Lord Templeman at 53.

[16] The Act requires judges to interpret English law consistently with the European Convention on Human Rights (1953, Cmd. 8969), including Art. 6, which establishes the right to a fair trial.

[17] *Agip v. Africa* [1990] Ch 265, *per* Millett J at 290H (affirmed CA [1991] Ch 547).

[18] Chapter 2, 'Tort'.   [19] *Parker-Tweedale v. Dunbar Bank plc* [1991] Ch 12, CA.

holds the defendant liable to account for the whole amount wrongfully received while allowing the defendant to deduct from the personal account such trust property as, still being in his possession, he is liable to surrender in satisfaction of the claimant's proprietary claim. Beyond this, a stranger will also be liable to account for personal gains made from the wrongful use of trust property in his possession or under his control. A stranger will also be liable for personal gains made from assisting or procuring a breach of trust even though he never had possession of trust property. On this basis, a solicitor would have to account for any fees paid to him by a company director for the drawing up of false documents for the purpose of misallocating the company's funds. The director would be committing a breach of trust[20] and the solicitor would be assisting in it.

From the claimant's point of view, the downside of personal liability against a stranger is that the claimant will have to 'join the queue' of personal claims against the defendant's estate in the event of the defendant's death or insolvency.

Liability 'as constructive trustees'

The fact that strangers are personally liable in equity '*to account as constructive trustees*'[21] does not mean that strangers are liable because they actually are trustees; rather, they are liable *as if* they were trustees. The description '*is nothing more than a formula for equitable relief. The Court of Equity says that the defendant shall be liable in equity, as though he were a trustee.*'[22] Where a stranger is liable for dishonest assistance in a breach of trust, he will frequently never have held trust assets at all, so he is clearly no trustee in the orthodox sense. Where a stranger wrongfully receives trust assets in the knowledge that someone else is beneficially entitled to them, he may properly be described as a constructive trustee of the assets as long as he retains them (the point is controversial),[23] but whether he is or is not a trustee of trust property in his hands, he is personally liable in equity for knowing receipt of trust property 'as if he were a constructive trustee'. Sir Robert Megarry VC made the following observation some years ago:

> Tracing is primarily a means of determining the right of property, whereas the imposition of a constructive trust [by reason of knowing receipt of trust property] creates personal obligations that go beyond mere property rights.[24]

Trusteeship *de son tort*

> [I]f one, not being a trustee and not having authority from a trustee, takes upon himself to intermeddle with the trust matters or to do acts characteristic of the office of trustee, he may

---

[20] See Chapter 2, 'Corporations'.

[21] Millett J in *Agip (Africa) Ltd v. Jackson* [1990] Ch 265.

[22] *Selangor United Rubber Estates Ltd v. Cradock (a bankrupt) (No. 3)* [1968] 1 WLR 1555, *per* Ungoed-Thomas J at 1582. Approved by Millett LJ in *Paragon Finance plc v. D. B. Thakerar & Co (a firm)* [1999] 1 All ER 400.

[23] See Chapter 14.   [24] *Re Montagu's Settlement Trust* [1987] Ch 264 at 285.

thereby make himself what is called in law a trustee of his own wrong—i.e. a trustee de son tort, or, as it is also termed, a constructive trustee.[25]

A number of features distinguish the constructive trustee *de son tort* from the stranger who is liable for knowing receipt or dishonest assistance. The former takes it upon himself to act for the benefit of the beneficiaries of an existing trust, he does not purport to act in his own right, and, if he properly discharges the trust that he has assumed, he will not be liable: a trustee *de son tort 'is just as much accountable and on substantially the same principles as the express trustee'.*[26] The latter, on the other hand, does not purport to act for the beneficiaries; he acts on his own account, and the nature of his liability 'as a constructive trustee' is essentially independent of the express trust: it simply arises at the moment of the knowing receipt or dishonest assistance.[27]

The fact that a trustee *de son tort* does not act in his own right, but in the right of another, means that a trustee *de son tort* cannot rely upon the passage of time to bar a claim against him. In this respect, a trustee *de son tort* resembles an express trustee, who is never able to plead passage of time to prevent a trust beneficiary from recovering property from him.[28] A trustee *de son tort* has even been referred to as an actual[29] or de facto trustee.[30]

Personal liability in equity for receipt

Under this heading, we are concerned with what Lord Nicholls referred to as '*the liability of a person as a* recipient *of trust property or its traceable proceeds*'.[31] His Lordship asserts that '[r]*ecipient liability is restitution-based*', but neither the Privy Council nor the UK Supreme Court has so far found an opportunity fully to explain what this means. The law concerning the personal liability of a recipient of trust property is in a decidedly unhealthy state and much in need of treatment by the highest court at the earliest opportunity; in fact, the problems are so entrenched that they may require a legislative solution.[32] Nearly everything about this head of liability is controversial, including theories as to its present nature and ideas as to its future reform. Most commentators agree that liability under this head is merely personal, but while some argue that liability should be based upon the stranger's wrongdoing,[33] others argue that unauthorized receipt of another's wealth is an

---

[25] *Mara v. Browne* (1896) 1 Ch 199, *per* Smith LJ at 209; *Soar v. Ashwell* [1893] 2 QB 390; *Burdick v. Garrick* (1870) LR 5 Ch App 233; *Re Barney* [1892] 2 Ch 265; *Williams-Ashman v. Price and Williams* [1942] Ch 219.

[26] *Bishopsgate Investment Management Ltd (in liquidation) v. Maxwell and Anor* [1993] Ch 1, CA, *per* Dillon LJ at 38.

[27] *Selangor United Rubber Estates Ltd v. Cradock* [1968] 1 WLR 1555.

[28] 'No time bars a direct trust as between cestui que trust and trustee' (*Beckford v. Wade* (1810) 17 Ves 87, *per* Grant MR at 97).   [29] *Taylor v. Davies* [1920] AC 636 at 651.

[30] *Dubai Aluminium Co Ltd v. Salaam* [2002] 3 WLR 1913, HL, *per* Lord Millett at para. 138.

[31] *Royal Brunei Airlines Sdn Bhd v. Tan* [1995] 2 AC 378 at 382D.

[32] C. Harpum, 'Accessory liability for procuring or assisting a breach of trust' (1995) 111 LQR 545 at 548.

[33] S. Gardner, 'Knowing assistance and knowing receipt: taking stock' (1996) 112 LQR 56 at 85–93.

unjust enrichment that should give rise to strict liability to make restitution, regardless of the recipient's honesty or state of knowledge, albeit that such strict liability should be subject to the usual restitutionary defence of innocent change of position.[34] Even amongst those who agree that a recipient's liability is only ever fault-based, there are those who argue that nothing less than dishonesty should give rise to liability, others who argue that actual knowledge that the property is trust property should suffice to render the stranger liable, and still others who argue that a stranger will be liable if he ought reasonably to have appreciated that he had received trust property in breach of the trust.[35] It is reassuring that at least one commentator sees a silver lining to this cloud of uncertainty: *'It may be that these unresolved conceptual difficulties are no bad thing as equity seeks flexible tools to rationalise the complex transactional environment of the modern commercial world.'*[36]

Knowing receipt

As things stand, a stranger who receives trust property will only be personally liable in equity if the relevant kind of knowledge and the relevant kind of receipt are proved against him. The relevant kind of knowledge is knowledge of the breach of trust and the relevant kind of receipt is receipt that is beneficial to the stranger. The essence of these requirements is that a stranger will be personally liable in equity if he receives assets for his own benefit knowing that he does so to the detriment of a person with better proprietary title to the assets. The remedy for knowing receipt is essentially compensatory *'notwithstanding that it may also be described as restitutionary'.*[37] Simon Gardner argues that knowing receipt should be seen to be *'simply the usual liability for failure to preserve trust property, applicable to all trustees, given particular application to those who are trustees because they receive illicitly transferred trust property'.*[38]

Knowledge

A person who receives property innocently, but later discovers that it was trust property, is liable to account as a constructive trustee from the moment he is aware of the true facts.[39] In other words, a recipient is not liable as a constructive trustee for knowing receipt until he knows about the breach of trust[40] and, if he parts with the property never having discovered that it was trust property, he will escape liability.

---

[34] Lord Nicholls of Birkenhead, 'Knowing receipt: the need for a new landmark' in *Restitution: Past, Present and Future* (W. R. Cornish et al., eds) (Oxford: Hart Publishing, 1999); P. Birks, 'Receipt' in *Breach of Trust* (P. Birks and A. Pretto, eds) (Oxford: Hart Publishing, 2002).

[35] C. Harpum, 'Liability for intermeddling with trusts' (1987) 50 MLR 217; S. B. Thomas, 'Goodbye knowing receipt, hello unconscientious receipt' (2001) 21 OJLS 239.

[36] S. Gardner, 'Knowing assistance and knowing receipt: taking stock' (1996) 112 LQR 56.

[37] *Charter plc v. City Index Ltd* [2007] 1 WLR 26, Ch D.

[38] (2009) 125 LQR 20 at 23 (a note on the decision of the Court of Appeal in *City Index Ltd v. Gawler* [2007] EWCA Civ 1382; [2008] Ch 313).   [39] *Re Montagu's Settlement Trusts* [1987] Ch 264.

[40] *Agip v. Africa* [1990] Ch 265; *Papamichael v. National Westminster Bank plc* [2003] 1 Lloyd's Rep 341 at 375; *Criterion Properties plc v. Stratford UK Properties LLC* [2003] 1 WLR 2108.

Degrees of knowledge

One of the more complex aspects of fixing liability on a stranger for knowing receipt of trust property is ascertaining the degree of knowledge that is required to give rise to liability: is it essential that the stranger actually knew of the trust, or is it sufficient that he turned a blind eye to the obvious, or even that he ought to have been suspicious? Presumably, there is a whole spectrum of states of knowledge ranging from actual complete awareness at one end to complete and utter ignorance at the other. One might have thought it beyond the wit of anyone to produce a comprehensive categorization of types of knowledge, still less to identify knowledge as falling within one of five degrees, but, according to the judges, not even this monumental task is beyond the skills of leading Chancery counsel. In the *Baden* case,[41] counsel submitted that knowledge is of five types for the purpose of liability:

(i) actual knowledge;

(ii) wilfully shutting one's eyes to the obvious (sometimes referred to as 'Nelsonian blindness'[42] or 'blind-eye knowledge'.[43] In *Manifest Shipping Co v. Uni-Polaris Shipping Co*, Lord Clyde held that such knowledge requires '*a conscious reason for blinding the eye. There must be at least a suspicion of a truth about which you do not want to know and which you refuse to investigate*'[44]);

(iii) wilfully and recklessly[45] failing to make such inquiries as an honest and reasonable man would make;

(iv) knowledge of circumstances that would indicate the facts to an honest and reasonable man;

(v) knowledge of circumstances that would put an honest and reasonable man on inquiry.

Peter Gibson J adopted the classification, adding the refinement that a stranger in (ii) or (iii) is to be treated as if he had actual knowledge, whereas a person in categories (iv) or (v) is to be treated as having constructive knowledge only. Although the *Baden* case did not concern liability for knowing receipt, but for knowing assistance (as dishonest assistance was then known), his Lordship expressly stated that he could see 'no justification' for treating the two bases of liability differently in this regard.[46]

Millett J adopted the same classification in *Agip (Africa) Ltd v. Jackson*,[47] another case concerned with dishonest assistance, but warned against '*over refinement or a too ready*

---

[41] *Baden v. Société Générale Pour Favoriser le Développement du Commerce et de l'Industrie en France* [1993] 1 WLR 509, Ch D, [1983] BCLC 325. The case was heard in 1983, but did not appear in the weekly law reports until 10 years later.

[42] Alluding to the famous incident at the Battle of Copenhagen when Admiral Lord Nelson is reputed to have placed a spyglass to his blind eye to avoid sight of a signal calling him to disengage from the Danish fleet.

[43] *Credit Suisse (Monaco) SA v. Attar* [2004] EWHC 374; *Manifest Shipping Co v. Uni-Polaris Shipping Co* [2003] 1 AC 469, HL.   [44] [2003] 1 AC 469 at 481.

[45] See, for example, *Cantor Fitzgerald International v. Edward Bird et al* [2002] WL 1446181.

[46] *Baden v. Société Générale pour Favoriser le Développement du Commerce et de l'Industrie en France* [1993] 1 WLR 509, Ch D; [1983] BCLC 325 at para. [249].   [47] [1990] Ch 265.

assumption that categories (iv) or (v) are necessarily cases of constructive notice only.[48] In his Lordship's judgment, '[t]*he true distinction is between honesty and dishonesty. It is essentially a jury question*'.[49] His Lordship suggested that a stranger who suspects wrongdoing, but fails to make inquiries because he does not wish to know the truth (category (ii)), or considers it to be none of his business (category (iii)), acts dishonestly and cannot complain if he is treated as having actual knowledge for the purpose of liability for knowing receipt. In this vein, Scott LJ observed in *Polly Peck International plc v. Nadir (No. 2)*,[50] yet another case concerning assistance rather than receipt, that the *Baden* categories are not '*rigid categories with clear and precise boundaries*' and that '[o]*ne category may merge imperceptibly into another*'.[51] For his Lordship, the real question is whether the stranger should have been '*suspicious of the propriety of what was being done*'.[52] Vinelott J in *Eagle Trust Plc v. SBC Securities Ltd*[53] confirmed that liability based on knowledge in categories (iv) and (v) is not appropriate to commercial transactions, because the basis of commercial transactions should be trust and not suspicion.[54] Certainly, a stranger is not expected to entertain every suspicion that might be aroused. A bank should be especially slow to refuse a deposit into a customer's account. In *Tayeb v. HSBC Bank plc*,[55] the court reminded banks that the proper way to respond to concerns about money laundering is to apply to court for a declaration of interim directions. That case concerned the transfer, on 21 September 2000, of £944,114.27 to an account recently opened by a Libyan business man at a Derby branch of the HSBC. The bank manager suspected money laundering, which in the circumstances was a reasonable suspicion, but his unreasonable response (as the court found it) was to send the money back to the transferring bank. In the event, the transfer was found to be perfectly legitimate and the claimant was awarded judgment in the sum of £944,114.23 with interest from 21 September 2000. The judge held that the anti-money laundering procedures to which banks are subject

> do not necessarily lead to the bank having to disengage from the transfer and they certainly do not normally involve the retransfer to the payor, a course which would be most unlikely to protect the rightful beneficiary of the fund and which might well involve tipping off those criminally responsible[56]

and

> [i]f banks are to be entitled to depart from their contracts with customers, on the basis of suspicion of unlawfulness and of general banking practice, that practice has to be clearly proved.[57]

Of course, whether the court would have been quite so censorious had the bank followed the same course exactly one year later—that is, 'post 9/11'—may be doubted.

---

48 Ibid. at 293.   49 Ibid.   50 [1992] 2 Lloyd's Rep 238, CA.   51 Ibid. at 243.
52 Ibid. at 244.   53 [1993] 1 WLR 484.
54 See also *Cowan de Groot v. Eagle Trust plc* [1992] 4 All ER 700.
55 [2004] EWHC 1529.   56 Ibid. at [77].   57 Ibid. at [66].

In *Bank of Credit and Commerce International (Overseas) Ltd v. Akindele*,[58] the Court of Appeal held that the *Baden* categories are not particularly helpful in cases, of knowing receipt. In such cases, a single test, asking whether it would be unconscionable for the recipient to retain the benefits of the receipt, is sufficient. This is reminiscent of the older formulation which asks whether the defendant's conscience became 'sufficiently affected for it to be right to bind him by the obligations of a constructive trustee'.[59]

Dishonesty, want of probity, and unconscionability

A leading authority on knowing receipt is still *Re Montagu's Settlement Trust*,[60] decided shortly after *Baden*. The action was brought by the remainderman of a trust (the eleventh Duke of Manchester) against the estate of the deceased life tenant, alleging that the life tenant (the tenth Duke of Manchester) had knowingly received trust property from the trustees during his lifetime, which he knew the trustees had transferred in breach of trust. The claim failed, because the situation resulted from an 'honest muddle' involving all concerned, including the failure by the trust solicitor to make a clear inventory distinguishing trust property from property to which the tenth Duke was absolutely entitled. It was held that the tenth Duke might have known in the past that he was not entitled to the property he received, but he was not liable for knowing receipt because he had 'genuinely forgotten' that fact by the date of the receipt.[61]

Megarry VC held that, for the purpose of fixing liability as a constructive trustee for knowing receipt, the claimant must establish 'want of probity' on the defendant's part. The claimant is not required to prove that the defendant was positively dishonest, but merely to establish that the defendant's actions are not consistent with how an honest person would have acted in his situation. 'Want of probity' literally means 'lacking in proof': the proof that is lacking is proof of honesty. His Lordship held that, of the *Baden* categories, only types (i), (ii), and (iii) would suffice for liability. He doubted that the accusation of negligence implicit in types (iv) and (v) is consistent with an accusation of 'want of probity'. It is notable, though, that even categories (iv) or (v) make reference to honesty.

In *Hillsdown Holdings plc v. Pensions Ombudsman*,[62] the plc was held liable for knowing receipt. It had persuaded the trustees of its employees' pension scheme to transfer a pension surplus to it. Upholding the Ombudsman's decision to require the company to refund the surplus, Knox J adopted the judgment of Megarry VC in *Re Montagu's*:

> In considering whether a constructive trust has arisen in a case of the knowing receipt of trust property, the basic question is whether the conscience of the recipient is sufficiently affected to justify the imposition of such a trust.[63]

---

[58] [2001] Ch 437, considered further later.

[59] *Relfo Ltd (In Liquidation) v. Varsani* [2012] EWHC 2168 (Ch), applying *Re Montagu's Settlement Trusts* [1987] Ch 264.   [60] [1987] Ch 264.

[61] Forgetting general knowledge of a fact can excuse a trustee, but forgetting a fact to which the trustee was put on actual notice will not be excused. (See *AON Pension Trustees Ltd v. MCP Pension Trustees Ltd* [2010] EWCA Civ 377; [2011] 3 WLR 455.)

[62] [1997] 1 All ER 862.   [63] [1987] Ch 264 at 285.

Although there was never any suggestion that the company had acted dishonestly, Knox J held that it had not been as innocent as the defendants in *Re Montagu's* and *Carl Zeiss Stiftung v. Herbert Smith (No. 2)*.[64]

In *Bank of Credit and Commerce International (Overseas) Ltd v. Akindele*,[65] the Court of Appeal confirmed that it is not necessary to prove that a defendant was dishonest in order to fix him with liability for knowing receipt. The liquidators of the bank had sought to recover US$6.79m from the defendant on the basis of personal liability for assistance in a breach of trust or wrongful receipt of trust property. In 1985, A had advanced US$10m to a company controlled by the bank under a false loan agreement. In 1988, A received US$16.79m under the agreement. The claimants argued that A's dishonesty could be inferred from his knowledge of the artificial character of the loan and from his receipt of the unusually high return of 15 per cent compound interest.

At first instance, the court dismissed the claim on the ground that the claimant had failed to prove that the defendant had been dishonest. The Court of Appeal held that it is not necessary to prove that a defendant was dishonest in order to fix him with liability for knowing receipt, but dismissed the appeal on the ground that the state of the defendant's knowledge in 1985 was not such as to make it unconscionable for him to enter into the transaction and, crucially, did not render it unconscionable for him to retain the benefits of the transaction in 1988, notwithstanding the rumours that were then circulating about the integrity of the bank's management.[66] In fact, their Lordships' judgments were concerned as much with 'unconscionable retention' as with 'knowing receipt'. This case can be compared with *Goldspan Ltd v. Patel*,[67] in which a third party received £100,000 in the course of a series of transactions the honesty of which had been called into question. The recipient was permitted to retain the money because he had been owed £100,000 by the transferor. Suppose that, in another case, a fake 'loan' were fabricated as part of a money-laundering scam? Do decisions such as this have the potential to play into the hands of fraudsters?

In *BCCI (Overseas) Ltd v. Akindele*, the defendant escaped liability because he could not be taken to know *for a fact* that the bank had been involved in a breach of trust; he could only be taken to have known that there were rumours to that effect. This raises a nice question: if a defendant has sure and certain knowledge of a rumour or allegation of breach of trust, is his conscience bound so as to give rise to personal liability in equity for knowing receipt? The court in *BCCI (Overseas) Ltd v. Akindele* thought not. It identified the crucial question to be whether the defendant himself had cause to believe the allegation. A similar approach was taken in *Carl Zeiss Stiftung v. Herbert Smith (No. 2)*.[68] An action was brought against one of the largest firms of solicitors in the UK, which was acting in litigation for a West German company against an East German company. Both companies shared a common ancestry before Germany was divided into East and West, but, some time after the division, the East German company alleged that profits made by the West German company had been made using intellectual property belonging to the East German company. The issue which concerns us arose because

[64] [1969] 2 Ch 276. [65] [2001] Ch 437.
[66] Ibid. at 455. [67] [2012] EWHC 1447 (Ch). [68] [1969] 2 Ch 276.

the East German company claimed that legal fees paid by the West German company to the firm of solicitors represented money that should have been held on trust by the West German company for the East German company. It was therefore claimed that the partners of the firm were personally liable for wrongful assistance in a breach of trust or for knowing receipt of trust property in breach of trust. The Court of Appeal found that the firm of solicitors had actual knowledge of the allegations made by the East German company against the West German company, but it held that knowledge of a *claim* that a trust existed was not enough to found liability as a constructive trustee.

The basis of the decision in *Carl Zeiss* appears to be the policy concern that we noted at the start of this chapter, that solicitors and other commercial agents should not be required to be forever '*watching their backs*'.[69] In *Carl Zeiss*, that policy concern was compounded by the policy concern to protect the due process of litigation, because solicitors would cease to act if every allegation were treated as established fact.[70]

None of this should be taken to suggest that a defendant will escape personal liability if it runs the risk of receiving misapplied trust assets. In *Armstrong DLW GmbH v. Winnington Networks Ltd*,[71] a fraudster tricked the claimant into transferring EU carbon emission allowances ('EUAs') to it, which the fraudster then sold on to the defendant. The court held that the defendant was personally liable for unconscionable receipt of misapplied trust property, the relevant trust being the constructive trust under which the fraudster was bound to exercise its legal possession and control of the EUAs for the benefit of the claimant. The finding of unconscionability was based on the fact that relevant personnel of the defendant company knew that the fraudster might not have been entitled to sell (either, applying the *Baden* categories of knowledge, because they had willfully shut their eyes to the obvious or because they had recklessly failed to make such inquiries as an honest and reasonable person would make[72]).

Overreaching, knowledge, and notice

The *authorized* sale of a trust asset by all of the trustees has the effect of transferring the beneficiaries' interest in the asset to the proceeds of sale. The process is called 'overreaching'. In the case of land, special statutory rules restrict overreaching to cases in which the trustees are at least two in number or a trust corporation.[73] However, in this chapter, we are concerned with the consequences for third parties when trust assets are transferred, whether by sale or voluntary transfer, without authority. In such cases, the doctrine of overreaching has no application.[74] Accordingly, the question of whether

---

[69] *United Mizrahi Bank Ltd v. Doherty* [1998] 2 All ER 230.

[70] See the comments of Pennycuick J at first instance in *Carl Zeiss Stiftung v. Herbert Smith (No. 2)* [1969] 2 Ch 276. See also C. Harpum, 'The stranger as constructive trustee' (1986) 102 LQR 114; P. Birks, 'Misdirected funds: restitution from the recipient' [1989] LMCLQ 296.   [71] [2012] EWHC 1; [2012] Ch 156 (Ch).

[72] Ibid. at para. [293]. Note that the descriptors of knowledge types are taken from the *Baden* case.

[73] Law of Property Act 1925, ss. 2 and 27(2).

[74] See further, the argument set out by David Fox in 'Overreaching' in *Breach of Trust* (P. Birks and A. Pretto, eds) (Oxford: Hart Publishing, 2002) 95 at 97.

or not the purchaser is bound by the beneficiaries' interests will fall to be determined according to the purchaser's state of knowledge or notice. Which it is to be, knowledge or notice, is our immediate concern.

When a person acquires legal title to *land* for valuable consideration in good faith he is generally held to take free of any equitable interests under trusts of which he had no notice. Notice includes notice of matters he *has* discovered (actual notice) or *would have* discovered (constructive notice) by carrying out the ordinary searches that a prudent purchaser would carry out. They include physical inspection of the land and investigation of title, which includes searches of relevant registers of title and interests. Notice is not the same thing as knowledge. A purchaser might have actual knowledge of an interest, but it will not be binding on him unless it is an interest that the usual conveyancing rules require him to take notice of.[75] Conversely, a purchaser

> may have actual notice of a fact and yet not know it. He may have been supplied in the course of a conveyancing transaction with a document and so have actual notice of its content, but he may not in fact have read it.[76]

The significant distinction between land conveyancing and other commercial transactions, such as the loan arrangement entered into by the defendant in *BCCI (Overseas) Ltd v. Akindele*, is the degree to which the transactions in both cases are governed by established investigation norms. In the majority of commercial transactions involving the transfer of property, the process of investigating whether or not the transferor is entitled to transfer the property is not as sophisticated as that which governs the purchase of land. Nevertheless, if the difference between the 'investigation norms' governing land transfer and other transactions is only a matter of degree, there is an argument for applying an adapted, less sophisticated, version of the doctrine of notice to a whole range of commercial transactions.[77] Accordingly, in relation to any transaction, two questions should be asked before it could be established that the defendant transferee did, or did not, have notice of the beneficiaries' interests: first, what investigative techniques do reasonable and honest commercial transferees of certain assets normally employ to determine whether the transferor of those assets was entitled to transfer them?; second, has the defendant complied with those investigation norms?

According to Lord Millett, as long as one accepts that, outside the context of land transfer, the investigation standards of an honest and reasonable person are likely to be undemanding,[78] there may be some scope to apply the doctrine of notice to other commercial transactions: '*There is no basis for requiring actual knowledge of the breach of trust, let alone dishonesty, as a condition of liability. Constructive notice is sufficient.*'[79] However, in the same case, Lord Millett acknowledged that there is

---

[75] An example is a non-registered land charge (Law of Property Act 1925, s. 199(1)(i)).

[76] *Eagle Trust plc v. SBC Securities* [1993] 1 WLR 484, *per* Vinelott J at 494A/B.

[77] '*There is no obvious reason why the doctrine of notice should not be employed as the test of liability for knowing receipt*' (C. Harpum, 'Liability for intermeddling with trusts' (1987) 50 MLR 217 at 221(iv)).

[78] A point that his Lordship made as the judge at first instance in *El Ajou v. Dollar Land Holdings plc* [1993] 3 All ER 717.   [79] *Twinsectra Ltd v. Yardley* [2002] 2 AC 164 at 194.

powerful academic support for the proposition that the liability of the recipient is the same as in other cases of restitution, that is to say strict but subject to a change of position defence.[80]

The strict liability argument is considered next, together with the author's own submission that the strict liability option may be more compelling if, in addition to the change of position defence, the defendant could raise in his defence the fact that he had complied with a recognized set of investigation norms. This would introduce the essence of the doctrine of notice into the strict liability test, without engendering the confusion that would arise from adopting the doctrine directly from orthodox land law.[81]

Strict liability

Professor Birks has proposed that if one leaves to one side as an independent question the recipient's personal liability for the wrongful nature of the receipt, a stranger who receives another's wealth, whether in the form of equitable or legal benefits, is unjustly enriched and personally liable to make restitution to the person at whose expense the unjust enrichment was acquired.[82] The liability to make restitution is strict, but subject to the usual restitutionary defences, including the recipient's innocent change of position and the claimant's consent.

In essence, Professor Birks' argument is that the restitutionary remedy that was made available to the legal owners in *Lipkin Gorman*[83] should be extended to equitable owners such as beneficiaries under a trust. However, even if Professor Birks' analysis is correct, in which he is by no means isolated,[84] it has to overcome an apparent conflict with the policy that commercial parties should not be required to be forever watching their backs. Nourse LJ in *BCCI (Overseas) Ltd v. Akindele*[85] considered the strict liability approach to be 'unworkable' in practice, but the likelihood remains that an appropriate version of it will be more workable than an approach based on the vague notion of unconscionability adopted in that case. The challenge is to identify an appropriate version of the strict liability approach.

It is submitted that an improved version of the strict liability approach would be one which incorporates a defence based on the defendant's compliance with investigation norms, in addition to the usual defence of change of position. The doctrine of notice is, in essence, a doctrine designed to protect purchasers who have complied with a set of investigation norms, the 'investigation norms' defence can therefore be seen to introduce a version of the doctrine of notice and thereby to offset the draconian character of strict liability. The relevant question in each case would be whether or not the defendant had complied with normal precautionary searches and made normal precautionary

---

[80] [2002] 2 AC 164. Therefore constructive notice 'may not be necessary'.

[81] See *Re Montagu's Settlement Trust* [1987] Ch 264 at 271.

[82] See, for example, P. Birks, 'Receipt' in *Breach of Trust* (P. Birks and A. Pretto, eds) (Oxford: Hart Publishing, 2002).   [83] See Chapter 14.

[84] Notably Lord Nicholls of Birkenhead, 'Knowing receipt: the need for a new landmark' in *Restitution: Past, Present and Future: Essays in Honour of Gareth Jones* (W. R. Cornish et al., eds) (Oxford: Hart Publishing, 1999) 231 at 238; see also P. Creighton and E. Bant, 'Recipient liability in Western Australia' (2000) 29 UWALR 205.

[85] [2001] Ch 437.

inquiries accepted in the industry for transactions of the sort he was engaged in. If he had carried out such inquiries and still had no knowledge of the trust, he will have a valid defence to liability. The defence might be good even if the set of investigation procedures carried out by the defendant is subscribed to only by a subset of the industry. This is similar to the test for medical professional negligence that immunizes a doctor from liability for unorthodox medical practice if he can show that his approach has the support of a responsible body of other practitioners.[86] A recipient, such as Chief Akindele, who acquires assets by a transaction for which he has given consideration, will usually find it easier to demonstrate that he has complied with transaction norms than a recipient who has given no consideration, because a buyer will usually be wary before parting with his money.

While we are on the subject of the giving of contractual consideration, it should be noted that in *Criterion Properties Plc v. Stratford UK Properties LLC*,[87] Lord Nicholls criticized the reasoning in *BCCI (Overseas) Ltd v. Akindele* on the ground that the Court of Appeal had been wrong to consider the law of knowing receipt in relation to the fully executed contractual transfer of assets in that case. However, Lord Nicholls was the only one of their Lordships to take that view and, although his Lordship purported to approve the reasoning of Lord Scott of Foscote (who delivered the leading speech in *Criterion*), Lord Scott of Foscote, in fact, acknowledged that the law relating to knowing receipt of assets may be applicable where assets have been transferred by a fully executed contract. Lord Scott of Foscote dismissed the appeal in *Criterion* on the basis that the contract in that case was merely executory—that is, it had not yet been fully executed by the transfer of the subject matter of the contract.

In Australia, the argument in favour of strict liability based on the reversal of unjust enrichment has been expressly disapproved.[88] There is, it is submitted, one context in which the proof of fault should certainly be a prerequisite to liability for receipt of trust property. That is where the claimant is claiming under a trust which was a bare trust at the time of misapplication of the trust property. In such a case the claimant, as beneficiary of a bare trust, had the power to bring the trust to an end before the misapplication of the fund. The beneficiary must therefore be taken to have run the risk of misapplication. Having run the risk that third parties might receive misapplied trust property, the onus should be on the claimant to prove that the recipient received with knowledge of the misapplication.[89]

The unconscionability error

In *BCCI (Overseas) Ltd v. Akindele*, the Court of Appeal declined to analyse the liability of a knowing recipient in terms of strict liability or the doctrine of notice. Instead, their Lordships held that Chief Akindele was not liable on the ground that his conscience

---

[86] *Bolitho v. City and Hackney Health Authority* [1998] AC 232, HL.   [87] [2004] 1 WLR 1846, HL.

[88] *Farah Constructions Pty Ltd v. Say-Dee Pty Ltd* [2007] HCA 22.

[89] G. Watt, 'Personal liability for receipt of trust property: allocating the risks' in *Modern Studies in Property Law* (E. Cooke, ed.) (Oxford: Hart Publishing, 2005) vol. III, 91.

was clear, or, to be more accurate, that he had not been shown to have acted 'unconscionably'. In short, the test that their Lordships adopted was 'unconscionability' pure and simple. The problem, of course, is that unconscionability is never pure and simple: when judges dispose of cases on the ground of unconscionability, the more simple the notion of unconscionability they apply, the more impure becomes the law.[90] We saw in Chapter 1 of this book that unconscionability has a very particular meaning in law. It refers to unconscionable reliance upon laws, legal rights, and legal powers. The wrong that is committed when a recipient wrongfully receives property belonging to another is not wrongful reliance upon any such law, legal right, or legal power. There is no right to misappropriate other people's property. In fact, it is sometimes called theft. The recipient of trust property is not abusing any legal power over the property, unless it is the power of possession (although where personal liability for knowing receipt is pursued, it is unusual for the defendant still to have possession of the property); his receipt of trust property is simply an abuse of the true owner's rights, rather than an abuse of any right that the recipient might be said to have. The defendant is committing a civil wrong (a tort), perhaps an equitable version of the common law tort of conversion or money had and received, if the language of unconscionability is retained to describe wrongful receipt; we must identify the factor that makes it unconscionable. That factor, it is submitted, is the *'conscious taking of commercially unacceptable risks to the prejudice of another'*.[91]

Receipt

As if the nature of the 'knowing' in 'knowing receipt' were not controversial enough, the reader will be dismayed to discover that even the nature of 'receipt' is not without controversy. It is even arguable that, if the trustees wrongfully disclose information about the trust to a stranger, the stranger should be treated as having received trust property.[92] However, we will confine our attention to receipt of more familiar assets such as cash and shares. Here the crucial distinction is between 'ministerial receipt' and 'beneficial receipt'. According to Millett J in *Agip (Africa) Ltd v. Jackson*, the essential feature of liability is that *'the recipient must have received the property for his own use and benefit'*.[93] According to his Lordship, this distinction is *'essential if receipt-based liability is to be properly confined to those cases where the receipt is relevant to the loss'*.[94] When a bank cashier passes cash to the security guard to be taken away, the security guard receives the cash in a purely ministerial capacity; he does not take possession of it for his own benefit so there is no liability. Correspondingly, the bank suffers no loss. If, on the other hand, the cashier had stolen the money from the bank and the guard was his accomplice, there would then be knowing receipt of property transferred in breach

---

[90] See Chapter 4.

[91] See G. Watt, 'Personal liability for receipt of trust property: allocating the risks' in *Modern Studies in Property Law* (E. Cooke, ed.) (Oxford: Hart Publishing, 2005) vol. III, 91 at 104.

[92] Lord Cohen has stated that information held by a fiduciary was not property *'in the strict sense of the word'* (*Boardman v. Phipps* [1967] 2 AC 46 at 102).   [93] [1990] Ch 265 at 292.

[94] Ibid.

of trust, because the security guard receives such money for his own benefit. However, matters become more complicated when we look at receipt by the bank itself. It has long been established that, when a banker takes deposits of customers' monies, he is permitted in the '*ordinary course of trade to make use of them for his own profit*'.[95] The bank becomes absolute owner of the deposit and the customer becomes absolute owner of a debt equivalent in size to the sums deposited plus interest at the account rate. One might have supposed, therefore, that if trustees were to deposit monies with a bank in breach of trust, the receipt by the bank would be beneficial receipt of the sort that may give rise to liability for knowing receipt. However, the authorities suggest a surprising basis for distinguishing ministerial and beneficial receipt in this context. According to Millett J in *Agip*:[96]

> In paying or collecting money for a customer the bank acts only as his agent. It is otherwise, however, if the collecting bank uses the money to reduce or discharge the customer's over-draft. In doing so it receives the money for its own benefit.[97]

When a bank pays money, it clearly receives nothing, but when it collects money as agent for a customer, the monies are presumably held in an account for the customer and the bank benefits from their being there. It is hard to read Millett J's statement without concluding that his Lordship regards deposits into a credit balance as being fundamentally different from deposits into an overdrawn account. If the distinction is sound, it would suggest that beneficial receipt is confined to receipt of capital benefits, because, in terms of income (or interest), banks profit more from overdrawn accounts than from accounts in credit.

Liability for inconsistent dealing with trust property

If trustees appoint an agent and transfer trust assets to his care within the terms of the trust, and if the agent receives the trust property lawfully and not for his own benefit, the receipt is purely ministerial and cannot give rise to liability for knowing receipt. If, however, he were subsequently to gamble the assets at a casino in a moment of impetuosity and lose it all, he would be personally liable for having dealt with the trust assets in a manner inconsistent with the trust.[98] In this example, the agent would also have appropriated the trust assets to his own use and benefit, but it seems that this is not necessary for liability for inconsistent dealing. Where an agent appropriates the trust assets to his own use and benefit, he commits a delayed form of knowing receipt in which he knew about the trust (although he need not have known its exact terms) and received the assets from the outset, but did not receive them beneficially until later. Where inconsistent dealing does not involve beneficial

---

[95] *Burdick v. Garrick* (1869–70) 5 LR Ch App 233 at 240.   [96] [1990] Ch 265.   [97] Ibid. at 292A.
[98] Ibid. at 291, following *Baden, Delvaux and Lecuit v. Société Générale pour Favoriser le Développement du Commerce et de l'Industrie en France SA* [1983] BCLC 325, *per* Peter Gibson J at 403.

receipt or appropriation, it is a head of liability distinct from both knowing receipt and dishonest assistance.

Is there a difference between receipt from trustees and receipt from absolute owners?

Property law has never considered equitable owners to be as deserving of protection as absolute owners.[99] The explanation for this is largely historical, but there is also a conceptual explanation: when property is held by trustees, the beneficial owner of the property is subject to the risk of trusting.[100] This means that the rights of trust beneficiaries are inherently qualified by the risk that their trustees' behaviour might cause the fund to suffer a loss; in this, and other respects, beneficial interests are 'limited' interests. This limited notion of ownership has implications for tracing and recovering property. Whereas an absolute owner is presumed to intend to recover his property under a resulting trust from a person to whom he has 'unintentionally' transferred it,[101] no such presumption operates in favour of beneficiaries when their trustees transfer trust property contrary to the intentions of the settlor as reflected in the terms of the trust. Professor Birks would like to see this state of affairs reformed, hence his support for, amongst other things, the imposition of strict restitutionary liability on recipients of trust property. He is committed, at a structural level, to the idea that wealth is deserving of equal protection whether owned absolutely or in trust.[102] Apparently, he does not accept that settlors—and, by extension, their beneficiaries—'assume' the risk of trusting. Instead, he considers it to be purely fortuitous in the modern investment environment that the claimant happens to be an absolute owner or a mere beneficial owner.[103] He neatly sidesteps problems associated with the claimant's assumption of the risk of loss by approaching the problem exclusively in terms of the just allocation of the defendant's gain or 'enrichment', the equitable or legal source of that enrichment being more or less irrelevant.

In the next section, we will see that acknowledging the fundamental difference between property held on trust and property held absolutely has the merit of elucidating the theoretical basis for the modern formulation of equitable liability for dishonest assistance in a breach of trust.

Equitable liability for assistance in a breach of trust

This head of liability has been dramatically reformed by the decision of the Judicial Committee of the Privy Council in *Royal Brunei Airlines Sdn Bhd v. Tan*,[104] where Lord Nicholls identified it as a form of 'accessory' or 'secondary' liability arising from assistance

---

[99] L. Smith, 'Unjust enrichment, property and the structure of trusts' (2000) 116 LQR 412.

[100] G. Watt, 'Personal liability for receipt of trust property: allocating the risks' in *Modern Studies in Property Law* (E. Cooke, ed.) (Oxford: Hart Publishing, 2005) vol. III, 91.   [101] See Chapter 5.

[102] P. Birks, 'Receipt' in *Breach of Trust* (P. Birks and A. Pretto, eds) (Oxford: Hart Publishing, 2002) at 214.

[103] Birks, ibid. at 214–15.   [104] [1995] 2 AC 378.

in a breach for which the trustee is primarily liable. According to his Lordship, it serves the dual purpose of '*making good the beneficiary's loss should the trustee lack financial means and imposing a liability which will discourage others from behaving in a similar fashion*'.[105] Previously, a stranger who assisted in, or procured, a breach of trust by the trustees was only liable if he knowingly assisted in a dishonest or fraudulent breach of trust. Since Lord Nicholls's judgment in *Tan*, the focus has very sensibly shifted from the nature of the primary breach to the nature of the assistance. Now, it is clear that an accessory will be liable even if he assists in, or procures, an innocent breach of trust. So if a solicitor were to deceive an innocent trustee into breaching his trust, or a director of a corporate trustee were to cause the corporation to commit a breach, the solicitor and director may be personally liable as accessories to the breach, despite the innocence of their respective trustees.

Tan involved a travel agent company that held customers' monies on trust for the claimant airline whenever customers bought flights on the claimant's aircraft. Instead of simply deducting its commission, the company took advantage of a rolling 30-day credit period to use the airline's money to relieve its own cash-flow problems. When the company became insolvent, the airline sought, amongst other things, to fix the managing director of the company with personal liability for assisting in the breach of trust. Lord Nicholls suggested that:

> if anything, the case for liability of the dishonest third party seems stronger where the trustee is innocent, because in such a case the third party alone was dishonest and that was the cause of the subsequent misapplication of the trust property.[106]

On the particular facts of *Tan*, however, where the defendant had complete control of the trustee company, his Lordship imputed the defendant's dishonesty to the company for good measure.

One aspect of the decision in *Tan* remains more controversial than any other: having very reasonably decided that liability does not depend upon the trustee's dishonesty, Lord Nicholls nevertheless decided to keep dishonesty within the total equation, with the result that, today, a stranger will not be liable as an accessory to a breach unless he himself had a dishonest state of mind. Apart from the desire to avoid vague notions of knowledge (and especially the '*Baden* scale' of knowledge), it is not clear why Lord Nicholls was not content that liability should be based on knowing assistance in a breach of trust, which would have brought this head of equitable personal liability in line with the common law tort of knowing interference with contractual rights.[107] Some years earlier, Millett J, as he then was, observed that the basis of the stranger's liability under this head '*is not receipt of trust property but participation in a fraud*'[108] and even earlier than that, Sachs LJ had held, in the *Carl Zeiss* case,[109] that there should be no liability without an element of '*dishonesty or of consciously acting improperly*'.[110] It may

---

[105] Ibid. at 387A.   [106] Ibid. at 384F–G.
[107] *Lumley v. Gye* (1853) 2 E & B 216 (118 English Reports 749).
[108] Millett J in *Agip (Africa) Ltd v. Jackson* [1990] Ch 265 at 292F.   [109] [1969] 2 Ch 276, CA.
[110] Ibid. at 298B.

have been with this thinking in mind that Lord Nicholls decided to require an inquiry into the honesty or dishonesty of the defendant's state of mind, rather than to abandon dishonesty entirely as an ingredient of liability. But *why* should this head of liability depend upon proof of a fraud? Is it to reflect the policy that commercial agents should not be personally liable for assisting in a breach of trust except in exceptional cases? This seemed to motivate Lord Selborne when he first formulated liability for knowing assistance in the great age of commerce immediately after the passing of the Judicature Acts,[111] but if that is the reason, then why are commercial agents so much more readily held liable at common law if they assist in breaches of contract? A possible answer is that the courts desire to discourage beneficiaries from pursuing actions against wealthy strangers before pursuing actions against their own trustees. Another related explanation may be an unspoken belief that equitable property rights under a trust are less deserving of protection than rights (even a mere contractual right of action) owned absolutely—a belief, in other words, that beneficiaries should bear an appropriate share of the risk that their trustee might commit a breach of trust and should bear an appropriate share of any loss caused if that risk materializes.[112]

Be that as it may, it is clear that, as a result of Lord Nicholls' speech in *Tan*, what had previously been personal liability for knowing assistance became personal liability for dishonest assistance.[113] It is also clear that the formula for liability under this head remains liability 'as a constructive trustee', even though there is no requirement that the stranger ever took possession of the trust property. There is, however, an argument for limiting accessory liability to situations in which the stranger had, at the very least, some degree of de facto control of the trust property, either by exerting undue influence on the trustee or by controlling the trustee's mind. *Tan* was a case in the latter category; a solicitor who misleads an innocent trustee might fall within the former.

If there had been any doubts about the status of this important decision of the Privy Council, they were put to rest when *Tan* received the unanimous approval of the House of Lords in *Twinsectra Ltd v. Yardley*.[114] It is notable that Lord Millett, the sole dissentient to the decision, wished to jettison dishonesty as a defining ingredient of liability, and, by implication, to reject his own earlier suggestion that this head of liability is fraud-based, in favour of a return to liability on the basis of the stranger's 'knowing assistance'. The majority held that the defendant, a solicitor acting for a trustee, had not been dishonest and was therefore not liable for dishonest assistance. Lord Millett, rejecting dishonest assistance as a basis of liability, held that the defendant was liable for knowing assistance. One of Lord Millett's reasons for rejecting dishonesty as a defining ingredient of liability was to bring this head of liability in line with the common law tort of knowing interference with contractual rights under which liability depends upon the defendant's knowledge, and '*negligence is not sufficient and dishonesty is not necessary*'.[115]

---

[111] *Barnes v. Addy* (1874) LR9 Ch App 244.   [112] See the earlier discussion under the heading 'receipt'.
[113] J. Snape and G. Watt, 'A Position of Trust' (1995) 92(28) LSG 20.   [114] [2002] 2 AC 164.
[115] Ibid. at 200H–201A. Lord Millett took another discrete step in that direction in *Dubai Aluminium Co Ltd v. Salaam* [2002] UKHL 48, HL, in which his Lordship held, at [10] that, because a person may be held vicariously liable for inducing a breach of contract, there is '*no rational ground*' for excluding similar liability in equity.

From an obligations perspective, there is certainly force in the view that procuring or assisting in a breach of another person's trust is at least as wrong as inducing a breach of another person's contract and should not be subject to the higher 'dishonesty' threshold of liability. Lord Millett even suggests that, due to the different thresholds of liability, claimants will be induced to '*spell a contractual obligation out of a fiduciary relationship in order to avoid the need to establish that the defendant had a dishonest state of mind*'.[116]

The elements of liability

In *Baden v. Société Générale*,[117] Peter Gibson J identified four elements that must be proved to establish that a stranger is liable as an accessory to a breach of trust. Having updated them to take account of *Tan*, we can say that there must be 'dishonest' (element 1) 'assistance' (element 2) in a 'breach' (element 3) of 'trust' (element 4): '*Taken together, those elements must leave the court satisfied that the alleged constructive trustee was a party or privy to dishonesty*.'[118]

Element 1: 'dishonest'

The complex question of the meaning of dishonesty in the context of accessory liability for 'dishonest assistance' finally came before the House of Lords in *Twinsectra Ltd v. Yardley*.[119] The facts of the case were fairly straightforward. Mr Yardley borrowed £1m from Twinsectra Ltd. Leach, a solicitor, acted for Mr Yardley in connection with the loan, but did not deal directly with Twinsectra. Twinsectra dealt with another firm of solicitors, 'Sims', which represented itself as acting on behalf of Mr Yardley. Sims paid the money to Leach and he paid it on to Yardley. Sims gave the following undertaking to Twinsectra:

> '1. The loan monies will be retained by us until such time as they are applied in the acquisition of property on behalf of our client.
>
> 2. The loan monies will be utilized solely for the acquisition of property on behalf of our client and for no other purposes.
>
> 3. We will repay to you the said sum of £1,000,000 together with interest calculated at the rate of £657.53, such payment to be made within four calendar months after receipt of the loan monies by us.'

The Court of Appeal[120] held that undertakings (1) and (2) created a *Quistclose* trust.[121] Contrary to the terms of the undertaking (and trust), Sims did not retain the money until Yardley had actually applied it in the acquisition of property. On being given a mere assurance by Yardley that it would be so applied, they paid it to Leach. He, in turn, did not take steps to ensure that it was utilized solely for the acquisition of property on

---

[116] *Twinsectra Ltd v. Yardley* [2002] 2 AC 164 at 201.

[117] *Baden v. Société Générale Pour Favoriser le Développement du Commerce et de l'Industrie en France* [1993] 1 WLR 509, Ch D, [1983] BCLC 325.   [118] Ibid. at 573D.

[119] [2002] 2 AC 164.   [120] [1999] Lloyd's Rep Bank 438.   [121] See Chapters 2 and 5.

behalf of Yardley: he simply paid it out upon Yardley's instructions. The result was that £350,000 or so was used by Yardley for purposes other than the acquisition of property. When, in due course, the loan was not repaid, Twinsectra sued all of the parties involved, including Leach. The claim against him was for the £350,000 that had not been used to buy property. The basis of the claim was that the payment by Sims to Leach in breach of the undertaking was a breach of trust and that Leach was liable for dishonestly assisting in that breach. The claimant did not pursue a claim for knowing receipt because, apart from his professional fees of £22,000, Mr Leach had never received or appropriated the claimant's monies to his own use and benefit; he had simply administered them. In the House of Lords, their Lordships allowed Mr Leach's appeal (Lord Millett dissenting). In reaching that decision, their Lordships had to identify the appropriate test for dishonesty in this context.

The test for dishonesty: subjective, objective, or 'hybrid'?

The test for dishonesty in this context is not the subjective test that applies in some criminal contexts,[122] so a defendant who dishonestly assists in a breach of trust will not escape liability by proving that he did not believe his actions to be dishonest.[123] Courts do not judge a defendant by his own moral standards, which is why a penniless thief who picks the pocket of a millionaire is guilty of theft[124] and why Robin Hood is liable for dishonest assistance in a breach of trust if he assists Friar Tuck to steal gold from the friary, even though he believes that Tuck will give the money to the poor. In *Starglade Properties Ltd v. Nash*,[125] the Court of Appeal confirmed that the standard by which 'dishonesty' is tested does not vary just because some people might think that the standard is set too high: '*There is a single standard of honesty objectively determined by the court. That standard is applied to specific conduct of a specific individual possessing the knowledge and qualities he actually enjoyed.*'[126] In *Tan*, Lord Nicholls held that the relevant question to ask is whether the defendant acted as an honest person would have acted in the defendant's circumstances. This, according to his Lordship, '*is an objective standard*',[127] albeit one that takes account of the defendant's personal characteristics. In this way, a junior bank clerk is judged by the standards of the hypothetical honest junior bank clerk and a senior bank manager is judged by the standards of the hypothetical honest senior bank manager.

The House of Lords considered the nature of Lord Nicholls's test for dishonesty in the case of *Twinsectra Ltd v. Yardley*.[128] The defendant was a solicitor who had acted as an adviser in a commercial transaction that involved a breach of trust and the question, as always, was whether the defendant had dishonestly assisted in the breach. Their Lordships were unanimous in their reluctance to stigmatize as 'dishonest' a professional adviser who had assisted in a complicated commercial deal, but Lord Millett, who was

---

[122] See, for example, *R v. Ghosh* [1982] QB 1053 in the context of obtaining money by deception.

[123] Lord Hutton in *Twinsectra*; Sir Christopher Slade in *Walker v. Stones* [2001].

[124] Sir Christopher Slade stated in *Walker v. Stones* [2001] Lloyd's Rep PN 864 at 877, [164]: '*the penniless thief, for example, who picks the pocket of the multi-millionaire, is dishonest*'.

[125] [2010] EWCA Civ 1314, [2010] All ER (D) 221.   [126] Ibid. at para. [25].

[127] [1995] 2 AC 378, PC, at 389–90.   [128] [2002] 2 AC 164 at 172–3, 196–8.

the sole dissentient, favoured a quite different approach to that adopted by the majority. For Lord Millett, the proper safeguard against inappropriate application of the 'dishonest' label is to remove dishonesty as a defining ingredient of accessory liability: 'knowing', not 'dishonest', assistance should be the touchstone of liability. Lord Millett noted that the gravamen of accessory liability is not that the accessory has handled stolen property, but that he has knowingly assisted a person, who he knows has been entrusted with the control of a fund, to dispose of the fund in a manner that the accessory knows to be unauthorized by the 'terms' of the trust. On this basis, Lord Millett held Mr Leach liable for knowing assistance, because he had put the claimant's monies at the free disposal of Mr Yardley knowing that Twinsectra had entrusted the money to Mr Sims for a specific purpose only and that Mr Sims had breached that obligation by paying the money to Mr Leach without ensuring that the obligation was fulfilled. In contrast to Lord Millett, the route favoured by the majority of their Lordships for avoiding the inappropriate imposition of the stigma of dishonesty on a defendant in Mr Leach's position was to relax the objective test proposed by Lord Nicholls in *Tan*.

Lord Nicholls clearly envisaged an objective test of dishonesty: the particular defendant is not to be judged by his own subjective standards, but by the objective standards of a reasonable onlooker. The onlooker is permitted to take into account the particular skills and experience of the defendant, and the particular circumstances which the defendant found himself in, but it is for the objective onlooker to determine whether an honest person with the defendant's characteristics could have acted the same way in the defendant's position. There is no subjective element to this test, as Lord Millett rightly observed in *Twinsectra*. However, the majority in *Twinsectra*, while ostensibly purporting to follow Lord Nicholls, favoured a test for dishonesty that appears to be a genuine hybrid of an objective and a subjective test. Lord Hutton called it 'the combined test'. According to this test, a defendant will only be personally liable as an accessory to a breach of trust if it can be shown that he appreciated that what he was doing was dishonest by the standards of honest and reasonable men. This gets a defendant 'off the hook' if he can prove, on the balance of probabilities, that he personally—that is, subjectively—did not realize that he had participated in a fraud, even though the majority of people in his position (represented by the figure of the objective onlooker) would have so realized. It cannot be denied that there are passages in Lord Nicholls's judgment that suggest that he may have had something like this 'combined test' in mind,[129] but that implication cannot stand in the face of Lord Nicholls's express rejection of the 'combined test' as it applies in the criminal case of *R v. Ghosh*.[130] In that case, Lord Lane CJ held that, in the law of theft, dishonesty requires '*that the defendant himself must have realised that what he was doing was dishonest by the ordinary standards of reasonable and honest people*'.[131] This test, expressly rejected by Lord Nicholls in *Tan*, is practically indistinguishable from the test adopted by Lord Hutton in *Twinsectra*. The Privy

---

[129] Lord Nicholls, *Royal Brunei Airlines Sdn Bhd v. Tan* [1995] 2 AC 378 at 389C, 391A–C.

[130] [1982] QB 1053. The case concerned obtaining property by deception.

[131] Lord Hutton's own summary of the judgment in *Twinsectra Ltd v. Yardley* [2002] 2 AC 164 at 173.

Council has acknowledged that Lord Hutton's analysis is 'ambiguous' and might appear to differ from Lord Nicholls's analysis in *Tan*.[132] However, their Lordships in the Privy Council adopted a generous construction of Lord Hutton's speech to reach the conclusion that Lord Hutton was, in fact, in agreement with Lord Nicholls in *Tan*. Despite this, the apparent distinction between Lord Hutton's 'combined' analysis and Lord Nicholls's purely 'objective' analysis remains, and will not be finally resolved until the House of Lords has another opportunity to consider the matter.

In *Republic of Zambia v. Meer Care & Desai (a firm)*,[133] the Court of Appeal held that where the defendant is, say, a solicitor, the test is whether an honest solicitor could have done what the defendant did given the knowledge of the facts that he had. It is not appropriate to apply the benchmark of an honest *and competent* solicitor, because it wrongly applies a test competency to determine honesty. The difference between negligence and dishonesty is not one of degree. As Lloyd LJ said:

> it is one thing to throw caution to the winds; that is likely to lead to negligent conduct. But even to do that to the nth degree does not involve crossing the dividing line and passing over to dishonesty.[134]

Dishonesty and knowledge

Although, in *Tan*, Lord Nicholls described 'dishonesty' as a necessary and 'sufficient ingredient' of accessory liability, and rejected 'knowledge' as a defining ingredient, and even suggested that '*the* Baden *scale of knowledge is best forgotten*',[135] his Lordship nevertheless relied heavily upon various (*Baden*-like) degrees of knowledge to explain what he meant by dishonesty:

> Honest people do not intentionally deceive others to their detriment. Honest people do not knowingly take others' property...an honest person does not participate in a transaction if he knows it involves a misapplication of trust assets to the detriment of the beneficiaries. Nor does an honest person in such a case deliberately close his eyes and ears, or deliberately not ask questions, lest he learn something he would rather not know, and then proceed regardless.[136]

It came as no surprise, then, when, in *Heinl v. Jyske Bank (Gibraltar) Ltd*,[137] Nourse LJ suggested that the *Baden* scale might still be useful in distinguishing different shades of knowledge.

Unconscionability

When we considered personal liability for knowing receipt, we criticized the approach currently prevailing in the courts, which is to rely upon ill-defined notions

---

[132] *Barlow Clowes International Ltd (in liquidation) v. Eurotrust International Ltd* [2006] 1 All ER 333; [2005] UKPC 37, at [15]; followed in *Abou-Rahmah v. Abacha* [2006] EWCA Civ 1492, CA. In *Abou-Rahmah*, Arden LJ opined, in somewhat optimistic vein, that *Barlow Clowes* 'shows how the Royal Brunei *case and the* Twinsectra *case can be read together to form a consistent corpus of law*'. [133] [2008] EWCA Civ 1007.
[134] Ibid. at para. [146]. [135] [1995] 2 AC 378 at 392F/G. [136] [1995] 2 AC 378 at 389.
[137] *The Times*, 28 September 1999. See also *Brinks Ltd v. Abu Saleh (No. 3)*, *The Times*, 23 October 1995.

of unconscionability as a basis for imposing equitable liability. The same error has occurred in the context of accessory liability. Consider, for example, the judgment in *Powell v. Thompson*: '*If the third party's conduct has been unconscionable...the third party is liable to be held accountable to the beneficiary as if he or she were a trustee.*'[138] Lord Nicholls disapproved of any such unbridled notion of unconscionability:

> If it is to be used in this context, and if it is to be the touchstone for liability as an accessory, it is essential to be clear on what, *in this context*, unconscionable *means*. If unconscionable means no more than dishonesty, then dishonesty is the preferable label. If unconscionable means something different, it must be said that it is not clear what that something different is. Either way, therefore, the term is better avoided in this context.[139]

The reason why equity imposes personal liability on accessories to breach of trust is not to restrain unconscionability; it is merely to follow the law. Equity is simply seeking to provide analogues to personal tortious (and possibly criminal) liability at common law.[140] It is too readily assumed that equity can only be aroused to the cry of 'conscience'.

Commercially unacceptable conduct

In *Cowan de Groot Properties Ltd v. Eagle Trust plc*,[141] Knox J held that dishonesty is evidenced by '*commercially unacceptable conduct in the particular context involved*'.[142] Lord Nicholls approved this dictum when attempting to capture the flavour of dishonesty in *Tan*, but, in a subsequent case, Lindsay J expressed reservations with this approach to establishing dishonesty in commercial contexts:

> It may, for example, be in one sense 'commercially unacceptable' for a bank to lend money without security or without investigating the title to the security it is offered by its borrower. It may thus be 'unacceptable' because too risky, [and therefore] 'commercially unacceptable', if at all, only in relation to the bank's own position.[143]

Element 2: 'assistance'

According to Gibson J in *Baden*, proof of 'assistance' is a simple question of fact. The payment of a company's funds by a bank on the instructions of fraudulent directors of the company may qualify as assistance.[144] There is no requirement for the assistance actually to have caused the breach, but it must have been of more than minimal importance. The 'assistance' requirement could be satisfied by proving that the stranger had been involved in an intermediate step in the process leading to the breach of trust.

Assistance seems to mean some kind of purposive conduct designed to advance and promote the unlawful object that breaches the trust. In *Brinks Ltd v. Abu-Saleh and Ors (No. 3)*,[145] the plaintiffs had been the object of a huge bullion heist that had been facilitated by the actions of one of its own employees who was, therefore, in breach of his fiduciary

---

[138] [1991] 1 NZLR 597, *per* Thomas J at 613. [139] [1995] 2 AC 378 at 392D–F.
[140] See the final section of this chapter. [141] [1992] 4 All ER 700. [142] Ibid. at 761H.
[143] *HRT Ltd v. J. Alsford Pension Trustees Ltd* (1997) 11(2) TLI 48 (noted in (1997) 6(2) J Int P 83).
[144] *Selangor United Rubber Estates v. Cradock (No. 3)* [1968] 1 WLR 1555 and *Karak Rubber Co v. Burden (No. 2)* [1972] 1 WLR 602. [145] *The Times*, 23 October 1995.

relationship with the claimants. The claimants' case was that Mrs E, as part of the laundering of the proceeds, had accompanied her husband on trips to Zurich, at the instigation of P, one of those convicted of the robbery. The allegation was of accessory liability against Mrs E. The judge found, as a matter of fact, that Mrs E had simply accompanied her husband in the capacity of his wife and that, on these facts, this did not constitute sufficient 'assistance' for the purposes of accessory liability. Lord Millett observed in *Twinsectra* that:

> Most of the cases have been concerned, not with assisting in the original breach, but in covering it up afterwards by helping to launder the money. Mr Leach's wrongdoing is not confined to the assistance he gave Mr Sims to commit a breach of trust by receiving the money from him knowing that Mr Sims should not have paid it to him (though this is sufficient to render him liable for any resulting loss); it extends to the assistance he gave in the subsequent misdirection of the money by paying it out to Mr Yardley's order without seeing to its proper application.[146]

Element 3: 'breach'

Before *Tan*, it had to be shown that a dishonest or fraudulent design existed and that the trustee or fiduciary had been a party to it. It had to be something more than a mere misfeasance or breach of trust, which, as we have seen from previous chapters, can be committed innocently. Since *Tan*, an innocent breach of trust on the part of the fiduciary or trustee will suffice.

Element 4: 'trust'

If a corporation holds monies on trust, the director of the corporation may be liable for dishonest assistance or procurement of a breach of trust by the corporation; this is what happened in *Tan*. However, '*the trust need not be a formal trust. It is sufficient that there should be a fiduciary relationship between the "trustee" and the property of another person*'.[147] So if a solicitor dishonestly assists a director to breach his duties to a corporation, the solicitor may be liable as an accessory even if he did not know that the corporation was a trustee[148] and, if the corporation was not a trustee, the solicitor may be liable if he dishonestly assisted the director to misapply the corporation's assets. What is not clear is whether a stranger can be liable as an accessory to breaches of trust that do not involve misapplication of any trust property. The answer to this question depends upon which common law analogue is deemed most appropriate to common law liability. If personal liability for dishonest assistance is the equitable analogue of being liable as an accessory to theft, misappropriation or misapplication of trust property ought to be prerequisite to liability. It is probably better, though, to regard dishonest assistance as an equitable analogue to common law conspiracy to defraud[149] or to the common law tort

---

[146] [2002] 2 AC 164 at 194.

[147] *Baden v. Société Générale Pour Favoriser le Développement du Commerce et de l'Industrie en France* [1993] 1 WLR 509, Ch D, *per* Peter Gibson J at 573E.

[148] Ibid. at 574D ('*a person beneficially interested in trust property held by a corporate trustee can rely on the fiduciary relationship between the directors and the trustee company as well as on the trust affecting the trust property in the hands of the company*').   [149] *Dubai Aluminium Co Ltd v. Salaam* [2002] 3 WLR 1913.

of wrongful interference with another's contract,[150] so that a stranger would be liable if he dishonestly assists in a breach even where trust property is absent. In support of the latter view, it has been held that '*in a case for accessory liability there is no requirement for there to be trust property*' and that '[s]*uch a requirement wrongly associates accessory liability with trust concepts*'.[151] This statement brings us neatly to the final section of this chapter.

Should accessory liability be a tort?

Professor Birks suggested some years before *Tan* that '[t]*here is no respectable modern reason why "knowing assistance" should not be regarded as a tort*'.[152] Support for that view can be found in the speech of Lord Millett in the House of Lords in *Twinsectra Ltd v. Yardley*.[153] Lord Nicholls had made express reference in *Tan* to the tort of procuring a breach of contract, even going so far as to suggest that the '*underlying rationale is the same*' for equitable accessory liability as for common law accessory liability,[154] but his Lordship did not take the step of assimilating the two. Nevertheless, it is surely a step that should be taken at the first opportunity, so as to remove an unnecessary distinction between law and equity.[155] The convergence of equitable liability for dishonest assistance and common law tortious liability has been advanced by recognition in the House of Lords that the partners of a solicitor liable for dishonest assistance may, like a tortious wrongdoer, be held vicariously liable where the acts of dishonest assistance were rendered in the ordinary course of the firm's business.[156] Another advance is the judicial suggestion that the equitable wrong should only be distinguished from tort for the purposes of domestic law and that '*its proper characterisation for the purposes of private international law is as a tort*'.[157]

Further reading

In addition to the following print sources, the Online Resource Centre accompanying this book contains web links to further reading as well as guide answers to assessment questions relevant to this chapter.

---

[150] See, generally, *Lonrho plc v. Fayed* [1990] 1 QB 490.

[151] *JD Wetherspoon plc v. Van de Berg & Co Ltd* [2009] EWHC 639 (Ch) (following the Court of Appeal in *Satnam Investments Ltd v. Dunlop Heywood & Co Ltd* [1999] 3 All ER 652).

[152] P. Birks, 'Civil wrongs: a new world', *1990 Butterworth Lectures* (London: Butterworths, 1991) at 100.

[153] [2002] 2 AC 164 at 200–1.

[154] [1995] 2 AC 378 at 387. Charles Harpum suggests that accessory liability is an equitable 'analogue' of the common law economic torts ('Accessory liability for procuring or assisting a breach of trust' (1995) 111 LQR 545).

[155] See, generally, A. Burrows, 'We do this at common law but that in equity' (2002) 22(1) OJLS 1.

[156] *Dubai Aluminium Co Ltd v. Salaam* [2002] 3 WLR 1913, HL.

[157] *OJSC Oil Co Yugraneft (in liquidation) v. Abramovich* [2008] EWHC 2613 (Comm).

ANDREWS, G., 'The redundancy of dishonest assistance' (2003) Conv 398.

BIRKS, P. B. H., 'Misdirected funds: restitution from the recipient' (1989) LMCLQ 296.

BRINDLE, M. J. and HOOLEY, R. J. A., 'Does constructive knowledge make a constructive trustee?' (1987) 61 ALJ 281.

BRYAN, M., 'The Liability of the Recipient' in *Equity in Commercial Law* (S. Degeling and J. Edeleman, eds) (Pyrmont, NSW: Lawbook Co, 2005).

CLARKE, SIR ANTHONY, 'Claims Against Professionals: Negligence, Dishonesty And Fraud' [2006] 22 Professional Negligence 70/85.

ELLIOTT, S. B. and MITCHELL, C., 'Remedies for dishonest assistance' (2004) 67(1) MLR 16.

GARDNER, S., 'Knowing assistance and knowing receipt: taking stock' (1996) 112 LQR 56, 85–93.

HARPUM, C., 'The stranger as constructive trustee' (1986) 102 LQR 114, 267.

HARPUM, C., 'Liability for intermeddling with trusts' (1987) 50 MLR 217.

HARPUM, C., 'Accessory liability for procuring or assisting a breach of trust' (1995) 111 LQR 545.

LOUGHLAN, P., 'Liability for assistance in a breach of fiduciary duty' (1989) 9 OJLS 260.

LORD NICHOLLS OF BIRKENHEAD, 'Knowing receipt: the need for a new landmark' in *Restitution Past Present and Future: Essays in Honour of Gareth Jones* (W. R. Cornish et al., eds) (Oxford: Hart Publishing, 1998) at 231.

MITCHELL, C., 'Dishonest assistance, knowing receipt, and the law of limitation' (2008) Conv. 226–37.

PANESAR, S., 'A loan subject to a trust and dishonest assistance by a third party' (2003) 18(1) JIBL 9.

PAYNE, J., 'Unjust enrichment, trusts and recipient liability for unlawful dividends' (2003) 119 LQR 583.

RIDGE, P., 'Justifying the Remedies for Dishonest Assistance' (2008) 124 LQR 445.

SALES, P., 'The tort of conspiracy and civil secondary liability' (1990) 49 CLJ 491.

SMITH, L. D., 'Unjust enrichment, property and the structure of trusts' (2000) 116 LQR 412.

THOMAS, S. B., 'Goodbye knowing receipt, hello unconscientious receipt' (2001) 21 OJLS 239.

WOODCOCK, A., 'Claims for dishonest assistance with breach of trust, and changes made by *Twinsectra v Yardley*' (2006) 57(3) NILQ 494.

PART V

Equity

16

Equitable maxims, doctrines, and remedies

Suppose that you have been chosen to sing in a newly created pop group after perform-ing on a TV talent show. All goes well at first, but your launch event is scheduled to take place on the day of your final examination in equity and trusts. Naturally, you wouldn't miss your examination for the world and you refuse to perform unless a new date can be arranged. The manager of the group knows that it would be pointless to sue you for common law damages, so he seeks the equitable remedy of specific performance instead. You are outraged and decide to seek the equitable remedy of rescission to bring the con-tract with the manager to an end, on the ground that the manager misrepresented before contract that you could continue with your studies. You also seek an injunction prohibit-ing any performance of the group's hit song without you (because you were the one who wrote it), and you seek a 'search order' to enter the manager's premises to seize the master discs of the studio recording in order to prevent the manager from distributing the song. By the end of this chapter, you will have a good idea of your prospects of success.

Strange as it may seem, the preceding scenario represents the 'real world' of equitable remedies: pop groups and artists figure prominently in the cases. That said, there is no hiding the fact that the leading cases on equitable doctrines and remedies are usually very old. That they still have the power to determine modern cases is a testament to the inherent adaptability of equity. We learned in Chapter 1 that equity is a body of law developed originally by the old Court of Chancery in constructive competition with the common law courts, but now applied (since the Judicature Acts 1873–75) by the unified Supreme Court of England and Wales. We also learned that equity, as a dimension of law, still performs the special function of restraining or restricting the exercise of legal rights and powers in particular cases, whenever it would be unconscionable for such rights and powers to be exercised to the full. In this chapter, we will examine particular principles (including maxims), doctrines, and remedies that have been developed over many cen-turies to help predict the way in which equity will operate in various types of case.

The maxims of equity

The recognition of equitable proprietary rights under a trust is characterized by the need for certainty in the ownership of property. In contrast, the grant of equitable remedies or relief is characterized by judicial discretion to disapply generally applicable legal and equitable rules on a case-by-case basis. Maxims tended to play a significant part in guiding the exercise of this judicial discretion in the old Court of Chancery and they are still employed today, although the suspicion is that they are not so much 'followed' as 'employed' to achieve the outcomes desired by the judges in particular cases. In the exercise of discretion, a principle or maxim is a more flexible and useful tool than a rule. It is true that some maxims, particularly those that relate to title and property, lay down something equivalent to a rule.[1] A common law maxim of this sort is the maxim *nemo dat non quod habet*, which, roughly translated, provides that no one can transfer title that he does not have. An equitable maxim of this sort is the maxim *qui prior tempore est potior est*, which provides that, if equitable claims or interests are equal, priority will go to whichever claim or interest arose first in time. Nevertheless, for the most part, maxims tend to guide the exercise of discretion without stultifying it in the way that rules do. Maxims should, however, be employed with caution. The risk is that they will become '*short dark oracles*'.[2] The most useful feature of equitable maxims—that they will sometimes outweigh a rule if there is a conflict between a maxim and a rule—is also their most dangerous feature. Maxims have no objectively assayable weight. There are no rules to determine when a maxim will outweigh a rule and there are no rules to determine which maxim should prevail when two maxims conflict. They have, as Simon Gardner has observed, '*a peculiarly Delphic quality, wrapped as they are in metaphor, grandly unqualified, and acknowledging no authority but transcendent wisdom*'.[3] Ultimately, the maxims of equity are useful to the extent (and perhaps only to the extent) that they guide what would otherwise be an even broader discretion, based upon that most enigmatic of ideas, 'unconscionability'.

Some of the key maxims are considered in the sections that follow. These, and others, have also been discussed in context throughout the book.

'Equity acts *in personam*'

At first, unconscionability was conceived along medieval ecclesiastic lines as a burden on individual or personal conscience. It was therefore assumed that equity, like private conscience, could only act against the individual defendant in person (*in personam*).[4] However, we have seen that equity came to accept that the rights of a beneficiary under a trust are binding not only upon the individual consciences of trustees and third parties, but also upon the trust assets themselves, so equity began to act by analogy to the common law idea of entitlement to property. Despite that development, the maxim 'equity acts *in personam*' is still used, just as it was in *The Earl*

---

[1] '*What are maxims but expressions of that which good sense has made a rule?*' (*Smith v. Baker & Sons* [1891] AC 325, *per* Lord Bramwell at 344).

[2] As Sir Francis Bacon warned in the preface to his 1630 work, *Maxims of the Law*.

[3] 'Two maxims of equity' (1995) 54(1) Camb LJ 60.

[4] S. F. C. Milsom, *Historical Foundtations of the Common Law*, 2nd edn (London: Butterworths, 1981) at 90.

of Oxford's Case,[5] to justify equitable intervention when the equitable jurisdiction comes into conflict with another jurisdiction.[6]

'Equity will not suffer a wrong without a remedy'

At first blush, this maxim would appear to suggest that equity is the healer of every form of wrongdoing. The reality, of course, is that equity is only concerned to remedy one type of wrongdoing, namely 'unconscionable' reliance on the common law. Apart from its special jurisdiction to relieve against unconscionability, equity will not remedy a wrong unless the wrong is already recognized as such in law. No matter how morally wrong a particular social action or behaviour might be, it is not appropriate for equity to label it as being generally wrong in law if the law itself will not. Consider the following facts concerning Diana, the late Princess of Wales, as a result of which legal proceedings were threatened, but never came to court.

Princess Diana was secretly photographed by a gymnasium owner while exercising in the gymnasium as his guest. He sold the photographs to the tabloid press for an alleged small fortune. There is little doubt that a court of morality would have required him to disgorge his ill-gotten gains, but would a court of law? At common law, it is hard to see that Princess Diana would have had any cause of action against the owner of the gym. There had been no contract between them into which terms could be implied and there was no general tort of infringement of privacy in English law. Possibly, there would have been an action in restitution for the reversal of unjust enrichment,[7] but the question for us is whether, in the absence of any established legal remedy for the moral wrong, this was a proper case for *equitable* intervention.

In its early history, it was the practice of Chancery to hear certain claims precisely because there was no established common law writ or 'form of action' covering the case. By analogy to that early practice, it could be argued that equity should have granted the Princess a cause of action due to the absence of any common law counterpart. The Latin form of the maxim presently under consideration harks back to the days when claimants petitioned the old Court of Chancery: *nullus recedat a curia cancellariae sine remedio* ('nobody will leave the Chancellor's court without a remedy'). However, the only reason why the old Court of Chancery exercised such creativity was to counter the fixed and inflexible nature of the old common law forms of action. Today, there is no such rigidity. The unified Supreme Court of Judicature is capable of recognizing new causes of action to take into account changing social practice. The most significant example of this may well be the recognition, in *Donoghue v. Stephenson,*[8] of a common law duty of care owed by a manufacturer of consumable goods to third-party consumers, despite the presence of a contract between manufacturer and retailer, and the absence of any contract between manufacturer and consumer. The decision formed the basis of the modern duty of care in negligence.

---

[5] (1615) 1 Rep Ch 1.   [6] See Chapter 1.   [7] See Chapter 2.   [8] [1932] AC 562, HL.

The decision in *Donoghue v. Stephenson* was a response to the modern practice of mass factory production and packaging of foodstuffs. The risk of contaminated food is a common risk and it therefore called for a common law solution. In modern times, secret photography of celebrities is also a common risk and it calls for a common law response. There is nothing to prevent the modern unified court from recognizing that the owner of private premises owes a duty to his guests (and perhaps especially his celebrity guests) not to photograph them secretly. In fact, the Court of Appeal approved such a development in *Douglas v. Hello! Ltd*,[9] a case involving photographs of the celebrity couple Michael Douglas and Catherine Zeta Jones. However, it is submitted that the reasoning in that case fell into error to the extent that it sought to remedy the well-established absence of a tort of privacy by '*plugging the gap*' with the old equitable doctrine of breach of confidence.[10] The House of Lords has acknowledged that the equitable label 'breach of confidence' is, indeed, inappropriate. Lord Nicholls suggests that '[t]*he essence of the tort is better encapsulated now as misuse of private information*'[11] (although that message appears to have been overlooked in at least one case in the *Douglas v. Hello!* litigation).[12] The significant step of providing a remedy to the celebrity who is secretly photographed should be taken, if it is taken at all, in the name of the 'common law' rather than 'equity'. It might have been different if the owner of the gym had been unconscionably abusing an established legal right to photograph the Princess, but, of course, he was doing no such thing.

'Equity follows the law'

Equity follows the law; it does not supplant it. If the law were a stone, the function of equity would be to smooth away the sharp edges by which the law causes injustice and to fill in the cracks where the legal remedies are inadequate. It would never be the function of equity to smooth away the law to the point of eroding it completely, or to overfill the cracks so as to render the stone uneven. Thus, when equity first recognized that a covenant (a promise made in a deed) by a landowner concerning the use of his land might be binding on his successors, it held that the successor will only be bound if, in addition to other factors, the successor had notice of the covenant and the covenant is 'restrictive' in the sense that it does not put the successor to any positive expense.[13] Had equity gone further than this, it would have threatened entirely to undermine the common law rule of privity of contract, instead of merely recognizing an exception to it.

If equity sometimes goes a little further than the common law, it does so only because the common law has carried it most of the way. As Aesop observed, even a wren can fly further than an eagle if the wren rides on the eagle's back until the eagle is exhausted. Thus equity's remedies for breach of contract (specific performance, rescission) are

---

[9] [2001] QB 967, CA.   [10] *Per* Sedley LJ at 1001.

[11] *Campbell v. MGN Ltd* [2004] 2 WLR 1232, HL at [13]–[14].

[12] *Douglas v. Hello! Ltd* [2005] EWCA Civ 595, CA.

[13] For further consideration of the restrictive covenant, see Chapter 2.

sometimes superior to the common law remedy of monetary compensation (damages), but equity's remedy is only given where it has first been established that the common law remedy is inadequate. If a common law remedy is adequate, equity will not substitute its own remedy, even though equity's remedy might be more convenient to the claimant.[14] Specific performance is considered in depth later in this chapter.[15]

Another respect in which equity 'follows the law' is in the recognition of estates in land. Whereas a valid *deed* confers legal title to a fee simple or a lease, a specifically performable *contract* for the transfer of a fee simple or a lease confers equitable title to an equivalent equitable estate: an equitable fee simple or an equitable lease, respectively.[16]

'Equity looks to substance, not form'

This maxim does not tell us very much about the functional distinction between law and equity, unless it is to say that equity will not permit a party to rely upon a legal form, or the formal wording of a law, in a way that would be substantially unconscionable. We should, however, be clear about what the maxim does *not* mean. It does not mean that equity looks solely to substance: equity respects the form of legal deeds and contracts, because equity follows the law. Furthermore, it does not mean that equity never *insists* upon form, thus statute now provides that equity cannot grant specific performance of a contract to sell land unless the contract is in writing, containing all relevant terms and signed by both parties.[17] Neither does it mean that the common law always insists upon form: so, for example, a lease of land, which is one of only two estates in land capable of being legal, can be created orally without any formality at all if it is for a term not exceeding three years.[18] Finally, it does not mean that the common law never looks to substance instead of form. In *Street v. Mountford*,[19] Lord Templeman held a form of 'licence' to be in substance a lease:

> [T]he manufacture of a five-pronged implement for manual digging results in a fork even if the manufacturer, unfamiliar with the English language, insists that he intended to make and has made a spade.[20]

This mirrors the approach taken in Equity, as exemplified by *Locking v. Parker*,[21] where the question arose whether a real security in the form of a trust for sale of land was or was not a mortgage. The judge held that:

> it is not for a Court of Equity to be making distinctions between forms instead of attending to the real substance and essence of the transaction. Whatever form the matter took, I am of the opinion that this was a solely a mortgage transaction.[22]

---

[14] See *Leech v. Schweder* (1873) LR 9 Ch App 463, *per* Sir G. Mellish LJ at 475.
[15] See 'Equitable remedies' later in the chapter.   [16] *Walsh v. Lonsdale* (1882) LR 21 Ch D 9, CA.
[17] Law of Property (Miscellaneous Provisions) Act 1989, s. 2.   [18] Law of Property Act 1925, s. 54(2).
[19] [1985] 1 AC 809.
[20] Ibid. at 819. Compare another famous gardening metaphor: '*What's in a name? That which we call a rose by any other name would smell as sweet*' (Shakespeare, *Romeo and Juliet* (II:2)).
[21] (1873) 8 LR Ch App 30.   [22] (1875) 8 LR Ch App 30 at 39.

'Equity will not permit a statute to be used as an instrument of fraud'

At first sight, it is hard to reconcile this maxim with the principle of parliamentary sovereignty. Ordinarily, a statute must be applied according to the proper construction of its words, no matter how just or unjust might be the consequences of so doing, and no court is entitled to disapply the statute or to admit exceptions to it. However, on closer examination, it is clear that this maxim is applied to uphold the integrity of the statute, not to undermine it. The maxim is usually applied in relation to statutory formalities. A party seeking to avoid an informal or insufficiently formal transaction is ordinarily entitled to refer to, and rely upon, the other party's failure to comply with the necessary statutory formalities, but the maxim prevents the defendant from so pleading where it would be unconscionable for him so to do.

In *Shah v. Shah*,[23] a signatory to a deed sought to argue that the deed was invalid, because it had not been attested (witnessed) in the signatory's presence. The argument was factually accurate, with the result that the deed was invalid according to the relevant statutory provision.[24] Despite this, the Court of Appeal held that the signatory could not deny the validity of the deed, because, in seeking to rely on the failure of statutory formality, he was acting unconscionably. Of course, equity cannot be permitted to undermine the central policy of the statute, so it was held that it would be inappropriate for equity to go so far as to prevent a party from relying upon the absence of a *signature* to a deed. The maxim was considered further in Chapter 6 in connection with the statutory formalities for trust creation.

A radical, and little known, variation on the theme of the maxim is the possibility that equity might prevent an unconscionable use of the power to apply to Parliament for the enactment of a new private statute. The possibility was acknowledged in *Re London, Chatham and Dover Railway Arrangement Act*,[25] although the court thought it difficult to conceive of a case in which it would ever be appropriate to intervene in this way.

'Those who come to equity must come with clean hands'

In *Lee v. Haley*,[26] the claimants sought the discretionary equitable remedy of an injunction, with a view to protecting their trade as coal merchants. The old Court of Chancery refused to grant the injunction, because the claimant had 'unclean hands', not because of the coal, but because he had 'systematically and knowingly' sold his customers short on weight. The judge held that equity would not grant a remedy for the protection of a fraudulent trade.[27] This maxim seems to be concerned as much with the risk that judicial process will be brought into disrepute as it is with justice between the particular parties.[28]

---

[23] [2001] 3 WLR 31, CA. [24] Law of Property (Miscellaneous Provisions) Act 1989, s. 1(3).
[25] (1869) LR 5 Ch App 671. [26] (1869) 5 LR Ch App 155. [27] Ibid. at 158.
[28] For the possibility that unconscionability operates at the level of policy, see Chapter 4.

This maxim only applies where discretionary relief is sought; it does not apply to prevent a claimant from enforcing his equitable *entitlement* to property [29] (although it has the potential to deny specific performance of an estate contract).[30] The maxim cannot be applied to deprive a defendant of his equitable interest in property, even though the defendant's behaviour towards the claimant may have been intolerably bad. This is so even where the defendant acquired his interest in the past in response to the unconscionability of the claimant or the claimant's predecessor.[31] In other words, when a property right is granted to B to prevent the unconscionable assertion of a legal right or power by A against B, B's right will continue to exist even if B subsequently acts in a manner injurious to A. The appropriate remedy for B's behaviour is damages in tort, not forfeiture of his property.[32] The only wrongdoing that can produce unclean hands in the eyes of equity is wrongdoing with '*an immediate and necessary relation to the equity sued for*'.[33]

'Those who come to equity must do equity'

This maxim, like the previous maxim, only applies to equitable remedies awarded at the discretion of the court, including the remedies of specific performance and rescission of contracts. It was in the context of these remedies that the following observation was made:

> the court will, in granting relief, impose such terms upon the party as it deems the real justice of the case require...The maxim here is emphatically applied—he who seeks equity must do equity.[34]

In *Vadasz v. Pioneer Concrete (SA) Pty Ltd*[35] the maxim was applied when a guarantor sought rescission of his guarantee on the ground that he had been induced by a misrepresentation to give a guarantee more extensive than he had intended to give. The High Court of Australia granted rescission, but held that the claimant would have to 'do equity' by returning, or paying for, goods that the defendant had supplied to the guarantor since the date of the guarantee. The High Court of Australia approved the English Court of Appeal decision in *O'Sullivan v. Management Agency Ltd*,[36] where their Lordships, having rescinded a contract that the claimant had entered under the defendant's undue influence, held that the defendant should be allowed to retain some of the profits he had made under the contract. Their Lordships employed the maxim as a means of achieving '*practical justice between the parties*'.[37]

---

[29] *Rowan v. Dann* (1991) 64 P & CR 202.

[30] *Coatsworth v. Johnson* (1866) 55 LJQB 220, [1886–90] All ER Rep 547.

[31] *Williams v. Staite* [1979] Ch 291.   [32] [1979] Ch 291 at 300B–C.

[33] *Dering v. Earl of Winchelsea* (1787) 1 Cox Eq 318, *per* Eyre CB at 319.

[34] Story's *Commentaries on Equity Jurisprudence*, 2nd English edn (London: Sweet & Maxwell, 1892) at 693.

[35] [1995] 69 ALR 678.   [36] [1985] QB 428.

[37] Ibid. *per* Dunn LJ at 458. See also Fox LJ at 466: '*the court will do what is practically just in the individual case*'. See further, *Sledmore v. Dalby* (1996) 72 P & CR 196; *Cheese v. Thomas* [1994] 1 WLR 129; *Re Berkeley Applegate Ltd* [1989] Ch 32.

In a number of cases, wives have successfully sought the rescission of mortgages charged to their homes on the ground that they had entered into them under the undue influence of their husbands.[38] In such cases, the practical balance of justice approach can be applied to rescind the mortgage and, at the same time, to allow the bank to enforce the wife's obligations under the mortgage to the extent that she would have assumed them even in the absence of undue influence.[39]

'Equity sees as done that which ought to be done'

'Ought' is a dangerous word in any branch of law. Equity knows nought about 'ought' in any moral sense: its only morality is that the law ought to be followed—what, then, is the import of this maxim?

The key does not lie in the identification of what ought to be done. Although equity will sometimes require an obligation to be performed when the common law would be content to award compensation for failure of performance, law and equity are basically in agreement that a legal obligation *ought* to be fulfilled. As has been said, '*contracts ought to be performed. To break them, and to propose compensation for the breach by damages, is not complete justice.*'[40] Rather, the key lies in equity's peculiar ability to see that which ought to be done as if it had already been done. Consider the example of a defendant who has entered into a binding legal agreement to convey unique subject matter, such as a piece of land. Common law damages for breach of the agreement will be inadequate, so equity will order specific performance of the agreement. The common law does not imagine that damages have already been paid (if it did it could hardly justify giving judgment in favour of the defendant), but equity adopts the fiction that a specifically performable contract has already been performed, with the result that the party entitled to the subject matter of a specifically performable contract becomes the owner of the subject matter, in the eyes of equity, the moment the contract is made. Where a contract is specifically performable, the following statement of Sir Peter Millett (writing extra-judicially) is perfectly true:

> The common law remedy for breach of contract is an award of damages...the promisor's legal obligation is *either* to perform the contract *or* to pay damages, at his option; he is free to break his contract if he chooses...but while the common law waits until the promisor has broken his contract and then awards damages for breach, equity adopts an entirely different approach...it refuses to countenance the possibility of breach.[41]

The seminal case of *Walsh v. Lonsdale* illustrates the point.[42] A landlord and tenant had entered into a contract for a seven-year lease and the tenant had gone into possession, but the parties had neglected to execute the formal deed needed for a valid legal lease.

---

[38] The line of cases that commenced with *Barclays Bank plc v. O'Brien* [1994] 1 AC 180, HL, are surveyed in *Royal Bank of Scotland plc v. Etridge (No. 2)* [2002] 2 AC 773.

[39] *Dunbar Bank v. Nadeem* [1997] 2 All ER 253.   [40] *Tilley v. Thomas* (1867) LR 3 Ch App 61 at 72.

[41] 'Remedies: the error in *Lister v. Stubbs*' in *The Frontiers of Liability* (P. Birks, ed.) (Oxford: Oxford University Press, 1994) vol. 1, 51 at 58.   [42] (1882) LR 21 Ch D 9.

Despite the absence of the deed, the landlord claimed rent in advance in accordance with the contract and attempted to enforce his claim by exercising the *legal* right to distress for rent (which is the right to take and sell the tenant's goods in lieu of rent). The tenant claimed that, in the absence of a legal deed, there could be no legal right to claim rent in advance and that rent should be payable in arrear. He sought an injunction against the distress.

Sir George Jessel MR held that, where specific performance is available, a tenant holding under an agreement for a lease holds '*under the same terms in equity as if a lease had been granted*'.[43] Ironically, the tenant had sought the aid of equity in the form of an injunction, but it was the landlord who received it in the form of an equitable lease and, paradoxically, the landlord was even permitted to exercise the traditional *legal* right to levy distress for rent despite the equitable nature of the lease. Equity regarded the agreement to grant a lease as being not only made, but fulfilled, at least so far as the immediate parties were concerned. Of course, equity would have refused to grant specific performance of the agreement *in favour of the tenant*, because, having breached a substantial term of the lease (regarding the payment of rent), the tenant would have come to equity with unclean hands.[44]

Although normally applied to private transactions, this maxim has occasionally been applied to treat a *court order* to transfer property as taking immediate effect in equity, so as to impose a constructive trust on the person subject to the order.[45]

'Equity imputes an intention to fulfil an obligation'

This maxim is similar to the last, but whereas the last allows the court to adopt the fiction that an obligation has been fulfilled which ought, in the future, to be fulfilled, this maxim introduces the 'lesser' fiction that an obligation has already been fulfilled which ought already to have been fulfilled. The essence of this maxim is equity's refusal to accept that a legal or equitable obligation has not been met, when the facts can be interpreted consistently with the obligation having been met. So when a trustee mixes trust money with his own money and spends part of the mixed fund, it is assumed that the trust money remains in the unspent part of the fund wherever such an assumption is necessary to fulfil the trustee's obligation to the trust.[46] The maxim can be applied in the face of clear evidence that the party subject to the obligation had no intention whatsoever of fulfilling it. This is because the requisite intention is imputed, not merely implied.

'Where the equities are equal the first in time prevails'

This maxim is sometimes paraphrased 'the first in time is the first in right' because it is typically employed to determine priority between competing claims to equitable

---

[43] (1882) LR 21 Ch D 9 at 14.   [44] On this maxim, see earlier.
[45] *Mountney v. Treharne* [2003] Ch 135, CA; *Re Flint (A Bankrupt)* [1993] Ch 319.
[46] *Re Hallet's Estate* (1880) LR 13 Ch D 696, CA, as discussed in Chapter 14.

proprietary rights in an asset, usually land. Whereas a *'legal owner's right is paramount to every equitable charge not affecting his own conscience'*, an *'equitable owner, in the absence of special circumstances, takes subject to all equities prior in date to his own estate or charge'.*[47] Suppose, for example, that A grants an equitable mortgage of property to B and later grants a mortgage of the same property to C. In the usual course of events, B's mortgage will have priority over C's, in accordance with the maxim. However, the principle that the first right in time will prevail only applies if the competing equities are equal, which raises the question: when are equities unequal and what is the effect of such inequality? An answer was provided by Kay J in *Taylor v. Russell*,[48] who held that nothing less than 'gross negligence' must be proved by a later equitable mortgagee against a prior mortgagee to give priority to a later one. The phrase 'gross negligence' is not an especially helpful one, but it does suggest that the behaviour of a prior mortgagee must be substantially worse than that of a later mortgagee for the usual order of priorities to be disturbed. Certainly, it casts doubt on earlier authorities,[49] which appeared to suggest that mere technical superiority of a later equitable title might be sufficient to establish priority over an earlier equitable title.

'Where equity and law conflict, equity prevails'

This is not so much a maxim as a rule that determines the jurisdictional priority of equity. The rule can trace its origins back to the *The Earl of Oxford's Case*, which we examined in Chapter 1, but it now appears in statutory form:

> Every Court exercising jurisdiction in England and Wales in any civil cause or matter shall continue to administer law and equity on the basis that, wherever there is any conflict or variance between the rules of equity and the rules of common law with reference to the same matter, the rules of equity shall prevail.[50]

The equitable doctrines

The equitable doctrines are rigid traditional precepts by which equitable discretion is guided and restrained. They are ultimately derived from the application of equitable maxims—most of the doctrines owing a good deal to the maxim 'equity imputes an intention to fulfil an obligation'—but, over time they have lost virtually all contact with the forces of principle and pragmatism which first gave rise to the maxims themselves. With the benefit of hindsight, the development of the equitable doctrines can be seen to be a project out of character for such a pragmatic branch of law as equity, since equity is not doctrinaire. As Lord Templeman put it: *'Equity is not a computer. Equity operates on conscience.'*[51] However that may be, it is precisely because responsiveness to

---

[47] *Liverpool Marine Credit Co v. Wilson* (1872) LR 7 Ch App 507 at 511.   [48] (1890) 1 Ch 8 at 17.
[49] See, for example, *Pease v. Jackson* (1867–8) LR 3 Ch App 576.   [50] Supreme Court Act 1981, s. 49.
[51] *Winkworth v. Edward Baron Development Co Ltd* [1986] 1 WLR 1512, 1516.

'conscience' has potential for arbitrary and unpredictable application that doctrines are so necessary.

It is not altogether clear what should and should not be included in the list of equitable doctrines: for example, should equitable estoppel (which we examined in Chapter 8) be included? It has been decided to include here only those well-defined doctrines that appear in the orthodox list. They were undoubtedly more significant historically than they are now, but we will examine them briefly because they still offer a valuable insight into the nature and operation of equity today.

Conversion

By the doctrine of conversion,

> money directed to be employed in the purchase of land, and land directed to be sold and turned into money, are to be considered as that species of property into which they are directed to be converted.[52]

According to this doctrine, equity will, in certain circumstances, regard personal property as real property and real property as personal. We have already considered an example of the operation of this doctrine in the context of a contract for the sale of land[53] and another example in Chapter 6 when we considered specific performance of an agreement to transfer shares in a private company. Taking the land example, we saw that, whereas, at law, the contract entitles the purchaser to a personal monetary remedy, equity will order specific performance of the contract and, because specific performance ought to be done in the future, equity will consider it as done now. By this feat of imagination, equity converts the purchaser's purchase money into a right in the land at the moment of contract.[54] The simultaneous effect upon the vendor is that his entitlement to the land is immediately converted into an entitlement to the purchase money. This can have impractical results. Thus it has been held that if A grants B a contractual option to buy A's land, the land becomes mere personal property of A from the date of the option if B elects to exercise it, with the result that, if A subsequently dies leaving all of his real property to C and all of his personal property to D, the identity of the person (either C or D) entitled to sell the land to B will turn upon B's election.[55] Thankfully, this problem is less acute in the case of intestacy, for in that context, there is no distinction between the passing of real property and personal property.[56]

The doctrine of conversion as it applies to convert land into money is now of reduced relevance. Previously, if a trustee held land under a 'trust for sale', the trustee was deemed already to have sold the land in accordance with the maxim 'equity sees as done that which ought to be done'. Section 3 of the Trusts of Land and Appointment of

---

[52] *Fletcher v. Ashburner* (1779) 1 Bro C C 497, *per* Sir Thomas Sewell MR at 499.
[53] See Chapter 1.   [54] *Jerome v. Kelly (Inspector of Taxes)* [2004] 1 WLR 1409, HL.
[55] *Lawes v. Bennett* (1785) 1 Cox Eq. 167; *Re Carrington* [1932] 1 Ch 1.
[56] Administration of Estates Act 1925, ss. 33, 45.

Trustees Act 1996 has now abolished the doctrine of conversion in relation to trusts of land, with the result that land is no longer deemed to be money and money is no longer deemed to be land, although a trust for sale of land created in a will taking effect before 1 January 1997 will still operate to convert the land into money or, where appropriate (as where personal property is subject to a trust for sale in order that the trustees may acquire land), to convert money into land.

Satisfaction

If A owes a sum of money to B, equity will require A to pay the debt while he is alive. However, if the debt has not been paid by the time of A's death and A's will contains no clause requiring his executors to repay his debts, a legacy (a bequest of a sum of money) left by A to B in his will is presumed to satisfy any outstanding debt for an equal or lesser[57] sum owed by A to B prior[58] to making his will. Equity sees as done that which ought to be done and imputes to A an intention to fulfil his obligation to B, provided that the legacy is on terms that are as beneficial to B as repayment of the debt. Another example of the operation of the doctrine is so-called 'ademption of a legacy by a portion'. Where a child is bequeathed a specific legacy (such as '£1,000') in the will of a parent, or person *in loco parentis*, and that person, having written the will, but before death, makes a lifetime donation in the same or greater sum and in substantially the same kind, the legacy can no longer be taken. It is said to have been satisfied by the lifetime donation through the process of 'ademption'. If the lifetime donation is for a lesser sum, the legacy can be taken to the extent of the difference only. Whether or not there is an ademption always turns, ultimately, on the presumed intention of the donor.[59]

Performance

The doctrine of performance is a close relation to the doctrine of satisfaction and both doctrines share a common root in the maxim 'equity imputes an intention to fulfil an obligation'. However, whereas one type of obligation, such as a debt, may be satisfied by something quite different, such as a legacy, performance always involves an action of the same kind as that which would be required to perform the particular obligation. Thus a promise by A that he will leave a legacy to B will be performed if A dies intestate (without making a valid will) and the money passes to B on A's intestacy.[60] Likewise, if A promises to acquire freehold land of a certain value and settle it on trust for the benefit of his wife-to-be, the purchase of freehold land of a lesser value may be held to be a partial performance of the promise.[61] In that case there would have been no performance if A had acquired leasehold land, because that is fundamentally different in type to the freehold land promised.

---

[57] *Crichton v. Crichton* [1895] 2 Ch 853, Ch D. [58] *Cranmer's Case* (1702) 2 Salk 508.
[59] *Hopwood v. Hopwood* (1859) 22 Beav 488. [60] *Blandy v. Widmore* (1716) 1 P Wms 323.
[61] *Lechmere v. Lady Lechmere* (1735) Cas t Talb 80.

Election

The doctrine of election requires a party to choose between mutually exclusive courses of action. The common law version of the doctrine requires a claimant to choose between mutually inconsistent remedies before judgment is entered in his favour. In equity, the doctrine provides that, where a court judgment or a written instrument (such as a will[62] or trust deed) confers a benefit on a certain person, that person must choose to take the benefit subject to all the requirements of the judgment or instrument, or else choose to reject the judgment or instrument and lose the benefits conferred by it.[63] Despite its name, the equitable doctrine does not confer a right to choose; rather, it restricts the right to choose in the interest of fairness between the parties by ensuring that no party takes a benefit without taking an associated burden.[64] The equitable doctrine of election has its roots in the maxim *quod approbo non reprobo* ('that which I approve, I cannot reject'). A modern example is provided by *First National Bank Plc v. Walker*,[65] where the Court of Appeal held that a wife, who was awarded the matrimonial home in divorce proceedings and had accepted the mortgage on the house as part of the award, was not permitted in subsequent repossession proceedings brought by the bank to allege that the mortgage was invalid. She had elected to take the house and could not in conscience take it free of the mortgage.

Equitable remedies

In *Co-operative Insurance Society Ltd v. Argyll Stores (Holdings) Ltd*,[66] Lord Hoffmann affirmed that equitable remedies are '*flexible and adaptable to achieve the ends of equity*'.[67] But what are 'the ends of equity'? His Lordship approved the view expressed by the Lord Chancellor in *Wilson v. Northampton and Banbury Junction Railway Co.*[68] that the purpose of equitable relief is to '*do more perfect and complete justice*' than would be the result of leaving the parties to their remedies at common law. The usual common law remedy for breach of contract or commission of a tort is an award of damages, but if, in a particular case or in a particular type of case, it would be unconscionable for the defendant to restrict the claimant to common law damages, the court may award an equitable remedy against the defendant. For example, an injunction may be awarded to remedy the tort of trespass and the court may decree specific performance of a contract to acquire land, because, in both of these cases, an award of damages is insufficient to achieve a just outcome. In the former case, damages are inadequate because they will be nominal unless real harm has been caused and in any event an award of damages does not prevent future trespass; in the latter case, damages are inadequate because

---

[62] *Codrington v. Codrington* (1875) LR 7 HL 854.
[63] See, for example, *Frear v. Frear* [2008] EWCA Civ 1320.
[64] *Nexus Communications Group Ltd v. Lambert* [2005] EWHC 345, Ch D.
[65] (2001) 1 FLR 505.   [66] [1998] AC 1, HL.   [67] [1998] AC 1 at 9.
[68] (1874) LR 9 Ch App 279 at 284.

even if damages were competent to meet the purchaser's legitimate expectations as to the investment value of the land, no amount of money will assist the purchaser to buy identical substitute land, because all land is unique.

Whereas common law remedies are available as of right, equitable remedies retain the discretionary nature of the early equitable jurisdiction. Having said that, the onset over the past two centuries or so of defined systems of precedent and law reporting have curtailed the historical discretion somewhat, so that discretion is now exercised in accordance with fairly clear and sometimes rigid principles. As Lord Hoffmann once put it[69] when considering the equitable remedy of specific performance: '[T]*here are no binding rules, but this does not mean that there cannot be settled principles . . . which the courts will apply in all but exceptional circumstances.*'[70] Furthermore, we have already noted that the discretionary nature of equitable remedies can lead to the refusal of a remedy where the defendant comes to equity with unclean hands, but entirely innocent claimants may also be denied a remedy if to grant it would put the other party in breach of a contract with a third party.[71] It is also the case that entirely innocent claimants will be denied a remedy if to grant it would prejudice an innocent third party, or require the defendant to commit an illegal act, such as breaching a contract with a third party.[72] Other grounds for refusing an equitable remedy are that unfair hardship might be caused to the defendant (reflected in the maxim 'those who come to equity must do equity'),[73] or, as in a contract action, that the contract was forced upon the defendant through unfair pressure (whether or not actual undue influence was also present).[74] Ultimately, the question whether to award an equitable remedy calls for the court to exercise a very broad discretion. The court asks itself: '[i]*s it just, in all the circumstances, that a plaintiff should be confined to his remedy in damages?*'[75]

An equitable remedy is awarded *in personam* against the particular defendant. It is not a law as such, but a direct order of the court against the individual. Failure to comply with the order is contempt of court punishable by fine or imprisonment. However, the fact that remedies are sought *in personam* does not always mean that the defendant must be named: it can be sufficient to identify the defendant by description provided it is certain enough to enable potential defendants to be identified and distinguished from persons who are not potential defendants.[76] The fact that equitable remedies operate *in personam* means that they bind the persons against whom they are addressed and do not bind other persons (but see the section on the 'Freezing order' later in the chapter).

Equitable remedies are sometimes awarded as part of the final judgment in a matter, but some can also be awarded as interim remedies. Amongst the interim remedies listed

---

[69] *Co-operative Insurance Society Ltd v. Argyll Stores (Holdings) Ltd* [1998] AC 1, HL.

[70] Ibid. at 16.   [71] *Warmington v. Miller* [1973] QB 877.

[72] *Harnett v. Yielding* (1805) 2 Sch. & Lef 549, *per* Lord Redesdale LC at 554; *Willmott v. Barber* (1880) 15 Ch D 96, *per* Fry J, at 107; *Warmington v. Miller* [1973] QB 877, CA.

[73] See earlier.   [74] On undue influence, see the section on 'rescission' later.

[75] *Evans Marshall & Co Ltd v. Bertola SA* [1973] 1 WLR 349, *per* Sachs LJ.

[76] *Bloomsbury Publishing Group Ltd v. News Group Newspapers Ltd* [2003] 1 WLR 1633; *Hampshire Waste Services Ltd v. Intending Trespassers upon Chineham Incinerator Site* [2004] Env LR 9.

as available under the Civil Procedure Rules 1999[77] are injunctions, freezing orders, and search orders, all of which are considered in detail in this chapter. In the process of examining individual remedies, we will discover that there are a great many safeguards in place to ensure that the claimant does not gain an unfair advantage and that the defendant does not suffer an unfair detriment from the award of interim remedies.

Specific performance

At common law, the person who makes a contractual promise has the option to perform or not to perform. He might choose to breach his promise and to pay damages. In this sense equity is something of a spoilsport, for equity requires a promise to be performed whenever damages would not be an adequate remedy. The inadequacy of common law damages is prerequisite; equity will only decree specific performance where '*it can by that means do more and complete justice*' than the common law.[78] However, because an order, or 'decree', of specific performance is (like all equitable remedies) discretionary, it will be refused if the claimant has not kept his side of the bargain. This is in accordance with the maxim 'those who come to equity must come with clean hands'. Where the court does order (decree) specific performance, the order is binding against the defendant *in personam* and breach of the decree is a contempt of court, which may be punished by imprisonment.[79]

We have already noted that specific performance is only available where damages are inadequate. The reason for this is that the decree of specific performance is ordered to remedy unconscionability and there is nothing unconscionable in offering damages where they are adequate. This leaves us with the task of determining when common law damages are and are not 'adequate'. In the following sections, we will see that the adequacy of damages turns to a large extent upon the nature of the subject matter of the contract that has been breached. The availability of specific performance can also turn on pragmatic considerations, such as extreme difficulty in quantifying damages, and political considerations such as the protection of free speech.[80]

Specific performance is a court order to perform a specific positive obligation—typically, a contractual obligation. Whereas some equitable remedies, such as certain injunctions, may be ordered as interim measures before the final hearing of a matter, specific performance is a final order that is made only at the conclusion of the full trial.

Land

We considered specific performance of land in Chapter 1. We noted there that all land is unique (even identical homes on modern housing estates are located in utterly unique

---

[77] Rule 25.1.　　[78] *Wilson v. N&BJ Rly Co* (1874) LR 9 Ch App 279 at 284.

[79] *C.H. Giles Co Ltd v. Morris* [1972] 1 WLR 307, *per* Megarry J at 318.

[80] Even if it is the free speech of a far-right group: see *Verrall v. Great Yarmouth Borough Council* [1981] QB 202, in which the court ordered specific performance of a licence to occupy premises in which it was intended to hold a 'National Front' conference.

portions of three-dimensional space, benefiting from subtly distinct views, lighting, shade, etc.) and this means that there is a very strong presumption in favour of specific performance of contracts for the sale of land.

Personal property

Damages will usually be adequate where the contract was to purchase personal property, such as chairs (even antique 'Hepplewhite' chairs, provided they could be considered *'ordinary articles of commerce'*).[81] Damages are adequate in such cases because, as the Vice-Chancellor put it in *Falcke v. Gray*,[82] *'you only have to go into the market'* to *'buy another equally good article'*. Damages will not be adequate if the property is unique or if equivalent property cannot be readily acquired on the open market. Such was the case in *Falcke v. Gray* itself, where the subject of the contract was a pair of antique china vases of *'unusual beauty and rarity'* (although specific performance was, in that case, refused on other grounds); nor will damages be adequate if the property is of *'peculiar and practically unique value to the plaintiff'*.[83]

Sale of goods

Specific performance of a contract to deliver specific or ascertained goods may also be ordered at the court's discretion, on such terms and conditions as seem just to the court.[84] According to the Sale of Goods Act 1979:

> In any action for breach of contract to deliver specific or ascertained goods the court may, if it thinks fit, on the plaintiff's application, by its judgment or decree direct that the contract shall be performed specifically, without giving the defendant the option of retaining the goods on payment of damages.[85]

Shares

For more on the application of specific performance in cases involving shares, see *Oughtred v. IRC*[86] and *Neville v. Wilson*[87] in Chapter 6.

Contracts of employment, contracts for services, and contracts for a particular service

The Trade Union and Labour Relations (Consolidation) Act 1992[88] prohibits any court order for specific performance of a contract of employment and any injunction that would compel an employee to do any work or attend at any place for the doing of any work. There are a number of reasons for this rule and the reasons explain why the courts will generally refuse to order specific performance of any contract to provide ongoing personal services, whether or not it is an actual contract of employment.

---

[81] *Cohen v. Roche* [1927] 1 KB 169.   [82] (1859) 4 Drew 651.

[83] *Behnke v. Bede Shipping Co* [1927] 1 KB 649. In this case, an experienced ship valuer gave evidence that he was aware of 'only one other comparable ship'.   [84] Sales of Goods Act 1979, s. 52(1), (3).

[85] Section 52(1).   [86] [1960] AC 206, CA.   [87] [1997] Ch 144, CA.   [88] Section 236.

One reason is public policy: '*Courts are bound to be jealous, lest they should turn contracts of service into contracts of slavery.*'[89] The risk of enforcing something akin to slavery is increased if the contract requires the service provider to work closely over a prolonged period of time with someone with whom they do not wish to work. Prolonged employment can be contrasted with a case in which Champion Jockey Kieren Fallon was required to ride a particular horse in a specific one-off race ('The Derby').[90]

Another reason is the problem of supervision. If the contract is to perform a defined task, the court will not order specific performance if the contract cannot practically be enforced: as the maxim says, 'equity will not act in vain'. So, for example, trying to force a pop star to produce an album will be pointless if he or she might deliberately produce a bad one. This point was made by Megarry J in *C. H. Giles & Co. Ltd v. Morris*:[91]

> If a singer contracts to sing, there could no doubt be proceedings for committal if, ordered to sing, the singer remained obstinately dumb. But if instead the singer sang flat, or sharp, or too fast, or too slowly, or too loudly, or too quietly...who could say whether the imperfections of performance were natural or self-induced?

If the contract is not to perform a defined task, but to perform ongoing duties over a prolonged period of time, the problem of supervision is an even more serious one. The court will not order specific performance of such a contract if that would require '*constant supervision by the court*'.[92] Constant supervision is not merely impracticable,[93] it also raises the spectre of the court system being clogged by repeated applications to renew or vary the order. In *Co-operative Insurance Society Ltd v. Argyll Stores (Holdings) Ltd*,[94] the claimants were landlords of a shopping centre and the defendant's supermarket was the main tenant. In the defendant's lease, the defendant had covenanted to keep its premises open for retail trade during the usual hours of business in the locality, but, when the supermarket became unprofitable, the defendant closed the supermarket, having given the claimants only one month's notice to find a new tenant. At first instance, the judge granted an order for damages to be assessed, but refused an order for specific performance. The Court of Appeal, by a majority, allowed an appeal by the claimants and ordered specific performance.[95] The settled judicial practice not to grant specific performance of an agreement to carry on a business was affirmed, although it was recognized that the grant or refusal of specific performance remains a matter for the discretion of the judge and the settled practice might be departed from in exceptional circumstances. The decision of the Court of Appeal was reversed by the House of Lords.[96] Lord Hoffmann distinguished '*orders which require a defendant to carry on*

---

[89] *De Francesco v. Barnum* (1889) 45 Ch D 430.   [90] *Araci v. Fallon* [2011] EWCA Civ 668.
[91] [1972] 1 WLR 307, Ch D.
[92] *J.C. Williamson Ltd v. Lukey and Mulholland* (1931) 45 CLR 282, *per* Dixon J at 297–8.
[93] *Ryan v. Mutual Tontine Westminster Chambers Association Ltd* [1893] 1 Ch 116.
[94] [1998] AC 1, HL.   [95] 1 August 1995, Ch D.   [96] [1996] Ch 286, CA.

an activity, such as running a business over a more or less extended period of time' from '*orders which require him to achieve a result*'.[97] The courts will be more willing to make the latter sort of order because the order is limited in time.

The courts have ordered specific performance of building contracts[98] and repairing covenants.[99] The courts have even ordered defendants to perform an obligation to appoint a porter to supervise an office block, on the basis that the task of finding the porter was well defined and had to be performed within two months.[100]

Damages in lieu of specific performance

Equity will decree specific performance in lieu of ('in the place of') a common law remedy of damages to achieve more perfect justice, but since the Chancery Amendment Act of 1858[101] (known as 'Lord Cairns' Act'), equity has been able to award common law-type damages in lieu of specific performance.[102] At first sight, this seems nonsensical. If specific performance is awarded where damages are inadequate, when can it ever be appropriate for a court to award damages instead of specific performance? The answer is that, sometimes, it is simply not practicable to award specific performance, even though the decree of specific performance would be just and desirable.

Even though damages may be awarded in lieu of specific performance, it has been held that there is no common law analogy to specific performance, and it is therefore inappropriate 'by analogy' to apply the common law limitation period for contract to bar an action for specific performance.[103] Lord Cairns' Act also applies to authorize the award of damages in lieu of an injunction.[104]

Subrogation

Subrogation means, literally, to ask for something under another person's right. The remedy is frequently described in metaphorical terms as 'standing in another's shoes'.[105] Like other equitable remedies, subrogation '*arises from the conduct of the parties on well settled principles and in defined circumstances which make it unconscionable for the defendant to deny* [the claimant's claim]'.[106] The well-settled principles of subrogation were set out clearly by Walton J in *Burston Finance Ltd v. Speirway Ltd*,[107] in which his Lordship observed that:

> [Subrogation] finds one of its chief uses in the situation where one person advances money on the understanding that he is to have a certain security for the money he has advanced, and, for one reason or another, he does not receive the promised security. In such a case he is nevertheless to be subrogated to the rights of any other person who at the relevant time had

---

[97] [1998] AC 1 at 13.   [98] *Wolverhampton Corporation v. Emmons* [1901] 1 KB 515.

[99] *Jeune v. Queens Cross Properties Ltd* [1974] Ch 97.   [100] *Posner v. Scott-Lewis* [1987] Ch 25.

[101] 21 & 22 Vict c 27.   [102] See now Supreme Court Act 1981, s. 50.

[103] *P & O Nedlloyd BV v. Arab Metals Co* [2006] EWCA Civ 1717. See, further, Chapter 13.

[104] See later.

[105] See, for example, *Banque Financière de la Cité v. Parc (Battersea) Ltd* [1999] 1 AC 221, 226.

[106] *Boscawen v. Bajwa* [1996] 1 WLR 328, CA.   [107] [1974] 1 WLR 1648.

any security over the same property and whose debts have been discharged, in whole or in part, by the money so provided by him, but of course only to the extent to which his money has, in fact, discharged their claim.[108]

This means that, if a third party (T) pays off a debt owed by a debtor (D) to a creditor (C), T will be permitted to claim any assets which were held by C to secure the payment of the debt by D, although T can only claim those assets to the extent that his money discharged C's claim against D.

So if a person lends money to assist in the purchase of a house and those moneys are paid to the vendor and used to discharge the vendor's mortgage, the lender is entitled to be subrogated to the mortgagee's rights under the mortgage even if the sale falls through before the lender can establish a mortgage of its own.[109] It is not necessary that T should intend to be subrogated to the rights of B, only that T should not intend to benefit C.[110] Subrogation has been described as a restitutionary remedy, whether in the sense of assisting in the recovery of trust property[111] or in the sense of reversing unjust enrichment.[112] Subrogation was held to operate in the latter sense in a case involving mortgage fraud.[113] A husband and wife had signed a mortgage deed, which they used to acquire their home, but, later, the husband forged his wife's signature on a second mortgage, which was used to discharge the earlier mortgage. The wife claimed that she was not bound by the first mortgage, but it was held that the later mortgagee had been subrogated to the rights of the earlier mortgagee. Those rights included the unsecured right (a right not against the land, but against the wife personally) to require the wife to pay arrears of instalments. Accordingly, the wife was ordered to pay unpaid arrears to the later mortgagee, plus 13 years of unpaid interest on the claim.[114]

Rectification

The equitable remedy of rectification is one aspect of the general equitable jurisdiction to relieve from the consequences of mistake[115] or fraud.[116] It has proved most useful in the case of mistakes in contracts and wills,[117] and in cases where a party's advisers should have appreciated that the party did not understand the terms of the arrangement.[118] The remedy must be specifically pleaded and proved.[119] If a formal document

---

[108] At 1652B–C.   [109] *Boscawen v. Bajwa* [1996] 1 WLR 328, CA.

[110] Ibid. (*Orakpo v. Manson Investments Ltd* [1978] AC 95, *per* Lord Diplock at 105; *Wylie v. Carlyon* [1922] 1 Ch 51 considered.)   [111] *Boscawen v. Bajwa* [1996] 1 WLR 328, CA.

[112] *Banque Financière de la Cité v. Parc (Battersea) Ltd* [1999] 1 AC 221 at 234 (but compare the contrary view of the High Court of Australia in *Bofinger v. Kingsway Group Limited* [2009] HCA 44).

[113] *Filby v. Mortgage Express (No. 2) Ltd* [2004] EWCA Civ 759, CA, *per* May LJ at [67].   [114] Ibid.

[115] *Gibbon v. Mitchell* [1990] 1 WLR 1304, *per* Millett J at 1307; *Gallaher Ltd v. Gallaher Pensions Ltd* [2005] EWHC 42 (Ch).   [116] *Collins v. Elstone* [1893] P 1.

[117] *Holtam v. Holtam* [2004] All ER (D) 408.

[118] In *Bhatt v. Bhatt* [2009] EWHC 734 (Ch) the mistake to be rectified arose from the party's poor grasp of the English language.

[119] *Chartbrook Ltd v. Persimmon Homes Ltd* [2009] UKHL 38, [2009] 1 AC 1101, House of Lords; *Cherry Tree Investments Ltd v. Landmain Ltd* [2012] EWCA Civ 736; [2012] 2 P & CR 10, Court of Appeal.

does not carry out the parties' (in the case of a trust, the settlor's or testator's) intentions, a court may order that it be rectified on the basis that 'equity looks to substance not form'.[120] This is in contrast to the common law, which construes documents according to their form without regard to the parties' prior intentions, as revealed by discussions or other acts preparatory to drawing up the relevant document.[121]

Lord Walker confirmed in *Futter v. HMRC Commissioners; Pitt v. HMRC Commissioners*,[122] that the court cannot decide the issue of what is unconscionable according to an elaborate set of rules. It must consider in the round the existence of a distinct mistake (as compared with total ignorance or disappointed expectations), its degree of centrality to the transaction in question, and the seriousness of its consequences, and make an evaluative judgment whether it would be unconscionable, or unjust, to leave the mistake uncorrected. The court may and must form a judgment about the justice of the case.[123] This approach was followed in *Pagel v. Farman*,[124] in which a businessman sought to recover millions of pounds paid to his business partner. The claimant alleged that the gift was made under the mistaken belief that the business partner needed the money to stave off the sale of his home. The court held that the gift had more likely been made by way of acknowledgment that the donor had caused the donee's financial problems in the first place.

Contracts

The status of rectification as an equitable doctrine means that even bilateral contracts may be rectified in favour of one party, if '*it is inequitable that* [the other party] *should be allowed to object to the rectification*', as might occur if the former party were to enter the contract under a unilateral mistake of which the latter party was aware.[125] For rectification to be ordered in such a case, the defendant's conduct in suppressing his knowledge of the mistake must be '*such as to affect the conscience*'.[126] The defendant's conscience is unlikely to be affected unless the mistake was one that was to his benefit.

The court also has jurisdiction to rectify an agreement if there was a common continuing mistake between the parties with regard to a particular provision of the agreement, but the court requires '*convincing proof*' that the concluded instrument did not represent the parties' common intention.[127]

Wills

If a court is satisfied that a will is so expressed that it fails to carry out the testator's intentions, in consequence of a clerical error or of a failure to understand his instructions, it

---

[120] The equitable remedy of rectification has lately been put on a statutory footing. Administration of Justice Act 1982, s. 20(1); *Re Segelman (deceased)* [1996] 2 WLR 173. See Chapter 9.

[121] *BCCI v. Ali* [2002] 1 AC 251, HL; *Cambridge Antibody Technology v. Abbott Biotechnology Ltd* [2004] EWHC 2974 (Pat), Ch D (Patents Ct).   [122] [2013] UKSC 26; [2013] 2 WLR 1200.

[123] Ibid. at para. [128].

[124] [2013] EWHC 2210 (Comm) Queen's Bench Division (Commercial Court).

[125] *Thomas Bates & Son Ltd v. Windham's (Lingerie) Ltd* [1981] 1 WLR 505, *per* Buckley LJ at 515–16; *George Wimpey UK Ltd v. V I Construction Ltd* [2005] EWCA Civ 77, CA (Civ Div).

[126] *George Wimpey UK Ltd v. VI Construction Ltd* [2005] EWCA Civ 77.

[127] *Joscelyne v. Nissen* [1970] 2 QB 86.

may order that the will shall be rectified so as to carry out his intentions.[128] Crucially, the court has the power to rectify a settlement to give effect to the intentions of the parties to an agreement. It is not necessary for the parties to have agreed precisely the form of words that they wished to be inserted into the settlement.[129] If a solicitor makes a mistake in drafting a will, the test to be applied is whether or not the solicitor had applied his mind to the significance and effect of the words used. An error through mere inadvertence *should* be rectified.[130] Sometimes quite remarkable mistakes are corrected, as in *Lawie v. Lawie*,[131] where a discretionary trust established for the benefit of the settlors' grandchildren accidentally omitted to include the settlors' children within the class of potential beneficiaries. Rectification was ordered in part because the trusts, as initially created, gave the trustees no practical choice of potential beneficiaries.[132]

Injunction

The effect of an injunction will be to stop the defendant from doing something (a 'prohibitory' injunction), or to require the defendant to do something (a 'mandatory' injunction), or, exceptionally, to prevent the defendant from committing a wrong that has not yet been committed, but which is threatened. The latter is the so-called *quia timet* injunction (*quia timet* means 'because he fears'). An example of a prohibitory injunction is one that prevents a trespasser from entering onto the claimant's land. An example of a mandatory injunction is one that requires a person to pull down a wall that was wrongly built on another person's land. The various types of injunction are considered in detail later.

As with the equitable remedy of specific performance, injunctions are only available at the court's discretion and where damages would not be adequate. It is also required that the party seeking the injunction has a legal (or equitable right) that the injunction would protect. In *Day v. Brownrigg*,[133] the claimant whose house had carried the name 'Ashford Lodge' for 60 years was refused the injunction he sought to prevent his next-door neighbour from giving his house the very same name. Sir George Jessel MR held that no right of the claimant was infringed by the defendant renaming his house in this way.

Injunctions operate *in personam*. This means, as we have already noted, that to breach an injunction is not to break a legal rule, but rather to act in contempt of court—an offence that is punishable by fine or even imprisonment. In *Shalson v. Russo*,[134] a fraudster was imprisoned for two years for breaching an equitable injunction freezing his assets.[135]

---

[128] Administration of Justice Act 1982, s. 20.   [129] *Stephenson v. Stephenson* [2004] All ER (D) 35 (Mar).
[130] *Re Segelman (decd)* [1996] 2 WLR 173.   [131] [2012] EWHC 2940 (Ch).
[132] Compare *Re Gibbon (Deceased)* [2013] EWHC 2862 in which a deed of variation in relation to a will was rectified to show that discretionary trust funds should vest in the trustees during the beneficiary's lifetime and would therefore fall outside of her estate for inheritance tax purposes. Compare, also, *Marley v Rawlings* [2014] UKSC 2, where a solicitor's failure to notice that the husband had signed the wife's will (and vice-versa) was rectified as a 'clerical error' under Administration of Justice Act 1982 s. 20(1)(a).
[133] (1878–79) LR 10, Ch D 294, 4 December 1878.   [134] [2003] EWHC 1637 (Ch).
[135] For 'freezing orders' see later.

Injunctions may be made at the final hearing of a matter, in which case they will often be made on detailed terms that are designed to ensure that the parties will not resort to litigation in the future; alternatively, injunctions may be made in a preliminary hearing before the hearing of the merits of the case, in which case it is said to be 'interim' (formerly, 'interlocutory', meaning 'between hearings'). Interim injunctions are frequently made to deal with some emergency and, for this reason, some may be sought by an 'application without notice' to the other party (previously called an *ex parte* application).[136]

The standard form of court order for an interim injunction contains the following fearsome warning to the defendant:

(1) This Order [prohibits you from doing] [obliges you to do] the acts set out in this Order. [You should read it all carefully. You are advised to consult a Solicitor as soon as possible]. You have a right to ask the Court to vary or discharge this Order.

(2) If you disobey this Order you may be found guilty of Contempt of Court and [any of your directors] may be sent to prison or fined [and you may be fined] or your assets may be seized.[137]

The defendant to an injunction has it tough, but the applicant does not have it all his own way. The applicant must give the court an undertaking to pay any damages that the respondent (and any third party) might suffer as a result of the injunction—for example, loss of profits if a business activity is brought to a halt—to the extent that the court considers appropriate.

The requirement to give an undertaking to pay damages is so onerous for applicants of modest means that they frequently prefer to delay their application until they are quite sure that they can prove their claim in the final hearing. In *Mortimer v. Bailey*,[138] the applicants delayed their application for an interim injunction to halt and remove building works until the building works were very nearly complete. The judge refused the interim order, because it was so close to the date of the final hearing, but at the final hearing awarded a mandatory injunction to have the building (it was an extension to their home) pulled down. Previously, it had been thought that delay in seeking an interim injunction would amount to acquiescence so as to prevent the applicant from seeking an injunction, but the Court of Appeal recognized that the applicant's modest means justified their refusal to risk an injunction until they were sure of their case. The court ordered the defendant to pull down the extension on the basis that they had run the risk that the court would order a mandatory injunction to that effect.[139] Indeed, the award of damages in lieu of an injunction is very much the exception to the rule,

---

[136] Judges sometimes still prefer the Latin (for example, Hughes LJ in *The Earl of Cardigan v. Moore* [2011] EWCA Civ 1011, in which his Lordship reminds us that there is '*a plain and high duty of full disclosure on any ex parte applicant and if it is not discharged, even if that is in good faith, the order is apt to be set aside*').

[137] Practice Direction on Interim Injunctions (25PD–10) (cited in *Customs and Excise Commissioners v. Barclays Bank plc* [2006] UKHL 28; [2007] 1 AC 181 at 192–3, HL).

[138] *Mortimer v. Bailey* [2005] Build LR 85, [2004] EWCA Civ 1514, CA.

[139] See G. Watt, 'Building at risk of injunction' (2005) 69 Conv 14.

but damages will be awarded where it would be unjust to give the claimant more—for example, if the claimant '*has shown that he only wants money*'.[140]

In *Regan v. Paul Properties DPF No. 1 Ltd*,[141] the fact that the defendant continued development in the face of the applicant's strong protests was given as a reason for refusing to enforce the applicant's undertaking to pay the defendant's damages. Usually, though, the court will enforce an undertaking to pay damages if, at the final hearing, it appears that the injunction should not have been awarded in the first place.[142]

Prohibitory injunction

An interim prohibitory injunction operates before the final hearing of the matter to stop the defendant from doing something that is infringing the applicant's legal or equitable rights. In the leading case of *American Cyanamid Co v. Ethicon Ltd*,[143] Lord Diplock laid down a number of helpful guidelines to the circumstances in which it is appropriate to award such an injunction. The respect in which his Lordship's guidelines are held has tended to imbue them with the status of statutory rules, but it should not be forgotten that the award of an injunction is ultimately discretionary, albeit guided by principle.

The claimant in the case was a US company that owned a patent covering certain medical products. The defendants, also a US company, were about to launch on the UK market a product that the plaintiffs claimed infringed their patent. The plaintiffs applied for an interim (then an 'interlocutory') injunction, which was granted by the judge at first instance, with the usual undertaking in damages by the plaintiffs. The Court of Appeal reversed his decision on the ground that no prima facie case of infringement had been made out. The House of Lords allowed the appeal.

Lord Diplock held that the court must be satisfied that '*the claim is not frivolous or vexatious, in other words, that there is a serious question to be tried*' and that the claimant has a '*real prospect of succeeding in his claim for a permanent injunction at the trial*'.[144] Once this preliminary threshold is passed, the court should then ask whether '*the balance of convenience*' favours the grant or refusal of interim relief. With regard to this question, the first consideration is to ask whether, assuming that the claimant will succeed in his claim for a permanent injunction at the final trial, damages would be an adequate compensation for continuing hardship suffered by the claimant between the present application for interim relief and the date of the expected award of a permanent injunction. If common law damages would be adequate and the defendant can pay them, the presumption is against an interim injunction; if common law damages would not be adequate to compensate for continuing hardship suffered by the claimant between the present application for interim relief and the date of the expected award of a permanent injunction, the first consideration for the court is to ask whether, assuming

---

[140] *Shelfer v. City of London Electric Lighting* [1895] 1 Ch 287, CA, *per* Lindley LJ at 315. See, also, *Gafford v. Graham* (1999) 77 P & CR 73, CA; *Midtown Ltd v. City of London Real Property Co Ltd* [2005] EWHC 33 (Ch) at [70]–[80].   [141] [2006] EWHC 2052.
[142] *SmithKline Beecham plc v. Apotex Europe Ltd* [2006] EWCA Civ 658.   [143] [1975] 2 WLR 316, HL.
[144] [1975] AC 396 at 407 and 408.

that the claimant will fail in his claim for a permanent injunction at the final trial, the defendant would be adequately compensated by the claimant's undertaking to compensate the defendant for the loss he will sustain if an interim injunction is awarded. If the adequacy of damages is evenly balanced in favour of defendant and claimant, '*it is a counsel of prudence to take such measures as are calculated to preserve the status quo*'[145]—in other words, an interim injunction should not be ordered—although where the scales are evenly balanced between the parties, an injunction might exceptionally be awarded if the claimant's affidavit evidence adduces an unusually strong chance of success at the final trial, with the qualification that, in an interim hearing, the '*court is not justified in embarking upon anything resembling a trial*'.[146]

Other factors that might bear on the balance of convenience between the parties include: the presence of hardship or extreme personal circumstances;[147] a loss of employment;[148] the closing of a business;[149] or the fact that a prohibitory injunction cannot be used to force an employee into a position of having to perform a contract of services.[150] Where the injunction restricts freedom of expression, it is usually required to demonstrate more than a 'real prospect' of success (although exceptions will be admitted if necessary).[151] The fact that 'equity will not act in vain', means that an injunction will not be granted if it can do no practical good.[152]

Mandatory injunction

> [T]he court is far more reluctant to grant a mandatory injunction than it would be to grant a comparable prohibitory injunction. In a normal case the court must, inter alia, feel a high degree of assurance that at the trial it will appear that the injunction was rightly granted and this is a higher standard than is required for a prohibitory injunction.[153]

The court will not grant an interim mandatory injunction if it would have an effect equivalent to specific performance, unless specific performance would itself be an appropriate order. In the *Page One Records* case,[154] the manager of sixties pop group

---

[145] *Cottage Foods Ltd v. Milk Marketing Board* [1984] 1 AC 130.   [146] [1975] AC 396 at 409.

[147] See, for example, *Patel v. Ali* [1984] Ch 283, in which the defendant underwent the amputation of a leg at a time when she was pregnant and her husband was in prison.

[148] *Fellowes v. Fisher* [1976] QB 122, CA: the injunction was refused on the balance of convenience, because there was no clear evidence that the claimants would suffer any damage if the injunction was refused, but, if it was granted, the defendant would lose his job.

[149] In *Potter Ballotini v. Weston Baker* [1977] RPC 202, an injunction was refused because it would have unfairly required closure of the defendant's business.   [150] See 'Specific performance', earlier.

[151] See *Cream Holdings Ltd v. Banerjee* [2004] UKHL 44, [2005] 1 AC 253, HL, and *Douglas v. Hello! Ltd (No. 3)* [2005] EWCA Civ 595; [2006] QB 125, CA.

[152] See *BBC v. HarperCollins Publishers Limited et al* [2010] EWHC 2424 (Ch), in which the BBC failed to secure an injunction to prevent publication of a book revealing the secret identity of 'The Stig' character in the TV programme *Top Gear*. The judge observed that: 'the identity of Mr Collins as The Stig is [already] in the public domain'.

[153] Per Megarry J in *Shepherd Homes Ltd v. Sandham* [1971] Ch 340, Ch D, approved in *Locabail International Finance Ltd v. Agroexport (The Sea Hawk)* [1986] 1 WLR 657, CA.

[154] *Page One Records Ltd. v. Britton and Ors (trading as The Troggs)* [1968] 1 WLR 157, Ch D.

The Troggs asked the court to award him an interim injunction to restrain the group from engaging any other manager. He had produced The Troggs' song, 'Give it to me',[155] but, when it came to an injunction, the court declined to give it to him. The applicant's request for an injunction to prevent the employment of another manager was interpreted as being, in effect, a mandatory injunction compelling the group to continue to employ the applicant, which would, in turn, be tantamount to ordering the applicant specifically to perform his contract for personal services. The applicant was therefore refused an injunction—for his own protection. With hindsight, the parties could have saved themselves a great deal of trouble and expense: The Troggs reunited with Page at a later date. If The Troggs are a little out of date, the reader may be interested to know that The Stone Roses' failure in the 1990s fully to capitalize on the immense popularity that they had achieved at the end of the 1980s can be put down, in large part, to the fact that they were trapped in a legal battle with their management and, from 1990, were prevented from releasing any music until the *Second Coming* album appeared in 1994.

Damages in lieu of injunction

Just as Lord Cairns' Act authorizes the award of damages in lieu of specific performance, so it authorizes the award of damages in lieu of an injunction.[156] Damages are awarded when an injunction would be desirable, but impracticable. Classic instances include cases where a vital industry is causing an ongoing nuisance to landowners and cases where houses have been built in breach of a restrictive covenant. In *Wrotham Park Estate Co v. Parkside Homes Ltd*,[157] Brightman J awarded damages in lieu of a mandatory injunction to pull down several houses because '[t]*he erection of the houses, whether one likes it or not, is a fait accompli and the houses are now the homes of people*'.[158]

However, the courts are ever mindful to ensure that the builders of houses and the creators of nuisance are dissuaded from thinking that they are immune to injunctions that would tear down their houses and close down their factories. In *Shelfer v. City of London Electric Lighting*,[159] Lindley LJ opined that the jurisdiction to award damages instead of an injunction should be exercised only in exceptional cases. In that case, an electric lighting company had erected powerful engines and other works on land near to a house, causing structural damage to the house. The Court of Appeal ordered the nuisance to cease. To have awarded damages instead would have sent out the message that the law allows tortfeasors to purchase the right to commit torts. For the same reason, courts are quite willing to order the demolition of buildings erected with reckless disregard for breach of restrictive covenants.[160]

Quia timet injunction

The Latin phrase *quia timet* means 'because he fears'. A *quia timet* injunction is ordered where a civil wrong is threatened, but has not yet been committed. Prevention is better

---

[155] Ibid.   [156] *Jaggard v. Sawyer* [1995] 1 WLR 269, CA.   [157] [1974] 1 WLR 798
[158] Ibid. at 811.   [159] [1895] 1 Ch 287.
[160] *Mortimer v. Bailey* [2004] EWCA Civ 1514, see earlier.

than cure when it comes to administering justice: *'justice that prevents excels justice that punishes'*, to paraphrase Coke.[161] From this, it follows that, '[a]*lthough the claimant must establish his right, he may be entitled to an injunction even though an infringement has not taken place but is merely feared or threatened'*.[162] The threshold requirement for the award of a *quia timet* injunction is *'convincing evidence of real danger of actual violation'*.[163] The claimant must establish a strong case: *'no one can obtain a* quia timet *order by merely saying "*Timeo*"'*.[164]

In *Redland Bricks Ltd v. Morris*,[165] Lord Upjohn summarized two types of *quia timet* action: First:

> where the defendant has as yet done no hurt to the plantiff but is threatening and intending (so the plaintiff alleges) to do works which will render irreparable harm to him or his property if carried to completion.[166]

Second:

> the type of case where the plaintiff has been fully recompensed both at law and in equity for the damage he has suffered but where he alleges that the earlier actions of the defendant may lead to future cases of action.[167]

The present case was a typical example of the second type. A judge had awarded a mandatory injunction requiring the defendant clay-digging company to fill in a pit so as to restore support to the claimant's neighbouring land. The defendant appealed. On ultimate appeal, the House of Lords discharged the injunction. It was held that, albeit that there was a strong probability of grave damage to the claimant's land in the future and damages were not a sufficient remedy, the appellants had not behaved unreasonably and, since the mandatory injunction imposed upon them an unqualified obligation to restore support without any indication of what work was to be done, the injunction would be discharged.

Search order (formerly 'Anton Piller order')

The search order allows a claimant to search the defendant's premises and seize things, especially documents, which the claimant will need to prove a legal claim against the defendant. In theory, the search is not forcible, but the defendant is ordered to give his permission to be searched and is provided with the incentive of prison for contempt of court if he refuses. Established by the Court of Appeal in *Anton Piller KG v. Manufacturing Processes Ltd*[168] on the basis of long-standing case law, this order now has a statutory basis. The Civil Procedure Act 1997, s. 7, provides that, in the case of

---

[161] *Coke's Institutes* states *'preventing justice excelleth punishing justice'*.

[162] *Snell's Equity*, 28th edn, at 630.

[163] *Angela Drury v. The Secretary of State for the Environment Food and Rural Affairs* [2004] EWCA Civ 200, CA.

[164] *A-G for the Dominion of Canada v. Ritchie Contracting and Supply Co Ltd* [1919] AC 999, *per* Lord Dunedin at 1005. *'Timeo'* translates 'I am afraid'. [165] [1970] AC 652, HL.

[166] [1970] AC 652 at 665. [167] Ibid. [168] [1976] Ch 55.

any existing or proposed proceedings the court may make an order for the purpose of securing (a) the preservation of evidence which is or may be relevant; or (b) the preservation of property which is or may be the subject matter of the proceedings or as to which any question arises or may arise in the proceedings. Such an order may direct any person to permit any person described in the order to enter premises in England and Wales, and, while on the premises, to take any of the following steps, so far as the terms of the order allow: to carry out a search for or inspection of anything described in the order; to make or obtain a copy, photograph, sample or other record of anything so described; to retain for safe keeping anything described in the order.

The Civil Procedure Rules 1999 summarize the search order as being an '*order requiring a party to admit another party to premises for the purpose of preserving evidence etc*'.[169] The order may also direct the person subject to the order to provide any information or article described in the order, but an order made under the 1997 Act does not affect any right of a person to refuse to do anything on the ground that to do so might tend to expose him or his spouse to proceedings for an offence.

So we know what a search order does, but when will it be granted? A search order is a draconian measure and will be granted sparingly. The decision whether or not to award a search order lies, as it does for all injunctions, in the discretion of the court, but the court will be guided by the wisdom of earlier cases.

In the original case, AP Ltd, a German company, claimed that MP Ltd, its English agent, had been passing on confidential information to certain of AP's rival German companies. AP Ltd applied for an interim injunction to permit, *inter alia*, entry of MP's premises to inspect documentation and to remove documentation to the custody of AP's solicitors. AP undertook to issue a writ forthwith to support the action for breach of confidence and AP was granted its injunction. MP appealed. The appeal was allowed. Lord Denning MR held that, in very exceptional circumstances, if the plaintiff has a very strong prima facie case to show that the defendant has caused, or will cause, very serious damage to the plaintiff and if there is clear evidence that the defendant possesses vital evidence that might be disposed of so as to defeat justice, the court could by order permit the plaintiff's representatives to enter the defendant's premises to inspect and remove such material. The order could, in such very exceptional circumstances, be made without notice to the other party (at that time, called an *ex parte* application). It was stated that, where such an injunction is granted, the plaintiff must act carefully and with full respect for the defendant's rights. One aspect of this is that the applicant's solicitors should photocopy confiscated documentation and return the originals to their owner. From this and subsequent cases, it is possible to identify the following factors as general prerequisites to an order: an extremely strong prima facie claim against the defendant; a real risk of serious damage to the defendant if the search order is refused; clear evidence that the defendant has the target assets in his possession; clear risk that the defendant will destroy, conceal, or dispose of the target assets.

---

[169] Rule 25.1.

The last factor is perhaps the most difficult. It has been held that a search order is inappropriate where the defendant will probably comply with an ordinary order to deliver up the assets; indeed, it has been said that the defendant must be akin to a '*fly by night pirate*' for a search order to be justified.[170]

The search order has proved to be most useful in dealing with cases of alleged audio and video piracy. In *Columbia Picture Industries Inc v. Robinson*,[171] the company sought an Anton Piller injunction against an alleged 'video pirate'—that is, a person who, according to the judge, '*manufactures and trades in video cassettes which infringe the copyright in cinematographic films*'. On one issue, the dispute ultimately came down to the films *For Your Eyes Only* and *Star Wars*. If there is some dispute as to the proper ownership of certain items, such as alleged pirate tapes, they should not be retained by the claimant or his solicitor; they should be passed, subject to an undertaking that they be produced in court, to the defendant's solicitor.

The beneficiary of a search order is not allowed to use force (not even when seeking to recover pirated *Star Wars* movies). Where a search order has been executed in an excessive and oppressive manner the court may order aggravated damages against the applicants and possibly, since solicitors executing such orders do so as officers of the court, exemplary damages.

As a result of the Human Rights Act 1998, we can add to the applicant's worries the risk that a disproportionate search may be a potential breach of Art. 8 of the European Convention on Human Rights.[172]

Freezing order (formerly 'Mareva injunction')

The freezing order is a prohibitory interim injunction by which the defendant is prevented from dealing with his assets in any way that might defeat the claimant's prospects of enforcing a legal judgment against the defendant. (In many cases the order nevertheless permits the party subject to it to continue to deal with its assets in the ordinary and proper course of business.)[173] Originally developed in judicial decisions, including the decision of the Court of Appeal in *Mareva Compania Naviera SA v. International Bulkcarriers SA*,[174] the order now has statutory force. The Civil Procedure Rules 1999 describe it as an order '*restraining a party from removing from the jurisdiction assets located there*' or '*restraining a party from dealing with any assets whether located within the jurisdiction or not*'.[175] It is not the purpose of the order to give a claimant security for his claim or to give him any proprietary interest in the 'frozen' assets.[176] As

---

[170] *Lock International plc v. Beswick* [1989] 1 WLR 1268.   [171] [1987] Ch 38.

[172] *Rank Film Distributors Ltd v. Video Information Centre* [1982] AC 380; *Chappell v. United Kingdom* 10461/83 [1989] ECHR 4 (30 March 1989).

[173] *Mobile Telesystems Finance SA v. Nomihold Securities Inc* [2011] EWCA Civ 1040; [2012] Lloyd's Rep 6.

[174] [1975] 2 Lloyd's Rep 509.   [175] Rule 25.1(f).

[176] *Gangway Ltd v. Caledonian Park Investments (Jersey) Ltd* [2001] 2 Lloyd's Rep 715, *per* Colman J at [14]. See, generally, S. Gee, *Commercial Injunctions*, 5th edn (London: Sweet & Maxwell, 2004) at 77–83, cited in *Fourie v. Le Roux* [2007] UKHL 1, HL, at [2].

Lord Bingham of Cornhill puts it: '*The ownership of the assets does not change. All that changes is the right to deal with them.*'[177]

In the original case, MCV owned a ship, '*The Mareva*', which it let to IB on a charter bound for the Far East. IB subsequently subchartered the vessel to the president of India on a voyage charter to India. The Indian High Commission paid £174,000 into IB's London bank. Out of these monies, IB paid two instalments of the fees that it owed to MCV, but failed to pay a third instalment that had fallen due. The judge at first instance granted an injunction against IB in favour of MCV, with a view to preventing dissipation of the balance of monies in the London bank. Lord Denning MR upheld the injunction on the basis that '*it is only just and right that this court should grant an injunction*'.[178] His Lordship stated that, if IB should have any grievance about the injunction when it came to hear of it, it would be permitted to apply to court to attempt to have it discharged.

We saw earlier that one can discern in the cases certain prerequisities to the grant of a search order. The same is true of a freezing order: a freezing order will not be awarded on an interim basis unless the claimant issues, or undertakes to issue, definable substantive proceedings;[179] the applicant must establish a good arguable case; the applicant must establish that the defendant has assets in the jurisdiction (where assets are abroad, the applicant may seek a worldwide freezing order);[180] the applicant must demonstrate that the target assets are likely to be destroyed, removed, or dissipated.

Although a freezing order is directed at the defendant and operates *in personam*, it can affect third parties. A standard form of injunction is annexed to the Practice Direction on Interim Injunctions.[181] The prescribed standard form contains the following stark penal notice (which, in the original, appears in capital letters):

> If you... disobey this order you may be held to be in contempt of court and may be imprisoned, fined or have your assets seized. Any other person who knows of this order and does anything which helps or permits the respondent to breach the terms of this order may also be held to be in contempt of court and may be imprisoned, fined or have their assets seized.

In *Customs and Excise Commissioners v. Barclays Bank plc*,[182] the House of Lords was called upon to determine whether a bank, notified by a third party of a freezing order granted to the third party against one of the bank's customers, affecting an account held by the customer with the bank, owes a duty to the third party to take reasonable care to comply with the terms of the injunction. Lord Bingham of Cornhill held that it would be

> unjust and unreasonable that the Bank should, on being notified of an order which it had no opportunity to resist, become exposed to a liability which was in this case for a few million pounds only, but might in another case be for very much more.[183]

---

[177] *Customs and Excise Commissioners v. Barclays Bank plc* [2006] 1 CLC 1096, [2006] UKHL 28, HL, at [10].
[178] [1975] 2 Lloyd's Rep 509 at 511.
[179] *Fourie v. Le Roux* [2007] UKHL 1, HL. In this case, it was held that the applicant should have failed at first instance, because, when he applied for the injunction, he had not even '*worked out what proceedings he was going to bring to which the freezing order would be relevant*'. [180] See later.
[181] 25PD.10.   [182] [2006] 1 CLC 1096; [2006] UKHL 28.   [183] Ibid. at [23].

In *Independent Trustee Services Ltd v. GP Noble Trustees Ltd*,[184] the applicant company applied to vary a freezing order made on a without notice application by the respondent company. The applicant wanted to release funds to help it to defend an action brought by the respondent company. It was held that a balance had to be found between permitting the applicant to spend funds which might belong to the respondent and refusing to allow the respondent to spend the funds. On the evidence, the respondent had an arguable proprietary claim to the monies and it was arguable that F was a vehicle for fraud. The variation was refused.

Worldwide freezing order

Although a freezing order is usually used to prevent assets from being taken outside the English Jurisdiction, it is effective *in personam* against any person made a defendant to proceedings in an English court and is not defeated by the mere fact that the assets subject to the injunction are based outside its jurisdiction. In *Derby & Co Ltd v. Weldon (Nos 3 & 4)*,[185] the claimant sought a Mareva injunction against a number of defendants, including a Panamanian company and a Luxembourg company, neither of which appeared to have any assets within the UK. It was held by the Court of Appeal that the purpose of the Mareva injunction was to prevent frustration of a court order and, although normally confined to assets within the jurisdiction, it could be used in relation to foreign assets, subject to the ordinary principles of international law. Because the injunction operated *in personam*, it did not offend against the principle that courts should not make orders to take effect in foreign jurisdictions. Their Lordships did suggest, however, that the existence of sufficient assets within the jurisdiction would be an excellent reason for refusing a worldwide injunction.

According to the *Lord Chief Justice's Practice Direction on Mareva Injunctions and Anton Piller Orders*,[186] the terms of a worldwide freezing order do not affect or concern anyone outside the jurisdiction of the court of England and Wales: except, and to the extent that, a court in a foreign jurisdiction declares it enforceable; except that the order is binding on the addressee and any agent or attorney of his; except also that the order will bind a person subject to the jurisdiction of the court of England and Wales if he has (i) been given written notice of this order at his residence or place of business within England and Wales; and if he is (ii) '*able to prevent acts or omissions outside the jurisdiction of this Court which constitute or assist in a breach of the terms of this order*'.

When a worldwide freezing order is made, the claimant is usually required to give an undertaking to seek the permission of the English court before actually enforcing it in a foreign jurisdiction. Detailed guidelines governing the grant of that permission were set down by the Court of Appeal in *Dadourian Group International Inc v. Simms*.[187] The

---

184 [2009] EWHC 161 (Ch).   185 [1990] Ch 65.

186 [1994] RPC 617; [1994] 1 WLR 1233, HC (Lord Taylor of Gosforth CJ, Sir Stephen Brown P., and Sir Donald Nicholls VC).   187 [2006] 1 WLR 2499.

case makes it clear that all of the relevant circumstances and options need to be considered. The '*Dadourian* guidelines' are as follows:[188]

1. the grant of permission should be '*just and convenient*' and '*not oppressive to the parties to the English proceedings or to third parties who may be joined to the foreign proceedings*';

2. consideration should be given to '*granting relief on terms*' (for example, extending to third parties the requirement of giving an undertaking for costs) and to '*the proportionality of the steps proposed to be taken abroad*' and to '*the form of any order*';

3. '*The interests of the applicant should be balanced against the interests of the other parties . . . and any new party likely to be joined to the foreign proceedings*';

4. '*Permission should not normally be given in terms that would enable the applicant to obtain relief in the foreign proceedings that is superior to the relief given by the WFO*';

5. the decision, whether or not to grant permission, should be based on all of the relevant information reasonably obtainable in the available time such as the judge would require to reach an informed decision (including evidence as to the applicable law and practice in the foreign court, the nature of the proposed proceedings to be commenced, the assets believed to be located in the jurisdiction of the foreign court and the names of the parties by whom such assets are held);

6. the standard of proof requires proof of a '*real prospect*' that such assets are located within the jurisdiction of the foreign court in question;

7. the risk of dissipation of the assets should be assessed;

8. '*Normally the application should be made on notice to the respondent, but in cases of urgency, where it is just to do so, the permission may be given without notice to the party against whom relief will be sought in the foreign proceedings but that party should have the earliest practicable opportunity of having the matter reconsidered by the court at a hearing of which he is given notice.*'

On the facts of *Dadourian*, the Court of Appeal held that, when the judge at first instance had given permission, he had failed to take adequate account of the law governing proceedings underway in Switzerland and of the possible oppression of a third party whom the claimant proposed to join to those proceedings. Nevertheless, the worldwide freezing order was allowed to stand because of the real prospect that the defendant had assets in Switzerland, and that it was reasonable and proportionate for it to seek to enforce the order there.

The worldwide freezing order is especially useful in an age when fraud crosses national borders. When the BCCI group of banks collapsed as the result of international fraud on a grand scale, a worldwide freezing order (then a 'worldwide Mareva injunction') was granted to the liquidators against a director and an employee of BCCI, with a view to making them personally liable for the losses which (it was alleged) had resulted from their fraud.[189]

---

[188] Ibid. at 2502–3.   [189] *Re BCCI (Overseas) Ltd (No. 9)* [1994] 2 BCLC 636.

Interim freezing injunctions (domestic and worldwide) may be made to support foreign courts, provided that the foreign state is a Regulation State[190] within the meaning
of s. 25(1) of the Civil Jurisdiction and Judgments Act 1982 or is a signatory to the
Brussels Convention or the Lugano Convention. In *Fourie v. Le Roux*,[191] the House of
Lords held that an interim injunction may be made in support foreign litigation only
if the injunction is genuinely acting as relief relevant to the final remedy sought. There
must also be a genuine nexus between UK territory and the interim relief sought. These
restrictions govern the circumstances in which it is appropriate to grant interim relief in
support of foreign litigation, but in no way restrict the extent of the relief awarded if it is
appropriate to exercise it.[192] In *Banco Nacional de Comercio Exterior SNC v. Empresa de
Telecomunicationes de Cuba SA*,[193] two orders were made at first instance: one to freeze
the defendant's assets in England and another (a WFO) to freeze assets elsewhere. The
orders were made to support a judgment made by a court in Turin. The Court of Appeal
set aside the WFO on the basis that there was no connection between the UK-based
assets and assets which might be covered by the WFO.[194] It may be a rare case in which
a WFO is ordered against a defendant who is not a UK resident.

Rescission

Rescission is an equitable remedy by which a specific contract or other transaction is
rendered unenforceable in law. It is, in a sense, a decree of specific *non*-performance.
It directly and comprehensively prevents unconscionable assertion of legal rights, and
has therefore been described as '*one of the most common and natural occasions for the
exercise of equitable jurisdiction*'.[195]

As a precondition to rescission, it must be possible to effect *restitutio in integrum* (that
is, to put the parties back into the position they were in prior to entering the rescinded
agreement). The requirement to effect *restitutio in integrum* is not absolute in relation to
transactions entered into by persons in breach of a fiduciary relationship. In such a case,
where rescission is called for on grounds of public policy, it will be ordered where the
court can '*do what is practically just, though it cannot restore the parties precisely to the
state they were in before the contract*'.[196] By the same token, a court might decide that a
fair agreement should stand, even if it was technically in breach of fiduciary duty.[197] The

---

[190] The term 'Regulation State' includes all Member States of the EU, with the exception of Denmark.
[191] [2007] UKHL 1.
[192] See, also, *Albon (t/a NA Carriage Co) v. Naza Motor Trading Sdn Bhd* [2007] EWCA Civ 1124.
[193] [2007] EWCA Civ 723.
[194] Cancelling the WFO also had the merit of avoiding conflicts with similar orders made in other jurisdictions (see Art. 47 of Council Regulation (EC) 44/2001).
[195] R. Woodeson, *A Systematical View of the Laws of England* (Dublin: Various subscribers, 1794) vol. III,
Lecture LVII.
[196] *Erlanger v. New Sombrero Phosphate Co* (1878) 3 App Cas 1218, *per* Lord Blackburn at 1278; followed in
O'Sullivan v. Management Agency and Music Ltd [1985] 3 All ER 351, CA, see Chapter 10.
[197] *Wilson v. Hurstanger Ltd* [2007] EWCA Civ 299; *Ross River Ltd v. Cambridge City Football Club Ltd*
[2007] EWHC 2115 (Ch).

remedy is, after all, discretionary. Rescission may be ordered on a number of grounds, including mistake and undue influence.

Mistake

The circumstances in which a transaction may be rescinded for mistake depend upon whether the transaction is contractual or non-contractual. In the case of a contract, a fundamental mistake as to the facts or their legal consequences may be a ground for rescission.[198] In the case of a non-contractual (unilateral) transaction, apart from cases of mistake induced by fraud, undue influence or misrepresentation, the transaction will stand unless there was such a serious mistake as to the nature and effect of the transaction as would render it unjust for the transaction to stand, although a mere mistake as to the '*consequences or the advantages to be gained by entering into*' the transaction will not be a ground for rescission.[199] This rather difficult distinction between 'effect' and 'consequence' has been criticized.[200]

Undue influence

Lifetime transactions and testamentary dispositions are liable to be rescinded on the ground of undue influence.

Lifetime transactions

Undue influence is a ground for rescinding many types of transaction, including contracts, mortgages,[201] and even the resignation of a trustee.[202] There are two broad forms of unacceptable conduct amounting to undue influence: the first comprises overt acts of improper pressure and coercion; the second is a relationship in which one party has taken unfair advantage of a position of strength.[203] In certain types of relationship, such as those in which it is '*the duty of one party to advise the other or to manage his property for him*', undue influence is presumed, provided the complainant can prove as a matter of fact that the trust-like relationship existed, and that the transaction was exceptional and therefore calls for an explanation.[204] Thus gifts from child to parent are liable to be set aside,[205] and an unfavourable contract entered into by a young and inexperienced pop star is liable to be set aside if the other party is, for example, a professional manager.[206]

---

[198] *Bell v. Lever Bros Ltd* [1932] AC 161, HL.

[199] *Gibbon v. Mitchell* [1990] 1 WLR 1304. This rather difficult distinction between 'effect' and 'consequence' has been criticized.

[200] J. Hilliard, '*Gibbon v. Mitchell* reconsidered: mistakes as to effects and mistakes as to consequences', Pts 1 and 2 (2004) 6 PCB 357; (2005) 1 PCB 31.

[201] See, for example, *Thompson v. Foy* [2009] EWHC 1076 (Ch).

[202] *Daniel v. Drew* [2005] EWCA Civ 507, CA (Civ Div).

[203] *Royal Bank of Scotland plc v. Etridge (No. 2)* [2002] 2 AC 773.

[204] *Allcard v. Skinner* (1887) 36 Ch D 145, *per* Lindley LJ at 181; See, also, *Zamet v. Hyman* [1961] 1 WLR 1442 at 1444–5; *Randall v. Randall* [2005] 1 P & CR DG4, Ch D.

[205] *Bainbrigge v. Browne* (1881) 18 Ch D 188. This contrasts with equity's approval of gifts from parent to child (as Willmer LJ observed in *Re Pauling's Settlement Trusts* [1964] Ch 303 CA at 336). For the presumption of advancement from parent to child, see Chapter 5.

[206] See, for example, *O'Sullivan v. Management Agency and Music Ltd* [1985] 3 All ER 351, CA.

However, benefits conferred by the vulnerable party will not be examined if they are unexceptional, otherwise no parent could confidently accept so much as a birthday present from their child.[207] It should be noted that the receipt of legal advice is usually sufficient to rebut the presumption of undue influence.[208] In *Brown v. Stephenson*,[209] an elderly businesswoman who had gone into partnership with a builder and agreed to give him a half-share of her land failed to establish undue influence, not only because she was not stereotypically 'vulnerable', but also because she had received legal advice and (echoing judicial respect for 'normal' behaviour)[210] because, in the judge's words, the benefit received by the builder was not 'so large that it cannot be reasonably accounted for on the grounds on which ordinary men or women act'.[211]

We should always bear in mind that the jurisdiction to set aside contracts for undue influence is used sparingly. A court of equity, it must be remembered, is not a court of morality. Professor Woodeson recognized more than two centuries ago that '[t]o *rescind every contract incompatible with the nicest principles of honor and morality, tends to terminate all commercial intercourse*'.[212]

Testamentary dispositions

The judgment of Lewison J, in *Re Edwards* (*desceased*),[213] contains a useful summary of the law concerning undue influence and wills. His Lordship concludes that it is not a question of whether or not the terms of the will are fair to all of those who might have expected an interest under it; rather, the '*question, in the end, is whether in making his dispositions, the testator has acted as a free agent*'. His Lordship observed that there is, in contrast with lifetime dispositions, no presumption of undue influence. It is determined as a matter of fact in the particular case whether or not the will was made under undue influence and the burden of proving undue influence lies on the person who asserts it. Proof requires a high civil standard of proof, which means proof of facts which cannot be explained except by positing undue influence. Undue influence might take the form of coercion, which overbears the will of the testator. The fact that the testator is physically frail or mentally fragile is relevant to determining whether will was overborne in this sense:

> Pressure which causes a testator to succumb for the sake of a quiet life, if carried to an extent that overbears the testator's free judgment discretion or wishes, is enough to amount to coercion in this sense.[214]

Undue influence might also take an insidious form known by the exotic label 'fraudulent calumny'. It entails knowingly telling lies about the proper beneficiary of the testator's bounty so as to poison the testator's mind against her. Shakespeare called it 'back-wounding calumny',[215] which just about sums it up.

---

[207] *Royal Bank of Scotland plc v. Etridge (No. 2)* [2002] 2 AC 773, *per* Lord Nicholls of Birkenhead at 798, approving *Allcard v. Skinner* (1887) 36 Ch D 145.

[208] But not always: see, for example, *Wright v. Hodgkinson* [2005] WTLR 435.

[209] [2013] EWHC 2531 (Ch).   [210] See earlier.

[211] [2013] EWHC 2531 (Ch) para. [5.1].   [212] *A Systematical View of the Laws of England* (Dublin, 1794).

[213] [2007] EWHC 1119 (Ch).   [214] Ibid. at [47].   [215] *Measure for Measure*, Act III:2.

Re Edwards (desceased) is typical of the unfortunate affairs that give rise to such claims. It is the tale of a mother and her three sons set in the Rhondda Valley, Wales. One son was married and lived nearby; the other sons lived with their mother until one of them died. The mother went to live with her married son and daughter-in-law, apparently because of the bad behaviour of the unmarried son. Her daughter-in-law drafted a letter for her by which she sought to evict the unmarried son from her home. The mother had a fall and admitted herself to a nursing home, but the unmarried son discharged her and took her back to her home against medical advice, and there, in apparent revenge against the married couple who had sought his eviction, he unduly influenced his mother to write them out of her will. The will was set aside.

Account

Account is a process by which the court assesses sums due from one person to another; it also describes the remedy of payment that is ordered at the end of the assessment process. An action for an account was, at one time, available at common law, but Chancery procedure for taking accounts, was *'so superior that by the 18th century the common law action for an account had come to be superseded by equitable proceedings for an account'*.[216] Account is most significant for present purposes as a remedy that may be ordered in favour of a beneficiary against a defaulting trustee.[217] It requires the production of the trust's financial accounts, and requires the trustee to give an account of his dealings with the trust property and to make up any shortfall to the fund. A trustee will also be required to account for unauthorized profits made by reason of his trusteeship.[218] Account is also very useful for requiring a defendant to disgorge profits made from unauthorized use of confidential information.[219] Like the remedy of injunction, the remedy of account is one of the 'interim' remedies that a court may employ to facilitate the expeditious conduct of litigation.[220] Account is the usual default remedy against a defaulting trustee or fiduciary, but as with all equitable remedies the award lies in the discretion of the court and a judge cannot be criticized simply because he or she preferred to make another award instead, for example of liquidated damages.[221]

Equitable set-off

It seems appropriate to conclude this book with the example of an equitable remedy which can work on a 'self-help' basis without judicial intervention. Before the Judicature Acts 1873–75 a court of equity would sometimes restrain a party who had brought an action at law from proceeding to trial if, for example, the defendant had an arguable cross-claim. Since the Judicature Acts, it is no longer possible to obtain an injunction to restrain a pending action but equity can instead order equitable set-off on the basis that

---

[216] *Tito v. Waddell (No. 2)* [1977] Ch 106.   [217] See Chapter 13.   [218] See Chapters 10 and 13.
[219] *AG v. Guardian Newspapers Ltd (No. 2)* [1990] 1 AC 109.   [220] CPR 1999, r. 25.1.
[221] *Walsh v. Shanahan* [2013] EWCA Civ 411; [2013] 2 P & CR DG 7, Court of Appeal (Civil Division).

neither the claim nor the counterclaim ought to be insisted upon 'without taking the other into account'.[222] To be precise, equitable set-off is available where a cross-claim is 'so closely connected with [the claim] that it would be manifestly unjust to allow [the claimant] to enforce payment without taking into account the cross-claim'.[223] The doctrine of equitable set-off is not simply a procedural defence, in the way that legal set-off is, but can be relied on outside the context of legal proceedings to prevent a person from exercising contractual or other legal rights which that person would otherwise be entitled to enforce.[224]

Further reading

In addition to the following print sources, the Online Resource Centre accompanying this book contains web links to further reading as well as guide answers to assessment questions relevant to this chapter.

DEVENNEY, J. and CHANDLER, A., 'Unconscionability and the taxonomy of undue influence' (2007) JBL 541.

GARDNER, S., 'Two maxims of equity' (1995) 54(1) CLJ 60.

GEE, S., *Commercial Injunctions*, 5th revd edn (London: Sweet & Maxwell, 2006).

GRIFFITHS, G. L. H., 'Part performance: still trying to replace the irreplaceable' (2002) Conv 216.

HARRIS, D. R., 'Specific performance: a regular remedy for consumers' (2003) 119 LQR 541.

KERRIDGE, R., 'Undue influence and testamentary dispositions: a response' (2012) 2 Conv 129–44.

KODILINYE, G., 'A fresh approach to the *ex turpi causa* and "clean hands" maxims' (1992) Denning LJ 93.

MASON, SIR ANTHONY, 'The place of equity and equitable remedies in the common law world' (1994) 110 LQR 238.

O'SULLIVAN, D., ELLIOTT, S. and ZAKRZEWSKI, R., *The Law of Rescission* (Oxford: Oxford University Press, 2007).

RIDGE, P., 'Equitable undue influence and wills' (2004) 120 LQR 617–39.

SMITH, M., 'Rectification of contracts for common mistake, *Joscelyne v. Nissen*, and subjective states of mind' (2007) 123 LQR 116.

SWADLING, W., 'Rescission, property, and the common law' (2005) 121 LQR 123–53.

TILEY, J., 'Deeds of covenant: equitable remedy of rectification' (1994) 53(3) CLJ 464.

---

[222] *Hanak v. Green* [1958] 2 QB 9, *per* Morris LJ at 26.

[223] *Federal Commerce & Navigation Co Ltd v. Molena Alpha Inc (The 'Nanfri')* [1978] 2 QB 927, *per* Lord Denning at 975; followed in *Geldof Metallconstructie NV v. Simon Carves Ltd* [2010] EWCA Civ 667, CA.

[224] *Gary Fearns (trading as 'Autopaint International') v. Anglo-Dutch Paint & Chemical Company Limited* [2010] EWHC 2366 (Ch) at para. [21].

Index